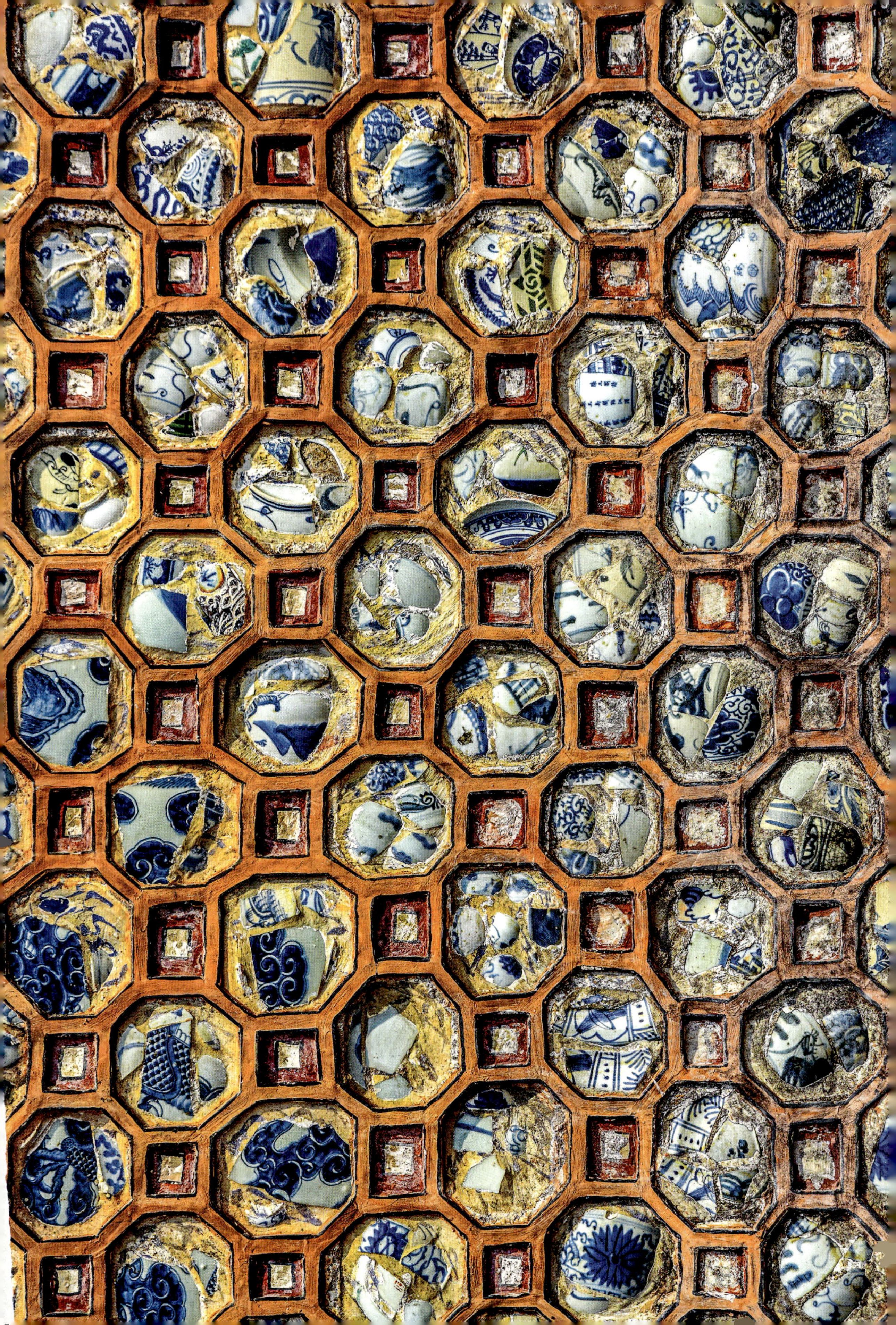

HIDDEN IN PLAIN SIGHT

THE UNTOLD MYSTERIES, MYTHS, AND MARVELS OF THE WORLD'S MOST POPULAR LANDMARKS

RONAN O'CONNELL

Hidden in Plain Sight

Published by Harper Celebrate, an imprint of HarperCollins Focus LLC.

Photography: Ronan Patrick O'Connell
Cover design: Gabriella Wikidal
Interior design: Michelle Lenger

Additional photography: Shutterstock, pages 222–223
Photograph of artwork on page 83 used with permission from the Botanic Gardens of Sydney.

ISBN 978-1-4002-5146-9 (HC)
ISBN 978-1-4002-5149-0 (audiobook)
ISBN 978-1-4002-5148-3 (ePub)

Printed in India

25 26 27 28 29 REP 5 4 3 2 1

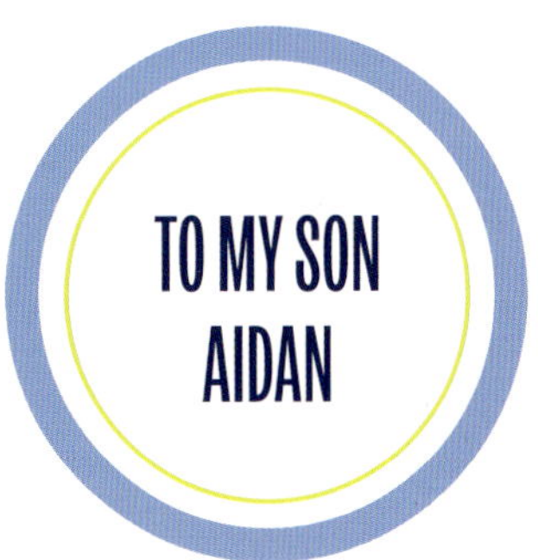

You are growing up in a society where technology promises to solve your every problem, to answer your every question. The internet powering your smart devices will continue to make our planet feel smaller and less mysterious. It will give the impression that all the earth's glory can be witnessed via a phone screen.

Always remember: This is an illusion. The real world remains so vast, varied, and volatile that it cannot be tamed, nor fully catalogued by the digital sphere. So please do harness technology. But use it to explore our planet on foot and discover the rare cultures, low-profile history, and complex craftsmanship that only truly lives on earth, not on the World Wide Web. Get out there, my boy.

ISTANBUL

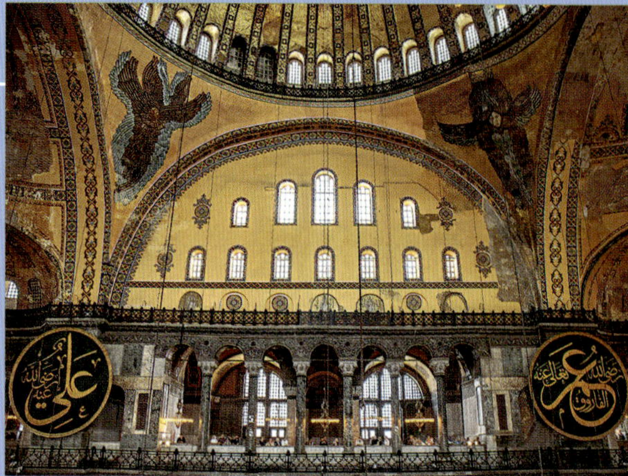

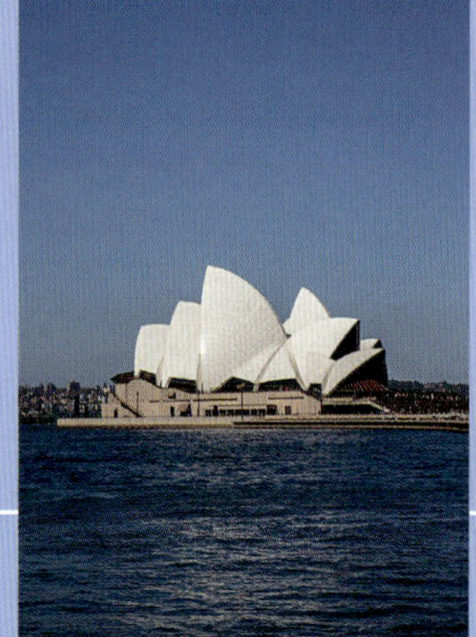

SYDNEY

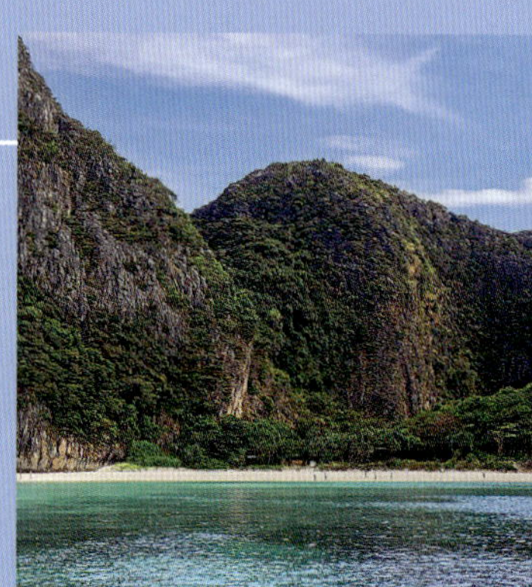

THAILAND

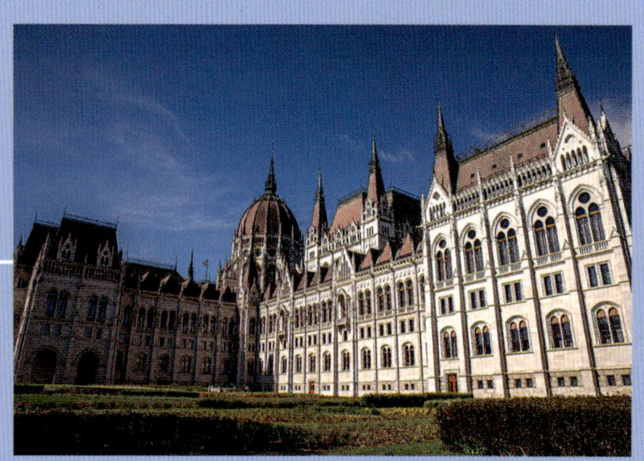

BUDAPEST

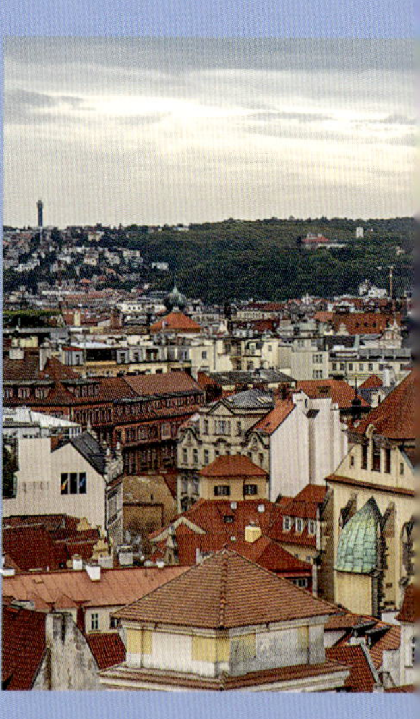

CONTENTS

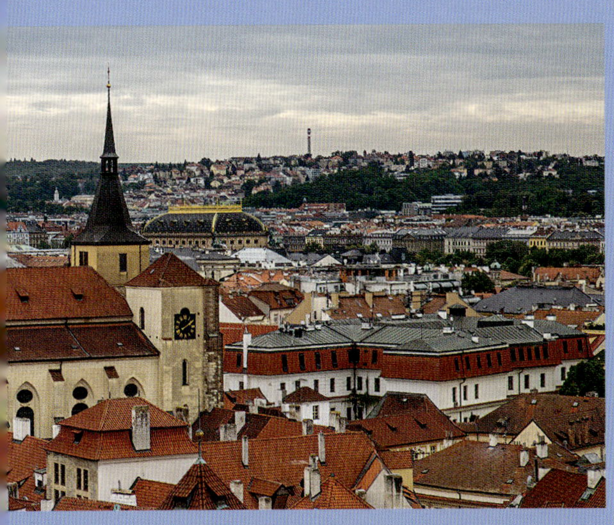

PRAGUE

INTRODUCTION

Wolves became political assassins in Japan. A stripper caused fifty thousand deaths in Europe. The sun disappeared for a year in Turkey. Naked cults hid beneath Rome. A city of treasure vanished in China. And a pope's three faces set Prague ablaze.

"Nonsense" is how most people would interpret such outlandish tales. Their skepticism would only grow if they were told that these bizarre stories are connected to world-renowned landmarks they have visited. Yet they would know that each of these stories is actually true, had they only spotted the clues to the history that was right in front of them at each landmark.

If they had noticed the dent on a Kyoto bridge.

Descended a dark staircase in Rome.

Looked closer at an odd statue in Macau.

Translated the sign on a Czech clock tower.

These hints hide in plain sight at bucket-list attractions swarmed by visitors from around the globe.

From childhood we've seen, heard, read, and talked about these iconic marvels: the Eiffel Tower, the Colosseum, the Berlin Wall, Angkor Wat, the Sydney Opera House. As a result, they feel so familiar that it's hard to imagine they hold any mystery. What more can be said about such photographed, studied, and celebrated landmarks?

That is a reasonable assumption, until you consider that some of these wonders are up to nineteen hundred years old, a timeline so vast that it's impossible for each of a beloved site's extraordinary moments to be well-known. Which helps explain why every day, tourists visiting these marvels walk in the wake of astonishing, yet factual, historical tales.

Before each visitor stands a revered castle, palace, temple, beach, or waterfall. Their senses flare as they touch a marble facade, stare at intricate murals, inhale the scent of incense, taste the salty air, listen to the thunderous flow of water. Amid this glut of sensory input, many overlook small details that unveil big stories. Sculptures, plaques, patterns, or paintings can act like a trail of breadcrumbs, leading an inquisitive mind toward an extraordinary find.

Since 2013, I have traversed the world in search of such riddles. That year I began a career in travel journalism after spending almost a decade as a newspaper reporter covering crime and politics, a job that demanded and rewarded curiosity.

I had already learned that big news stories rarely land in your lap. Instead they must be hunted. Most journalistic investigations begin with discovering one piece of a puzzle, then following paper trails. Such detective work can earn reporters what we call a "great yarn," a news story that's not only impactful, but also intricate and engrossing.

When I switched to travel writing, my journalistic approach remained similar. I had limited passion for writing summaries of cities, reviewing luxury hotels, or listing a destination's top-five bars, spas, or restaurants. Instead, what ignited my passion was delving into foreign environments in search of a great yarn, one that would explain a little-known element of a location's culture or history.

So while reporting for the likes of *National Geographic*, the BBC, CNN, and *Smithsonian*, I hunted down remarkable places. Ireland's "hell cave," where Halloween was invented. Cambodia's training center for "hero" rats. Scotland's graveyard where corpses became cash. India's long-lost temple uncovered by a tsunami. Japan's shrine to the Samurai who "caused" COVID-19.

Along the way, experts taught me to cook tarantulas, perform exorcisms, carve crossbows, harvest worms, make death masks, mix sacred yogurt, interpret dolphin sounds, trick an audience, and blend "ghost" whiskeys.

All of which inspired me to write this curious book. I scoured twenty-two countries across four continents to photograph global landmarks and uncover their most startling secrets. Why? To remind you that even in our internet age, when smartphones can seemingly answer any question, mysteries still abound. And some of these enigmas reside in the world's highest-profile locations, just waiting for you to notice them and investigate.

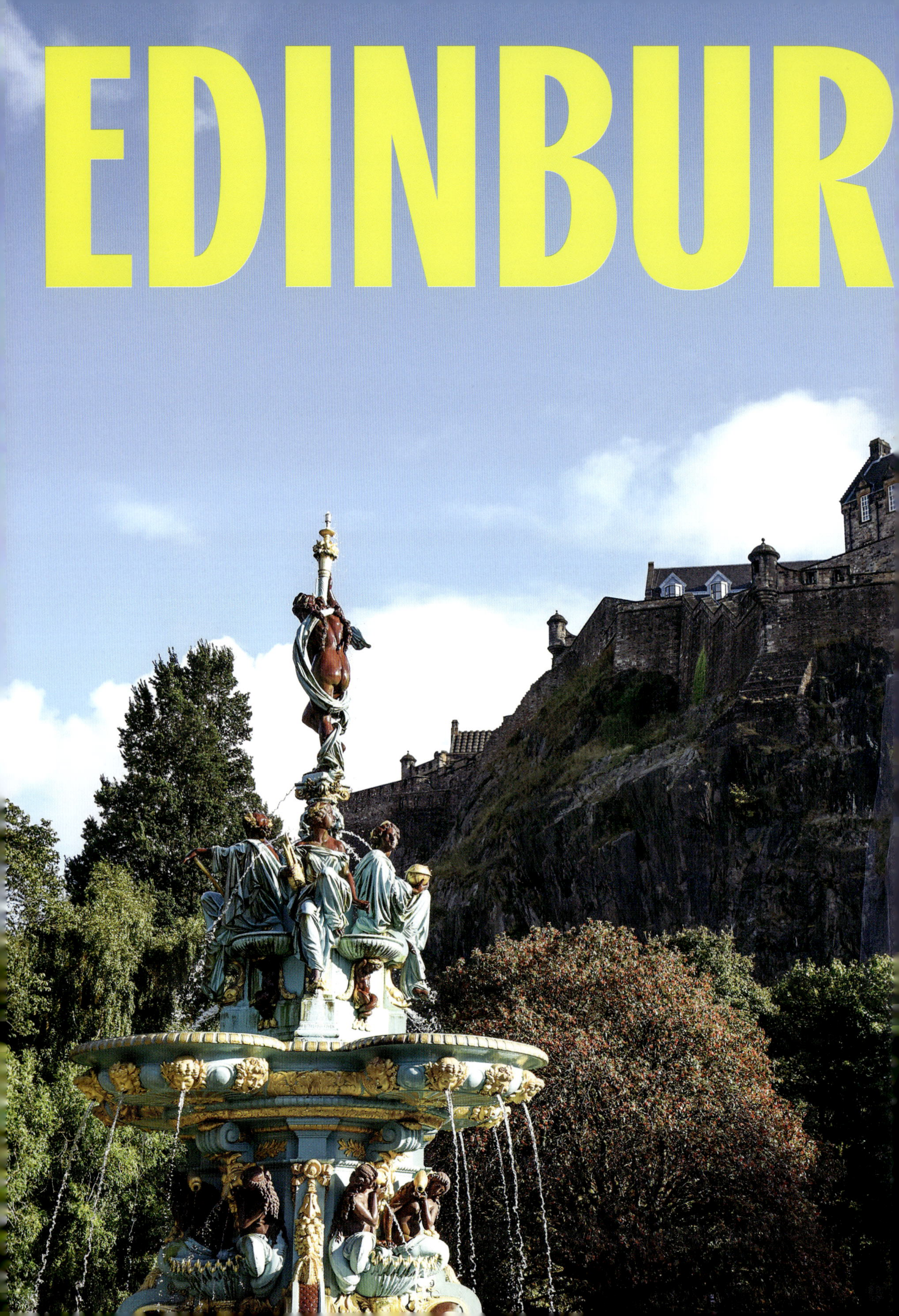
EDINBUR

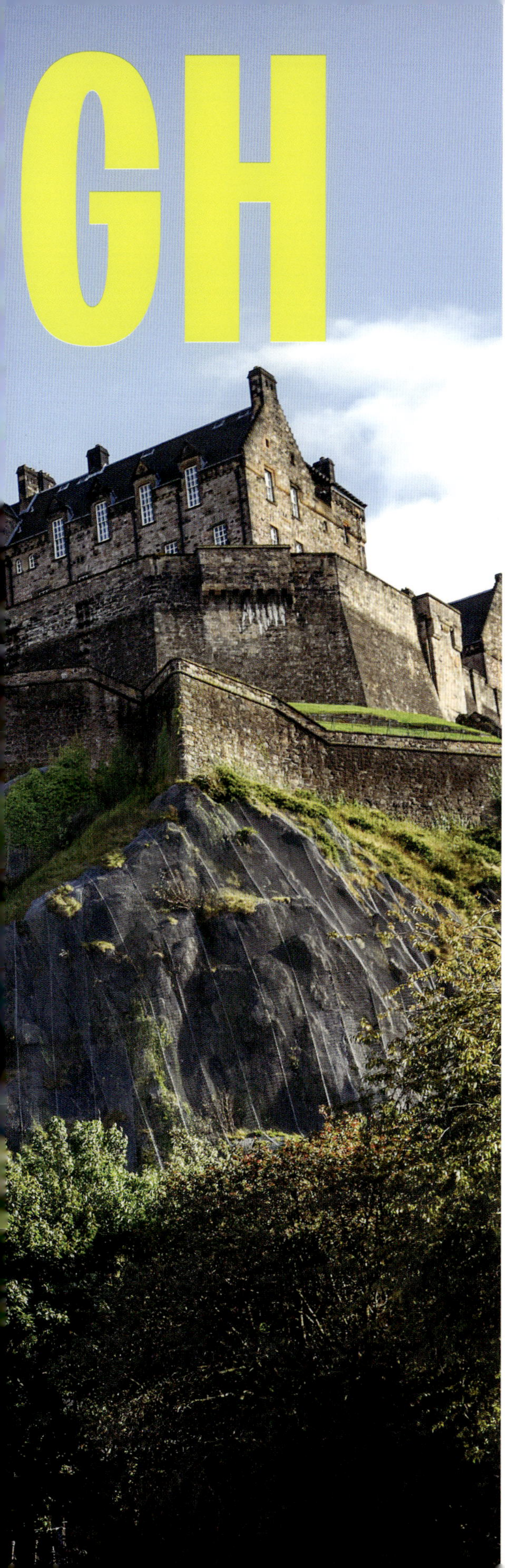

GH

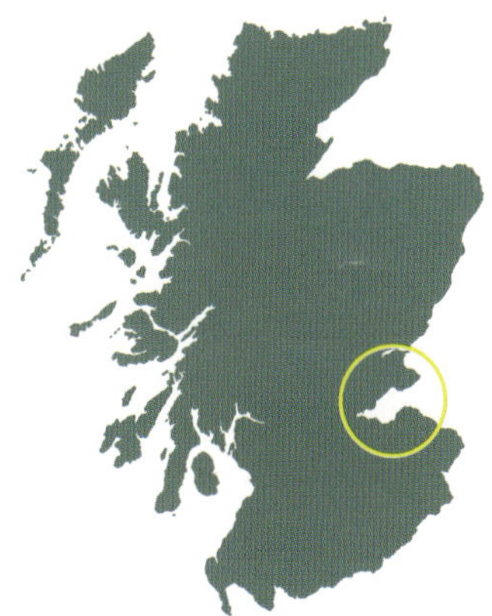

While royals, celebrities, and politicians looked on in London's Westminster Abbey, magic swirled unseen beneath King Charles III as he was crowned monarch of the United Kingdom. Amid the pomp of this 2023 event, a supernatural stone sat inconspicuously under the king's coronation chair.[1]

Few observers likely noticed the slab. Probably fewer still realized that it's imbued with millennia of controversy, mystery, and violence. Called "the Stone of Destiny," its extraordinary history has been similarly overlooked by many visitors to Scotland's Edinburgh Castle, where this priceless artifact has been frequently displayed in the heavily guarded Crown Room.[2]

Seven centuries after the slab was first featured in a British coronation, there is no consensus on its age, where it originated, or why so many empires throughout history have believed that the stone possesses magical qualities. To this day, researchers are continuing a long academic effort to decipher this enigma.[3]

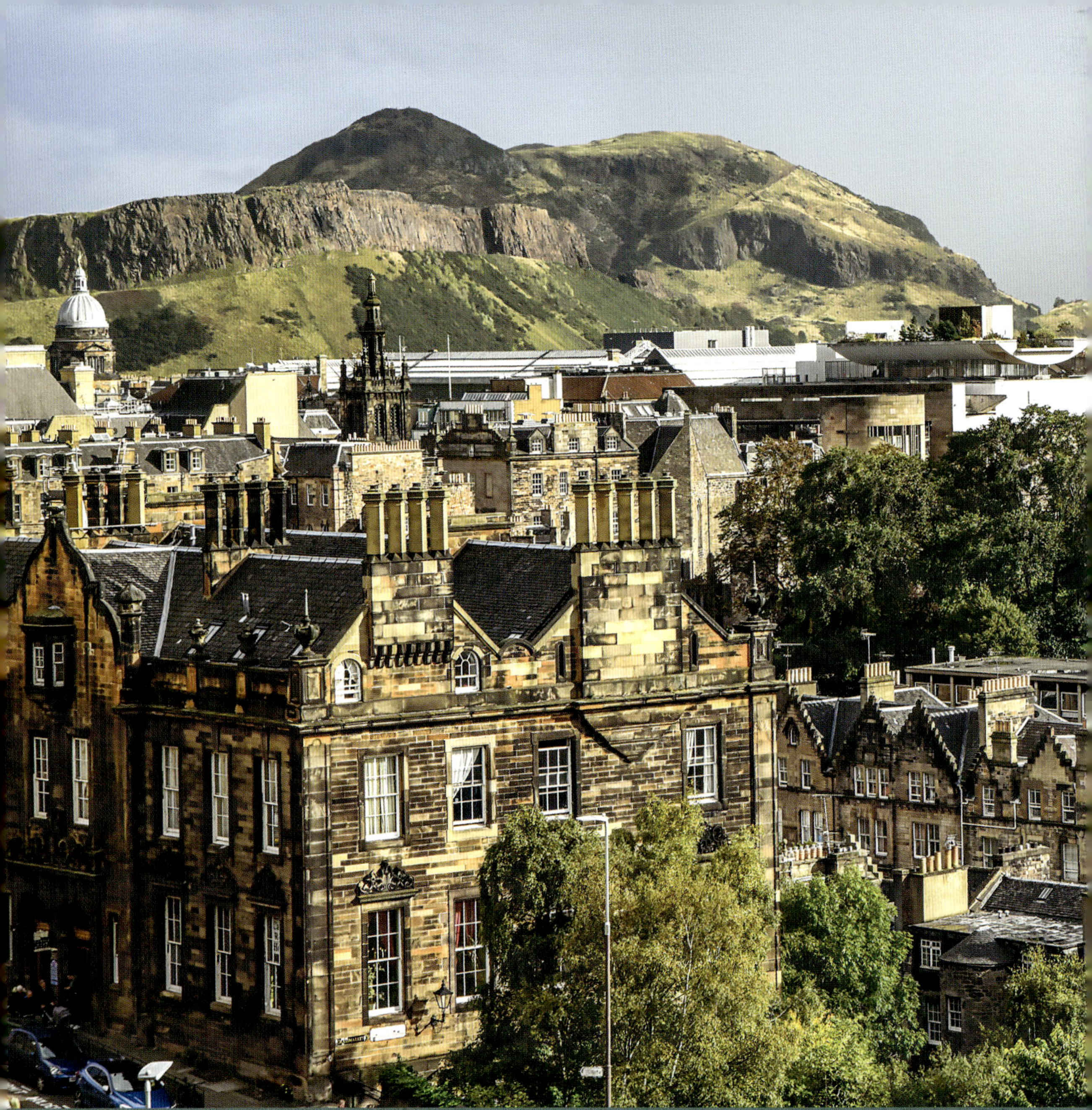

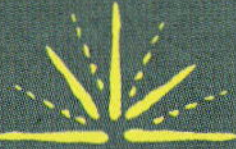

Edinburgh Castle is connected to many key moments in the history of Scotland, which, despite being within the United Kingdom and therefore governed partly from London, is a sovereign nation with its own illustrious past. Dating to the eleventh century, this commanding stone fortress looms above Scotland's capital, a hilly, storied city on the nation's southeast coast. The castle was a royal headquarters and military installation until 1819, when it was opened to the public and transformed into a tourist attraction.[4]

Roosted atop a 443-foot-tall volcanic bluff called Castle Rock, Edinburgh Castle has a suitably auspicious location in the city center. It is frequently in the eyeline of people as they explore the parks and art galleries of Edinburgh's New Town, beneath the fortress, and the museums of the cobblestoned Old Town, where the castle sits.[5]

Edinburgh's oldest building, the twelfth-century St Margaret's Chapel, is nestled behind the castle's thick, lofty walls.[6] This Romanesque private chapel commemorates Queen Margaret, whose husband, Malcolm III Canmore, was the first Scottish king to make Castle Rock his home.[7]

Across the many centuries since, parts of the castle were damaged and rebuilt. Scotland was repeatedly invaded, most frequently by English forces, making Edinburgh Castle the most besieged site in Europe.[8] A row of formidable cannons protected this citadel, including Mons Meg. This six-ton giant was capable of firing a 330-pound cannonball as far as *two miles*. Occasionally Mons Meg was moved to other locations to attack castles, particularly by Scotland's King James IV. This took great effort, as oxen couldn't haul it more than three miles a day.[9]

In 1511, James IV witnessed the completion of the castle's most memorable building, the Great Hall, which he used to host banquets and state events. Its ceiling features an intricate nest of wooden beams that contrast with its deep red walls, on which imposing weaponry is exhibited.[10]

Within the adjacent Royal Palace, complete with a graceful clock tower, is the room where King James VI was born. Still hanging there is an original, hand-carved sign bearing the year of that event: 1566.[11] It is a lasting marker of this influential man, who became the monarch of Scotland as a baby and, nearly four decades later, was crowned King James I of England. Visitors can also access the palace's lavish Royal Apartments, with their decadent wooden paneling and immense chandeliers.

Such ostentatious settings could distract from some of Europe's most unique and valuable artifacts, displayed deep within the castle at its Crown Room. Scotland's crown jewels rest there behind thick glass. Called the Honors of Scotland, they consist of a crown, sword, and scepter, are almost five hundred years old, and are heavy with gold, silver, and gemstones.[12]

If we peer into these relics' past, we find a rollicking tale. In the mid-seventeenth century, when Oliver Cromwell's English troops threatened to invade Scotland, authorities quickly gathered the Honors of Scotland and hid the jewels in an isolated fortress. After the Treaty of Union was signed in 1707, uniting England and Scotland, the jewels weren't considered to be needed anymore. And so the Honors remained locked away and, amid the ravages of time and war, were forgotten. But more than a hundred years later, the nation rejoiced as these jewels were discovered, quite remarkably, after novelist Sir Walter Scott brought about a search for them. All the while, they were just sitting in a secure box inside Edinburgh Castle.[13]

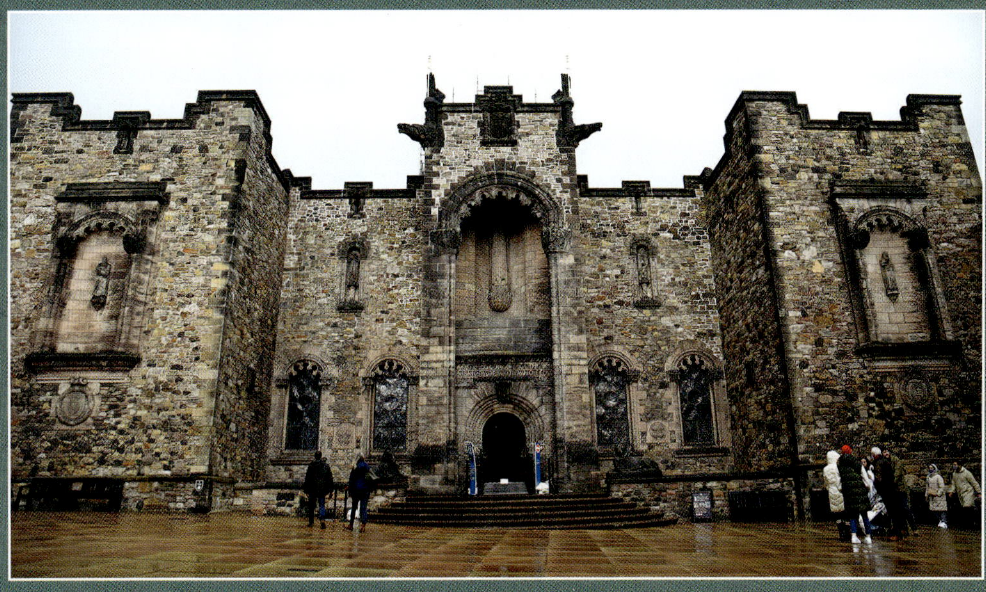

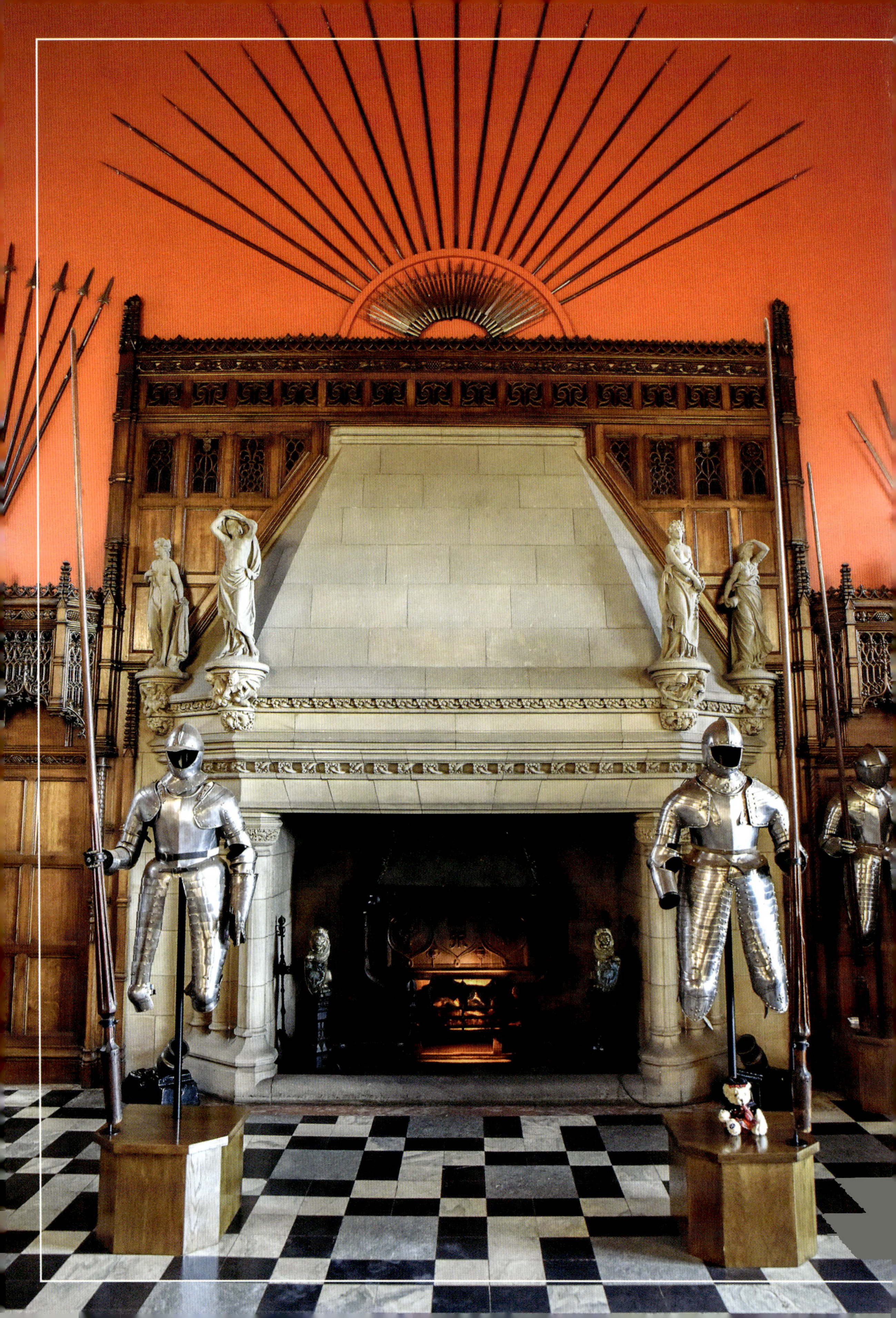

THE STONE OF DESTINY BY THE NUMBERS

So what do we actually know about this auspicious artifact? What is universally accepted is that it's a 330-pound chunk of sandstone that measures twenty-six inches long, sixteen inches wide, and eleven inches deep. Beyond such facts, myriad theories of the stone's origins come into conflict. This matchbox-shaped rock exists within a dense matrix of folk tales that variously trace it to the Middle East, North Africa, Ireland, Spain, and Scotland.[14]

AN IRISH CONNECTION

Some historic accounts track the stone to Ireland's County Antrim. There it was apparently central to the crowning of Celtic monarchs, who called it the *Lia Fáil*, or the "speaking stone." According to Irish lore, the Lia Fáil was more than a ceremonial decoration. The Celts believed it possessed an otherwordly ability to identify the next rightful monarch, and only when a true king sat on Lia Fáil would this slab release its famous wailing sound. In that dramatic moment, the artifact granted them supernatural powers, including the capacity to prophesy future events.[15]

TIES TO SCOTLAND'S FOUNDING FATHER

Other legends link this slab to fifth-century leader Fergus Mór.[16] He commanded Dál Riata, a Gaelic kingdom that formed in what is now Ireland and then expanded to western Scotland. Mór's own mythology is intriguing. As the folktale goes, he became acquainted with that most renowned of holy men, St. Patrick, who prophesied that Mór would forge a royal dynasty.

Mór went on to do just that. He is now widely considered to be a founding father of Scotland, bringing the Gaelic language and establishing the royal line of Scottish kings for hundreds of years to come. In the late fifth century, Mór moved the seat of Dál Riata's power from Ireland to western Scotland, around modern-day Argyll. Legend has it that he brought with him the Stone of Destiny, where it was used for coronations of his descendants and gradually became known as the Stone of Scone.[17]

A BIBLICAL THEORY

Not all folklore lines up with the accounts of the stone's European origins, or how it found its way to Scotland. Some, in fact, suggest that the stone's significance began thirty-six hundred years ago as a key artifact of a well-known story from the Old Testament. According to the book of Genesis, Jacob, who would become the father of the Israelites, laid his head on a rock at Bethel, an ancient city of Palestine. Suddenly a vision of God appeared in his dreams.[18]

It is said that this precious rock, which became known as "Jacob's Pillow," was moved later to Jerusalem in Israel. Legend goes that it spent centuries acting as a table for the Ark of the Covenant, perhaps the most sacred of all Old Testament objects.[19]

Then entered Scota. According to the medieval text *Scotichronicon*, she was born to an Egyptian pharaoh in the fourteenth century BC and married a Greek prince named Gaythelos. Scota and Gaythelos resided in Egypt, where their royal status afforded them vast wealth and power. But their luxurious life in North Africa was ended abruptly by an uprising. Scota and Gaythelos fled to Spain, then north to Ireland, where they settled in the land now reputedly named after her: Scotland. Despite leaving Africa under duress, Scota kept possession of the Stone of Destiny, transporting it all the way to her new home.[20]

Her tale contradicts the other theories and has long been considered myth. Although in recent years, academic research found Scota's story in the ancient historical text, *The History of Egypt*, written by Egypto-Greek historian Manetho, suggesting she may not have been a mythical figure after all.[21]

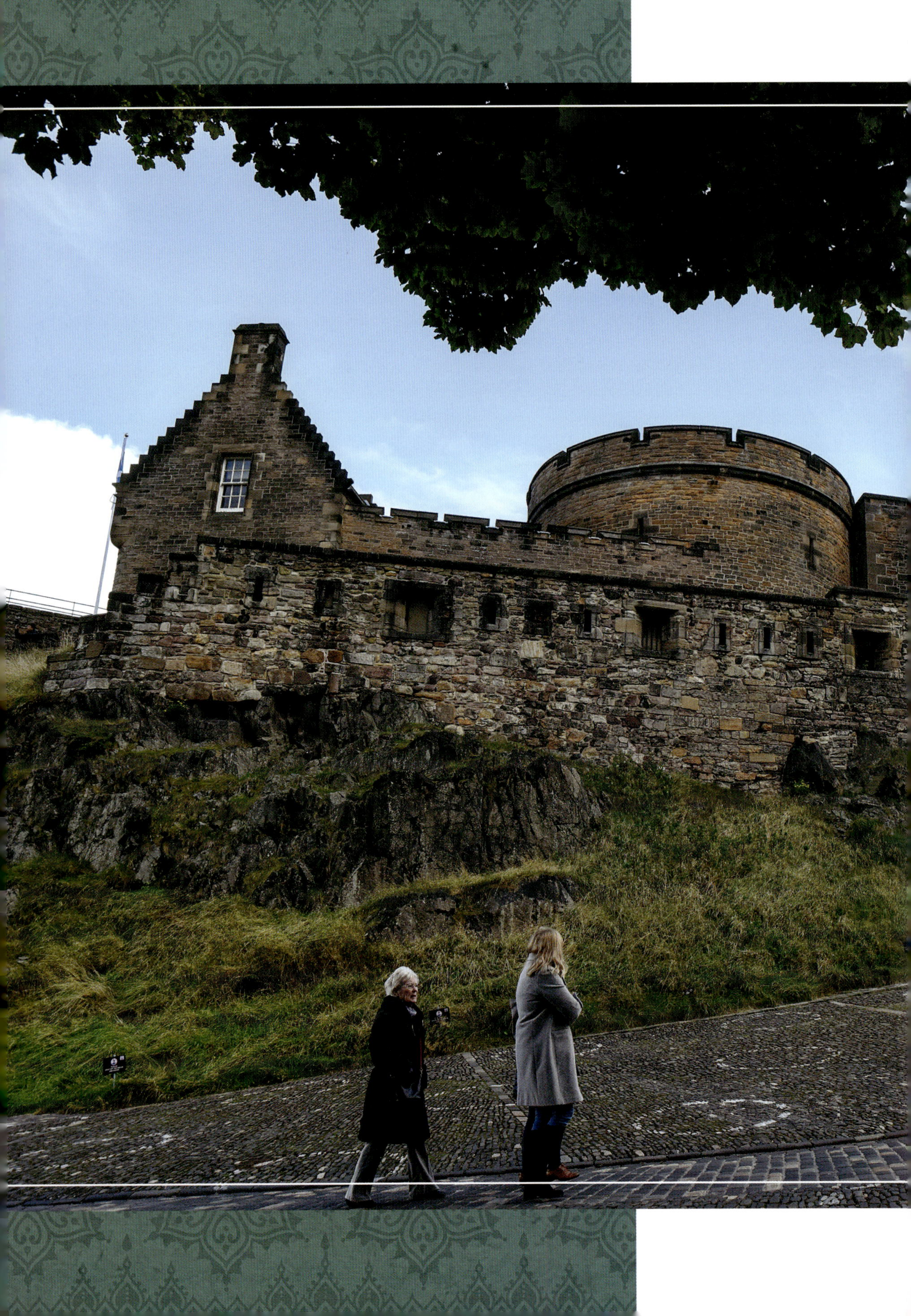

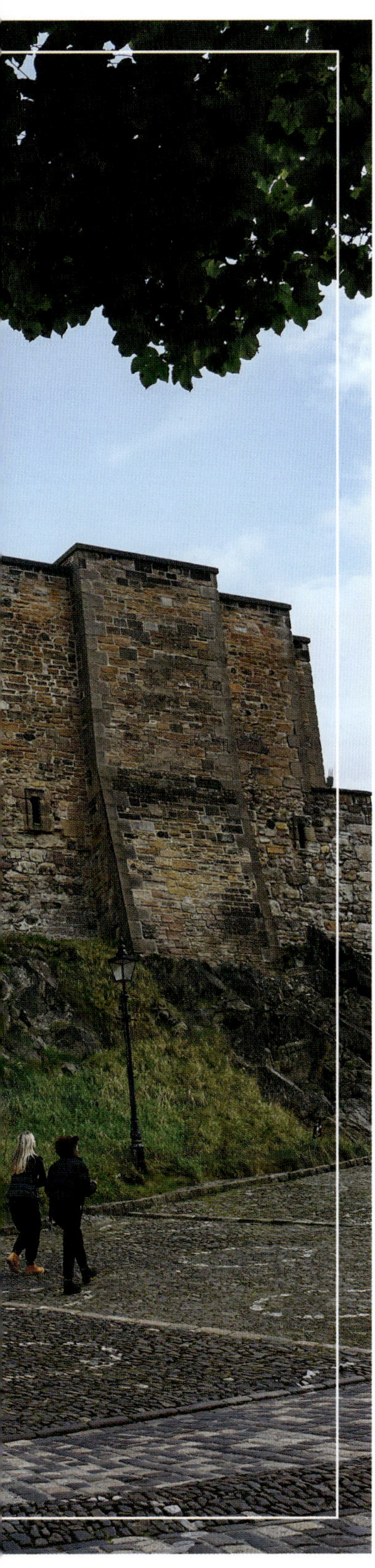

ACADEMIC ATTEMPTS TO EXPLAIN THE STONE

Amid conflicting historical accounts, scientists have also tried to pinpoint the Stone of Destiny's origins. In 1998, the British Geological Survey determined that the stone is about four hundred million years old. Their analysis indicated that it was likely quarried from the Scone Sandstone Formation near Scone Palace, thirty-five miles north of Edinburgh.[22]

Then in 2023, researchers using 3D technology introduced a new wrinkle in the debate about the slab's origins. This tool revealed the Roman numerals XXXV etched on the slab. However, those marks alone couldn't confirm if the inscription was made during the Roman era or whether the stone has any ties to the Roman Empire. So ironically, rather than clarifying the stone's backstory, scientific studies have only introduced new layers of uncertainty.[23]

HOW THE STONE BECAME A ROYAL AMULET

Realistically, the origins of the Stone of Destiny may remain murky for generations to come. But further along its timeline, the mists of mystery begin to clear. It is widely believed that this artifact was brought to the town of Scone in the ninth century AD by the first king of the united Scots, Kenneth MacAlpin. There it was used to crown Scottish kings.[24]

In yet another twist, it was later thieved in 1296 by the English king, Edward I. He prized the stone both as a trophy from his invasion of Scotland and a symbol of his right to rule that nation. Edward I then requested a new coronation chair, beneath which the stone has been positioned during every crowning of a British monarch for the past seven centuries.[25]

Finally, in 1996, the revered artifact was given back to Scotland, where it rested in Edinburgh Castle before finding a new home about forty miles north at Perth Museum in 2024. The stone returned to London for the coronation of King Charles III. And until the next royal-in-waiting summons it for their coronation, it will sit on display in Scotland, appearing to be a mere rock, yet consisting of layers of sedimentary intrigue.

BALI

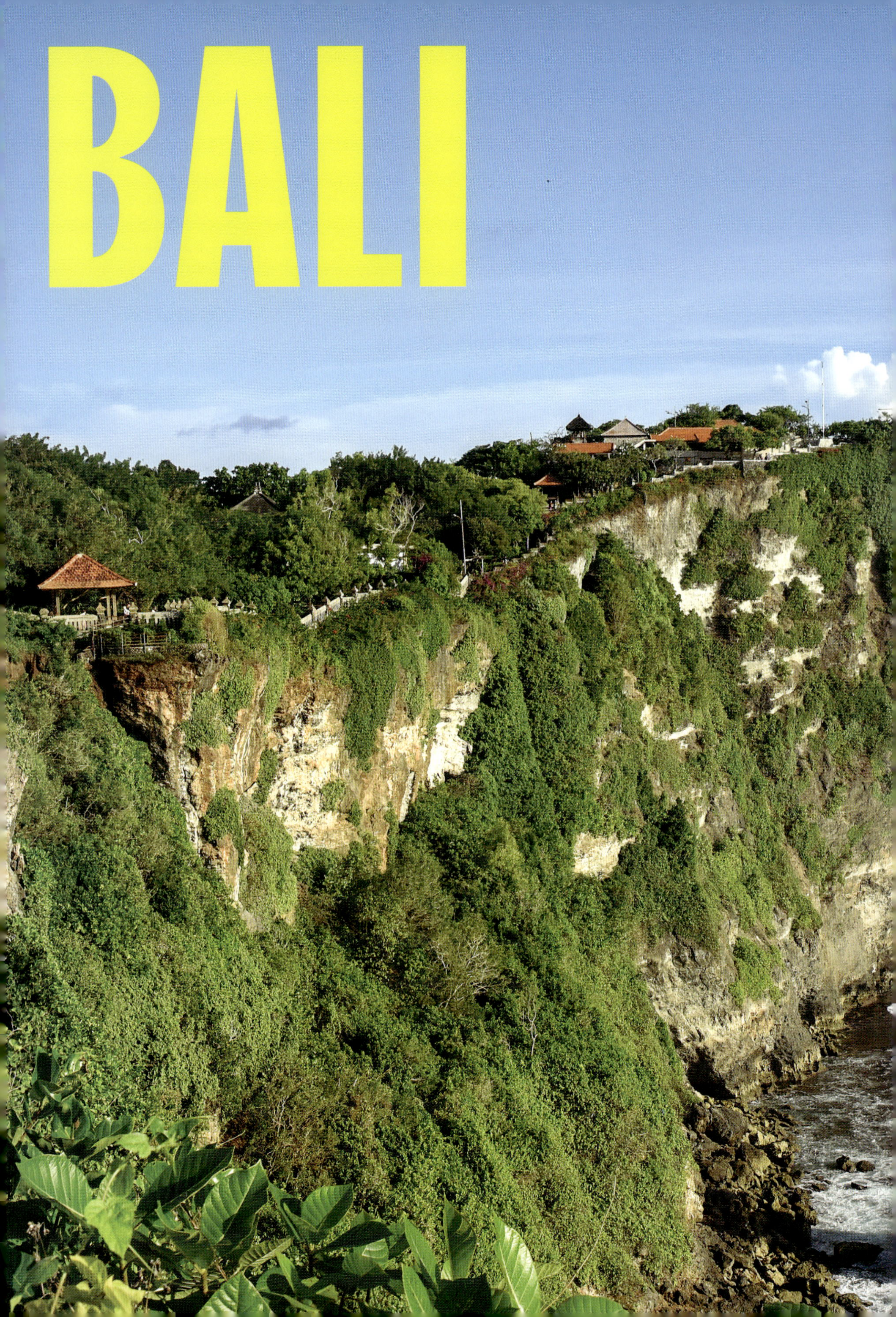

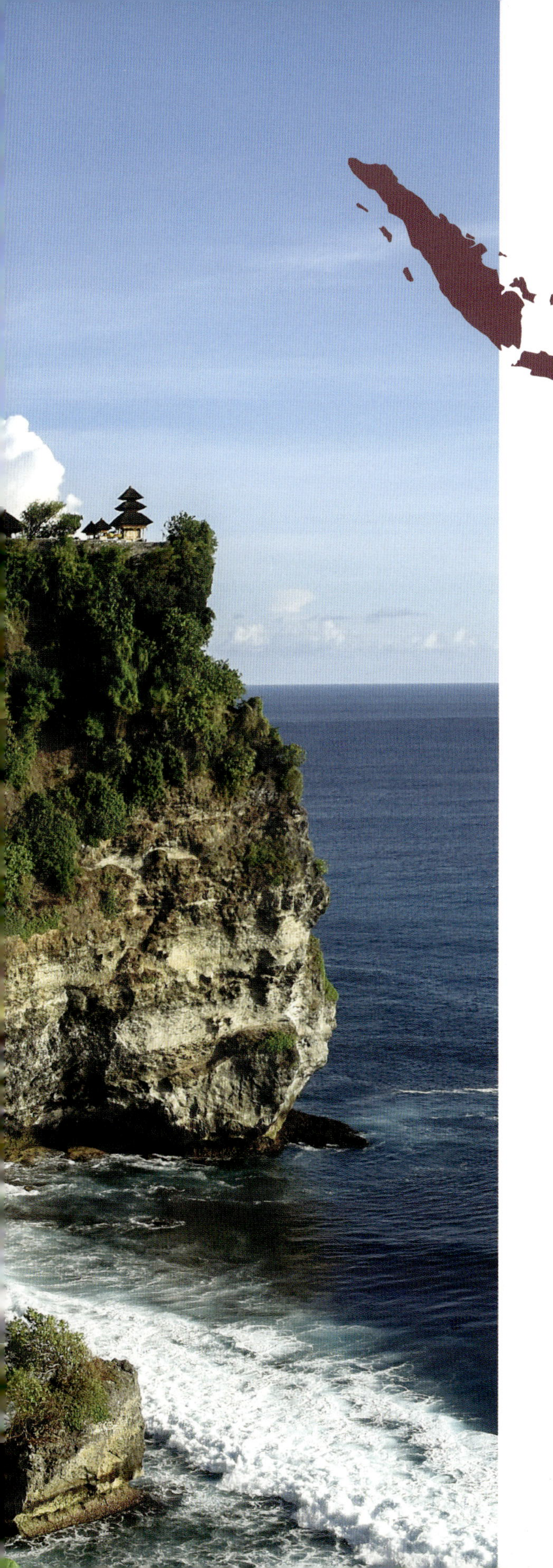

Encircled by flames, bare-chested men sway in unison as they enter a trance atop a Balinese cliff. Hundreds of spectators look on as the sun slips into the Indian Ocean, casting orange and pink hues on the nearby shrine, which acts as a bodyguard for all in attendance.

Dramatically perched three hundred feet above torrid waters, Uluwatu Temple is among the most visited sites on the dreamy Indonesian island of Bali.[26] Tourists flock to witness the temple's nightly Kecak fire show, an ancient Balinese ritual that incorporates chanting, dancing, and the retelling of Hindu legends.[27] Other visitors come to peer down Uluwatu's sheer cliffs. And where foreigners see only foaming waves below them, locals spot a liquid realm riddled with demons.

In Bali's Hindu mythology, the direction toward the ocean is known as *kelod*, and toward the mountains is called *kaja*. While kaja is a sacred place, home to the island's deities, kelod is an underworld brimming with dangerous spirits. If left unattended, kelod's devils could rise from the water to disrupt Indonesian society.[28] So for centuries, the Balinese have monitored them via seven so-called Sea Temples, including Uluwatu. Part places of worship, part mystical lookouts, the temples are strategically positioned around Bali's coastline.[29]

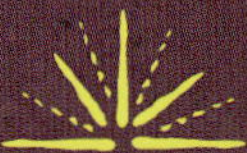

Bali is the most visited destination in vast and vastly varied Indonesia. Stretching 3,200 miles from west to east, this Asian nation is an archipelago home to 284 million people, who collectively speak hundreds of native languages.[30] Indonesia is governed from Jakarta, a megalopolis with 35 million people in its metro area.[31] As it's choked by traffic and shrouded by smog, Jarkarta is not a major tourist draw. Instead, most foreigners step off the plane at Bali and into a tropical daydream.

Bali epitomizes the equatorial haven many people fantasize about while stuck at work or enduring a harsh winter. Sunny beaches, secluded bays, cinematic sea cliffs, and luxurious yet affordable resorts dot its 411-mile coastline.[32] In the interior, volcanoes loom above rainforests, pierced by pristine rivers that feed emerald rice fields. All of which is enhanced by year-round warmth fit for shorts and swimsuits. Tourism is concentrated along Bali's southwest coast, where unfortunately, many of the beaches are now blighted by overdevelopment, especially at Kuta, Legian, and Seminyak.

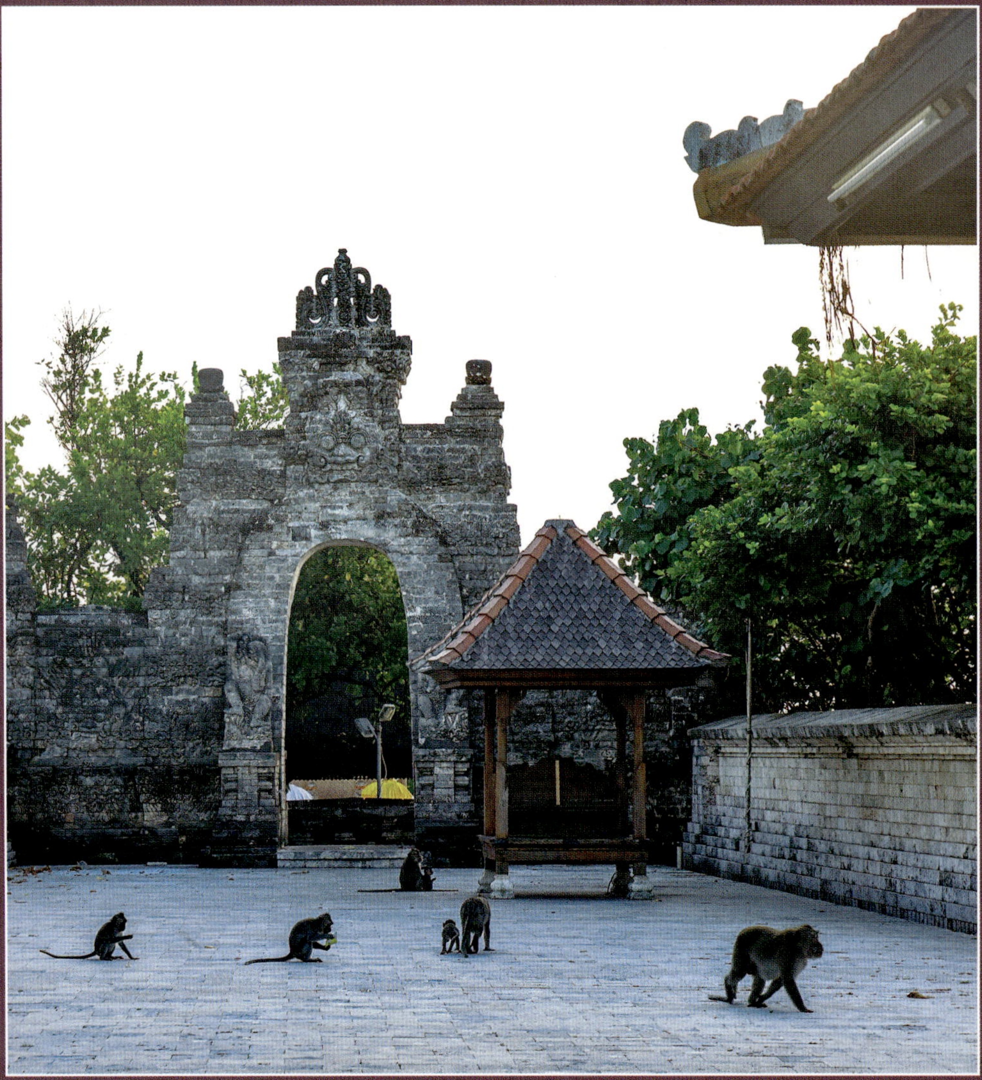

BALI'S NEVER-ENDING SPIRITUAL BATTLE

According to local lore, Uluwatu is central to an esoteric war. Bali is said to be locked in an eternal conflict between kindly deities that reside in its peaks and the evil spirits that lurk in oceans, rivers, forests, valleys, and graveyards. But these clashing forces do not represent a simple yin and yang dichotomy. Instead, each deity and spirit is part of a universal living energy called *Shakti*.

To Balinese Hindus, demons are hostile and menacing, yet can also be placated. Many residents of the island try to pacify malevolent spirits by showing them respect via daily ritual offerings. They weave coconut leaves into triangular bowls, called *segehan*, fill each one with ginger, onion, salt, and rice, and leave these gifts outside houses, restaurants, hotels, and temples across the island, including at Uluwatu.[33]

KEEPING THE DEMONS AT BAY

Lining the road to Uluwatu Temple are dozens of traditional Balinese structures featuring anti-demon measures. Many of these buildings employ *asta kosala kosali*, a local design concept that organizes spaces to promote harmony. Asta kosala kosali dictates how homes or hotels should be laid out to prevent infestation by harmful spirits.

Buildings made according to this philosophy employ layers of defense: first to confuse demons, then to placate them, then finally to block them. The outermost layer is called *tembok penyengker*, tall stone walls that ring the structure. Should a demon manage to breach the sole gate in these walls, the next ancient tactic is to kill it with kindness. Directly inside that entrance is an ornate half wall, called an *angkul-angkul*, where residents leave gifts for the spirits. If the demon remains displeased, it will move deeper inside the building to the *aling-aling*, a half wall meant to act as a final barrier preventing negative spirits from entering the home.

Asta kosala kosali designs also aim to harvest positive energy. Homes are oriented to face toward the mountains and away from the beautiful, yet devil-ridden sea. Although Balinese Hindus observe great beauty and positivity in the ocean, many remain wary of its underworld of evil spirits.[34]

A FIERY CLIFFTOP SHOW

The Balinese belief in the supernatural also shapes Uluwatu's popular Kecak fire dance. Wearing vibrant sarongs and Udeng headdresses, the all-male dance troupe performs a tale intended not just to enthrall the crowd, but also to honor their ancestors and Hindu deities. This spectacle unfurls seven nights a week at a cliffside amphitheater about five hundred feet south of the temple's main entrance.

Its story derives from the *Ramayana*, an epic Indian text of twenty-four thousand verses laden with Hindu philosophy and parables. Kecak's tale begins when Prince Rama and his wife, Sita, are exiled into a forest. While navigating the dark jungle, they encounter demon king Ravana, who kidnaps Sita and hides her in his castle.

This sets up the Kecak dance's thrilling final act, during which Prince Ayodhya Rama and his brother embark on a perilous mission to rescue Sita from one of Bali's most feared demons. Predictably, and satisfyingly, they succeed.

Spectators learn that what they are witnessing is no mere tourist exhibition. Rather, Kecak is a flamboyant depiction of a ceaseless war between forces of light and dark—lore that still influences the beliefs and behavior of many Balinese Hindus.

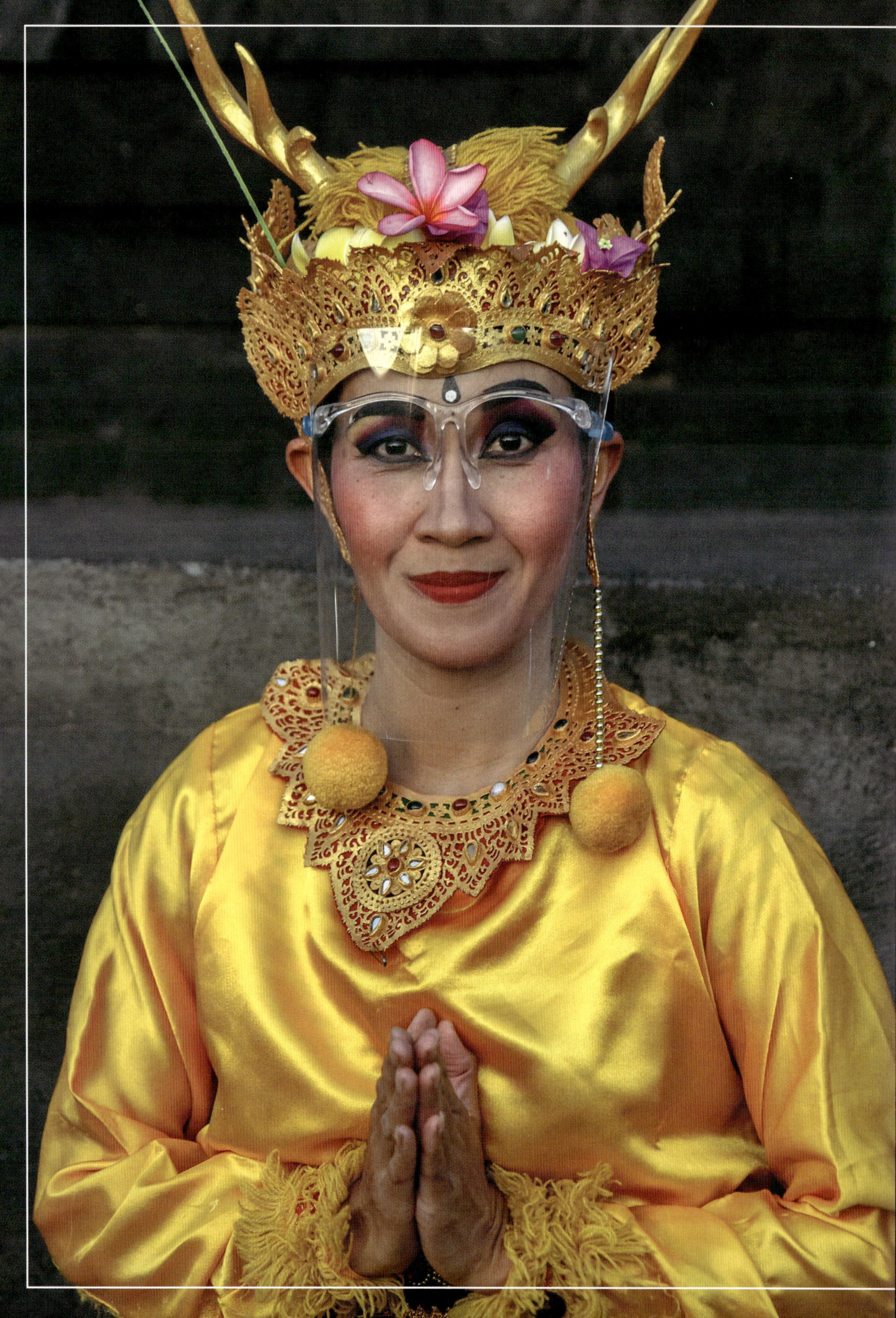

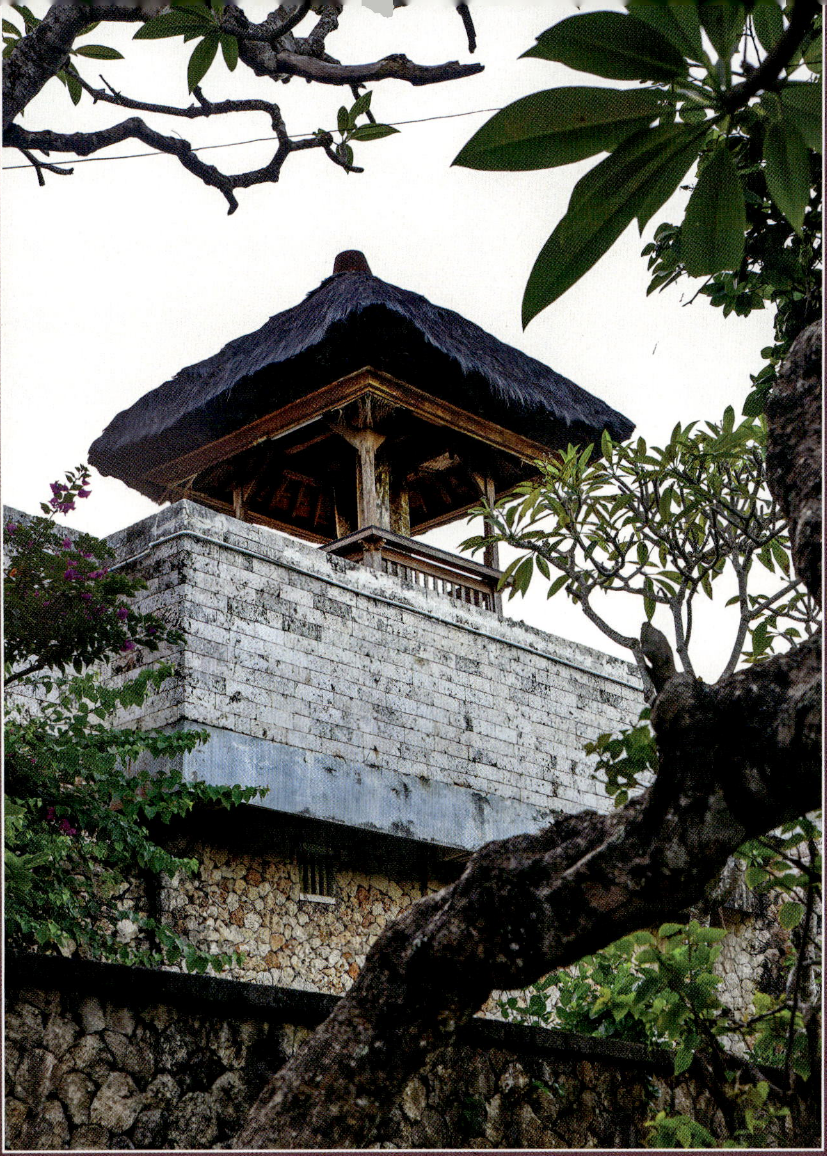

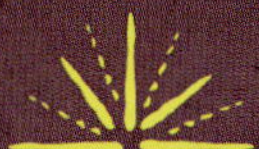

Uluwatu retains some rugged grandeur thanks to greater seclusion and rougher seas than the nearby tourist hubs of Kuta, Legian, and Seminyak. Many visitors come to witness Uluwatu's prodigious cliffs, especially at sunset, when the Indian Ocean is ignited by blistering yellows, searing pinks, and scorching oranges.

Flanked on three sides by sheer plunges, Uluwatu Temple is a prime perch from which to witness the sky's daily spectacle. Paths hug these cliffs for hundreds of yards north and south, winding through jungle awash with brazen long-tailed macaques that are infamous for thieving hats, phones, and snacks.

After the Kecak show finishes, many spectators take one more look over the cliffs of Uluwatu. They stare down toward kelod, an underwater world that, to them, is invisible yet to locals is eternal and perilous.

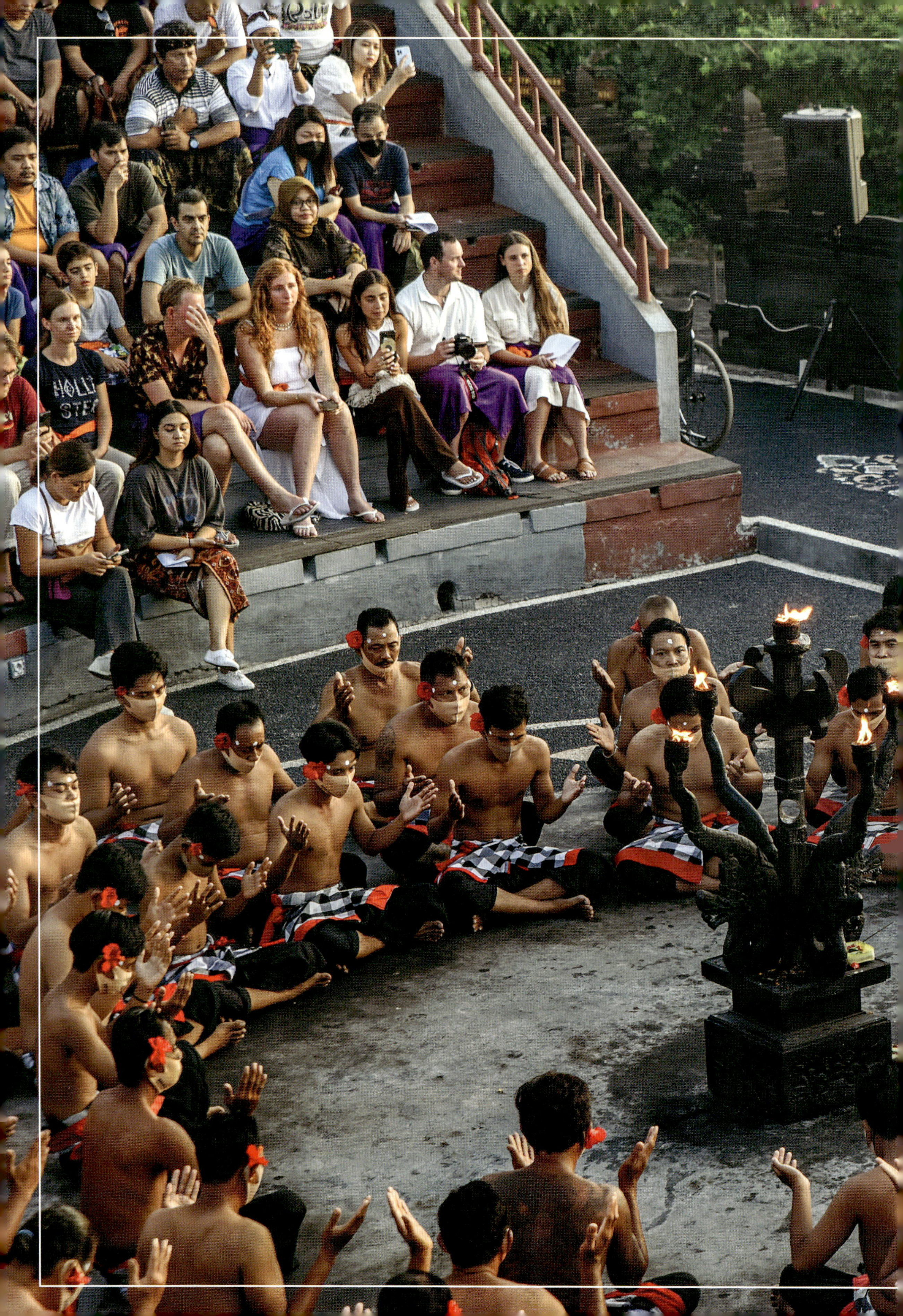

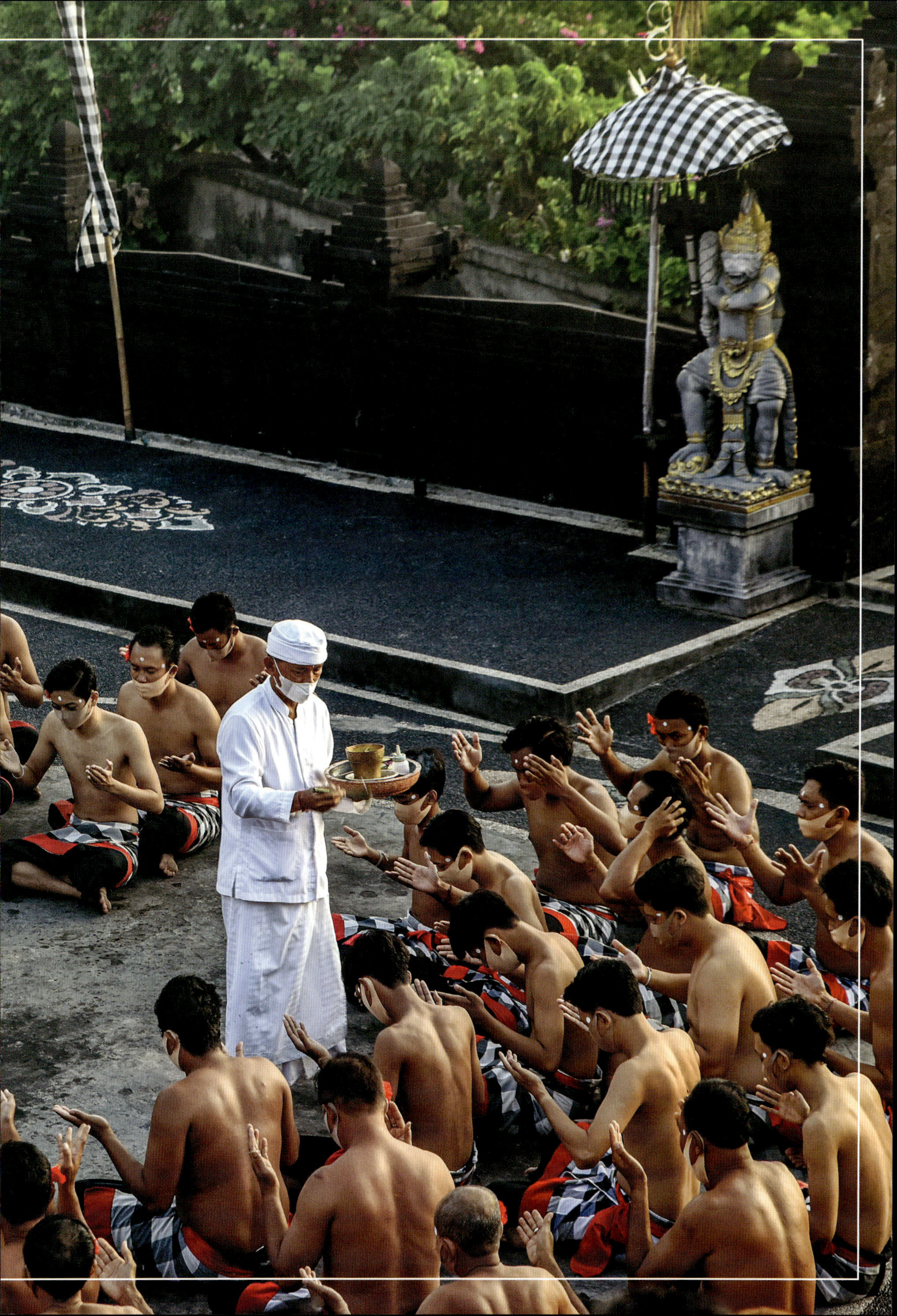

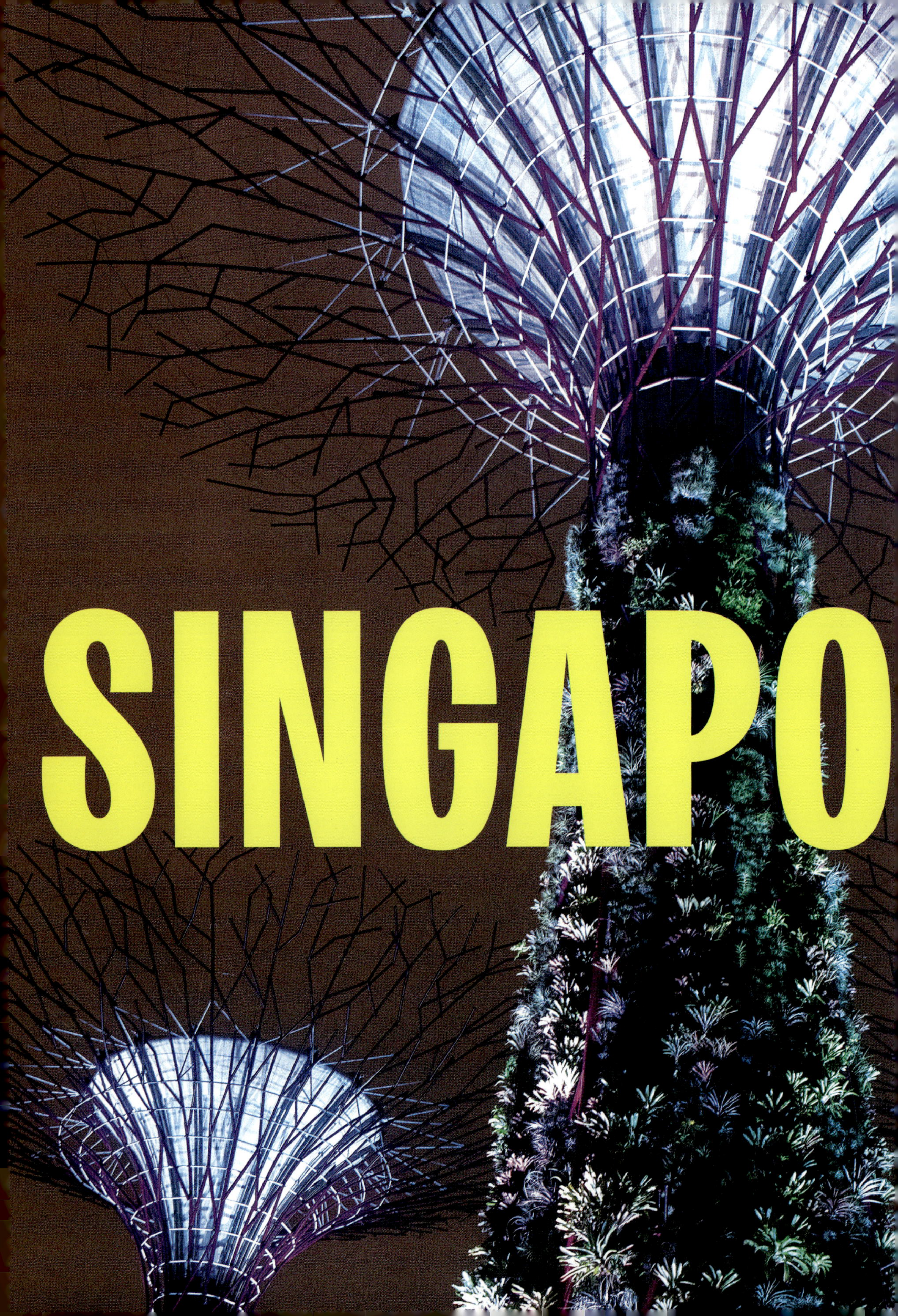
SINGAPO

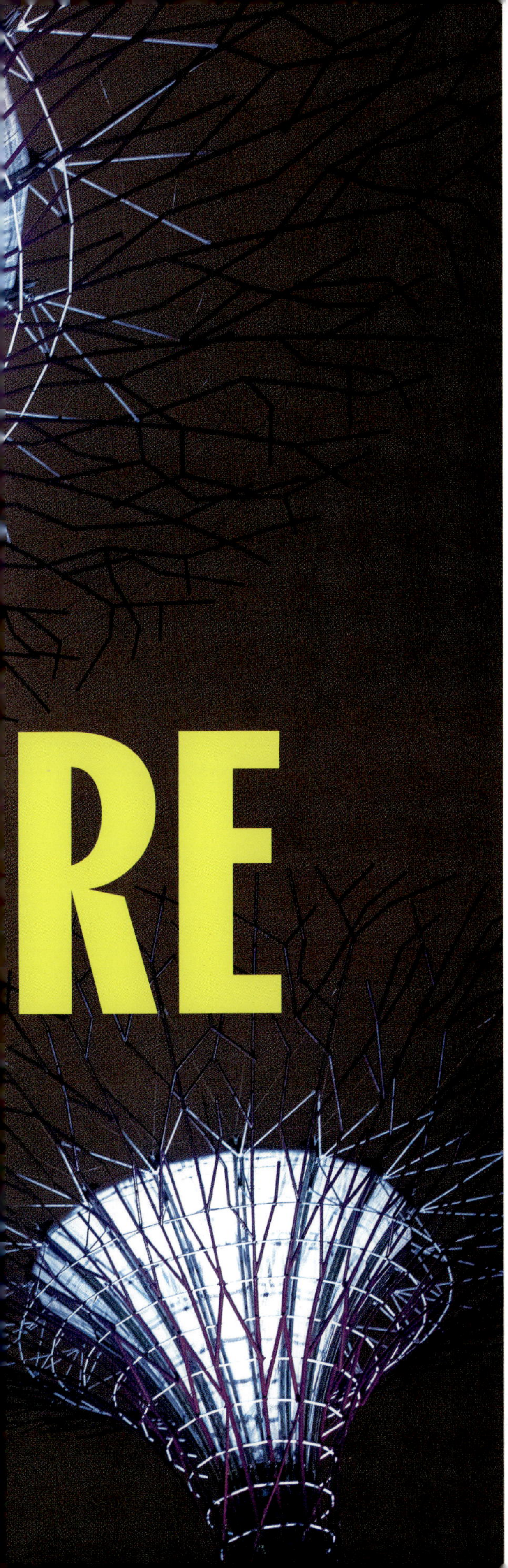

RE

Even darkness can't dull the radiance of Gardens by the Bay. As night shrouds its acres of glorious greenery, visitors become entranced by the man-made spectacle that glows above their heads. The world's most futuristic botanical garden fuses natural majesty and human ingenuity.

Each evening, onlookers gather here beneath space-age Supertrees, towering metallic structures cloaked in blossoms and bathed in fluorescent light. By day, visitors marvel at this site's other distinctive architectural features, like its glass-roofed Flower Dome and Cloud Forest.

What isn't apparent to visitors is that, behind the scenes, scientists at Gardens by the Bay are using this 250-acre botanic complex as a tool in a wildly ambitious project. The aim? To make Singapore the world's greenest city.

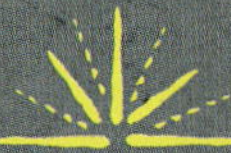

Since opening in 2012, in the shadow of Singapore's iconic Marina Bay Sands building, Gardens by the Bay has become a globally recognized attraction. Within this vast botanic complex are three sprawling gardens: Bay Central, Bay East, and Bay South.

Bay South is its tourist hub. Visitors gravitate there to peruse its huge conservatories and ogle its eighteen Supertrees. Each Supertree is a vertical garden of sorts, measuring up to 164 feet tall and draped in thousands of orchids, ferns, bromeliads, and flowering climbers.[36]

Elevated walkways connect several of the Supertrees and expose visitors to memorable views. The tallest path features an observatory, augmented reality panels explaining climate change, and a rooftop deck with sweeping vistas of the marina and the Singapore skyline.

From that lofty vantage, visitors may also spy Gardens by the Bay's two glass-roofed conservatories: Cloud Forest and Flower Dome. Inside these structures are hundreds of foreign plants that otherwise couldn't survive in Singapore's scorching climate. The Flower Dome, which held the Guiness World Record for the world's largest glass greenhouse when it was built, is especially drenched in color. Golden azaleas vie for attention alongside orange tulips, magenta roses, red petunias, purple pincushions, blue hydrangeas, and pink cherry blossoms.[37]

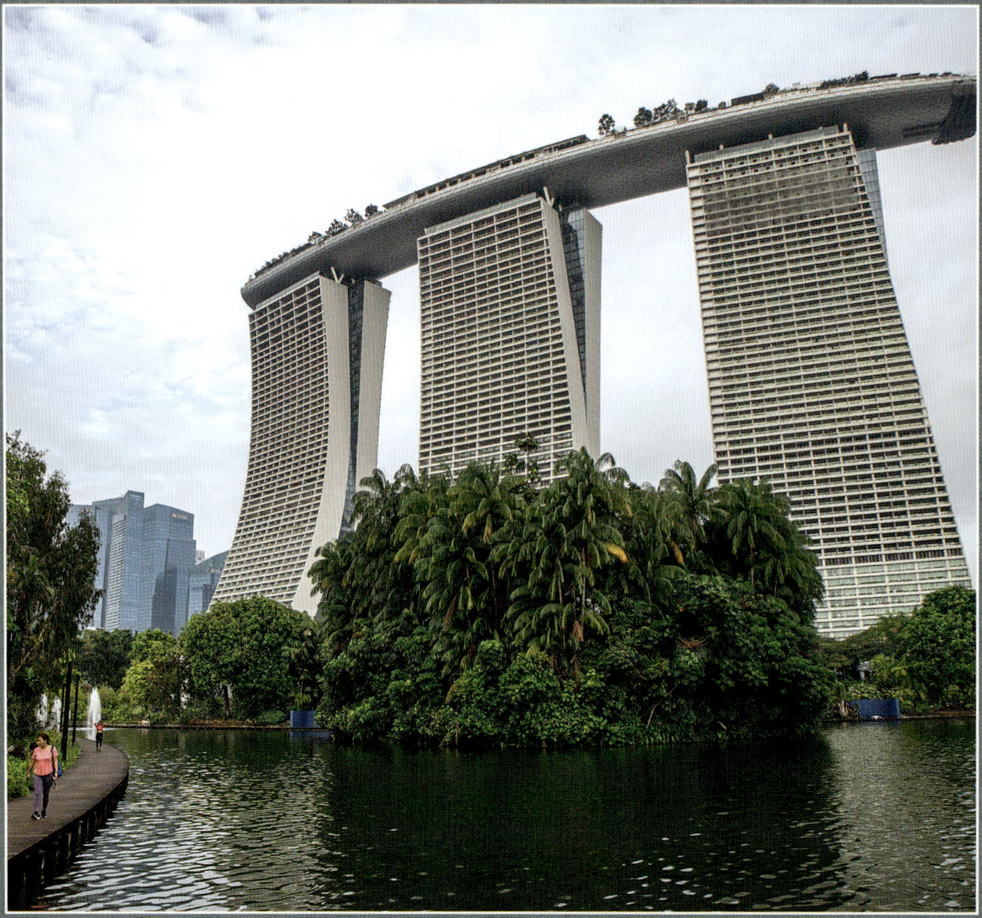

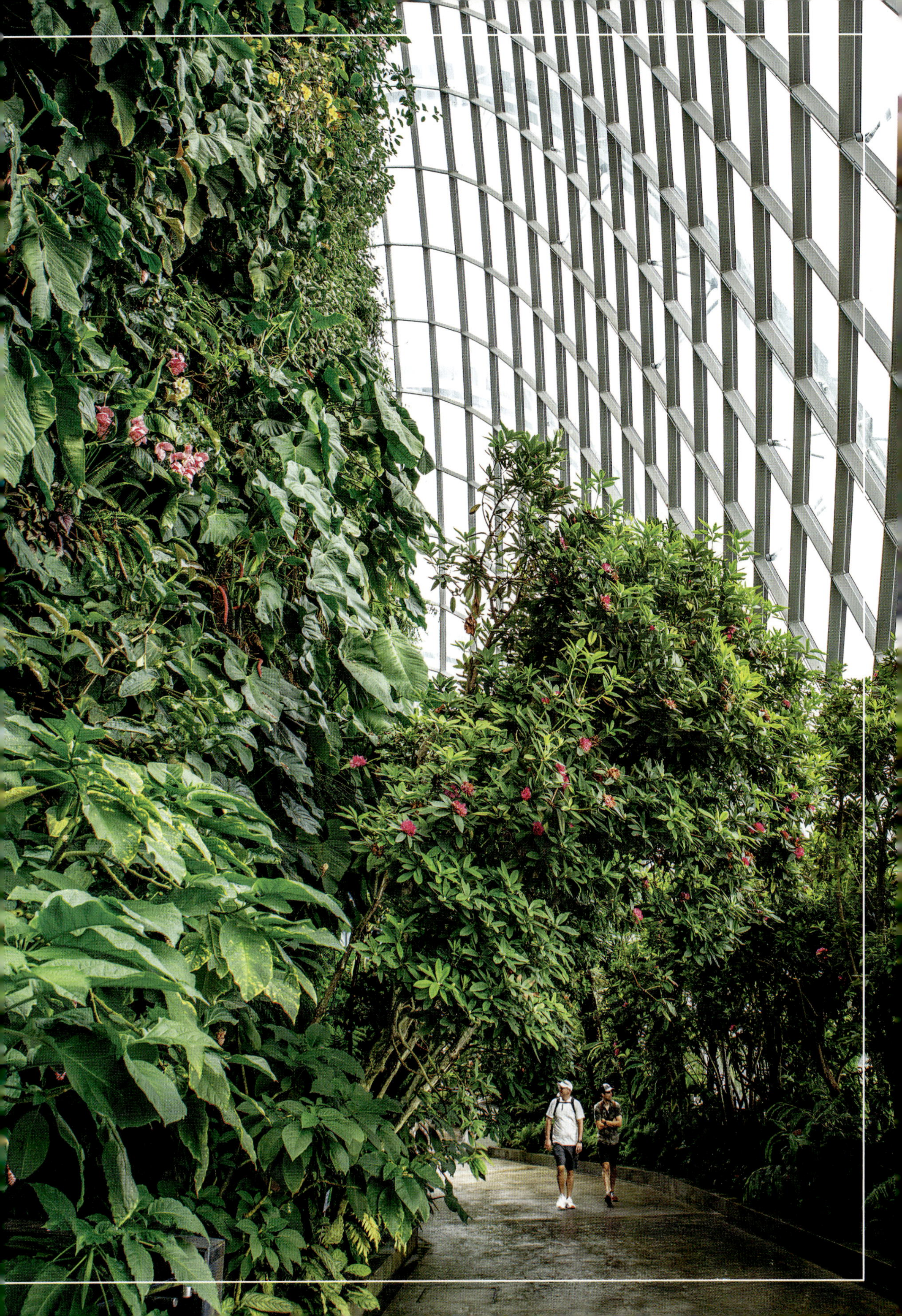

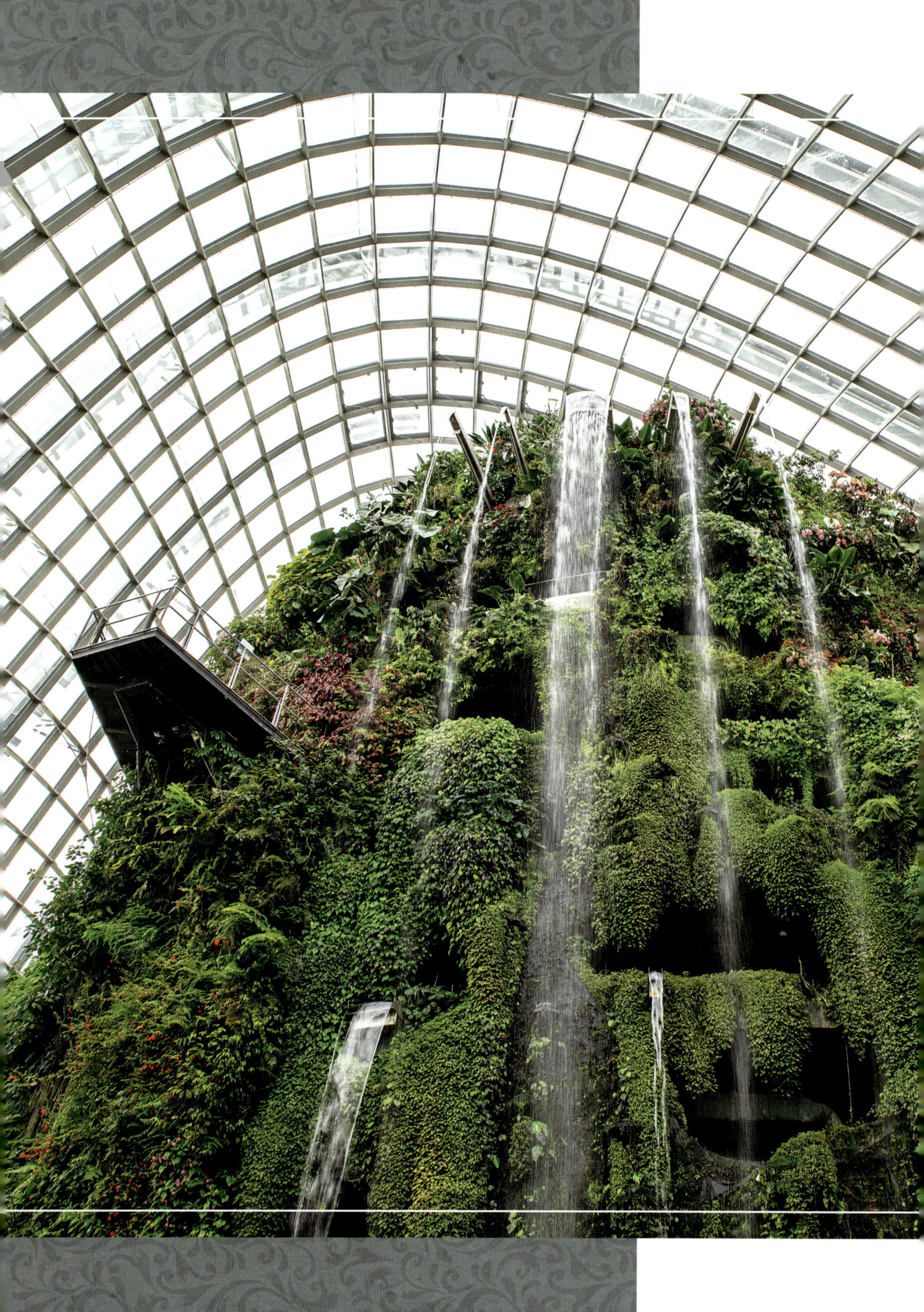

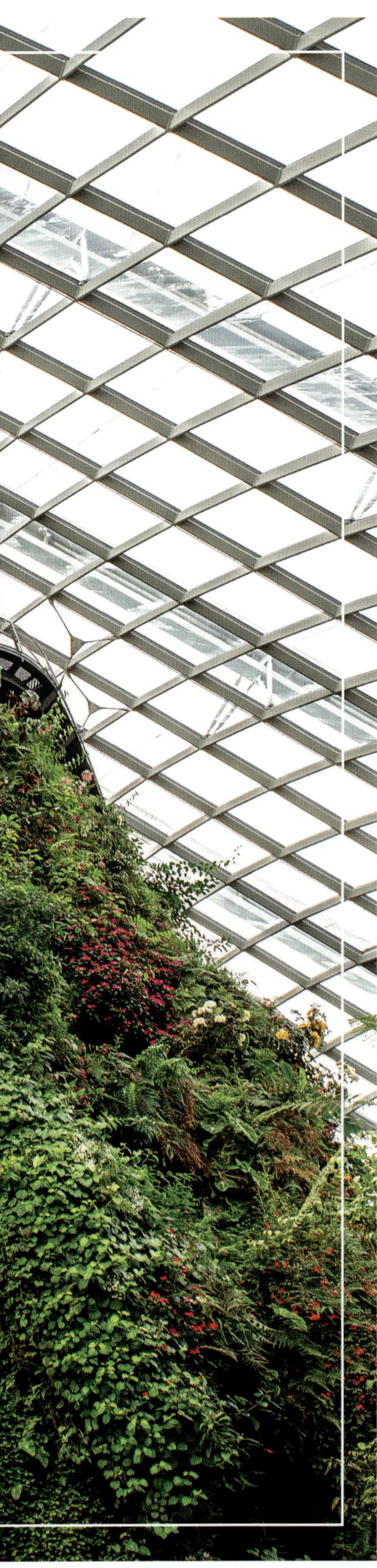

CREATING A GARDEN CITY

As of 2024, more than 40 percent of Singapore is covered by green space.[38] That compares favorably with the global city average of 14 percent, according to figures from the United Nations.[39] While there are no official world rankings on this topic, an MIT University study found Singapore to be the greenest city it analyzed.[40]

Singapore's uncommonly lush environment can be traced back to 1967, when its government began an ongoing campaign to create what it dubbed a "Garden City."[41] The remarkable success of this project is due to communal tree planting, hundreds of community gardens, investment in nature-based attractions like Gardens by the Bay, and thousands of volunteers who help maintain it all. In fact, many locals work for free at Gardens by the Bay, doing basic tasks like planting, weeding, and watering.[42]

TECHNOLOGY AND NATURE COMBINE

How is Gardens by the Bay furthering Singapore's grand green goals? Concealed amid its bold architecture are multiple eco-friendly technologies. For instance, its pair of conservatories stay cool in the sweltering Singapore climate partly due to spectrally selective glass. These glazed panels, which cover the roof of each structure, let natural light reach plants while reducing heat from sunrays. Further temperature control is provided by cold-water pipes beneath the domes and air-chilling systems powered by horticultural waste.

Renewable energy also drives the garden's nightly Garden Rhapsody light and sound show. Once the sun sets, onlookers snap photos of its luminous Supertrees, seven of which are topped by solar panels that power their illumination.

These structures cast rainbow reflections across the surface of adjacent lakes, which also hide green technologies. Scientists crafted Gardens by the Bay's interconnected lakes to function as a thriving ecosystem. Water from the botanic garden runs off into these lakes, where it is cleansed by aquatic plants such as reeds, which filter out phosphorus and nitrogen to minimize algae bloom. In turn, that fosters a healthy environment for thriving fish and dragonfly populations.

At Kingfisher Wetlands, meanwhile, more than two hundred mangrove trees reduce greenhouse gases and store blue carbon. In this way, they mimic the method by which rainforests combat climate change. Mangroves here also act as a protective habitat for birds and otters.[43]

LOOKING TO A GREENER FUTURE

Despite such notable progress, Singapore has not become complacent in their environmental efforts. Rather than leaning on its leafy laurels, this nation is doubling down. Opposite Gardens by the Bay, it is building Bay East Garden, a massive sister facility with a museum, walking trails, and a botanic garden boasting seven hundred thousand plants.[44]

Meanwhile, the nation is continuing to expand its nature park network. Singapore has an ongoing campaign to increase vegetation density in parks, restore natural habitats, create gardens atop its skyscrapers, and build pathways that connect existing green spaces.

This nation's four nature reserves—Labrador, Bukit Timah, Central Catchment, and Sungei Buloh—consist of key rainforests and habitats for native flora and fauna. So protective barriers are being built around them in the form of nature parks, which act as green buffers against urbanization.[45]

Complementing all of this is a bold project called OneMillionTrees. At least seventy-five thousand Singaporeans have contributed to this campaign, which aims to increase the city-state's total tree population by a million.[46]

Tourists, too, benefit from all of this environmentally minded labor. Many arrive in Singapore expecting to enter a futuristic urban environment dominated by concrete and glass. Instead, they are welcomed into one of the most verdant cities in existence. And at the center is Gardens by the Bay, which is not just a prominent attraction but a surprising center of eco-innovation.

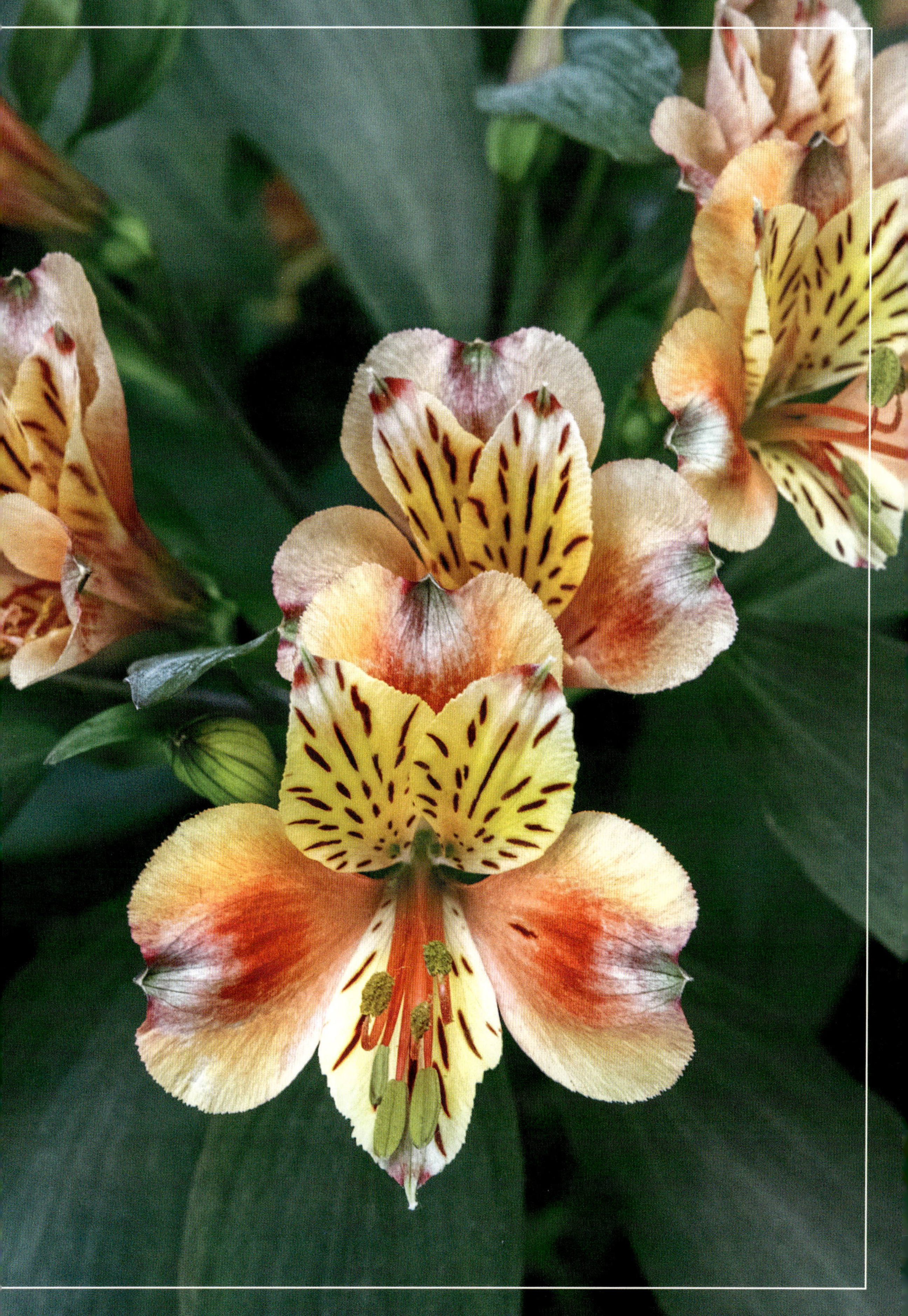

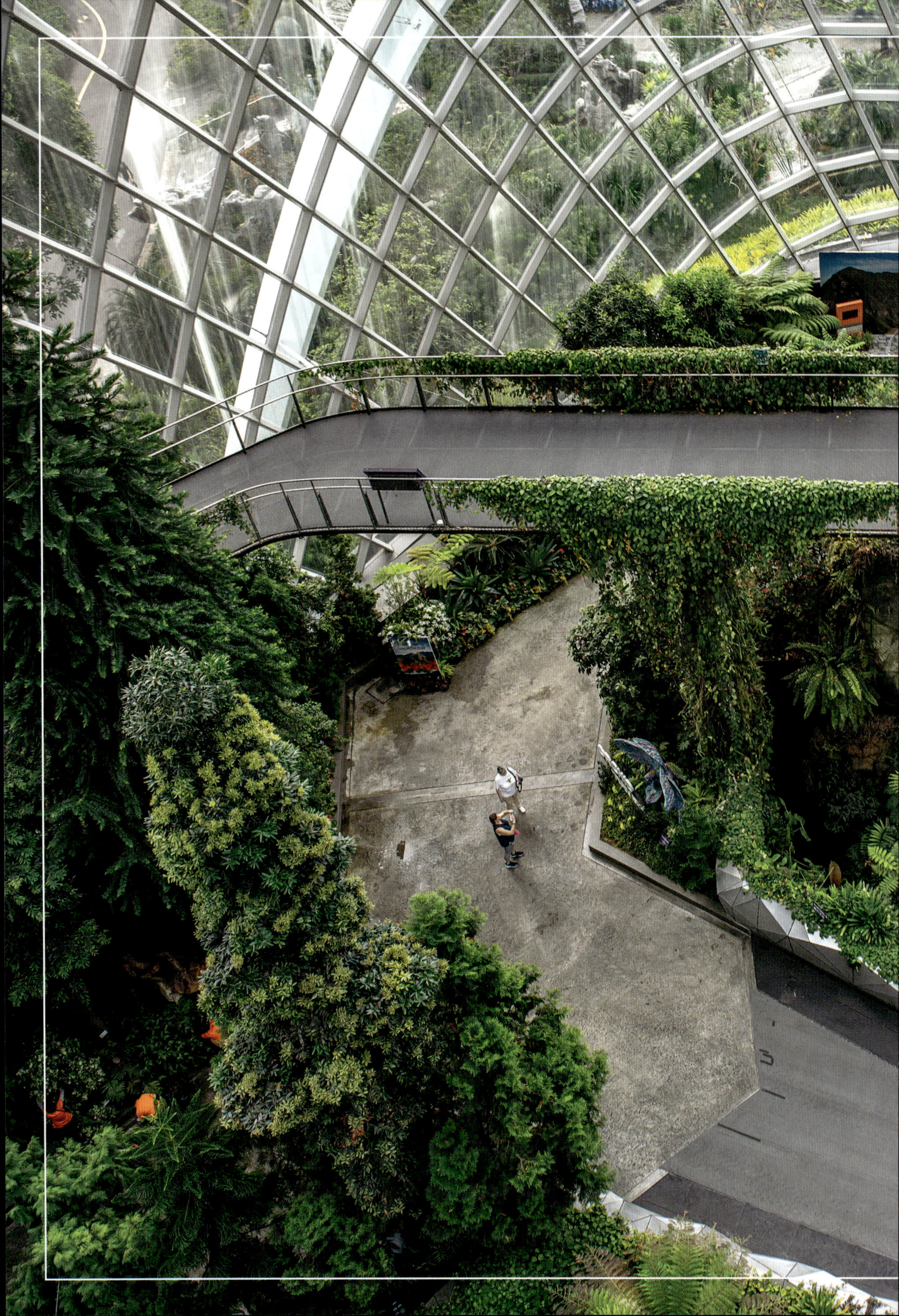

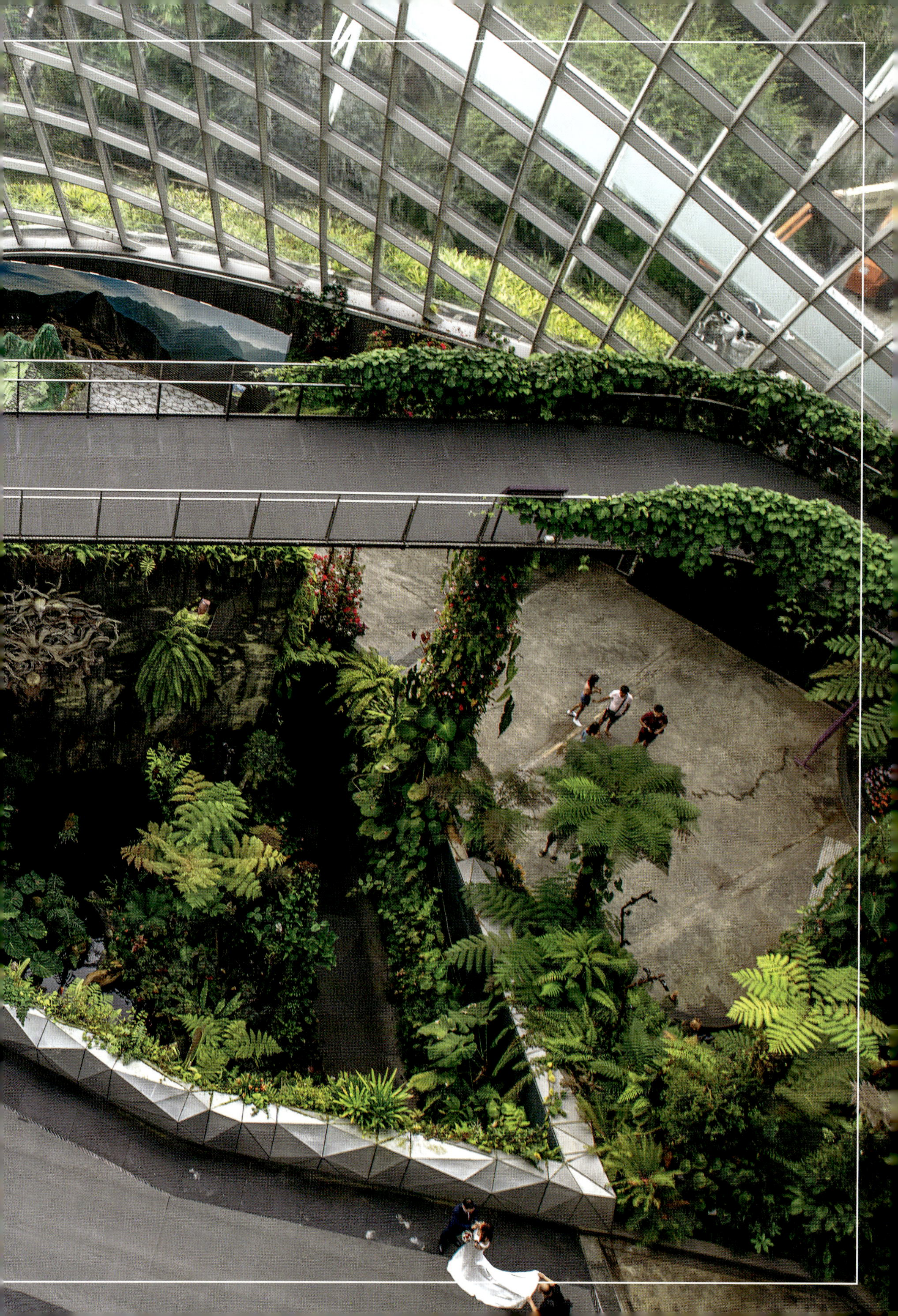

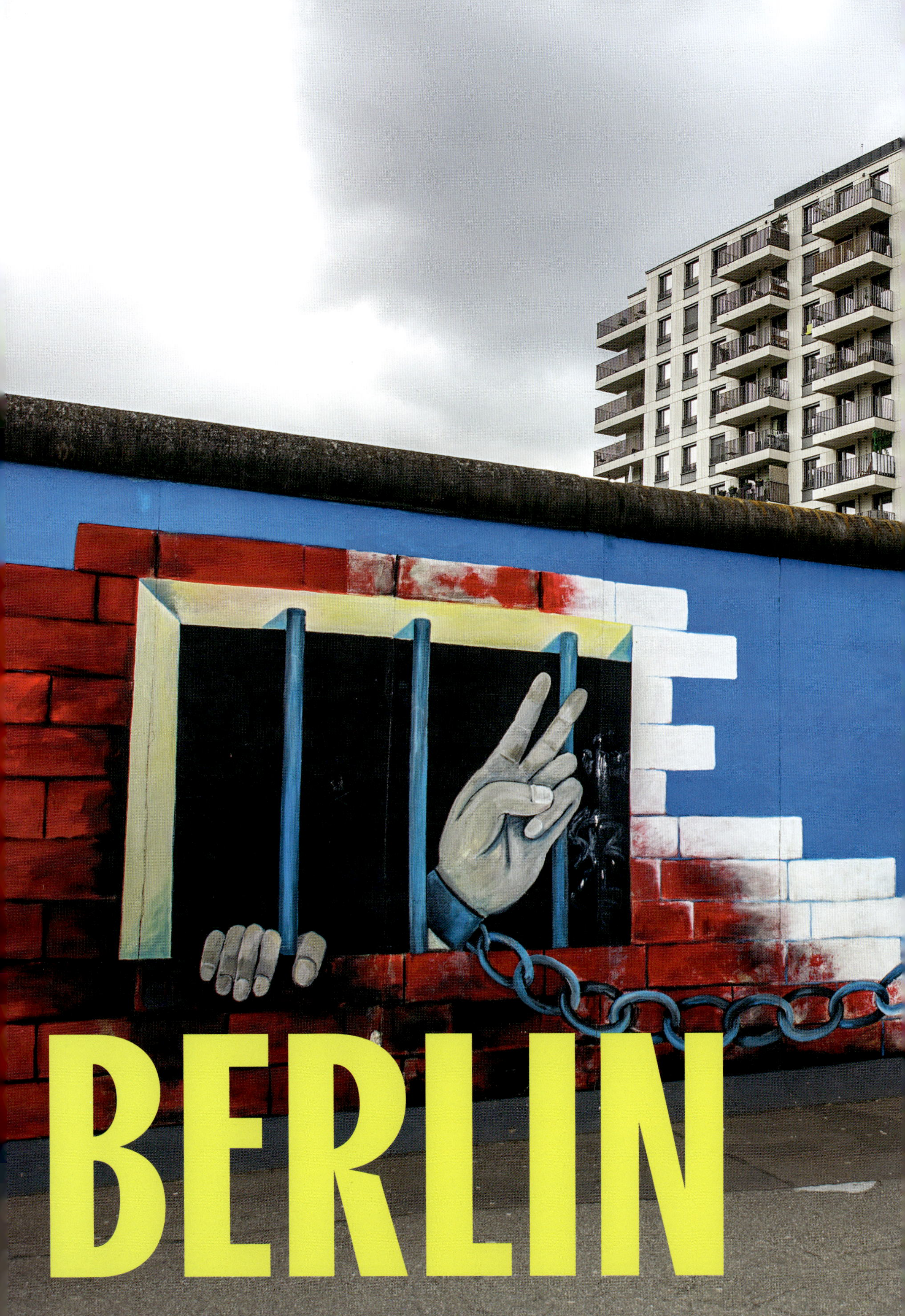
BERLIN

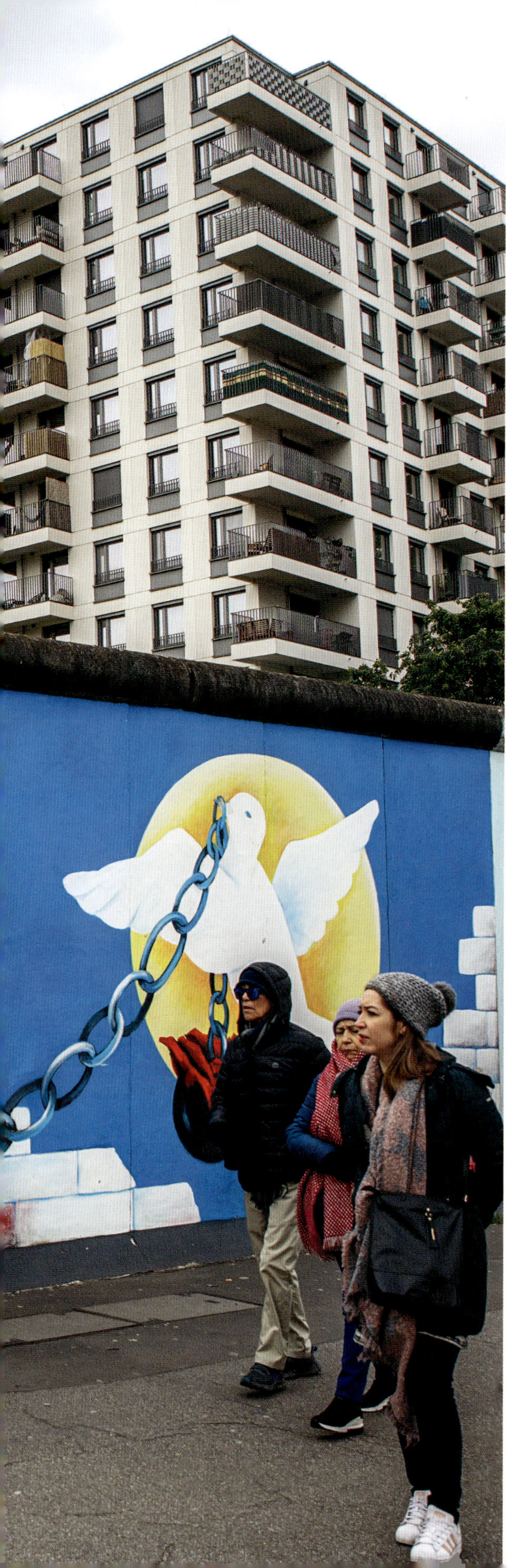

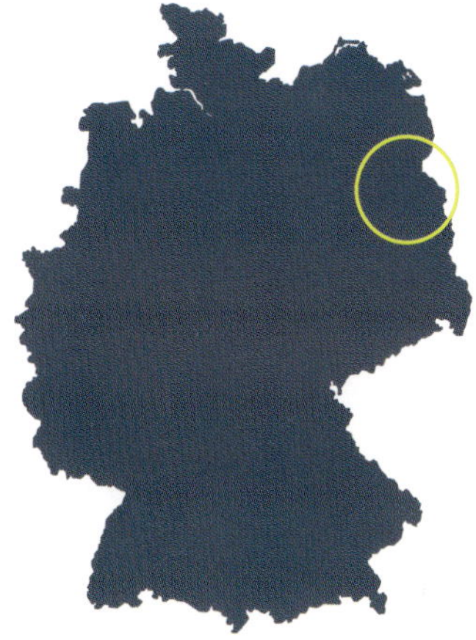

Painted on gray stone, a hand in shackles extends from behind prison bars to raise two fingers into the peace symbol. But the chain is not fixed to the cell. Rather, it is gripped in the beak of a white dove, whose wings are outstretched as it ascends into the sky.

Liberty sought from captivity. Resilience even in injustice. Hope in the face of despair. Such weighty symbolism marks this and countless more murals painted along the Berlin Wall, formerly a barrier built to divide a nation, now a global icon of humanity's fight for freedom.

From 1961 to 1989, this ninety-six-mile-long blockade split Berlin in two. It was erected by the communist state of East Germany to stem mass defections of its residents to the more liberal and modern West Germany. The Berlin Wall further fractured German society by separating families, and at least 140 people were killed or died at the wall.[47]

Most of those victims were East Germans trying to breach the barricade to West Germany when they were shot by East German soldiers.

Crossing the wall was a hugely difficult task. The Berlin Wall was, in fact, two walls that ran parallel to each other, in between which was a narrow ribbon of ground colloquially called the "death strip." As escapees sprinted across this no-man's-land, they had to evade attack dogs, thousands of land mines, and gunfire from East German soldiers manning three hundred guard towers.

Even still, many East Germans accepted those risks in pursuit of emancipation. Inspiring tales of daring escapes shine amid the gloomy history of the Berlin Wall. Yet one of the most extraordinary breaches of this fortification involved an American Civil Rights legend and remained secret for five decades.[48]

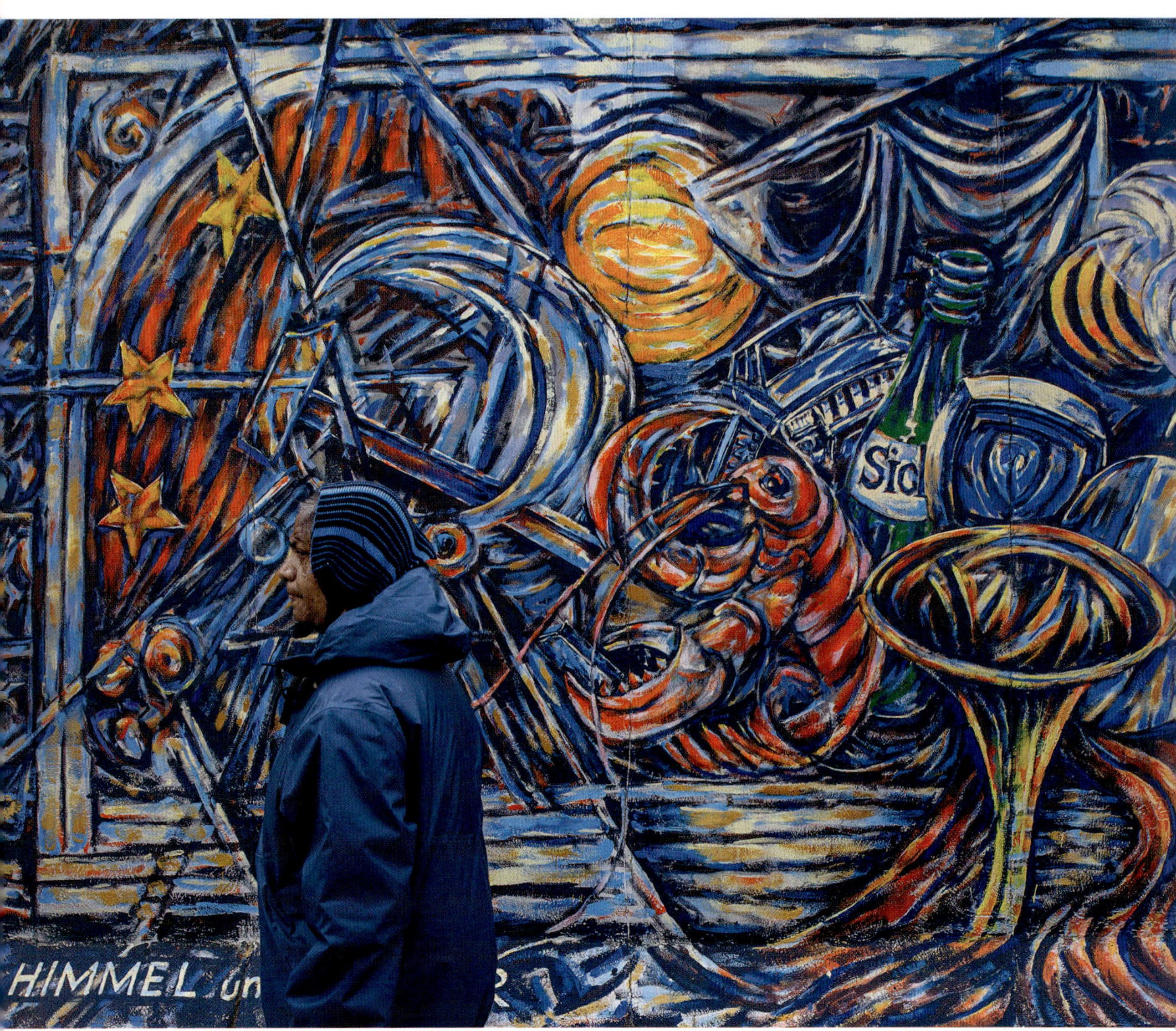

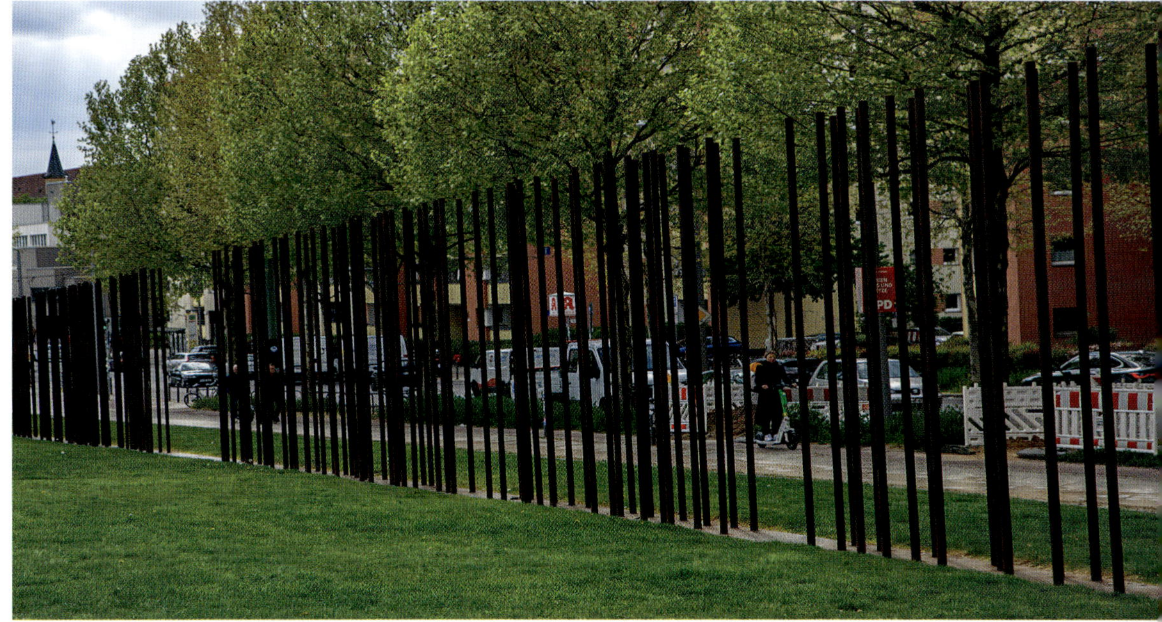

ORIGINS OF THE BERLIN WALL

Visitors to the Berlin Wall Memorial learn that the structure had its genesis in World War II. In 1949, four years after Germany's Nazi Party was defeated and its dictator, Adolf Hitler, met his doom, a rebuilding Germany was divided into four quarters by the Allied powers. Eventually two independent nations emerged: West Germany and East Germany. Soon this split became a focal point of the simmering Cold War. Wealthier, more progressive West Germany was supported by Western democracies, whereas impoverished and repressive East Germany had the backing of the communist Soviet Union and its allies.

Tensions came to a head in August 1961. Over the previous decade, more than two million intellectuals and skilled workers had left East Germany and headed west. Fearing a lasting blow to their economy, East German leaders decided they couldn't accept any more defections. So overnight, the East erected a lofty wire fence through Berlin's spine. Many Berliners awoke to find relatives and friends marooned on the opposite side of that barrier.[49]

TWO FRACTURED NATIONS

By 1964, the Berlin Wall divided an entire populace. Meanwhile, across the Atlantic Ocean, Martin Luther King Jr. had a contrasting purpose: He was trying to act as a bridge, connecting American communities riven by racism. This fostered a powerful link between the courageous activist and downtrodden Germans.

To King, Germany was a reflection of the subjugation long suffered by Black Americans. In return, many Germans drew inspiration from this American campaigner. Furthermore, West Germany was an ally of the US and grateful for the security presence of American soldiers, a large number of whom were Black. As a result, America's Civil Rights Movement was covered extensively by West German media. On both sides of the wall, Germans were buoyed by King's uplifting books and rousing speeches.[50]

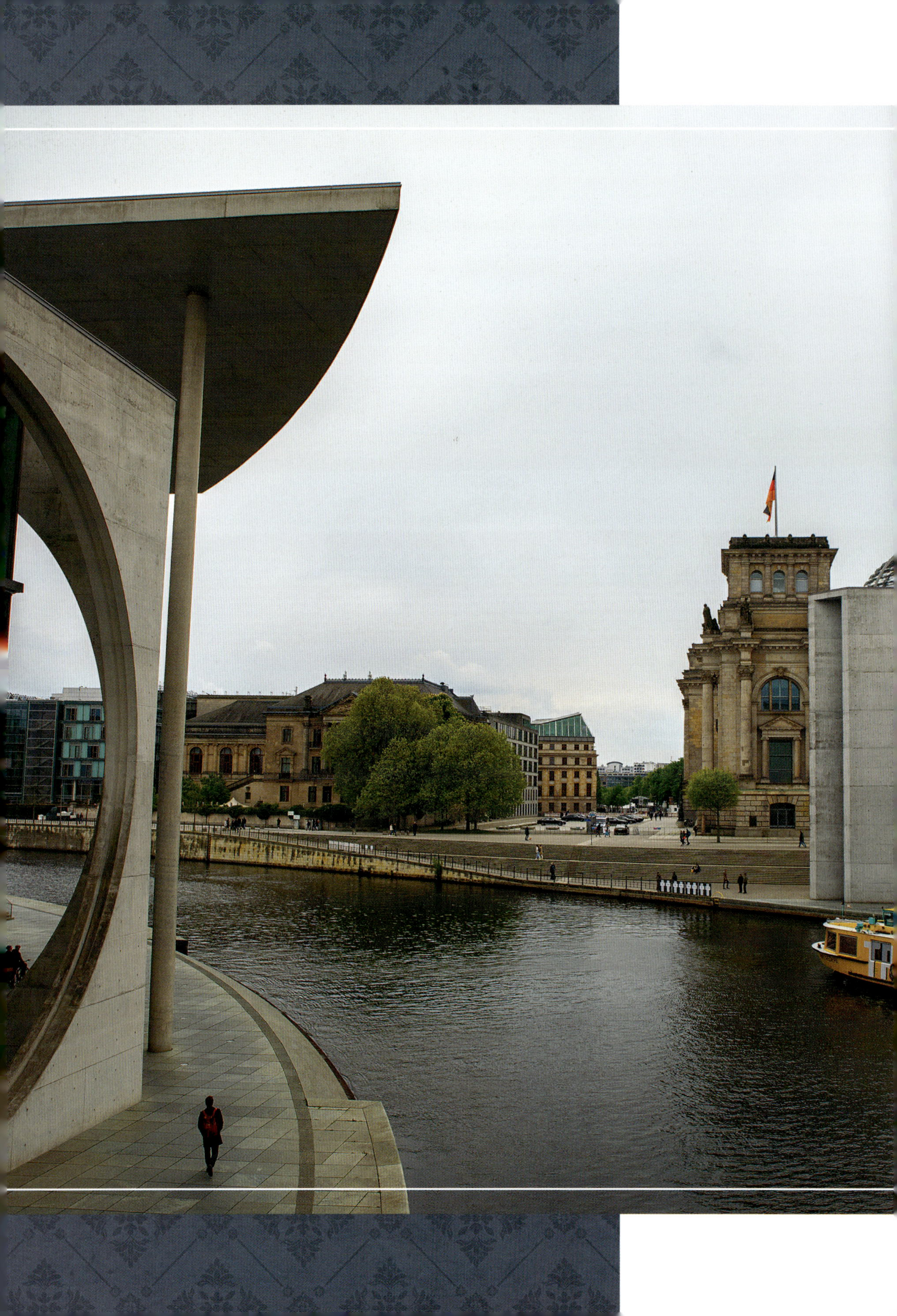

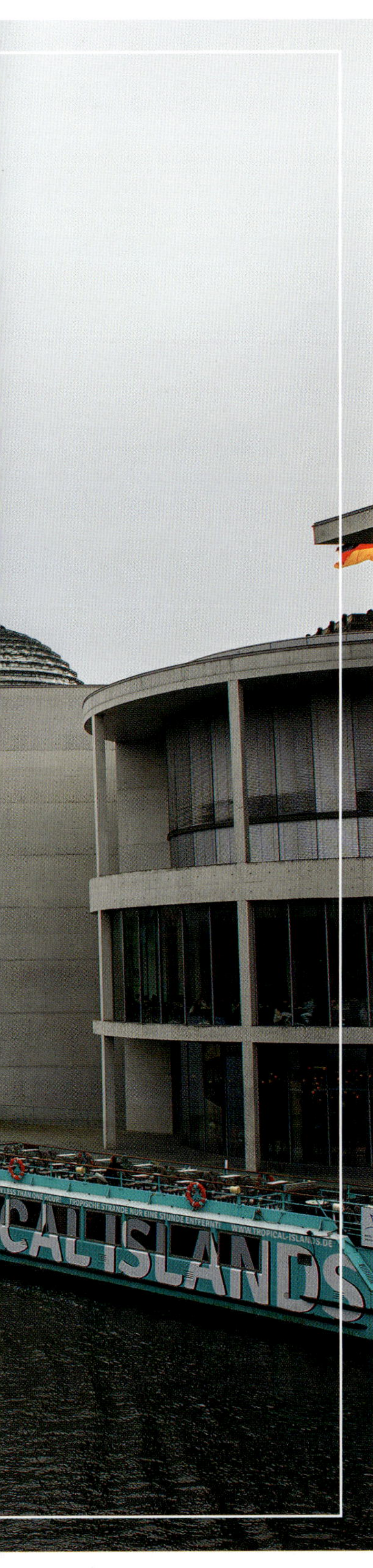

KING ARRIVES IN BERLIN

In September 1964, King landed in West Berlin, a city he'd never visited, unaware of the scale of his local celebrity. The Mayor of West Berlin, Willy Brandt, publicly embraced King and described him as an iconic freedom fighter who set an example for every community battling persecution.

The American then walked into a place with an evil history to paint it in shades of peace. Inside the Waldbühne amphitheater, a venue built by the Nazis, twenty thousand West Berliners listened as King drew parallels between the divisions harming the US and Germany. They clapped and cheered as he spoke of love, acceptance, and commonality.[51] King finished this triumphant appearance by categorizing Berlin as a "symbol of the divisions of men on the face of the earth."[52]

Yet this upbeat event was soon soured by sorrowful news. King heard that an East German solider had just shot someone as they tried to cross the wall into West Berlin. He asked to be taken to the site of this tragedy. There he and fellow Civil Rights hero Ralph Abernathy stood on an elevated spot, peering over the partition into East Berlin, where King had planned to visit later that evening. Although King would be gambling with his freedom, possibly even his life, he felt compelled to smuggle supplies of optimism across the border to a needy people.[53]

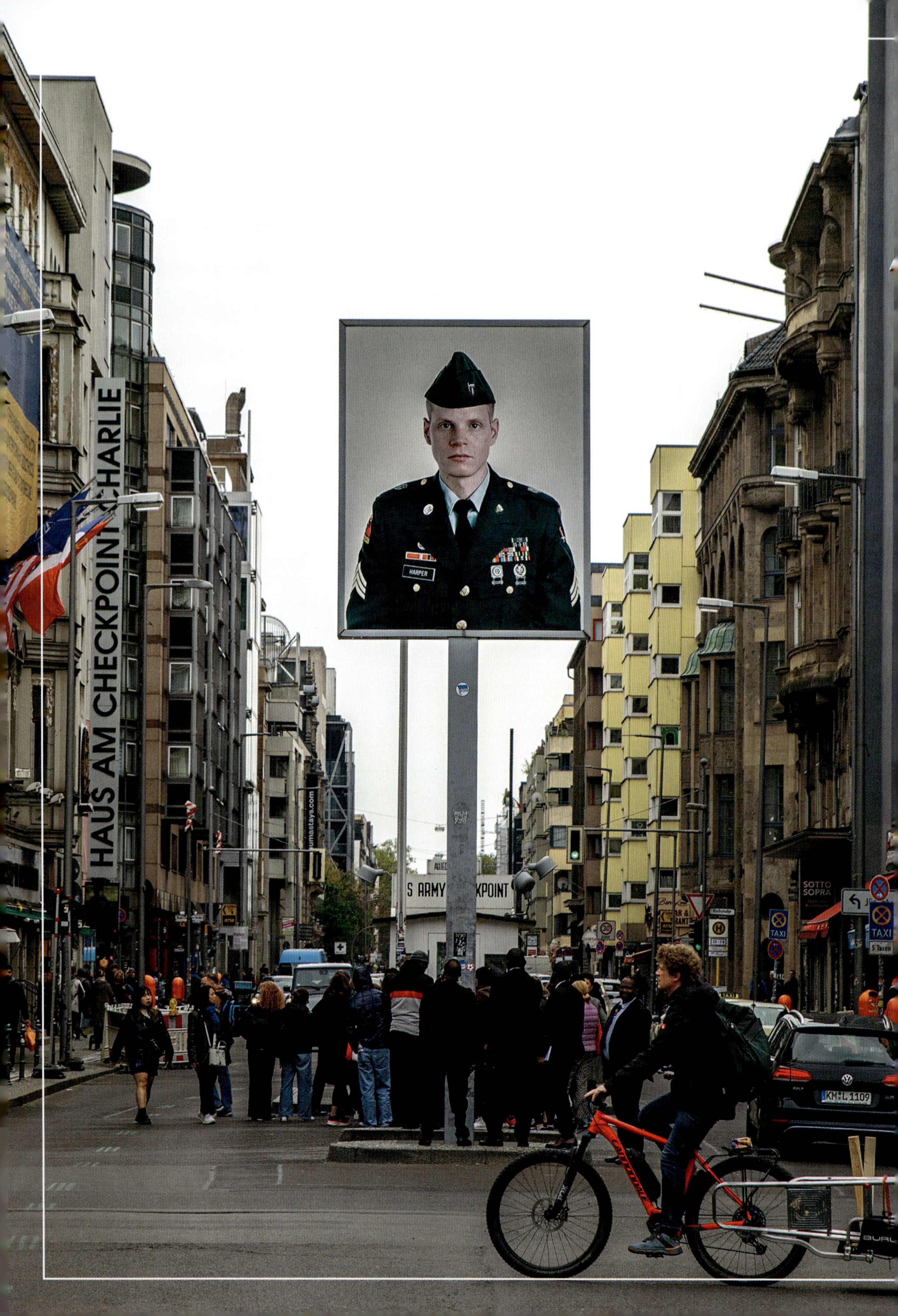
HAUS AM CHECKPOINT CHARLIE
HARPER
SOTTO
SOPRA
TAXI
TAXI

SNEAKING THROUGH THE BERLIN WALL

According to declassified documents from the Central Intelligence Agency, King was invited to give a speech in East Berlin by Heinrich Grüber. King accepted the invitation of this former church pastor from East Germany, who had escaped to the West. Grüber appeared to have gotten word to his connections in East Germany, where excited whispers about the American's upcoming visit circulated.[54]

Soon these rumors also reached US government officials. When they learned of King's plan to breach the wall, they confiscated his passport to try to prevent him from entering East Germany. He was warned that, as an outspoken political figure, his safety was not guaranteed in East Germany and his presence could stoke controversy.

Regardless, King intended to keep his promise. So that evening, he went to the Berlin border crossing, Checkpoint Charlie, where foreigners and West Germans could request to pass through the wall. King was accompanied by his interpreter, Alcyone Scott, a twenty-four-year-old West German literature graduate.[55]

They told the checkpoint guards that King was a US citizen and presented the only identification he had left, an American Express credit card. After some negotiating, this was accepted as proof of his nationality. King and Scott were allowed into East Germany.

With Scott's help, King quietly made his way through rundown East Berlin to St. Mary's Church, a red-brick gothic building that is Berlin's oldest parish church, dating to the 1200s. Waiting inside its spacious prayer hall was an eager audience, hoping the rumors of King's visit were true.[56]

Though this large church was filled to its brim, another two thousand East Germans lined the building outside. After transfixing the crowd with his passion and eloquence, King did the same at nearby Sophien Church. During both speeches, he reminded the East Germans in attendance that the barriers around them were only temporary.

"There is no East, no West, no North, no South, but one great fellowship of love throughout the whole, wide world," his voice bellowed. Fortunately, the East German government decided against breaking up these events or detaining King. Why they made that choice remains unclear. Historical accounts of King's bold journey also don't outline whether any East Germans were punished for attending or helping to organize his sermons.

What is documented is that after about three hours in East Berlin, King slipped through the city in the darkness and returned to Checkpoint Charlie. There he retrieved his American Express card, which had been held by border guards. He then reentered West Germany, completing a daring foray across a deadly barrier, and leaving behind legions of East Germans buoyed by his inspirational words.[57]

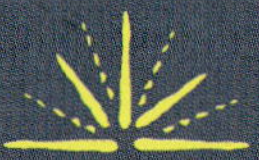

After King's extraordinary visit, another twenty-five years passed before the Berlin Wall was demolished in 1989. Several sections of it remain and collectively have become Berlin's defining landmark.

No section is more evocative than the East Side Gallery, where hundreds of artworks emblazon a nearly one-mile stretch of the original barricade. This art was conceived amid Germany's rebirth. Days after the wall came down, more than a hundred artists from twenty-one countries started decorating this riverfront remnant. Today the East Side Gallery is a heritage site, the longest surviving part of the wall, and a captivating open-air museum.[58]

For visitors looking to see where the wall once stood, they can follow the Berlin Wall Trail. This walking and cycling path weaves past Berlin Wall monuments, memorials, and museums, as well as former watchtowers, border crossings, and documentation centers. To make it more manageable, the trail is split into fourteen sections, each of which is clearly signposted and can be reached easily via public transport.

In the downtown area are several prominent Berlin Wall sites. Brandenburg Gate is appealing in its own right, a regal stone structure at the east entrance of Tiergarten, the city's biggest green space. For almost thirty years, Germans couldn't access this monument, which was marooned in an exclusion zone. After the Berlin Wall crumbled, more than one hundred thousand people gathered there to rejoice at its reopening.[59] A short walk south of that gate is Potsdamer Platz, where original slabs of the wall sit at the feet of glimmering skyscrapers. Just east of that busy plaza awaits Checkpoint Charlie. People queue for photos in front of its small booth, which was the most famous border crossing during the Berlin Wall era, and the same site where King crossed.[60]

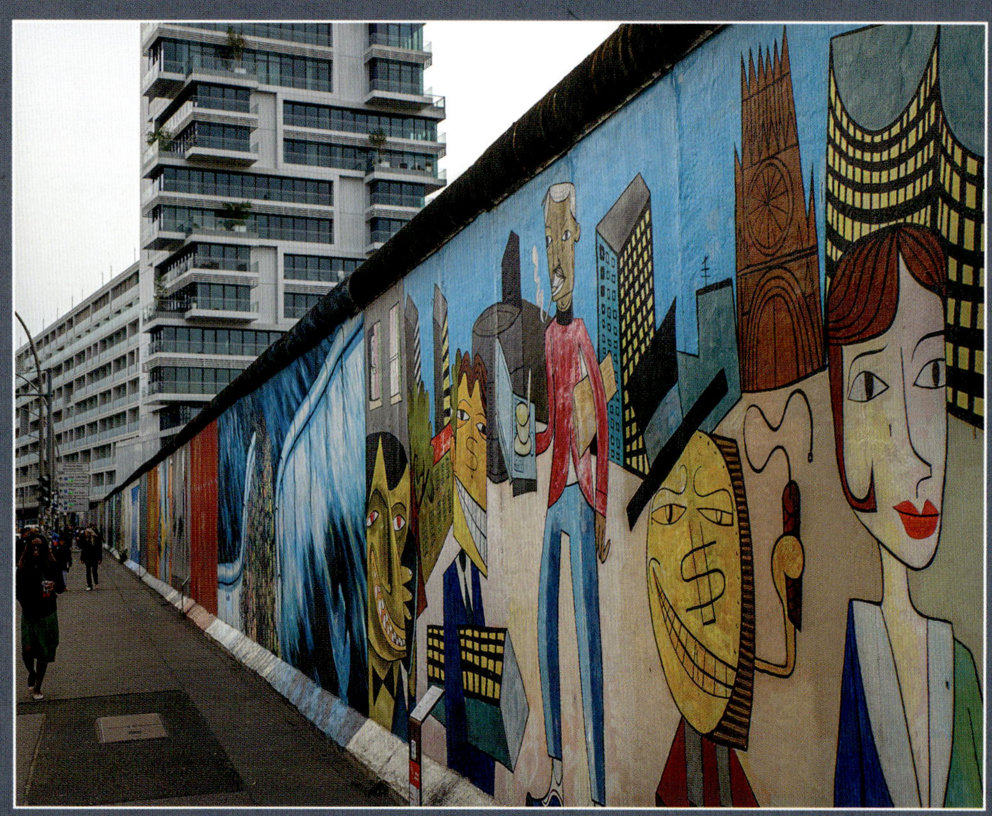

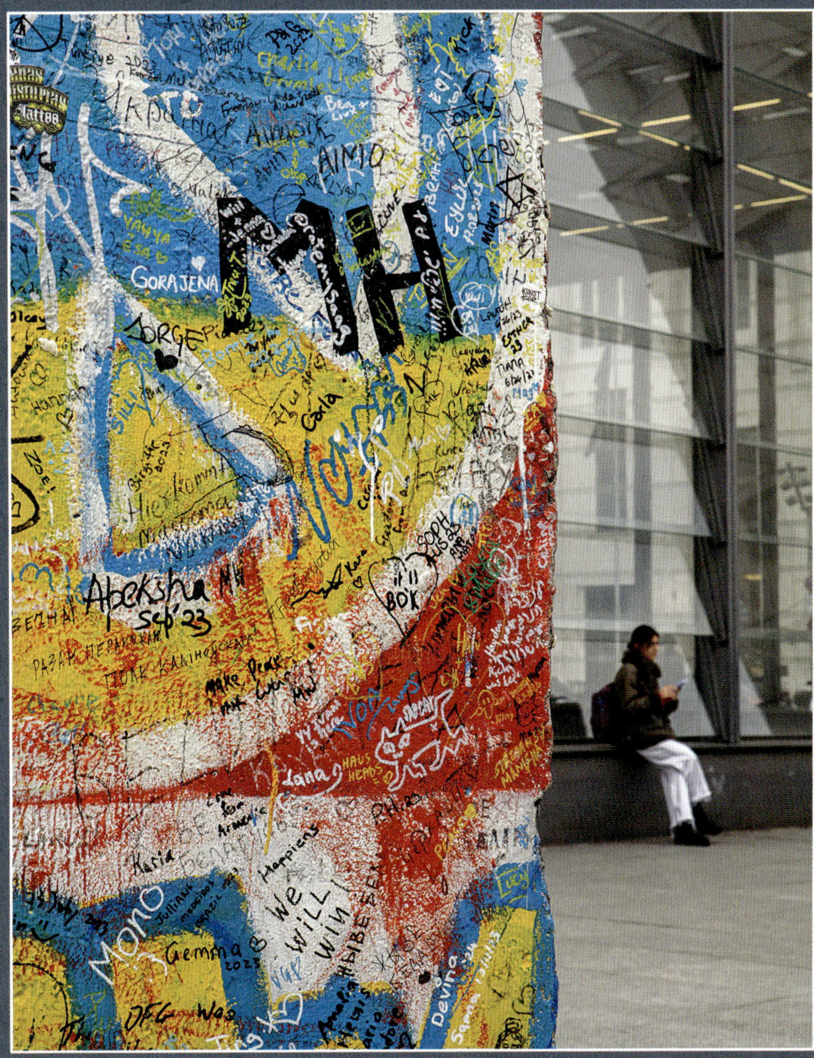

The trail is, at turns, serene and unsettling. Some sections are filled with soothing scenery, like the glassy lakes and flower-filled fields of Babelsberg Park, the tranquil forest of Bieselheide, and the wildlife sanctuary of Tegeler Fliess.

Other sections of the trail jolt visitors with their grim history, revealed via text and photo displays. Twenty-nine spots along the route tell the haunting biographies of Germans killed at the Berlin Wall.[61] That human toll is further detailed on a shorter, alternative trail, called the Berlin Wall History Mile. Along the History Mile are thirty-two stops, marked by signs and historical images that explain the wall's origins, impact, and downfall.[62]

None of the stops is more impactful than the Berlin Wall Memorial. This open-air site has a cluster of art installations, photo galleries, history exhibitions, a chapel dedicated to victims, and a five-story former watchtower. Its location is deeply significant because, in 1961, TV audiences worldwide saw distressing footage from this very spot, Bernauer Strasse, where the Berlin Wall directly divided East and West Berlin. Desperate Germans were shown scaling barbed wire fences, or climbing down the sides of buildings to try to cross the newly erected wall.[63]

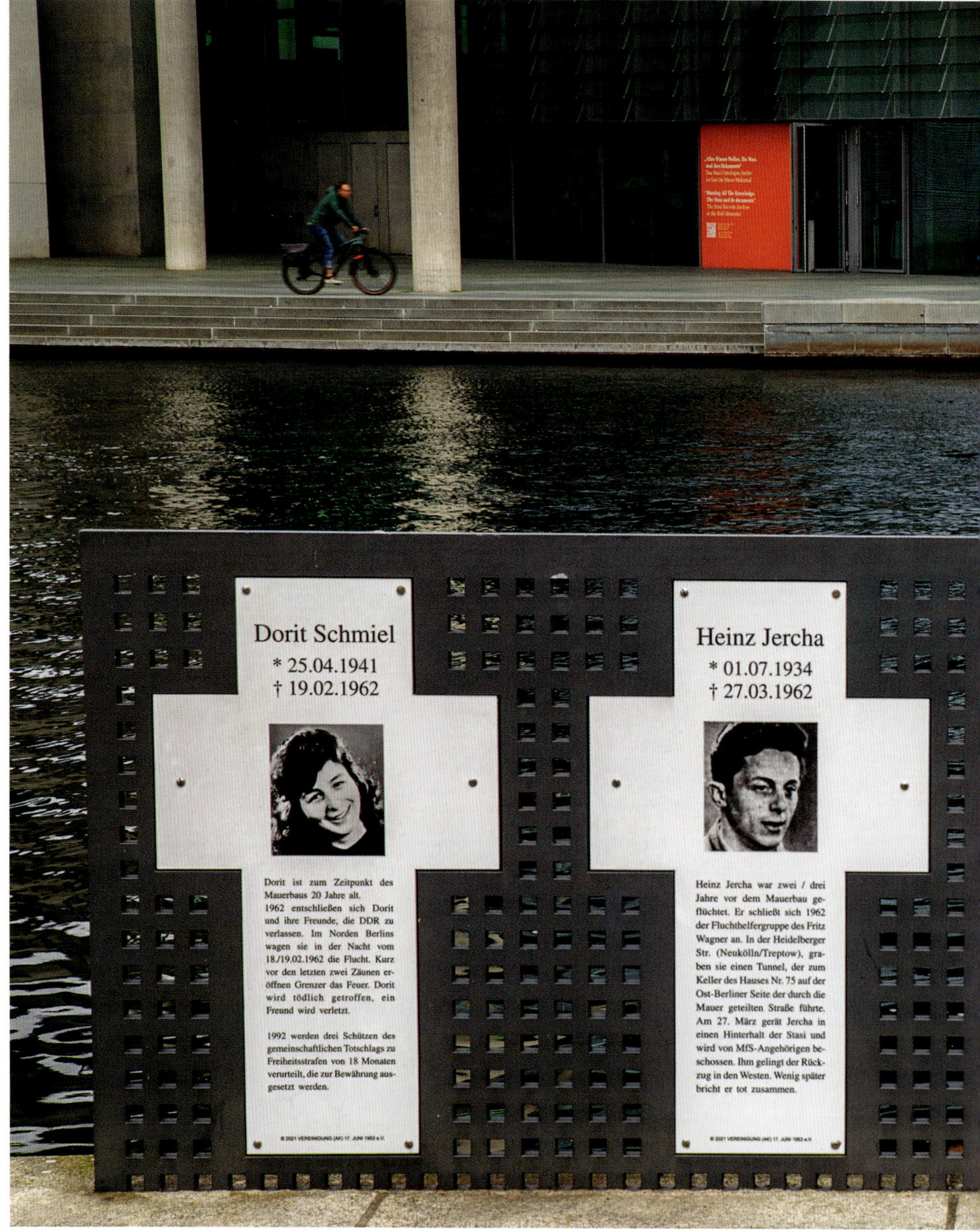

A DEADLY LEGACY

Many East Germans perished attempting the same crossing King made. They are commemorated along the River Spree through the ultra-modern cityscape of downtown Berlin. There, eight white crosses are fixed to a railing. Each one bears the photo, name, and story of a German

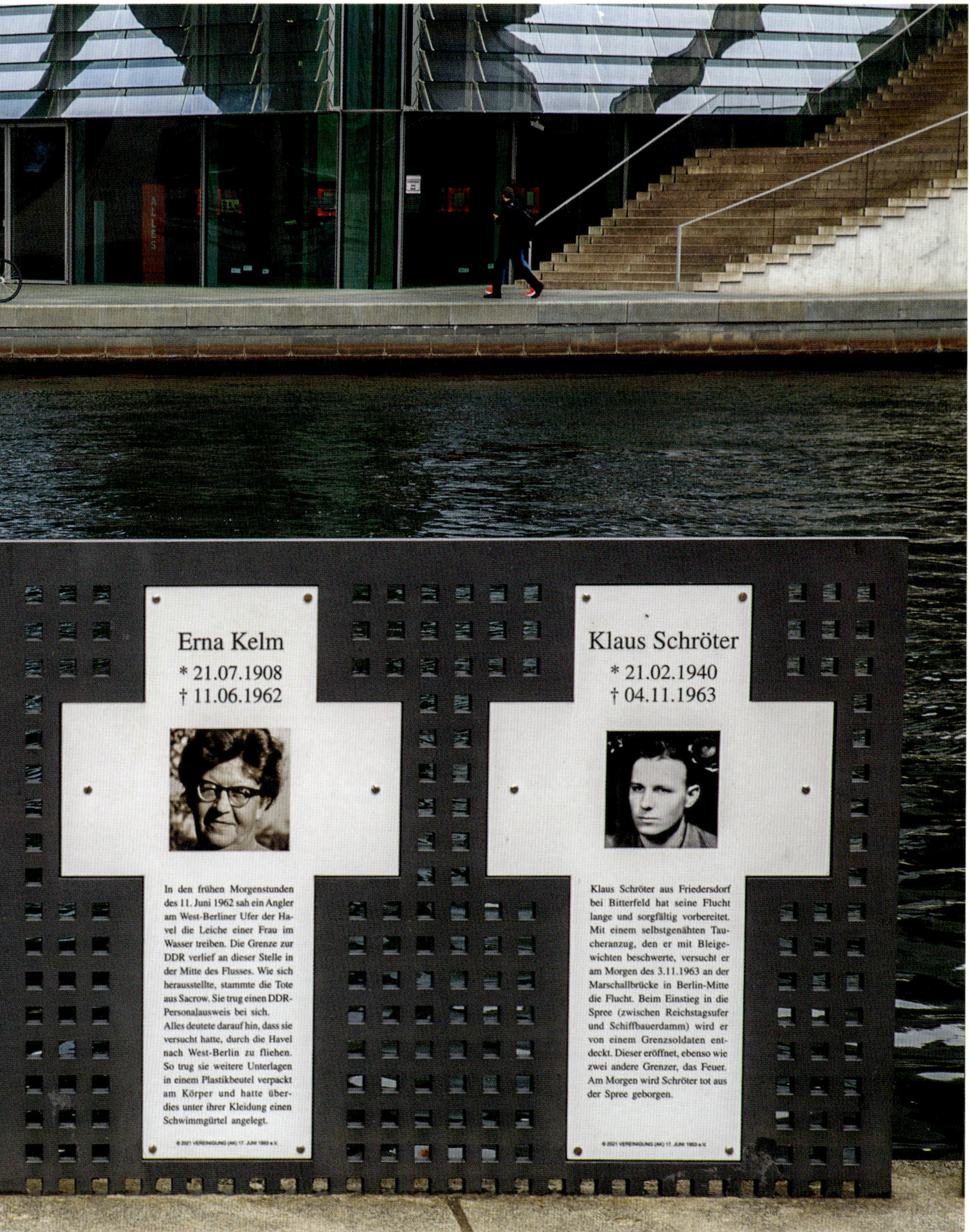

murdered while trying to flee over the Berlin Wall. Their harrowing tales illuminate the depth of tragedy that engulfed a divided Germany. They also underscore King's bravery during his long-secret breach of the Berlin Wall. A bold gamble, made in the name of peace.[64]

ISTANBU

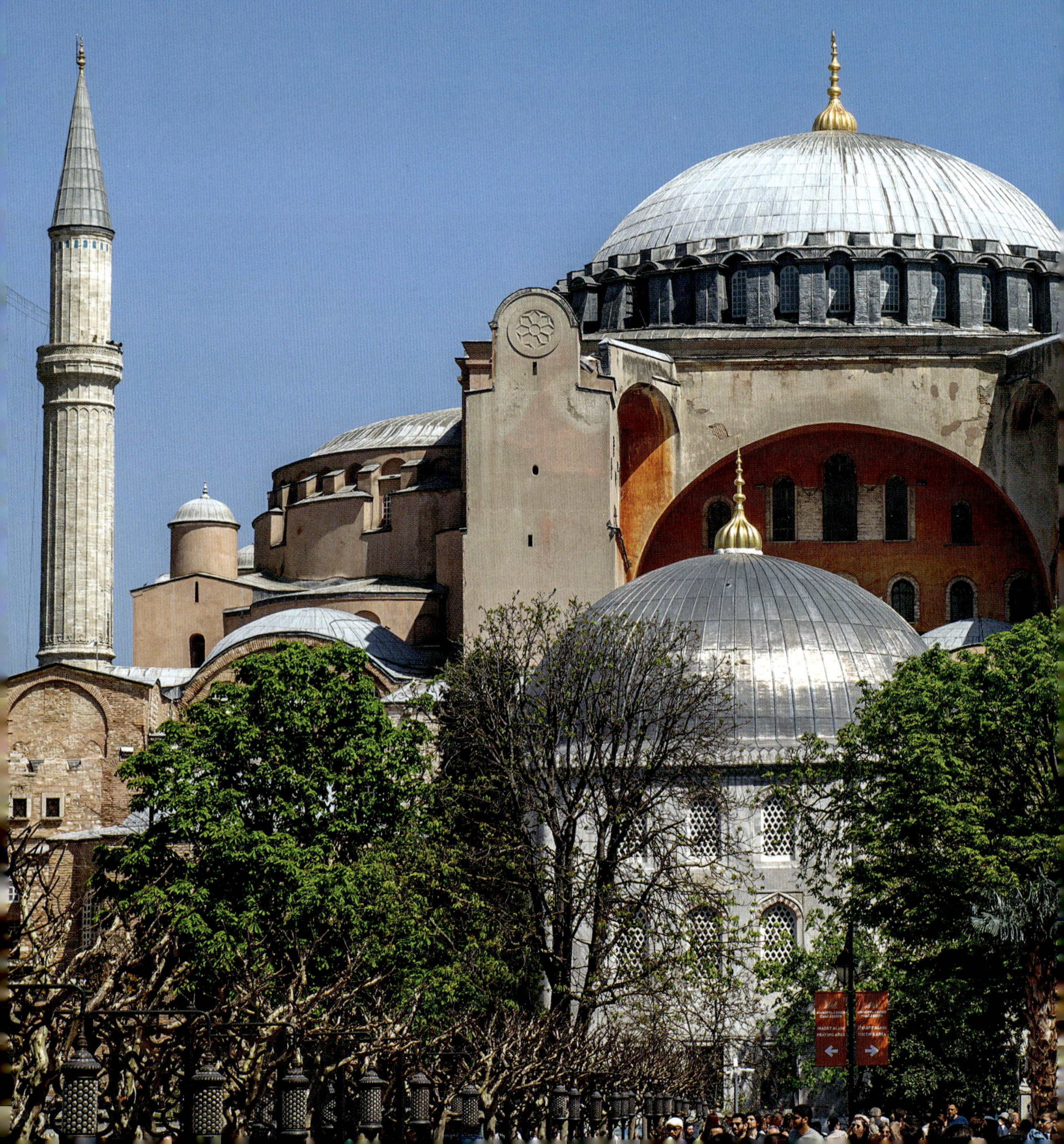

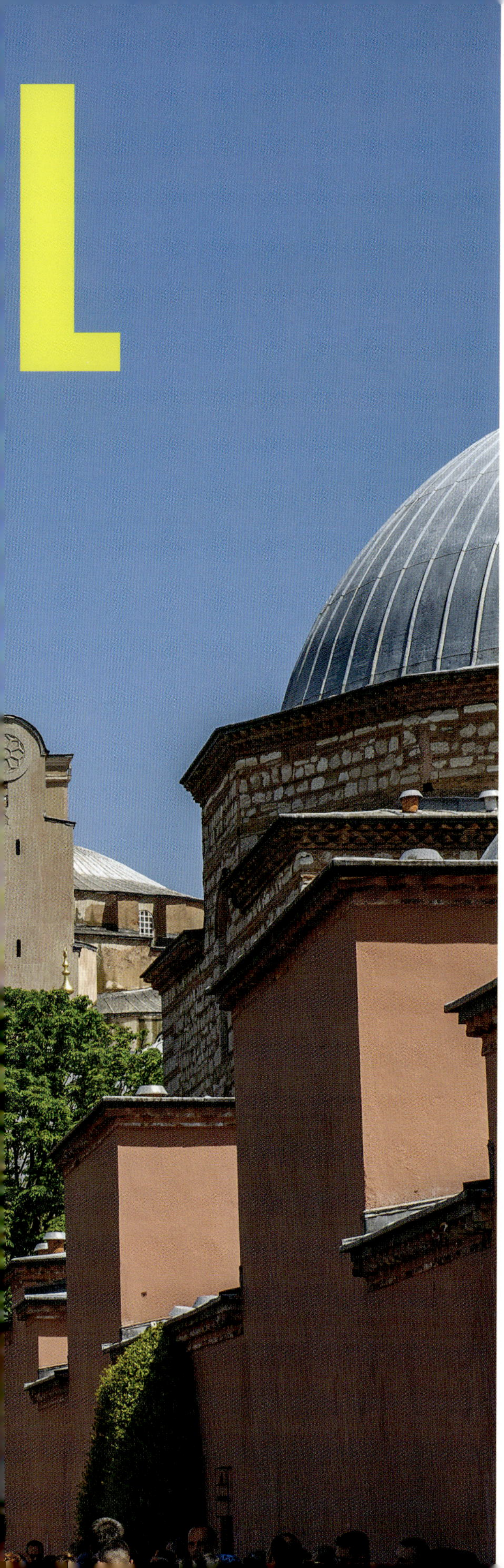

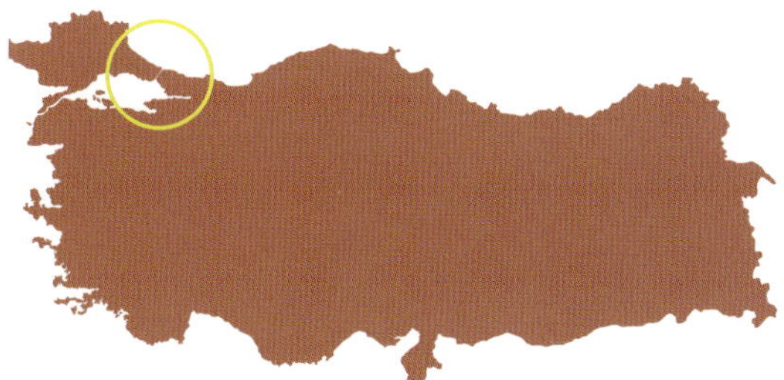

Nearly fifteen hundred years ago, as craftsmen were erecting Istanbul's iconic Hagia Sophia, the sun disappeared from view. Locals watched the sky, first expecting, then hoping, and finally praying for full daylight to return.

Days passed, then weeks and months, as citizens of the city then known as Constantinople went about their lives in permanent near-darkness. Each day, the light shone dimly through a mysterious fog that enveloped the city. The persistent gloom blanketing Constantinople caused unseasonable cold, drought, famine, disease outbreaks, and a mounting death toll.

Imagine how you'd feel waking to find the world plunged into darkness. Even today, when academics are able to clarify nearly all natural phenomena, such an event would prompt panic around the globe. Consider, then, the impact of a hidden sun in an era without scientific explanation.[65]

What caused this curse of darkness?

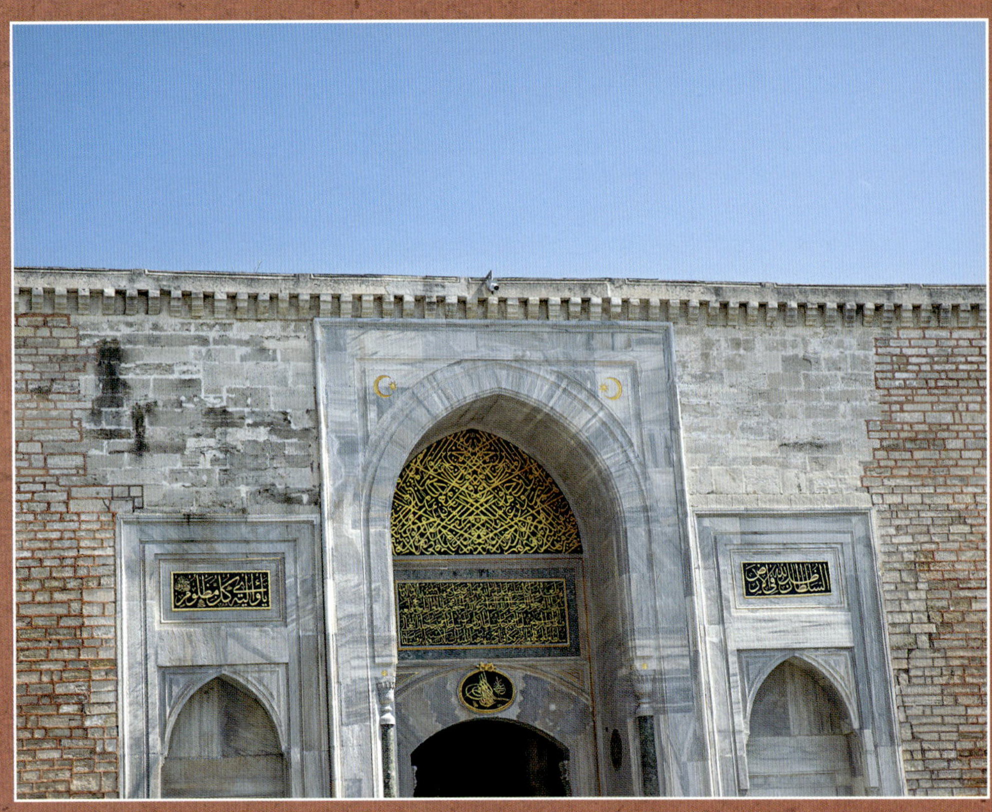

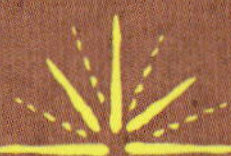

Now home to nearly sixteen million people, modern-day Istanbul is one of the most populous cities in the Middle East. Interestingly, the city straddles two continents: The western part of Istanbul is in Europe, while its eastern section is in Asia. This division is formed by the Bosporus Strait, which connects the Black Sea and the Sea of Marmara and slices through central Istanbul. This twenty-five-hundred-year-old city was known for sixteen centuries as Constantinople, named for Roman Emperor Constantine the Great, who declared "Constantinopolis" as the new capital of his empire. The city's name was changed to Istanbul in 1930.[66]

WILL THE SUN EVER RETURN?

The enduring dusk obscured Hagia Sophia's blooming beauty. Construction on the colossal structure had begun in AD 532, four years before the sun vanished. It was designed to be the world's largest church: a crowning achievement for Emperor Justinian I of the Byzantine Empire, which had its capital at Constantinople.

Hagia Sophia was at least three-quarters complete when the bizarre catastrophe unfolded. For the next eighteen months, as natural light remained scarce, Hagia Sophia's army of craftsmen had to work by lamplight.[67]

Constantinople was a nightmarish setting in AD 536 according to Byzantine scholar Procopious, who lived through the darkness. "It came about during this year that a most dread portent took place," he wrote. "For the sun gave forth its light without brightness, like the moon, during this whole year, and it seemed exceedingly like the sun in eclipse."[68] Roman politician Cassiodorus described the lack of light this way: "We marvel to see no shadows of our bodies at noon."[69]

Further descriptions of this eerie environment came from twelfth-century chronicler Michael the Syrian. He wrote of the hidden sun that "each day it shone for about four hours, and still this light was only a feeble shadow. Everyone declared that the sun would never recover its original light. The fruits did not ripen, and the wine tasted like sour grapes."[70]

For eighteen months, this was the dim reality of those living in Constantinople.

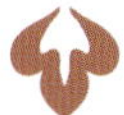

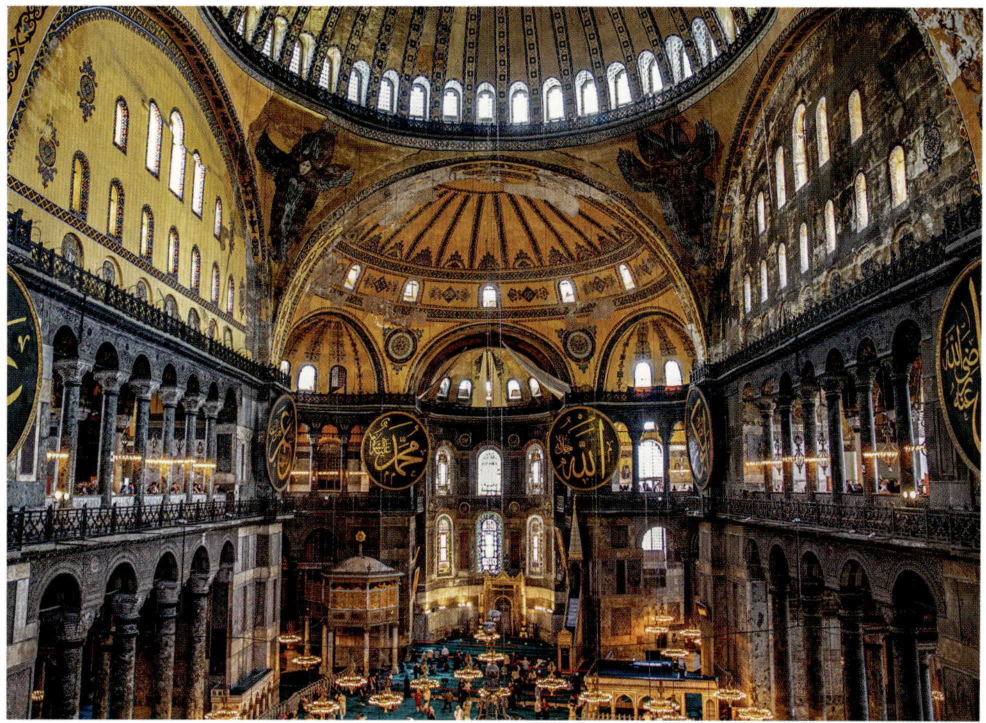

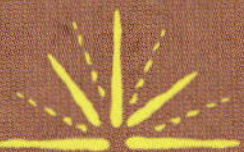

Hagia Sophia now stands as both a marvel of Istanbul and an icon of the city's tumultuous history. When the building as we know it today was constructed, Christianity was the chief religion of the Byzantine Empire, which formed the eastern half of the Roman Empire and commanded parts of what are now Turkey, Greece, southern Italy, and the Balkans.[71] The original church where Hagia Sophia stands was constructed by Constantine I in AD 325, but was ravaged in subsequent decades by fires. Seeing an opportunity to create a monumental replacement, Byzantine Emperor Justinian I decided to construct what was then the world's largest Christian house of worship.

So splendid was the finished product that Hagia Sophia overshadowed the adjacent Great Palace of Constantinople. These days, the landmark eclipses a different imperial complex: the fifteenth-century Topkapi Palace, which sits just north of Hagia Sophia.

After Constantinople was conquered by the Islamic Ottoman Empire in the mid-1400s, Hagia Sophia became a mosque, with many of its Christian decorations removed and replaced by Islamic iconography. Its function changed again in the mid-1930s, when the building was secularized and began operating as a museum. In 2020, Turkish president Recep Tayyip Erdoğan converted Hagia Sophia back to a functioning mosque.[72]

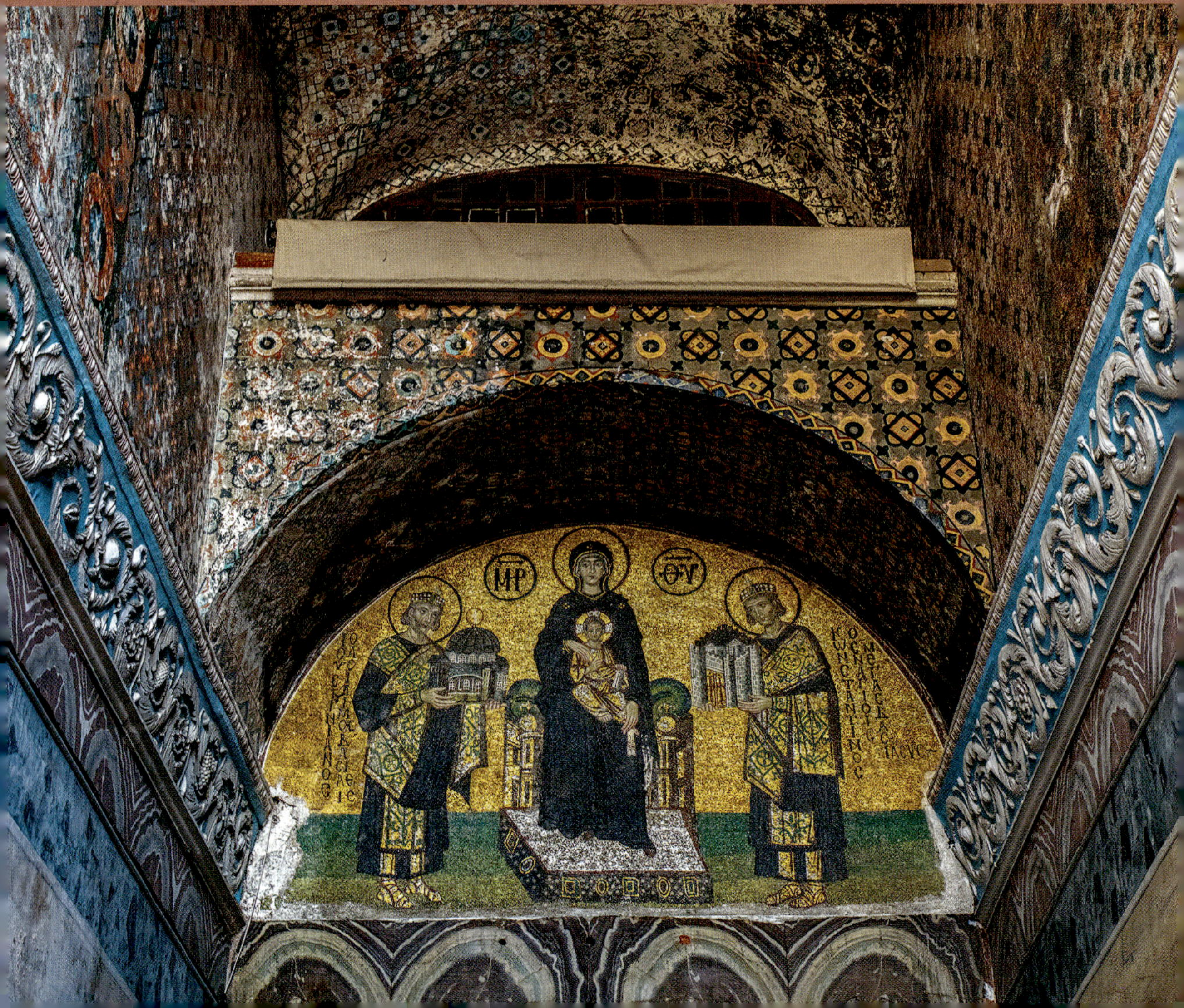

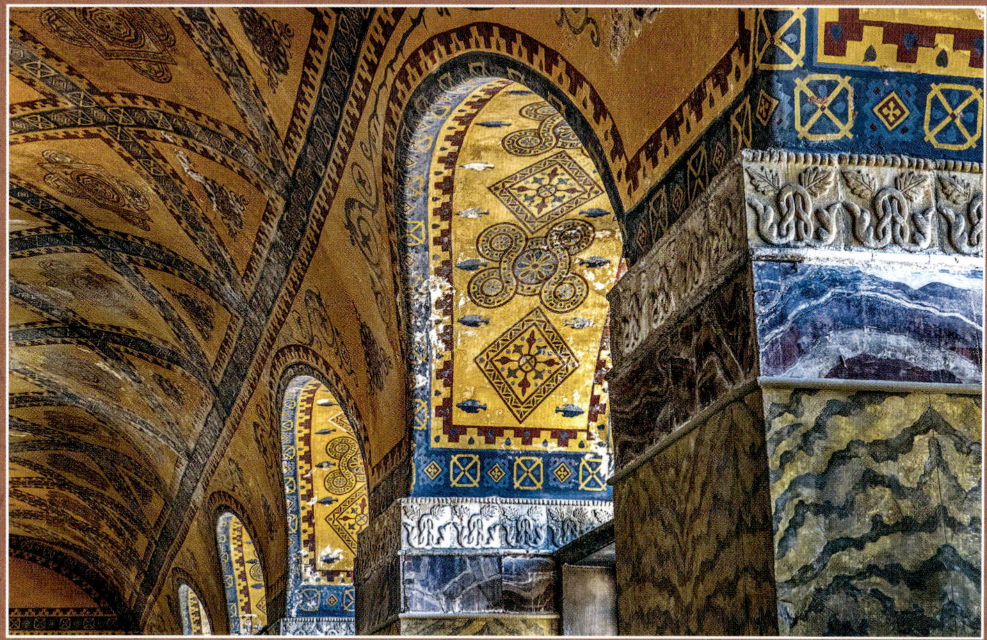

As a result, visitors can no longer access the building's ground floor. This hallowed space is reserved for worshippers, who pray on intricate handwoven carpets beneath a 182-foot-tall dome. Visitors can, however, still absorb Hagia Sophia's brilliance from its upper galleries, which overlook the prayer hall.

Many tourists begin their visit to Hagia Sophia in a strange manner: by inserting a finger in an ancient hole. Called "the weeping column," the base of the pillar is encased in metal, which has an opening that visitors poke during an ancient wishing custom.

One legend goes that the column was originally part of the home of the Virgin Mary. When she learned of the torture of her son, Jesus Christ, she held on to the column and cried. Her tears were so potent that they burned the famous hole in this pillar.[73] Now the mysterious column is but one of a forest of more than one hundred pillars inside Hagia Sophia. Each is carved from marble in shades of pink, yellow, and white.

Up above, meanwhile, polychromatic paintwork swirls across the ceiling. Similarly inspiring creative flourishes abound in the prayer hall. Near the crest of the domed ceiling hang giant black panels decorated by gilded Islamic calligraphy. This is one of the Islamic design features added to Hagia Sophia after it became a mosque in the 1400s, along with its four tall, spear-shaped minarets, one positioned on each corner of the complex.

Many of the building's Christian elements were erased at that time—but not all. An array of sumptuous mosaics created from silver and stone tiles depict angels, Christian crosses, and biblical figures. Two in particular draw visitors' attention.

The Virgin and the Child mosaic illustrates Mary sitting on a throne with her son, the boy Jesus, in her lap. Nearby, Byzantine leader John II Comnenus and his wife, St. Irene of Hungary, are the focus of a similarly elaborate mosaic thought to be at least nine hundred years old. In another artwork, an adult Christ is shown perched on a bejeweled chair, receiving gifts from Empress Zoe, the daughter of eleventh-century Byzantine Emperor Constantine VIII.[74]

Such Christian flourishes set Hagia Sophia apart in a city overflowing with mosques designed entirely in Islamic style. The intricacy and glory of this church-turned-mosque make it even more remarkable to consider the darkness in which it was born.[75]

MODERN-DAY EXPLANATIONS

This is no science fiction script. Modern researchers have analyzed myriad historical accounts of the darkness event, which for centuries thereafter was simply called a "mystery cloud." They found this phenomena caused drought, failed crops and famine, and animal deaths—not just in Turkey, but across swaths of the northern hemisphere.[76]

So what prompted this destructive eighteen months of darkness? Harvard University historian Michael McCormick and University of Maine glaciologist Paul Mayewski may have answered that question. Their analysis of ice at a Swiss glacier showed evidence of a giant volcanic eruption in AD 536 in Iceland, which scattered massive amounts of ash over Europe, including Constantinople. For eighteen months, the airborne ash caused massive disruption to climates across the Northern Hemisphere. It lowered summer temperatures by as much as thirty-seven degrees Fahrenheit and caused summer snowstorms in China.[77]

McCormick and Mayewski reached their conclusion by interpreting clues embedded within the glacial ice. When volcanoes erupt, they disperse huge volumes of chemical elements in their ash, such as sulfur and bismuth. These substances can remain intact in soil or ice for millennia, providing physical evidence of past eruptions. During their research, McCormick and Mayewski used a laser to cut ribbon-like microlayers of ice from the glacier, each layer corresponding with a specific year in history. While analyzing an ice layer from AD 536, they identified substances that not only indicated an eruption but also matched volcanic activity in Iceland, pinpointing the likely location of this volcanic event.[78]

NATURE CONTINUES TO PLAGUE ISTANBUL

By AD 538, the sun was finally shining again on Istanbul. Its welcome rays illuminated the city's new wonder, Hagia Sophia, which had just been completed by a team of ten thousand laborers. But the fortunate Istanbul residents who survived the volcanic fallout had, unfortunately, not seen the last of Mother Nature's wrath.

Just five years after that mystery cloud parted, the Plague of Justinian besieged the city. One of the worst pandemics in history, this outbreak of bubonic plague killed up to one hundred million people across Europe and Asia. Nowhere was more devastated than Turkey's biggest city, where up to ten thousand people died each day.[79]

When this eight-year pandemic finally ended in AD 549, those who had endured a world of darkness and illness were further terrorized by natural disasters. Over the following decade, Istanbul was rocked by two major earthquakes. Scientists believe that the latter may have sent a giant tsunami crashing into the city. What is certain is that this earthquake so badly damaged Hagia Sophia's dome that it soon collapsed (then was promptly rebuilt).[80]

ISTANBUL'S RESILIENT MASTERPIECE

Despite a devastating sequence of natural hardships, Hagia Sophia still stands after nearly fifteen hundred years. All these centuries later, visitors pour through this architectural wonder's marble galleries to observe its heft and appreciate its majesty. To them, this landmark's existence must appear inevitable. But history tells a different tale of resilience in the midst of darkness.

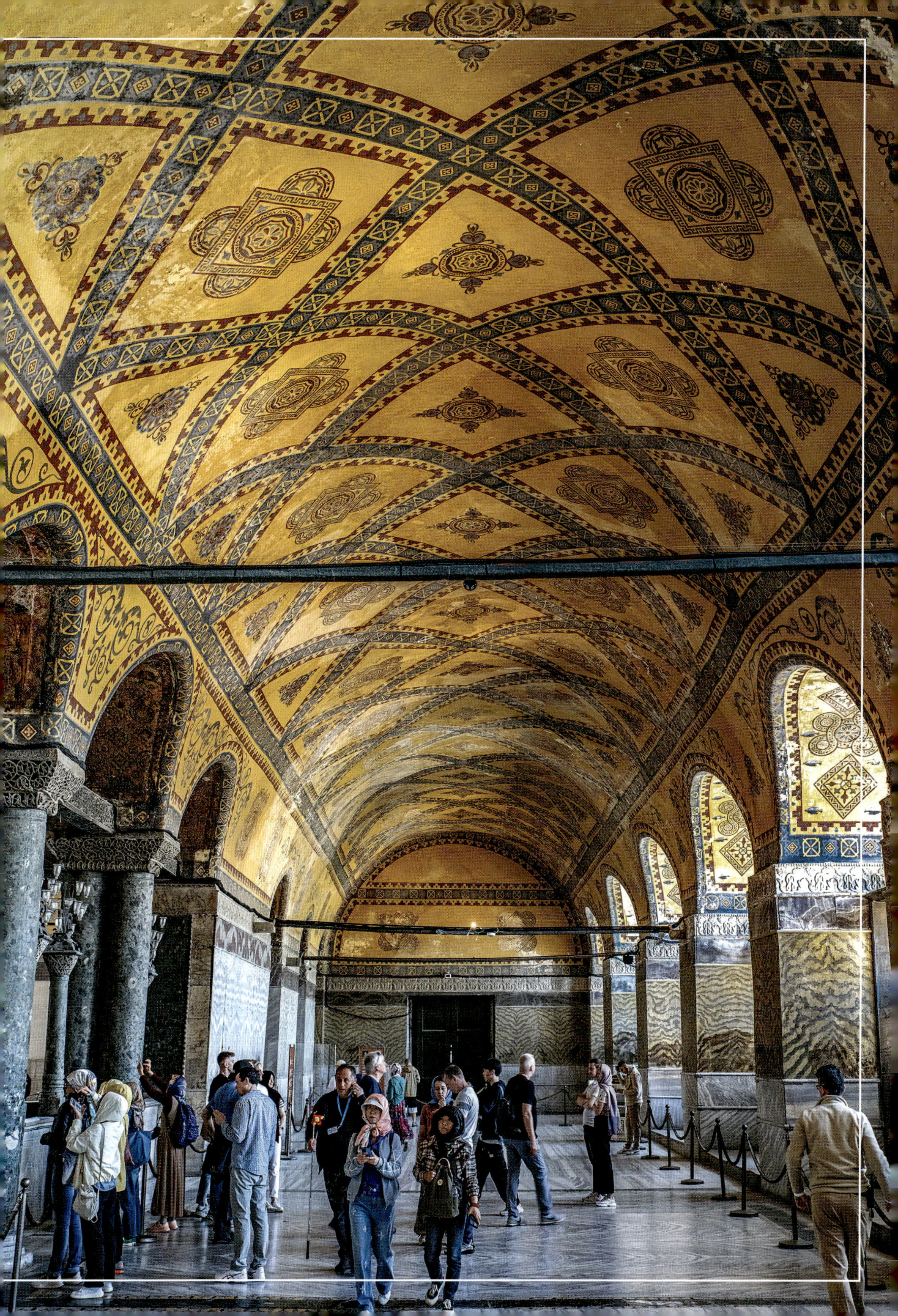

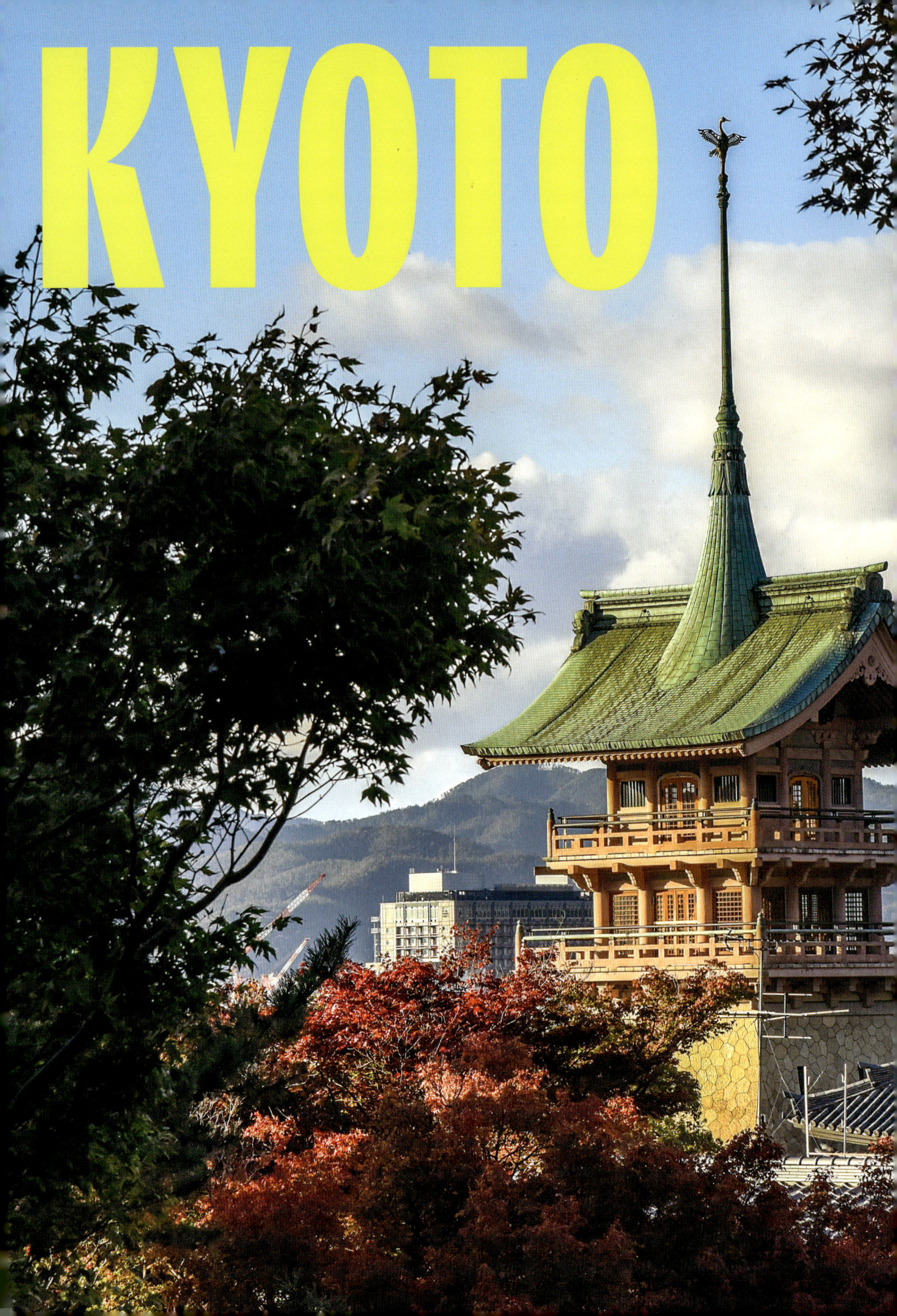
KYOTO

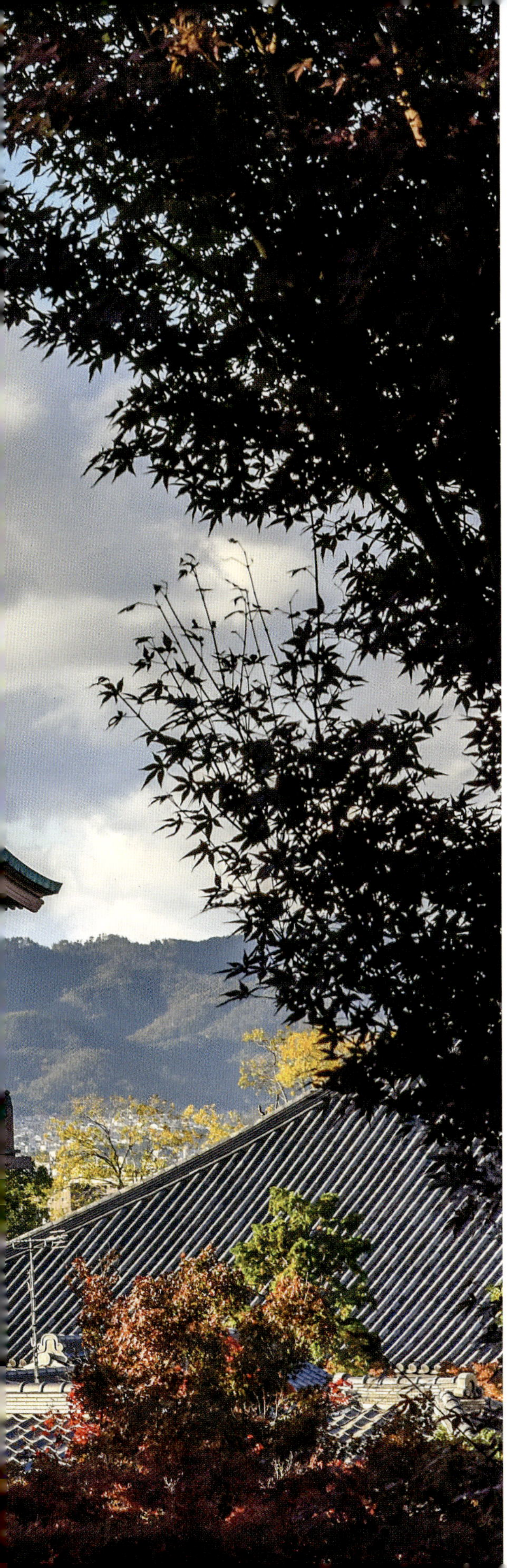

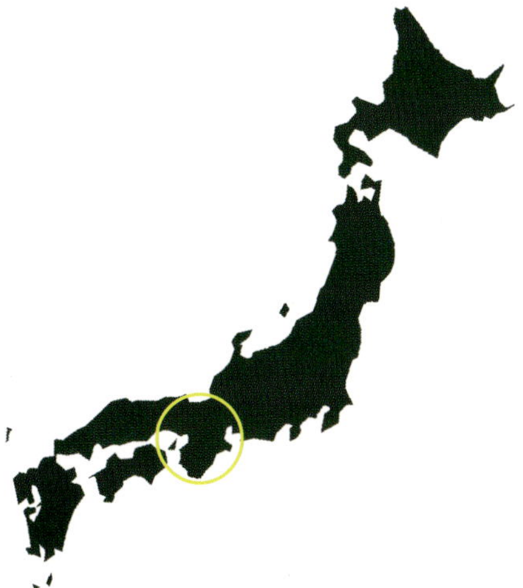

Higashiyama embodies the traditional Japan that beguiles so many Westerners. Threaded through the forested hills of Kyoto and lined by wooden homes, Buddhist temples, classical gardens, ceramics studios, and timeworn teahouses, this quaint neighborhood is a pretty portal to a bygone Japan.

Amid such beauty and serenity, it's hard to believe that Higashiyama was once splattered with blood. To blame? A pack of wolves. No, not wild beasts wielding sharp teeth and slicing claws. Rather, this violence was meted out by a shadowy police squad that mimicked the predation of wolves, using cunning and patience to track and ambush prey. This squad's chief objective was to quell a vicious rebellion by rogue Japanese samurai warriors, who were intent on overthrowing Japan's government.

Called "the Wolves of Mibu," this police squad prowled Kyoto in the 1860s, slaughtering dozens of enemies. Fear and paranoia mounted in the city as decapitated heads littered its streets. In Higashiyama, the wolves' six-year torrent of violence affected many sites that are now landmarks, such as commanding Kodai-ji Temple and tranquil Maruyama Park.[81]

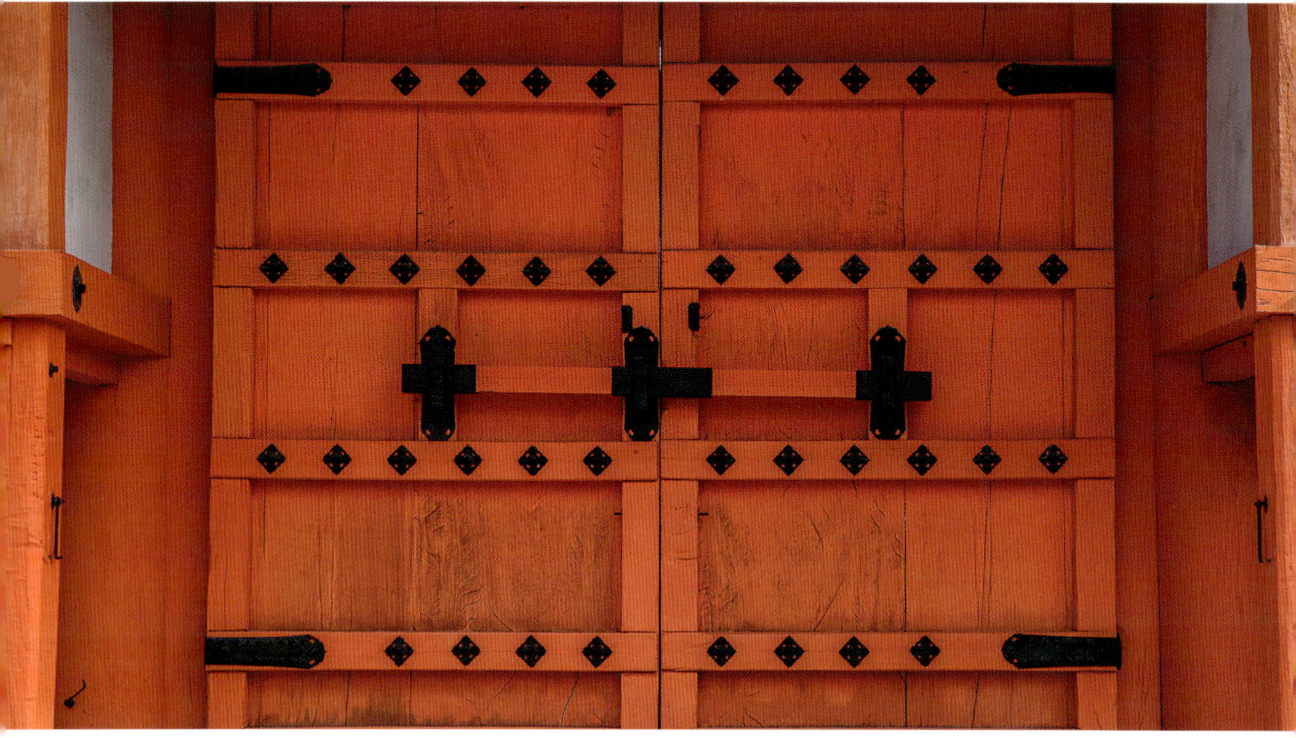

THE REVENGE OF THE SAMURAI

The Wolves of Mibu were birthed, in part, due to actions of the United States. Having recently seized California from Mexico, the US wanted to increase commerce at its new Californian ports. Boosting maritime trade with Asia was the key, it believed. So America looked to Japan and China, the two wealthiest Asian nations, to expand trade relations.

While the US and China were already doing steady business, Japan had isolated itself from the world since the early 1600s and only traded with China and the Netherlands. So the US decided to use its military to strong-arm Japan into a trade deal.[82]

In 1853, US Commodore Matthew Perry sailed with four ships into what is now called Tokyo Bay. Intended as a show of intimidation, the US vessels arrived heavily armed. Perry delivered a forceful letter from US President Millard Fillmore, demanding that Japan's emperor give the US access to a Japanese port. The looming threat of US military aggression convinced Japan to negotiate a treaty with the US in 1854, which effectively reopened its borders.[83]

Samurai were incensed by these events. To this fiercely patriotic class of Japanese warriors, who had long swayed the country's politics, the US incursion was a humiliation. It became a breaking point for many samurai, who already felt marginalized due to their gradual loss of wealth and status under the government of the Tokugawa Shogunate (1603–1868).

Prior to the Tokugawa period, Japan had experienced centuries of murderous turf battles. This war-torn environment had greatly benefited samurai, who had been paid generously to protect the domains of rich Japanese lords. But then that vicious era ended and was replaced by the peaceful Tokugawa period. This sudden dearth of violence across Japan was good news for most citizens, but left many samurai adrift. Without battles to be fought, these warriors experienced a steep decline in purpose, income, and influence.[84]

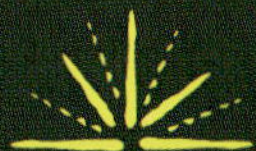

Home to 1.5 million people Kyoto is flanked on its north, east, and west by forested mountains. Looming to its south and southwest, meanwhile, is a colossal urban sprawl that encompasses port metropolis Kobe and hypermodern Osaka. Although Tokyo is easily Japan's largest and most visited city, Kyoto has the greater legacy. It was the capital of Japan for more than a thousand years, from 794 to 1868, and to this day, Kyoto is considered the cradle of Japanese culture.[85]

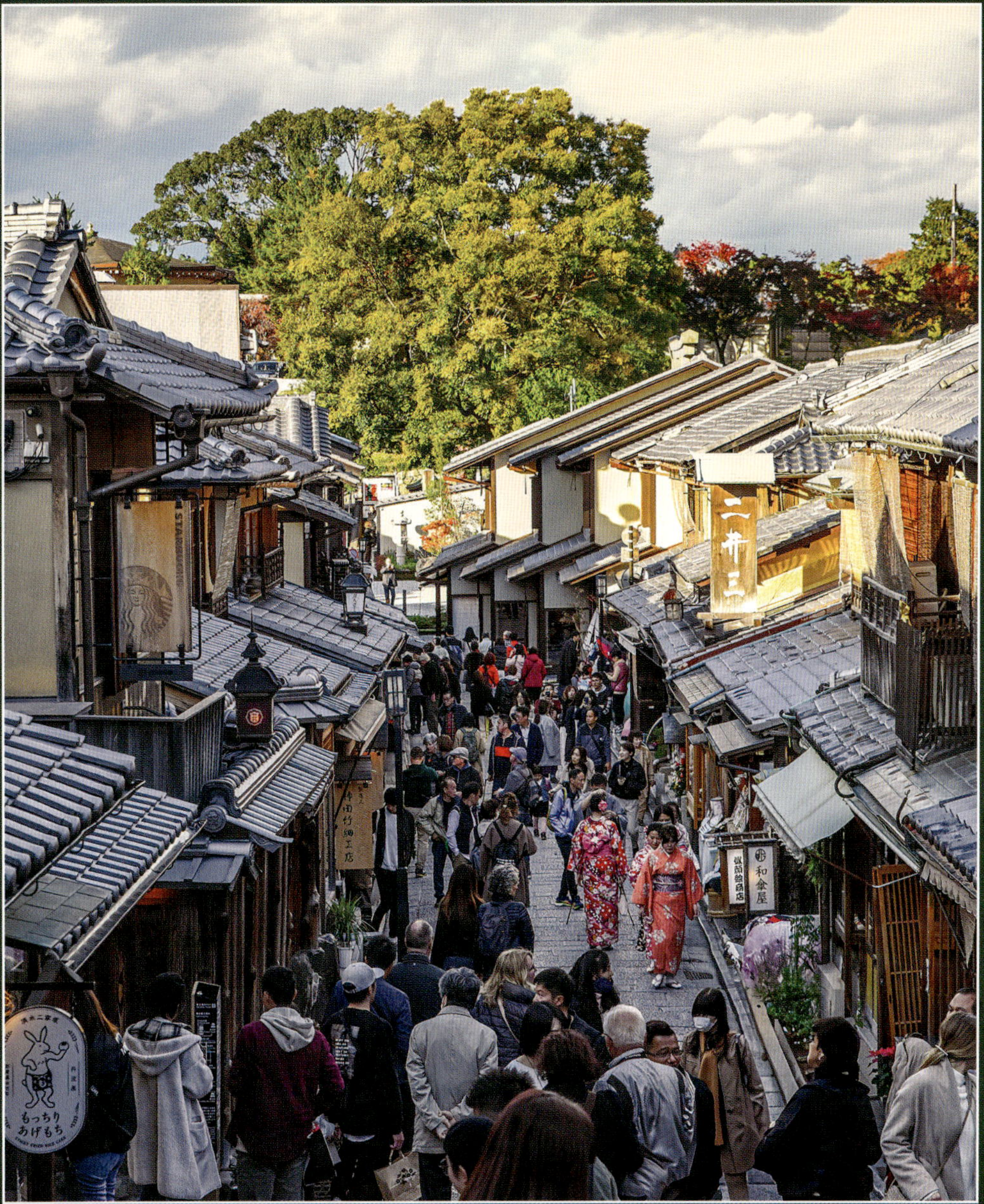

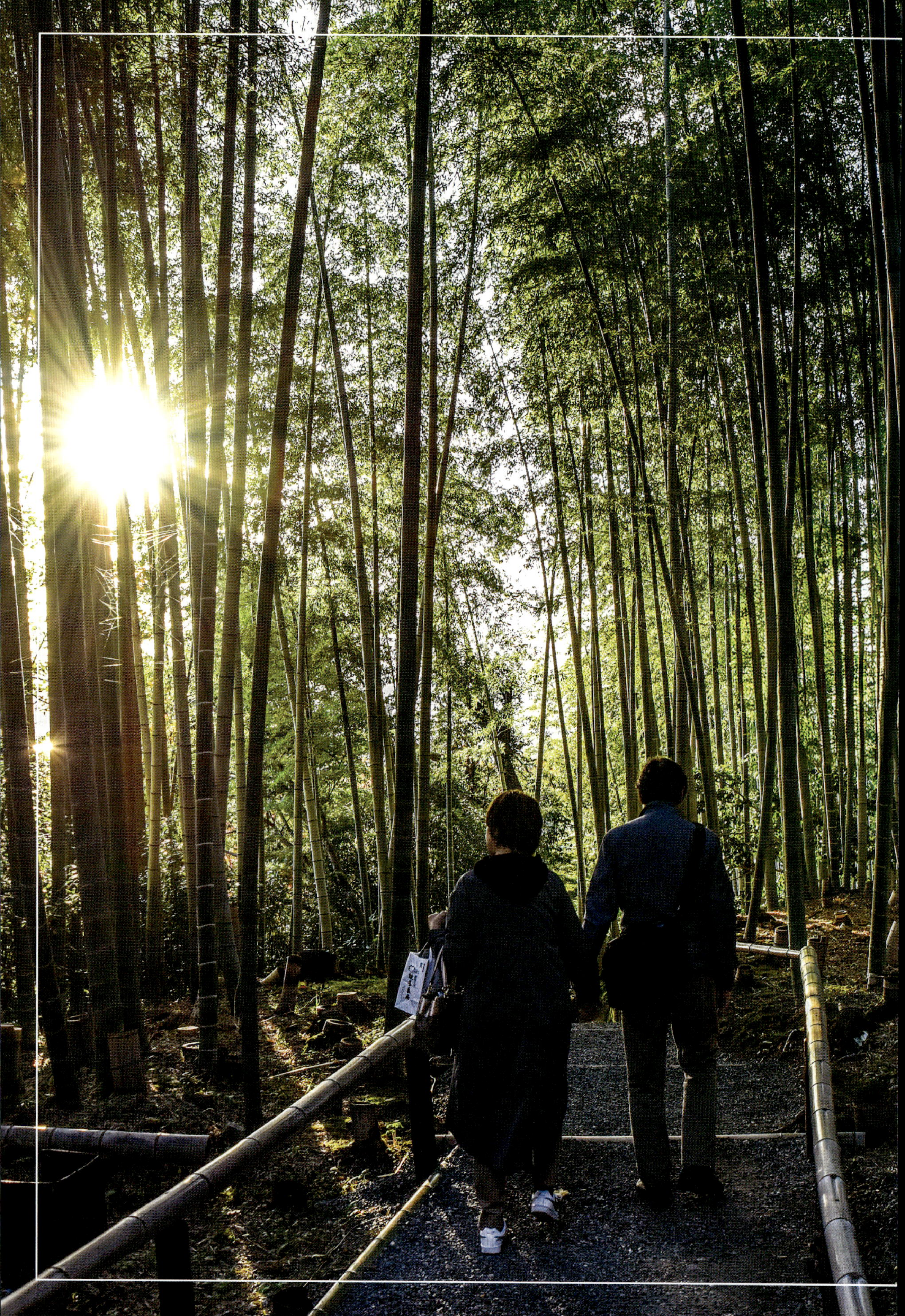

Called *ronin*, or "masterless samurai," those disaffected men refused to dissolve into obscurity.[86] This was especially true of one particular group, the mighty Choshu clan. Its hundreds of samurai craved revenge against the Tokugawa Shogunate, which these warriors blamed for their loss of status. So the Choshu samurai launched a long, brutal campaign on the streets of Kyoto. Their aims were to destabilize the Tokugawa, reduce foreign influence, and reinstate the power and prestige of samurai.

Decapitation was the Choshu's calling card. Along the Kamo River, near Kyoto's now-busy train station, they created an open-air gallery of death. Sharpened sticks were planted in the earth, each topped by a skewered skull. Passersby were startled to make eye contact with these latest Choshu victims, who most commonly were officials of the Tokugawa Government or supporters of the regime.[87]

MAYHEM ENGULFS KYOTO

Japan's leaders were dismayed by the bloodshed, yet not shocked. Samurai revolts had been anticipated by the Tokugawa government, which recognized that some of these warriors were furious about their diminished standing in Japanese society. The government's response was emphatic. It shunned diplomacy and instead communicated with the Choshu via their own language: extreme violence. Soon, these dissident samurai were being tracked by the government's newly formed Wolves of Mibu.

Elite and ruthless swordsmen, the Wolves also consisted mostly of samurai. From 1863 to 1869, this police unit waged many battles against foes of the Tokugawa government. None was fiercer than the wolves' lengthy war with the Choshu terrorizing Kyoto.[88]

This conflict reached a barbaric zenith in June 1864, when the Wolves learned that their Choshu foes were secretly meeting at the Ikedaya Inn, near Sanjo Bridge. So they hunted down, detained, and tortured two Choshu. Eventually these rogue samurai confessed that the Choshu were planning to invade Kyoto's Imperial Palace, set it ablaze, and abduct the figurehead they blamed for their loss of status: Emperor Komei.

Days later, the Wolves stormed the inn and surprised the plotters. A blur of slinging swords ended with a heavy body count. Although the Wolves' victory burnished their fearsome reputation, the Choshu continued their ruthless campaign to try to unseat the government. More than a century and a half later, the blood spilled by these warriors has been washed from the picturesque streets of Higashiyama.[89] But sword marks from this conflict can be observed on the Sanjo Bridge, connecting Higashiyama and busy Central Kyoto across the Kamo River, where deep gashes from this murderous maelstrom still mark the city.[90]

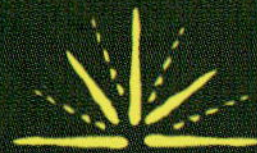

Many foreigners imagine Japan as an ancient land, where white-faced geisha conduct tea ceremonies inside weathered wooden halls. Others picture a cutting edge, neon-drenched nation of skyscrapers, robots, and bullet trains.

Rather thrillingly, both of those settings coexist in Japan. Megalopolis Tokyo showcases the country's future, whereas ultratraditional Kyoto offers crystalline views of its past. The former reputedly has more than 170 skyscrapers,[91] and the latter has at least that many shrines and temples.[92]

Kyoto is a city that fiercely protects its heritage, such that in 2024 it banned tourists from parts of Gion, a small neighborhood within Higashiyama. A key aim of this policy was to restore the privacy of geisha, who could no longer move freely without being pestered. Foreigners in Gion were incessantly photographing these traditional Japanese entertainers,[93] who don silk kimonos while playing the *shamisen*, a stringed instrument, during private performances.[94]

Travelers who wish to observe geisha respectfully can buy tickets to such a show.[95] Higashiyama also offers myriad options for delving into Kyoto's ancient art scene. Visitors can attend a Noh musical drama or Kabuki theater or learn how to create Ikebana flower arrangements, Onigawara tiles, or karakami wallpaper.

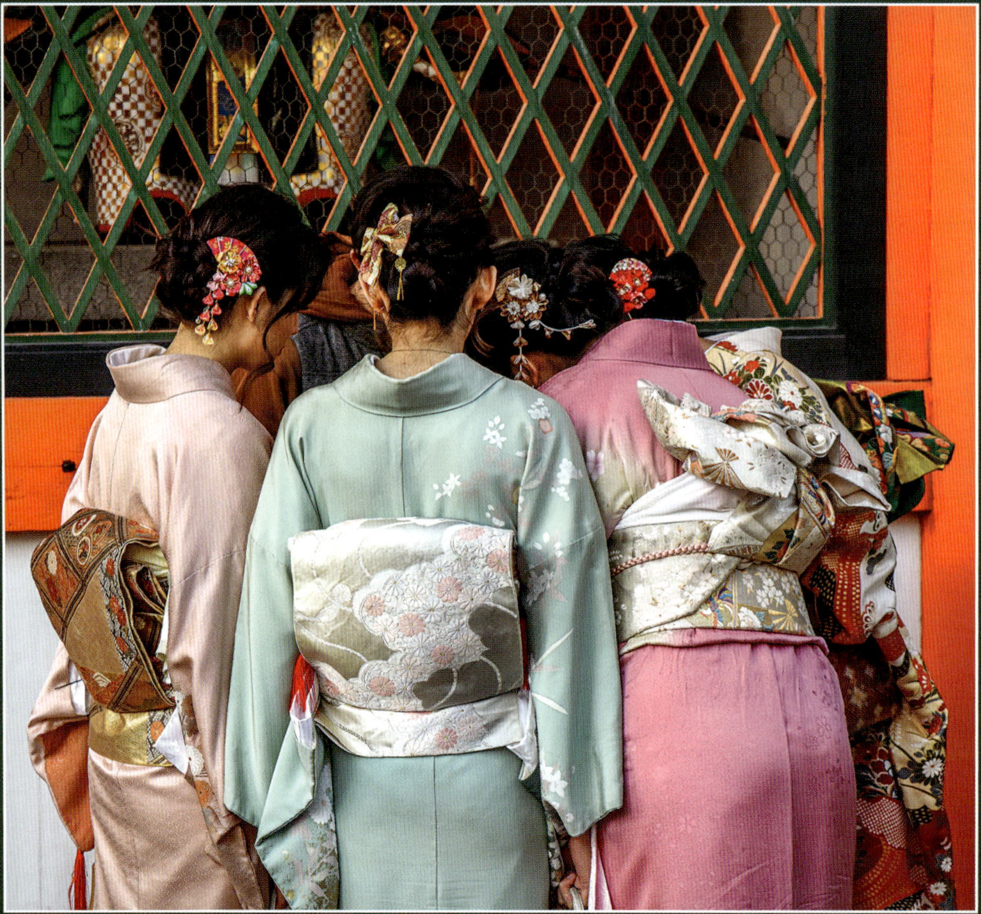

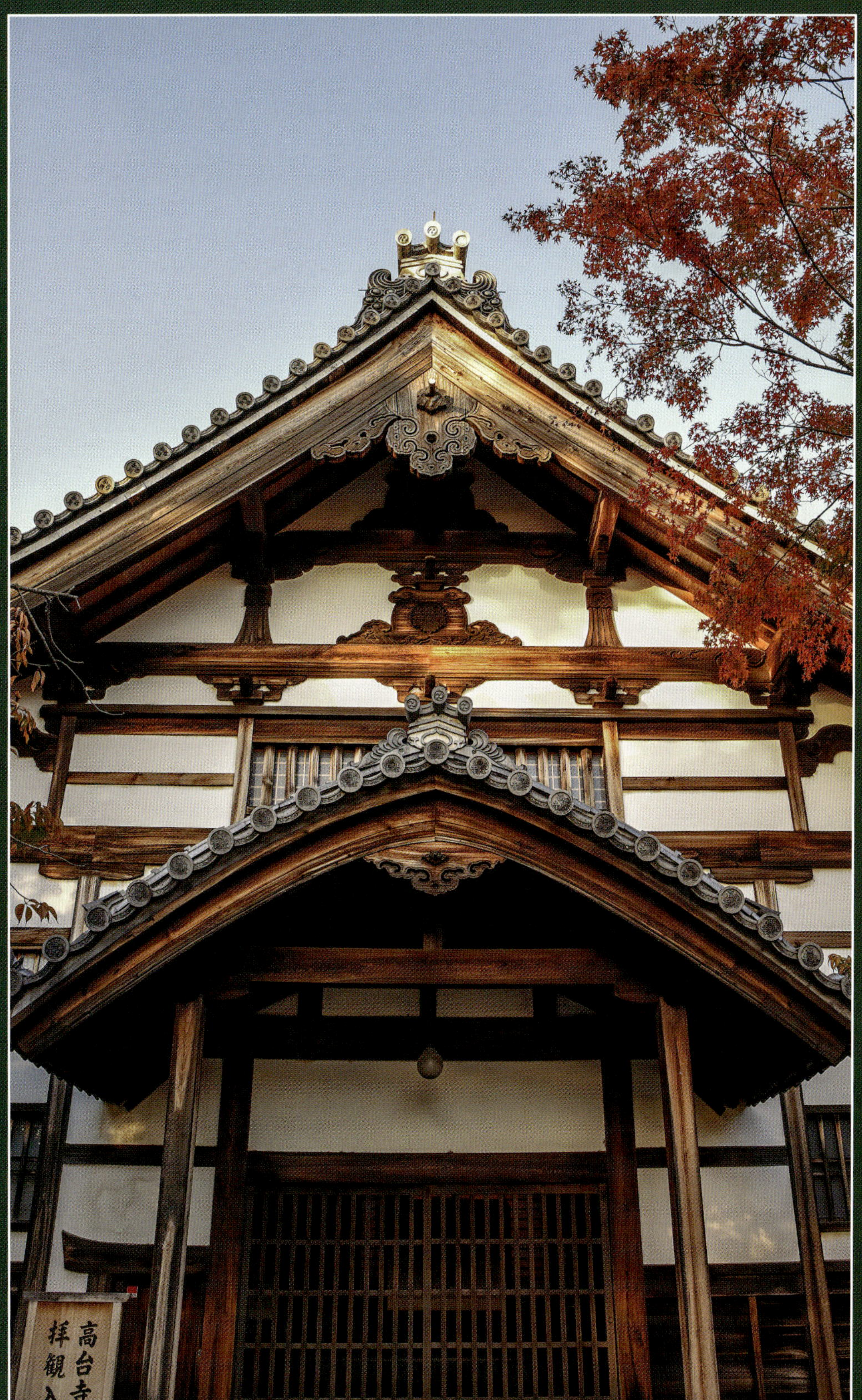
高台寺
拝観入

A FORMER WOLF IS DEVOURED

Three years after their violence shrouded Sanjo Bridge, the Wolves were still hunting. In June 1867, Kodai-ji became the base for the Guardians of the Imperial Tomb. This group of samurai was dedicated to protecting the soul of Emperor Komei, who was laid to rest in a grand mausoleum alongside Kodai-ji.[96] In reality, however, they were secretly assisting the Choshu campaign to unseat Japan's Tokugawa government.[97]

Led by legendary swordsman Kashitaro Ito, the Guardians of the Imperial Tomb earned fear and respect throughout Kyoto. They appeared almost untouchable. Until, that is, Ito's checkered past descended upon them like thunder.

Some months previous, Ito had defected from the Wolves of Mibu and recruited a dozen fellow Wolves to join his new unit. This was an insult destined to earn an intense response from the tight-knit brotherhood of secret police.

Rather foolishly, Ito accepted an invitation to go drinking with one of his former police colleagues. Inebriated and vulnerable, he was wobbling home through Higashiyama when the Wolves pounced. After Ito's comrades rushed to the scene, they, too, were lethally ambushed.[98]

A few months later, the Wolves committed perhaps their most infamous assassination. They slayed two of Ito's associates, who are now commemorated by a statue in Higashiyama's tranquil Maruyama Park. This tall metallic artwork depicts samurai Sakamoto Ryoma and Nakaoka Shintaro,[99] friends and key leaders in the Choshu uprising against the Tokugawa government.

Several times previous, the Wolves had tried and failed to murder Ryoma and Shintaro until, in December 1867, they cornered this pair at their hideout, Kyoto's Omiya Inn. By the time Ryoma and Shintaro heard clamor on the inn's staircase, it was too late to escape. Wolves burst into their room and swiftly delivered death.[100]

Although the Wolves claimed this battle, Ryoma and Shintaro helped win the Choshu war against the shogun. Because just weeks later, in January 1868, the cause they had died for finally came to pass. Japan's Tokugawa government was toppled, ending 264 years of military dictatorship and returning the nation to imperial rule. Called the Meiji Restoration, the period ushered in a new era for Japan during which the country was rapidly modernized and Westernized.[101] By 1869, the Wolves of Mibu were extinct, their masters having been ousted.[102]

Most people wandering Kyoto's streets admiring the many physical remnants of its past are oblivious to this bloody past. Yet to this day, keen observers can spy evidence of the Wolves' hectic reign etched into the majesty of Higashiyama. A pair of ronin immortalized in statue at a tranquil park. An ancient bridge scarred by swords. A serene temple marked by murder. And a calm river where skulls were once placed as symbols of chaos and terror.

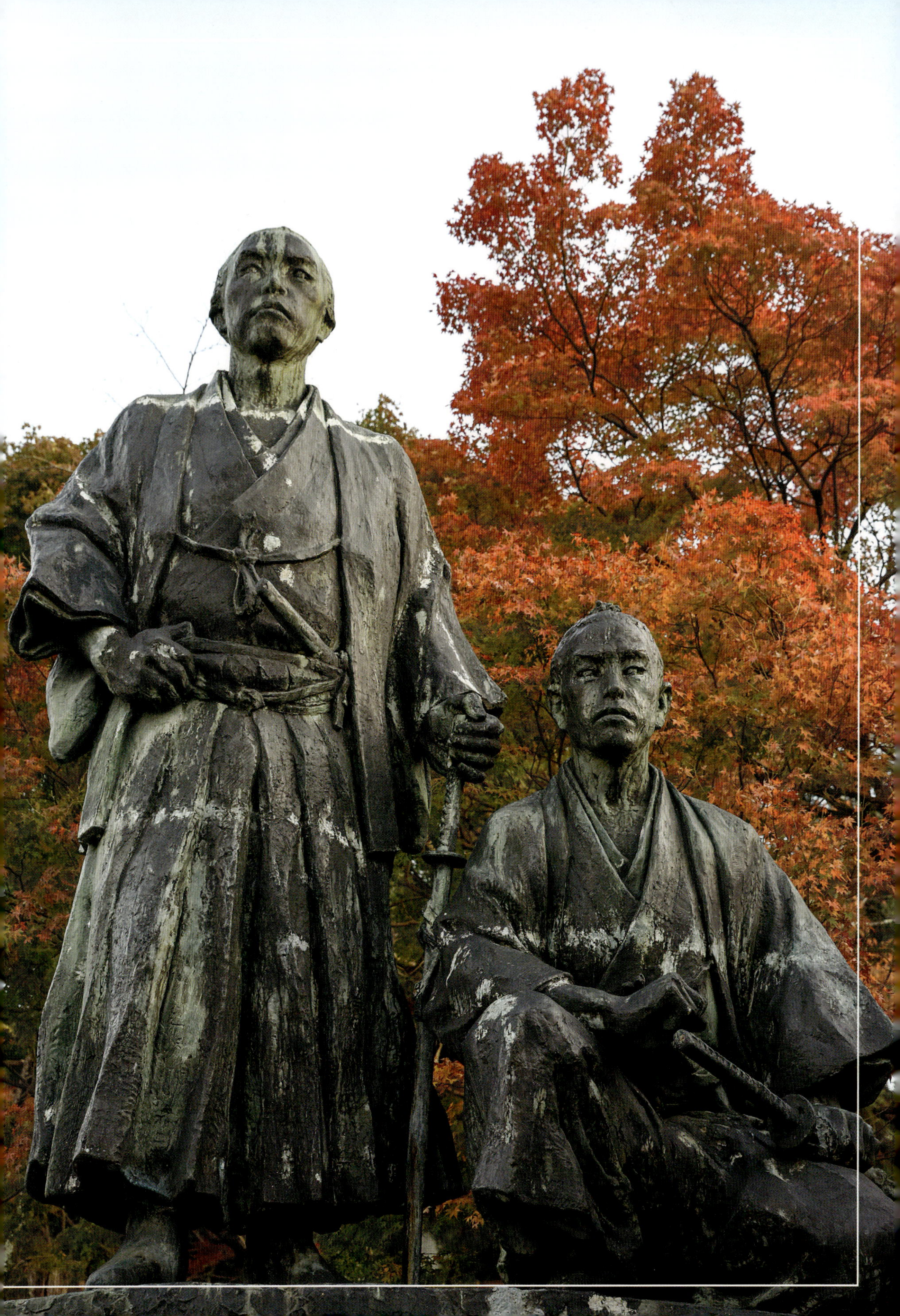

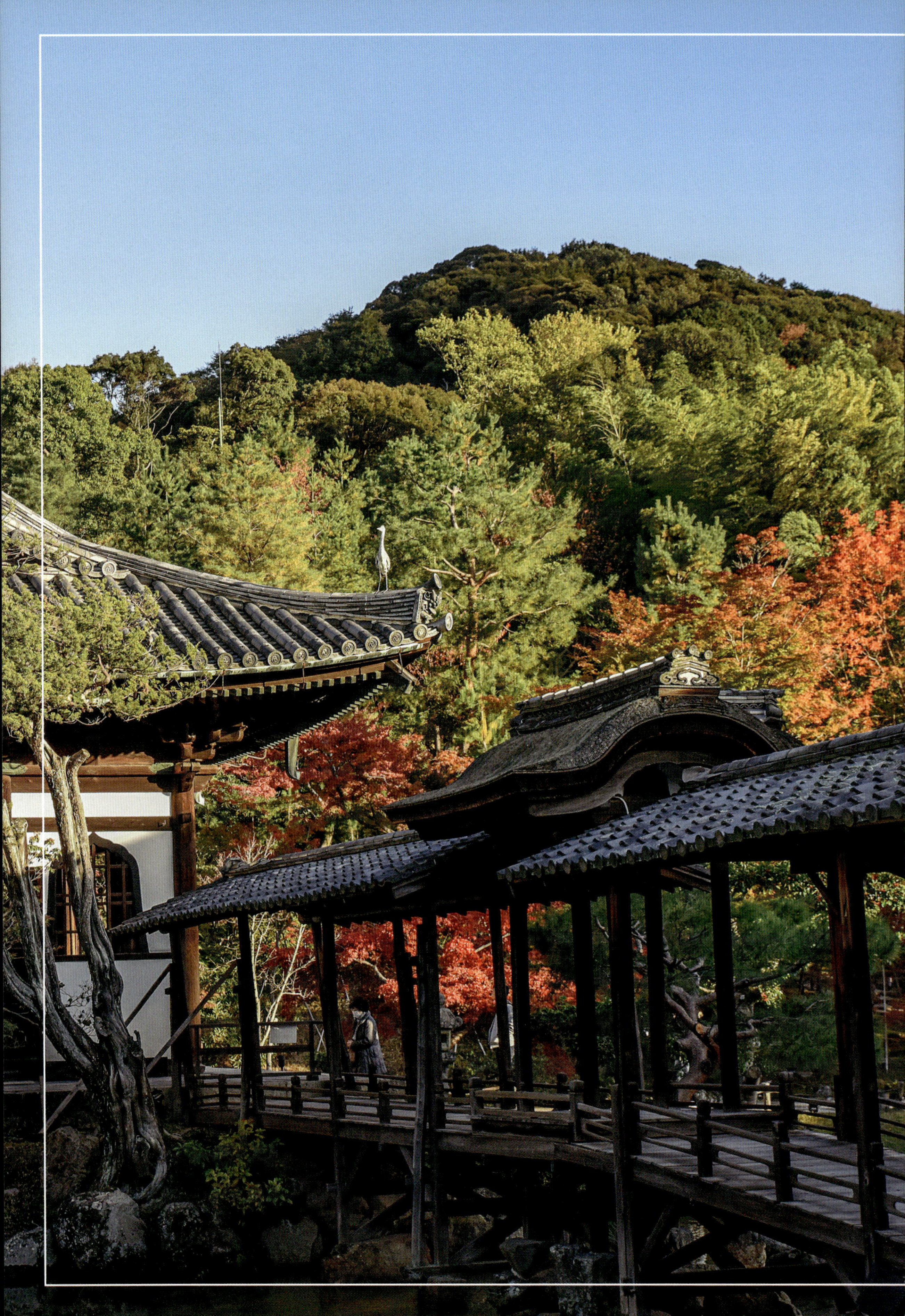

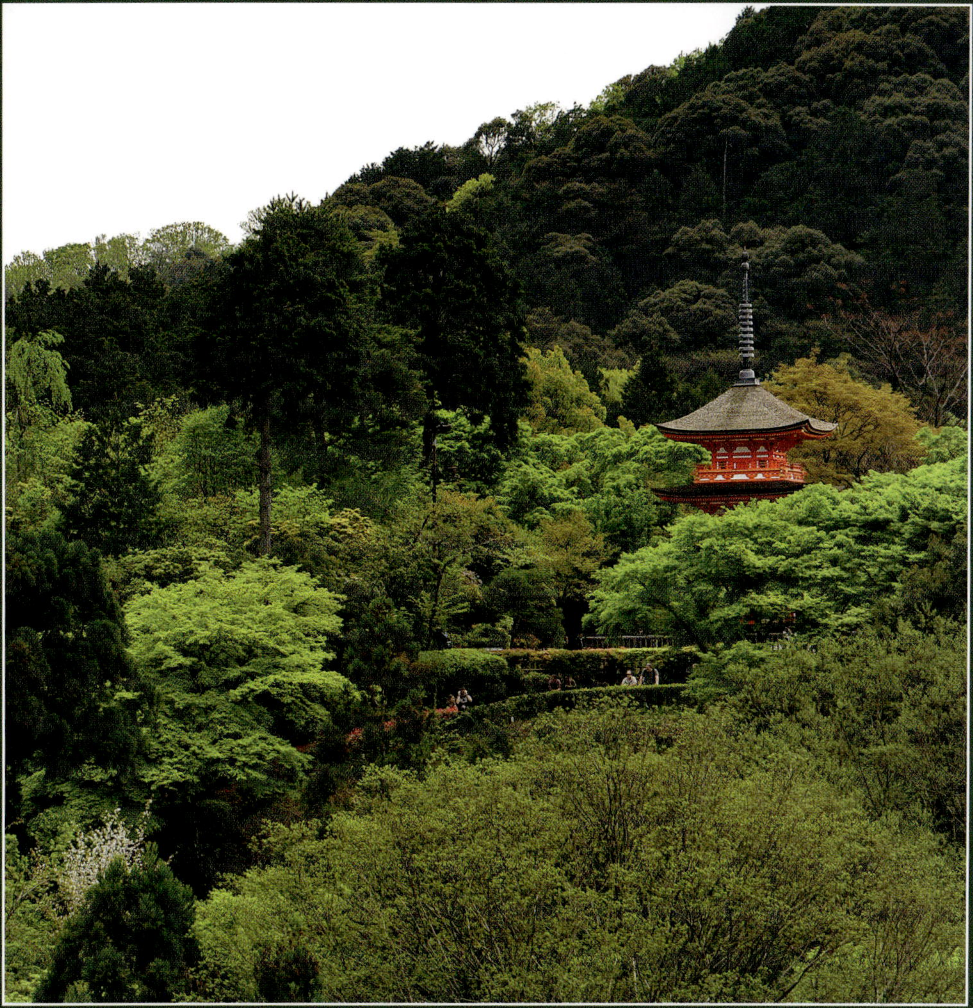

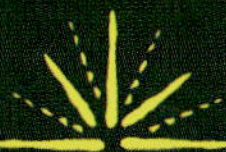

Japan's mastery of architecture and landscaping is showcased at Higashiyama's many sublime Shinto shrines and Buddhist temples, including Kodai-ji. This iconic Zen Buddhist complex is ensconced in forest, nearly a mile southeast of the Sanjo Bridge.

Built in the early 1600s, Kodai-ji's timeworn stone paths and bridges lead visitors over ponds and through manicured gardens, which are especially fetching during cherry blossom season (late March to early April) and the autumnal bloom (mid-October to early December). Meanwhile, Kodai-ji's bamboo grove is divine year round and peaks in beauty each evening, as the setting sun directs glowing rays between bamboo shoots.

All of this natural splendor envelops the temple's heritage structures, such as Kasa-tei and Shigure-tei, a pair of graceful teahouses embellished by fine woodwork and gold-flecked furnishings. And Kaisan-do, a hall dedicated to the temple's founding priest, is flanked by water and can be reached via a small, covered bridge.[103]

VIETNAM

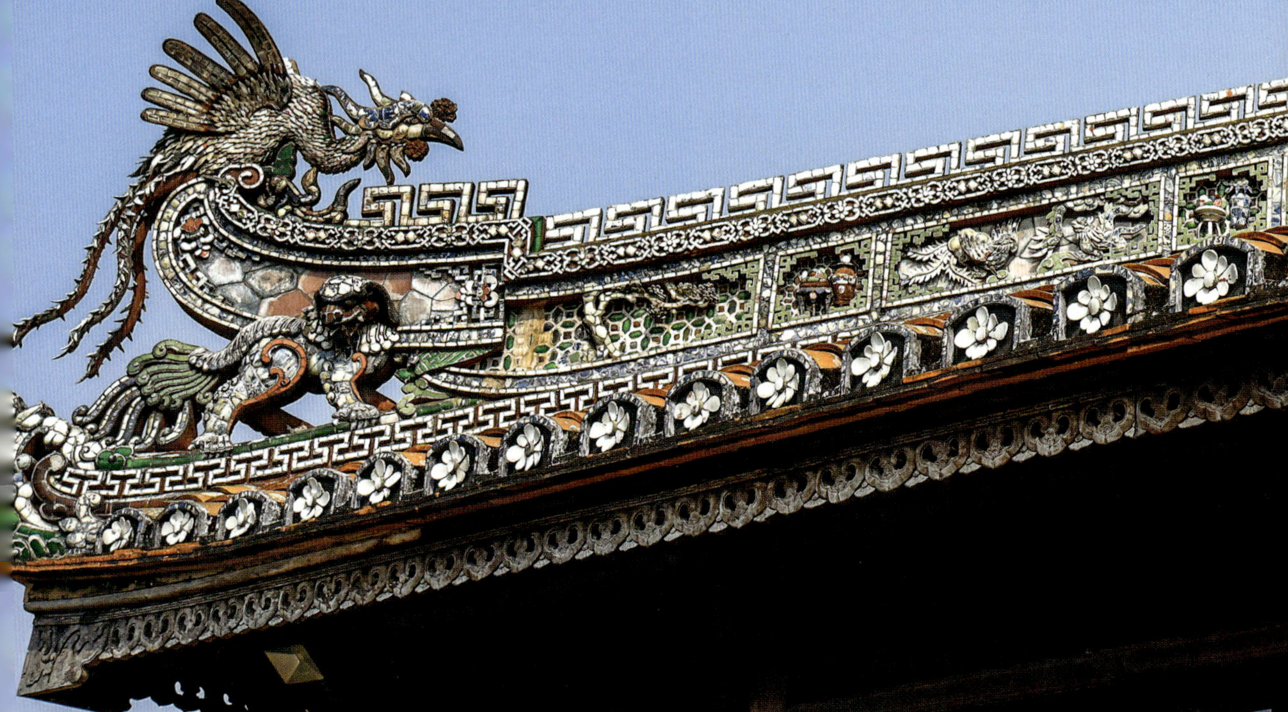

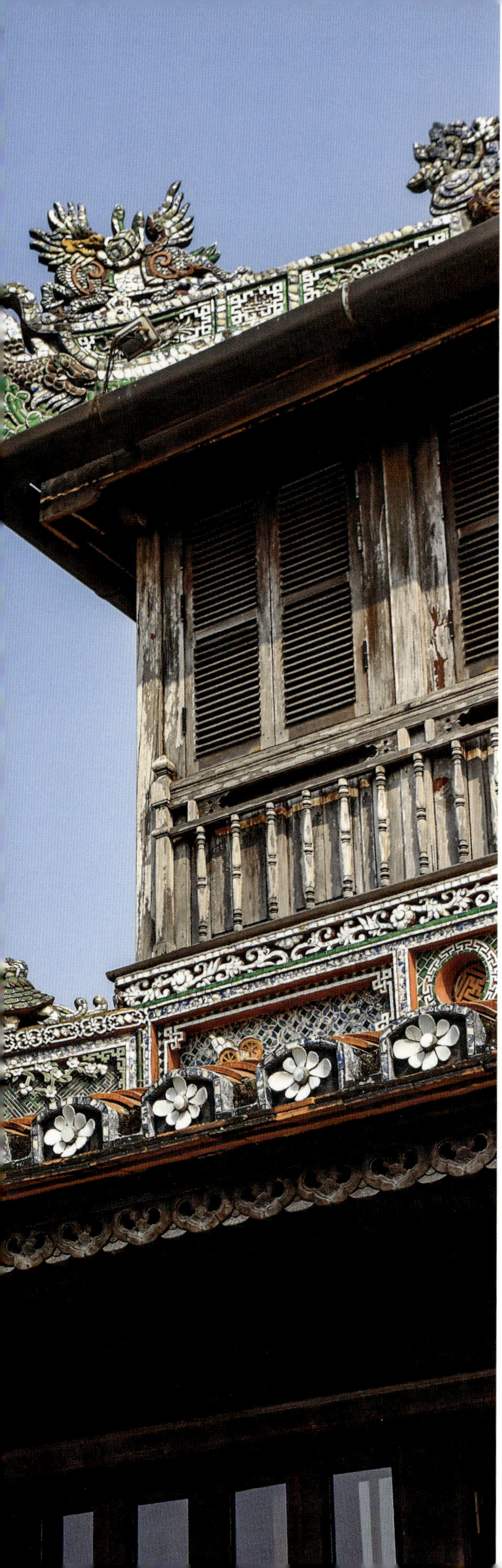

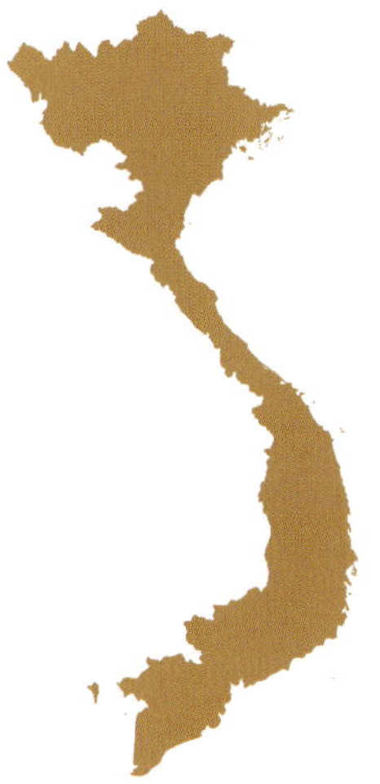

Visitors don't realize they're being watched as they wander Hue Citadel. While they explore the lavish palaces, halls, and shrines of Vietnam's grandest fortress, their every action is closely monitored and assessed for potential threat. But it's not CCTV cameras that are documenting their behavior. Instead, they are surveilled by creatures painted, etched, or sculpted within the sprawling grounds.

Although two miles of towering walls enclose this former royal complex, its actual protection comes from the four mystical animals that guard it.[104] In the eight decades since Vietnam's final dynasty ruled from Hue Citadel, these curious beings have remained on eternal patrol, scanning the earth for mortal foes and watching the skies for supernatural threats.

And as they keep their watch, these creatures also symbolize a twenty-five-hundred-year-old faith—one that staged an extraordinary comeback right here at Hue Citadel two centuries ago and continues to quietly shape Vietnamese society.[105]

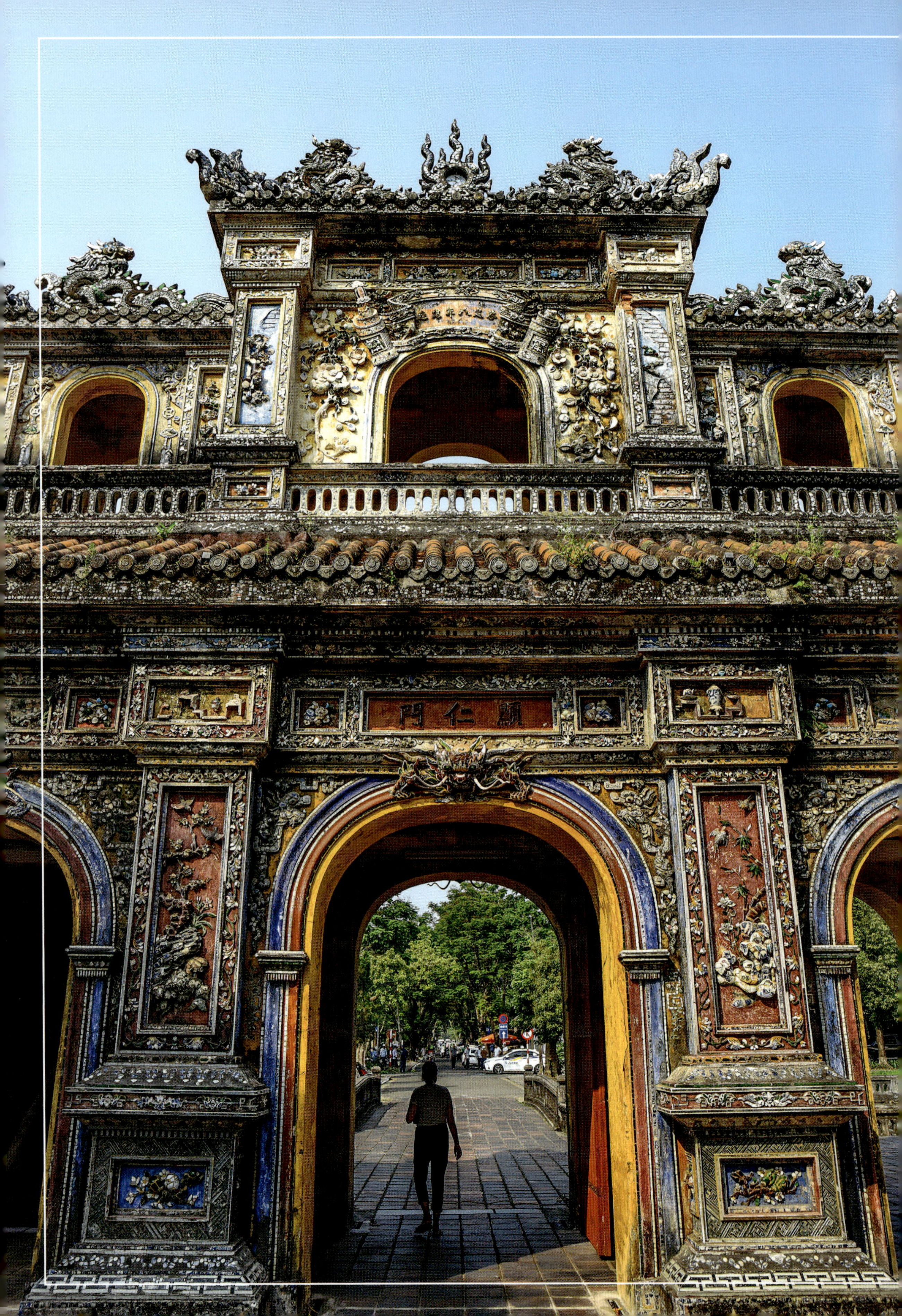
顯仁門

A NATION OF FORTRESSES

Vietnam is uniquely laden with citadels. At least a dozen walled cities remain in varied conditions throughout this southeast Asian nation. They are the product of more than two thousand years of savage turf wars across the country.

From the first century BC, Vietnam was repeatedly invaded, most frequently by its ultra-powerful northern neighbor, China, which occupied its lands for several long periods. All the while, dynasties within Vietnam often feuded over territory, splitting the country among multiple rival kingdoms. Military might was key to holding and defending territory, so these dynasties typically fortified their capitals against attack.[106]

Vietnam's oldest remaining fortification is the twenty-three-hundred-year-old Co Loa Citadel, the former hub of the legendary Au Lac kingdom on the outskirts of Hanoi. Long destroyed are most of its four tall walls, each of which were two and a half miles long. But Co Loa Citadel still preserves about sixty heritage sites, including ancient pagodas, temples, and communal homes.[107] In even better condition is Hanoi's Imperial Citadel of Thăng Long, which was besieged by military forces belonging to China's mighty Ming Dynasty in the 1400s. None, however, can match the heft and splendor of Hue Citadel.[108]

HOW DYNASTIES DIVIDED VIETNAM

The Ming invasion was the last time Vietnam was under Chinese rule. In 1428, Ming forces were permanently driven out of Vietnam by its longest-ruling empire, the Lê Dynasty.[109] From then until 1778, this dynasty commanded most of Vietnam, before being brought down by the short-lived Tay Son Dynasty, whose quick downfall in 1802 ushered in Vietnam's final dynasty, the Nguyen. A rich, powerful family, the Nguyens had waited generations for their turn to shape Vietnam. To celebrate their ascension to the throne, they commissioned the construction of the most magnificent citadel in the nation's history.[110]

ORIGINS OF HUE CITADEL

The Nguyen Dynasty chose Hue as its national capital. There, Emperor Gia Long selected a site for the new fortress that was both scenic and strategic. Hue Citadel was constructed on the leafy banks of the Perfume River, which flowed into the nearby East Vietnam Sea and provided swift passage for the Nguyen Dynasty's naval vessels. So ambitious was this construction project that it took nearly thirty years to finish.[111] By the time it was completed in 1833, this gargantuan fortress boasted around three hundred halls, palaces, temples, tombs, and offices. These spaces were protected by four massive walls ringed by moats.

Despite such fortifications, large swaths of Hue Citadel were later razed or badly damaged. First, Hue was besieged in 1885 by the French, who had been gradually colonizing Vietnam for the past two decades. They allowed the Nguyen Dynasty to remain in place, but only as a toothless, symbolic regime.[112]

Even greater harm was inflicted on Hue Citadel in 1968 during the Vietnam War, when it was swarmed by soldiers from North Vietnam and the Viet Cong. The latter group blindsided their enemy, South Vietnam, who fought alongside the US military. This ambush was part of the nationwide campaign called the Tet Offensive, which saw five South Vietnamese cities attacked and swung the momentum of victory away from the US and its South Vietnamese allies.[113]

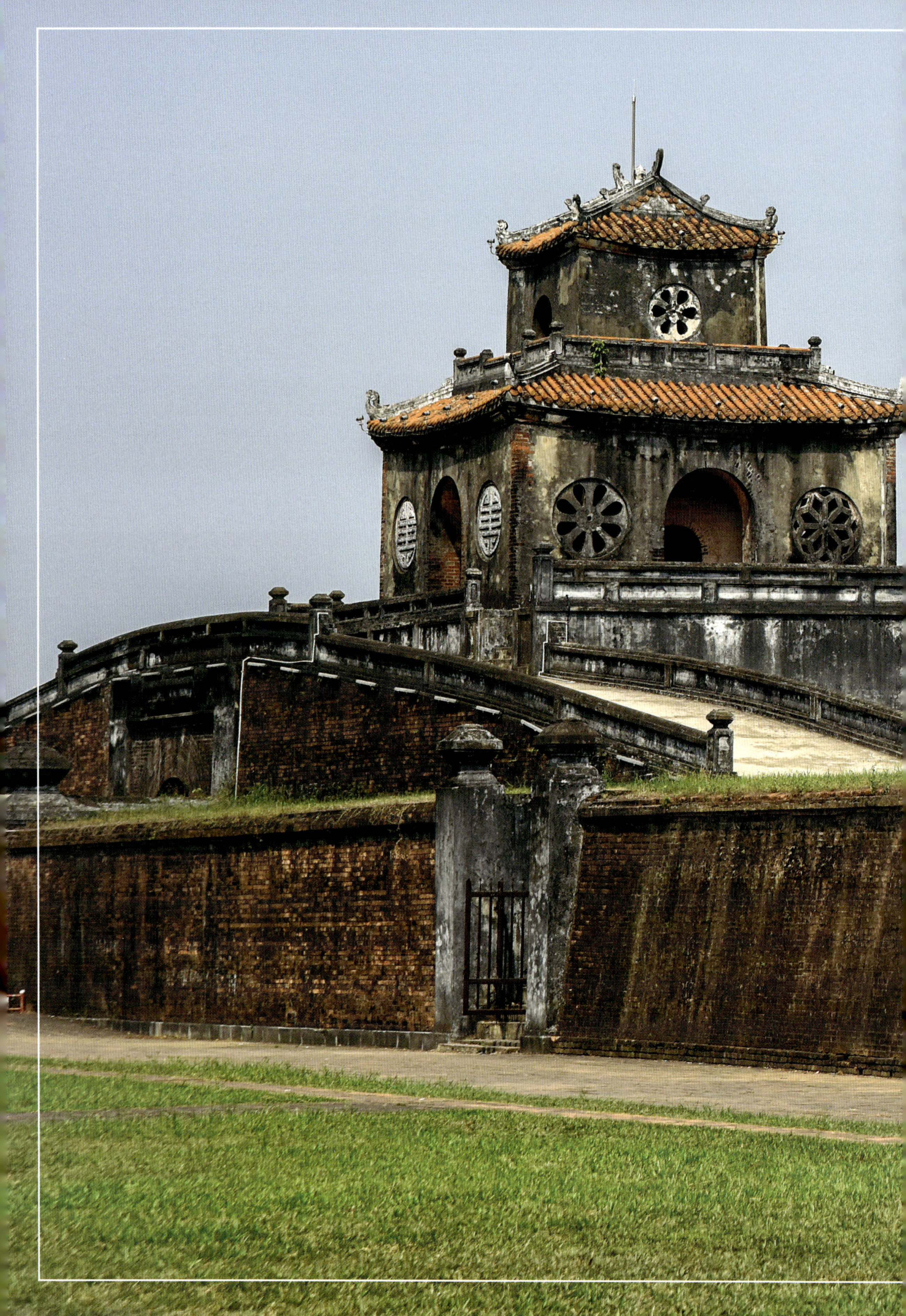

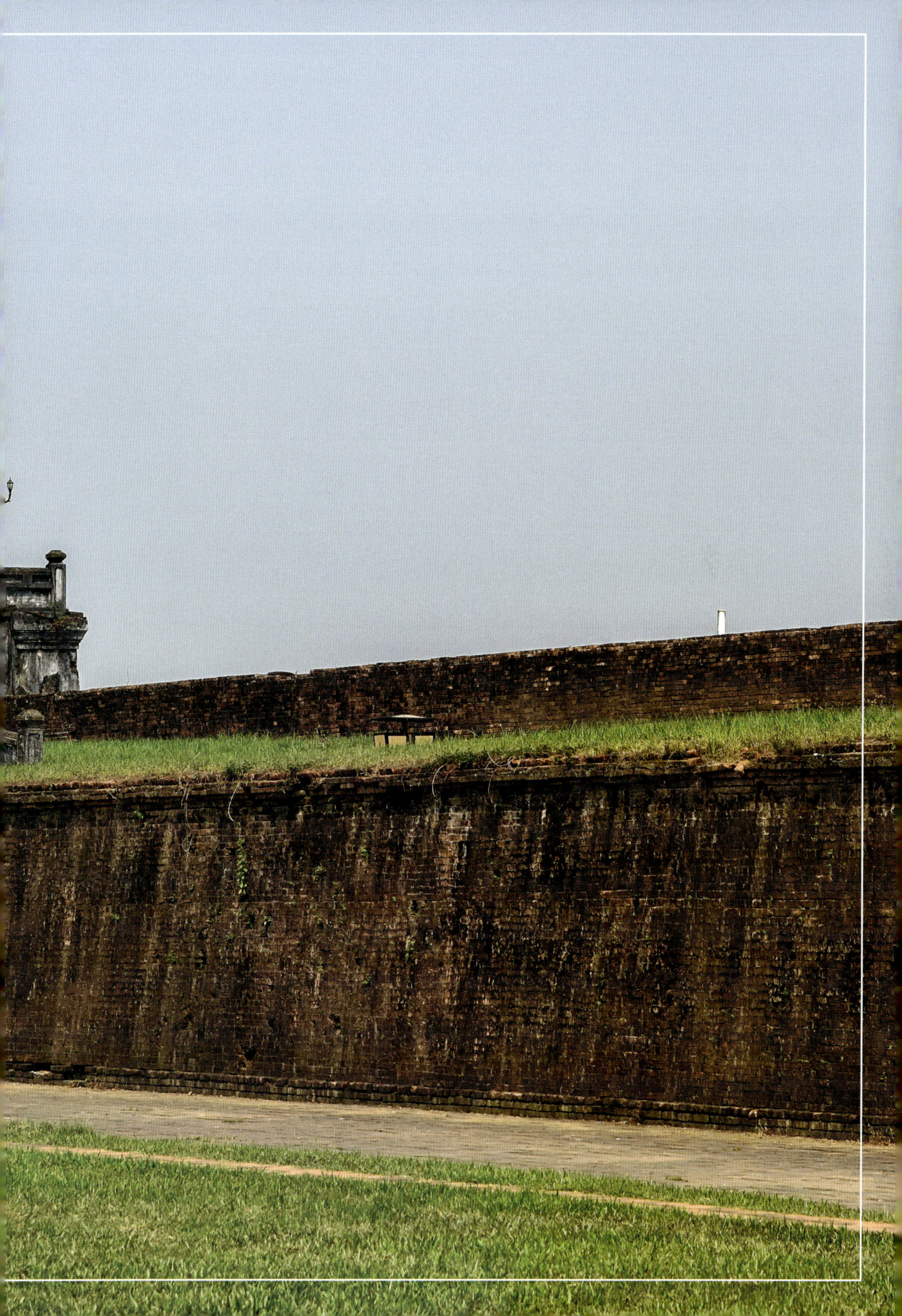

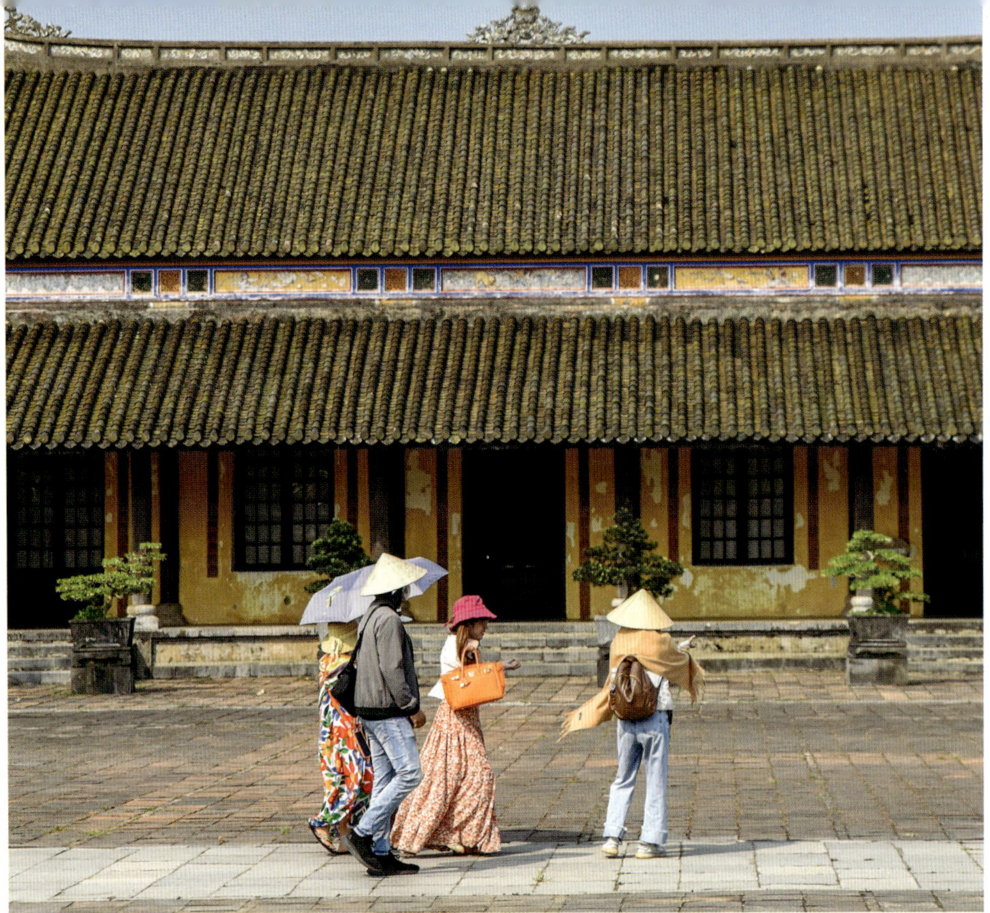

REMAINS OF A ROYAL COMPOUND

Today, visitors to Hue Citadel can still admire dozens of intact, restored buildings. First, they cross a bridge over the citadel's moat and enter the complex through the grand Ngo Mon gate, a thick stone structure topped by a two-story pavilion. This places visitors at the foot of Thai Hoa Palace. Inside its red-and-gold interior sits the original throne of the emperor, where Vietnam's monarch would preside during festivals and state visits. Four royal temples flank this imperial building, each accessed by shady paths.

Visitors can also walk atop a section of the citadel's twenty-foot-high original walls, alongside the main entrance. From that elevated vantage point, they can survey the grounds of the fort, then look south across the Perfume River to downtown Hue city.

A QUARTET OF MAGICAL CREATURES

Scattered through the stately architecture and sublime landscaping of Hue Citadel are dozens of images of dragons, phoenix, turtles, and unicorns. Some are sculpted in stone. Others are painted on ceilings, carved into wooden eaves, woven through vibrant murals, or glazed onto ceramics.[114]

But these beasts are no mere decorations. Instead, they are the mystical protectors of the complex, having been placed here for that very reason by the founders of Hue Citadel. Collectively, the dragon, phoenix, turtle, and unicorn are known as Vietnam's "Four Sacred Creatures." Many Vietnamese associate those beings with honorable character traits and believe that, by venerating them, they can earn their spiritual protection.[115]

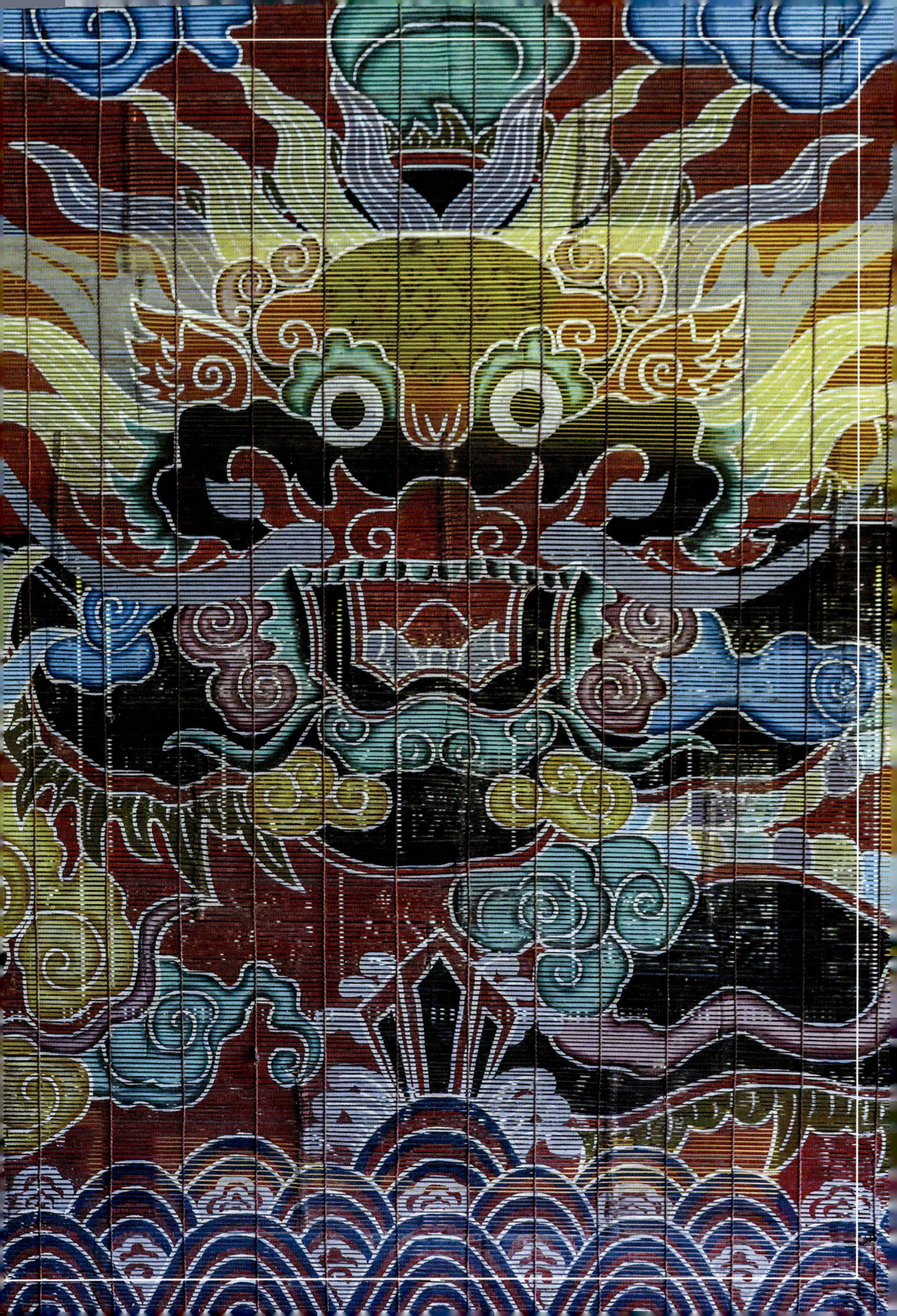

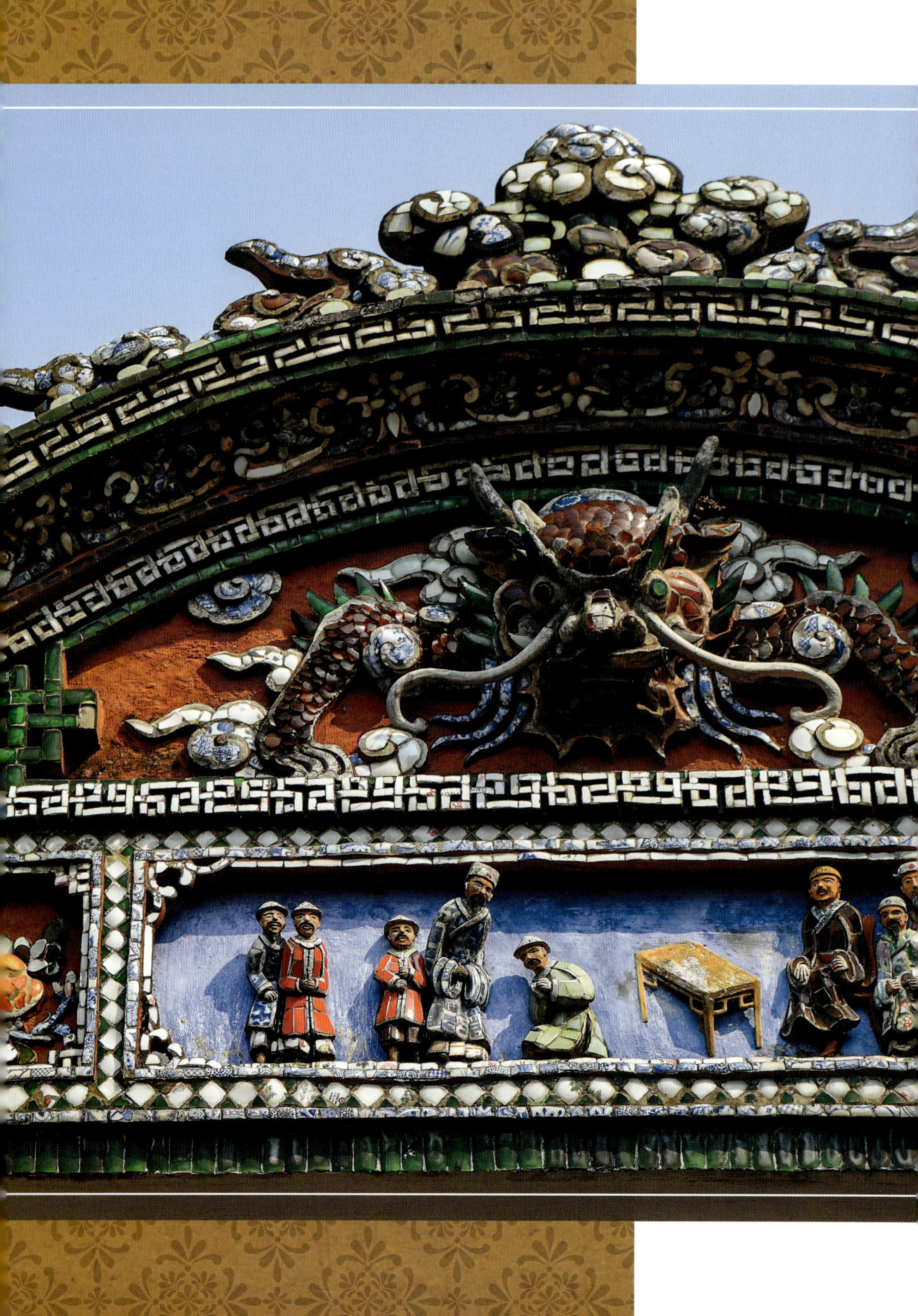

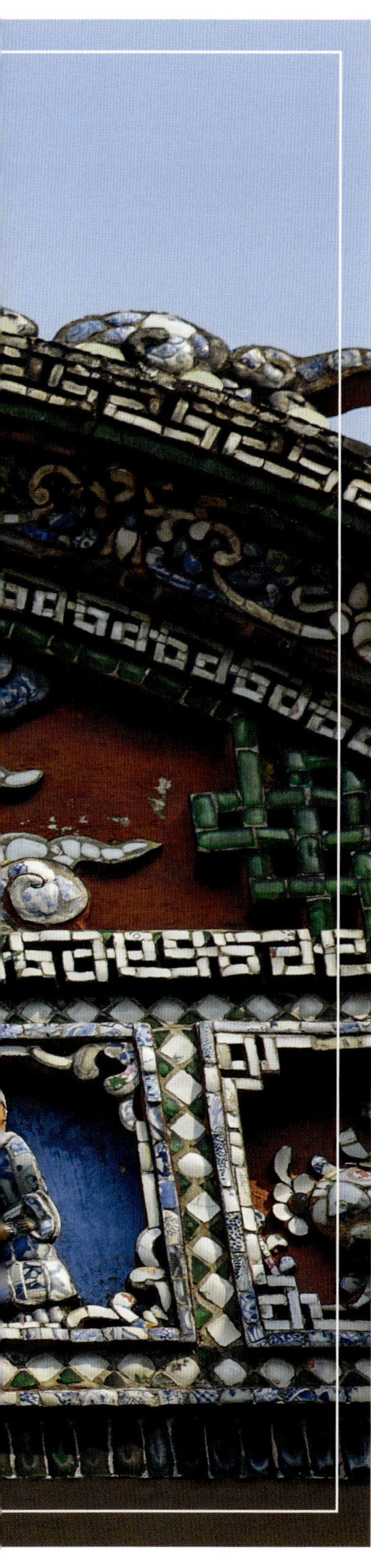

THE SPIRITUAL REASON HUE CITADEL IS PROTECTED BY ANIMALS

Hue Citadel appears to have more images of the sacred beasts than any other location in Vietnam. The reason for this is spiritual.

Buddhism and Christianity are now Vietnam's chief religions. Both have millions of followers who attend the country's hundreds of churches and Buddhist temples. Yet many of those Buddhists and Christians hold beliefs shaped by Confuscianism. This faith gained popularity in Vietnam from the tenth century onward, before it faded from relevance amid the rise of other religions, including Christianity. That is, until Hue Citadel helped spark Confuscianism's resurgence.[116]

When the Nguyen Dynasty took control of Vietnam in 1802, its leaders made two key decisions. First, Hue Citadel was constructed as the new imperial headquarters. Second, Confuscianism was declared the national religion. The Nguyen Dynasty rulers believed strongly in Confuscianism, which promotes morality, ethics, and seeking harmony with one's community, as a set of values that would promote a citizenry devoted to peace.[117] So they banned Christianity, which they associated with encroaching Western colonialism, and instead heavily promoted Confuscianism and began building monuments to celebrate this religion.

This was especially true within its new hub at Hue Citadel. There they tasked artisans with painting, sculpting, and carving attractive artworks of the four sacred creatures, who would act as the citadel's spiritual guardians. The concept of this mystical quartet originated in China, via Confucianism, but Vietnam placed its own spin on their mythology.[118]

HOW A DRAGON CREATED VIETNAM

According to legend, Vietnam's existence traces back to a dragon. Scaly and lethal, this beast features in Vietnamese art up to twenty-two hundred years old and defines the rollicking tale of the country's birth.

This national origin story begins with De Minh, an ethnically Chinese king, who married a fairy from Vietnam's mountains. Their son then mated with the daughter of the Dragon Lord of the Sea. Soon the couple produced a boy, Lac Long Quan, considered the first Vietnamese citizen. According to the legend, he not only fathered a hundred children himself but went on to rule the original Vietnamese dynasty. So beloved were dragons in Vietnamese lore that they were later used to adorn the robes of Vietnamese emperors.[119]

AN ASPIRATIONAL BIRD

The empresses, in contrast, often donned garments featuring a graceful feathered creature: the phoenix. The Vietnamese phoenix differs significantly in appearance from the common bird-like depictions in Western texts and folklore. Vietnam's version is a more unusual being. Thick plumage sits beneath its long reptilian neck. To its rear, a fish tail pokes from under a turtle shell. Many Vietnamese believe the phoenix embodies attributes all humans should strive for—poise, integrity, and honor.[120]

THE BELOVED TURTLE

Turtles displayed throughout Hue Citadel are not only icons of wisdom, resilience, and strength. They also represent Vietnamese independence. In the early 1400s, the nation was being pillaged by forces of China's Ming Dynasty, which was so wealthy and powerful that it appeared invincible.

No mere mortal could halt these rampant invaders. Or so it seemed, until in 1428 they encountered a real-life Vietnamese rebel named Le Loi. According to lore, Le Loi's valiant efforts to banish the Chinese were noticed by Vietnam's dragon king, Lac Long Quan, who gifted Le Loi a magical sword. This weapon let Le Loi slice his way through the Chinese army, who were forced to flee Vietnam once and for all. As Vietnam celebrated this military victory, its new emperor, Le Loi, visited Hanoi's Hoan Kiem Lake. There he passed the sword to a supernatural turtle, who has supposedly kept it safe ever since.[121]

VIETNAM'S MOST ELEGANT SACRED ANIMAL

The fourth of the Four Sacred Animals is the unicorn, an icon of beauty and tranquility. Locals kneel before its likeness in many temples and may pause to show respect to the unicorns depicted throughout Hue Citadel. Praying to this elegant creature is said to earn the worshipper safety and good luck. Unicorns are also believed to have the power to bestow patience, kindness, and intelligence.[122]

To this day, beyond the walls of the citadel, Confucianism still influences this Southeast Asian nation. The Vietnamese strongly respect their elders, highly value social harmony, and keep strong ties with their community—all of which are core tenets of the faith. For domestic visitors who come to Hue Citadel, they can be seen pausing in contemplation before depictions of the Four Sacred Animals. Foreigners, too, can close their eyes and call upon them for divine assistance. For no matter who requests help, this mystical cohort remains on eternal security duty and symbolizes how Hue Citadel helped revive Confucianism in Vietnam.[123]

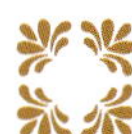

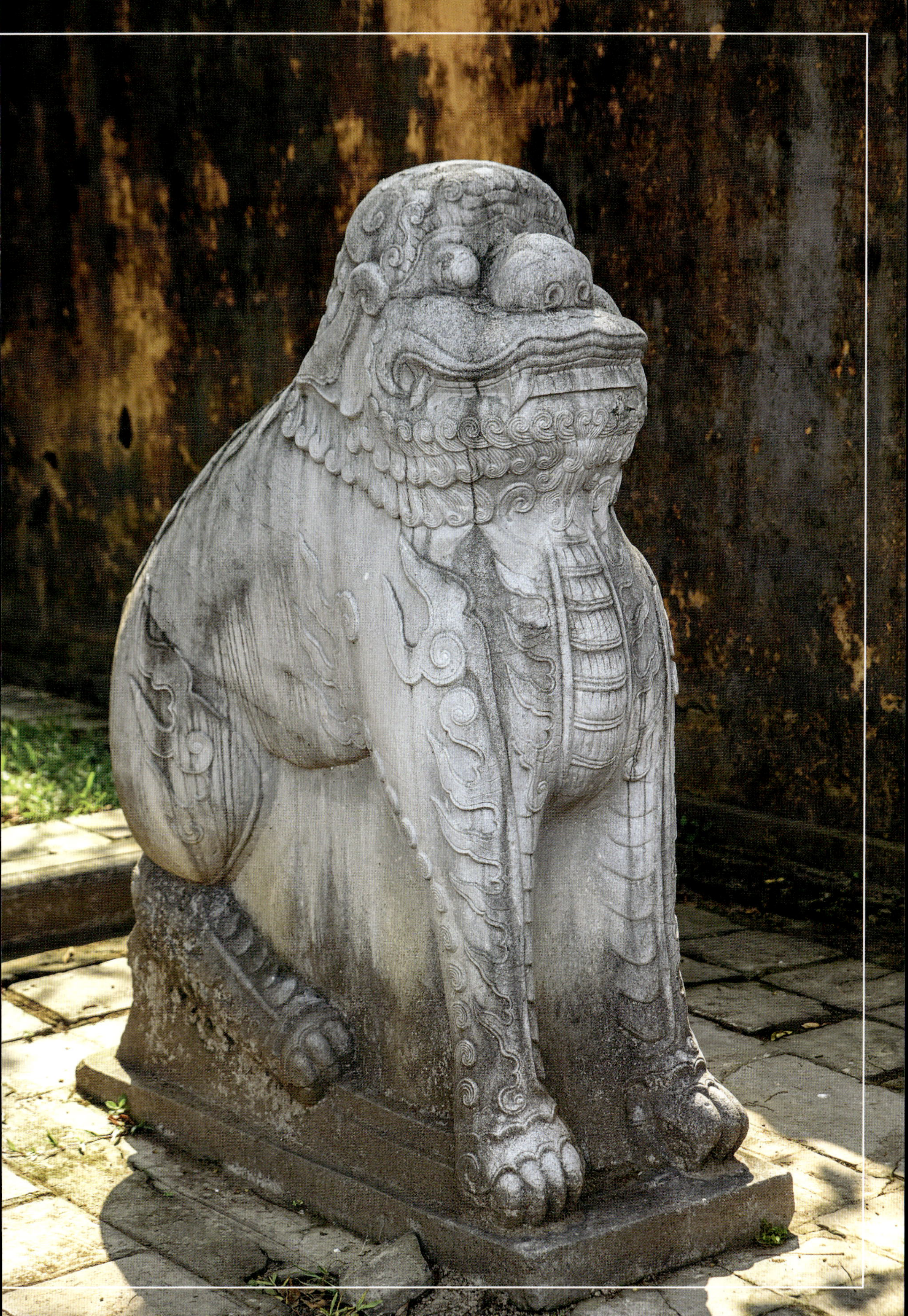

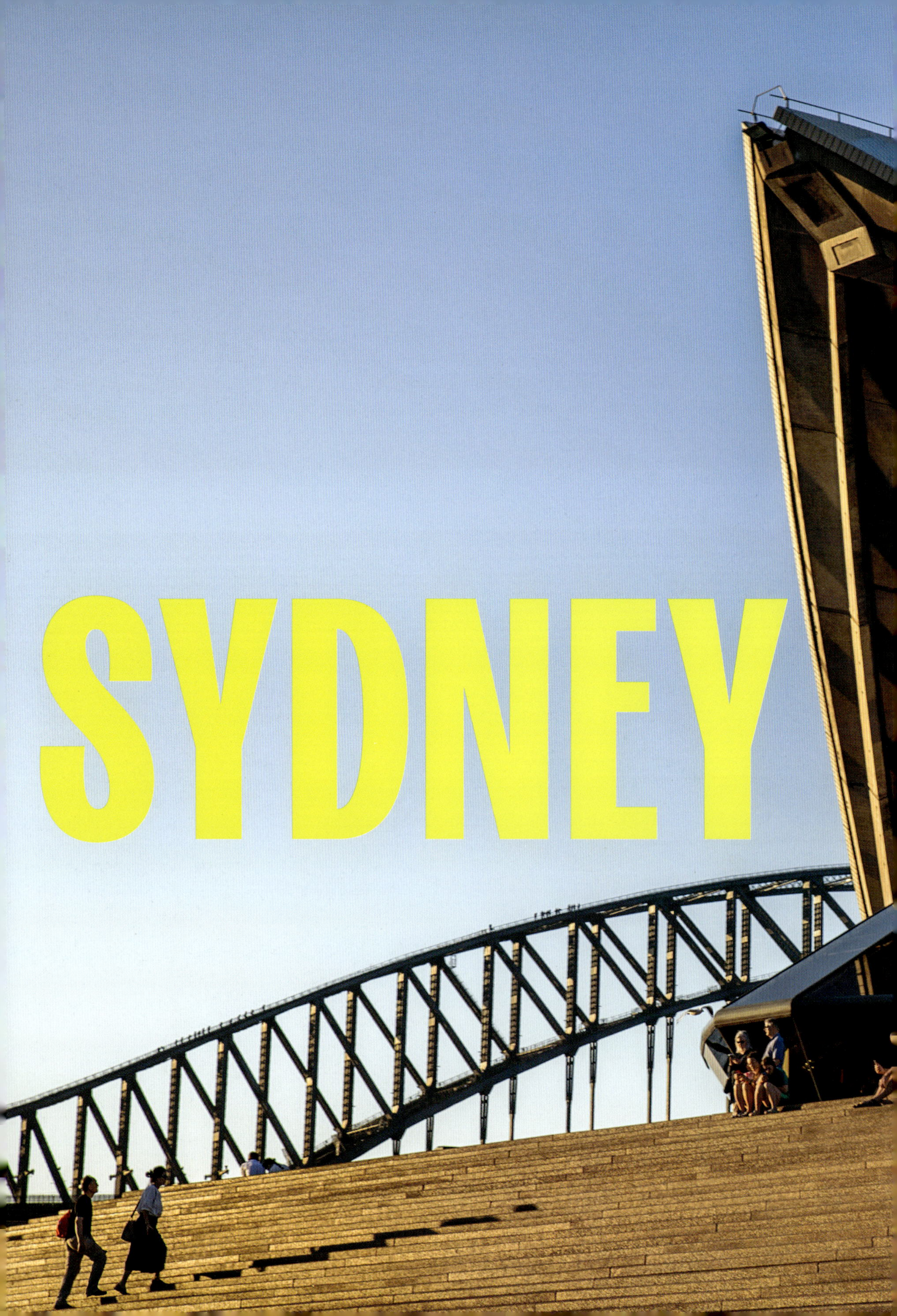
SYDNEY

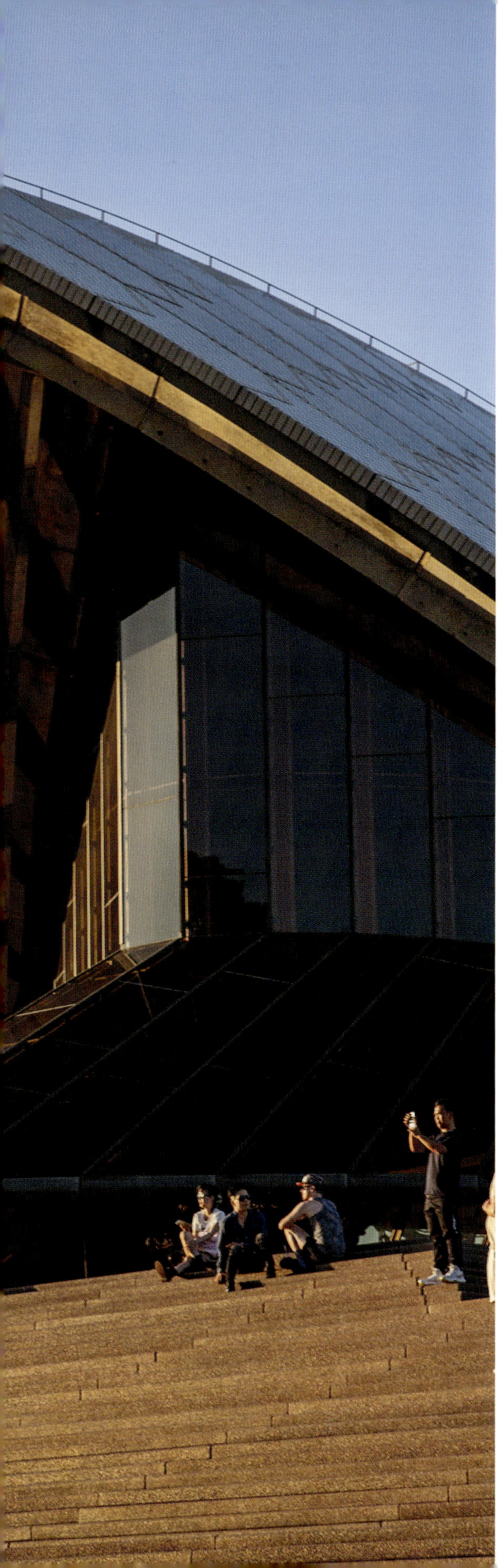

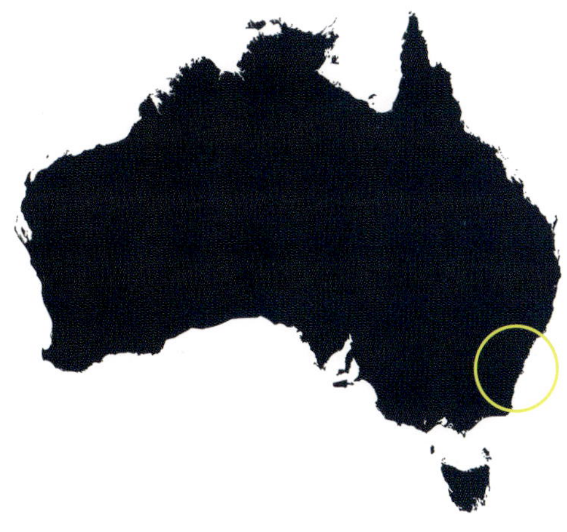

His name is all over Sydney. It graces parks, restaurants, businesses, and even the peninsula where the world-famous Sydney Opera House stands. Yet Woollarawarre Bennelong somehow remains mysterious, even to most Australians. Broad-shouldered, curly-haired, and daubed with body paint, a small painting of this Indigenous warrior stares at people wandering through the Royal Botanic Garden Sydney toward the revered concert hall.

Alongside that image is a heading which summarizes his crucial and heartbreaking legacy. "Bennelong: hero or traitor?" it asks. The answer has been debated for two centuries because Bennelong's controversial story is central to the defining moment in Australia's modern history: its ruthless colonization by Britain.

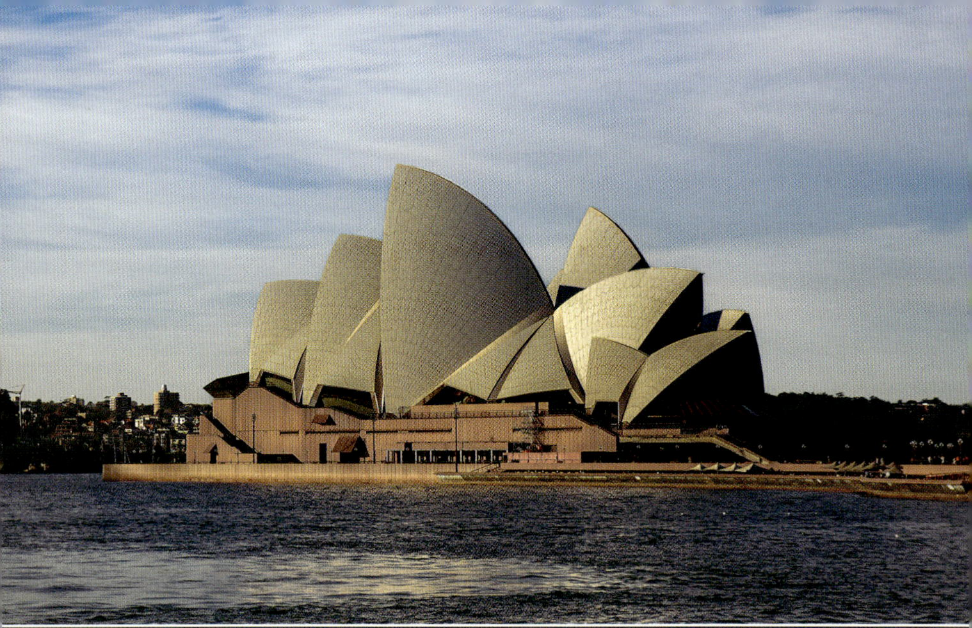

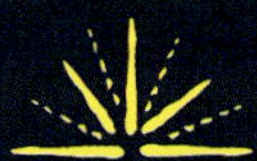

The Sydney Opera House is simultaneously timeless and modern. Although designed by Danish architect Jørn Utzon in the 1960s, the opera house is still distinctive and cutting-edge. Utzon's concept was among 223 concepts from across the globe submitted to Sydney authorities. The Dane had never stepped foot in Sydney, yet from his small European office, he envisaged a way to transform the city's harbor front. Competition judges said that amid a deluge of similar submissions of modernist-style glass boxes, they were struck by Utzon's daring and sculptural design.[124]

When looking at the opera house, some see a set of sails, billowing in the wind that whips across Sydney's waterways. Others spy a cluster of shells, like those dotting the city's sublime beaches. More still find that they're looking at branches of a palm tree, the crests of ocean waves, or the arching wings of a bird.

The truth is that Utzon's design drew on a wealth of sources. The opera house's iconic roof consists of fourteen interlocking, vaulted shells, with more than one million roof tiles.[125] So intricate was Utzon's design that, even with the input of ten thousand construction workers, the opera house took fourteen years to build.[126] Delays and budget blowouts triggered public backlash. Remarkably, given how beloved the building is now, the opera house was once widely considered an overpriced eyesore.[127]

Visitors can experience the beauty of the Sydney Opera House in a multitude of ways. They can simply wander its perimeter on foot, marvelling at how its facade seems to morph based on shifts in vantage point and natural light. Or visitors can peer at it from the deck of a boat during a scenic harbor cruise. Then, as the sun sets each night, Indigenous art is projected onto the building's exterior. Guided tours of its interior, meanwhile, detail the building's origin, history, grandest events, and complex architectural concepts.

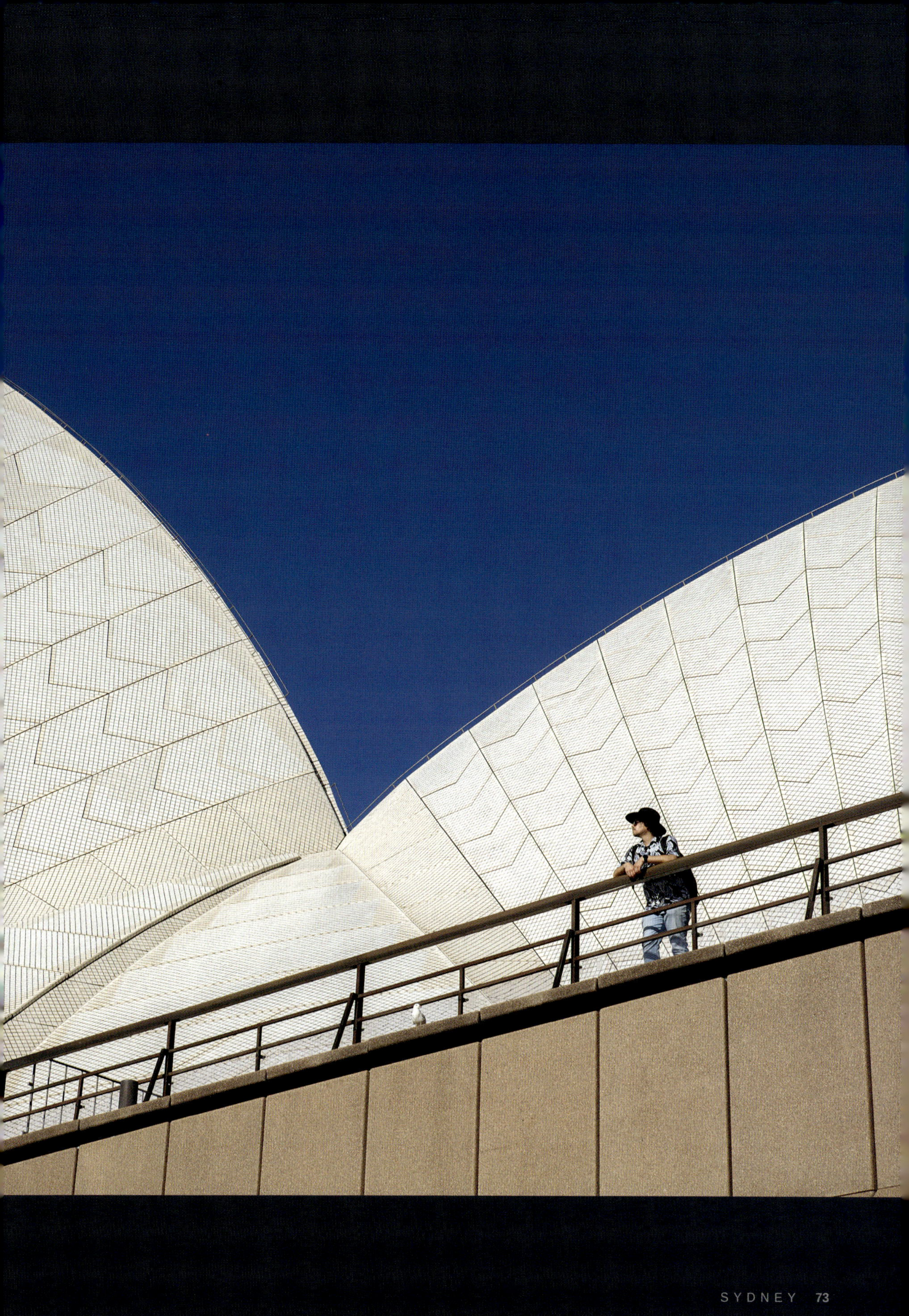

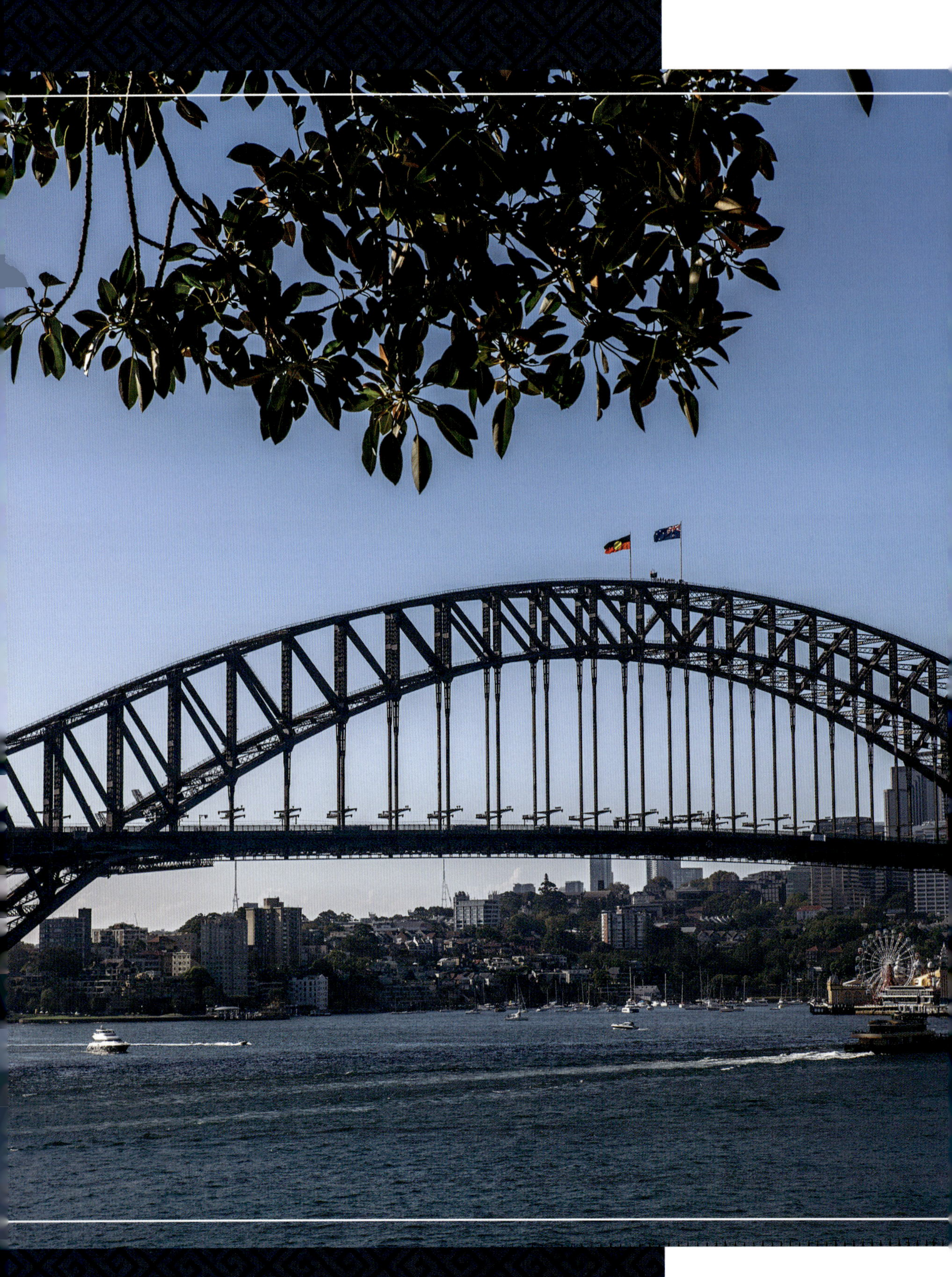

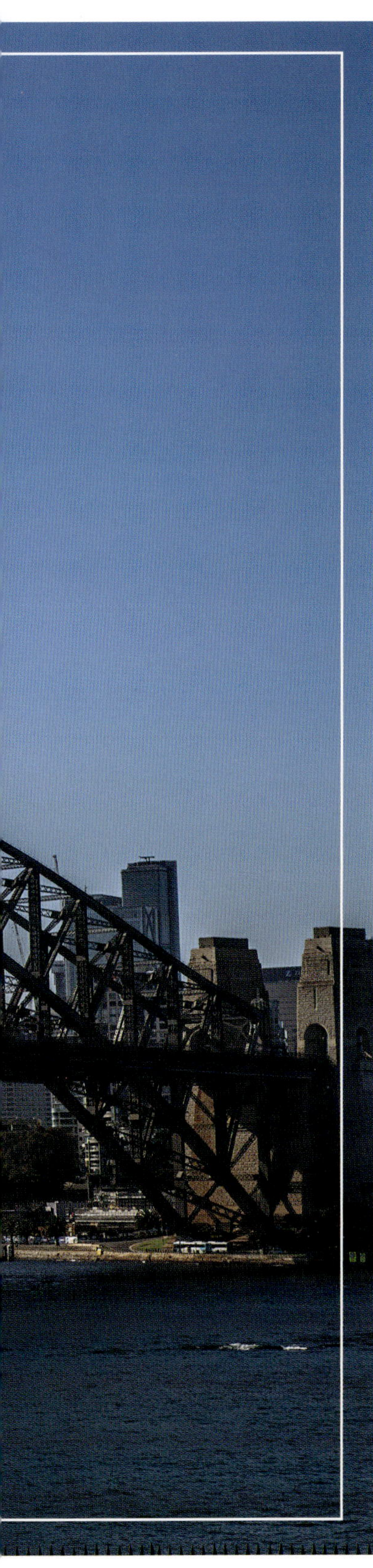

BRITAIN INVADES AUSTRALIA

From the opera house's balcony, concertgoers have a clear view of Circular Quay. Now a hub for harbor ferries and bulging with tourists, this quay was where eleven British ships landed in January 1788. Collectively, these vessels were called the First Fleet. On board were about seven hundred convicts and three hundred British soldiers and officials whose mission was to create a convict colony.[128]

Britain's invasion and seizure of Sydney was undeniably brutal to the Indigenous people, who had inhabited the area for fourteen thousand years. The Eora Nation—comprised of twenty-nine distinct Aboriginal clans—soon found itself dispossessed of its land, starving due to exhaustion of local food sources and dying en masse from smallpox introduced by the colonizers.

Less clear and still disputed is just how much effort the foreigners made to coexist with Aboriginals. Some history texts state that the British governor of the colony, Arthur Phillip, was ordered to build cordial relations. He supposedly encouraged his men to be kind to the locals and avoid disputes.[129] And there is evidence that the British attempted such diplomacy. During their earliest meetings in 1788, at Sydney's Port Jackson and Botany Bay, the newcomers shared meals, exchanged gifts, and danced with Indigenous people according to British documents. Adding to this spectacle were musket shots fired from British guns, a supposed exhibition of modern technology but, in reality, a revelation of rare power.

In the initial months after the British First Fleet landed, Sydney's Indigenous people did not know that the visitors intended to form a long-term colony.[130] But they began to avoid the foreigners when they saw them building a significant settlement less than a year after arriving, directly alongside where the Sydney Opera House now stands. Occasionally, Eora Nation people had violent encounters with convicts or British soldiers who roamed near Indigenous camps.[131]

Meanwhile, Governor Phillip forged ahead with a naive policy that had harsh consequences. He desired to integrate Indigenous families into his British settlement, where they'd be taught European ways while imparting Eora language and customs to colonists. Phillip believed this would improve relations between the two groups and help the British expand their colony. However, he didn't consult the Indigenous people about the plan. Had he done so, Phillip would have learned that the Eora had no interest in abandoning their culture for a new way of life. By December 1788, when not a single local family had agreed to join the British settlement, Phillip took drastic action.[132]

BRITAIN'S DESPERATE ABDUCTIONS

The British began to kidnap Aboriginal people, who were forced to join Phillip's colony. The first to be held captive was Arabanoo. This thirty-year-old Indigenous man was abducted from Manly Cove on New Year's Eve 1788 and died of smallpox in the colony in May 1789. By November that year, the Brits had seized two more Aboriginal males at Manly and imprisoned them on land now occupied by the Museum of Sydney. One of these captives, Coleby, managed to escape after just seventeen days. Not so fortunate was the man he left behind, a twenty-five-year-old from the Wangal people, Woollarawarre Bennelong. Reputedly, he was named after a fish, which proved appropriate since he grew up to become a skilled spear fisherman who provided sustenance for his community.[133]

During Bennelong's five months in captivity, he tried to make the best of a grim predicament. He impressed the colonizers by swiftly learning English and donning their fashions.[134] Bennelong also taught the British about local Indigenous culture, including the names and locations of Aboriginal clans, the intricate hierarchies within local communities, and traditional hunting methods.[135]

He was an impressive man according to diary accounts by leaders of the British colony, Captain Watkin Tench and Captain John Hunter. They described Bennelong as tall, athletic, muscular, and handsome with piercing dark eyes and wavy hair. His character also made a fine impression on them. Tench and Hunter praised Bennelong's bold, intrepid attitude, pleasant manners, generous sense of humor, and shrewd diplomacy.[136]

An unlikely kinship blossomed between Bennelong and Governor Phillip. Affectionate Indigenous names were exchanged. Bennelong referred to Phillip as *Beanna*, meaning "father," while in return the governor called him *Dooroow*, which translated as "son." During regular walks together along the waterfront now dominated by the Sydney Opera House, they discussed the contrasts between their cultures.[137] In doing so, many historians characterize Bennelong as Australia's first diplomat. They believe he recognized that the British were not leaving, so it was in the best interests of the Eora people to work with them.[138]

Yet all the while, Bennelong pined to return to his community and did just that at the first opportunity. Due to the trust developed with Governor Phillip, Bennelong's leg shackle was removed, and in the early hours of May 1790, he pretended to be ill, asked to be allowed outside his accommodation for some fresh air, and then escaped into the darkness.[139]

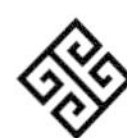

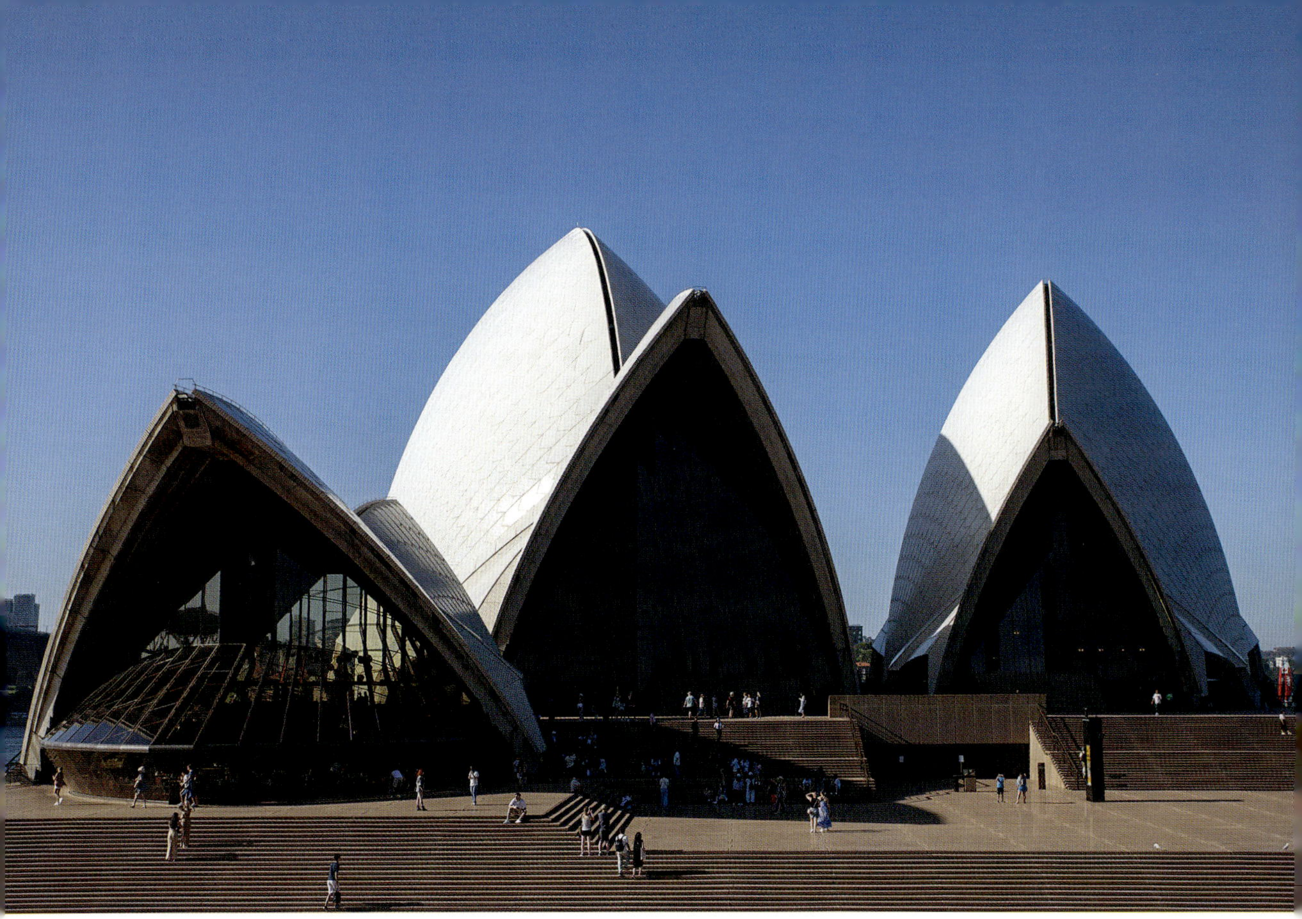

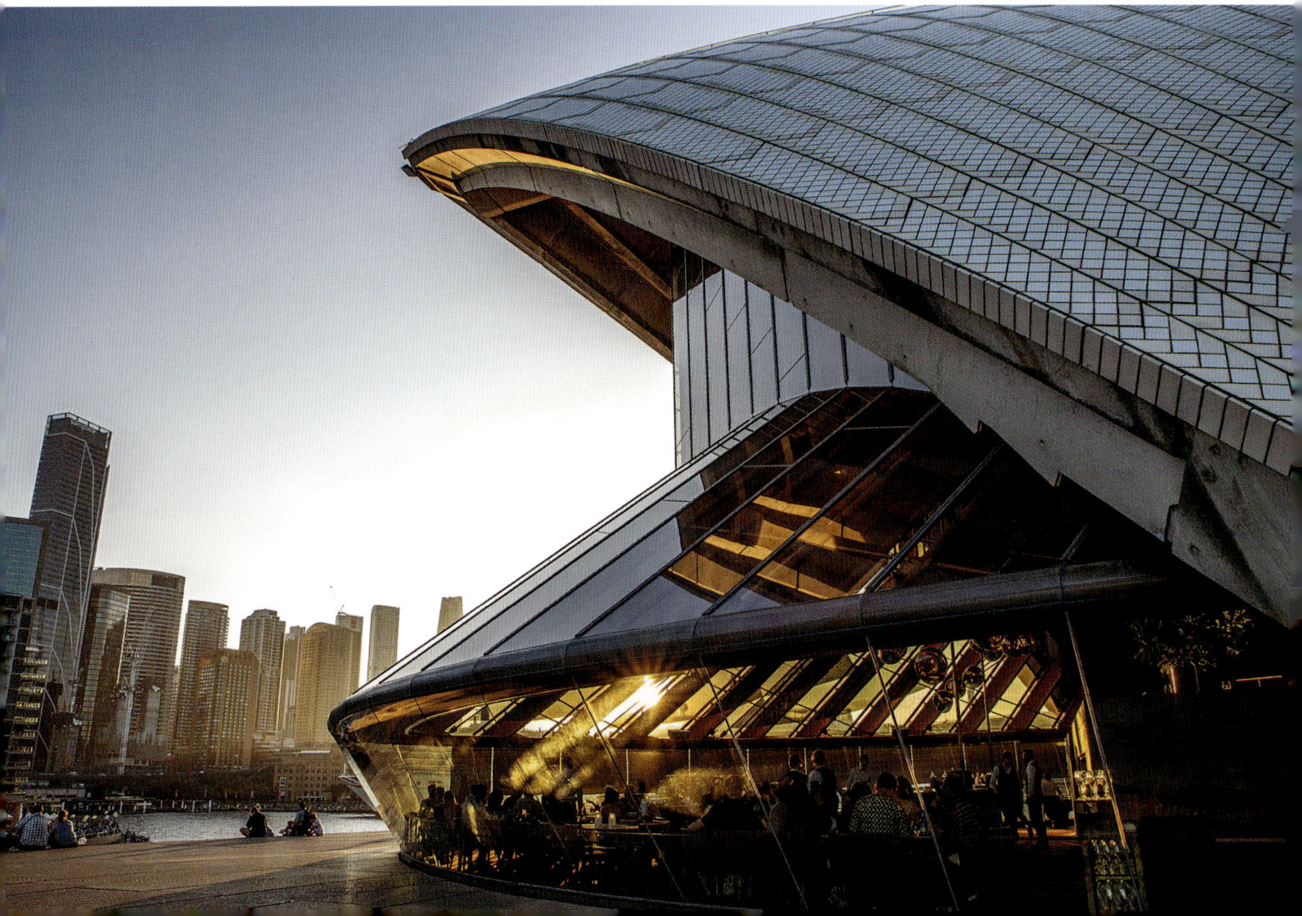

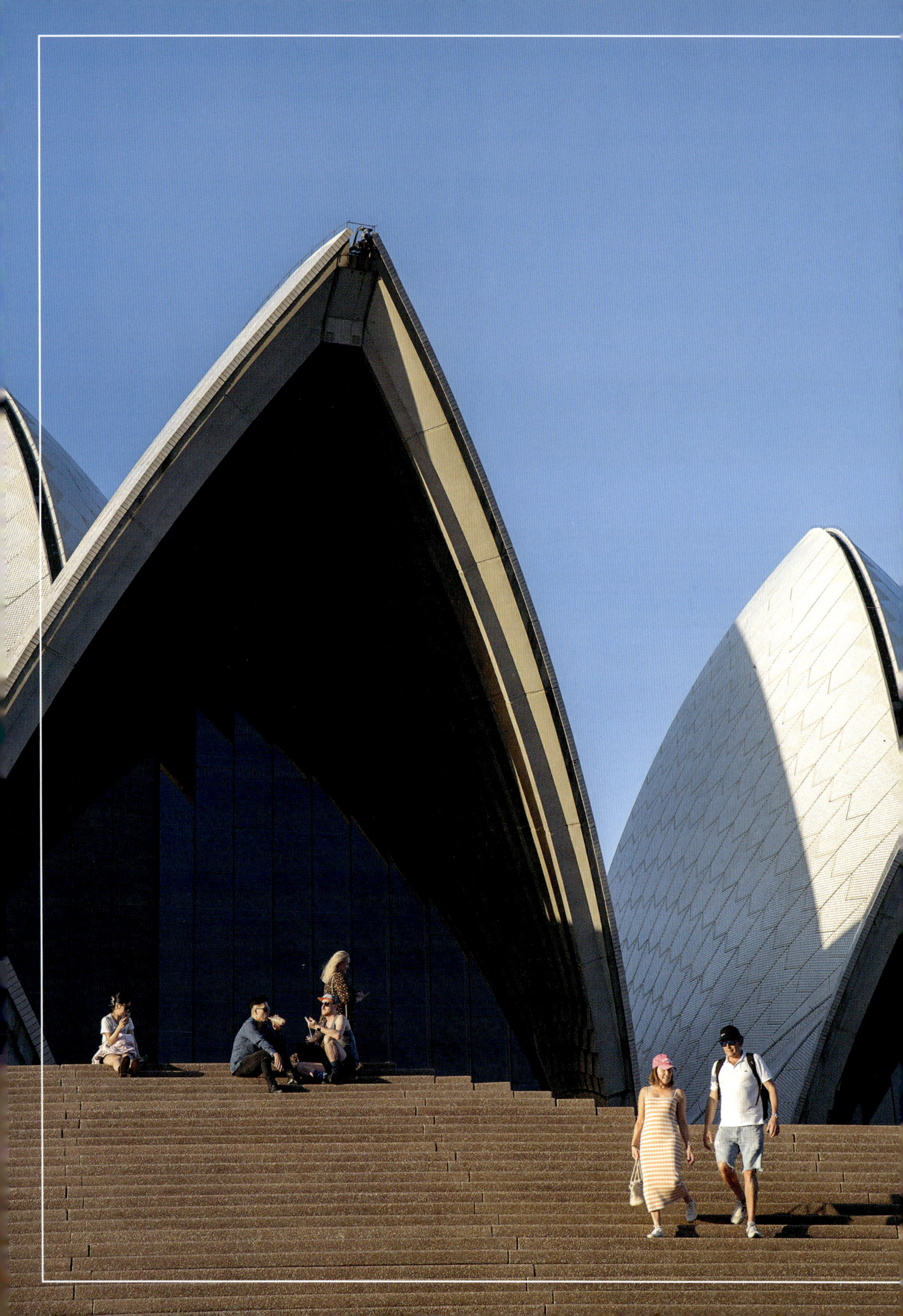

REVENGE IS HURLED AT THE BRITS

Four months later, the Eora asked Governor Phillip and his men to join them for a meal in Manly, now one of Sydney's most visited beach suburbs. There the Governor was first met with smiles, then by a spear. Thrown by Eora warrior Willemering, the weapon pierced Phillip's shoulder. Many historians describe this as retribution for his crimes punishable under Eora law, including the kidnappings of Arabanoo, Bennelong, and Coleby.[140]

In fact, Bennelong and Coleby were present and watched as Phillip's blood spilled. Bennelong did not intervene, and it remains unclear whether he knew about or approved of Willemering's attack. What is documented is that, about ten days later, Phillip recovered sufficiently from his wound to receive a visit from Bennelong. Once again, acting as an unofficial diplomat, Bennelong assured the governor that Willemering had acted only in self-defense, fearing that he was to be abducted by the British.[141]

Surprisingly, the spearing didn't trigger war between the two groups. Perhaps the colonizers believed Bennelong's explanation. He was so valuable to the British that they moved on from the incident swiftly.[142]

Meanwhile, the Eora people were satisfied that a degree of justice had been meted out. Only a month after the incident, relations between the groups had improved to the extent that Bennelong and several other Eora people repeatedly accepted invitations to enter the colony and dine with Phillip. In December 1790, Bennelong even visited the British with his wife, Barangaroo.

FROM INMATE TO EMISSARY

At the request of Bennelong, Phillip's men constructed a brick home for him on the land now known as Bennelong Point, where the Sydney Opera House was later built. Most historians don't interpret this as an indicator that Bennelong was devoted to the colonizers. Rather, his return to the colony is widely interpreted as a dedication to diplomacy. The better Bennelong helped the foreigners understand his people, the more likely it was that peace might be achieved.[143]

Bennelong's role as an emissary for the Eora people took him all the way to the United Kingdom. In 1792, he and a younger Eora man, Yemmerrawanne, became the first Aboriginals invited to England. During his three years in the UK, Bennelong visited Parliament, attended formal government events, and met English dignitaries, including King George III. Exactly what diplomatic role Bennelong played while in England, if any, has not been documented in great detail and continues to be debated by scholars today.

Some suggest that Bennelong was an ambassador of Australian Aboriginals, trying to advance their cause by explaining their beliefs and practices to English leaders. Others believe he was merely paraded around as a mascot by the Brits while he embraced a luxurious European life and drifted away from his roots.

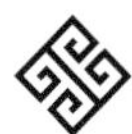

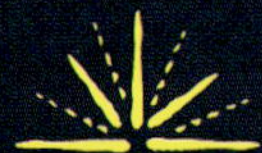

Visitors to the Sydney Opera House see a huge, distinctive flag fluttering near the structure. Black and red with a gold circle in the center, this is the banner of Australian Aboriginals, who number almost one million,[144] belong to more than two hundred language groups,[145] and have inhabited the continent for sixty-five thousand years.[146]

The flag was installed on top of Sydney Harbour Bridge in 2022 alongside the Australian national flag as part of nationwide efforts to pay greater respect to the country's original owners. Such progress is slow and terribly belated, but encouraging nonetheless.[147]

That same year, a sublime sculpture celebrating the Indigenous Eora people was unveiled alongside the opera house. Ancient Eora Nation fishing traditions inspired this shimmering metallic artwork. About twenty feet tall, it represents a *bara*, or shell fishing hook, used by Eora Nation women and adds to the generous aesthetic appeal of Bennelong Point.[148]

In addition to these installations, Australian cities are increasingly using their Indigenous names alongside English versions, such as Warrane (Sydney) and Naarm (Melbourne).[149] Major public events commonly begin with Aboriginal "Welcome to Country" ceremonies during which an Indigenous leader verbally consents to that event taking place on their traditional lands.[150] More national parks are being jointly managed by government authorities and traditional owners.[151] Indigenous tourism ventures are flourishing, especially in Sydney, the first land seized by the colonizing British in 1788.

Visitors to Australia's oldest city can now participate in Indigenous music sessions, cooking classes, and botany tours. They can also follow Yananurala, a 5.6-mile Aboriginal history walking trail that hugs Sydney Harbour and passes tourist hubs like the opera house, Harbour Bridge, and Art Gallery of New South Wales.

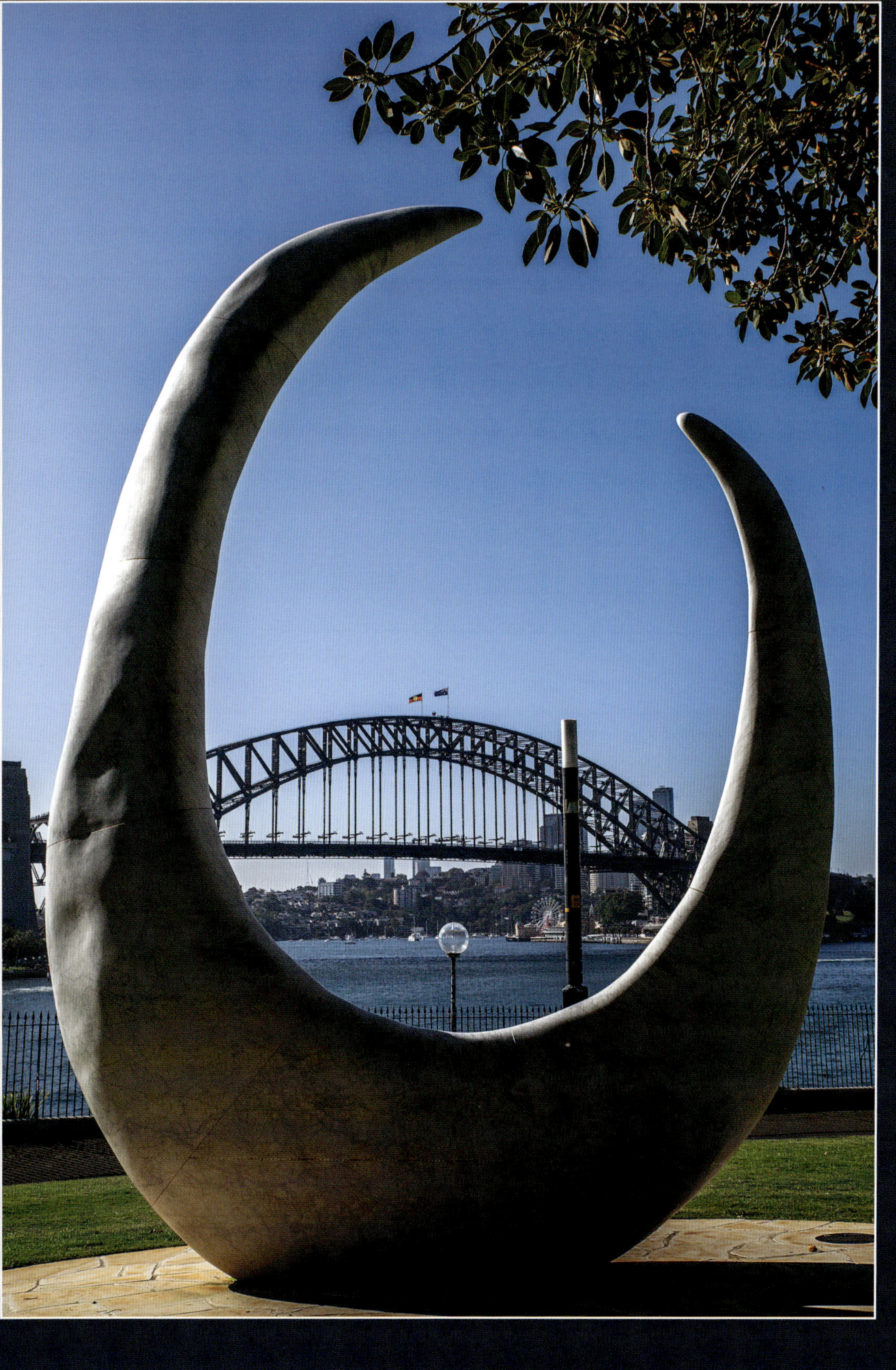

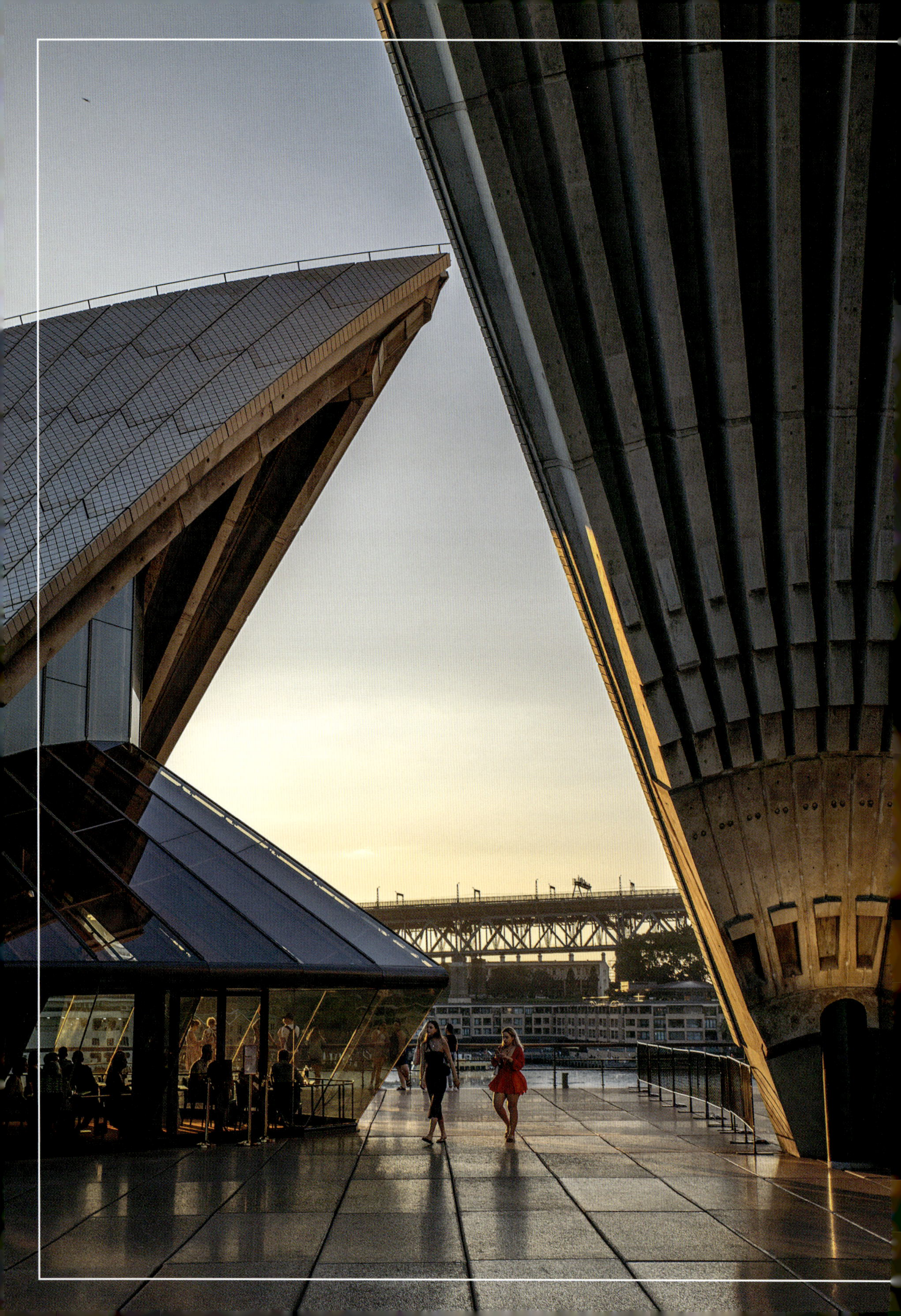

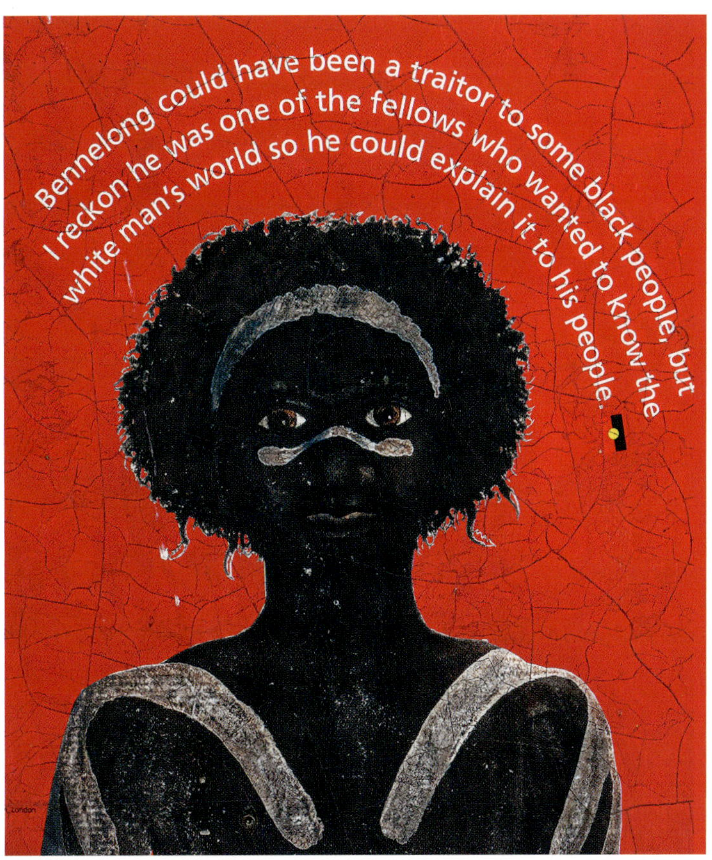

BENNELONG'S OUTCAST STATUS

After years abroad in the UK, Bennelong finally came home to Sydney in 1795. But it was not a joyous return. His wife had taken a new partner in his absence,[152] and the Eora people were inundated with hardships. Disappointment engulfed him as he saw that conditions hadn't improved for his community while he was gone. British forces continued to occupy and pillage Indigenous lands, and they had committed several massacres of Aboriginal people. Bennelong realized that his diplomatic efforts had been futile.[153, 154]

So Bennelong departed the British colony and rejoined his community. But he soon realized that his reputation was tarnished with his own people. Many of them were suspicious of him, sure he'd betrayed the Eora Nation by cooperating with the British and living a lavish life overseas. Bennelong's ostentatious new style of Western dress and command of the English language only fueled Indigenous perceptions that he had taken up allegiance with their enemy. This accusation left him feeling devastated and isolated for the rest of his life.[155]

Bennelong's is a pivotal story that illustrates the challenge many Australian Aboriginals currently face in trying to balance Indigenous and Western customs, laws, and beliefs. Yet Bennelong has remained mostly anonymous to white Australian society, such that his grave wasn't even discovered until 2010, almost two hundred years after his death.[156]

And whether tourists know it or not, while wandering the Sydney Opera House, they tread on the former home of Australia's original statesman. A trailblazing man, Bennelong now embodies the tensions and flaws of a Western society constructed on stolen Indigenous lands.

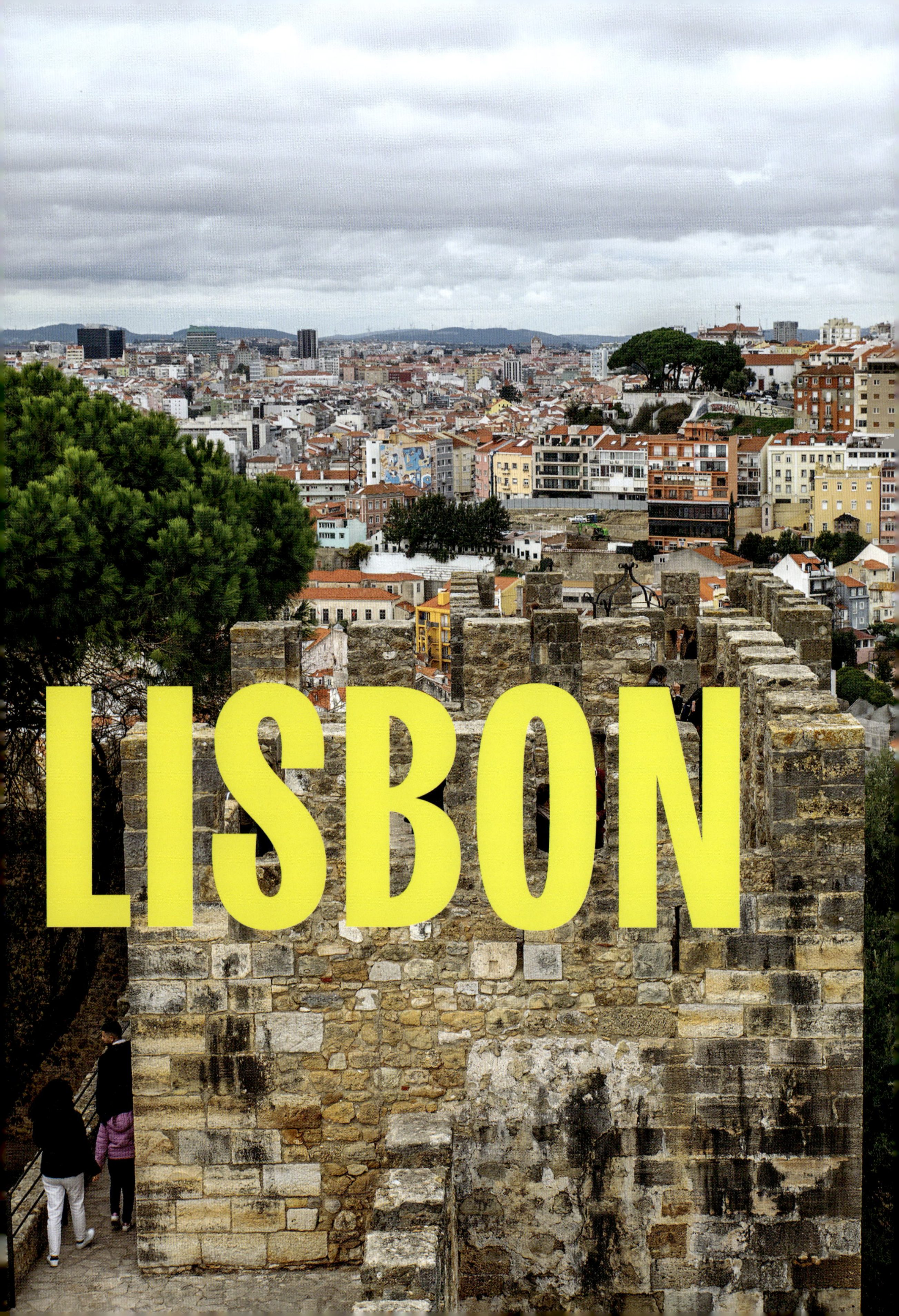
LISBON

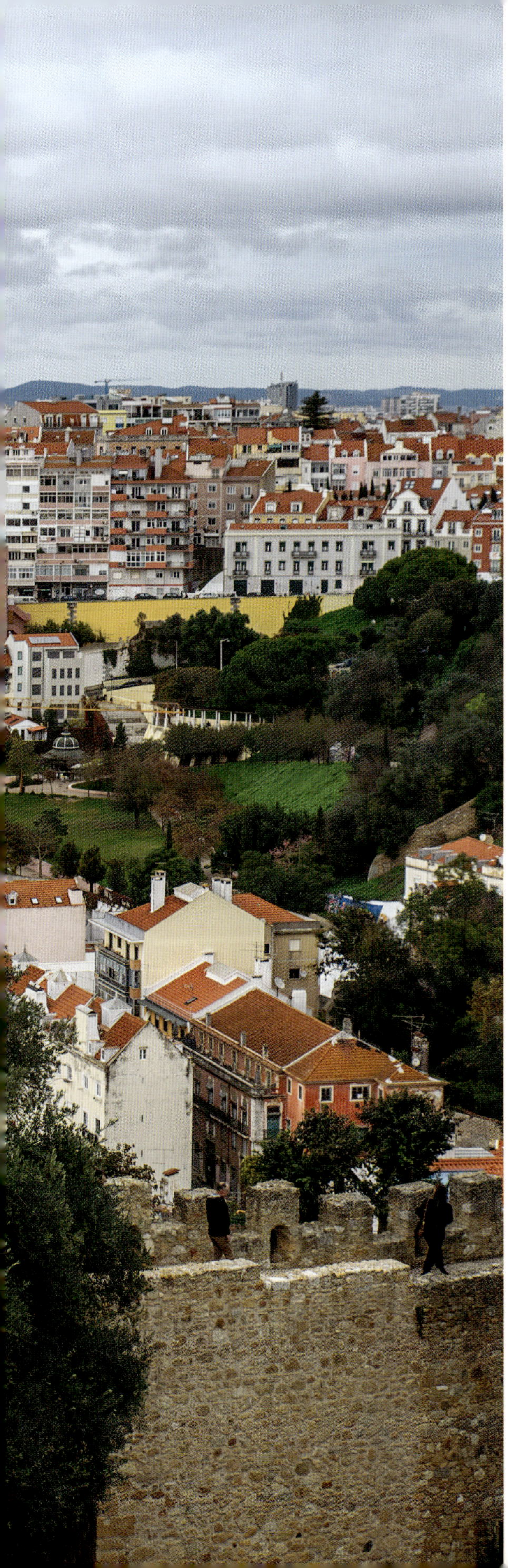

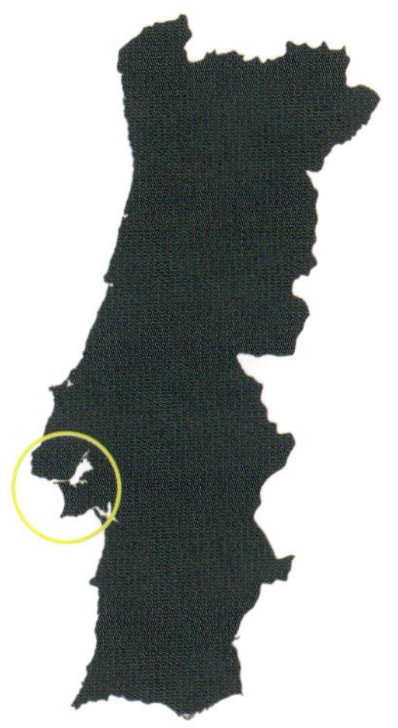

Lisbon attracts droves of visitors with its potent mix of addictive cuisine, graceful architecture, distinctive arts, mesmerizing music, and myriad historic sites, all set against an attractive backdrop overlooking the wide Tagus River.

Lisbon's old-world neighborhood Alfama is a labyrinth of steep roads and alleys scattered across a hillside, at the crest of which looms one of this city's oldest surviving structures, Castelo de São Jorge. Behind its bastions, turrets, and towers are many attractions, including an archaeological museum showcasing ancient artifacts collected from the castle. The weathered tiles, ceramics, coins, kitchenware, chamber pots, and artworks on display reveal the castle's one thousand years of history, explaining its evolution in design and purpose.

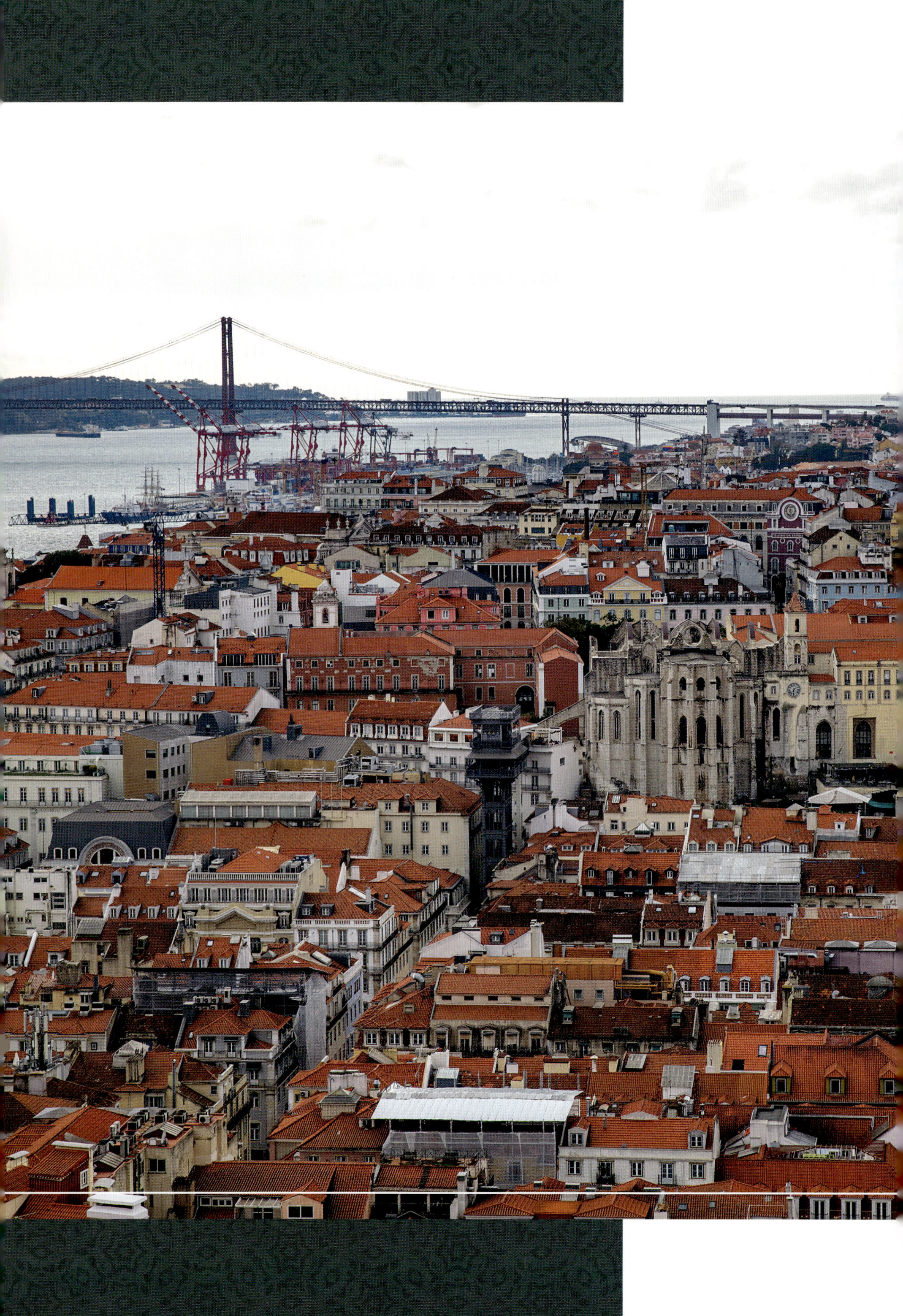

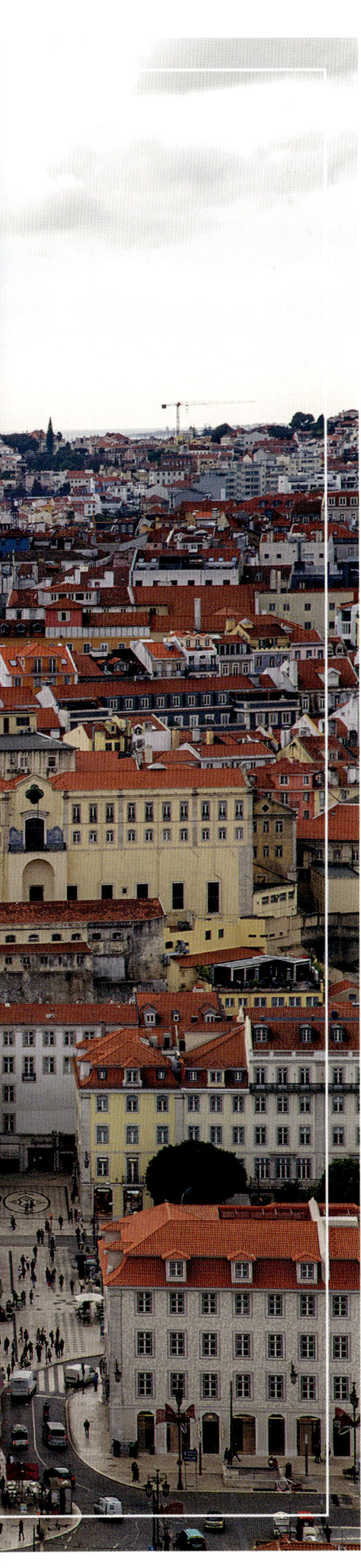

Visitors see items linked to many of the rulers who walked the castle walls, including one of its key characters, Portuguese King Manuel I. But they don't learn about a momentous puzzle forever connected to Manuel I's reign five hundred years ago.

Absent from this castle's museum is a retelling of the the long-lost city he established. This riddle still floats in the ocean thousands of miles east of Lisbon and confounds historians from China and Portugal: Where in the world is Tamão? The city was forged by Manuel I seemingly only to disappear. To this day, Tamão's location, and reputed trove of treasure, is being hunted by researchers from across the world.[157]

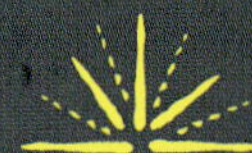

Central Lisbon remains shaped by a natural disaster that occurred in 1755. That devastating earthquake and subsequent tsunami caused sixty thousand deaths, razed twelve thousand buildings, and prompted Portugal's Royal family to relocate their Lisbon headquarters from seaside Baixa to hillside Alfama.

Nowadays, Lisbon revolves around its historic downtown, Baixa, which is arranged in an orderly grid of streets. This tourist district is lined by shops, cafés, bars, sweeping plazas, and historic buildings such as the San Justa Lift, a neogothic 148-foot-tall elevator tower with 360-degree city views from its rooftop platform.[158]

Forming Baixa's spine is Rua August, a lively and elegant pedestrian street that flows south before terminating at the grand waterfront plaza of Praça do Comércio.[159] King Manuel I built a royal palace here in the early 1500s before it was erased by the 1755 catastrophe.[160]

The hills of the adjacent neighborhood, Alfama, escaped much of the earthquake's damage. Its narrow streets, colorful buildings, and wall murals make it a time capsule of sorts where tourists can see how the city looked prior to that disaster. The impressive National Tile Museum, dedicated to the traditional Portuguese art of tile making, called *azulejo*, hosts a seventy-five-foot-long mural depicting a panorama of Lisbon's cityscape from circa 1750.[161]

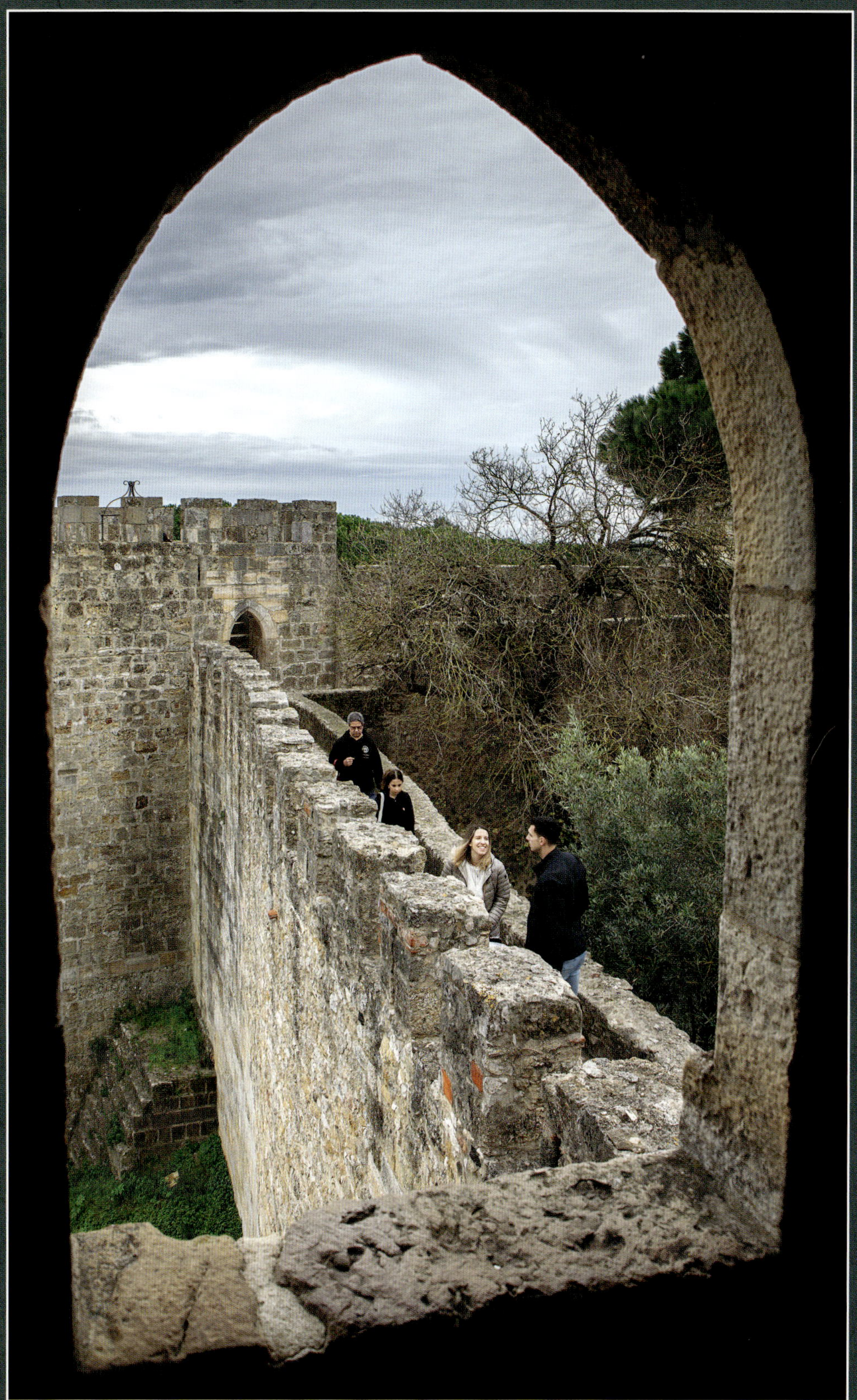

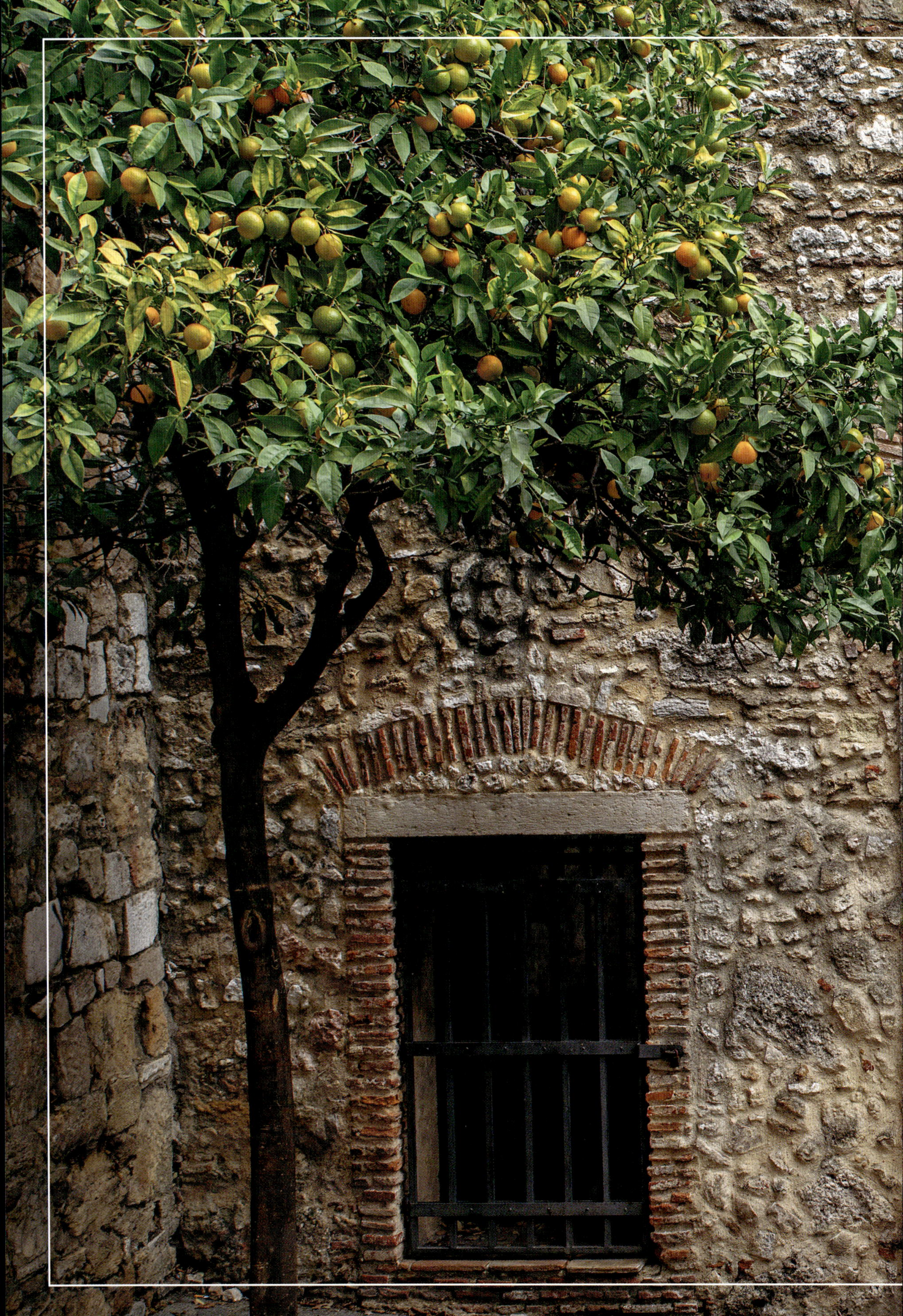

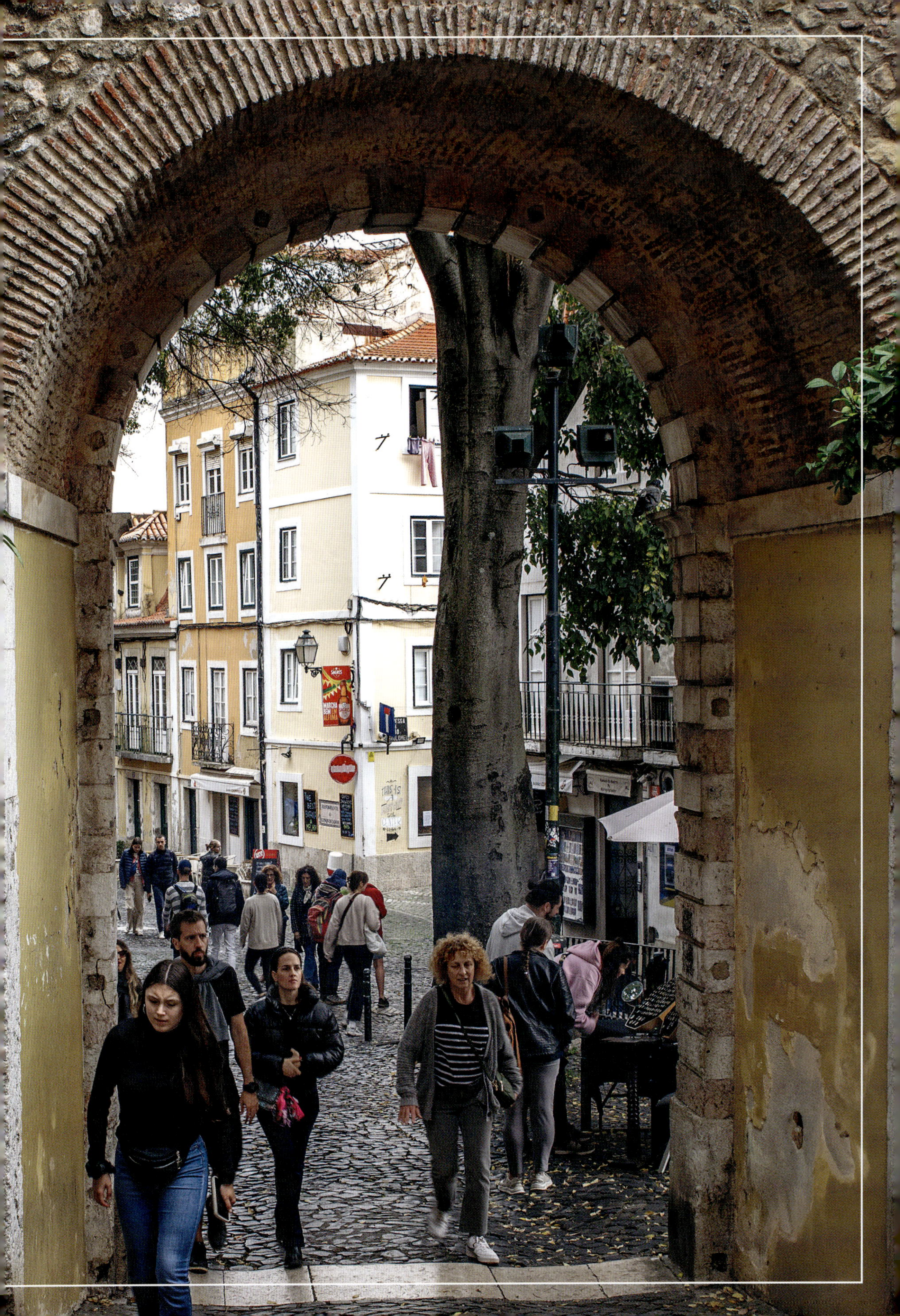
SAGRES
MARCHA BEM EM ALFAMA
THIS IS

PORTUGAL'S EXPANDING KINGDOM

Manuel I was just twenty-six years old when he took Portugal's throne in 1495. Beyond the power and wealth the position provided, Manuel also inherited an expanding horizon. Portuguese ships were sailing farther from their homeland than ever thanks to advancements in navigational technology. Seven years before Manuel came to power, Portuguese explorer Bartolomeu Dias led the original expedition to round the southern tip of Africa, establishing the first-ever maritime route between Europe, the Middle East, and Asia.

Manuel I's royal predecessors had invested in exploring new lands and creating fresh maritime trade routes. Adventurers they sponsored had laid claim to or established contact with the Canary Islands, Atlantic archipelagos, and West Africa. But Manuel I yearned to upstage them all by creating a trade relationship with Asia. Soon he did just that. Portuguese explorers reached India in 1498 and then began to trade with, and colonize, vast tracts of southern Asia.[162]

Fiercely driven, Manuel I set his sights even higher. Looming to the north of these new Asian colonies was a shadowy giant possessed of vast riches. His grand aim was to achieve something no European power had: attaining a foothold in China.[163]

At this time, China was arguably the world's greatest superpower. Its Ming Dynasty had the planet's largest armed forces, most populous city (Beijing), and operated an economy larger than all of Western Europe's combined.[164, 165] Yet China remained largely closed to the outside world. Initiating maritime trade with this goliath would catapult the status and influence of any European nation.

PORTUGUESE SAILOR EARNS HIS KING A STAKE IN CHINA

In 1513, Portuguese explorer Jorge Alvares set out to achieve this goal for Manuel I. That year, Alvares visited China on a fact-finding mission. Soon, Manuel I received detailed reports of what Alvares had discovered. China was found to be a rich, advanced society with a vast trade network, particularly via mammoth ports like Canton, which today is the sprawling port city of Guangzhou in the country's south, near Hong Kong.[166]

Alvares also learned that China was all but locked to foreigners. Centuries of devastating attacks by Mongol hordes and Japanese pirates had convinced China's Ming Emperor Zhengde that outsiders were malicious. Under his rule, the Great Wall of China was expanded, many new forts were erected along the country's coast, and foreigners couldn't freely do business on its mainland.[167]

However, a select few international merchants were permitted to sail into the Pearl River Delta, near Canton, to trade with the Chinese. Alvares and his crew followed suit. Their Portuguese spices and wine proved to be popular—so popular, in fact, that in late 1513, Alvares received a message from Manuel I praising his efforts.[168]

Soon, the king was even more pleased because Alvares negotiated an agreement with the Chinese to let him build a settlement for him and his Portuguese workers on a small, uninhabited island in the delta. Called Tamão, this trading outpost was a swift financial success. Once Alvares proved that his men were merchants, not would-be colonizers, Chinese clients inundated them with orders.

Over the following years, Tamão sprawled further and further. Yet to this day, historians are not sure exactly what it looked like, how large it became, and how many Portuguese lived there. Also uncertain is whether Tamão was a center of trading activity that welcomed Chinese merchants ashore or merely a depot and home for the Portuguese. Only one authoritative book has ever been authored on this topic.[169]

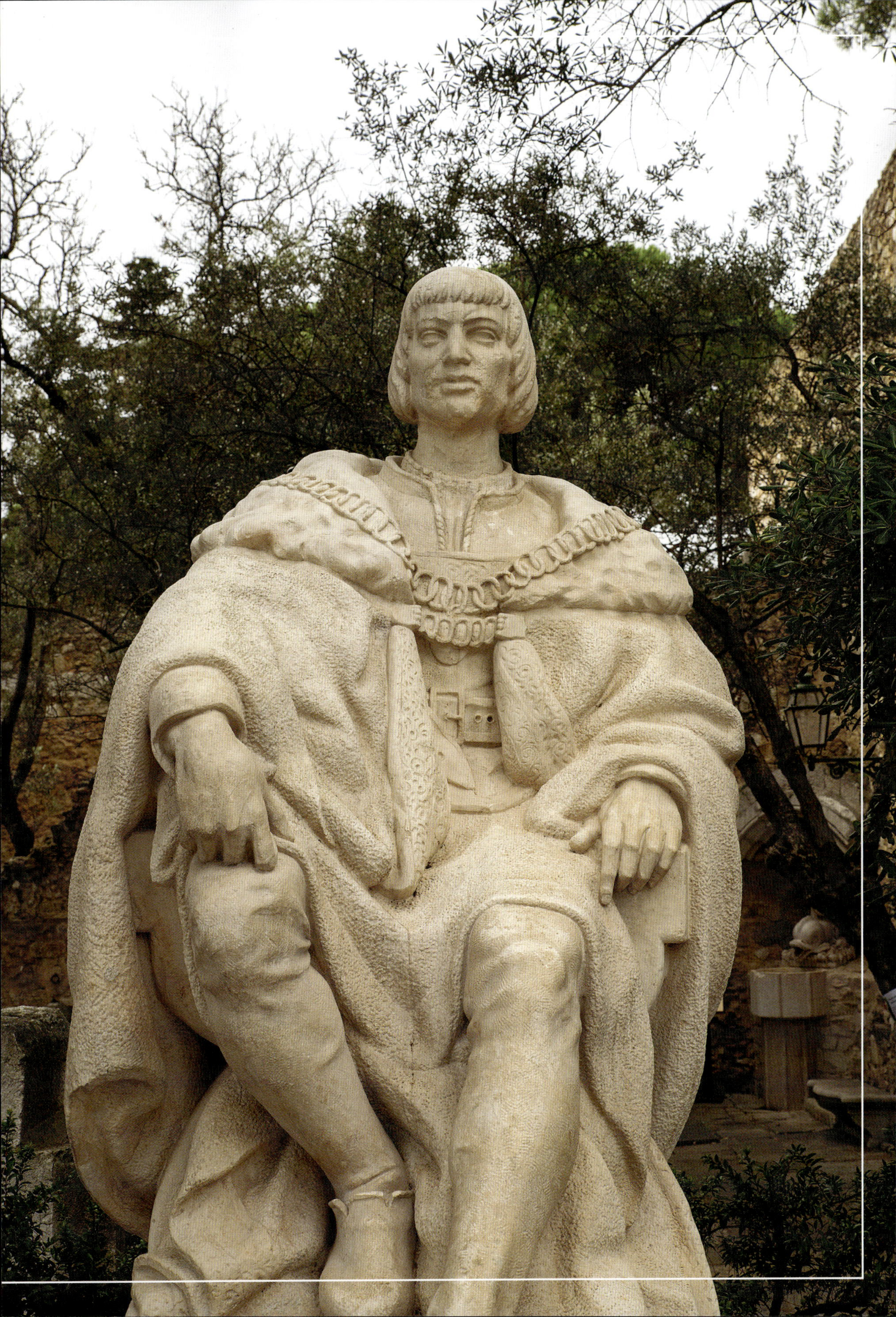

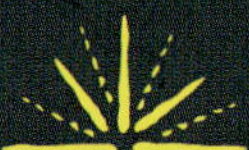

Lisbon's imposing Castelo de São Jorge is ringed by thick, lofty walls and topped by ten medieval towers. Beyond its fortified exterior are tranquil manicured gardens. These green spaces lead to perhaps the finest view in all of Lisbon: the sprawling vista from Place-of-Arms square, which overlooks the city and the River Tagus.[170]

The first iteration of the citadel was built more than a millennia ago by the Moors. Back then, they referred to their kingdom on the Iberian Peninsula where Portugal and Spain are located as *Al-Andalus*, which they controlled from AD 711 to the eleventh century.

Deeper inside the castle, more treasures abound: a fine artillery collection, the graceful Gate of the Holy Spirit, and the Torre de Ulisses, the complex's largest tower, which is named after the mythical hero Ulysses.[171]

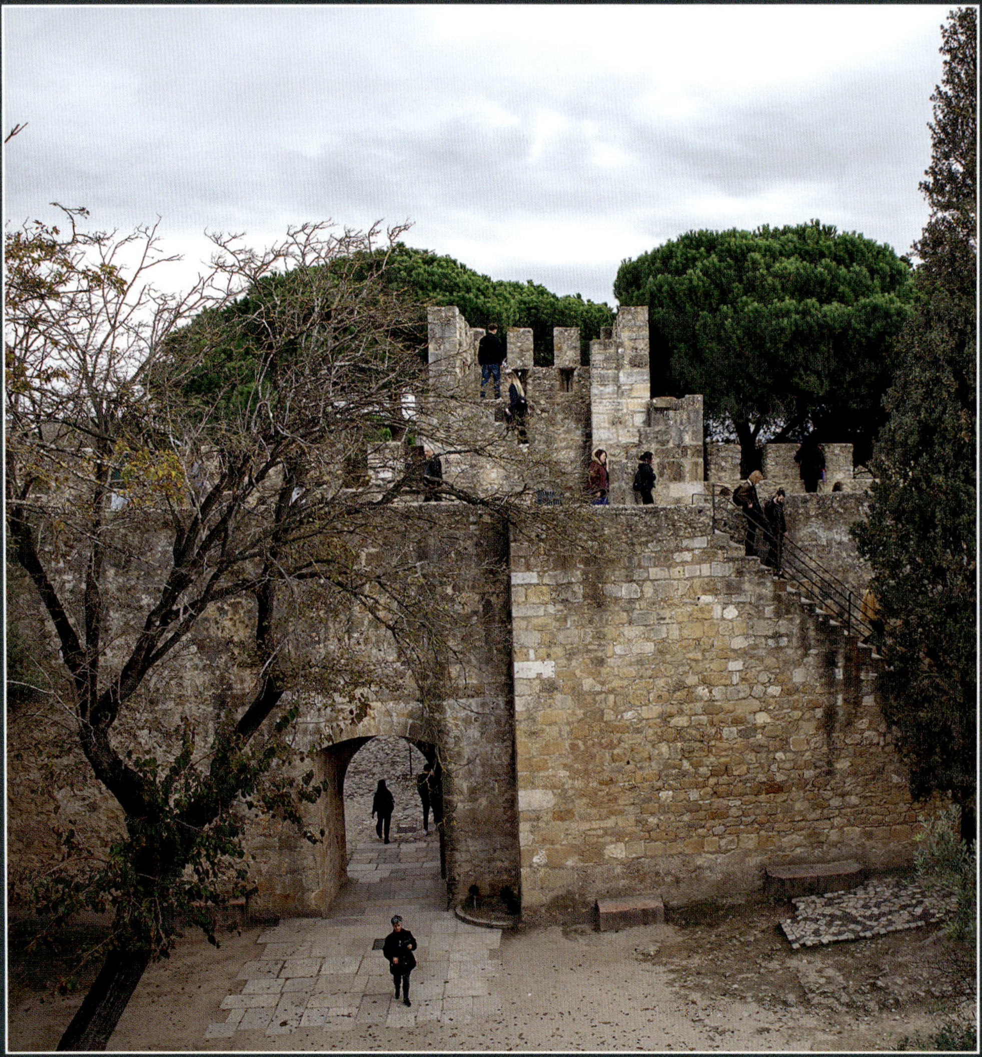

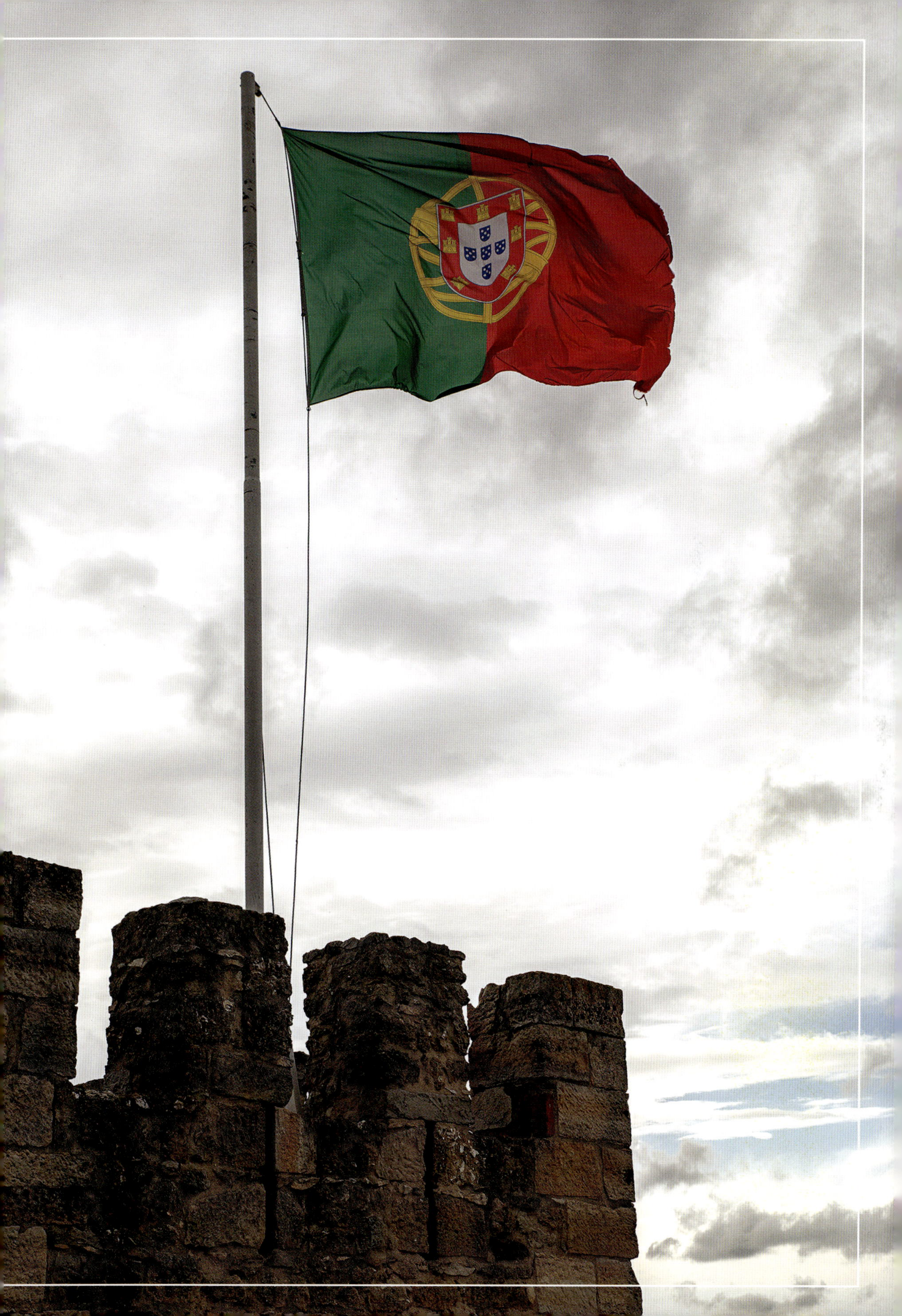

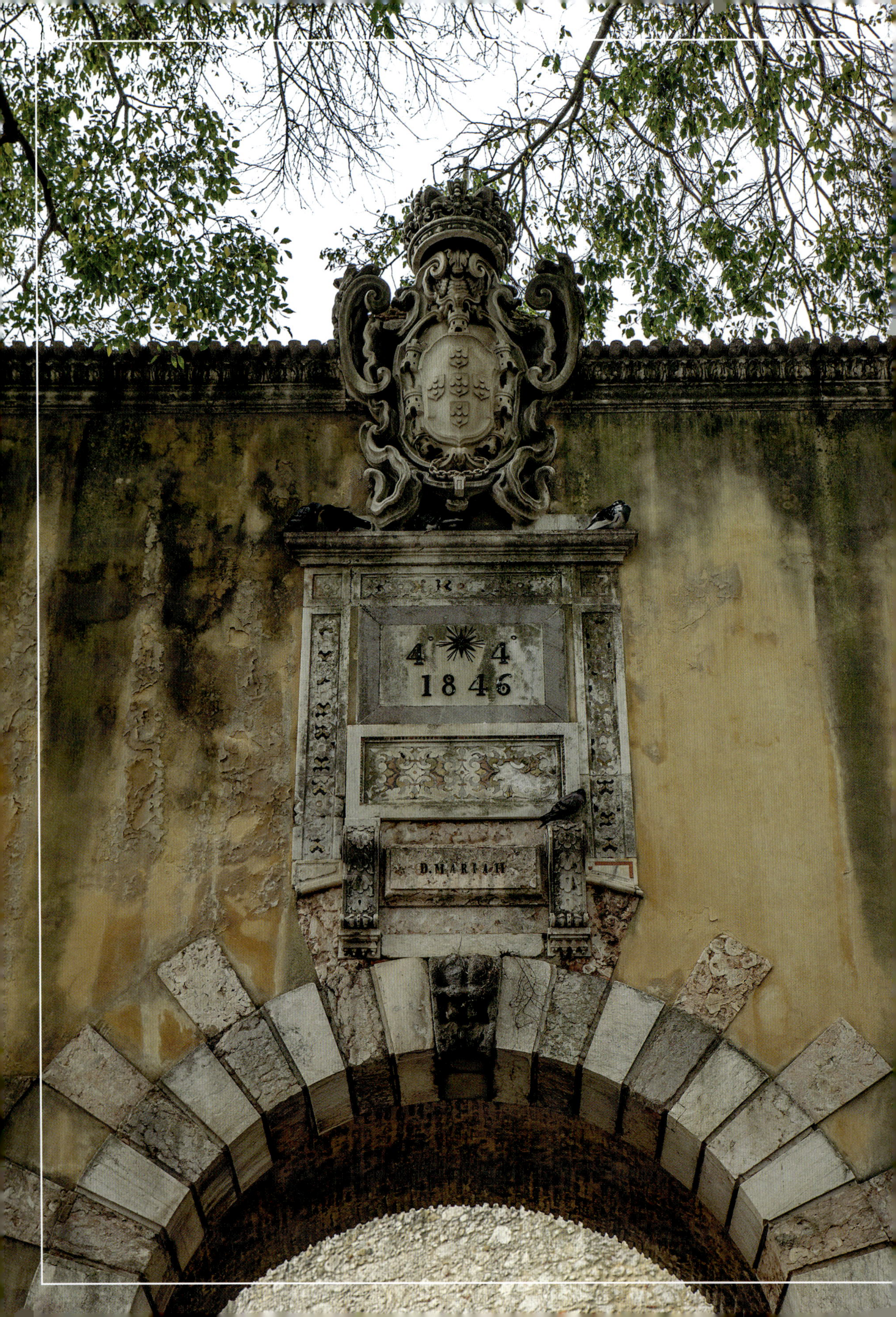
4 4
1846
D. MARIA II

BLOOMING TAMÃO ENDS WITH A BOOM

But Tamao's sharp rise was followed by an even steeper fall. Five years of Alvares's careful diplomacy was shattered by a rogue Portuguese captain named Simão de Andrade. De Andrade took command of Tamão in 1518 while Alvares was thousands of miles away in the southeast Asian port of Malacca, taking care of separate matters on behalf of Manuel I. A few months later, when Chinese tax collectors arrived at Tamão, de Andrade refused to pay them their normal toll. Then he added injury to insult by assaulting one of these men.

Yet what most alarmed the Chinese officials was the unsanctioned activity they witnessed on Tamão. Seemingly without the blessing of his king, Manuel I, de Andrade had decided to build a military fort. As a result, Tamão no longer resembled a peaceful trading settlement but rather an aggressive military outpost.

Hearing of the Chinese displeasure, the Portuguese went into damage control. Manuel I signed an official letter to China's ruling Ming Dynasty in which he condemned de Andrade's disrespectful actions and explained that the fort at Tamão was intended only as a line of defense against pirates. To Portugal's relief, China accepted their apologies.

But when Emperor Zhengde died in 1521, his agreement with the Europeans became void. The political winds shifted, and Chinese officials soon demanded that the Portuguese immediately and permanently leave Tamão. When this command was ignored, a bloody maelstrom ensued. Chinese military boats swarmed Tamão and engulfed it with cannon fire. Massively outgunned and outnumbered, Alvares and his men fled. As their boats set sail for Malacca, behind them Tamão lay in ruins. So, too, did Portugal's relationship with China.

Tamão's trade had been so lucrative that it reputedly housed great wealth, which had been stashed away, waiting to be shipped back to Lisbon. Legend has it that some of Tamão's treasure never left its shores. Following the Chinese attack, Tamão was abandoned. It has never again been located, despite fervent efforts by historians from Asia and Europe.

Just nine months after this setback, Manuel I died in late 1521, killed by the Black Plague outbreak that had inundated Lisbon.[172] Portugal eventually repaired its relationship with China via decades of cautious diplomacy, and in 1557, China permitted the Portuguese to establish Macau, a new trading territory.

Over the following centuries, Macau bloomed into a prosperous and independent colony, remaining under Portugese control until 1999, when it returned to the Chinese.[173] The world's only significant marker of Alvares is a statue of this forgotten explorer in a downtown Macau garden, called Praca de Jorge Alvares.[174] As of 2025, Portugal still has no grand monument to Alvares. Maybe he would receive his due if someone, anyone, could finally locate Tamão. Perhaps the site still bears the stone Christian cross erected by Alvares in 1513.[175] Planes and boats must unknowingly pass this sliver of land many times a day. But its whereabouts remain a mystery.

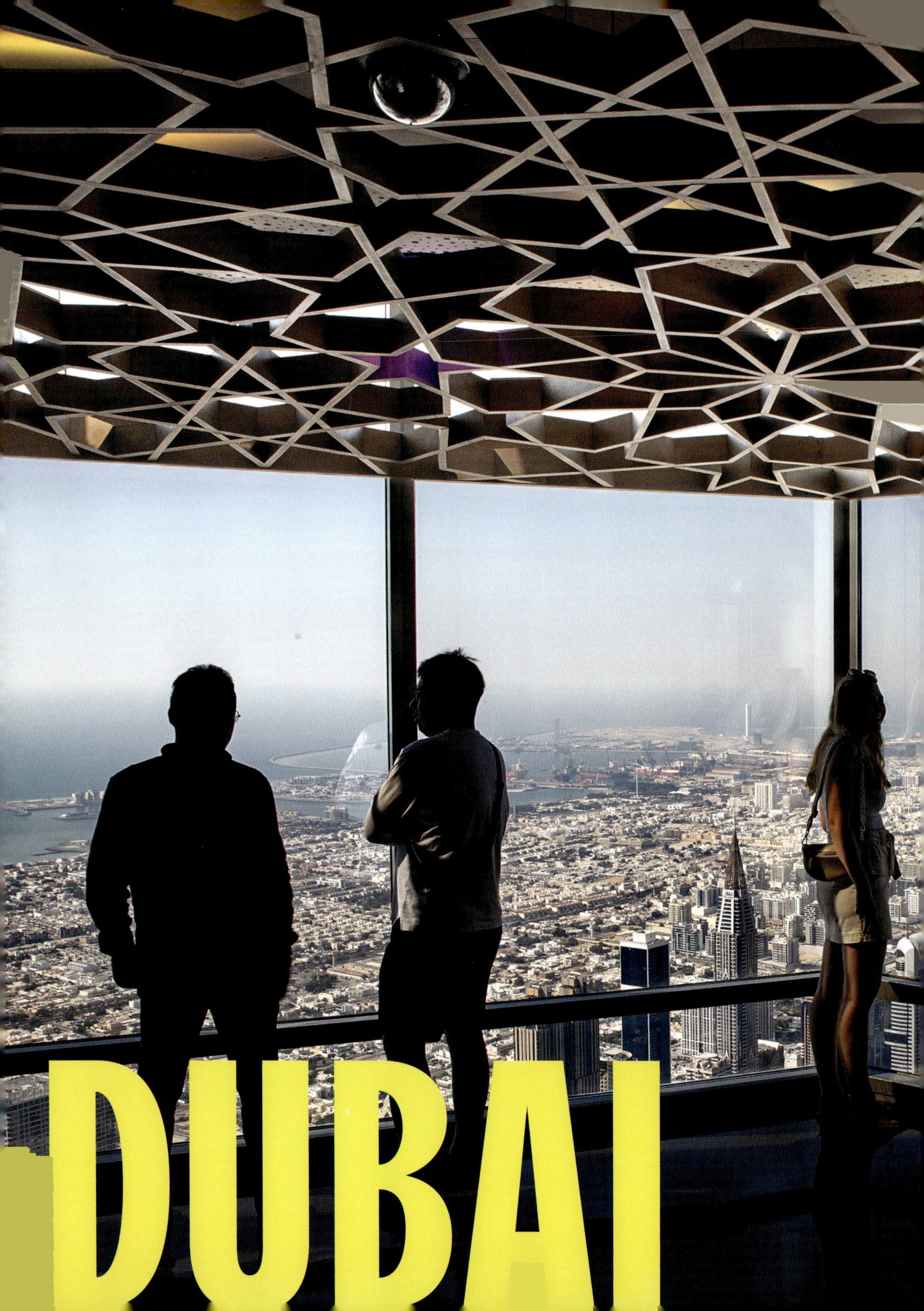

DUBAI

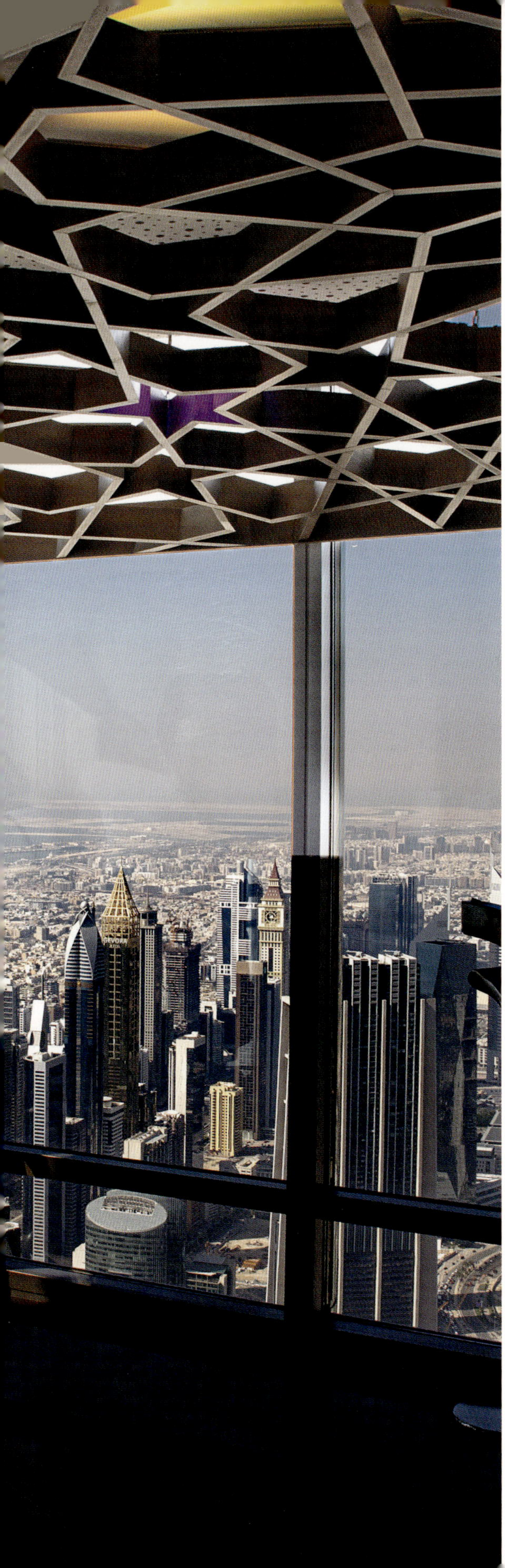

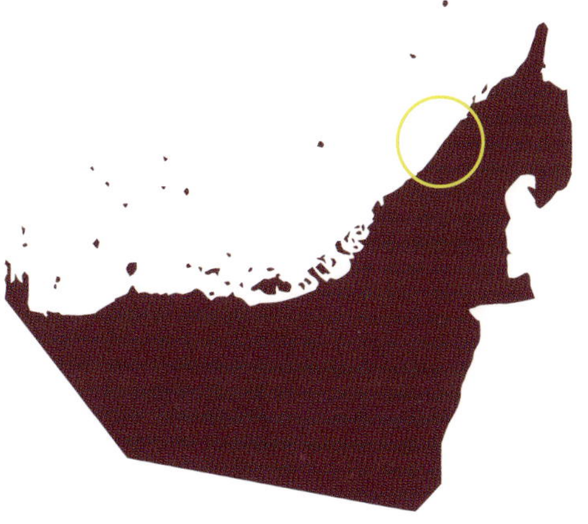

From the observation deck of Burj Khalifa, the world's tallest building, visitors earn startling views across Dubai's skyline and the sandy coast of the United Arab Emirates. Laid out beneath them is a space-age city that showcases the prosperous future of the Middle East.

Above their heads, meanwhile, hangs a celebration of this region's glorious past. A thousand-year-old Islamic art form decorates the deck's ceiling. This once-dying art form was revived in part by Burj Khalifa and its promotion of Arab cultural heritage.[176]

This skyscraper wasn't designed only as a monument to Dubai's wealth. It was also intended to be a source of pride for the Arab world, which hadn't boasted the planet's tallest structure since Egypt's Great Pyramid of Giza was overtaken seven hundred years earlier.[177] So rather than erecting a generic tower, Burj Khalifa's creators decided to make the building an informal gallery of Middle Eastern art forms.

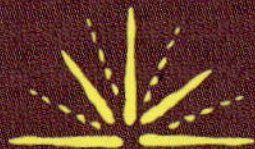

Although the United Arab Emirates (UAE) has been inhabited for six thousand years, most of its visitors are drawn by attractions that didn't exist three decades ago. Dubai is the largest city in this oil-rich nation on the east coast of the Arabian Peninsula, between Iran to its north, Saudi Arabia to its west, and Oman to its east.

That strategic location, midway between Europe and East Asia, has helped the UAE to transform itself into a global air travel hub and tourist hotspot. But before vast oil reserves were tapped in the 1960s, Dubai was just a petite port city. It wasn't until the 2000s that it embarked on a building boom aimed, in part, to make the city magnetic to tourists.

Before then, sand filled many of the sites now occupied by gleaming structures. Dubai's parched land has become studded by avant-garde skyscrapers, goliath shopping malls, world-class museums, five-star hotels, and cutting-edge theme parks. Some of these impressive constructions lie on unique, man-made archipelagos flanking the city's coast.

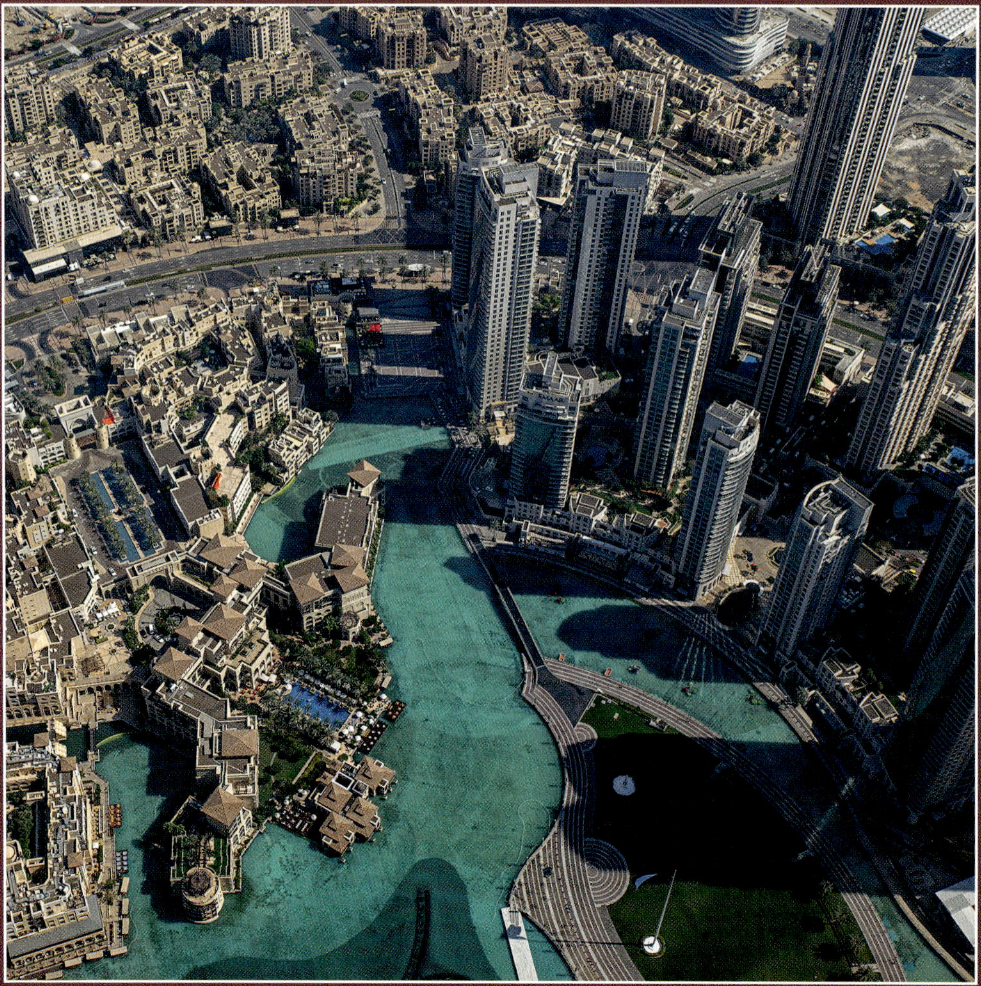

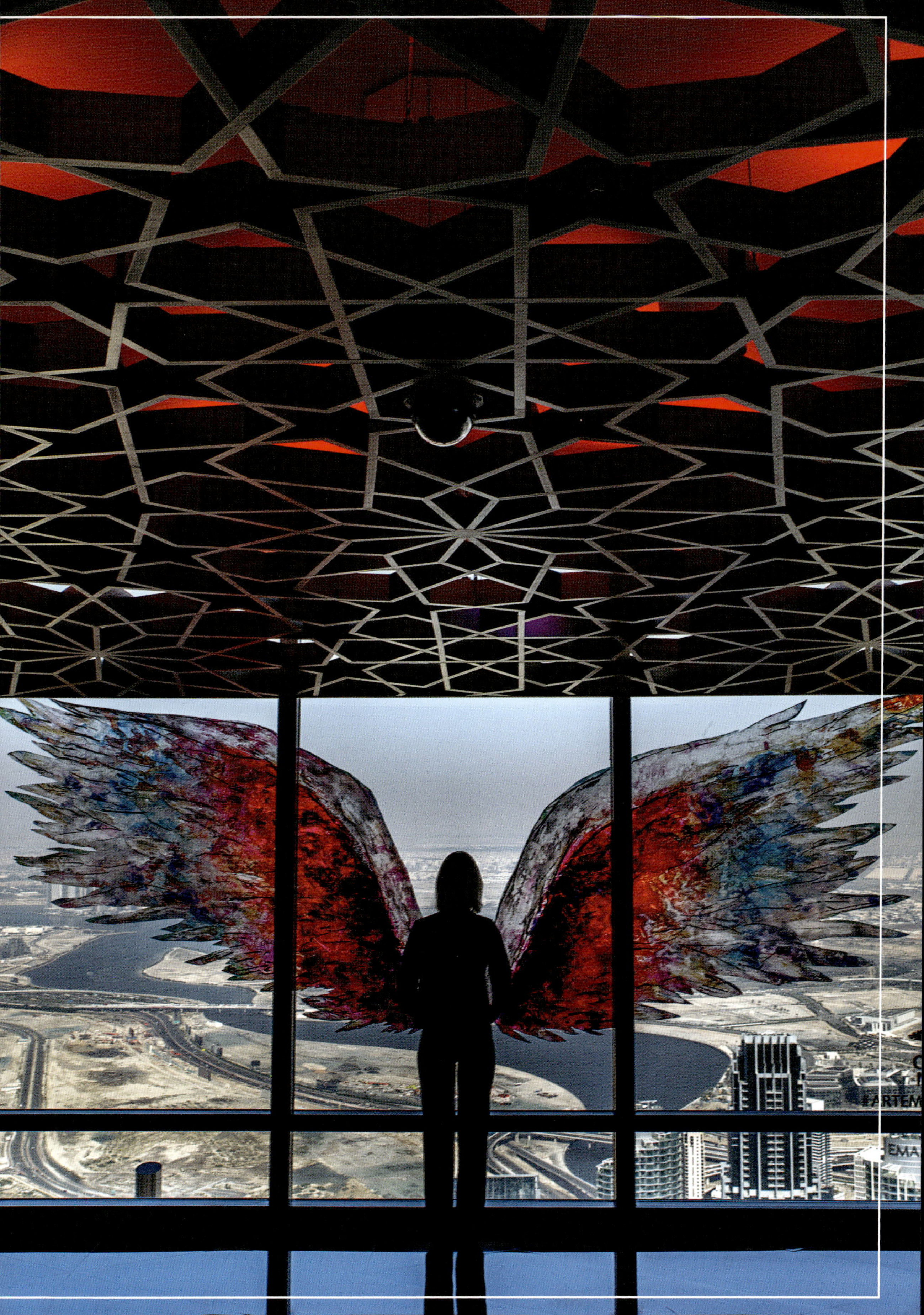

To achieve this, they embedded the skyscraper with dozens of Islamic features: spirals inspired by mosque minarets, cladding that mimics ancient Arab motifs, a footprint the same shape as a Middle Eastern spider lily flower, and the latticework on the deck's ceiling.[178] None of these regional flourishes is more fascinating than the latter, called *mashrabiya*. This geometric latticework was invented in the Middle East a millennia ago to be not only high art but also one of the world's earliest forms of air-conditioning. Modern cooling technologies almost made it irrelevant. But now mashrabiya is resurging, partly thanks to Burj Khalifa's championing of Islamic design.[179]

ORIGINS OF AN ANCIENT ART FORM

Mashrabiya was invented more than a millennia ago with an ambitious triple purpose: to provide functionality, beauty, and seclusion. Firstly, these lattice screens covering windows and balconies kept buildings cool by blocking sunlight and funneling breezes into homes. Secondly, they were were adorned with graceful geometric motifs, which enhanced a building's appearance. Lastly, mashrabiya prevented strangers from seeing into a home, affording its residents greater privacy than glass windows.[180]

Some historians trace this art form as far back as the ninth century. They believe that mashrabiya was created by the Tulunid Dynasty (AD 868–905), which ruled parts of Egypt and Syria, and that this architectural element graced many Tulunid buildings. Mashrabiya's popularity then boomed in that same region during the Mamluk Dynasty (1250–1517). It was the Mamluks who heightened the artistry of this latticework, adorning it with increasingly intricate motifs.[181]

By the 1500s, mashrabiya was used widely in Iraq and its capital Baghdad, then one of the world's largest, most sophisticated cities. Dozens of homes in the ancient Iraqi city of Basra still feature such latticework. By day, these abodes are dazzling due to the mashrabiya that frames their stained glass windows. Once darkness falls and house lights take effect, a kaleidoscope of patterns is beamed onto the Basra streetside.[182]

Historic examples of mashrabiya still grace homes and mosques in Muslim nations across North Africa and the Middle East. Some buildings utilize the Iraqi style of wooden mashrabiya screens, which enclose windows or balconies.[183] Others are latticework carved into stone. This style is particularly common in mosques and mausoleums, including India's Taj Mahal.[184]

MASHRABIYA'S MODERN RENAISSANCE

Despite being a proud Islamic innovation, mashrabiya faded in relevance during the 1900s due to the emergence of modern technologies.[185] Rather than using this latticework, many new Middle Eastern buildings were built with air-conditioning for comfort and tinted windows for privacy.

By the turn of the twenty-first century, mashrabiya was in terminal decline.[186] But in 2004, it launched a rousing comeback when designs for the Burj Khalifa unveiled mashrabiya as one of the most photogenic elements of the building. This skyscraper proved that, although mashrabiya's cooling and privacy functions are no longer necessary, its geometric patterns remain beguiling.

Since then, this latticework has begun adorning many new buildings across the Middle East, continuing the celebration of Arab cultural heritage kick-started by Burj Khalifa. While visitors stand on its 125th floor, transfixed by the futuristic view, mashrabiya looms in their peripheral vision, a marker of Islamic innovation that flourished long before the Middle East began to build toward the clouds.[187]

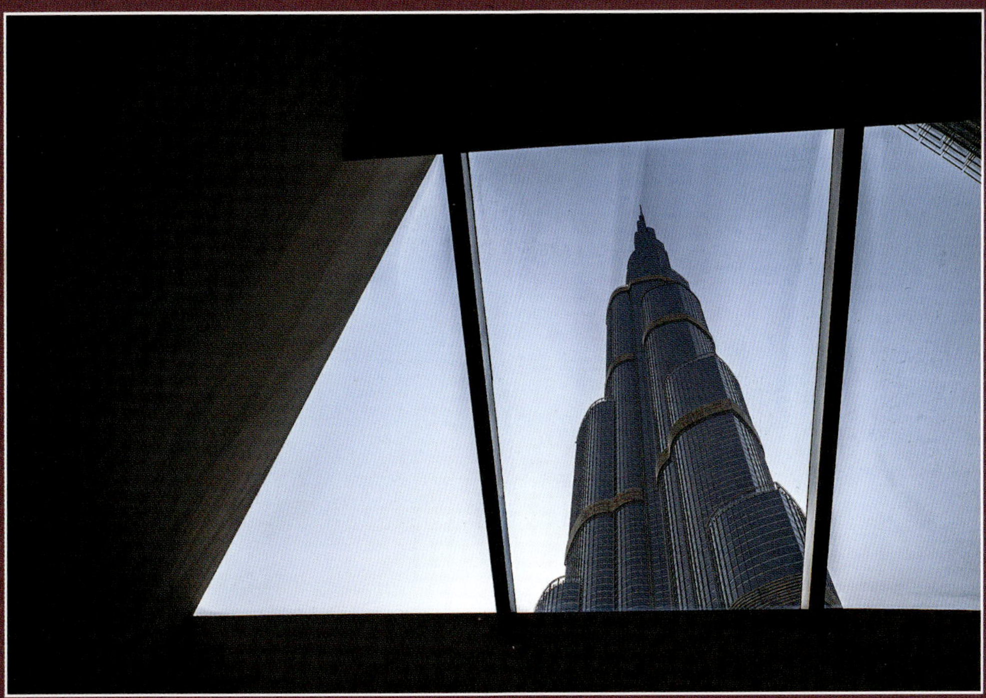

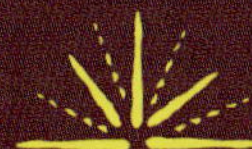

The world's greatest landmarks encapsulate their home cities. The Colosseum underscores Rome's deep history. The Eiffel Tower symbolizes Paris's timeless elegance. The Statue of Liberty signifies New York's multiculturalism. And looming above the city's more than 250 skyscrapers, Burj Khalifa embodies Dubai's commitment to gaudy excess.

Ostentatious, hypermodern, and record-breaking, Dubai strives to build the biggest, best, and boldest of everything. Given that fierce ambition, it was natural the city would reach further into the sky than any other civilization.

Before the twentieth century, the evolution of the world's tallest building had been slow and steady. Then skyscrapers started sprouting. Forty-one years after New York's Empire State Building opened (1,250 feet high), its record-setting height was eclipsed by the nearby World Trade Center's North Tower (1,368 feet), followed one year later by Chicago's Sears Tower (1,450 feet). Soon Kuala Lumpur's Petronas Towers (1,483 feet) stood taller, followed by Taiwan's Taipei 101 (1,667 feet).

Then in 2010, Dubai entered the race. Rather than merely taking the crown, Burj Khalifa made its competitors look like toys. Standing at 2,717 feet, the skyscraper is so lofty that, ocassionally, its spire disappears into fog.

Most days, however, visitors to its observation floors get a clear, 360-degree perspective of Dubai through soaring windows. This viewing experience is so memorable that Burj Khalifa has become a tourism goliath, visited by millions of people each year.[188]

AMSTERD

PEEK&CLOPPENBURG
MADAME TUSSAUD
PEEK&CLOPPENBURG
HOTDOGS

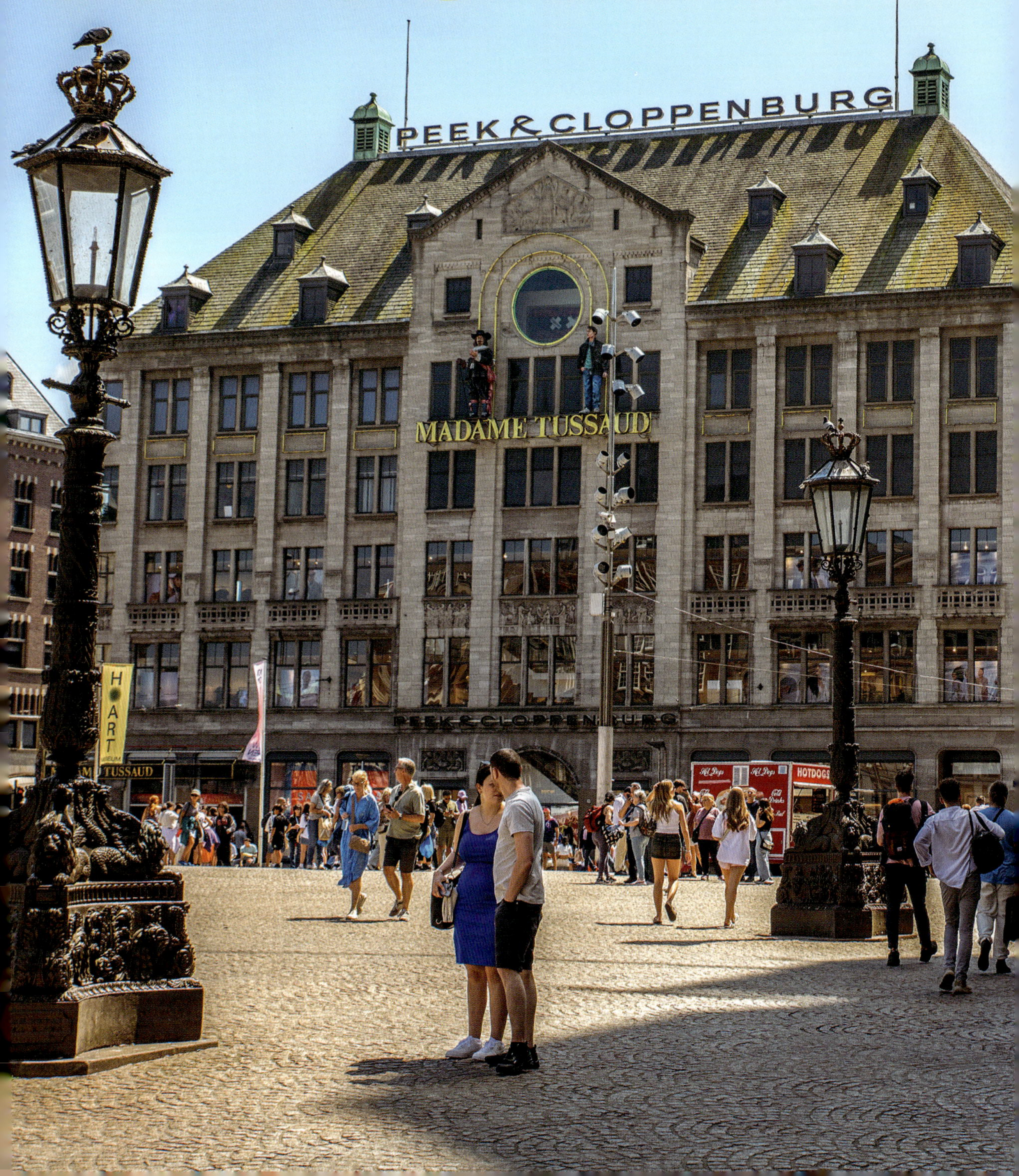

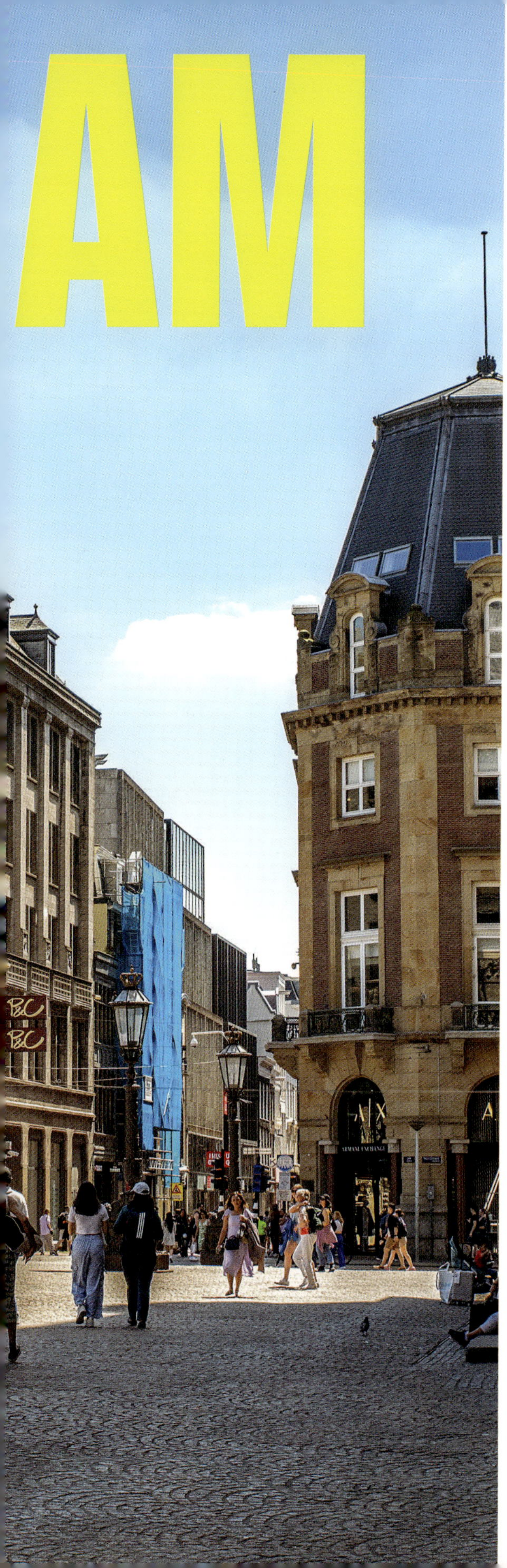

AM

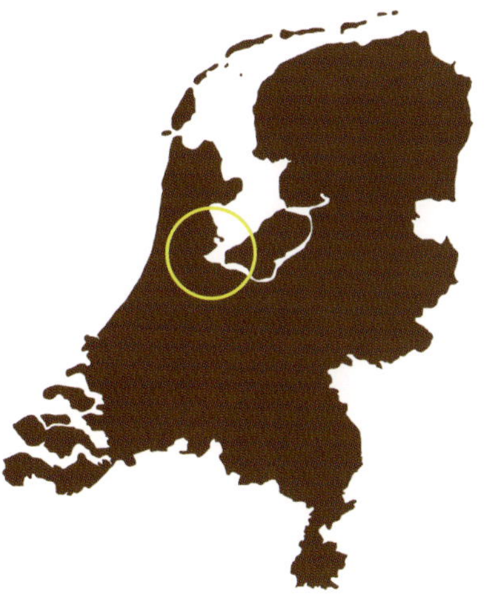

Superstitious barbarity is imprinted on Amsterdam's most famous plaza. Tourists visit Dam Square to admire its Royal Palace, National Monument, and fifteenth-century church De Nieuwe Kerk. Yet even a million prayers in that house of worship couldn't cleanse the evil that stained this site.

Dam Square sits at the core of Amsterdam's Royal Mile. Museums, historic sites, retail precincts, and dining enclaves dot this attractive strip, which stretches south from heaving Central Train Station through the downtown area. But concealed behind the square's austere appearance is a savage past.

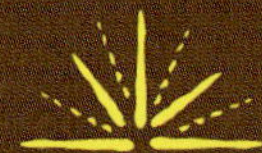

As hinted by its name, Dam Square originated in AD 1270 as a dam. What we now call Amsterdam was, in the thirteenth century, a petite fishing village on the Amstel River. Concerned about flooding risk, the residents constructed dykes on each riverbank and a dam in between. Over subsequent generations, a plaza developed alongside the dam, hosting events and markets.

By the early 1400s, Amsterdam blossomed into one of Europe's most prosperous cities. Dam Square at this time received its first grand landmark, De Nieuwe Kerk, a church where festivals, concerts, royal ceremonies, and Christian services were held for many centuries.[189]

Today the church is a museum that hosts exhibitions on art, photography, and history. Visitors to De Nieuwe Kerk can appreciate its colossal organ, lavish funerary monuments, shimmering brass choir screen, and the intricately carved woodwork of its pulpit.

Standing opposite that church is Amsterdam's top luxury department store, De Bijenkorf Amsterdam, equivalent to New York's Saks Fifth Avenue or London's Harrods. Dozens more high-end boutiques and jewelery stores occupy the cluster of heritage buildings and handsome arcades surrounding Dam Square.

After their shopping sprees, many tourists refuel at the trendy cafés and restaurants that fringe the north of this plaza. As evening approaches, these venues become shaded by the longest shadow cast across Dam Square: that of the Royal Palace Amsterdam. While the Dutch royal family resides thirty miles away, in the wooded wonderland of Huis ten Bosch Palace, they host galas and state visits at this seventeenth-century Amsterdam mansion.

Each day, thousands pose for photos in front of this stately building. Embellishing its giant stone facade are more than one hundred windows, above which sits a graceful bell tower. Royal Palace Amsterdam is also regularly open to visitors. They can admire its array of sculptures and painting and enter its chandelier-draped reception hall, where the Dutch monarch meets foreign presidents and prime ministers.[190]

As those leaders enter Dam Square, they spy Amsterdam's National Monument. Cream-colored and seventy-two feet tall, this pretty pillar has dark connotations. It commemorates the more than three hundred thousand Dutch people who died in WWII, during which the Nazis occupied the Netherlands, committing massacres and deporting most of its Jewish population to death camps.[191]

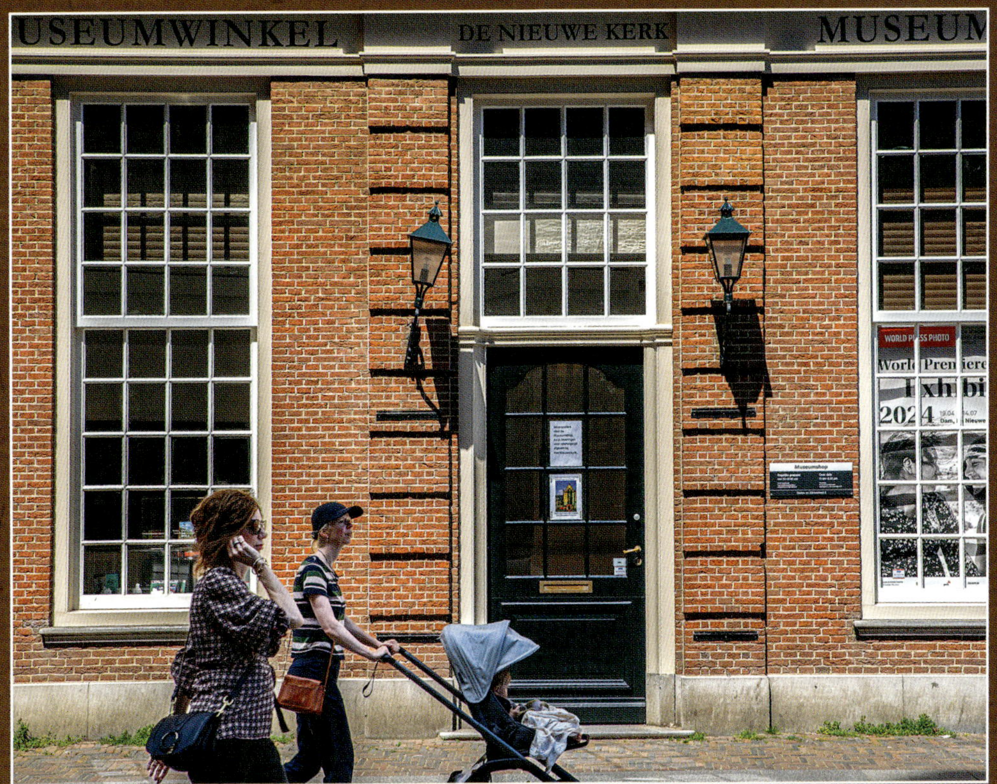
DE NIEUWE KERK
WORLD PRESS PHOTO

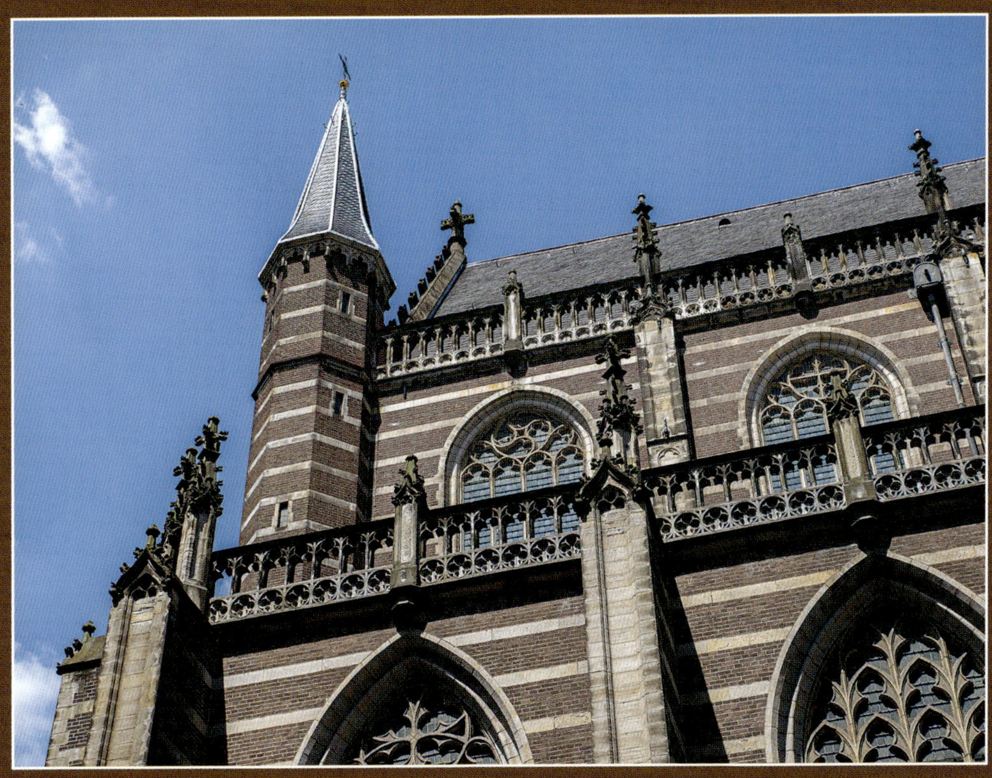

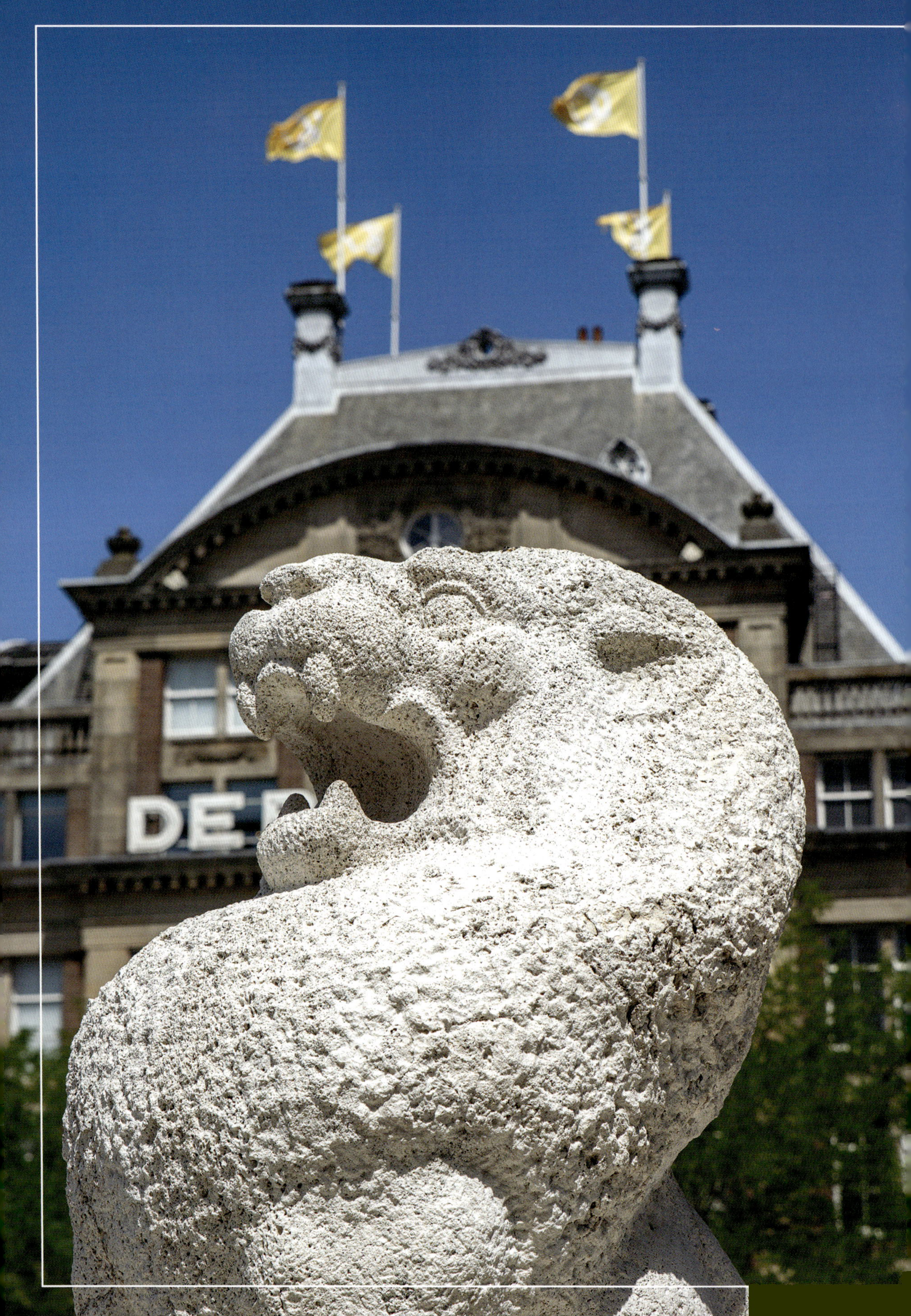

THE WITCH HUNT THAT SPANNED A CONTINENT

In the mid-1500s, Europe's Christian churches became obsessed with eradicating a supposed glut of dangerous mystical women and men. Witch hunts and trials exploded across the continent, fueled by superstition, paranoia, misogyny, and religious zealotry.

Between the fifteenth and eighteenth centuries, forty thousand people were executed in twenty-one European countries for alleged witchcraft. Such panicked persecution was not uniform across the continent. Instead it was most common in Germany, France, Switzerland, and the Netherlands.[192, 193]

WITCH HYSTERIA TAKES HOLD IN THE NETHERLANDS

Witch hunts proliferated from the mid-1400s to the 1600s in the area we now know as the Netherlands, which back then was split into the Dutch Republic and the Spanish Netherlands.[194] Often in Dam Square, Dutch women and men were tied to stakes and set ablaze.[195] Those accused typically had a low social standing; many unmarried women and widows were marginalized since they didn't have a male protector to "vouch" for them.[196] Also common in the era was the belief that women were weaker than men and were therefore more susceptible to succumb to possession by the Devil. Often this ensured that the public more readily assumed their guilt. All that was needed to condemn them was mere suspicion of possessing mystical powers. Hundreds of innocent Dutch people were hunted, tortured, and executed during these witch hunts.[197]

Paranoia became so intense that the Dutch opened a building in Oudewater, a town twenty-four miles south of Dam Square, for weighing witches. It operated on twisted logic. Since witches supposedly flew through the air on broomsticks, they surely must be featherlight. So when a true witch stepped on the scales at Oudewater and barely registered a reading, they would be exposed.

Fortunately, this weighing device was accurate, and no accused witch was ever convicted based on its readings. In fact, many had their names cleared after this bizarre process. Once their weight was proven normal, they were given a document that acknowledged this fact and could then use it as evidence that they were not in league with the Devil.[198]

Otherwise, accused witches rarely received anything close to a fair hearing. The burden was on them to prove their innocence. In many instances, there was no need for their case to be heard, as they'd already confessed to being a witch while under extreme duress.

Many of the heinous devices used to torment alleged witches during the interrogations are now displayed at the Torture Museum Amsterdam, an unnerving facility near Dam Square. Museumgoers learn how these poor souls suffered amid the cruelty. Some victims had their skin stripped by whips. Others lost body parts to amputation. More still were stabbed, choked, stretched, flogged, burned, or nearly drowned. These were not acts of punishment but rather ghastly coercion, intended to elicit whatever admission was deemed necessary. Desperate to end their misery, most victims would admit to anything—even having sex with the Devil. Such forced confessions were commonly followed by blazing acts of injustice.[199]

DAM SQUARE'S GRISLY WITCH CONNECTION

Dutch authorities often ordered these witches burned alive. Sometimes the flaming executions occurred publicly, in front of a sadistic audience. At least eight accused witches were put to death in this style at Dam Square during the 1500s and 1600s. Their names were featured on posters pinned throughout Dam Square during a 2023 event to commemorate witch hunt victims.[200]

Finally, in 1684, the Spanish Netherlands ended its witch trials, as the Dutch Republic had done several decades prior. In each territory, hysteria about supposed sorcerers had subsided. As a result, the public had become more aware of the lack of judicial process involved in witch trials.[201]

That year, the Netherlands' final such execution underscored the barbarism of the era. Heavily pregnant Martha van Wetteren was tortured until she confessed to being a witch. Soon she was tied to a stake and consumed by flames.[202]

A RECKONING WITH ITS VIOLENT PAST

Today the Netherlands is a socially progressive country[203] and consistently ranks highly on the global gender equality report by the World Economic Forum.[204]

Dutch people now widely recognize that the tortured, who were mostly women, were victims of gender-based violence. However, at the time of writing this book, no sign, statue, or sculpture in Dam Square acknowledges its shameful past.[205] The Netherlands' only museum specifically addressing the topic is in the now-serene town of Oudewater. The institution is called Museum de Heksenwaag, which translates to "Museum of the Witches Weighing House."[206]

There is, however, a growing public campaign to right that wrong and build a National Witch Monument in Amsterdam. During June 2023, about eight hundred people gathered to lay white flowers at Netherlands locations where witch burnings occurred, including Dam Square. They are continuing to lobby the Dutch government for this cause via the National Witch Monument Foundation.[207]

Until that happens, visitors to Amsterdam's main plaza surely would be shocked to learn that they're walking atop the execution site of alleged witches, blameless women and men hunted, tormented, and then burned to ash in Dam Square.

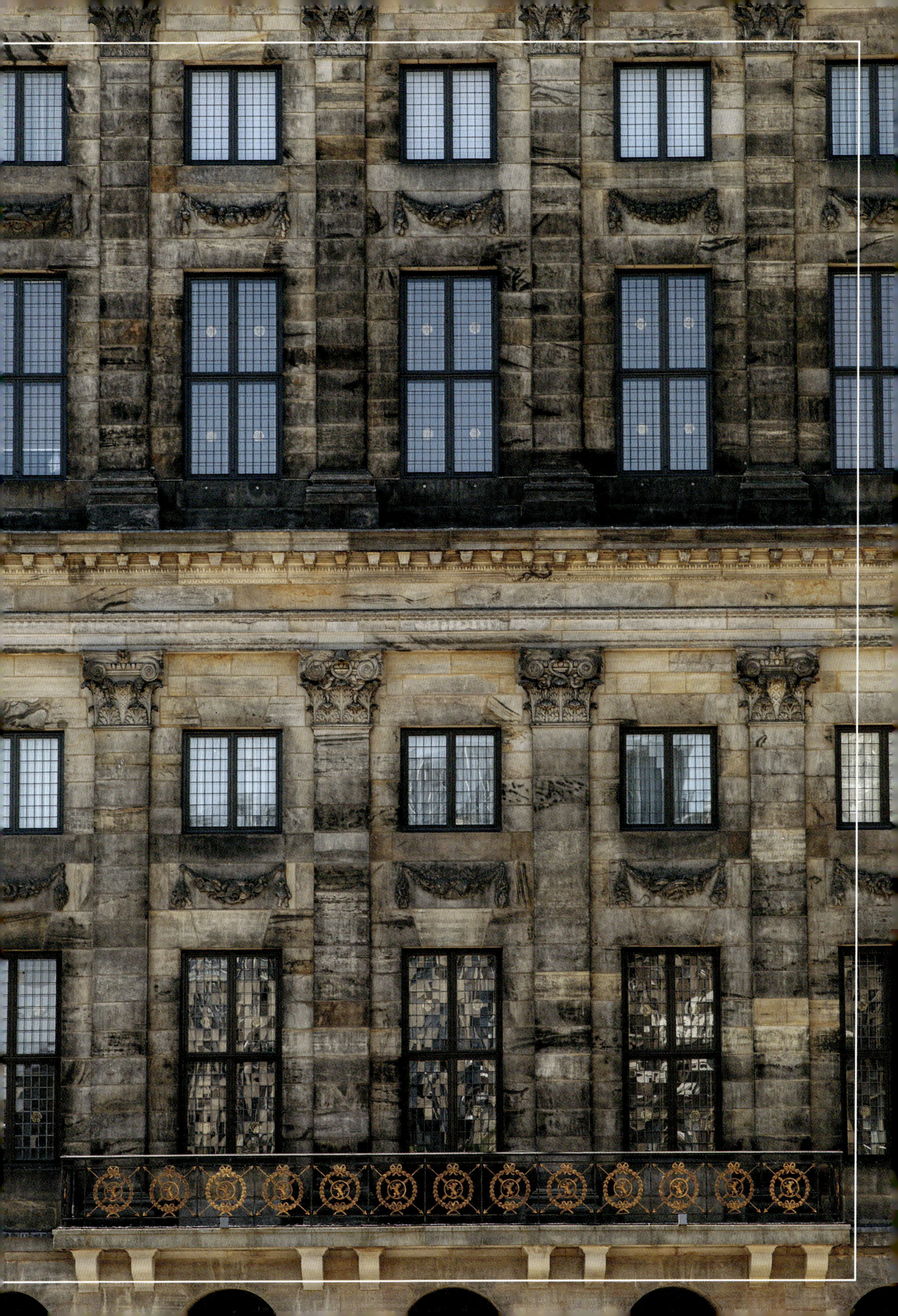

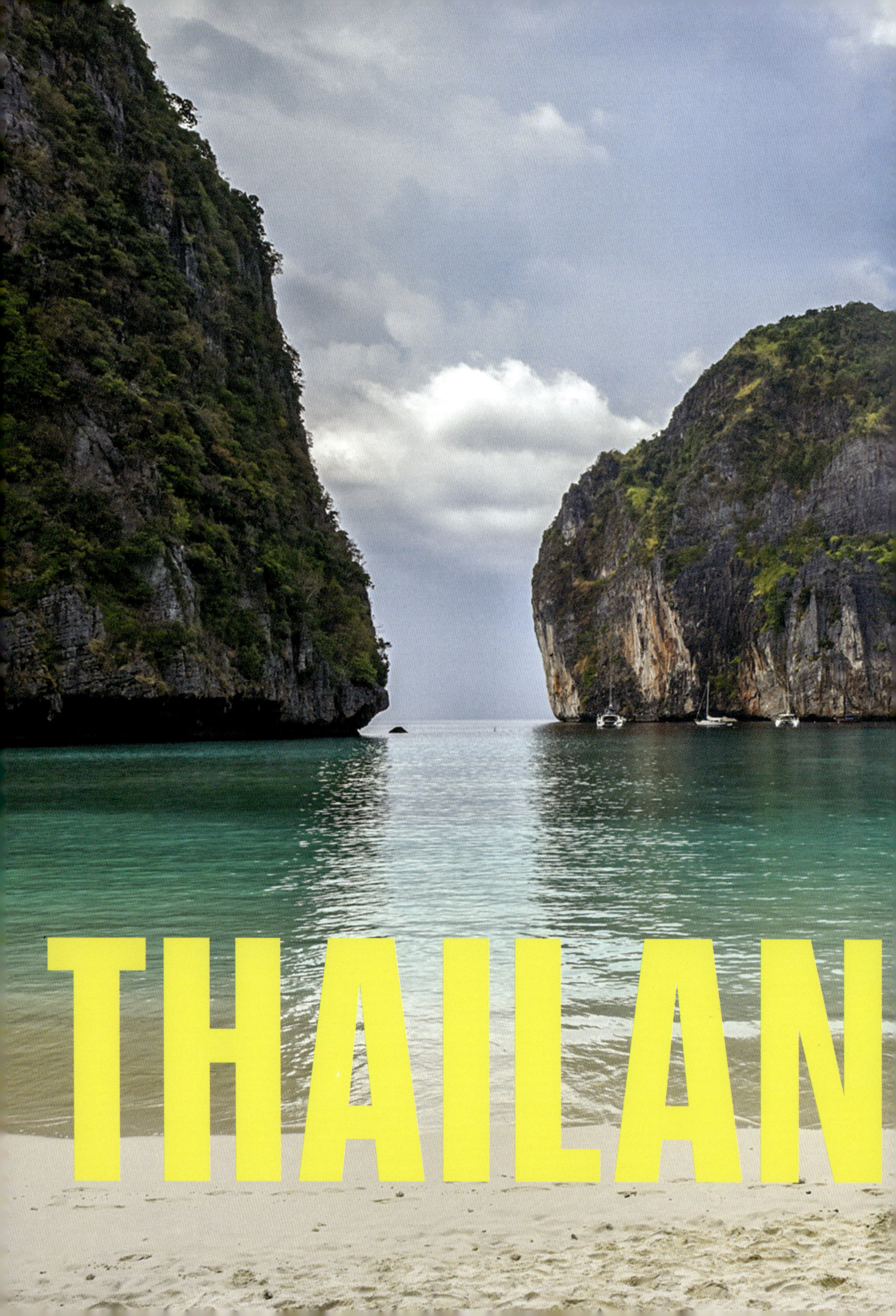
THAILAN

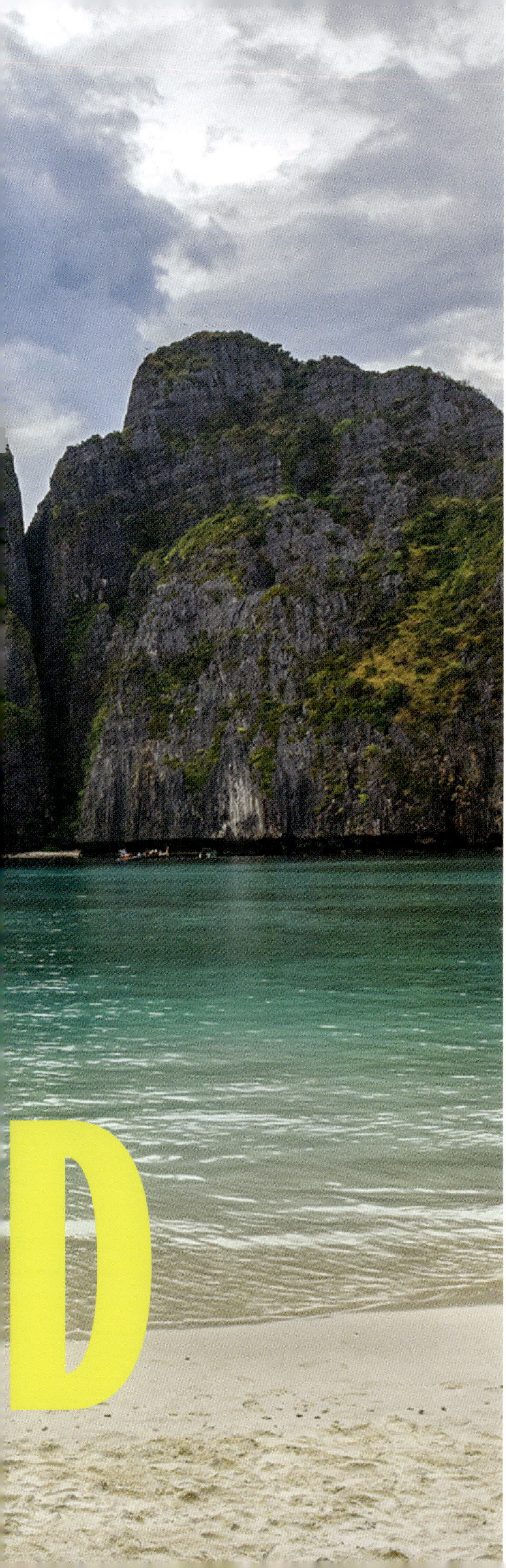

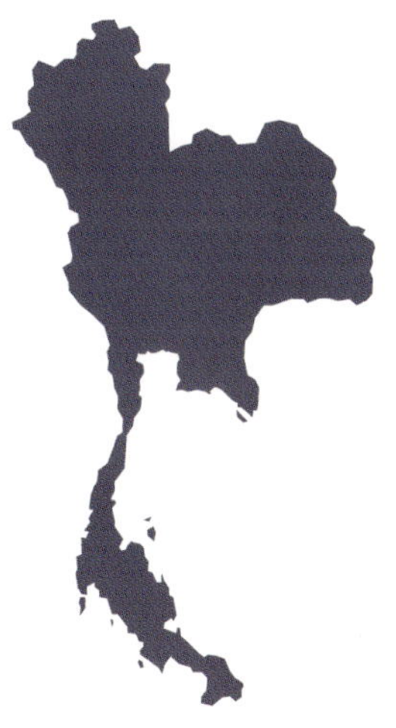

Surrounded by cliffs, flanked by jungle, and marooned in turquoise seas, Maya Bay is perhaps Asia's best-known strip of sand. Yet this tropical wonder in southern Thailand's Phi Phi Islands was largely anonymous until its star turn in *The Beach,* a 2000 American film that became a cult favorite, especially among viewers gripped by wanderlust.

Most visitors to Phi Phi are familiar with that movie. But few know of the area's remarkable link to one of the planet's last surviving nomadic sea cultures. Floating through the Phi Phi Islands' humid air is an Indigenous tale even more engrossing than the Hollywood script that made Maya Bay world famous.

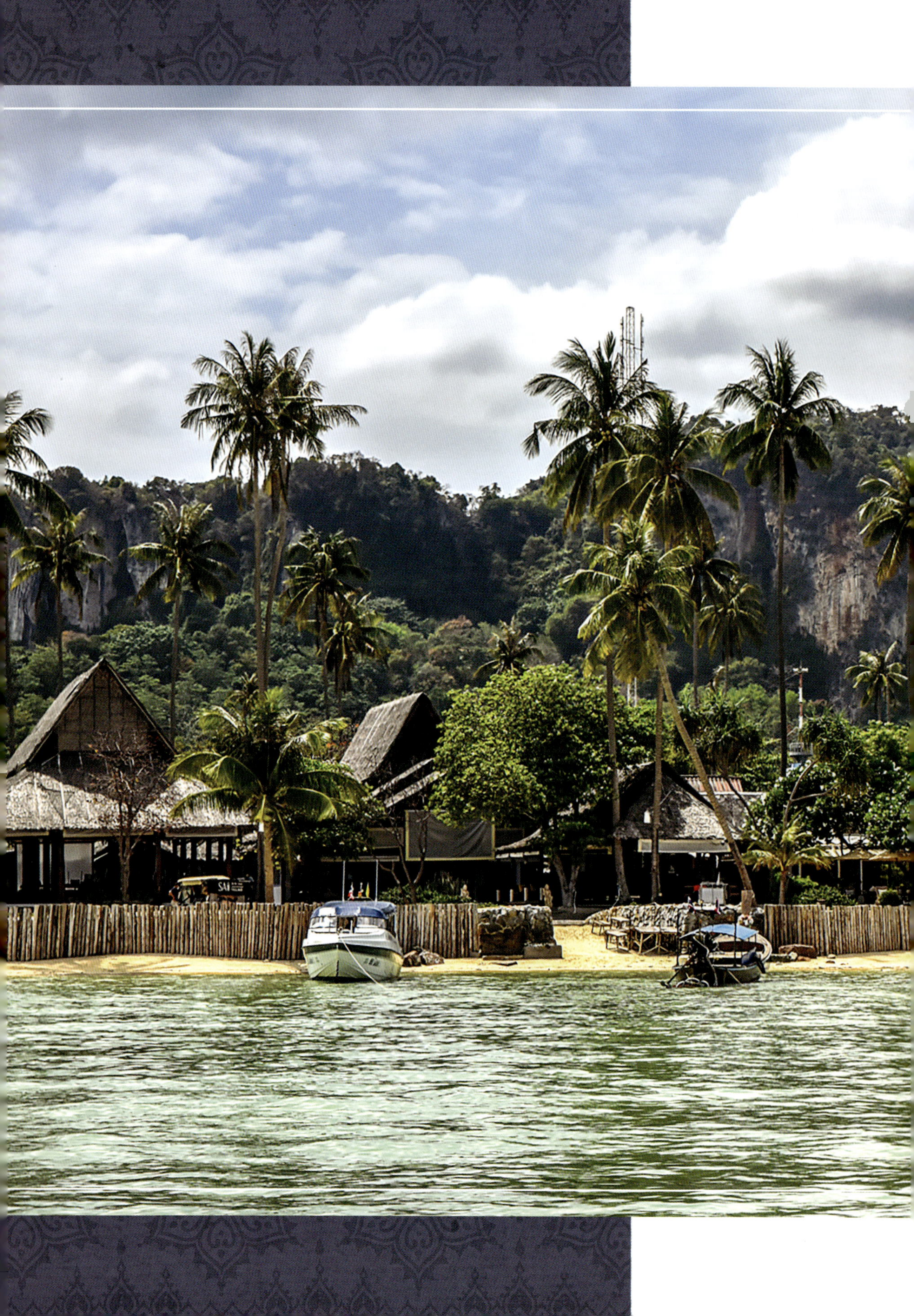

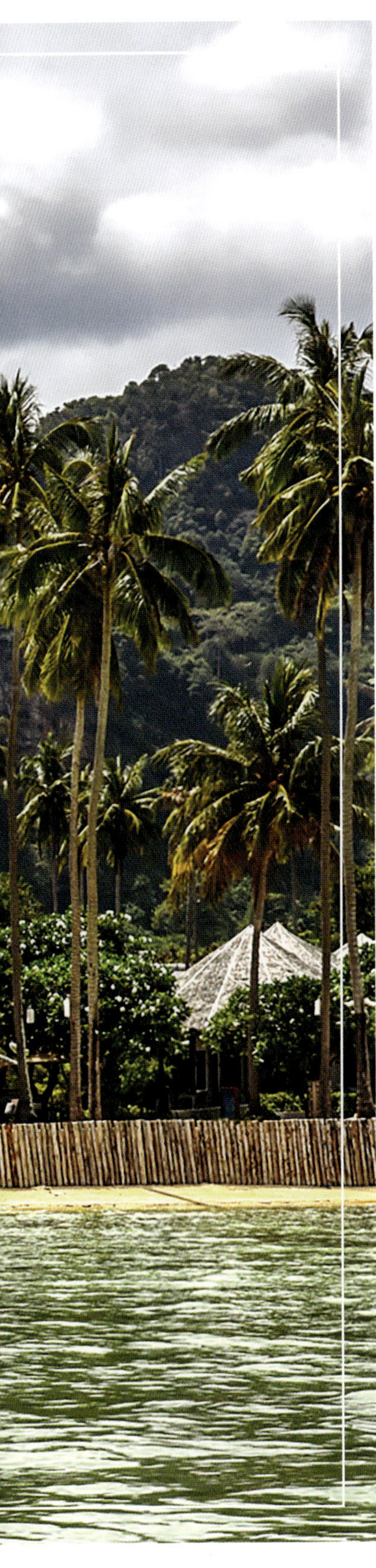

PHI PHI ISLANDS' NOMADIC PEOPLE

For generations, Phi Phi has been a seasonal hub of the Urak Lawoi, a unique community that roams Thailand's Andaman Sea. Many of these nomadic fishermen reside on boats and in makeshift coastal villages. Now, however, this community is on the verge of dying out.[208]

Some academics trace the Urak Lawoi's presence in the Andaman Sea back five centuries, to Kedah, a state in northwest Malaysia. Others pinpoint their origins in the eastern Malaysian region of Borneo. Another has Urak Lawoi roots stretching even further, fifteen hundred miles southeast of Phi Phi, to the Indonesian island of Sulawesi.

A fourth theory, meanwhile, is perhaps the most popular. Certainly it is the most riveting. It revolves around a revered adventurer named To Kiri, who, in the early 1900s, guided the Urak Lawoi to the paradise of southern Thailand before being assassinated by a jealous admirer of his wife.[209, 210]

THE ARRIVAL OF A LEGEND

To Kiri was from the Indonesian province of Aceh. Soon after entering adulthood, in the early twentieth century, he launched a bold voyage with his brothers, rowing more than 150 miles across the Malacca Strait in search of a new home.

After landing in Malaysia, near what is now the popular tourist island of Penang, To Kiri wed a local Chinese Malay woman, who gave birth to a daughter. Not long after, the young family cruised farther north, looking for the most fertile land in the region. They passed through the Phi Phi Islands and settled upon its neighbor, Koh Lanta.

A few years after his first wife died, To Kiri remarried in Koh Lanta, this time to an Urak Lawoi woman. Together they had a son and a daughter. While To Kiri was not an Urak Lawoi descendent himself, he embraced his second wife's heritage and raised his children to be proud of it. Gradually, the Urak Lawoi community accepted him. To Kiri became a trustworthy leader and protector of their culture, and a loving husband to his third wife.

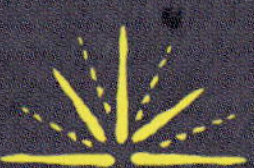

Phi Phi refers to six islands clustered together in southern Thailand's Hat Noppharat Thara-Mu Ko Phi Phi National Park.[211] The largest of these islands, Phi Phi Don, is lined with hotels, bars, restaurants, and souvenir shops. It is also the hub for boat tours that drop visitors at Phi Phi Leh, a few miles to the south. Here begins a pulse-raising walk.

Visitors pierce a narrow gap in Phi Phi Leh's steep cliffs and continue through dense greenery occupied by long-tailed macaques. Finally, the trees thin out to reveal the startling beauty of Maya Bay. Sparkling teal waters and silken sand appear to be enclosed by limestone peaks, as if visitors are within a dreamy caldera. Walk north along its half-moon beach, and an opening in those peaks comes into sight. So, too, does the glittering expanse of the Andaman Sea.[212]

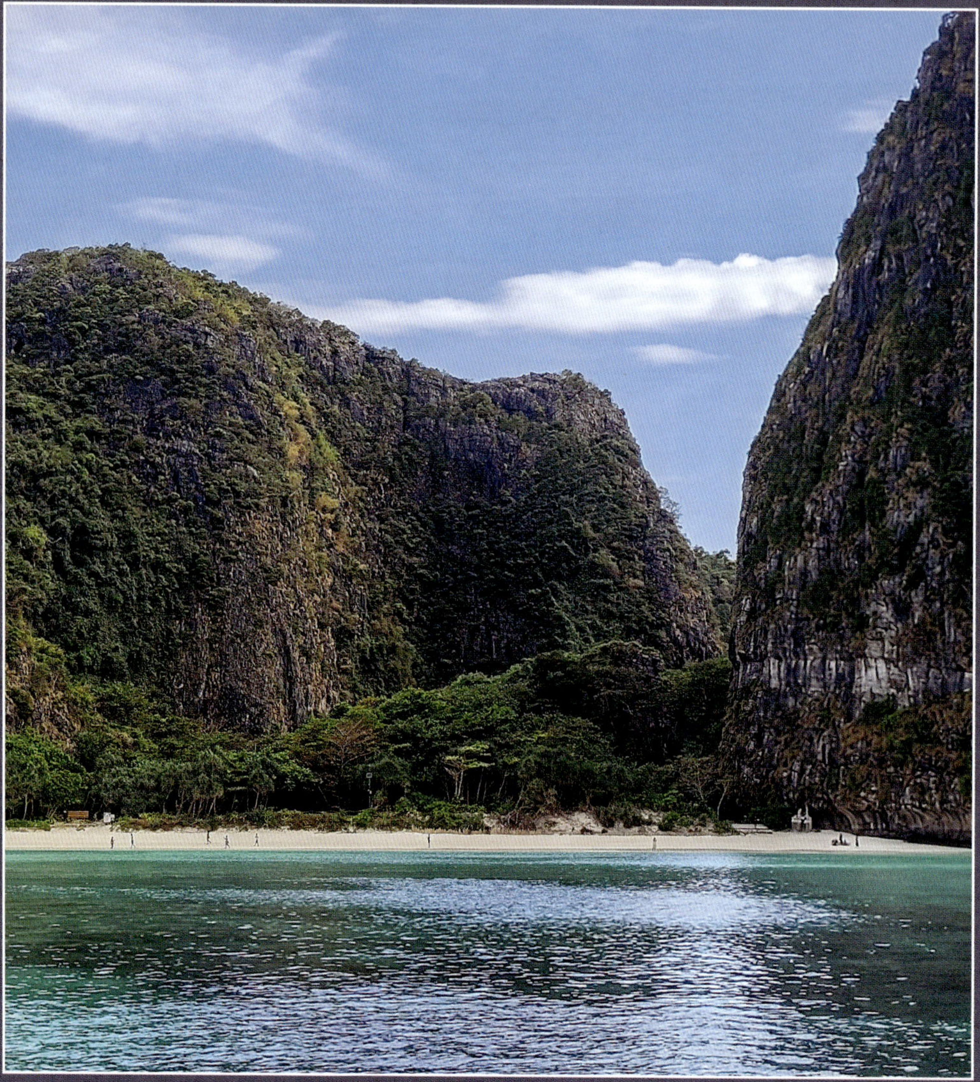

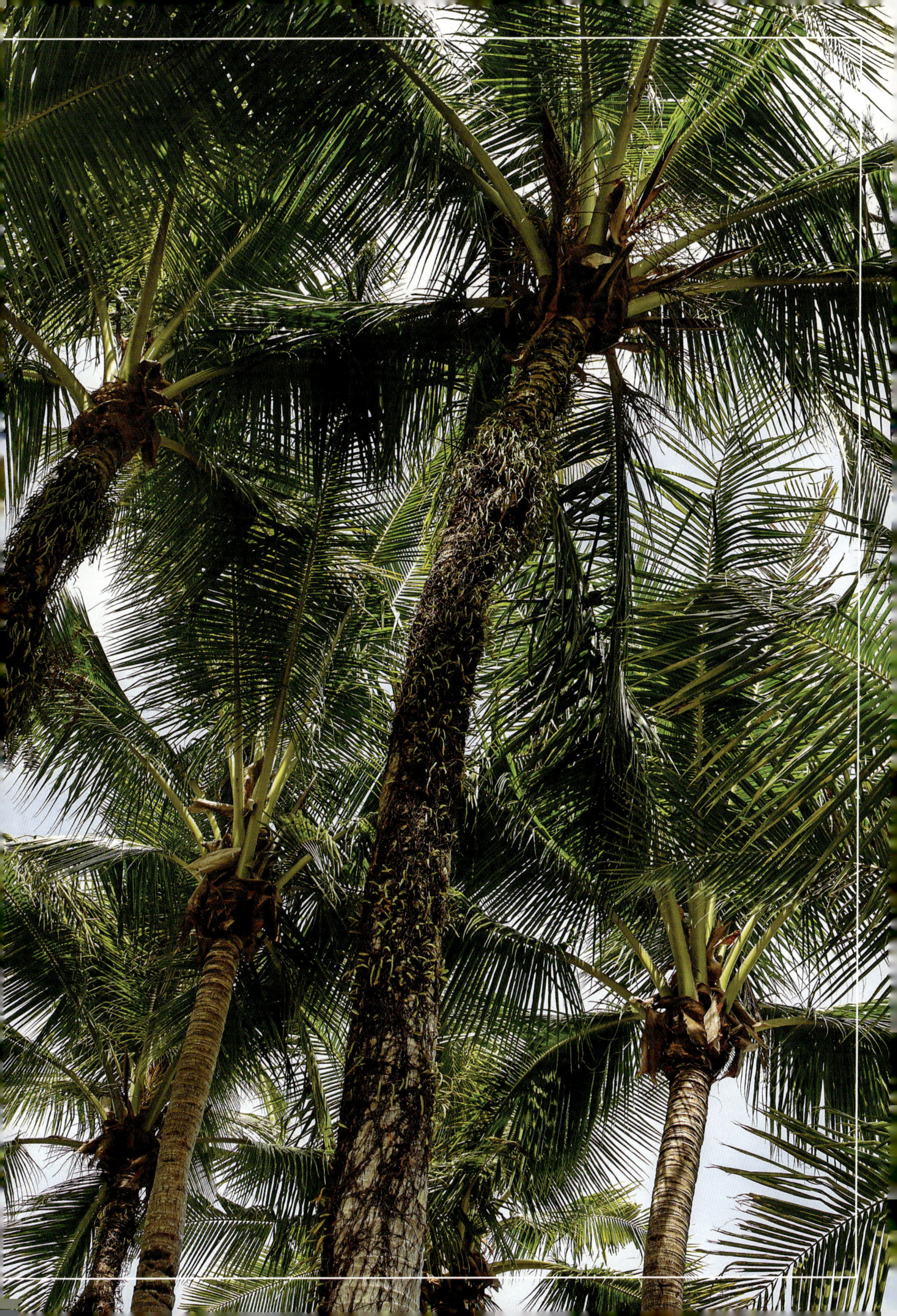

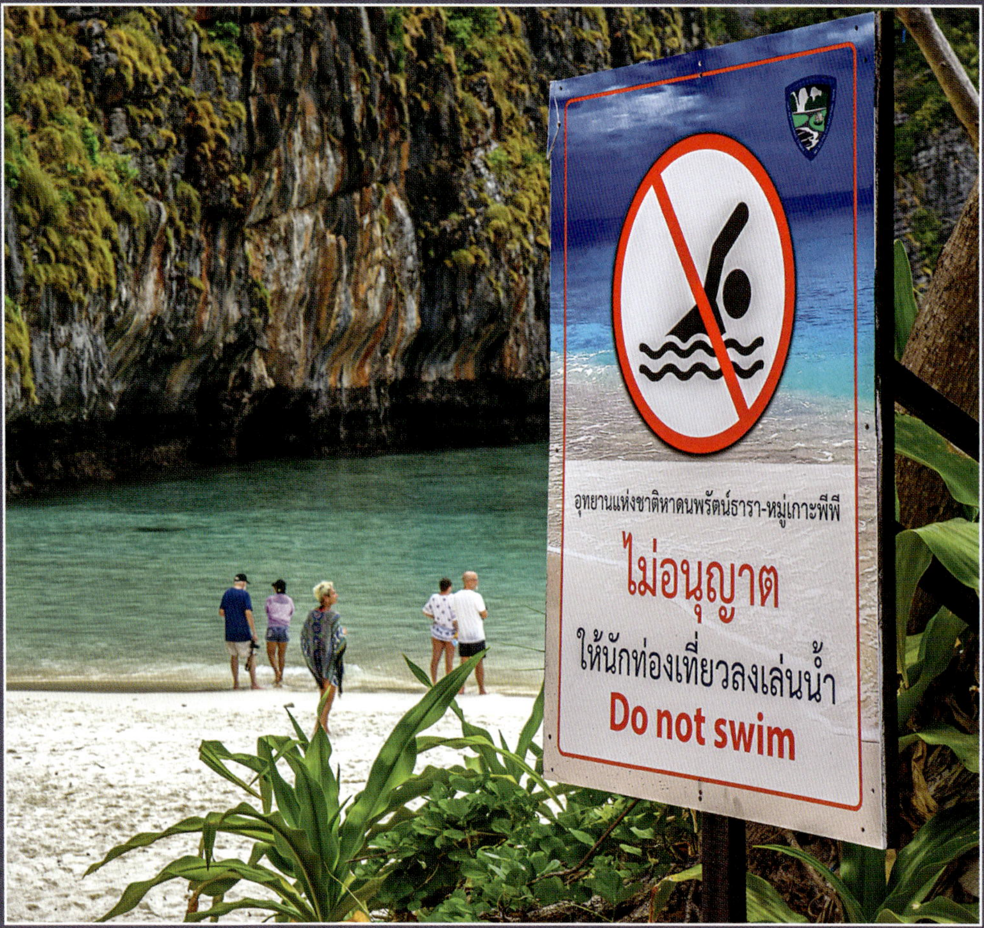

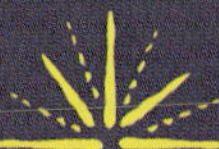

Hollywood changed the Phi Phi Islands forever. While *The Beach* technically starred Leonardo DiCaprio, its actual leading character was Maya Bay. Audiences around the globe were astonished by the majesty of this 655-foot-long stretch of sand lapped by azure waters on one side, embraced by jungle on the other, and ringed by limestone peaks. Overnight, the same natural glory that convinced To Kiri to stay in this region prompted an avalanche of travelers. Phi Phi swiftly morphed from little-known wonder to a bucket list destination of the most visited country in Southeast Asia.[213, 214]

Phi Phi Leh is tiny and uninhabited, yet in 2017 it received an extraordinary 1.7 million tourists. Such heavy human traffic put its coral reefs and marine life in dangerous decline. So starting in 2018, it was shut to visitors for almost four years, to give its ecosystem time to recuperate.

When it finally reopened for tourism, stricter rules were enforced. Boats were banned in Maya Bay, as was swimming.[215] In an attempt to prevent a backslide, Thai authorities in 2024 decided to close Maya Bay annually, each August and September, during the wet season. As a result, its coral is in better health, and some of its rare fauna has returned, including the endangered bamboo shark. And it is still possible to dive, snorkel, and swim at other sublime spots on Phi Phi Leh.[216]

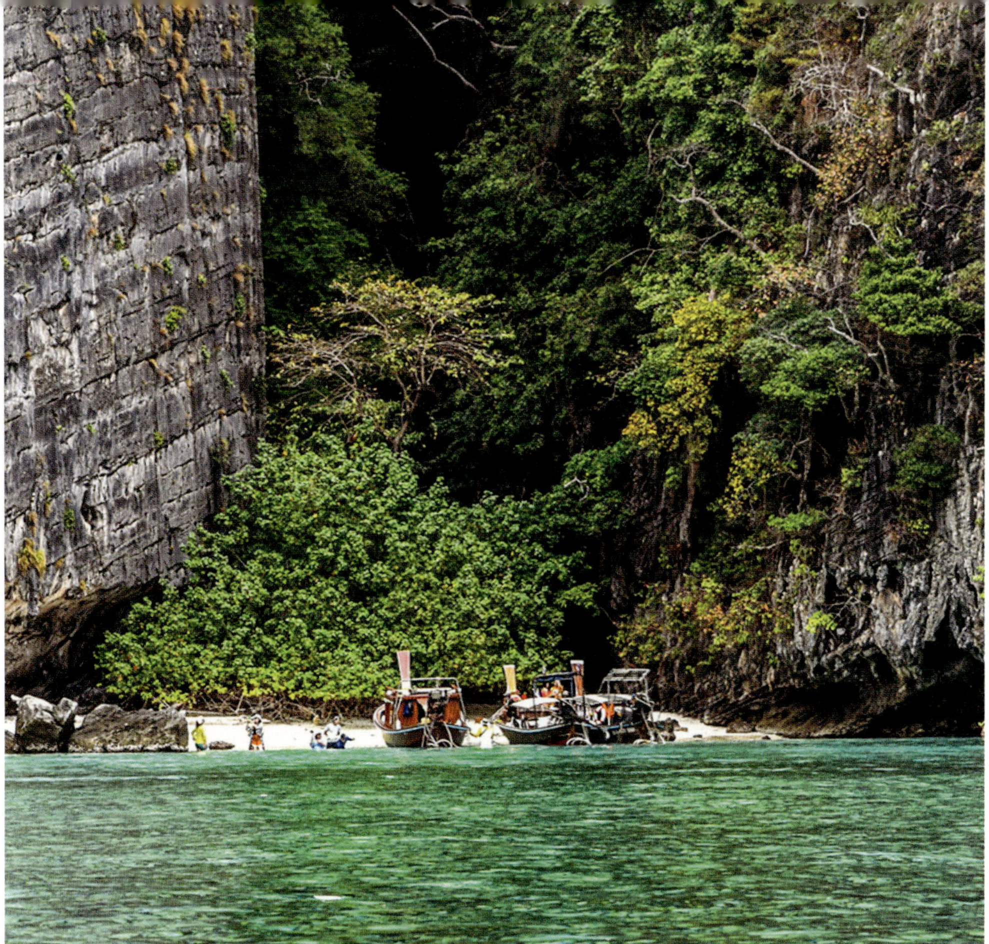

MAGICAL RISE AND FALL OF AN URAK LAWOI CHAMPION

In Urak Lawoi folklore, To Kiri is a miraculous man. He rode sharks with ease, rowed boats at blazing speeds, and controlled creatures with his mind. Schools of fish darted to his feet if he called out to them.

To Kiri used his supernatural abilities to safeguard the Urak Lawoi. When bad weather approached, his will repelled the storms. When disease arrived, he halted its spread. When pirates loomed, he made Urak Lawoi settlements invisible. When Japanese soldiers invaded Thailand during World War II, he reached out and caught their bullets.

But even with those incredible feats, the man was not invincible. Just four years after the war, To Kiri fell prey to a snake's bite, and his heart was stopped by its poisonous venom. Legend has it that this toxic creature was set upon him by a jealous man who was in love in with his third and final wife.[217]

THE URAK LAWOI UNCERTAIN FUTURE

Several generations later, To Kiri's tale of resilience and might remains central to Urak Lawoi mythology while they fight to preserve their culture and secure greater rights under Thai law.[218]

As tourism swells in the Andaman Sea, their story echoes ever more faintly. Right now, and likely in decades to come, the tale most widely associated with Maya Bay will be one crafted in Hollywood. But Phi Phi will forever be marked by the theater of To Kiri's life, and the unique legacy of the Urak Lawoi community that roams Thailand's Andaman Sea.

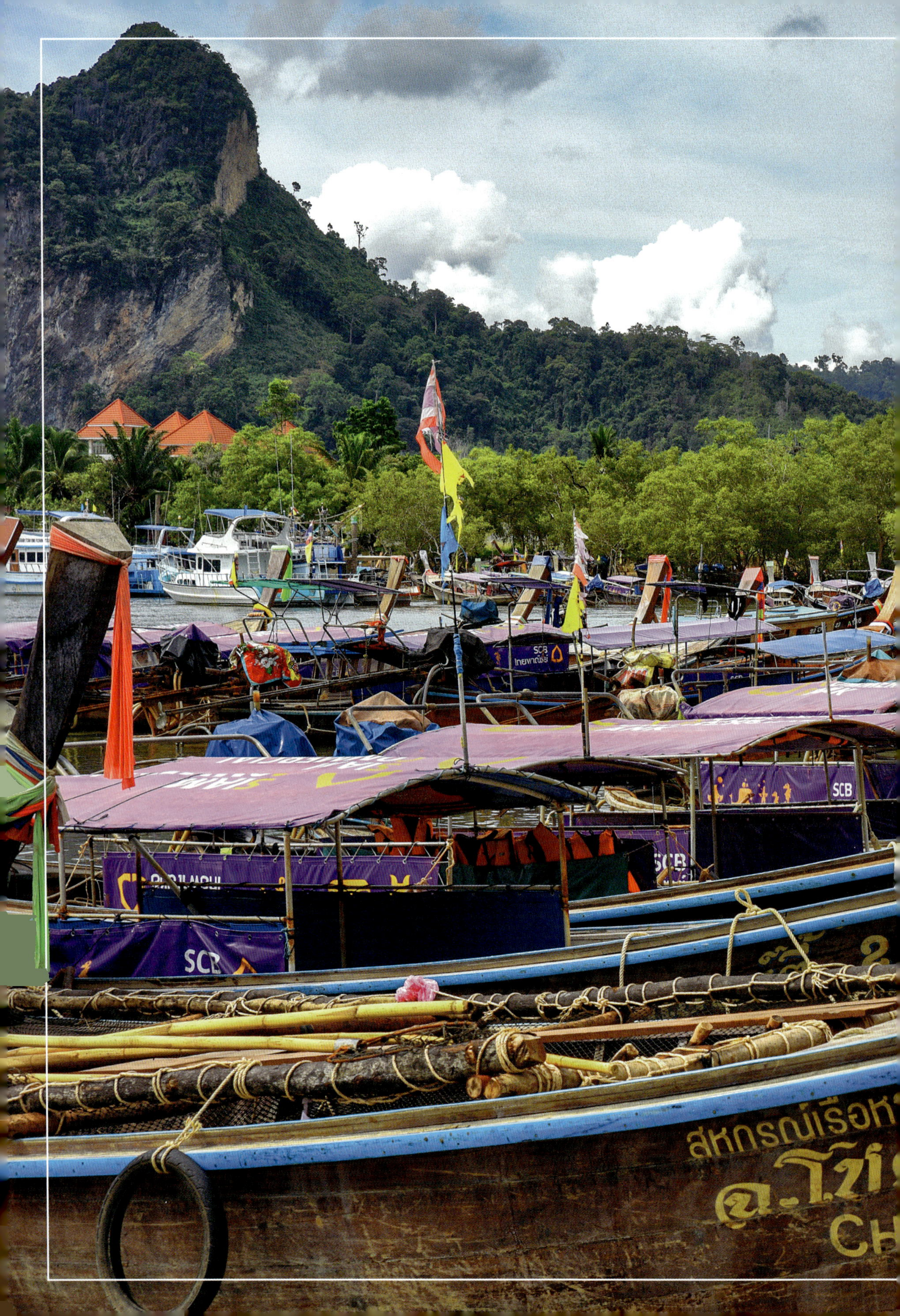
SCB
SCB
SCB

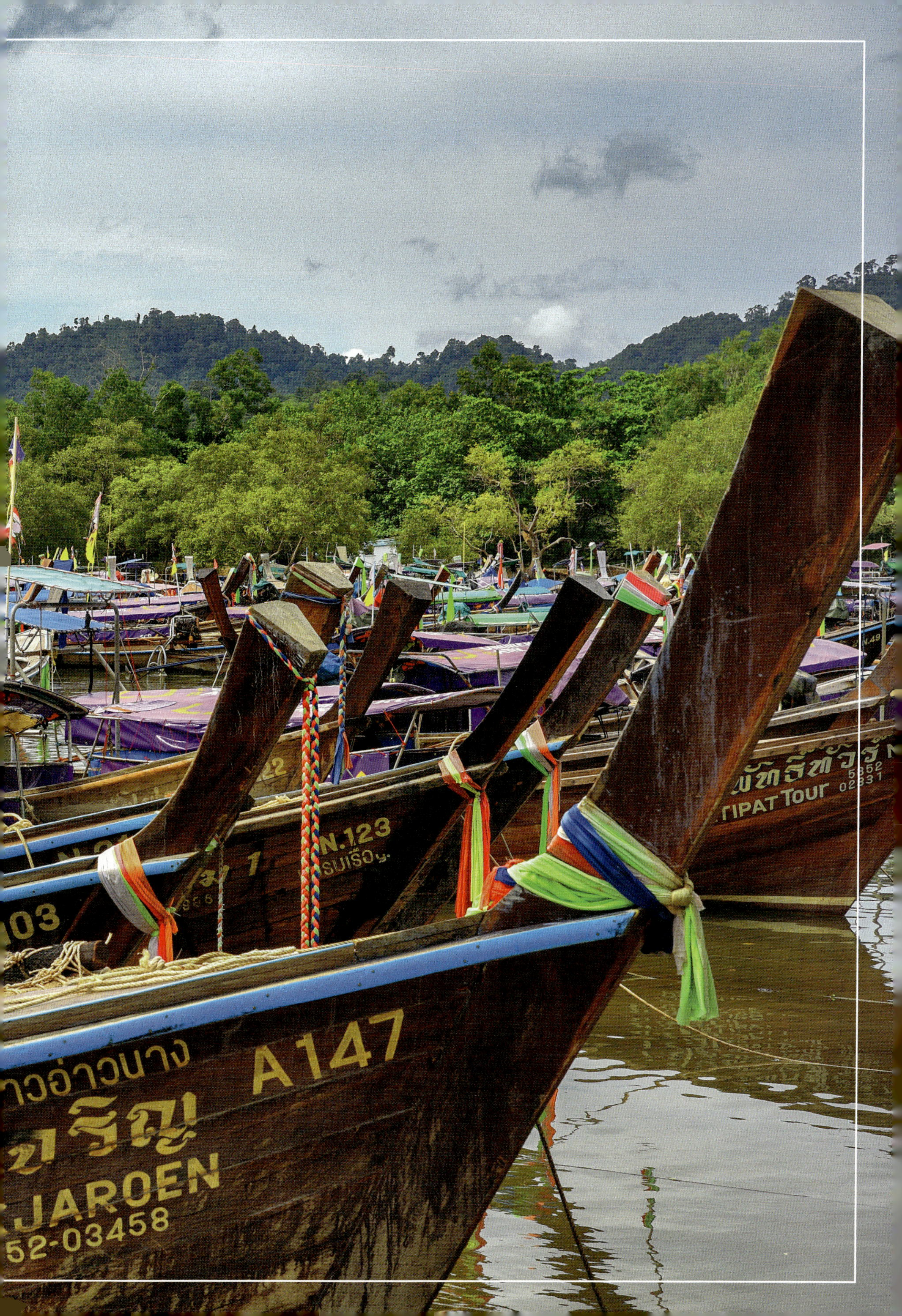

A147
JAROEN
52-03458
N.123
TIPAT Tour

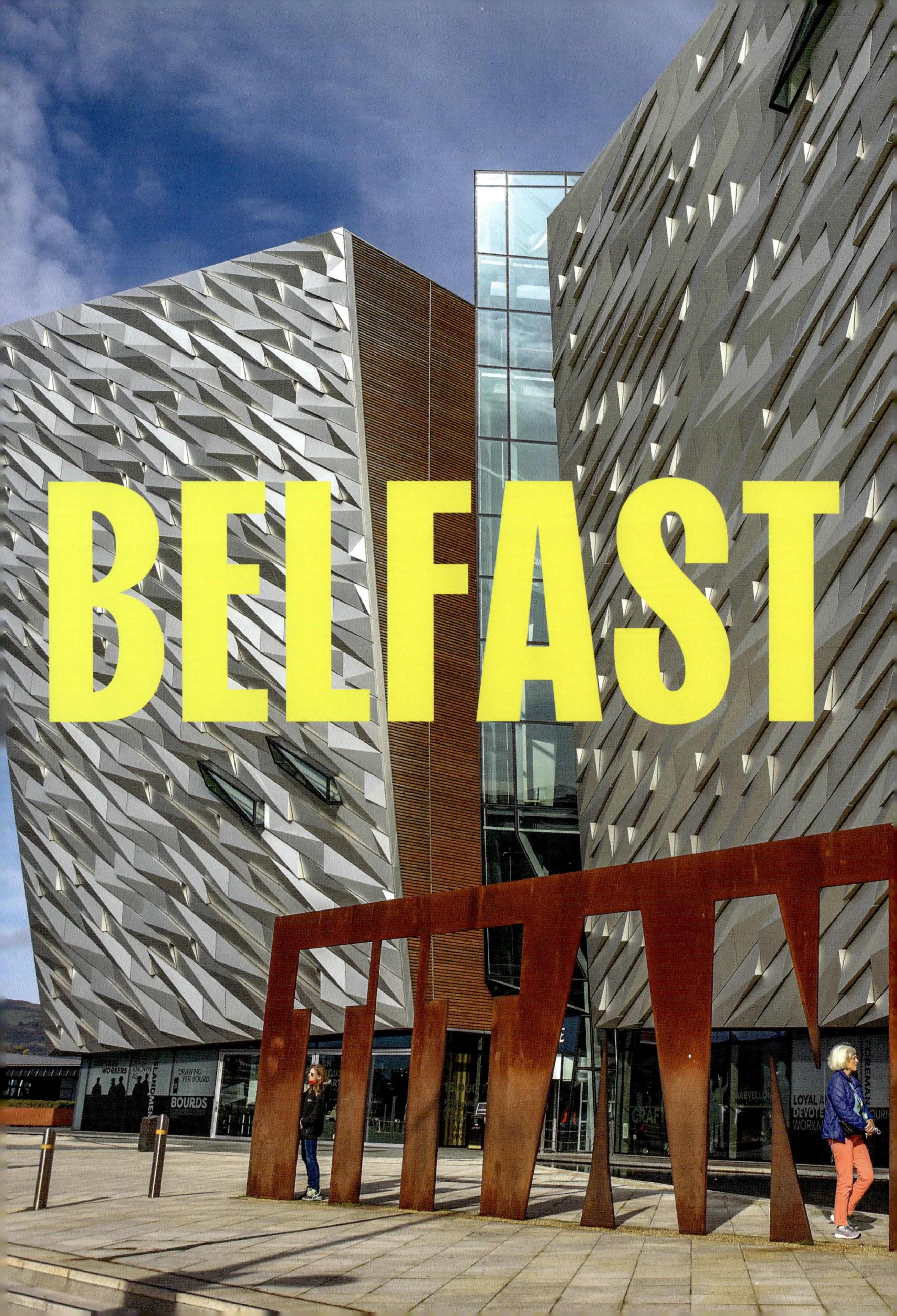
BELFAST
DRAWING YER BOURD.
BOURDS

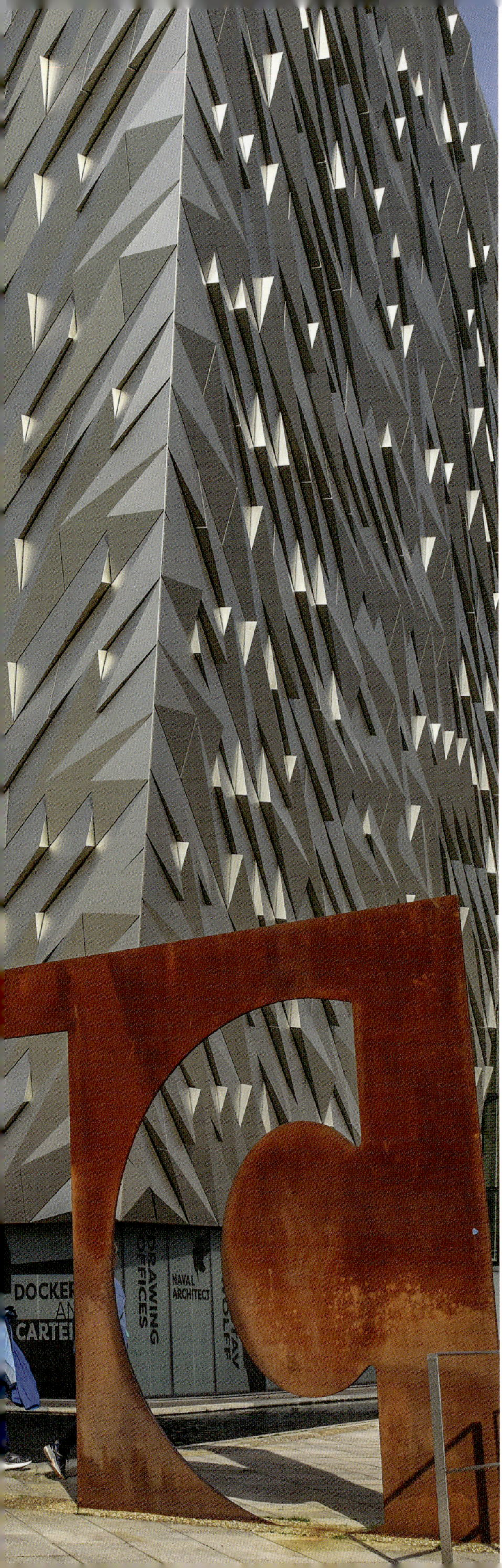

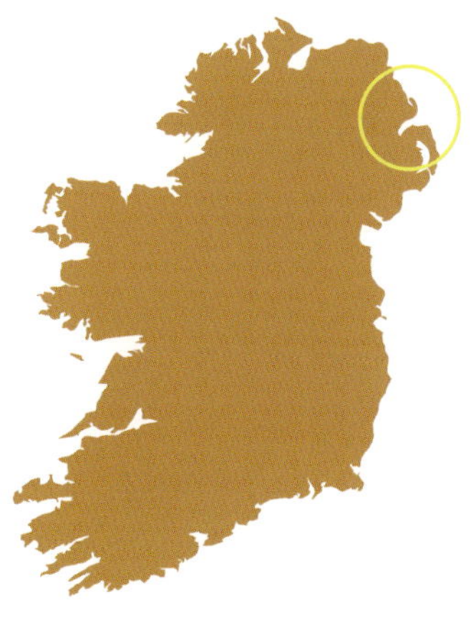

Belfast's deepest riddle claimed fifteen hundred lives, enthralled a global audience, and spawned the city's top tourist attraction. The most famous ship ever to ride our oceans was built here in Northern Ireland in the early 1900s. As visitors explore Titanic Quarter, home to an impressive museum and sprawling shipyards, they also navigate an enduring mystery: Why did the *Titanic* so clumsily collide with an iceberg? After dark, look up. A possible clue to this question hangs in the sky every night.

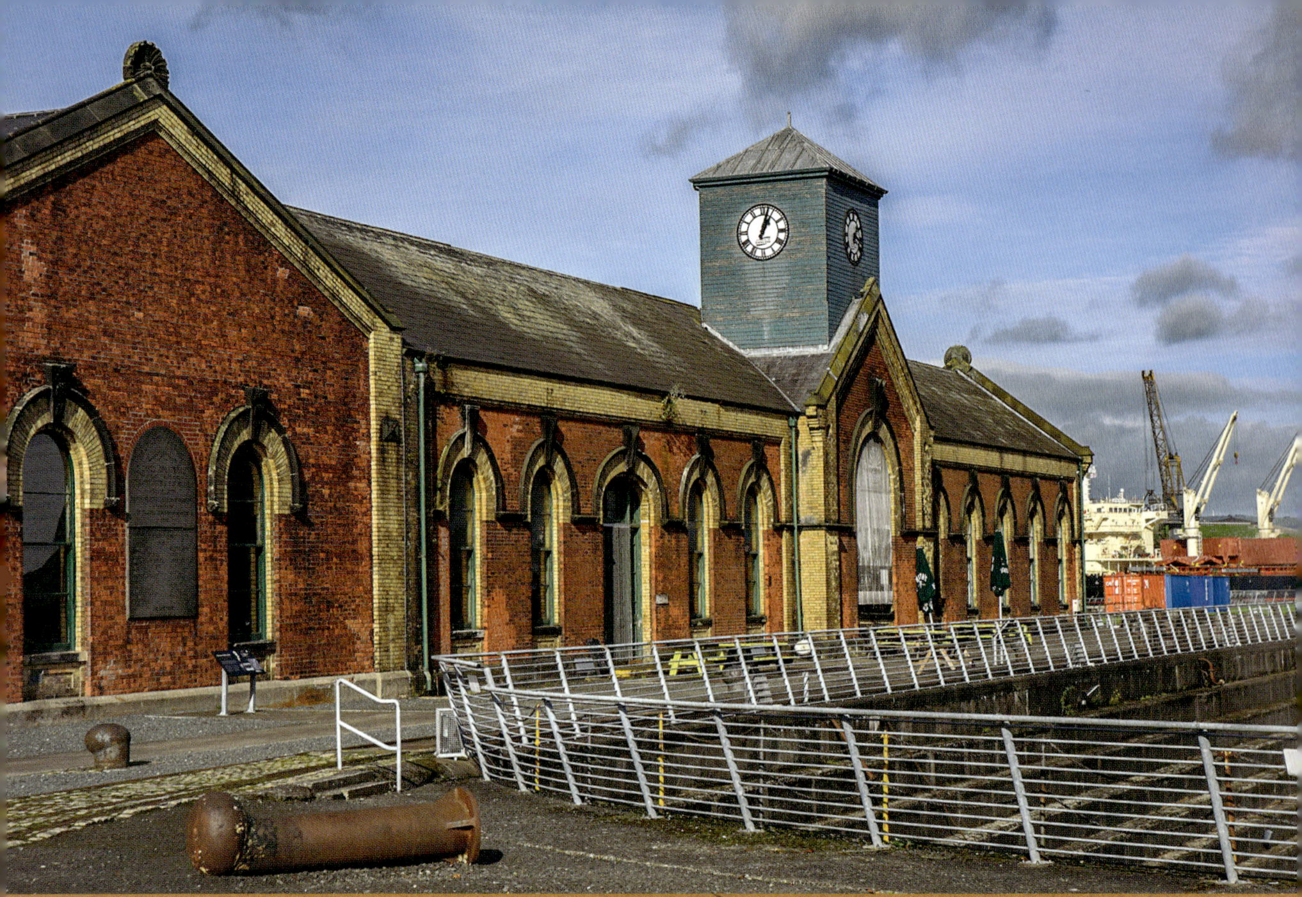

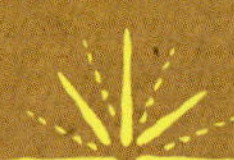

The £100 million Titanic Belfast Museum is not just the city's top attraction but also enscapsulates how the capital of Northern Ireland has evolved since the ship sank into the icy waters of the Atlantic.[219] Its ten interactive galleries tell the story of the *Titanic*'s monumental voyage and how this ship changed Belfast forever.

The eight-story museum has four sharp points, each resembling a ship's bow, and is clad in three thousand aluminum sheets.[220] Inside are informative signs, artifacts, and archival imagery. These are complemented by immersive exhibits, like re-created cabins that show how *Titanic* passengers lived aboard the ship, or the high-tech passenger car that transports visitors through a facsimile of the Belfast shipyard where the *Titanic* was birthed.[221]

Titanic Belfast excels at explaining the rise, fall, and revitalization of the shipyards. This giant industrial center blossomed in the wake of a national catastrophe. Half a century before the *Titanic* sank, more than one million Irish had died during the Great Famine (1845–1849). The agrarian blight was more devastating to people living in rural areas, forcing millions more to flee to Irish cities or emigrate to survive.[222] Belfast's waterfront welcomed many of these desperate farmers, and their labor helped power the shipyards' boom.

As the twentieth century arrived, Belfast's economy began to rely on the shipyards, which employed more than thirty-five thousand workers. The city earned global renown as an unparalleled hub of shipbuilding.[223] In early 1912, homegrown shipbuilding firm Harland & Wolff unveiled a brand-new luxury steamship called RMS *Titanic*. No vessel had ever been so vast, so advanced, so revered. Yet even the finest craftsmanship could not make the steamship impervious to the unpredictable fury of the ocean.

After the *Titanic* sank, so too did Belfast's shipyards. But this disaster was far from the only factor in the shipyards' gradual decline. Ireland's fight for independence, sectarian violence, and a global recession following World War I all contributed to the downturn. This industrial precinct's fortunes waxed and waned over many years before it hit the skids permanently in the 1960s.

For the next few decades, industry around the shipyards continued to struggle, leaving a gulf in Northern Ireland's economy. The docks became a blight on the city. By the turn of the twenty-first century, Belfast's reputation had shifted from proud shipbuilding hub to a hotbed of religiously motivated bloodshed. Worldwide media coverage of its fierce sectarian fighting during the Troubles deterred visitors.[224]

And then, quite remarkably, the shipyards came back from the dead and revived Belfast. In 2009, work began on what was billed as the biggest regeneration project in Northern Ireland's history. Almost £650 million has since been poured into the Titanic Quarter. Some 185 acres of its expanse host new hotels, offices, condos, bars, restaurants, a marina, an exhibition center, film and TV studios, and an array of attractions.[225]

Torrents of tourists now stroll the banks of Belfast's River Lagan, following its Maritime Mile. This walking route passes historic vessels, docks, pump houses, and lighthouses. Modern additions also spike its path such as art installations, sea-themed hotels, the Belfast Harbour Heritage Room museum, and Titanic Belfast.

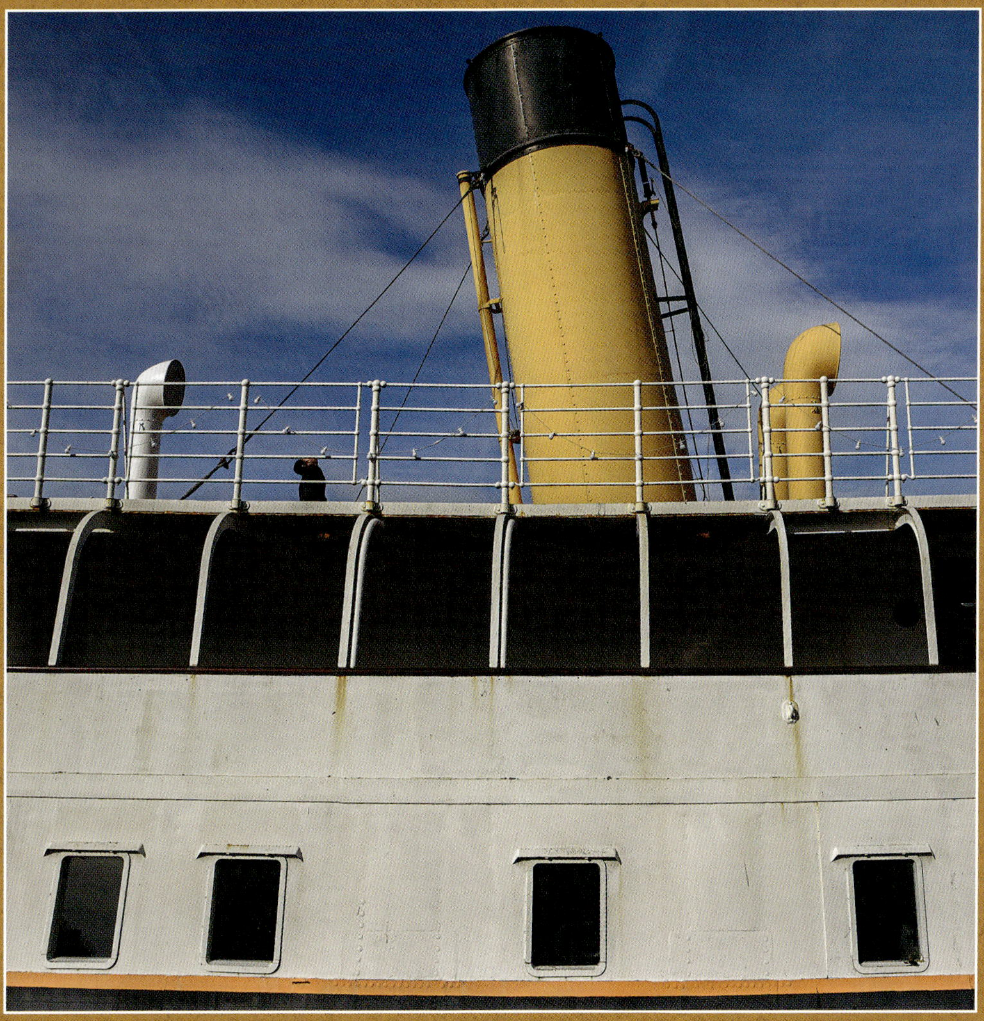

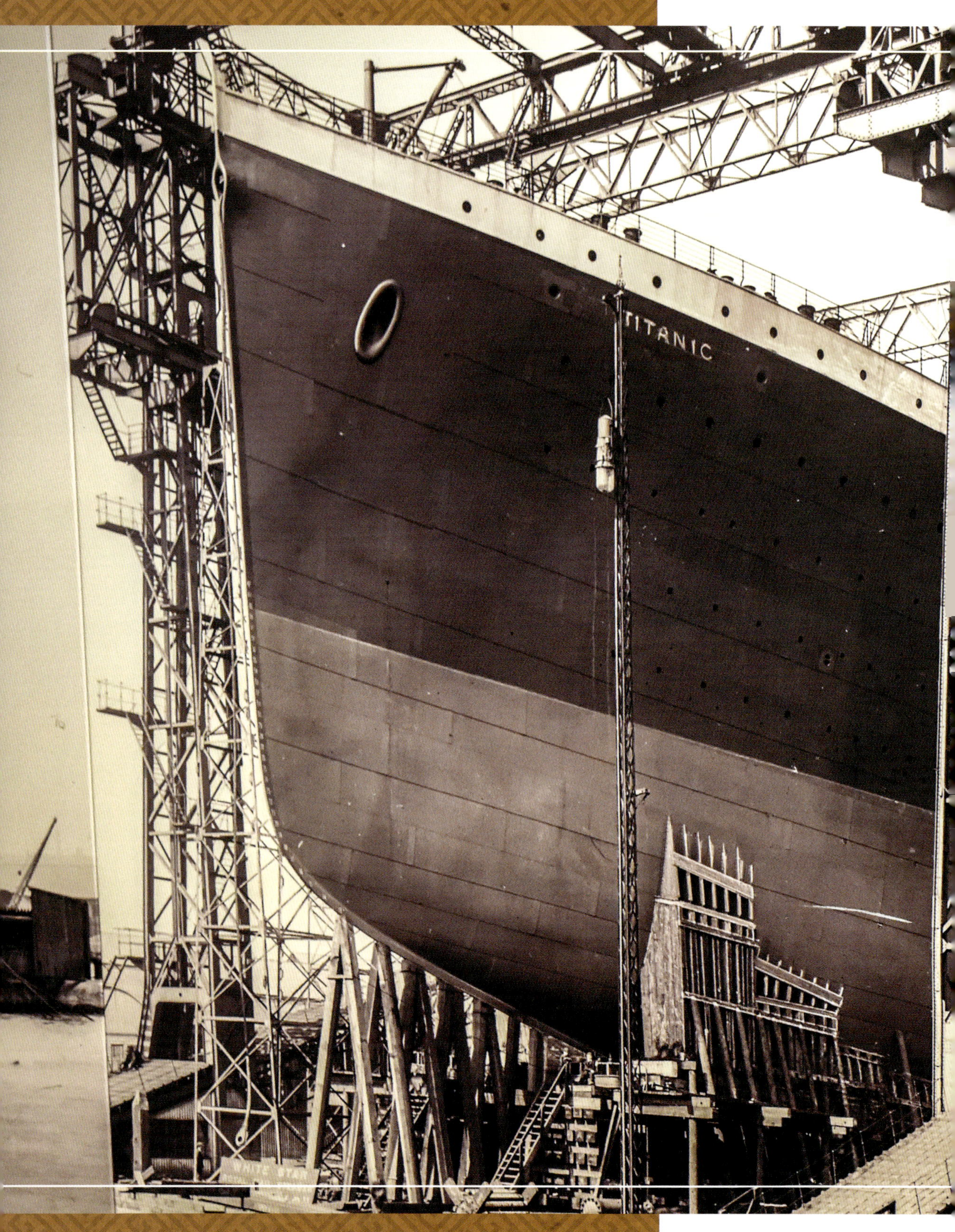
TITANIC

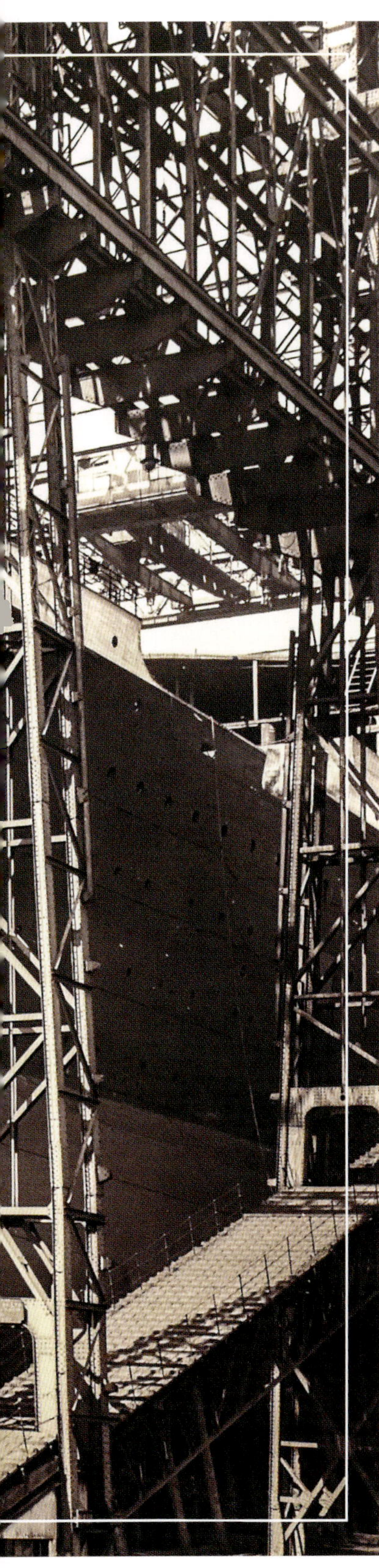

BELFAST BUILDS THE WORLD'S GREATEST SHIP

Built between 1909 and 1912, the *Titanic* was a luxury passenger liner commissioned by British shipping company White Star Line and built by Belfast shipbuilding firm Harland & Wolff. Measuring 882 feet long and 174 feet tall, the *Titanic* was small compared to many modern-day cruise ships, which typically stretch more than a thousand feet long. But the steamliner was a goliath in its era—so much so that the *Titanic* earned global headlines when it began its maiden voyage from Southampton, England, to New York. On board were more than twenty-two hundred passengers and crew. Guests ranged from wealthy tourists with first-class suites to working-class folk immigrating to North America who had to squeeze into third-class cabins in the bowels of the cruise liner.[226]

THE NIGHT *TITANIC* VANISHED

While ships now monitor hazards via satellite,[227] in 1912, they relied on more basic methods. At night, their lookout staff used binoculars to scan the horizon for foam created by ocean swells crashing against an iceberg.

On the evening of April 14, 1912, abnormally calm conditions kept the *Titanic's* lookouts from spotting any such froth. So, too, did the absence of moonlight, which made the ocean waters even harder to survey. The towering iceberg went undectected until it was too late.

At 11:40 p.m., about four hundred nautical miles southeast of Newfoundland, *Titanic's* starboard side struck the iceberg. The impact ruptured its hull, allowing ocean water to flood six of its sixteen watertight compartments. Thomas Andrews, the ship's designer, was on board and warned its captain, Edward Smith, that the *Titanic* would sink within hours.

Twenty lifeboats were launched. But they had space only for slightly more than half of the twenty-two hundred people on board, with priority given to women and children. Not even three hours after the collision, the *Titanic* snapped in two. It was claimed by the sea, along with the lives of about fifteen hundred people.[228]

INVESTIGATIONS PROVIDE NO ANSWERS

The catastrophe became a global news juggernaut. Readers from Australia to Argentina followed media reports of the multiple investigations into its sinking.[229] The US government's initial inquiry blamed lax ship inspection by British authorities and Captain Smith's slow reaction to the iceberg warning.[230] Meanwhile, the British investigation faulted the *Titanic's* "excessive speed."[231] Yet neither inquiry, nor any studies since, have brought about a clear consensus of which controllable factors, if any, led to the tragic collision.

ASTRONOMICAL INTERFERENCE

The moon may be largely to blame for the disaster, according to findings by Texas State University-San Marcos scientists David Olson and Russell Doescher. Their 2012 research found that the *Titanic's* sinking could have been due to an ultrarare trio of astronomical factors combining to supercharge the tides on that fateful night.[232]

Tides are the regular rise and fall of sea levels. Each day, most of the planet's coastlines experience two high tides (when ocean water moves closest to shore) and two low tides (when that water recedes). The moon's gravitational pull influences these tides.[233]

Shortly before the *Titanic* sank, the moon tugged at the planet with uncommon vigor, Olson and Doescher found. That was because Earth, sun, and moon were in perfect alignment. This further increased gravitational forces and created a stronger than normal tide, called a spring tide.

Additionally, both the sun and moon had reached their closest points to Earth that night. This, too, amplified the pull exerted on ocean waters. Very rarely, the scientists explained, do all of the these astronomical factors coincide. When they do, the ocean experiences savage forces. Even if its surface appeared calm, the waters below could have moved back and forth ferociously enough, the researchers believe, to potentially force a submerged iceberg to rise, protrude from the sea, and unexpectedly float in front of the *Titanic*.[234]

Uncertainty persists, though, because the theory is just that—a theory. The idea is plausible, no doubt, and originates from a respected source. But for now, no definitive answer exists for why the world's most famous cruise liner met an infamous demise.

Whatever the cause, this phenomenal vessel and its extraordinary tragedy continue to captivate the many visitors drawn to explore Belfast's shipyard and trace the tale of a maritime mystery.

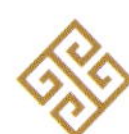

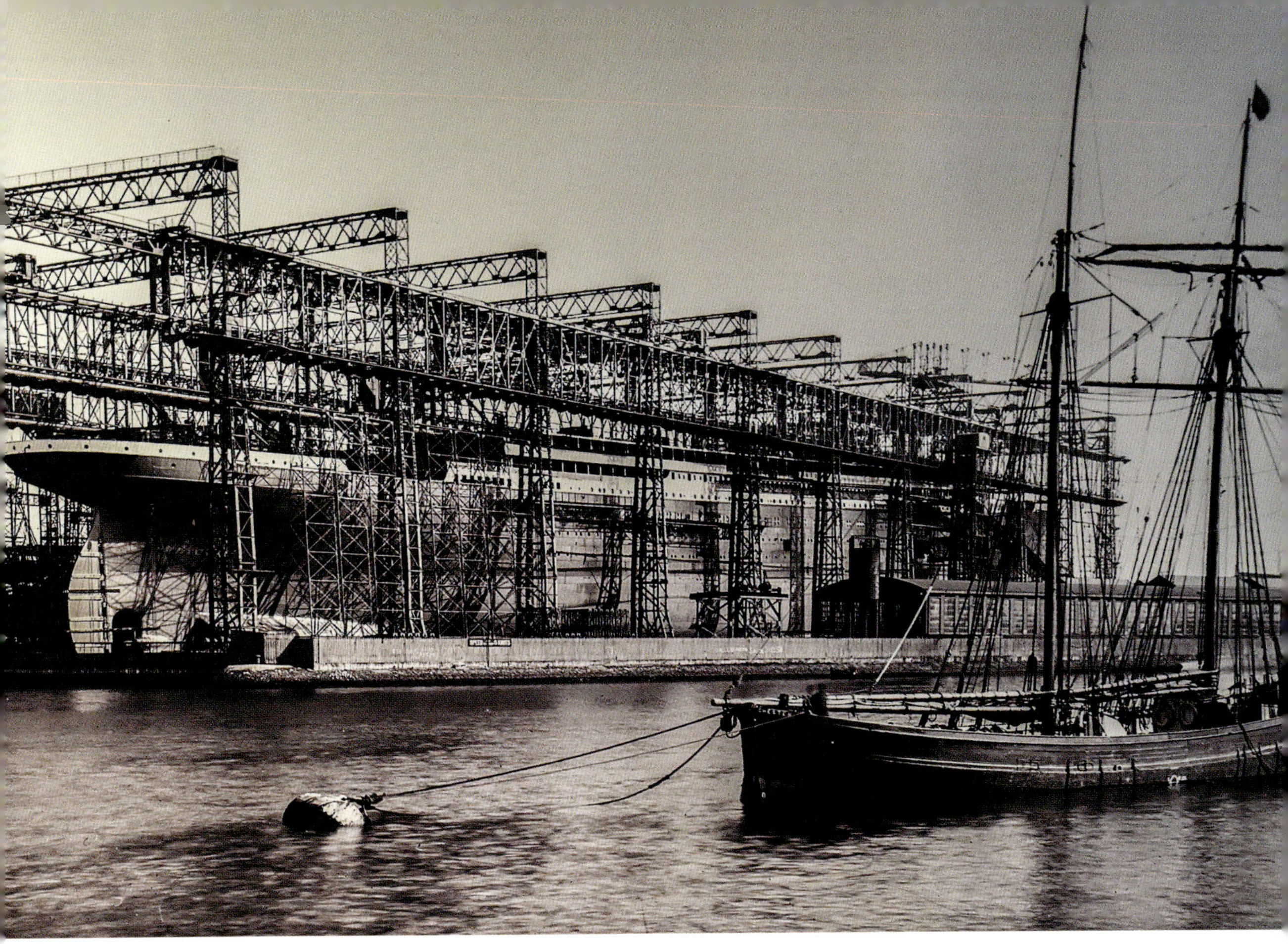

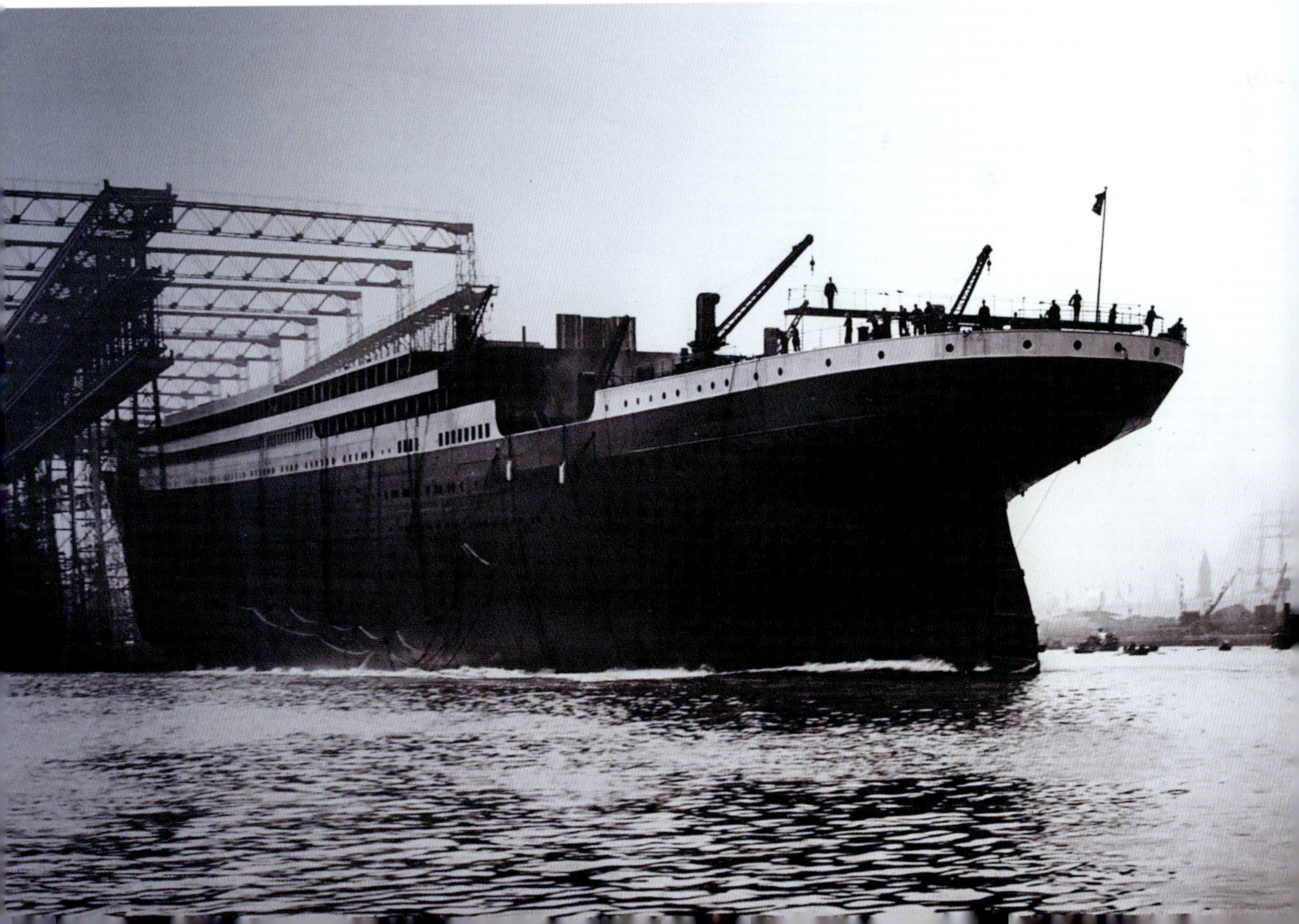

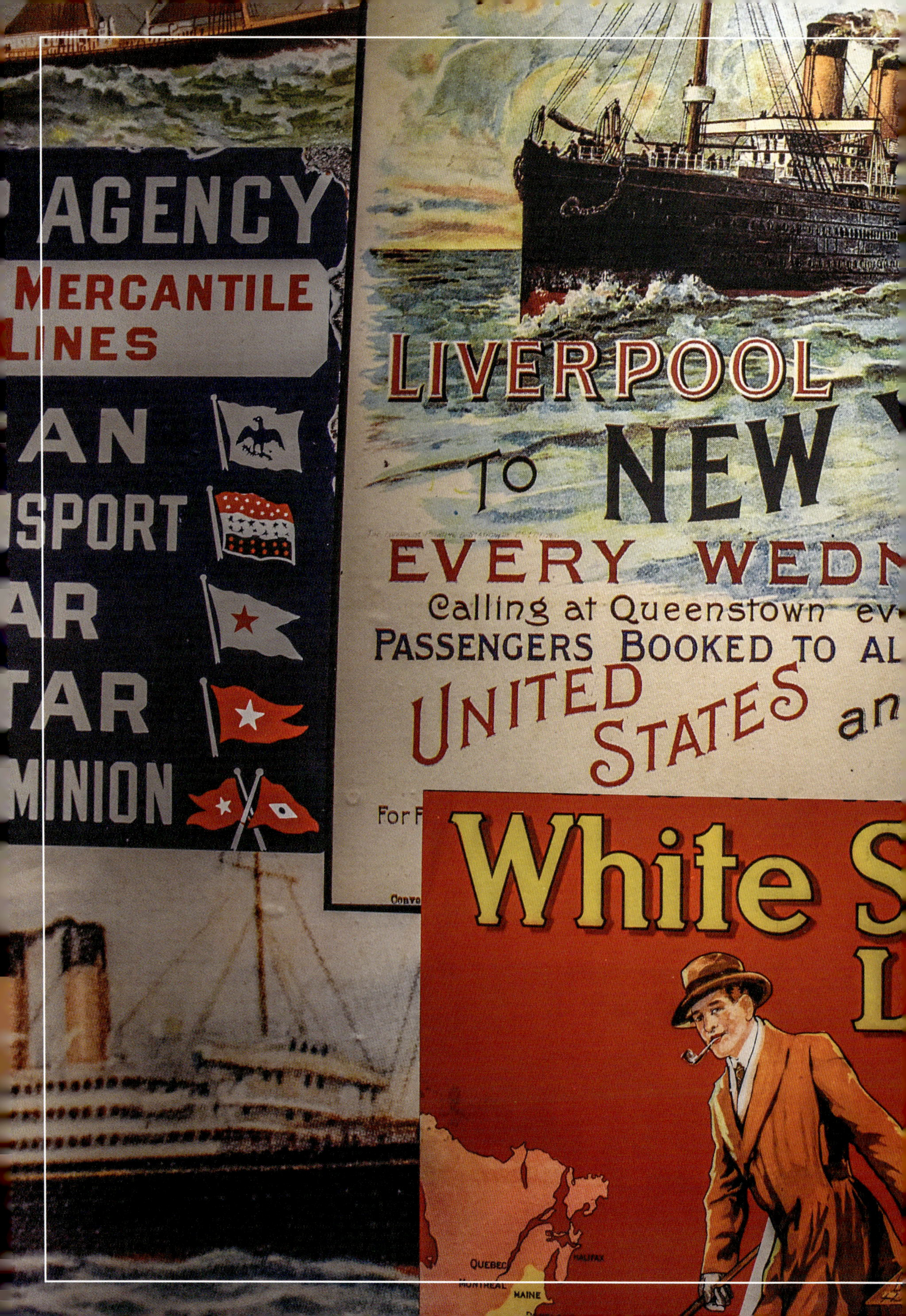
AGENCY
MERCANTILE
LINES
AN
SPORT
AR
TAR
MINION
LIVERPOOL
TO NEW
EVERY WEDN
Calling at Queenstown ev
PASSENGERS BOOKED TO AL
UNITED STATES an
White S
L
QUEBEC
HALIFAX
MONTREAL
MAINE

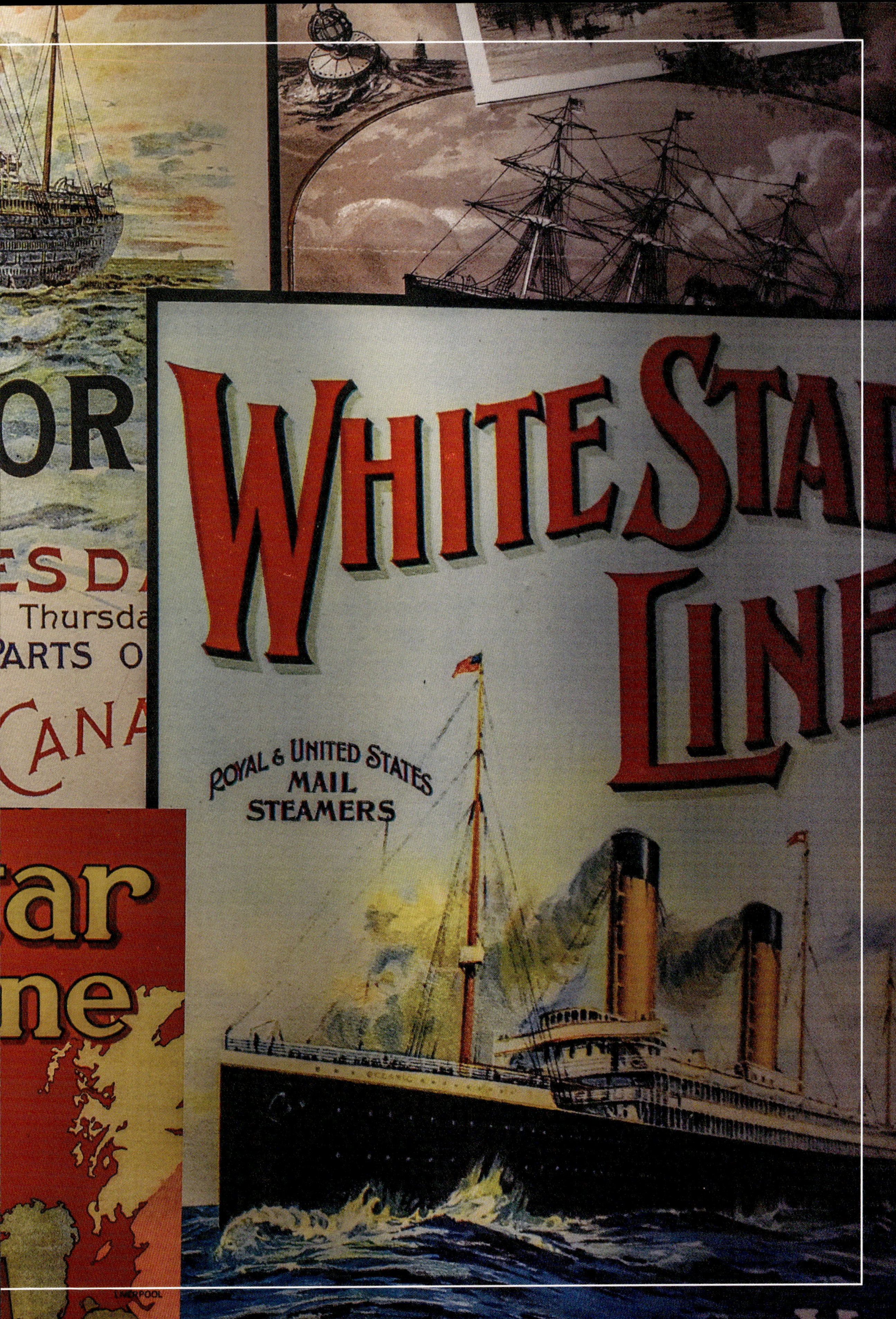
WHITE
ROYAL & UNITED STATES
MAIL
STEAMERS

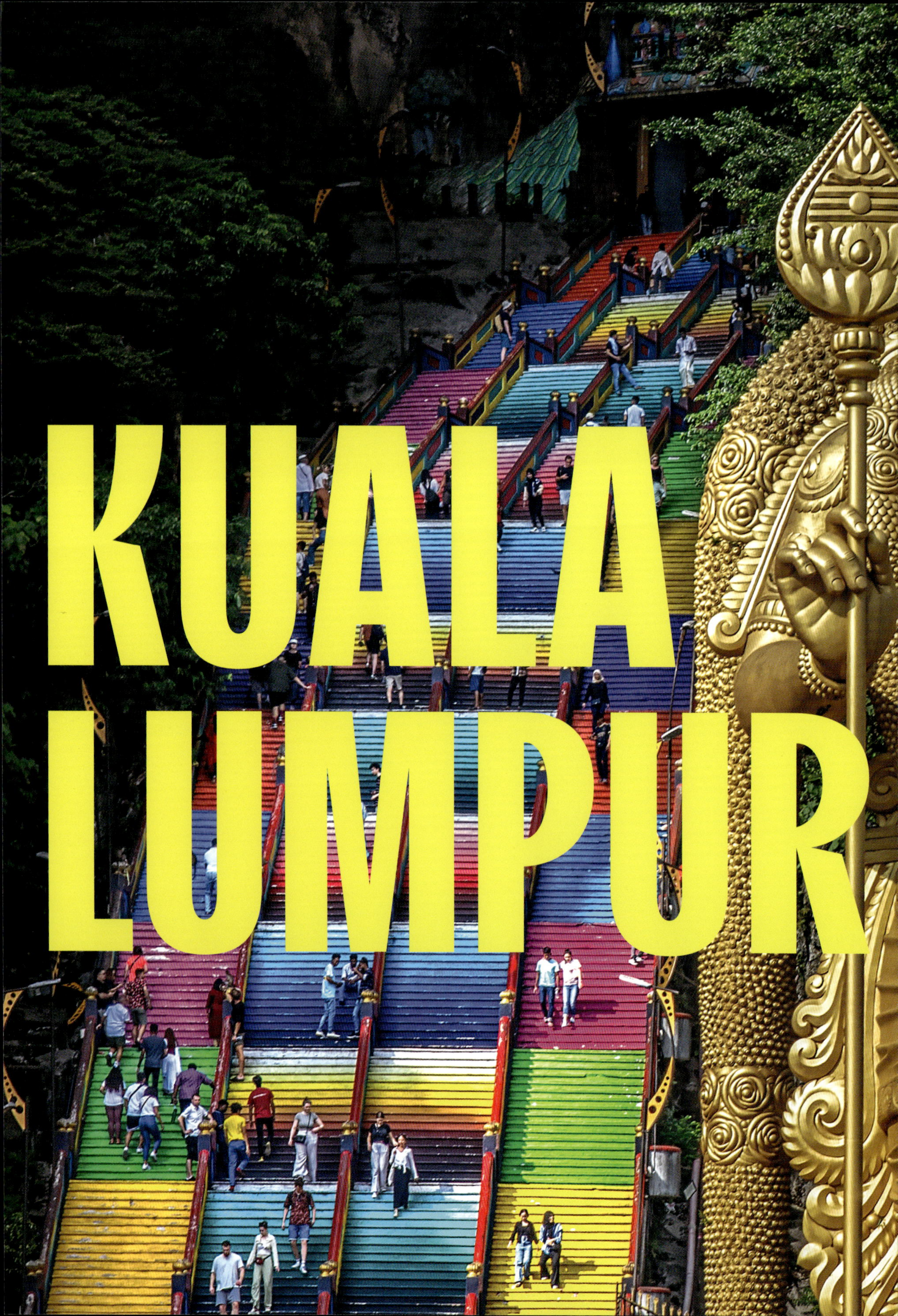

KUALA LUMPUR

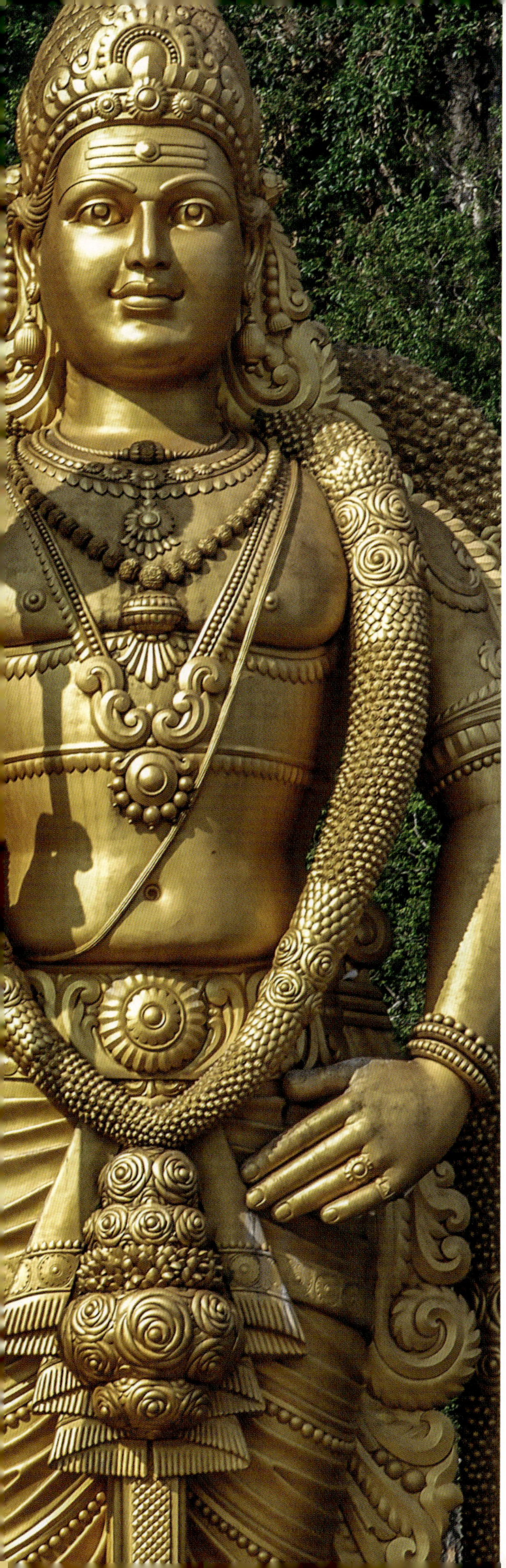

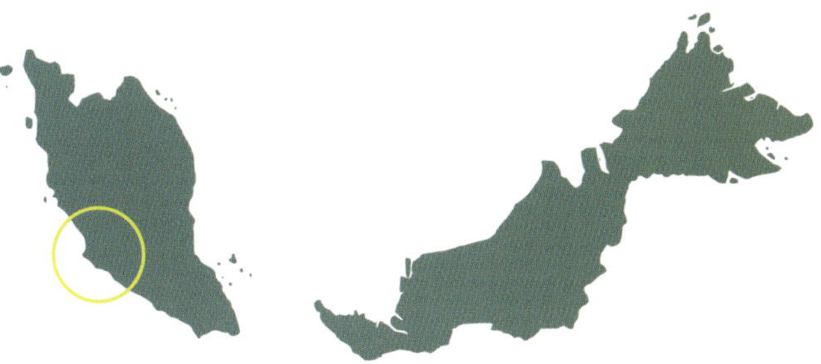

Lathered in gold, laden with jewelry, and brandishing a spear, a Hindu giant guards Malaysia's four-hundred-year-old geological wonder. Thousands of visitors each day ascend the steps to Batu Caves, passing beneath that 140-foot-tall statue of Murugan, which was erected in 2006 and took a team of craftsmen three years to build.[235]

Some come to this hallowed site as part of a religious pilgrimage. Others are drawn by its dazzling, neon-drenched setting. And for those who wish to learn more, there's an enthralling Hindu fable hidden in these dark, jungled caves—one that revolves around a magic peacock, rampaging devils, and a god of war's triumph over evil.[236]

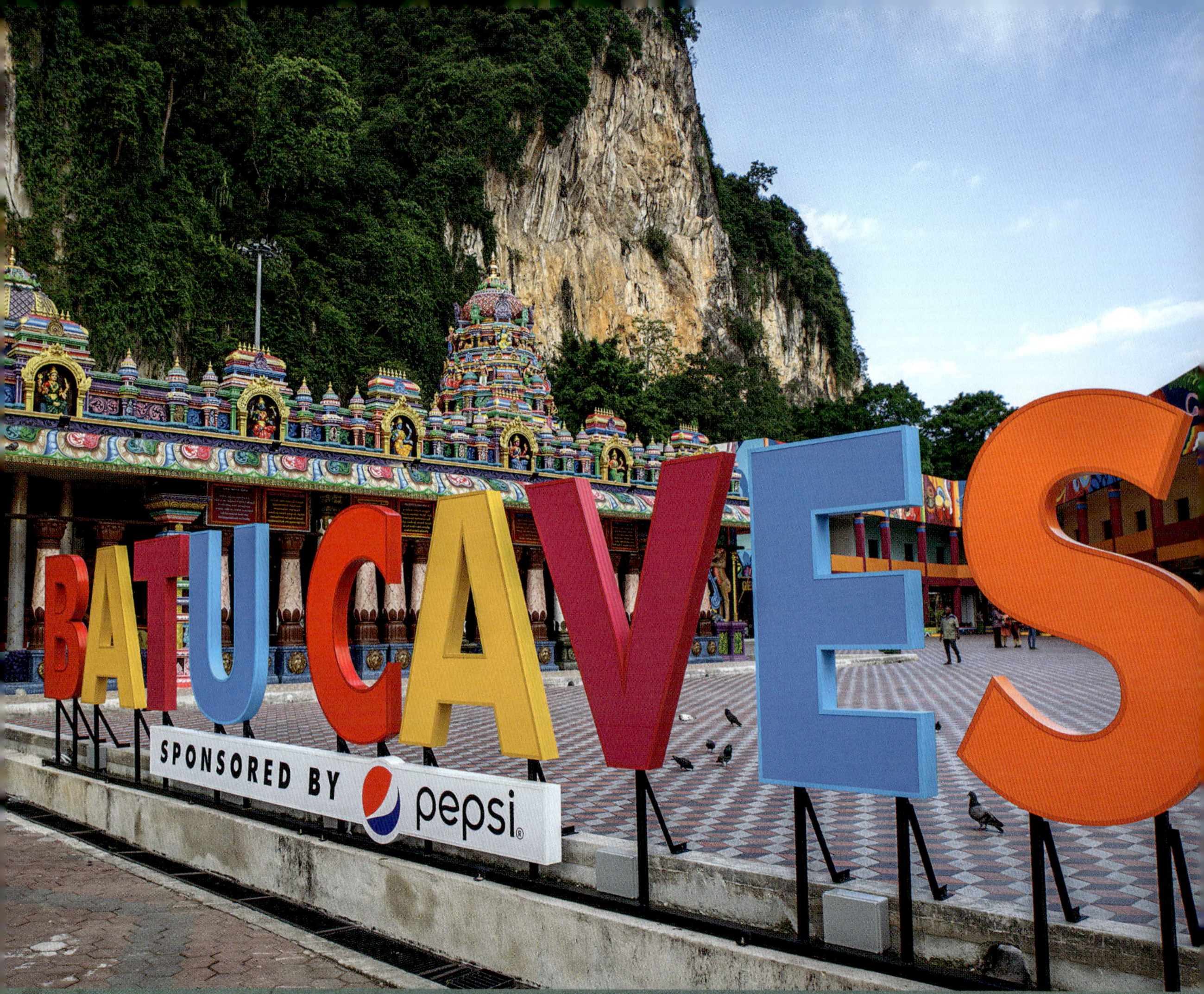

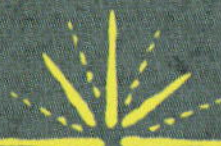

The visually arresting Batu Caves are well suited to Kuala Lumpur, a city scattered with memorable architecture. Almost nine million people occupy this modern metropolis, which sprawls through the Klang Valley, where trees have given way to a forest of skyscrapers.[237] Near the crest of this man-made canopy sit the 1,483-foot-tall Petronas Twin Towers. They once held the title of the world's tallest buildings, although that designation now belongs to Dubai's Burj Khalifa. Still, the Petronas Twin Towers continue to lure visitors with their iconic silhouettes, scenic skybridge, giant shopping center, and photogenic KLCC Park at their base.[238]

Dwarfing them now is the nearby Merdeka 118 tower. Currently the second-tallest building in the world, it stands at a woozy 2,230 feet. From its cloud-nudging observation decks, viewers earn panoramic views of Kuala Lumpur. They may glimpse labyrinthine Chinatown, where incense smoke wafts from timeworn Taoist and Buddhist temples, or spy magnificent Islamic houses of worship, like the commanding National Mosque of Malaysia, ornate Jamek Mosque, and modern Federal Territory Mosque.[239]

THE GIANT DEITY WHO GUARDS THE BATU CAVES

Murugan, the Hindu god of war, first appeared in Indian sacred texts more than twenty-five hundred years ago. Also known as Skanda or Kartikeya, he is the son of Goddess Parvati and Lord Shiva, the central deity of Hinduism. Murugan is a key character in many Hindu legends, including the triumphant tale celebrated by Thaipusam, a massive religious festival held annually at Batu Caves.[240]

The story begins with a group of Hindu deities, known as *Devas*, approaching Lord Shiva for help. They beg the god to vanquish the supernatural demons called *Asuras*, who have long tormented them. Shiva accepts their request and hands this momentous task to his son. Before Murugan sets off to battle the demons, his mother gifts him the same *Shakti Vel* (magical spear) that visitors to Batu Caves can see his likeness clutching.

Then, the legend goes, as the crowd of Murugan's followers has their heads bowed in prayer, they look up to see wind rustling the plumage of a giant peacock. Murugan is riding the bird like a horse. Soon the peacock's flapping wings land Murugan face-to-face with Surapadman, the ferocious boss of the Asuras.

Murugan and his spear are so effective that Surapadman resorts to shape-shifting, trying to create confusion. But his righteous foe sees through the ruse and continues to attack the demon lord. In desperation, Surapadman changes into a mango tree and tries to hide in the depths of the sea. When Murugan slices the tree open, a peacock and a rooster emerge and attack him under orders of Surapadman. However, Murugan immediately subdues both birds and turns them into his allies.

Soon he is riding the peacock in pursuit of the ultimate demon, who he follows across vast swaths of India before finally vanquishing Surapadman. When Murugan returns from this successful battle with the forces of darkness, his devotees dance and cheer. He stands before them gripping his gilded spear and draped in jewelry, which is how he is depicted here at Batu Caves.[241, 242]

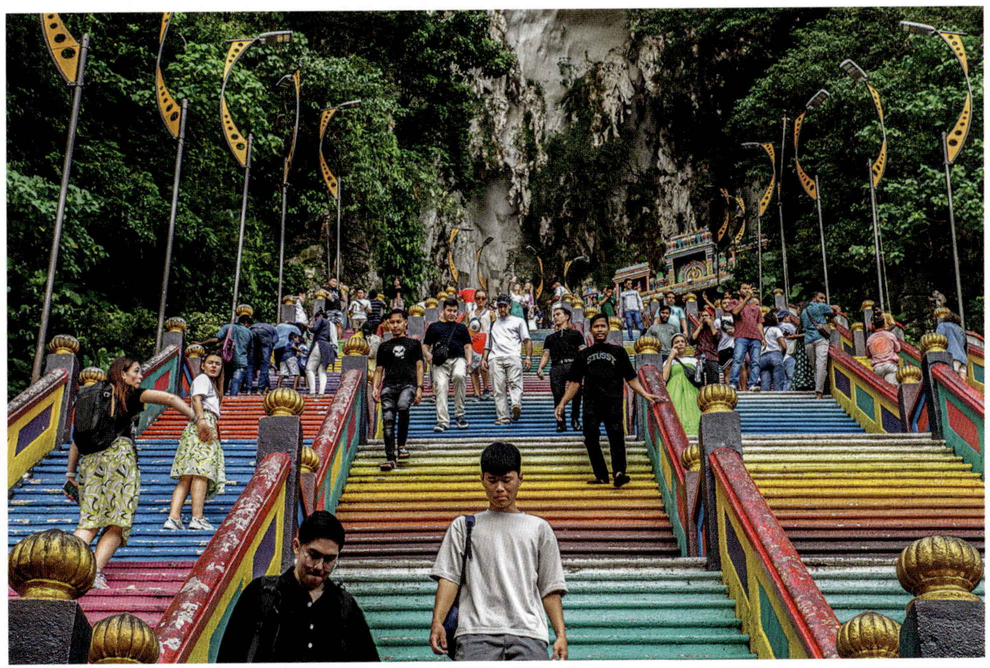

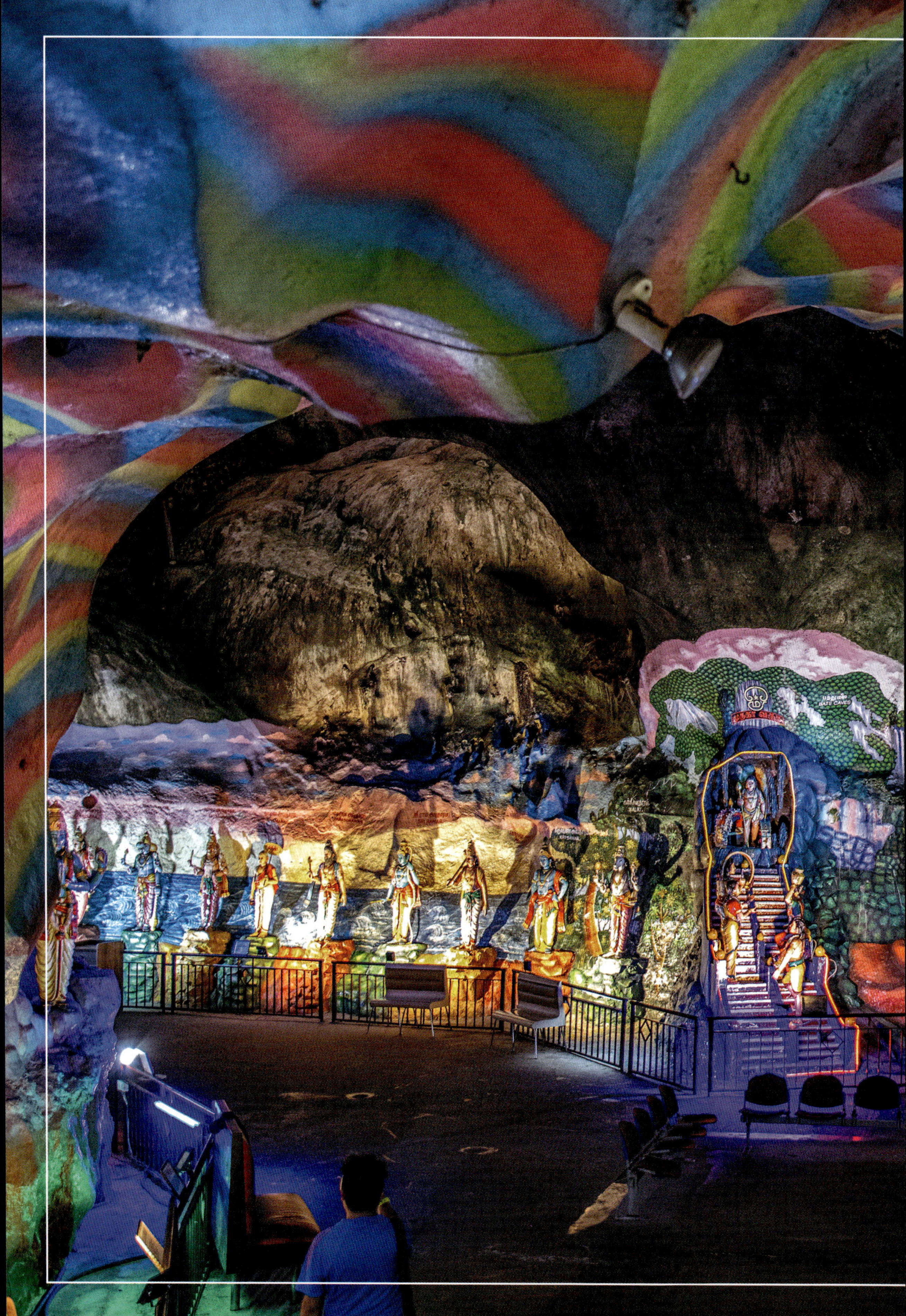

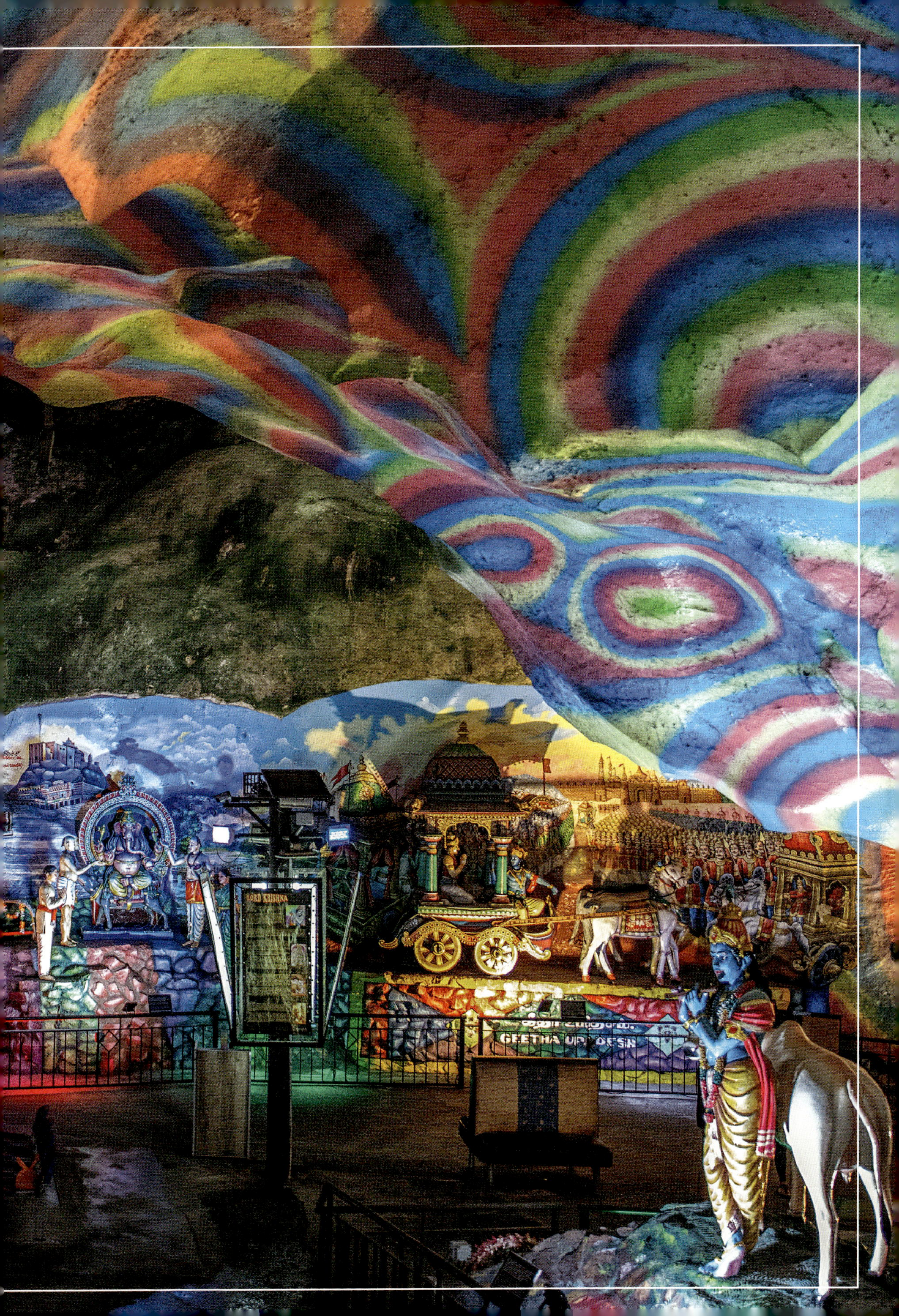
LORD KRISHNA
GEETHA

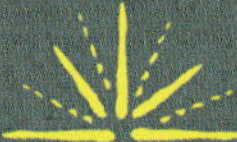

In the northern suburbs of Kuala Lumpur lie the forested hills that host Batu Caves. After a twenty-five-minute taxi ride from downtown, the city's endless high-rises finally part to expose the towering figure of Murugan. Visitors to Batu pass through a rainbow-hued gate etched with Hindu deities to enter its huge complex of temples and limestone grottoes. Here, they climb 272 steps to the main cave in the year-round swelter of this equatorial city.

The ascent tends to go slowly—not just due to its physical demands or the distraction caused by armies of long-tailed macaques trying to steal visitors' snacks. Rather, it's slow because most people repeatedly pause on the staircase to snap photos of this landmark's vivid paintwork and the panoramic views of Kuala Lumpur's cityscape to their backs. As visitors reach the top, they land at the entrance to enormous Cathedral Cave. Any breath they've managed to catch is soon snatched away.

About 320 feet high, Cathedral Cave is startling in its size. Comparatively tiny yet similarly photogenic is the cave's century-old Hindu temple, which is covered with red-and-white candy-striped walls and iridescent Hindu sculptures. This cavern is a key site of Hindu pilgrimage, especially during annual festivals. Behind Cathedral Cave, a smaller staircase leads to another spectacular grotto, this one illuminated by sunlight that rushes through its open ceiling.

Adventurous visitors to Batu can also choose to disappear beneath the earth by joining a guided tour of Batu's largest grotto, Dark Cave. About 1.3 miles deep, it's one of Asia's most heavily researched subterranean spaces.

Many scientists have entered this blackened environment to study the world's rarest arachnid, the trapdoor spider, a small, mildly venomous species that is elusive, typically hiding away in its burrow.[243] Visitors to Dark Cave witness an array of rock formations, from helictites to cave curtains, flowstones, and columns that glow in torchlight due to heavy crystal concentrations.[244]

The Batu caves also boast another two remarkable grottoes. Ramayana Cave is splashed in radiant murals and dioramas. Collectively, these artworks depict scenes from the *Ramayana*, an epic Indian text more than two thousand years old. Nearby, visitors follow a walkway across a koi pond to Cave Villa, a grotto that brims with spiritual statues and paintings and hosts regular live Hindu dances.[245]

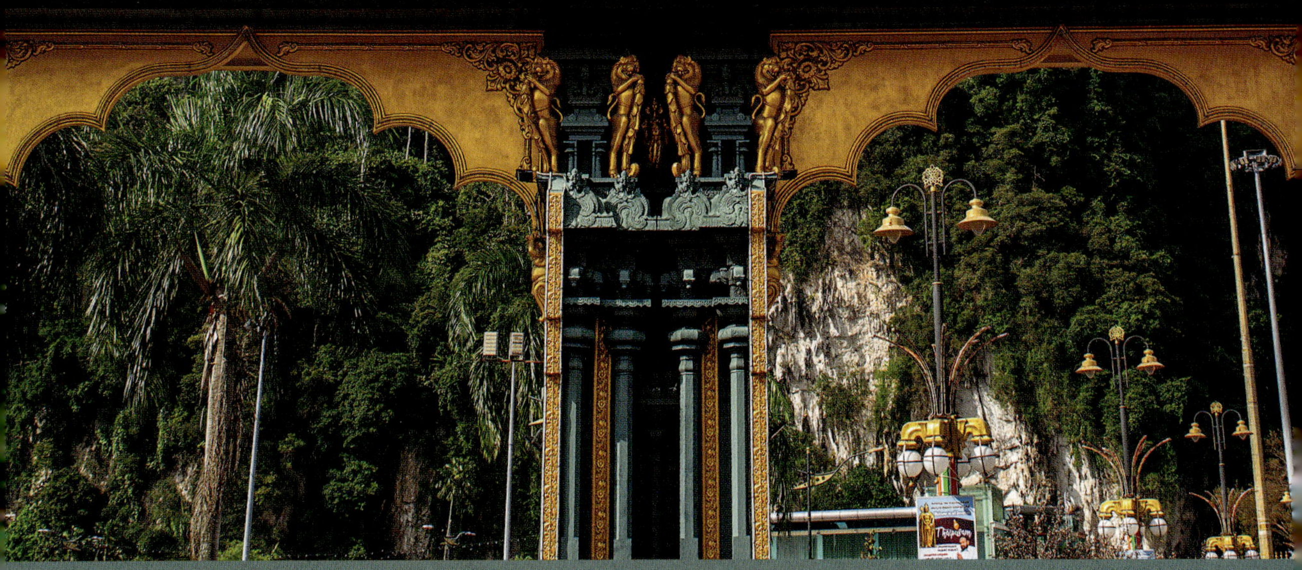

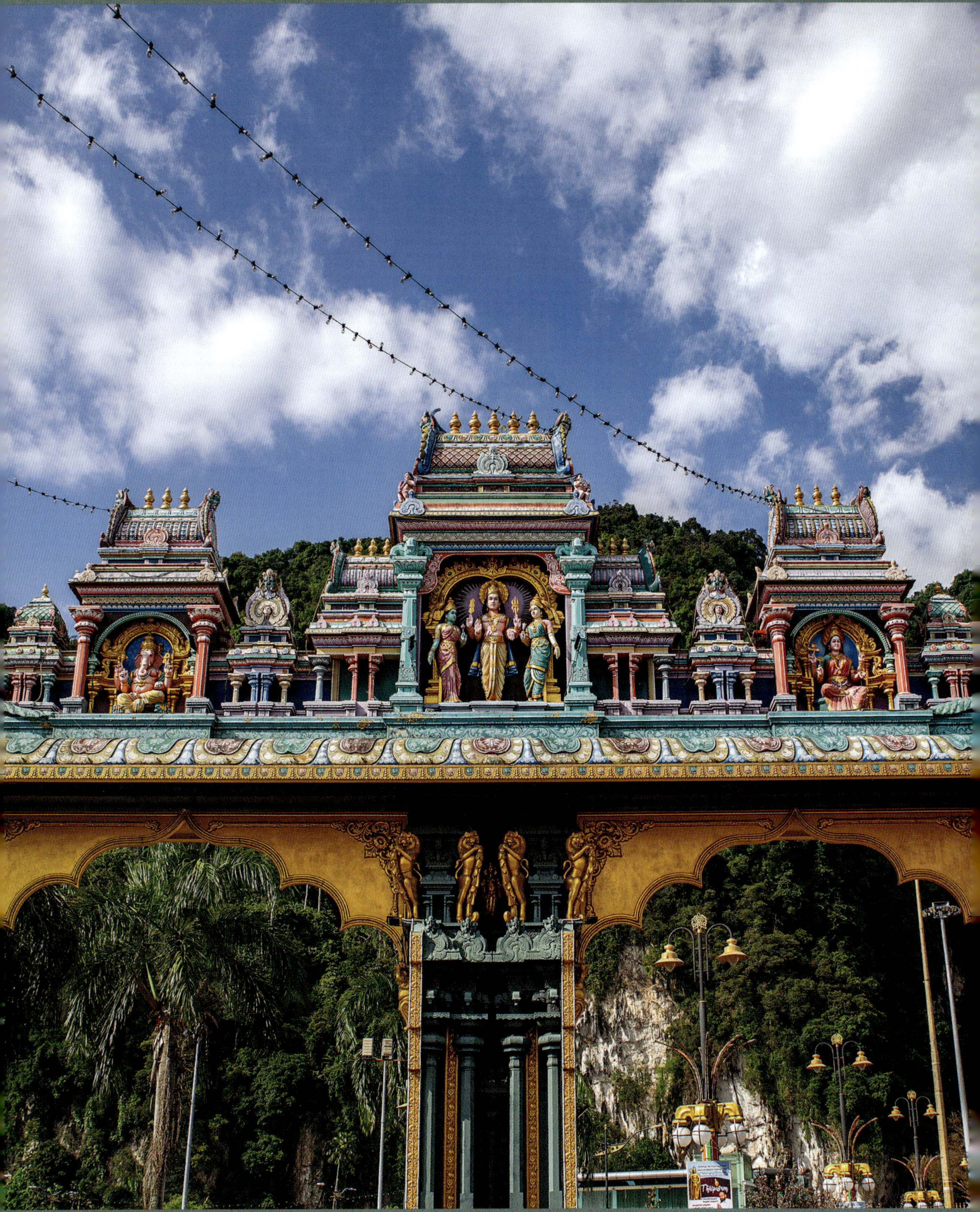

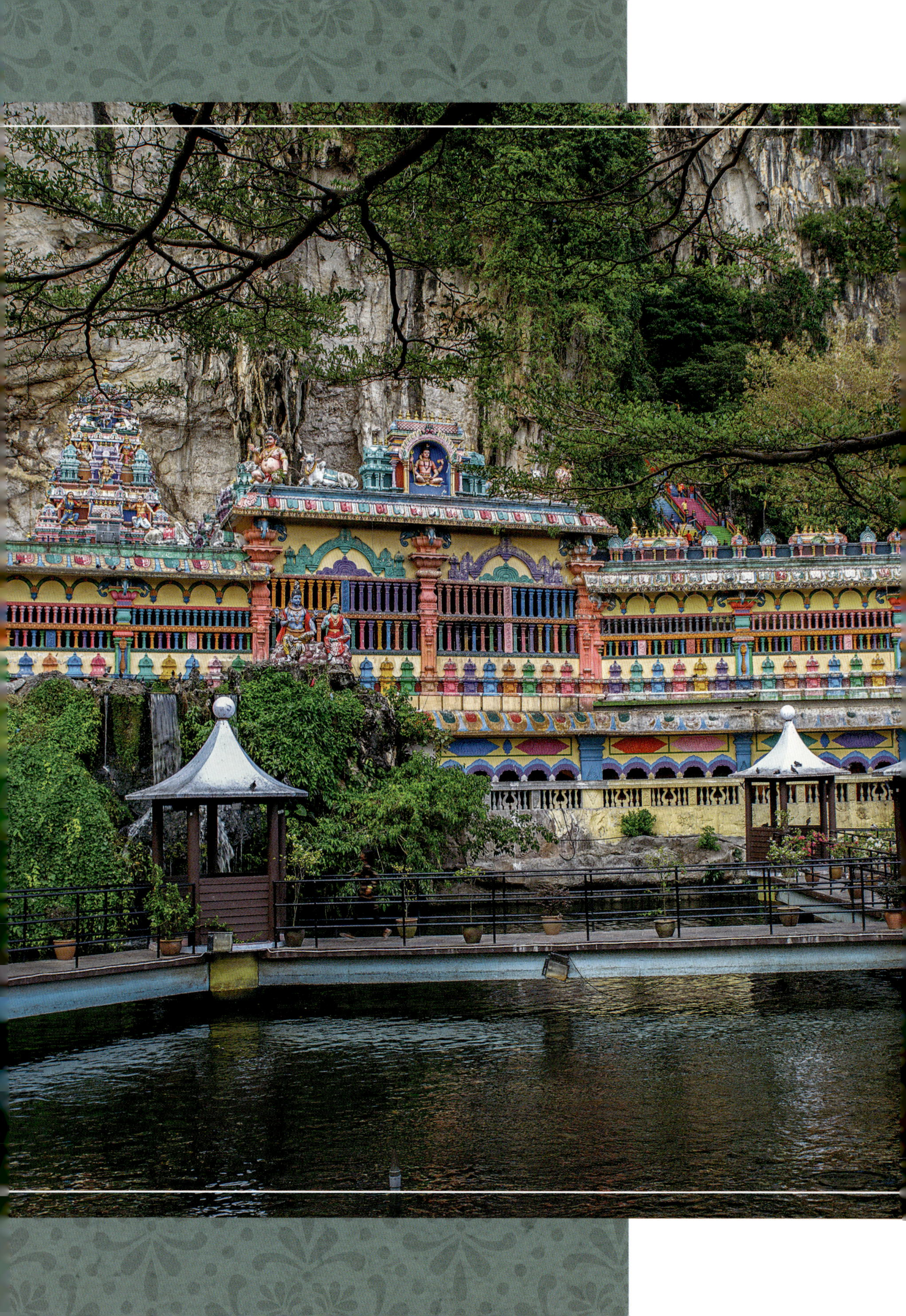

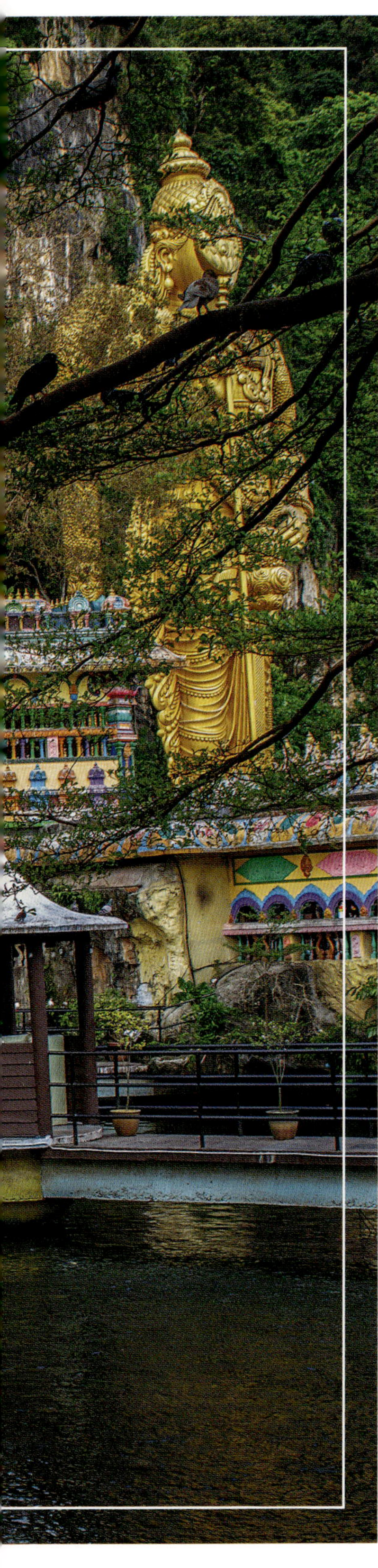

BATU CAVES' MASSIVE ANNUAL SPECTACLE

Worshippers visit Batu Caves to request the assistance of Murugan, who, as well as being a god of war, grants his faithful both fertility and prosperity. Their devotion is never more pronounced than during Thaipusam, which has been held at Batu Caves early each year since the 1890s.[246] Over two days, in either January or February, one million worshippers flood the site for the largest Thaipusam festival on the planet.[247] Percussive tunes rumble through the caverns, emanating from hundreds of *urumi*—double-headed jackwood drums pounded in unison by troupes of musicians honoring Murugan.[248] This provides a hypnotic aural backdrop for startling displays of spirituality.

During Thaipusam, thousands of worshippers thread their cheeks and tongues with razor-sharp rods, an act that exhibits their allegiance to Murugan. Other men pierce their backs with large hooks and use their body weight to pull behind them a *kavadi* wooden canopy. Embellished by peacock feathers, the kavadi commemorates Murugan's mighty victory.

Worshippers who put themselves through such discomforts are believed to receive from Murugan a spiritual cleansing. Many devotees spend weeks fasting and praying to prepare themselves physically and spiritually for the ritual. As part of the festival, women carry offerings of fruit, milk, and flowers while streaming past the monolithic statue of Murugan.[249]

At the same time, this god of war lures many tourists to the caves, all thanks to the gilded glory of his likeness and the contrast it creates with this site's fluorescent stairs, sculptures, and temples. As people tread those colorful steps, however, most are unaware that they've entered a setting dedicated to a wild tale of demons, deities, and a magic spear.

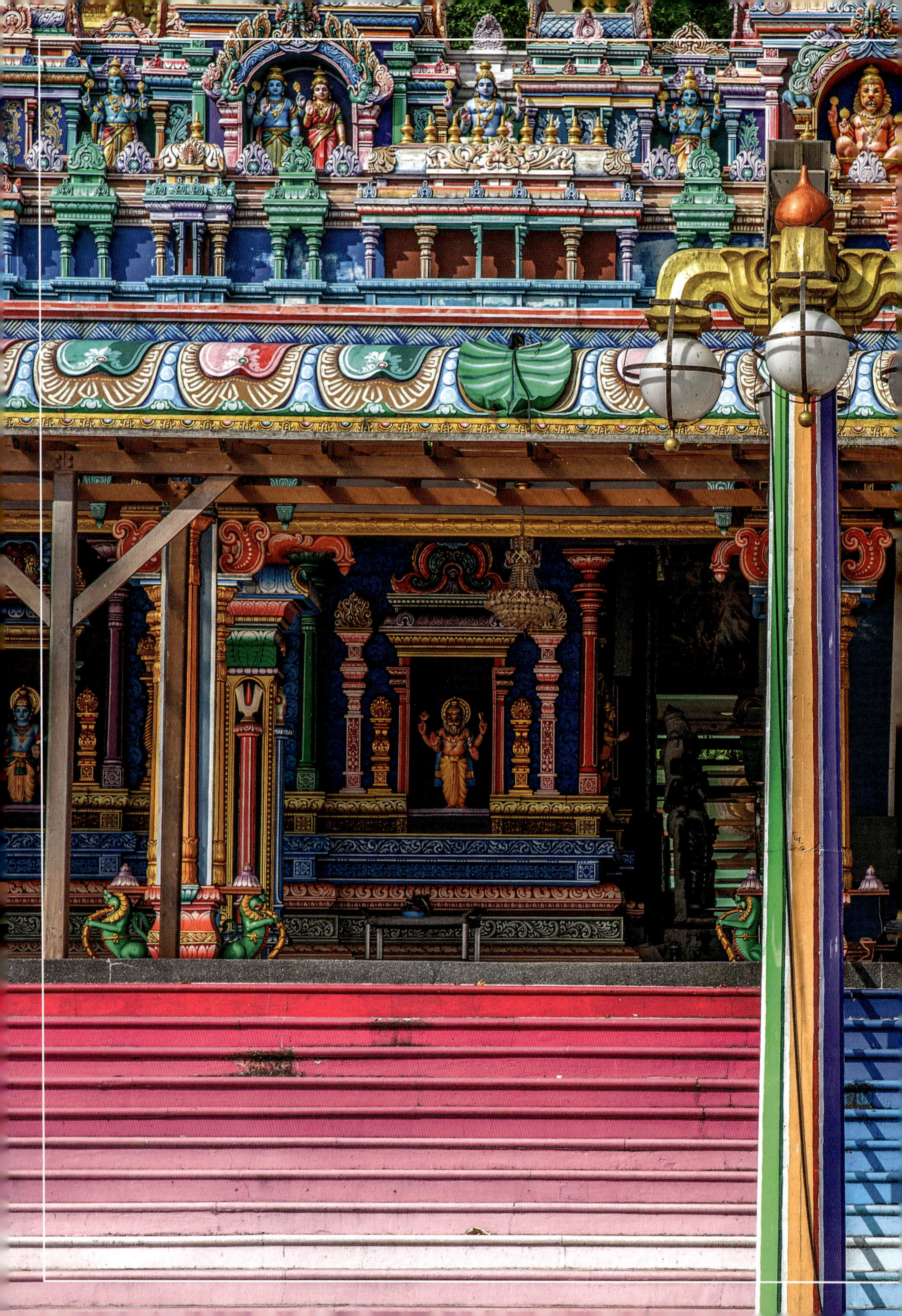

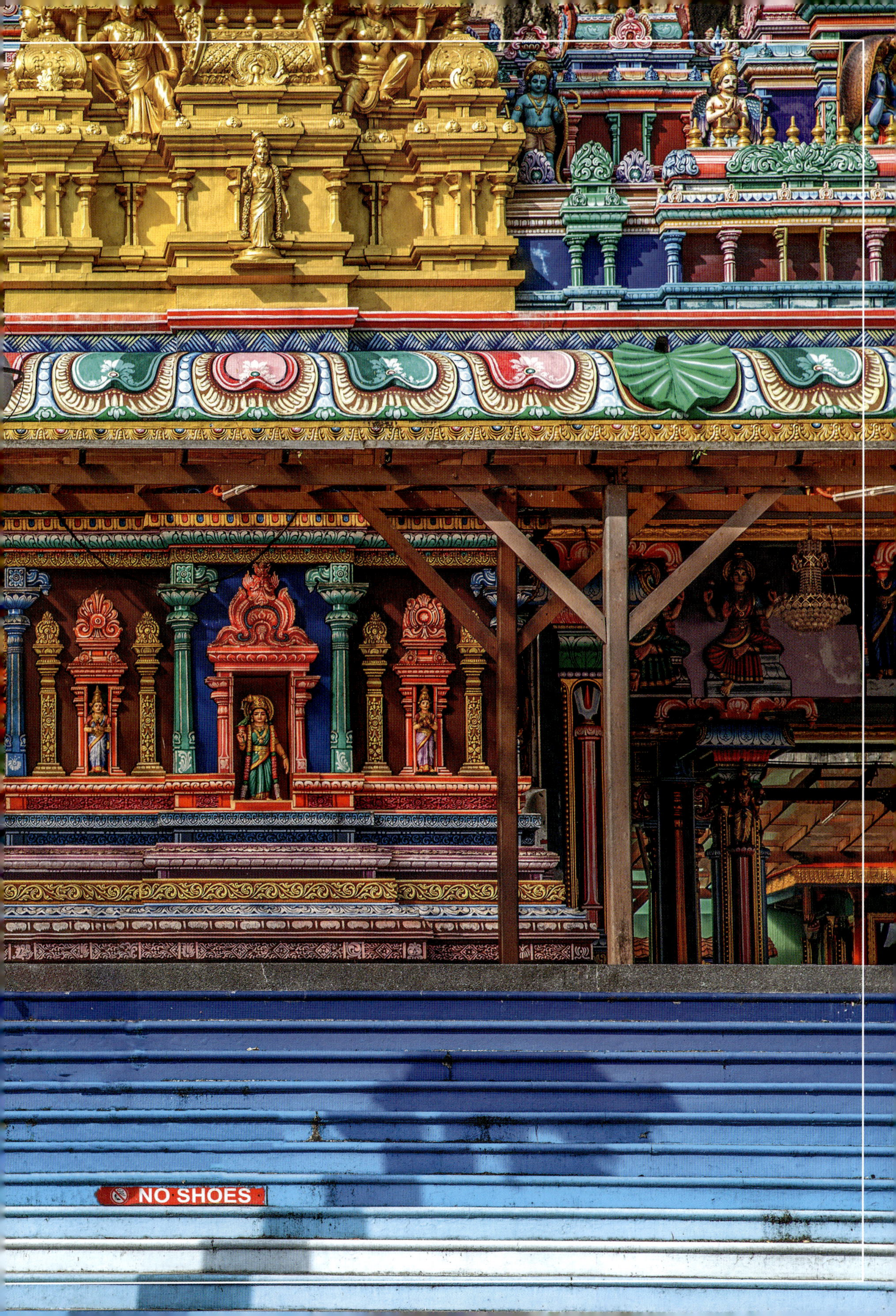
NO SHOES

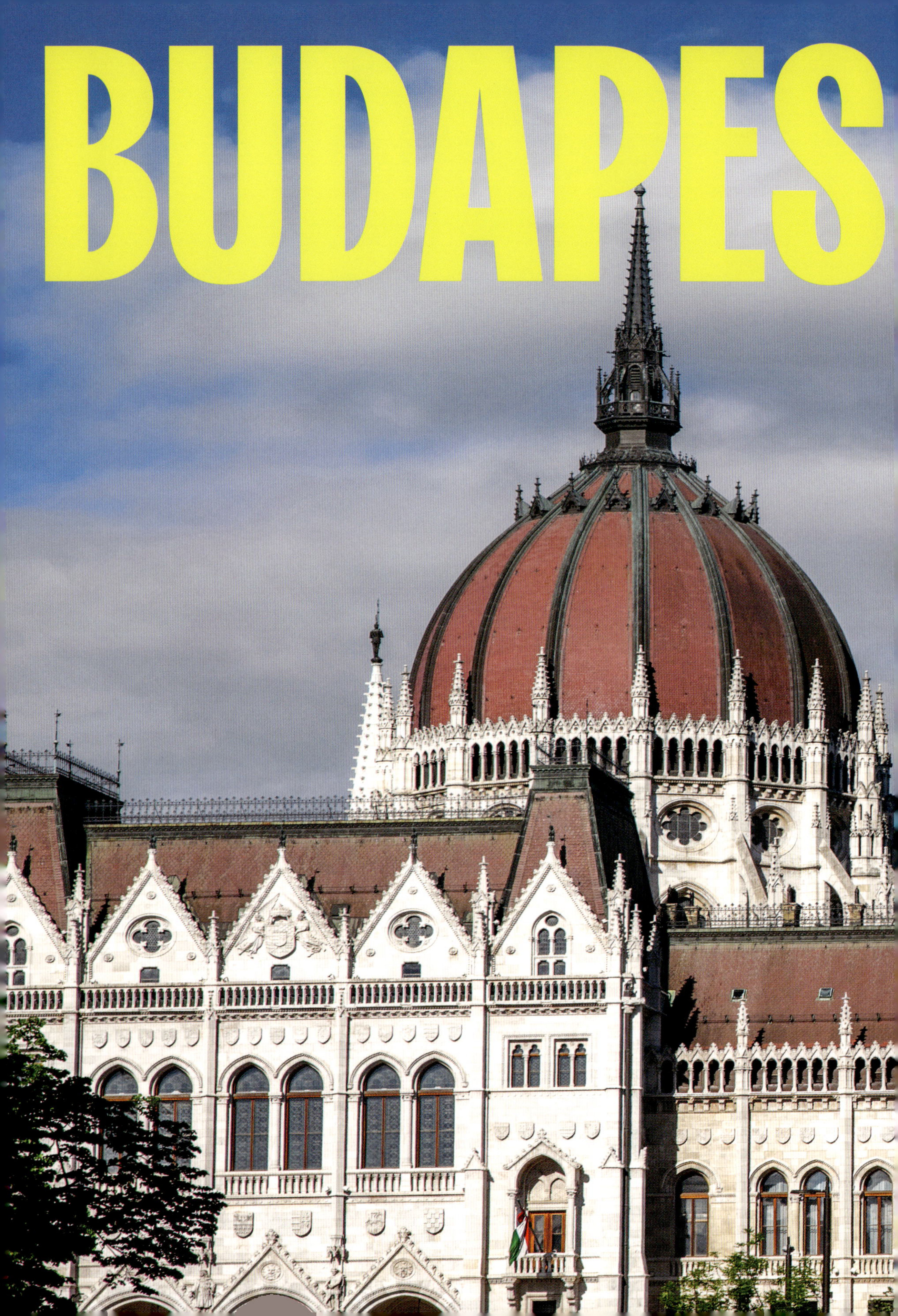
BUDAPES

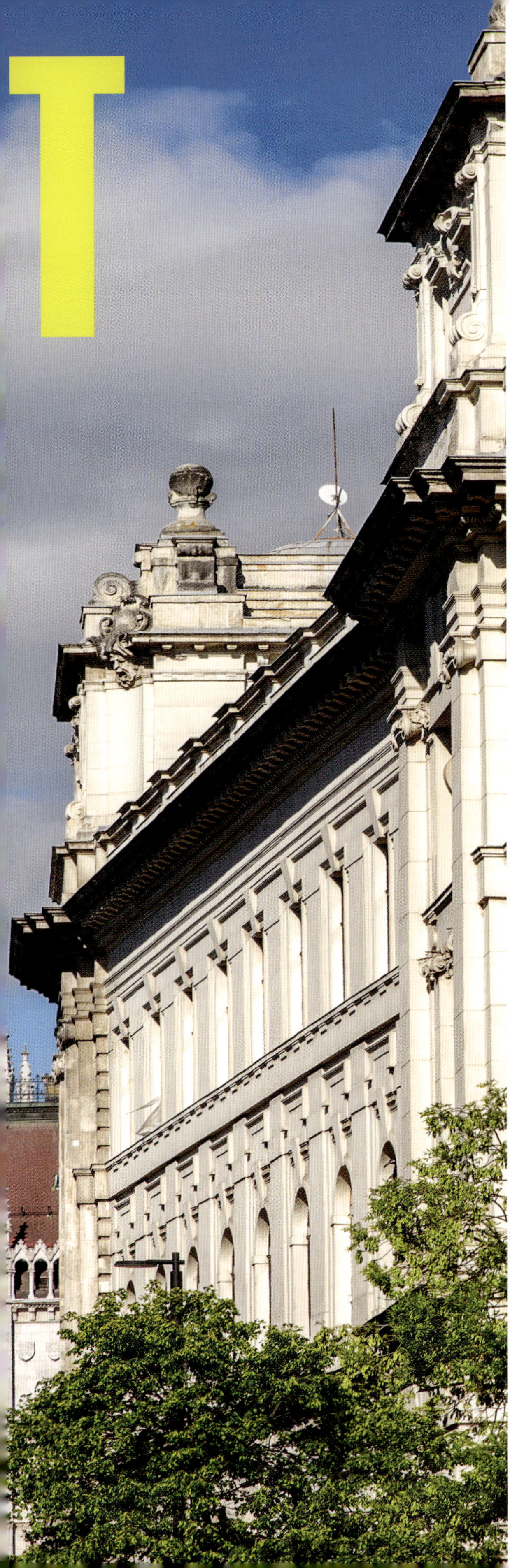

T

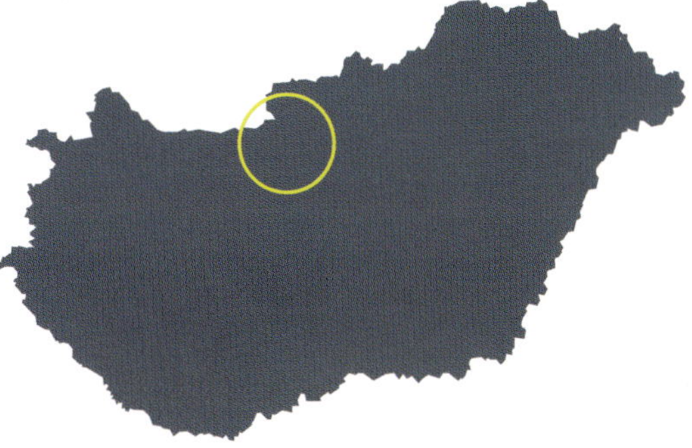

A prince, a bishop, and a sock stuffed with cash. What sounds like the beginning of a hacky joke instead describes a harebrained scheme that enraged one nation and humiliated another.

The halls of Budapest's Hungarian Parliament Building—which these days astounds tourists with its heft, beauty, and ritzy interiors—have hosted political debates for more than a century. Visitors to this complex learn much of its history during guided tours.

What they don't hear, however, is the comical tale of how powerful Hungarians, including a royal and a senior priest, once bungled a revenge plot so badly that they embarrassed the very country they were trying to honor. Seeking furious payback is always risky and ill-advised. Rarely, however, does such an attempt at retribution reach the level of farce that marked Hungary's counterfeit franc scandal in the 1920s.[250]

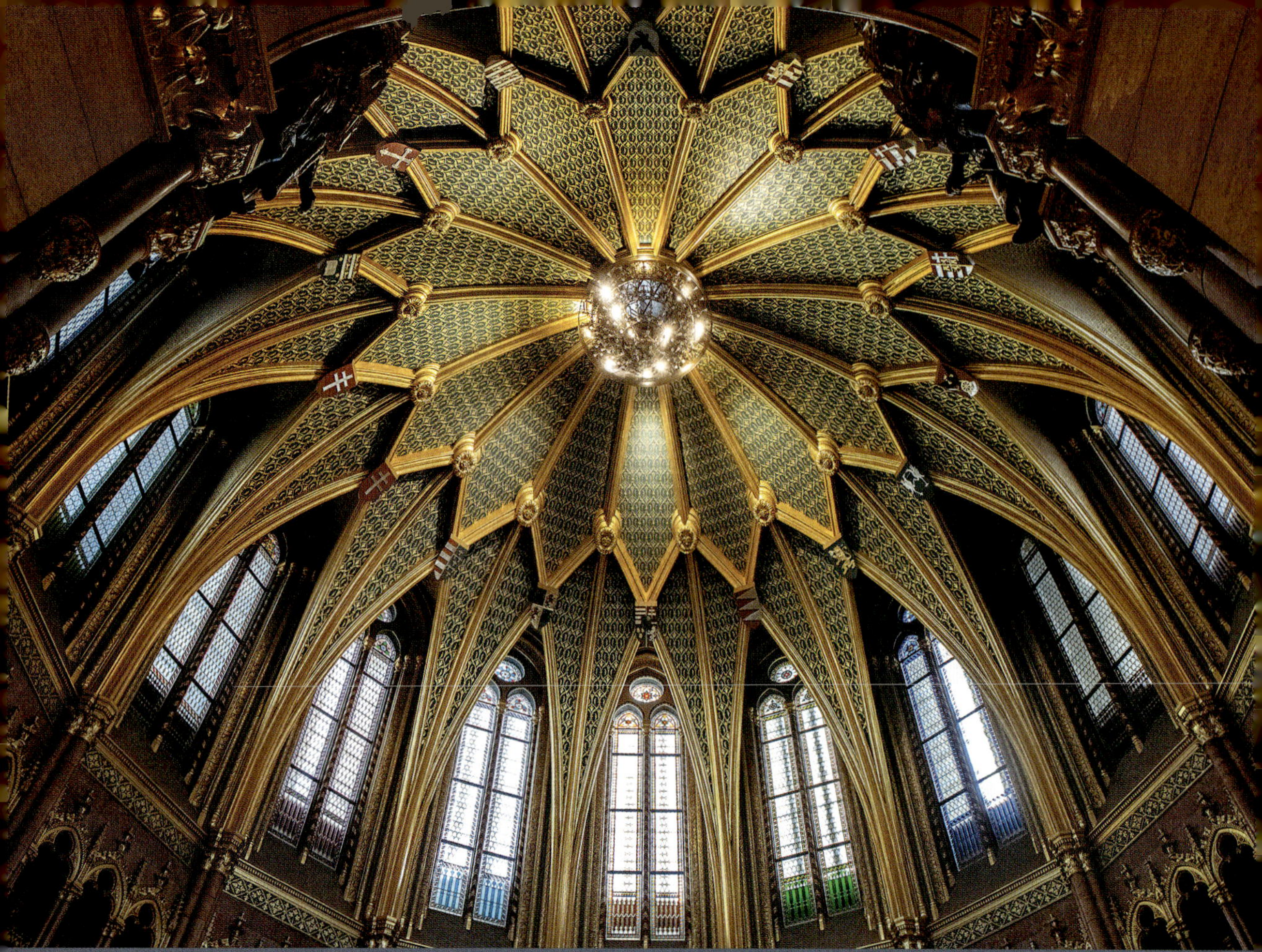

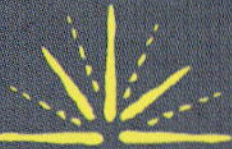

As a rule, the buildings that house parliaments tend to be uninspired, monolithic structures. Some, however, are dazzling in form, such as the ostentatious Hungarian Parliament Building.

The building stands out amid Budapest's trove of stately architecture along the picturesque Danube River, which once separated the royal center of Buda, on its western bank, from the town of Pest to its east. Buda and Pest combined in 1873 to create Budapest, which swiftly bloomed into an impressive city of three hundred thousand people.[251] Such was the optimism and ambition coursing through Budapest when, rather than building a boxy new parliament, the city shot for the stars.

In 1885, architects sketched what would be one of the world's largest buildings. The Hungarian Parliament Building stands at 889 feet long and 404 feet wide and is crowned by a 315-foot-tall dome.[252] It consists of almost forty million bricks, has 194,000 square feet of floor space, and was built over seventeen years by an army of one hundred thousand workers.[253]

What those figures don't portray is this landmark's wildly lavish embellishment. It shunned the old maxim of design that dictates "less is more." Instead, the architects of the Hungarian Parliament Building went all in on both quality and quantity of decoration.

Close to three hundred sculptures occupy its grand hallways, foyers, meeting rooms, banquet halls, and political chambers. Competing for attention are dozens of complex murals and vivid stained glass windows. Not to mention jumbo chandeliers, 1.8 miles of fine handwoven carpet, eighty-eight pounds of gold accents, endless intricate woodwork, and a quarry's worth of marble flooring.

On paper, those collective elements sound excessive. Yet, in person, it somehow works. This visual banquet is mesmerizing, both to the naked eye or when captured in images. The City Side Staircase XVII is laden with gleaming gold panels and leads to a corridor drenched in rainbow-hued light, filtered through yet more stained glass windows. Similarly stunning is the Grand Stairway, a colossal foyer framed by eight granite columns and crested by three ceiling frescoes, each rich with detail.

Alongside looms Dome Hall, home of the Hungarian Holy Crown. Armed soldiers monitor visitors and protect these priceless royal jewels, exhibited in a box beneath the eighty-nine-foot-tall dome, which boasts a hypnotic geometric motif. Also accessible to visitors are several spaces where Hungarian politicians debate and collaborate, such as the enormous Chamber of Peers. The chamber features oak paneling, gilded accents, dozens of archways, murals of Hungarian nobility, and seating for 453 members.[254]

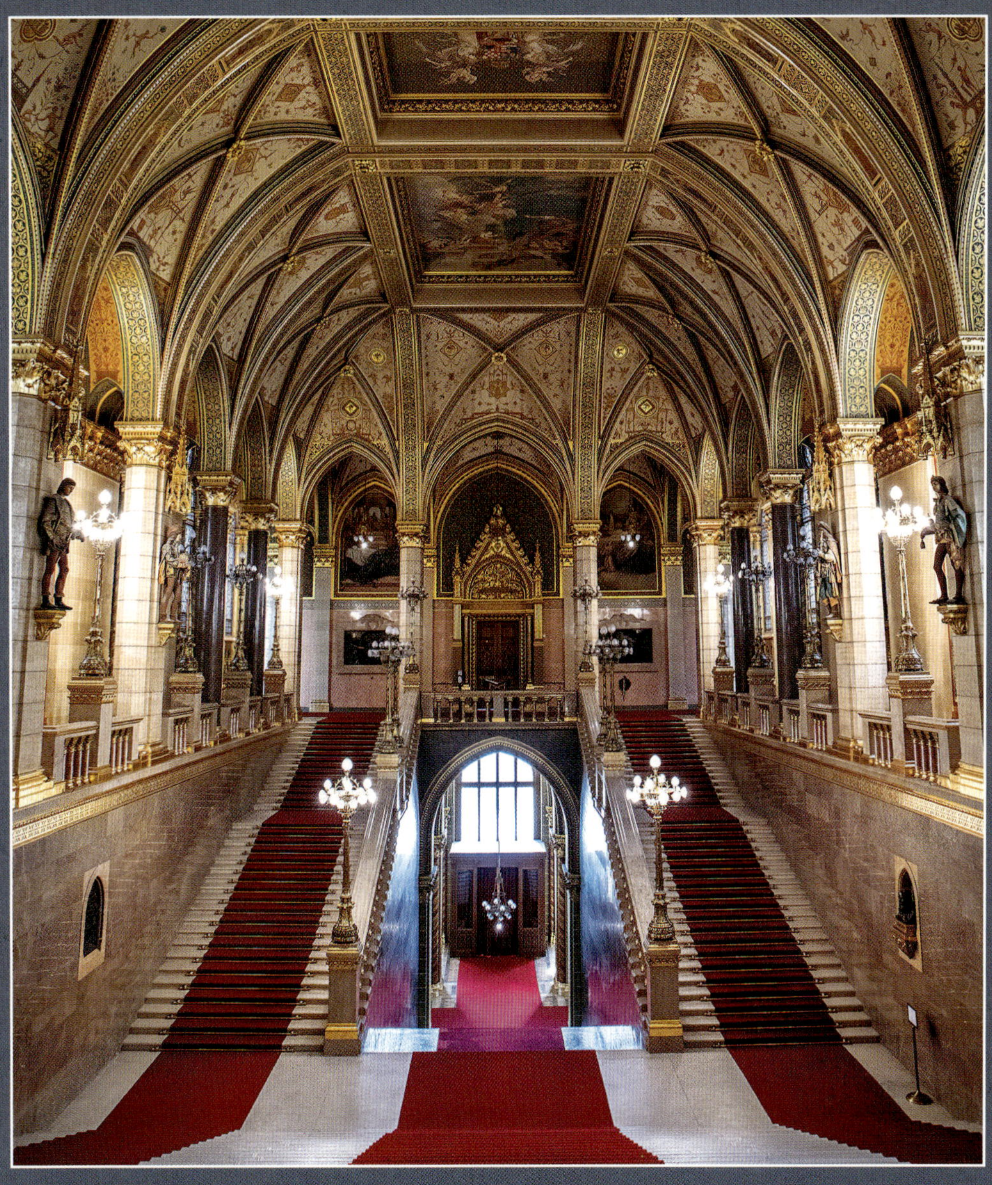

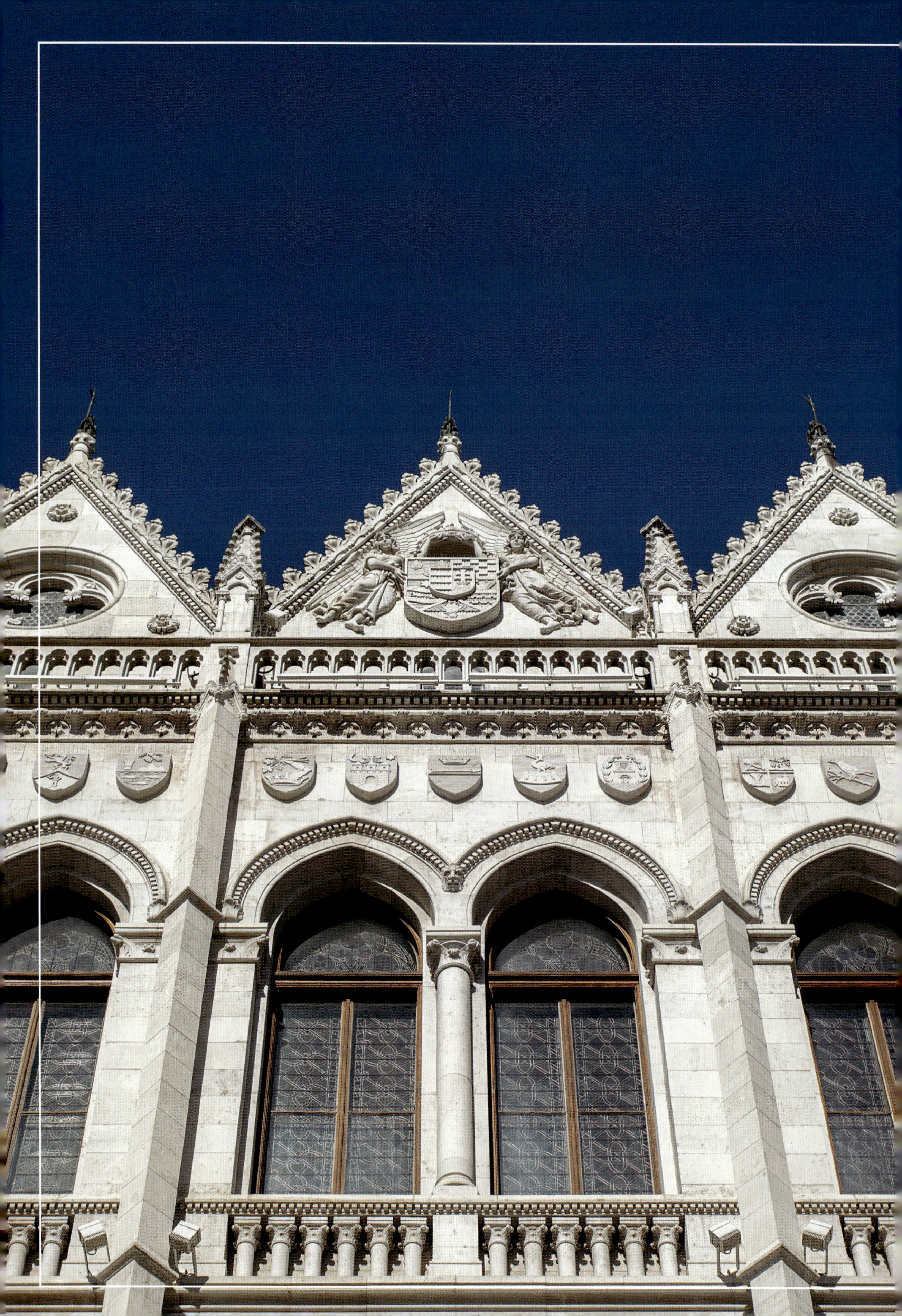

A NATION IN TURMOIL

Hungary was in tatters after being on the losing team in World War I. From 1914 to 1918, the Central Powers (Germany, Turkey, and Austria-Hungary) battled the Allies (Great Britain, France, Russia, Japan, Italy, and the US). Some sixteen million deaths later, the Allies were triumphant. Hungary, meanwhile, lost more than two-thirds of its territory.[255]

What remained of this fractured land was then rocked by years of savage domestic conflicts and a struggle for governing power. During a brief communist rule, beginning in March 1919, Soviet paramilitary groups launched the Red Terror, executing hundreds of alleged dissidents.[256]

Revenge swiftly manifested in the form of White Terror. This was supposedy a revolt against Soviet occupation. In reality, it sprawled into indiscriminate executions, assaults, and imprisonment of anyone deemed a foe of the burgeoning Hungarian state, including Hungary's Jewish community. By 1921, the violence finally had slowed, but this nation remained in turmoil, and resentment among its citizens was thick.

Much of its spite was directed toward France, which, despite being only one of several enemies from World War I, became a lightning rod for right-wing Hungarian hate. In this fertile ground for hostility, a scandal sprouted.[257]

A SCAMMING PLAN TO PUNISH FRANCE

In 1925, bitter, enraged Hungarian nationalists decided to use counterfeiting to seek payback on France. This revenge plot was led by Prince Lajos Windischgraetz. A known political agitator who had previously plotted a coup in Hungary, he believed they could ruin the French economy by saturating Europe with fake francs. A then-feeble France supposedly would be powerless to prevent Hungary from regaining all it had lost after World War I.

Prince Windischgraetz assembled a team of influential Hungarian nationalists to take part in his plot, including the country's highest-ranked police officer, Imre Nádosy. Senior staff at Hungary's National Cartographic Institute were recruited to offer printing expertise. And State Postal Savings Institute boss Gábor Baross advised them how to best circulate the fake francs.

Counterfeiting the currency proved simple. By September 1925, they had printed about thirty million francs. This haul was stored at the mansion of another influential coconspirator: Hungarian army chaplain Bishop István Zadravetz. The next step was to send the fake francs into the world to cause havoc. The powerful men behind this plot thought that if they executed this plan, Hungary's lost territory could be recovered and its glory restored.[258]

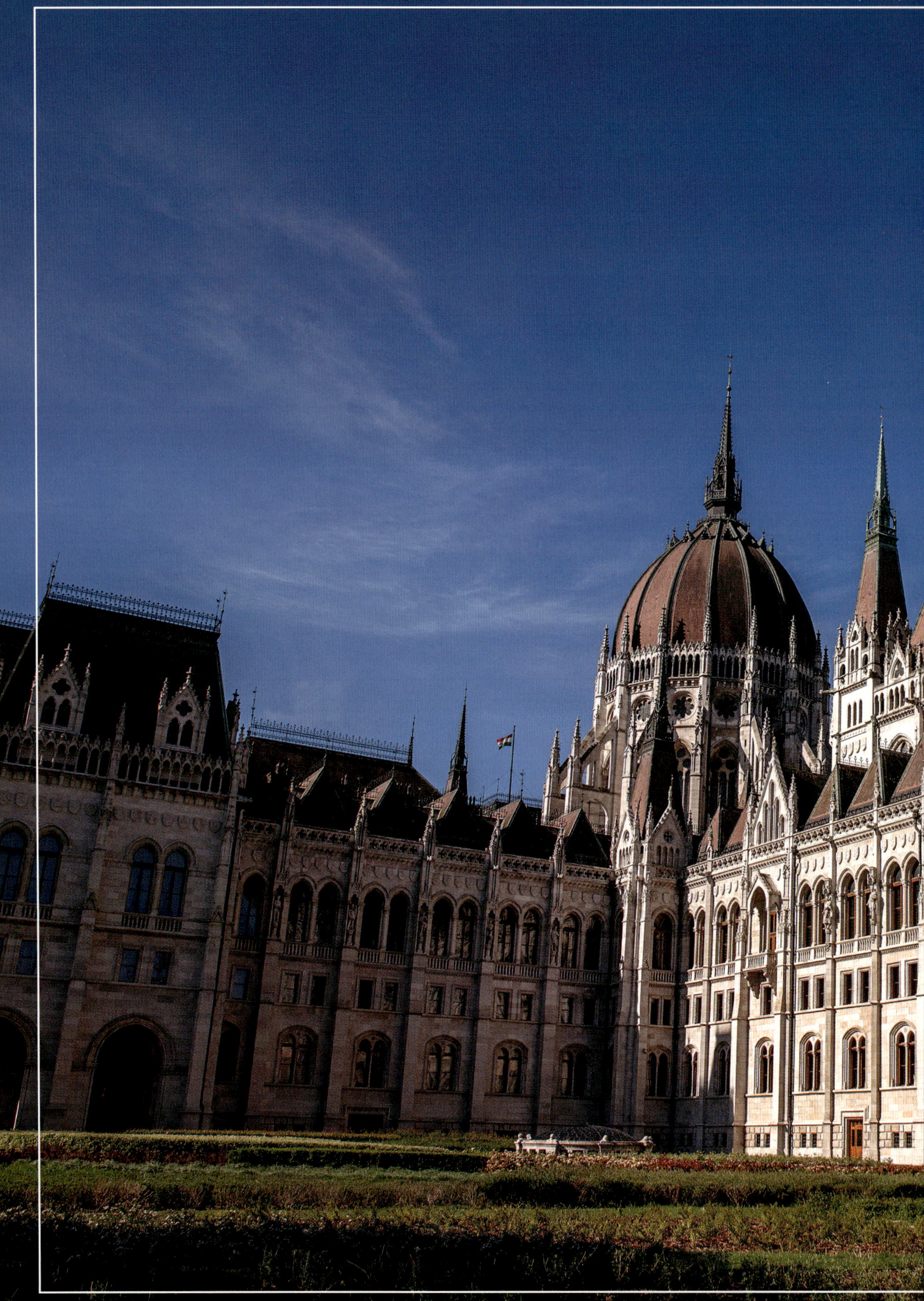

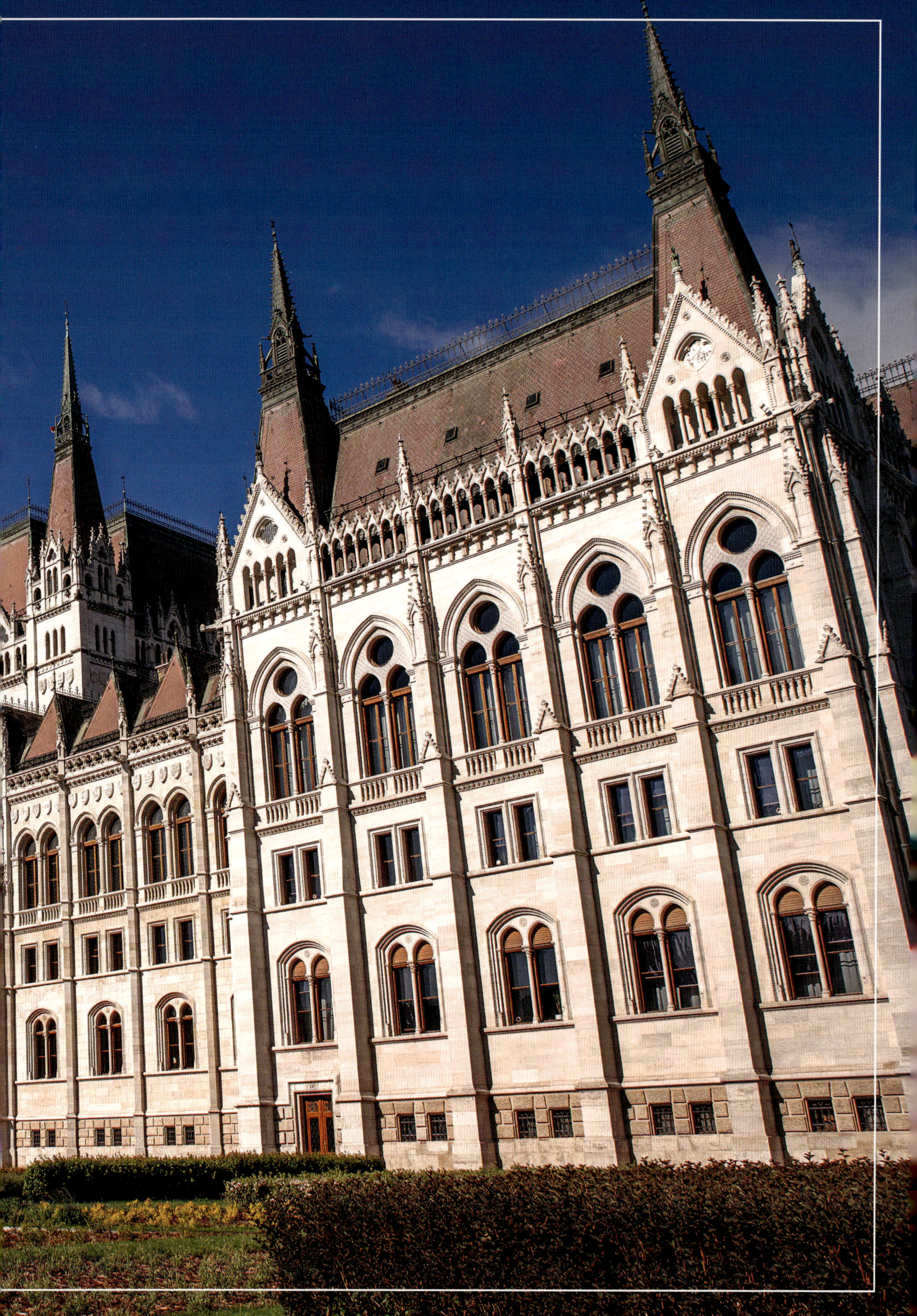

COMEDY OF ERRORS FOILS FORGERY PLOT

Prince Windischgraetz and his powerful accomplices had made a grave mistake. They handed great responsibility to a bumbling man, Arisztid Jankovich. This Hungarian colonel, who had many influential friends in Budapest, was chosen to begin smuggling the fake currency out of Hungary. In December 1925, he committed clownish errors while sneaking a suitcase of counterfeit cash into the Netherlands.

Dutch border police stopped and questioned Jankovich, not because they suspected that he was a smuggler but because he'd forgotten to apply for an entry visa. Fortunately for the colonel, police let him visit Amsterdam to get the required border clearance. But there Jankovich made another blunder.

As he tried to exchange currency at an Amsterdam bank, he accidentally handed staff some of the counterfeit francs that he had, bizarrely, left in his wallet alongside legitimate notes. Instantly, red flags were raised. The bank's manager inspected the cash, identified it as forged, and called the Dutch police.

When officers questioned Jankovich, he claimed ignorance. "Check his sock," instructed bank staff, and there police found his stash of fake francs. Dutch law enforcement was well trained in tracking such fraud. Soon they caught a pair of Jankovich's coconspirators and reported the scam to European crime-fighting agencies.

It wasn't long before the arrested trio caved under questioning and revealed the details of their plot. Dutch and French investigators were startled to hear the names of high-profile coconspirators. They learned that Prince Windischgraetz hatched the plan, Bishop Zadravetz helped warehouse the fake francs, and Hungary's senior police officer Nádosy approved diplomatic passports used by the smugglers.[259]

WHO'S HELD TO BLAME FOR A HUNGARIAN SHAME?

Such a sensational cast of characters ensured media coverage across Europe. The wide exposure shamed a nation still trying to recover from World War I and stabilize its society. Heated debates bellowed through the plush rooms of the Hungarian Parliament Building. Eventually, more than twenty alleged conspirators were put on trial. Most were found guilty to some degree of helping to organize or carry out the counterfeit plot, including the prince, the bishop, the cop, and the bumbling man who mucked it all up by stuffing his sock.[260]

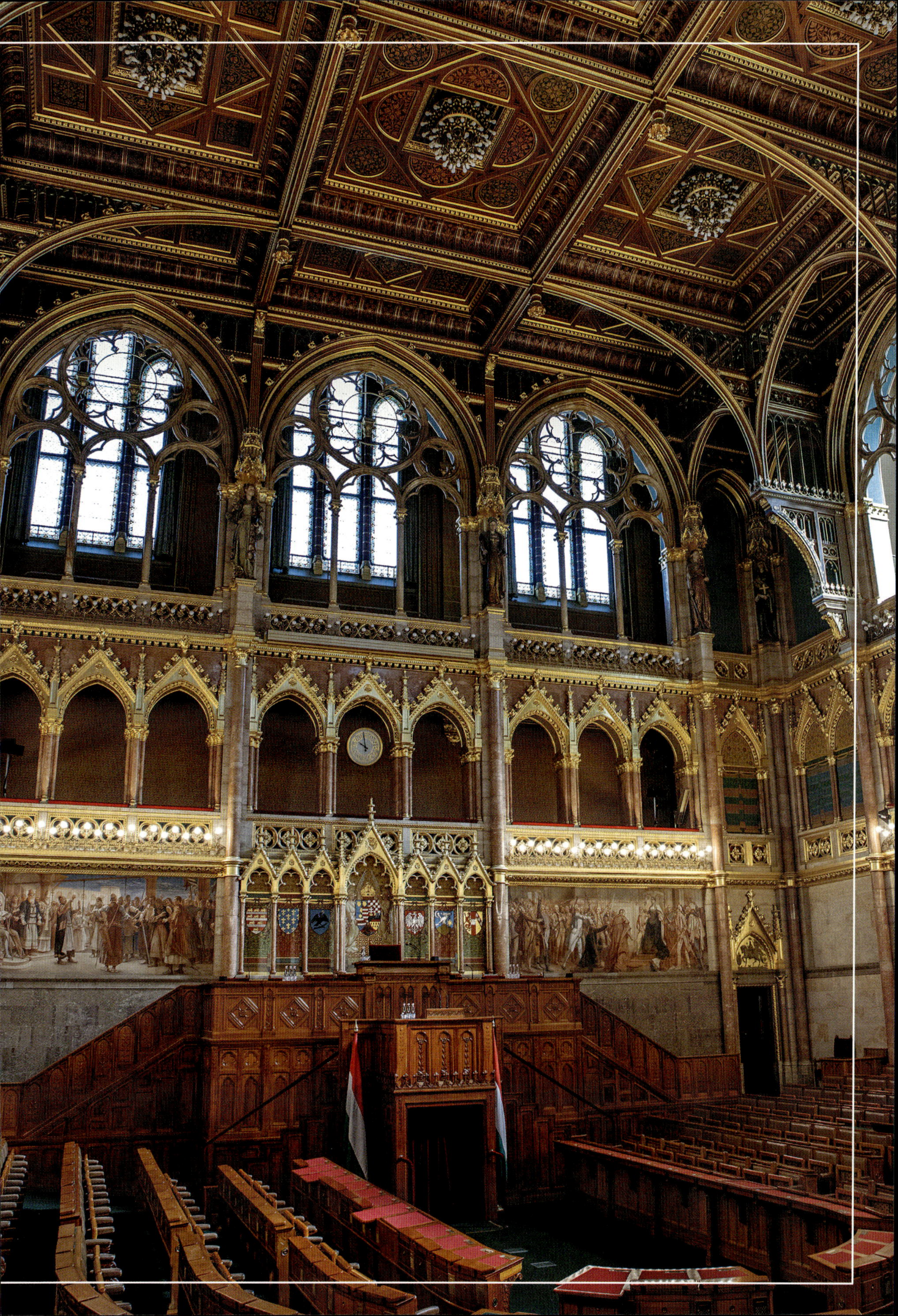

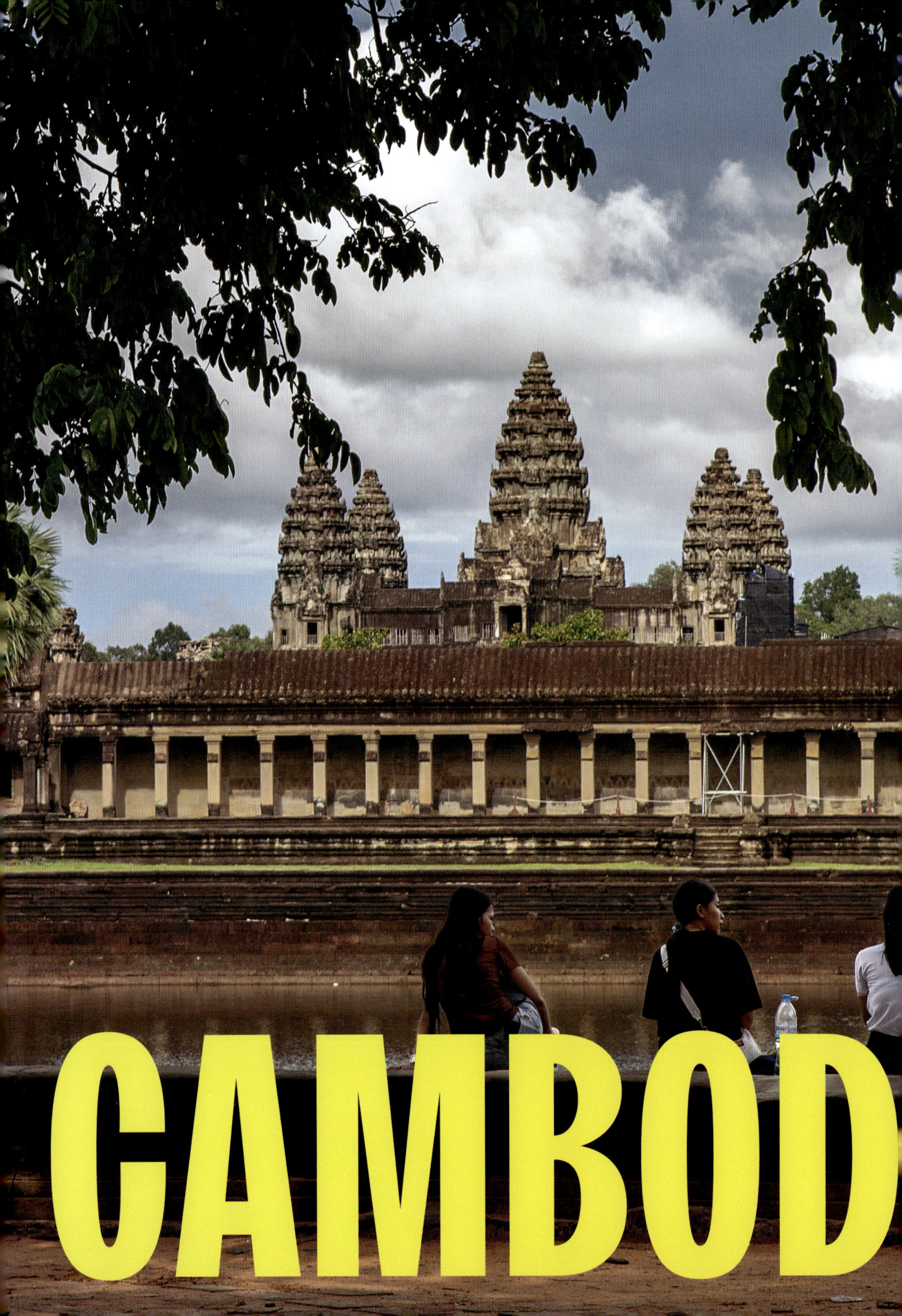
CAMBOD

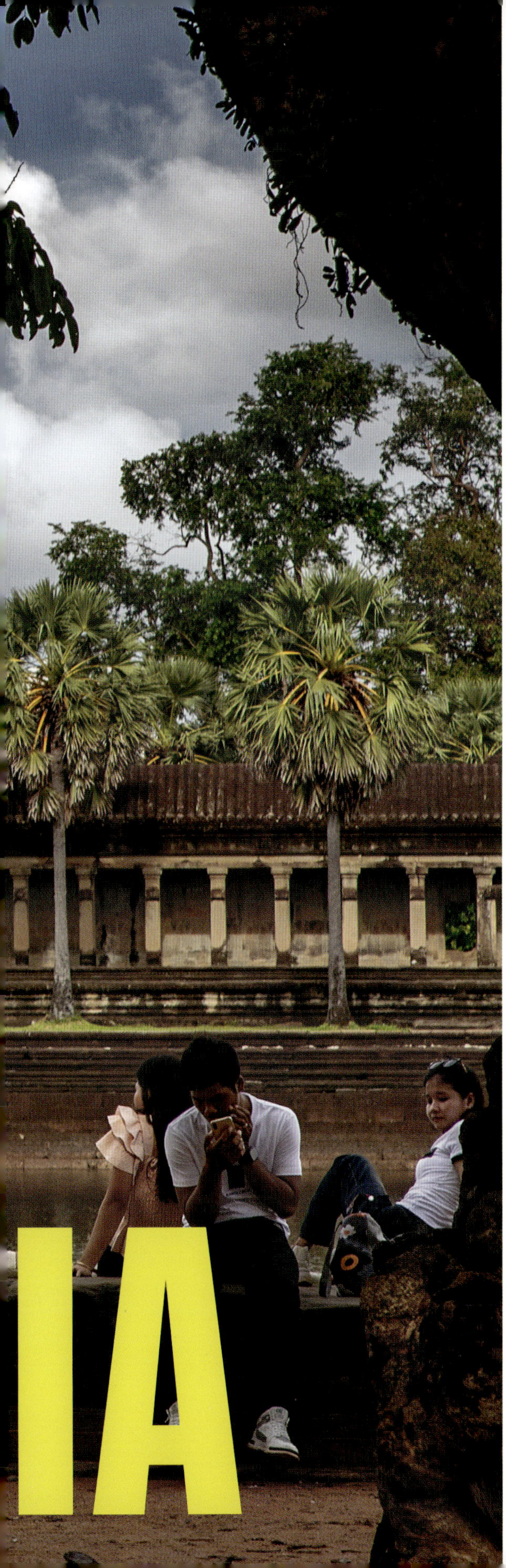

IA

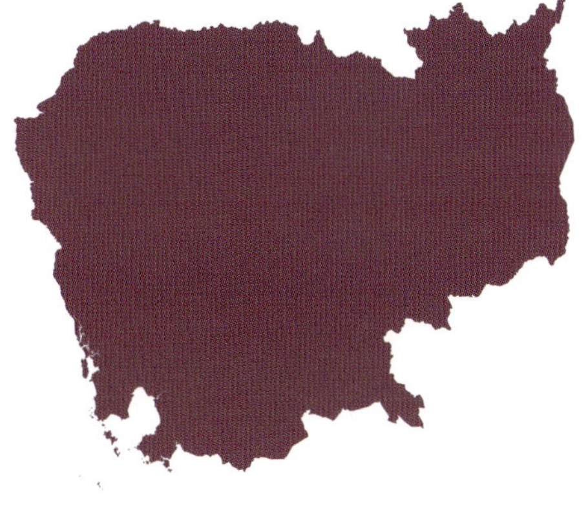

For centuries, only the birds could see, and the deities could know, that Angkor Wat was more than a temple. Asia's most famous religious complex thrills visitors via its grand scale, intricate stonework, and jungle setting. But only from high in the Cambodian sky is the temple's most unique feature apparent.

Because the creators of nine-hundred-year-old Angkor Wat were so ambitious, so creative, and so skilled, they designed the layout to represent a miniaturized version of something truly enormous. When Angkor Wat and the grand city surrounding it were abandoned in the fifteenth century, the jungle consumed this temple and obscured the divine secret of its blueprint. Only in the twentieth century did scientists finally reveal its hidden symbolism.[261]

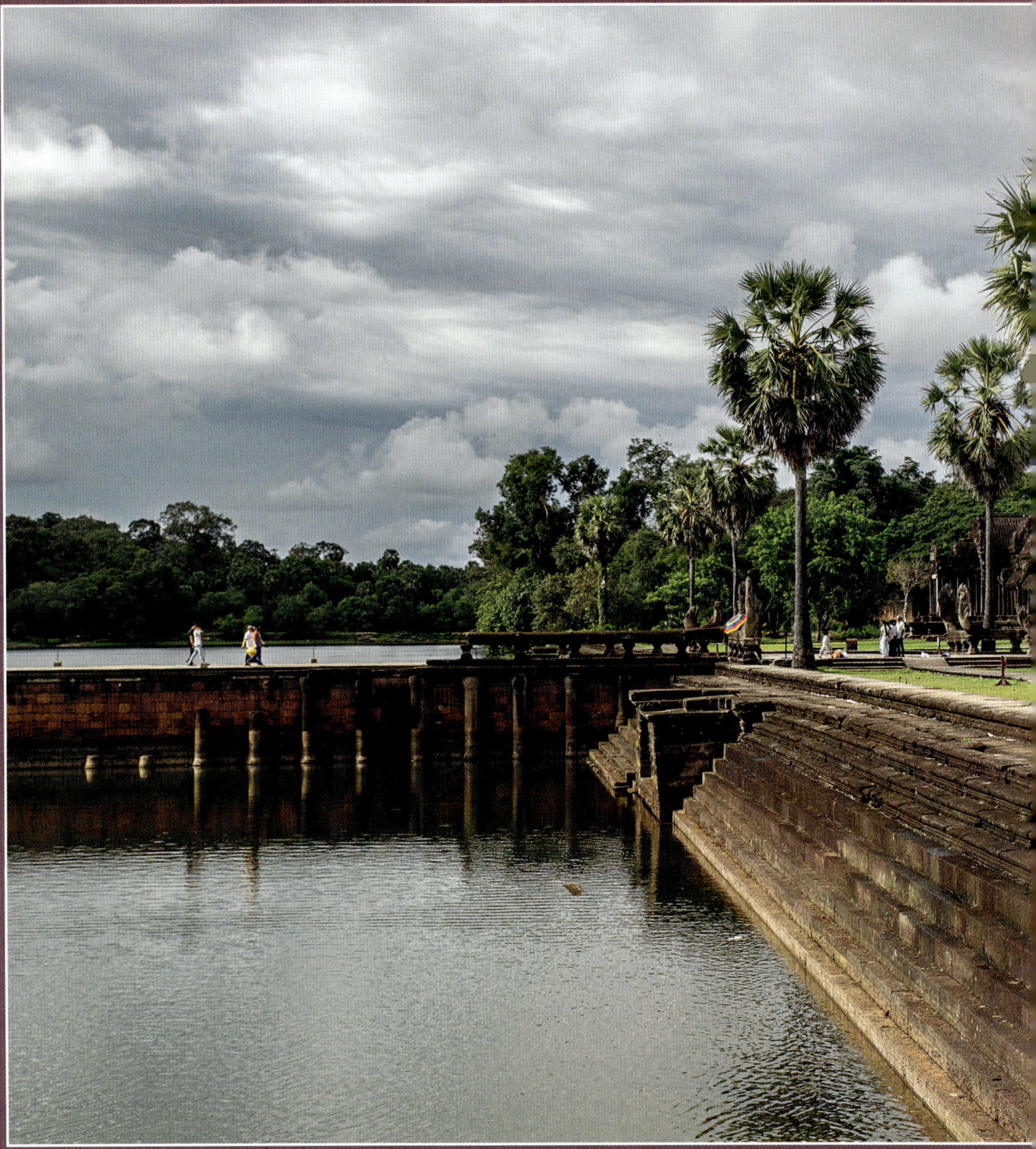

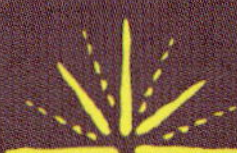

Angkor Wat sits amid forest on the northern outskirts of Siem Reap, a small city laden with hotels, bars, and restaurants aimed at foreigners. Yet throughout Cambodia, this temple is omnipresent. Tourists will spy its likeness on the national flag fluttering above their hotel and on five different Cambodian riel banknotes in their wallet.[262]

Why? Not just because this temple is the most visited attraction in Cambodia, a Southeast Asian nation

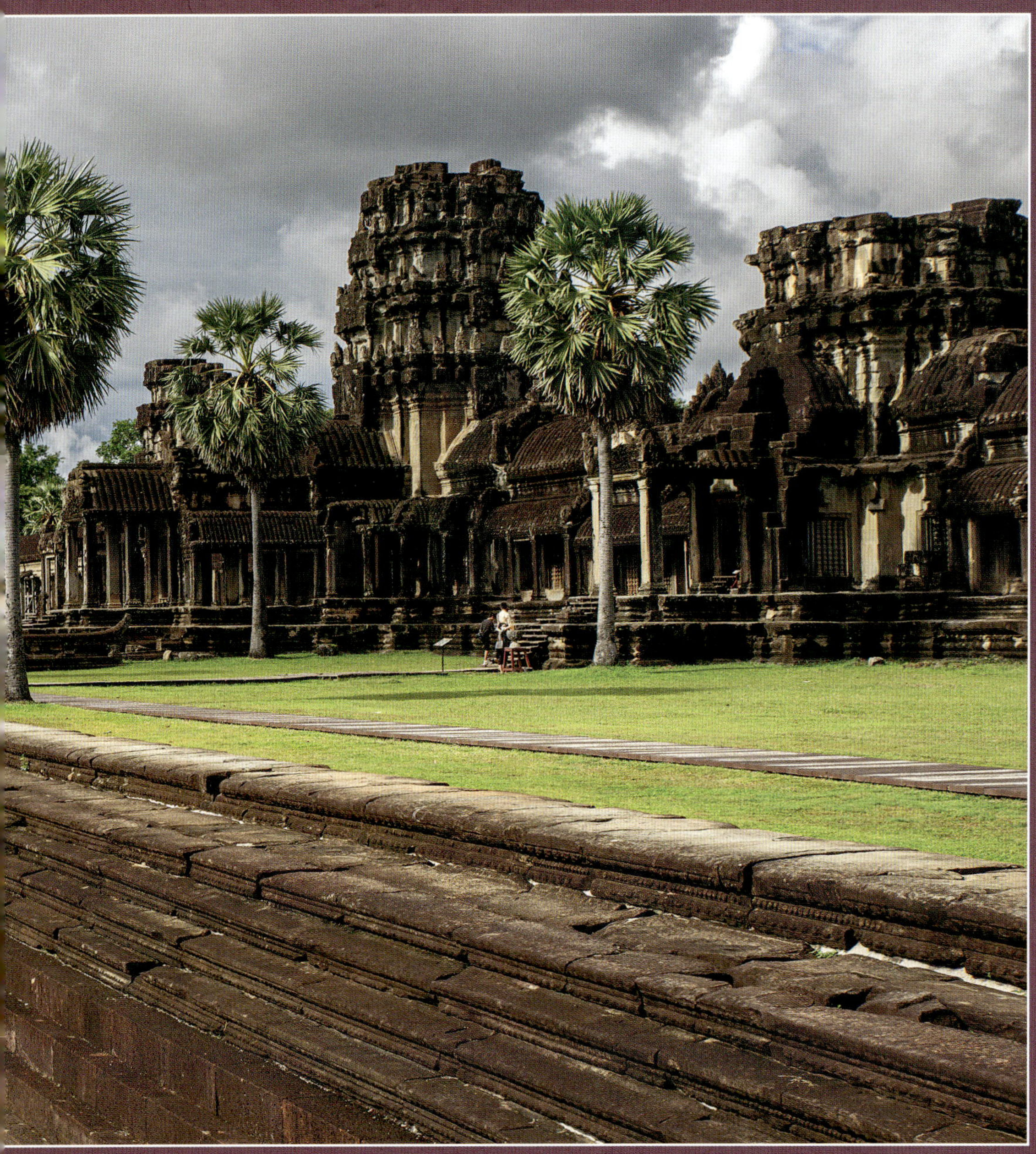

of seventeen million people, wedged between Thailand to its west, Laos to its north, and Vietnam to its east.

Rather, Angkor Wat is ubiquitous due to its symbolism.

Angkor Wat signifies the deep spirituality of this country. Even more importantly, it celebrates the proud heritage of its Khmer people, who account for more than 90 percent of Cambodians, showcasing their skill, flair, and ingenuity.[263, 264]

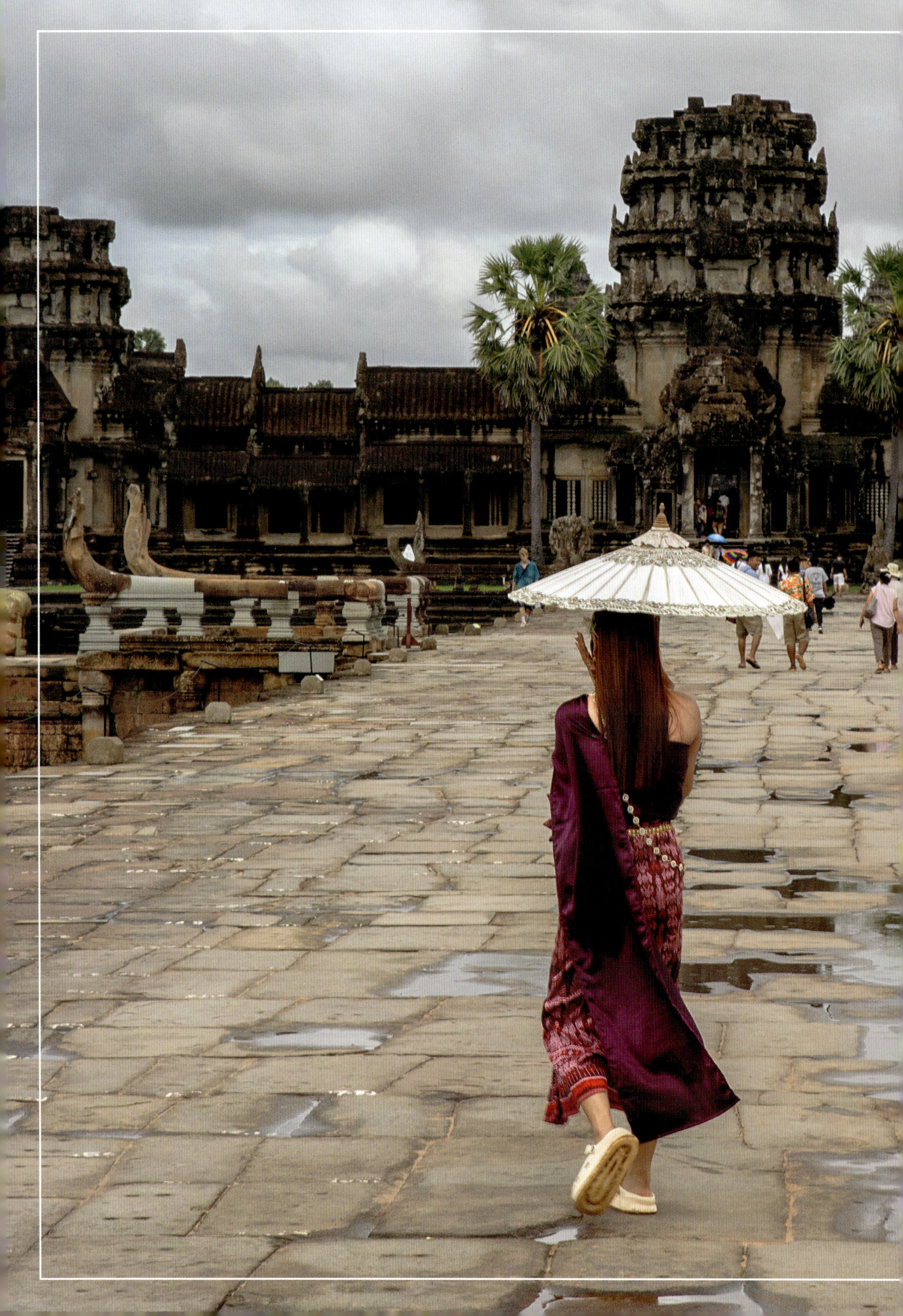

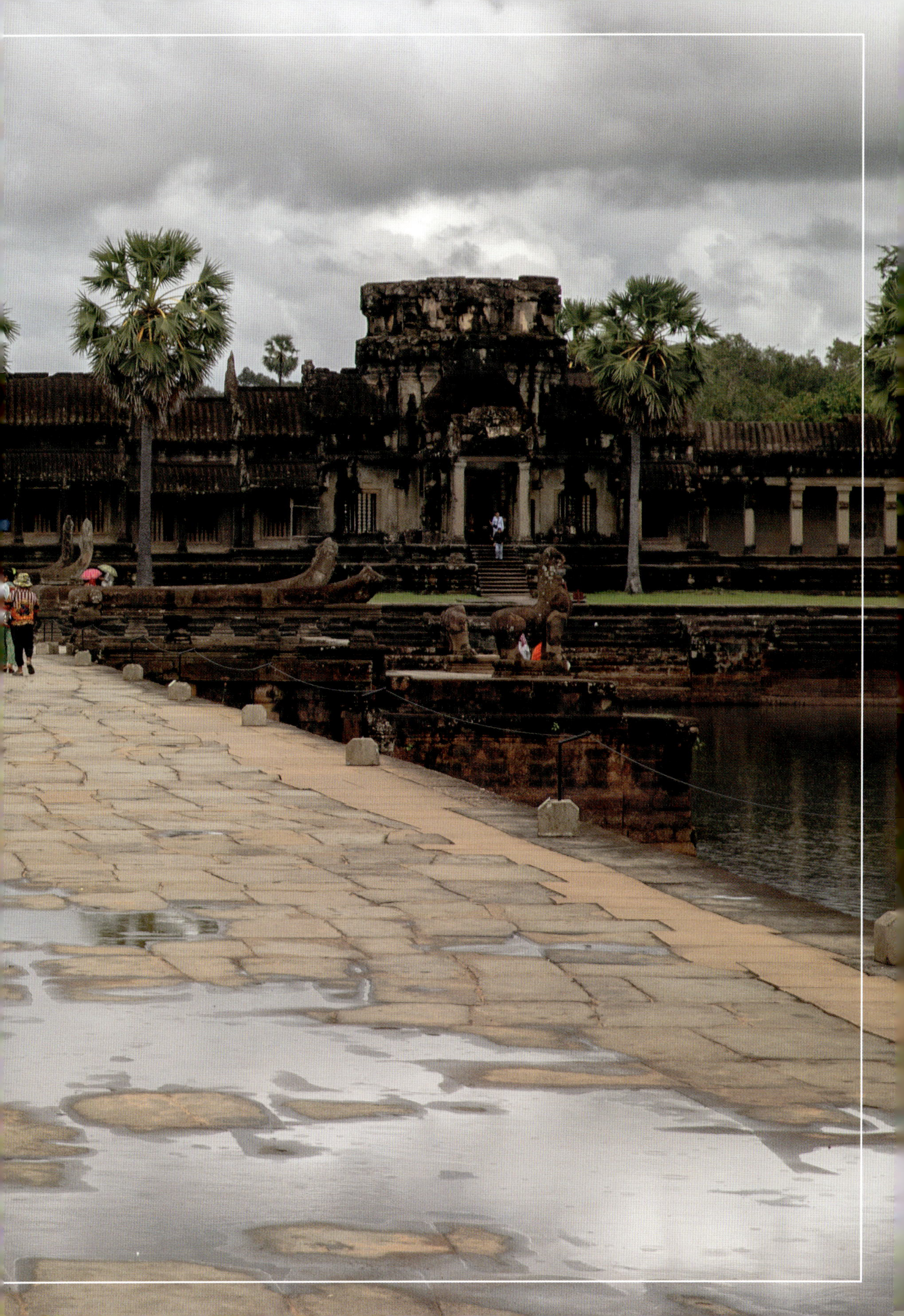

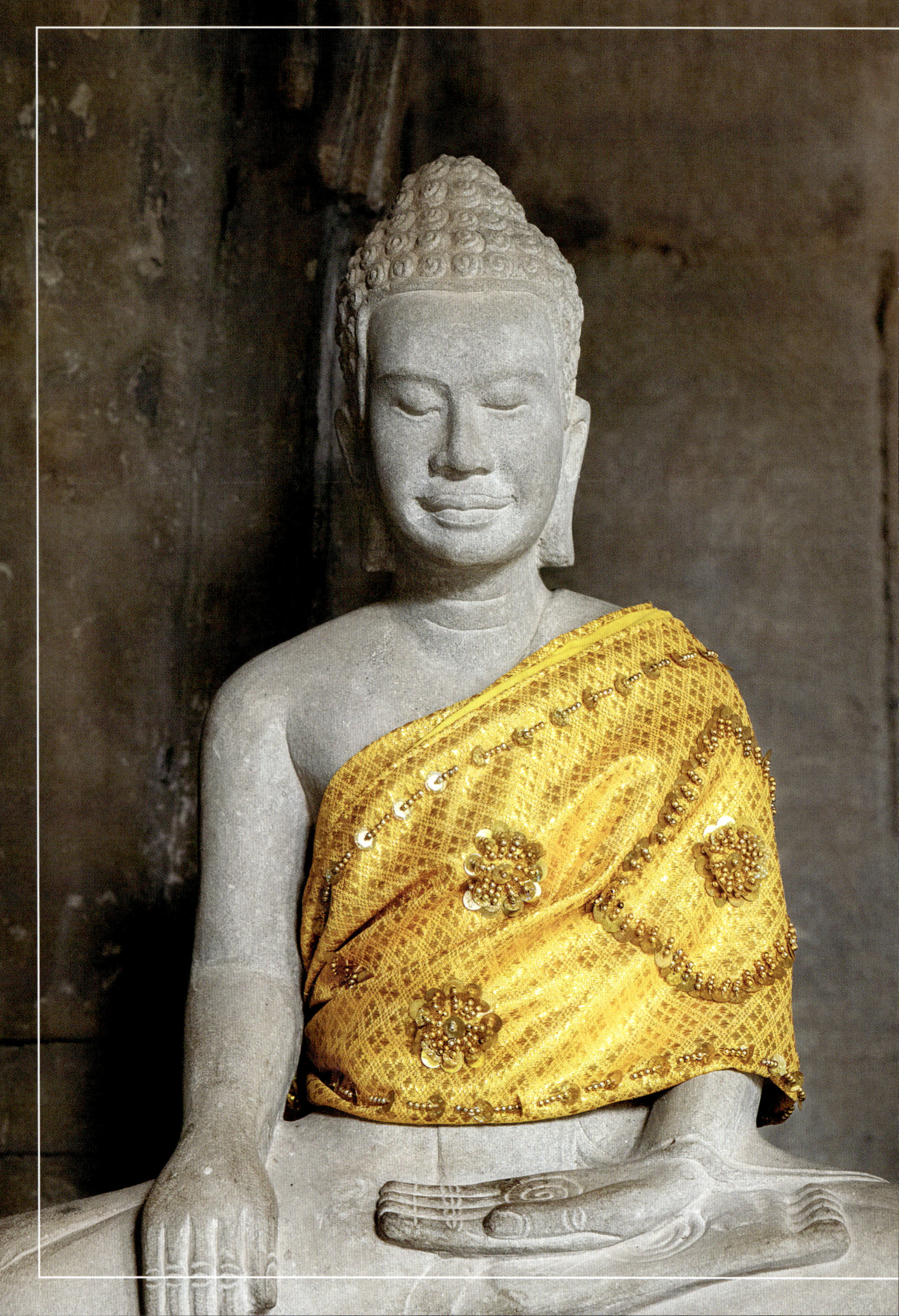

ANGKOR WAT IS BORN

What visitors see at Angkor Wat is the dazzling legacy of the ancient Khmer Empire, which emerged in the ninth century AD, expanded greatly, and then disappeared in the fifteenth century. This was no small, regional kingdom. Rather, the Khmer Empire was an enormously powerful and advanced civilization. During its peak in the thirteenth century, the empire covered areas of what is now Cambodia, Vietnam, Laos, Thailand, and Myanmar.[265]

The entirety of these lands was commanded from behind the lofty walls of what was once the world's biggest city. Called Angkor, it was a metropolis of rare sophistication, beauty, and wealth. In the 1200s, at a time when London's population numbered around eighteen thousand, Angkor housed up to 750,000 people.[266] Now a UNESCO World Heritage Site, Angkor is praised by that global body as an "exceptional civilization," which showed a high level of social order and extreme talents in art and architecture.

That creativity is abundantly clear within Angkor's vast remains. Named the Angkor Archaeological Park, this site covers almost one hundred thousand acres. Dotting its forest sprawl are more than fifty Buddhist and Hindu temples, in various states of decay, complemented by dozens more halls, pagodas, sanctuaries, reservoirs, canals, and dykes.[267]

Angkor Wat is the star. It was commissioned approximately AD 1116 by King Suryavarman II to venerate Vishnu the Protector, one of the three chief gods of Hinduism. Angkor Wat's grandeur and complexity is as much a monument to his ambition as it is to his devotion. Khmer leaders built such colossal wonders to symbolize, and legitimize, their power over this wealthy kingdom.

Compared to modern standards, its construction was extraordinarily long and complex. The world's current tallest building, Dubai's Burj Khalifa, took twelve thousand workers six years to build. Angkor Wat, meanwhile, was erected by three hundred thousand sets of hands over more than three decades.

Whereas many religious structures around Southeast Asia are marked by gilded accents, rainbow palettes, or geometric motifs, Angkor Wat is all but drained of such color. Yet this gray, stone monolith eclipses them all. Its scale and grandeur do have robust competition from other sacred houses of worship in the region: Indonesia's ornate Borobudur Temple, Myanmar's golden Shwedagon Pagoda, and Thailand's lavish Wat Phra Kaew temple.

What makes Angkor Wat most notable, however, is its confounding size and exotic setting. Wilderness is forever trying to reclaim this masterpiece. Angkor Wat is encircled by jungle and striped by tree roots that grow out of and along its floor and facade. These natural decorations underscore the sheer age of this site.

In addition to being remarkably old, Angkor Wat is also comfortably the world's largest religious structure. To reach this fortified sanctuary, one must cross a six-hundred-foot bridge that spans the temple's huge moat.[268]

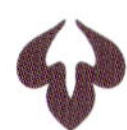

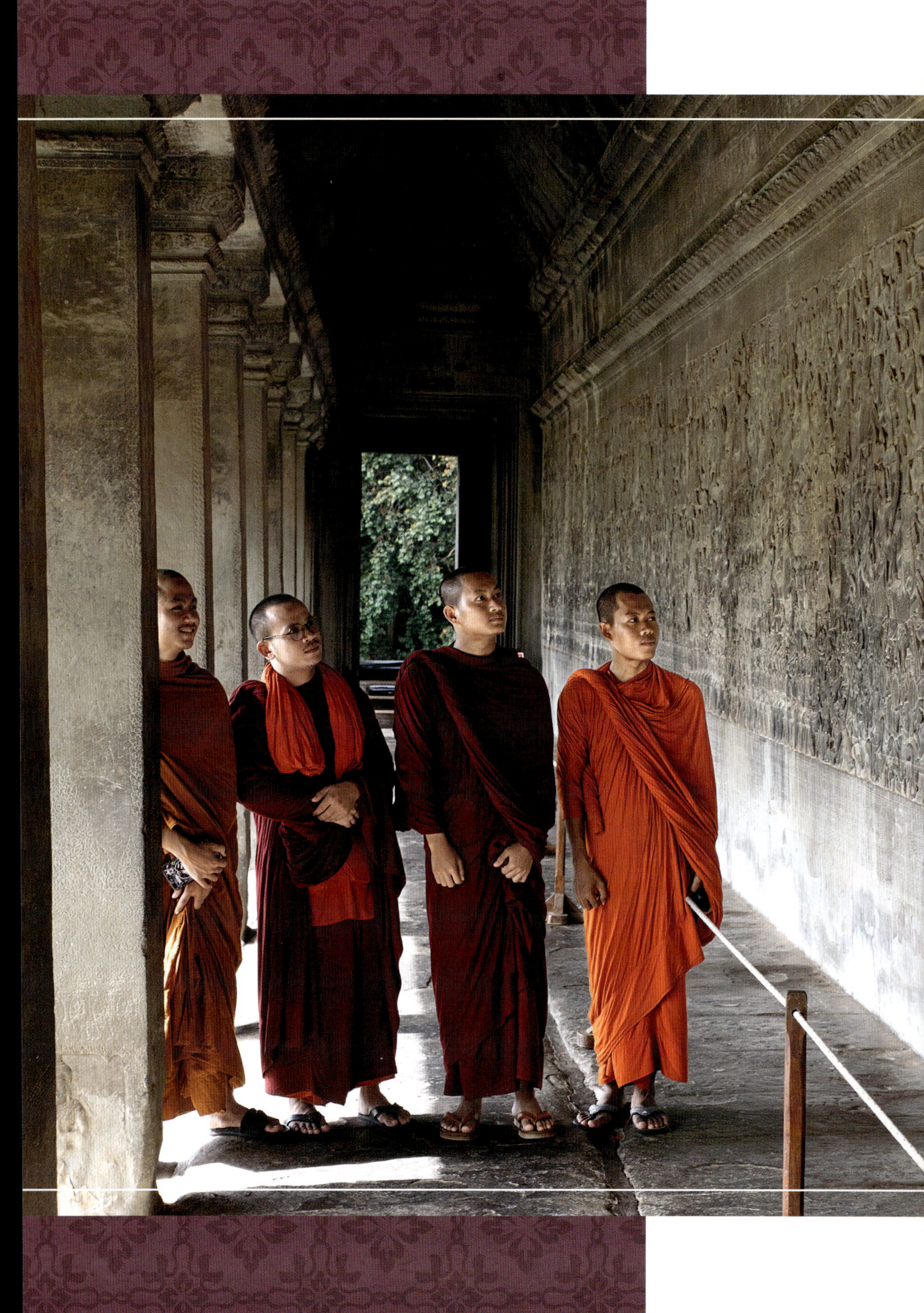

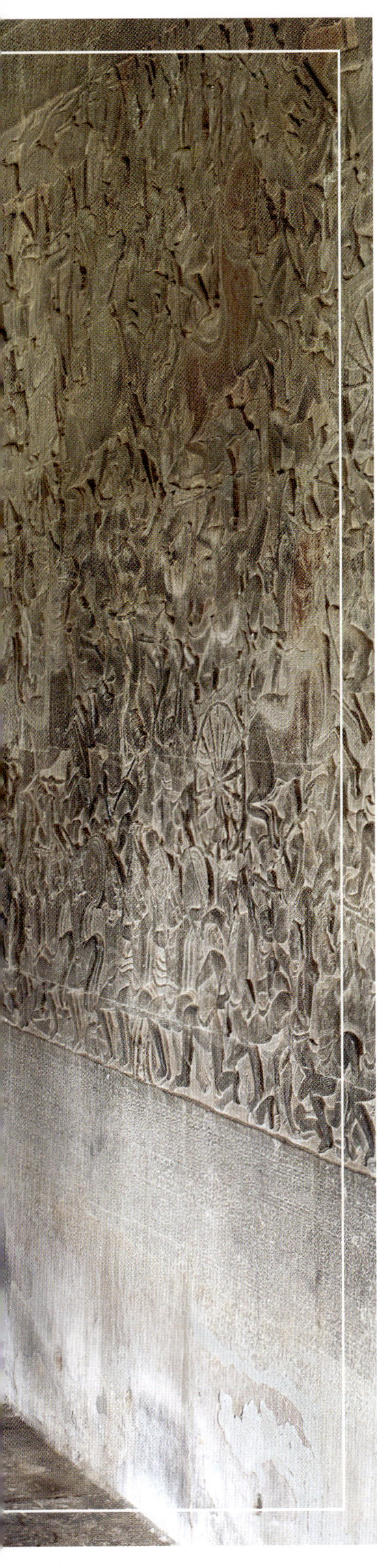

ANGKOR WAT'S DAZZLING ARTISTRY

Once inside its thick outer walls, visitors are transfixed by Angkor Wat's craftsmanship. Hundreds of thousands, if not millions, of man-hours are represented by the elaborate bas-reliefs hand-etched into its spires, halls, and corridors.

Some of these artworks are so massive that they unravel entire tales from Hindu mythology, like the 160-foot-long Churning of the Ocean of Milk.[269] Carved into a wall, it depicts Deva gods and Asura demons waged in a savage fight for control of an immortality potion, which lies beneath the cosmic sea.[270]

The temple's five central towers, each decorated by dozens of Hindu figures, were designed to collectively represent Mount Meru, the mythical seat of Hindu gods. Meanwhile, the moat that visitors cross to enter Angkor Wat symbolizes the cosmic ocean that encircles Meru.[271]

Such an array of thoughtful decorations gives the temple an awe-inducing appearance from ground level. But what can't be seen from this vantage is that Angkor Wat's square formation and geometric divisions resemble a mandala. In Hindu and Buddhist traditions, this is a diagram of the infinite universe.[272]

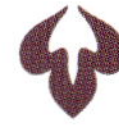

A MATHEMATICAL MYSTERY

It was not until 1976 that Western scientists finally saw Angkor Wat's layout clearly. After years of studying its composition, University of Michigan researchers had a revelation: This complex was arranged according to principles of astronomy and cosmology. Scientists determined that it wasn't built only for beauty and austerity but also to act as an observatory.

Angkor Wat was designed so that sunrise would align with its western gate on equinox or solstice days. This allowed Khmer people to track the changing seasons—and in turn plan their harvests more accurately—since equinoxes take place when the sun is directly above the equator and solstices when it is most distant from that imaginary line.

Further architectural alignments throughout the complex offered daily feedback on lunar and solar cycles. All of this means that Angkor Wat's core beauty resides in numbers, as its architectural splendor is rooted in, and reliant upon, the clinical clarity of mathematics. Scientists still marvel at the precision the Khmer achieved in such an ancient era.[273]

Angkor Wat is phenomenal at first sight, but it is even more astounding once you consider its complex scientific design elements. To this day, humans struggle to create structures so spectacular in appearance, efficient in purpose, and inspiring in symbolism. Truly wondrous and rarely equaled, Angkor Wat is only recently becoming understood by foreigners, almost nine centuries after its construction.

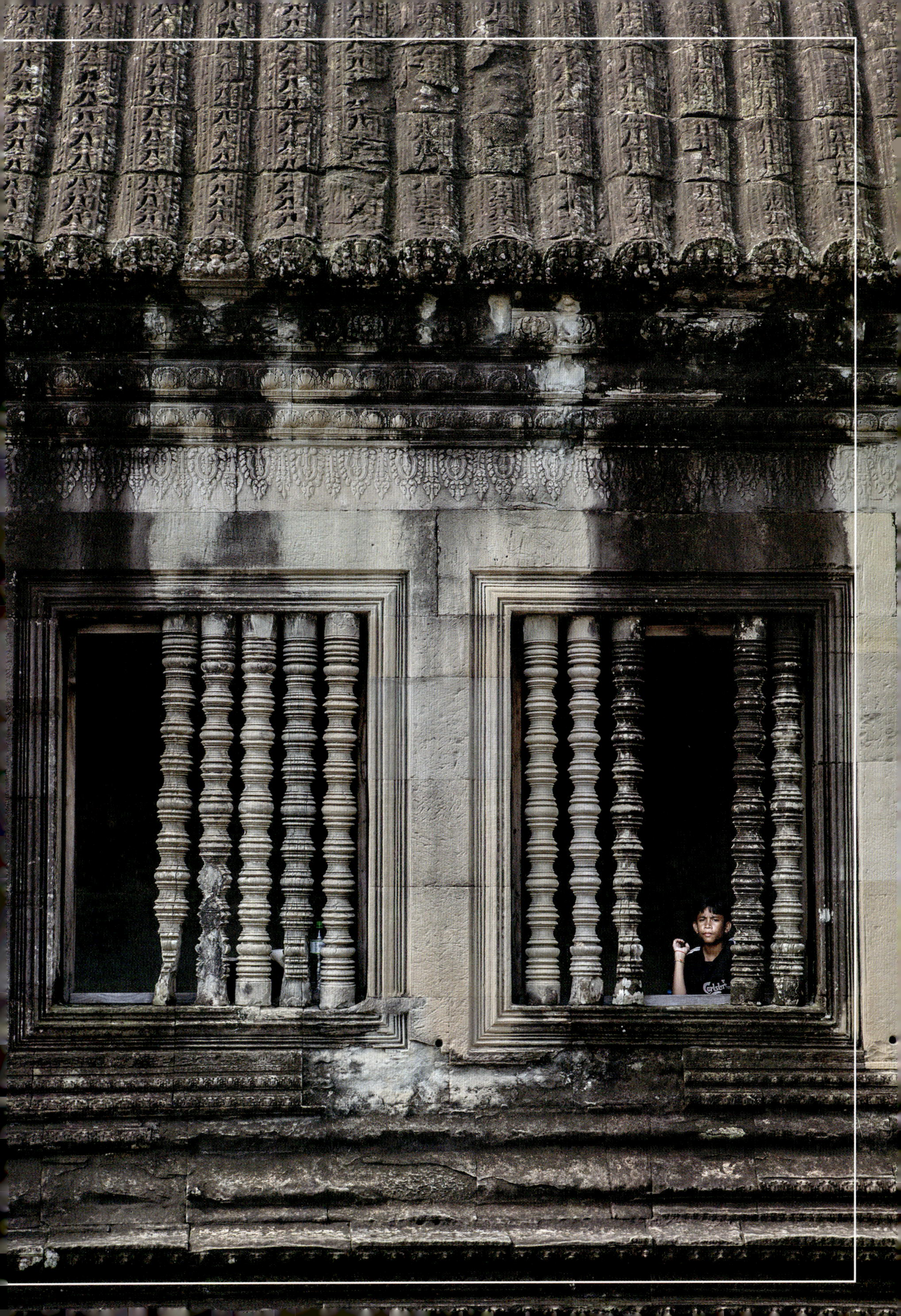

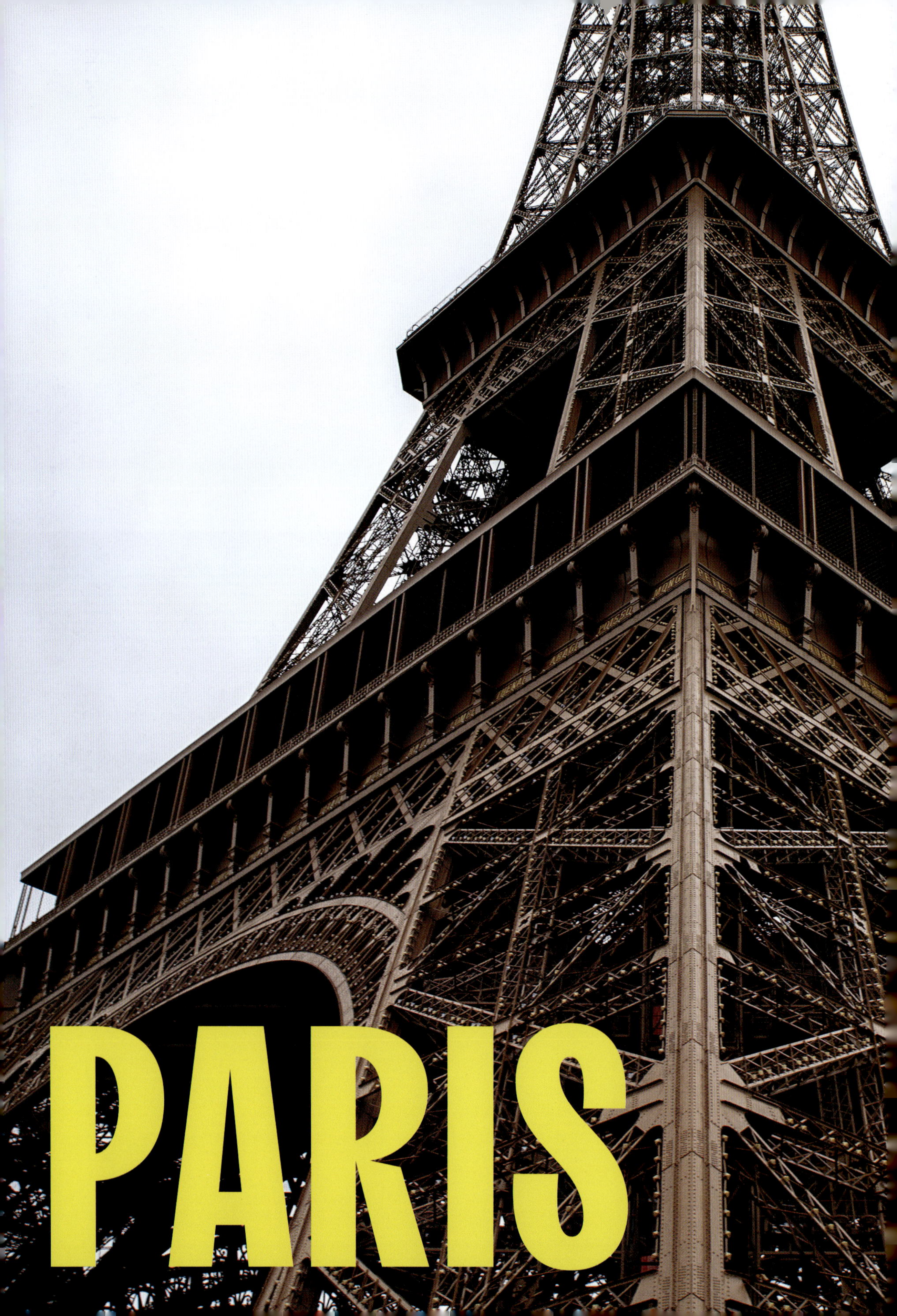
PARIS

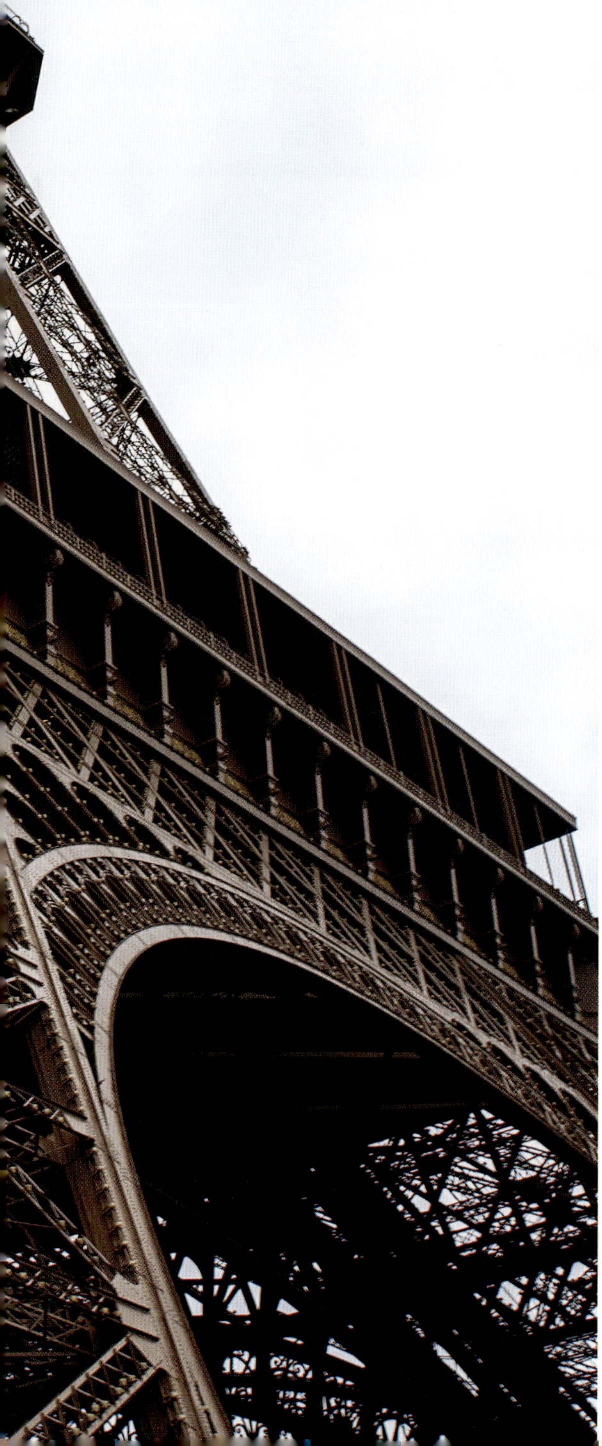

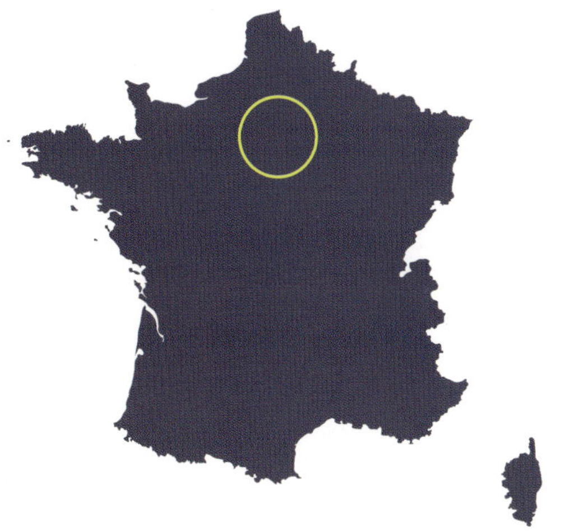

Her naked body mesmerized audiences and entranced powerful men. It also allegedly helped kill fifty thousand French soldiers and shape a global conflict. Few women have ever used their beauty with such cunning, and such catastrophic effect, as the beguiling burlesque performer who haunted France during World War I. She called herself Mata Hari.[274]

Making this tale even more bizarre, the Eiffel Tower played a key role in ending this Dutch exotic dancer's supposedly deadly influence. Before that landmark became a beacon for tourists, it lived a double life rooted in the shadowy world of espionage. In fact, it was Paris's revered tower that helped trap Mata Hari.[275]

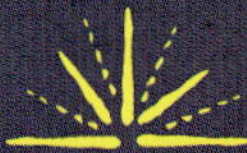

Many people don't feel like they've arrived in this city until they spy its A-framed tower. The French capital is uniquely laden with famous landmarks. People worldwide recognize the glass pyramid of the Louvre, the graceful curves of the Arc de Triomphe, the square towers of Notre-Dame Cathedral, and the tree-lined elegance of the Champs-Élysées.

Yet it is the Eiffel Tower that defines Paris. This city's name often isn't even written on posters, T-shirts, souvenirs, or ads promoting the French capital. Instead, like a form of emoji, the Eiffel silhouette equals Paris.

Its whole or partial form can be seen from many other parts of this chic metropolis. At 1,083 feet high, it dominates the low-rise skyline of Paris, which now disallows new buildings taller than 121 feet.[276] The Eiffel Tower owns a prime perch on the River Seine's south bank. There it rests in the 7th arrondissement neighborhood, where visitors can savor many more sights, such as the impressive Monument to Human Rights, the sculptures of the Rodin Museum, and the military museums of Hôtel des Invalides.

All these attractions can be seen, at a bird's-eye perspective, from the upper levels of the Eiffel Tower. Some 905 feet tall, its top floor offers two platforms with 360-degree vistas. This vantage is so high that the streets below feel miniaturized. So, too, do typically imposing landmarks like Musée d'Orsay and Palais Garnier opera house.

Understandably, given all that sprawls before them, tourists tend to be preoccupied by this vista. Once they break from its hypnotic grip, they'll find more to appreciate on the Eiffel Tower's top floor, such as a ritzy champagne bar and a reconstruction of Gustave Eiffel's office.[277] Ticket holders can also access what are called the first and second floors, perched at a height of 187 feet and 380 feet respectively.[278]

Each year, almost one million people ascend to one of those three floors,[279] an extraordinary figure that is partly due to the tremendous accessibility of the Eiffel Tower. Many other landmarks around the world are closed for dozens of days a year and have strict daylight opening hours. But Paris's jewel typically operates 365 days a year, from morning until late at night.[280]

The majority of tourists never even scale this landmark. Instead they linger at its base, capturing endless images. A photographer's delight, its design is at once starkly simple and deeply complicated. The former is evident to anyone who has viewed the Eiffel Tower from afar, whether in person, photo, or video. But its intricacies are revealed only to those fortunate enough to stand in its shadow.

Up close, this French wonder's ironwork is astoundingly complex. Thousands upon thousands of metallic bars, girders, trusses, chords, clips, struts, and wings combine to create both an engineering marvel and a work of art. Collectively, these features give the facade a mesmerizing lattice effect, which plays with natural light by day and night.[281]

In fact, the Eiffel Tower only grows in glamour and prominence once the sun departs. As surrounding buildings darken, it glows against a blackened sky, thanks to more than three hundred sodium-vapor spotlights. Then, for a few minutes each hour, up until 1:00 a.m., another twenty thousand small bulbs sparkle across its exterior, like a twinkling galaxy.[282]

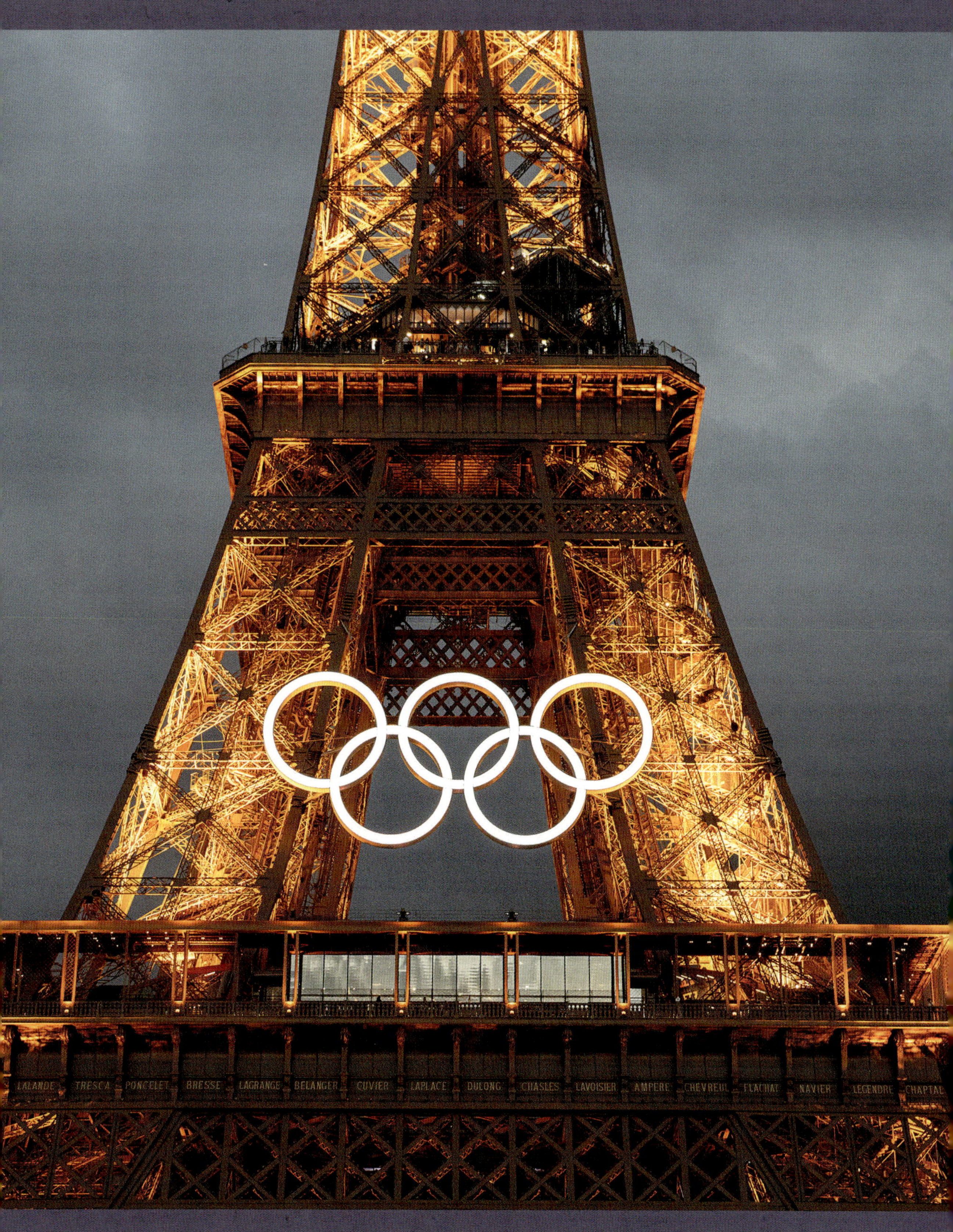
LALANDE TRESCA PONCELET BRESSE LAGRANGE BELANGER CUVIER LAPLACE DULONG CHASLES LAVOISIER AMPERE CHEVREUL FLACHAT NAVIER LEGENDRE CHAPTAL

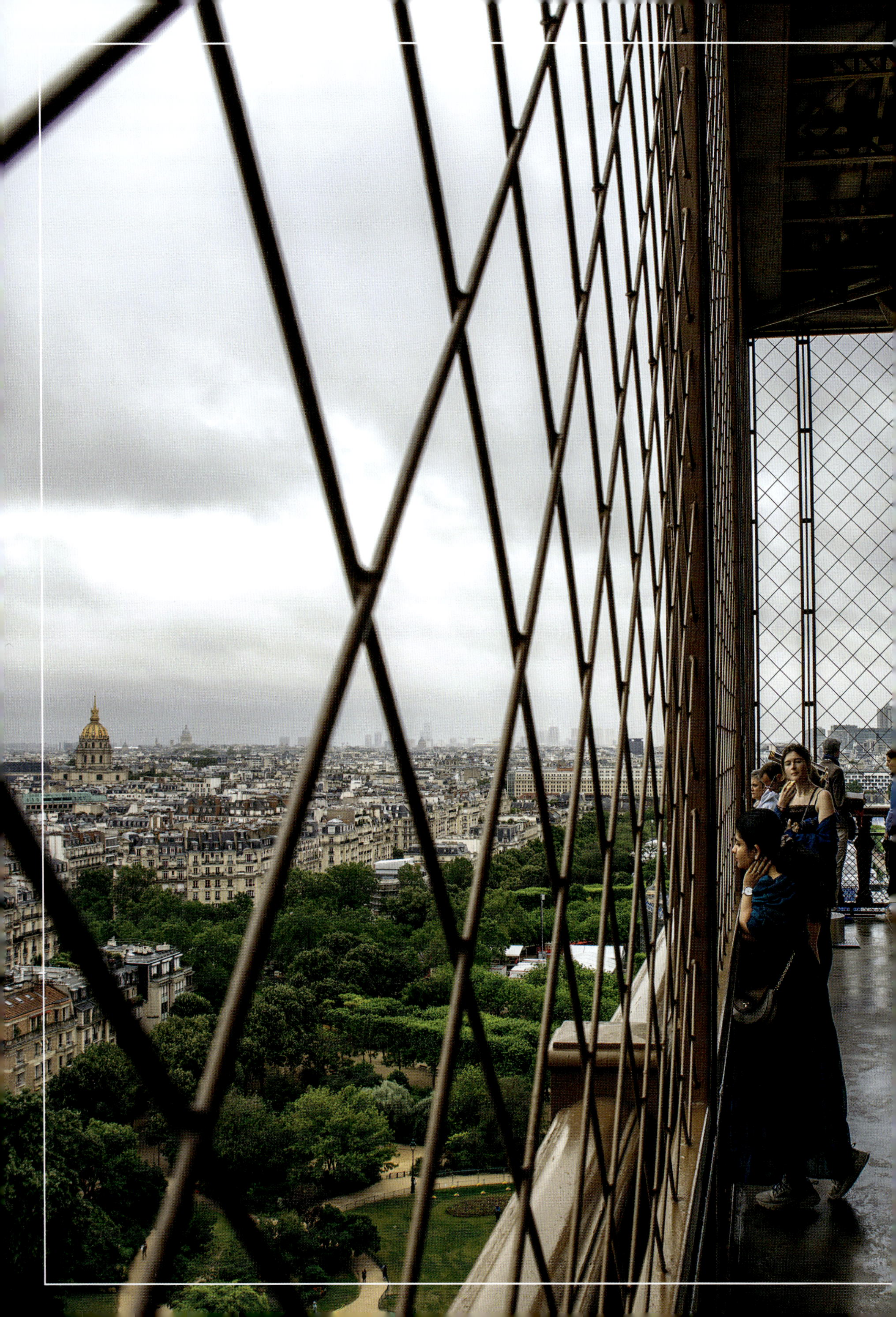

A YOUNG WOMAN STARTS TAKING RISKS

Born in Leeuwarden, Netherlands, in 1876, Margaretha Zelle was only eighteen when she took her first major gamble.[283] She read a newspaper ad placed by a Dutch army captain named Rudolph John MacLeod, who was seeking a wife. He was more than twice her age and planning a move back to Indonesia, the far-flung Dutch colony where he'd been stationed. Seeing an opportunity for adventure, she decided to leap into the unknown.

Margaretha met MacLeod for the first time in Amsterdam, and within weeks they were married. Four years later, while living in Indonesia, the couple was struck by tragedy. Their two-year-old son, Norman, became ill and died. At the time, Margaretha and MacLeod accused their nanny of poisoning both Norman and his younger sister, Nonnie, who survived. However some historians now believe that Norman may have died from mercury treatment he received for a venereal disease contracted from his parents.

The devastated couple soon returned to Europe and divorced. Margaretha was awarded custody of Nonnie, but MacLeod allegedly refused to pay alimony to his ex-wife. As a result, she was left in poverty, and couldn't provide for their daughter. Margaretha was forced to give up custody of Nonnie, who went to live with MacLeod.[284]

A BURLESQUE SUPERSTAR IS BORN

In 1905, to help her make enough money to win back her daughter, Margaretha created a densely layered alter ego. Overnight, she became an exotic dancer from the Far East. The name she chose was Mata Hari, a Malay term for the sun.[285]

It didn't take long for the dancer to land a breakthrough performance in her new home city of Paris. She danced before a wealthy mixed-gender audience at luxurious Musée Guimet. Her audience was instantly bewitched. Never had they witnessed such a spectacle.

Mata Hari's trademark was revealing outfits designed in Orientalism, a style of fashion that fused elements of dress from across Asia. Her classic combination was an ornate headdress, bejeweled bodice, sarong-style skirt, and see-through veil. As she danced, these garments gradually disappeared, and another roomful of fans was earned.

So, too, were large sums of money. At the peak of her popularity, in 1907, Mata Hari was paid the equivalent, in modern terms, of up to forty thousand dollars per performance. Such riches, and the lavish lifestyle they afforded, furthered her celebrity, although she had a tendency to spend money as soon as it came in. Mata Hari also lived large thanks to a sequence of wealthy lovers, who showered her with gifts and dates at exclusive venues, where paparazzi were often waiting.

French newspaper reports swooned about the long-limbed beauty's spellbinding shows. Gradually, her potent blend of boldness and faux exoticism earned attention from afar. She began making headlines in the US and starred at revered venues in Monaco and Italy.[286]

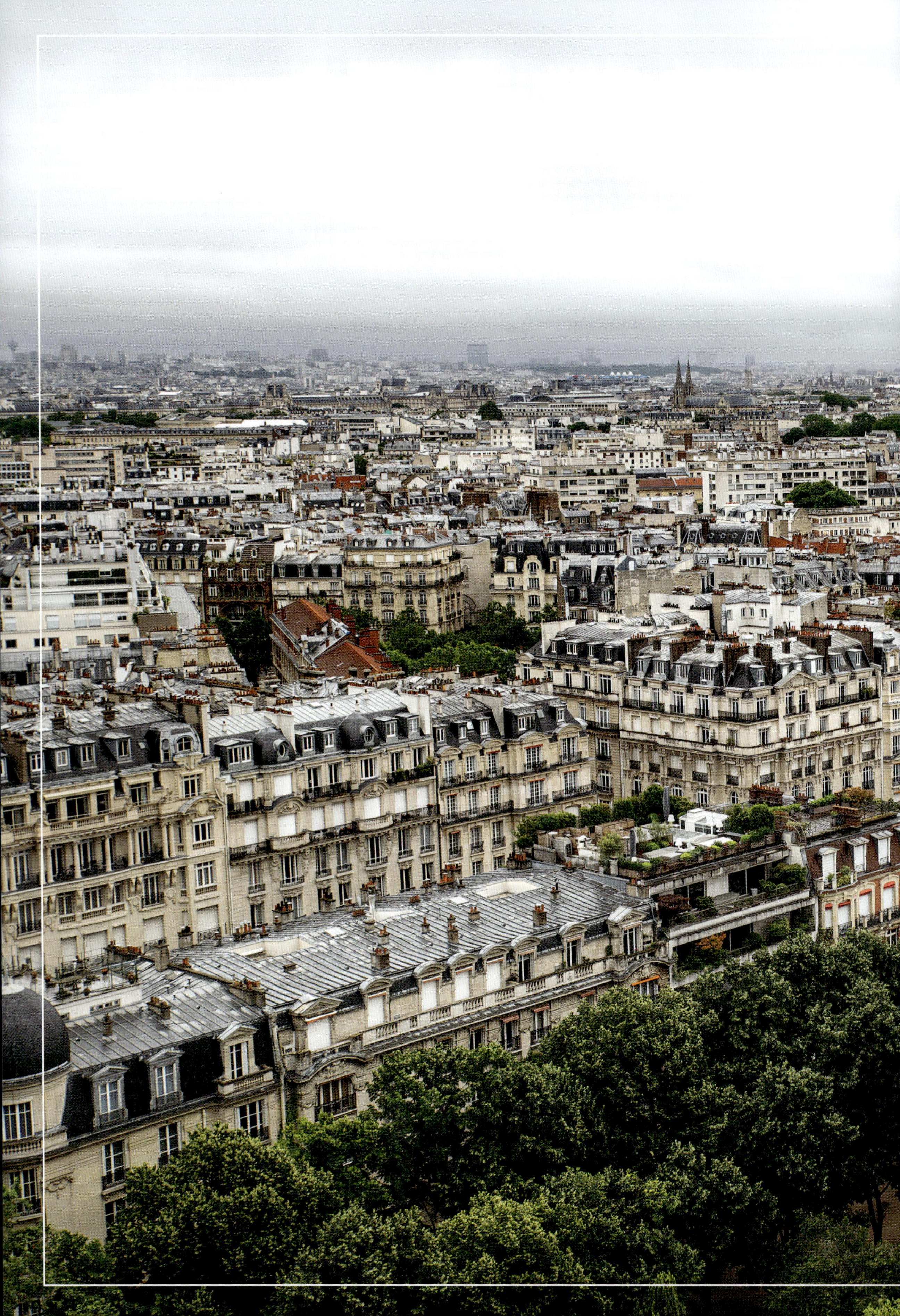

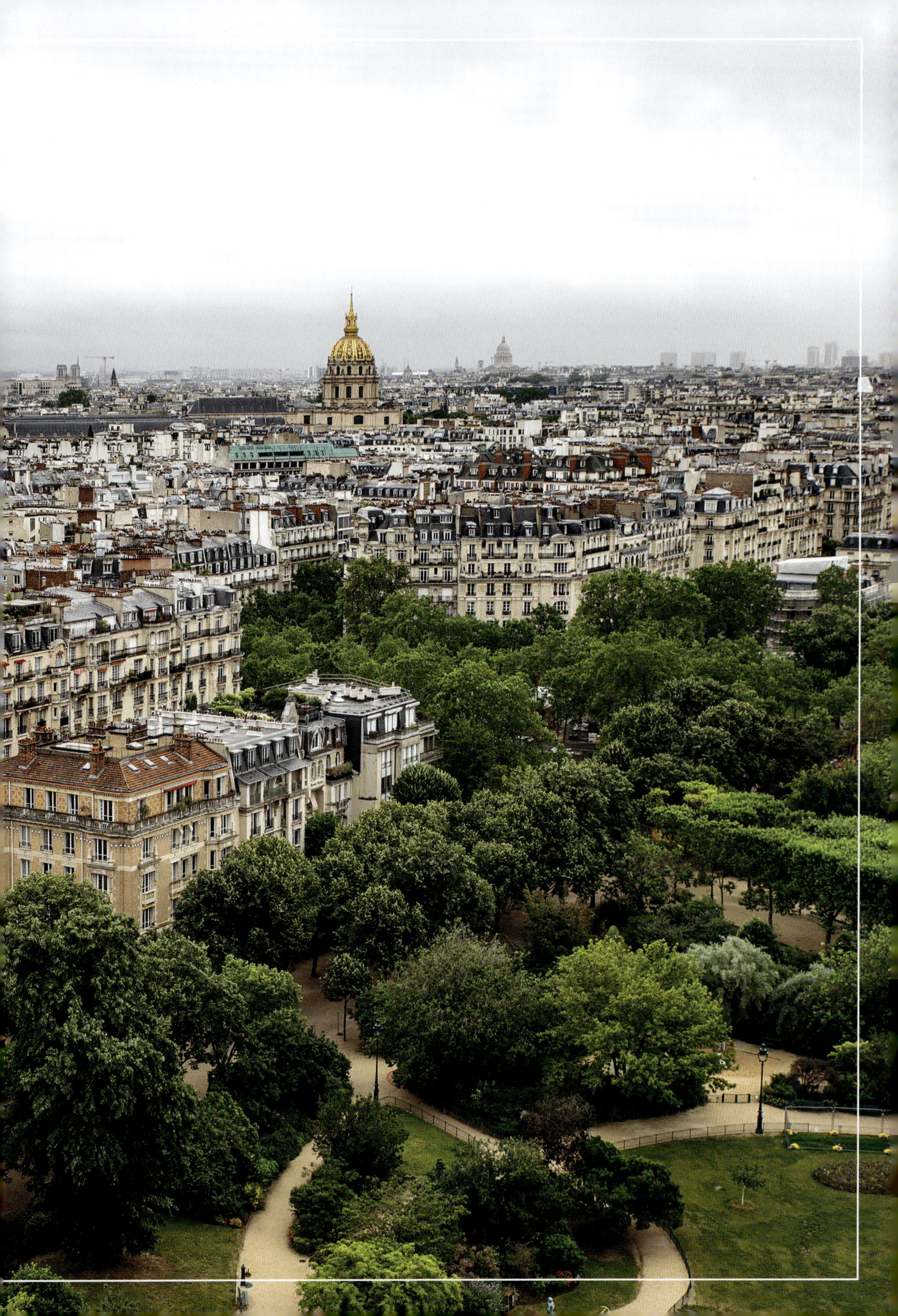

WAR LEADS MATA HARI IN A NEW DIRECTION

By 1914, however, the outbreak of WWI slowed the dancer's ambition. With bloodshed erupting across Europe, most entertainment venues closed or greatly reduced their opening hours. Mata Hari continued to travel across the continent to perform but had far less stage time and therefore greatly reduced income. Initially she relied on the generosity of her wealthy lovers. Then she made a daring career change.[287]

In May 1916, Mata Hari was secretly approached by a German official in The Hague. He saw her as a perfect potential spy. First because of her natural ability to seduce powerful men and second because although Europe's borders were tightly controlled amid the war, Mata Hari could roam widely without causing great suspicion due to her neat cover story as a traveling dancer.

She quickly accepted the German's offer. Mata Hari was to provide on-the-ground intelligence reports from their enemy territory of France in return for payment. Perhaps she took a liking to the work. Or maybe she enjoyed the pay. Before long, Mata Hari also began spying for France, without disclosing to them her German links.

When she was arrested by French police in February 1917, they accused her of being a double agent. It was a light charge compared to what followed.[288] According to the French, Mata Hari's espionage for the Germans had led to the deaths of some fifty thousand soldiers from France.[289] And they caught her only because of the Eiffel Tower.

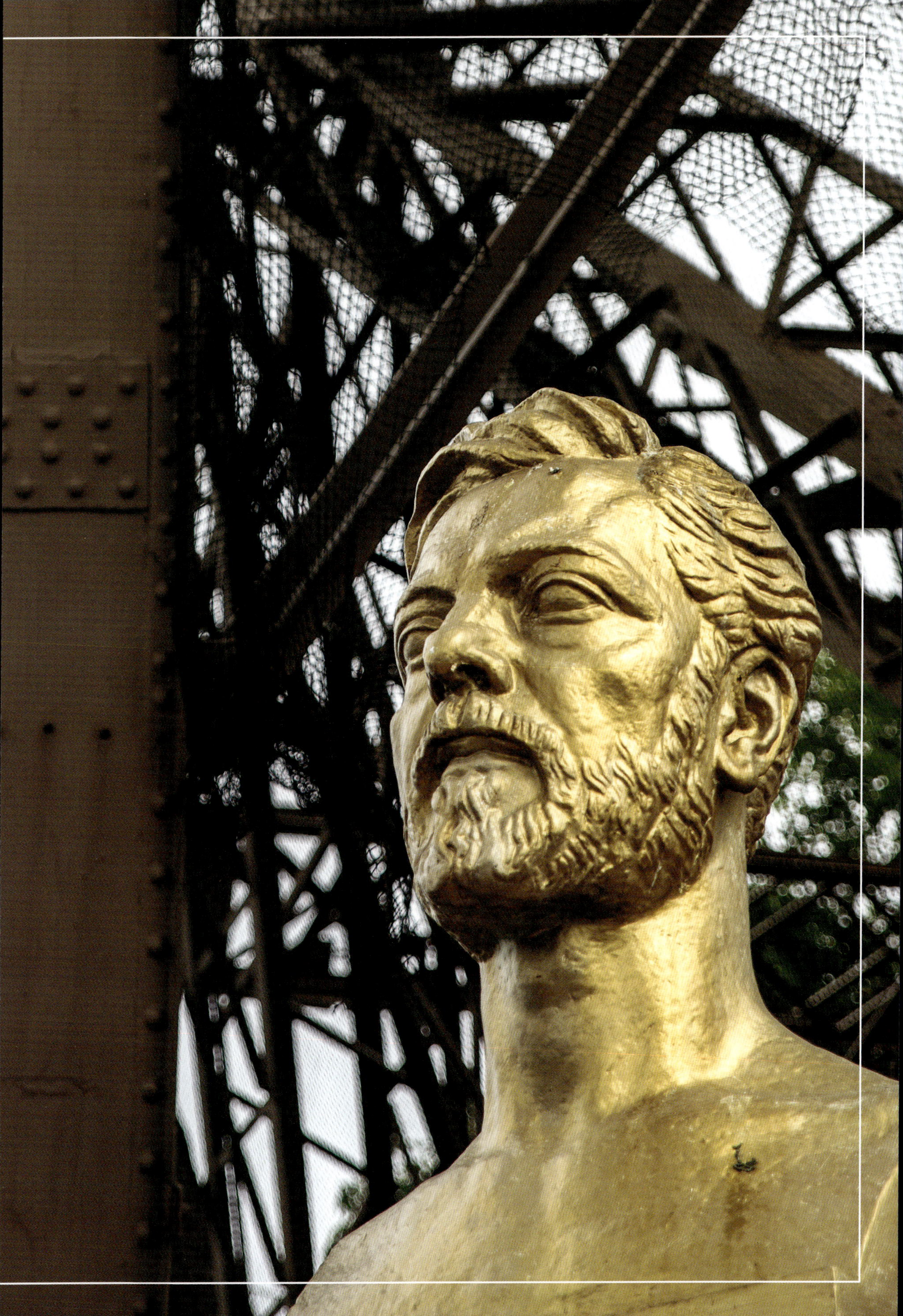

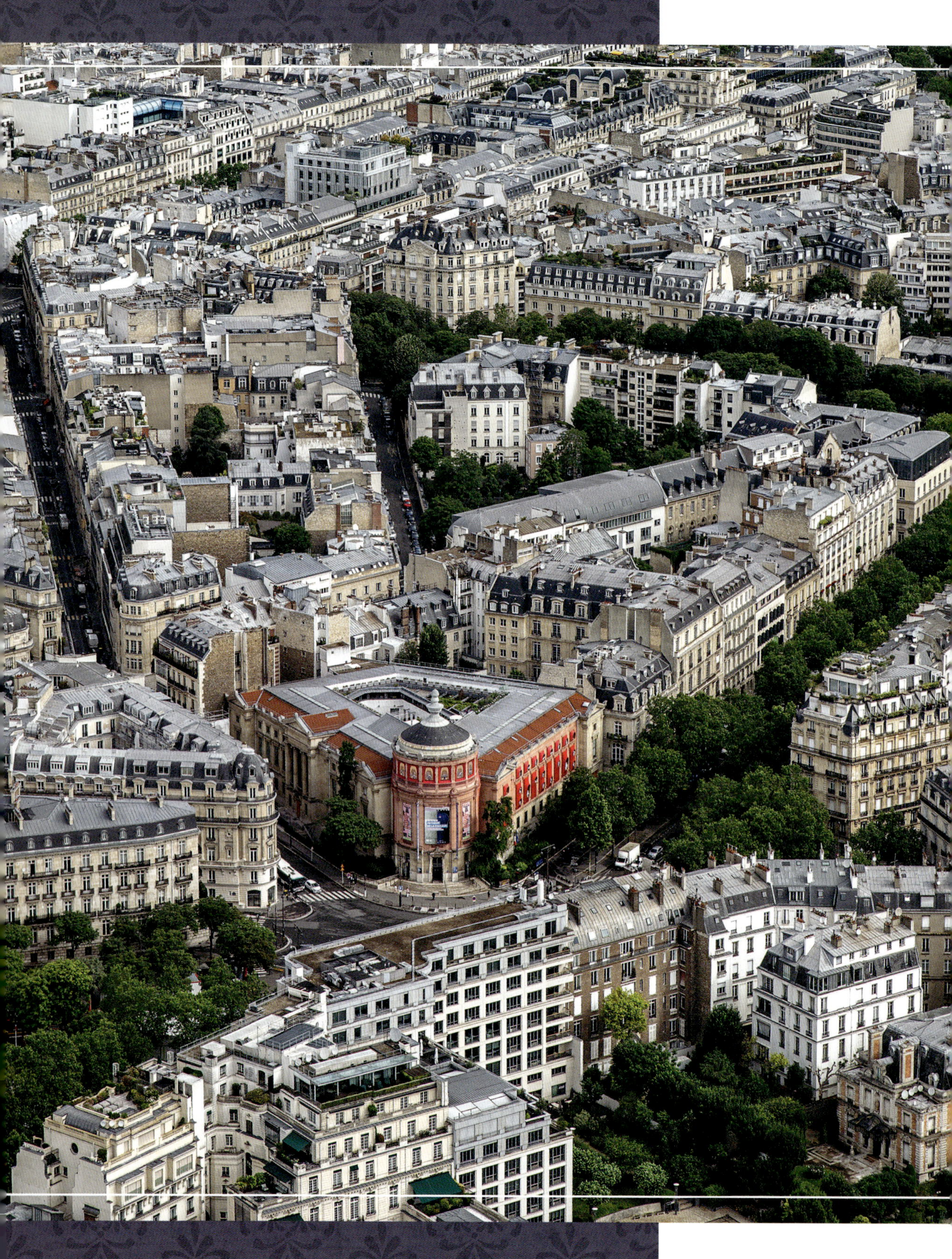

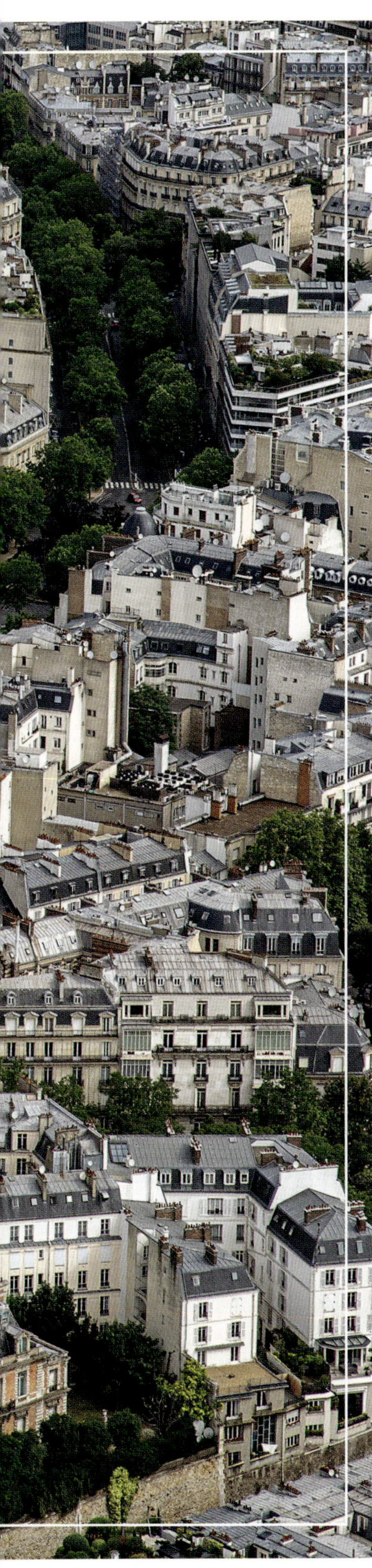

EIFFEL TOWER EXPOSES MATA HARI THE SPY

In retrospect, it sounds unbelievable, but this Parisian marvel was slated for demolition in the early 1900s. Desperate to save his masterpiece, French engineer Gustave Eiffel proposed a solution: Convert the structure into a communications pylon. Five years later, this new purpose went from useful to crucial as Europe became embroiled in World War I.

The French military used the Eiffel Tower's powerful radiotelegraphic station not only to message its troops and ships but also to intercept high-level directives sent by German forces. Decoding such enemy messages let the French operate a step ahead of their foes.

In 1916, the Eiffel Tower's radiotelegraphic station captured one such German communication, which had massive ramifications for Mata Hari.[290] German military attache Major Arnold Kalle sent this message back to Berlin. In it, he detailed several clandestine discussions with a spy in Spain, whom he simply called "H21." Unbeknownst to Major Kalle, the French had already cracked the code he used in these messages, and the major had disclosed enough information that the French were able to identify operative H21 as none other than Mata Hari.

They waited until she returned to France, in February 1917, and then arrested her on espionage charges. A French court convicted Mata Hari, who it described as "one of the greatest spies of the century, responsible for the deaths of tens of thousands of soldiers."

Just a few months later, her extraordinary life was ended by court-ordered gunfire execution in Paris. All of Mata Hari's fame, wealth, and success had never earned her what she most coveted—to regain custody of her daughter.

Despite being salacious and shocking, this sliver of Eiffel Tower history reaches few tourists to Paris. Mata Hari's blood trail leads all the way to that landmark, an icon of Parisian style, with inconspicuous links to espionage.[291]

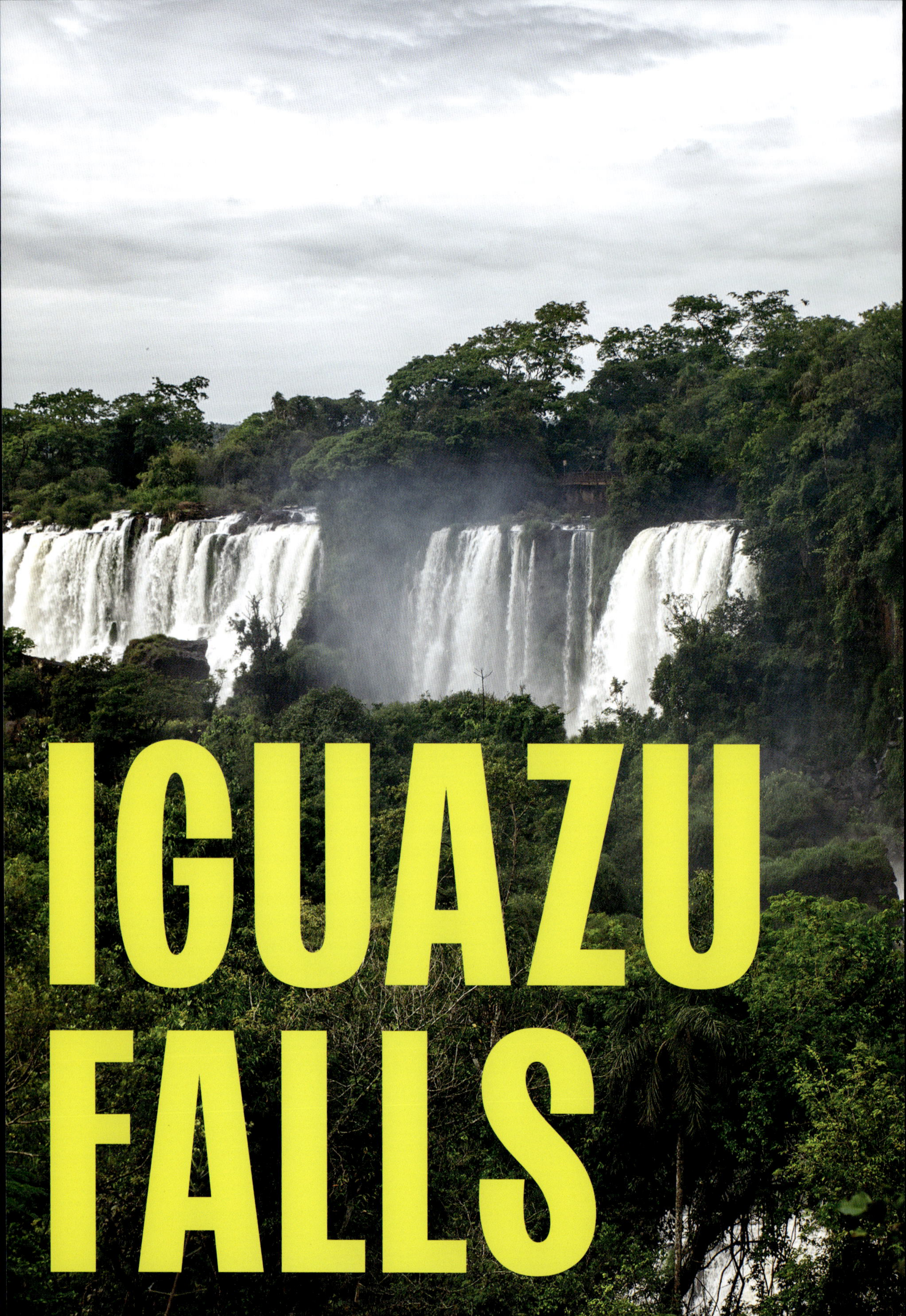
IGUAZU
FALLS

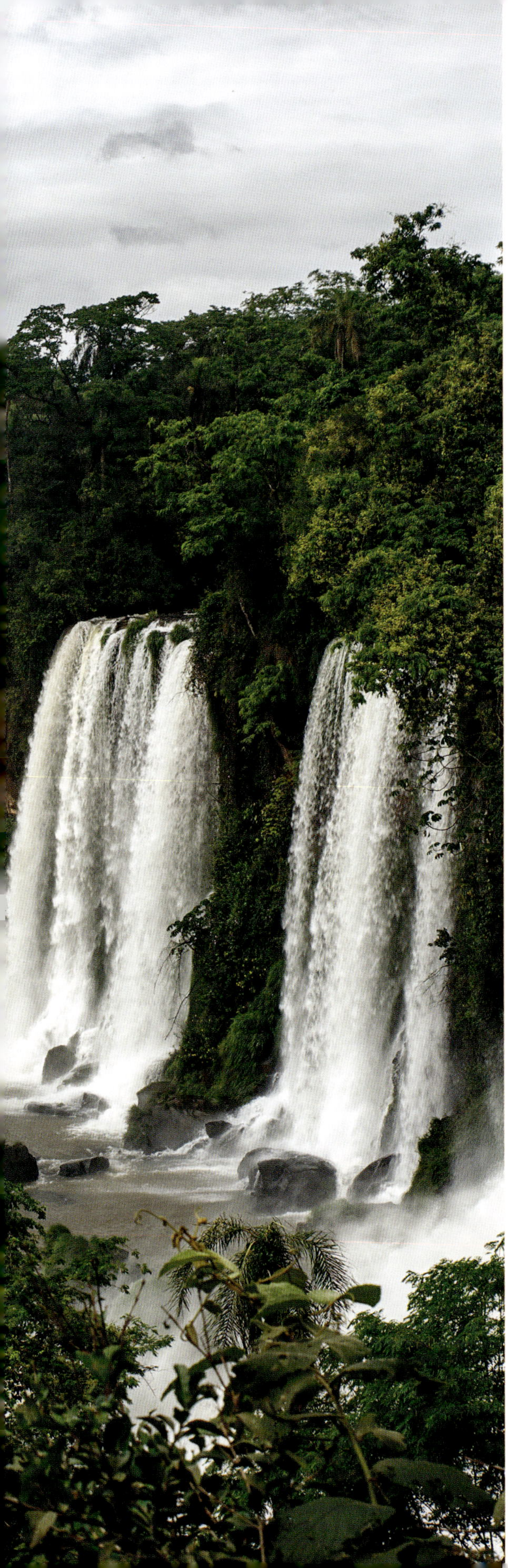

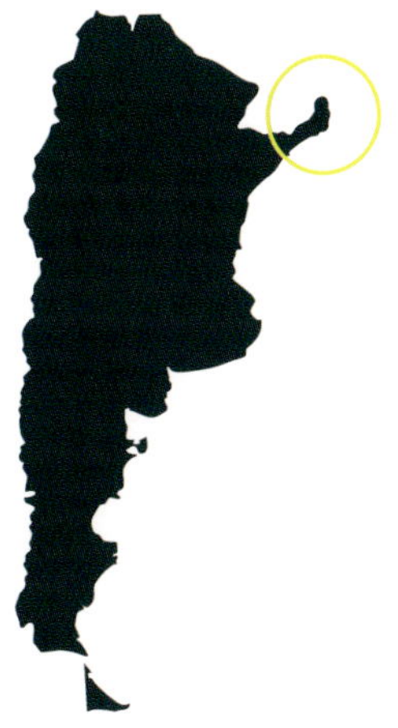

Every second of every day, a heartbroken rock and a mourning tree are drenched by the natural marvel that cruelly ended their romance. This odd, melancholy scenario plays out in front of one million tourists a year. Yet none notice. What they perceive, instead, is a swollen river charging over cliffs to create one of the world's biggest waterfall systems.

Located at the border between Argentina and Brazil, Iguazu Falls has become an iconic attraction of South America. About 1.7 miles long, this horseshoe formation consists of 275 waterfalls, spans the Iguazu River, and is almost triple the width of North America's iconic Niagara Falls.[292]

But this natural phenomenon was revered long before its tourist facilities were built. Up to ten thousand years ago, the Indigenous Guarani people viewed this site with awe and a degree of fear. They understood that Iguazu Falls was created by a furious being who wished to curse those aforementioned lovers.[293]

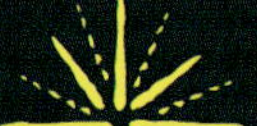

Mother Nature's creativity at Iguazu extends well beyond the falls. Flanking that watery wonder is a pair of rainforest national parks, one on either side of the international border.

Amid this wilderness, jaguars prowl, toucans perch, alligators lurk, howler monkeys frolic, and more than two thousand plant species flourish. Together, Argentina's Iguazu National Park and Brazil's Iguaçu National Park cover 593,000 acres.[294]

With canopies up to a hundred feet tall, the parks encompass what the World Wildlife Fund describes as "part of the most important area of forest in the Central-South region of South America." Sheltered within them are more than 250 plant species, 635 butterfly species, 550 bird species, 120 mammal species, 79 reptile species, and 55 amphibian species.[295]

Some of this natural environment is explained at the Iguazu visitor center in Argentina. The Argentine side of the falls is particularly neat and well organized.[296] An open-air train offers passengers memorable views as it shuttles back and forth to Devil's Throat. Known as Iguazu's most spectacular section, these falls are the star attraction on both sides of the border.

From the Devil's Throat train station, a 0.7-mile-long pedestrian bridge spans the Iguazu River. It terminates at a viewing platform that sits above Devil's Throat, cloaked in wet mist. There is no more dramatic vantage from which to absorb the raw vigor of Iguazu Falls.

Visitors may complement that adrenaline surge with the calming effect of a hike back to the single train stop between Devil's Throat and the visitor center. Called Cataratas Station, its key attraction is a pair of loop walks. One winds 1.1 miles through throbbing rainforest and exposes several of Iguazu's smaller, lesser-visited falls. Another is slightly longer and leads past eight falls, finishing with an overwater balcony at enormous San Martin Waterfall.

A short distance north of Iguazu Falls, visitors can traverse a bridge to Brazil to view this landmark from a fresh perspective. Here, too, is a memorable raised walkway, the end of which is surrounded by more than a dozen falls.[297]

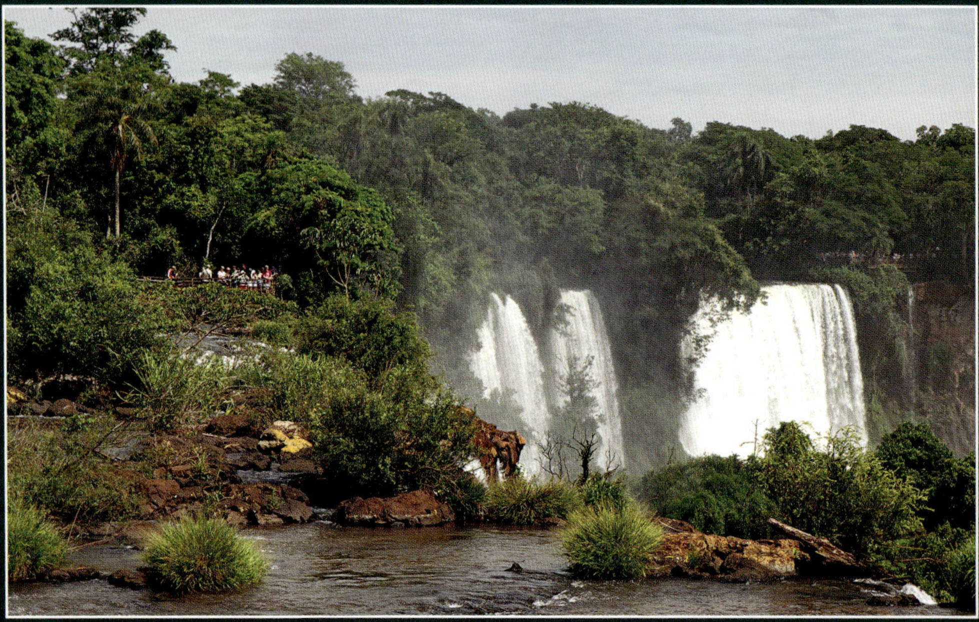

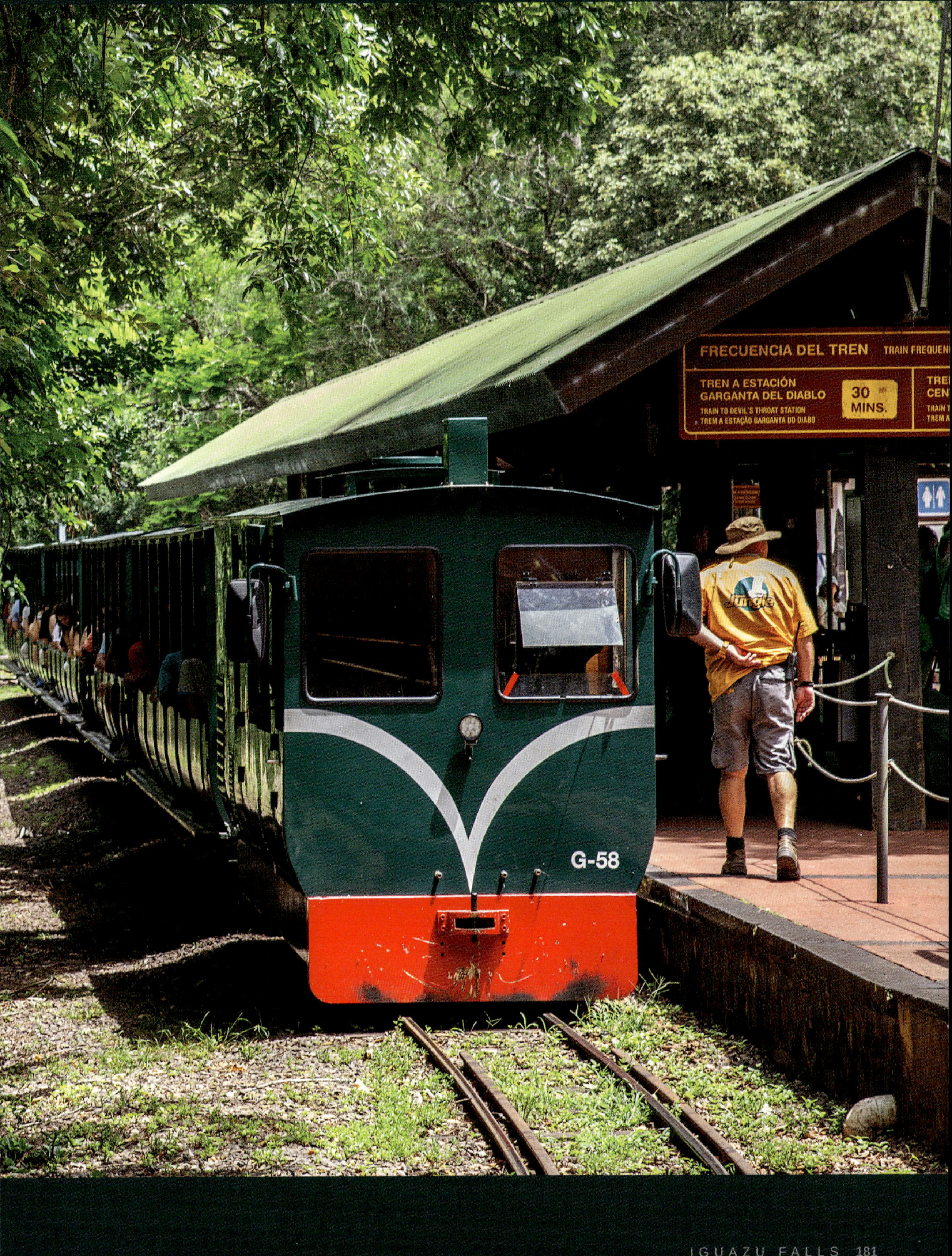
FRECUENCIA DEL TREN
TREN A ESTACIÓN
GARGANTA DEL DIABLO
TRAIN TO DEVIL'S THROAT STATION
TREM A ESTAÇÃO GARGANTA DO DIABO
30
MINS.
Jungle
G-58

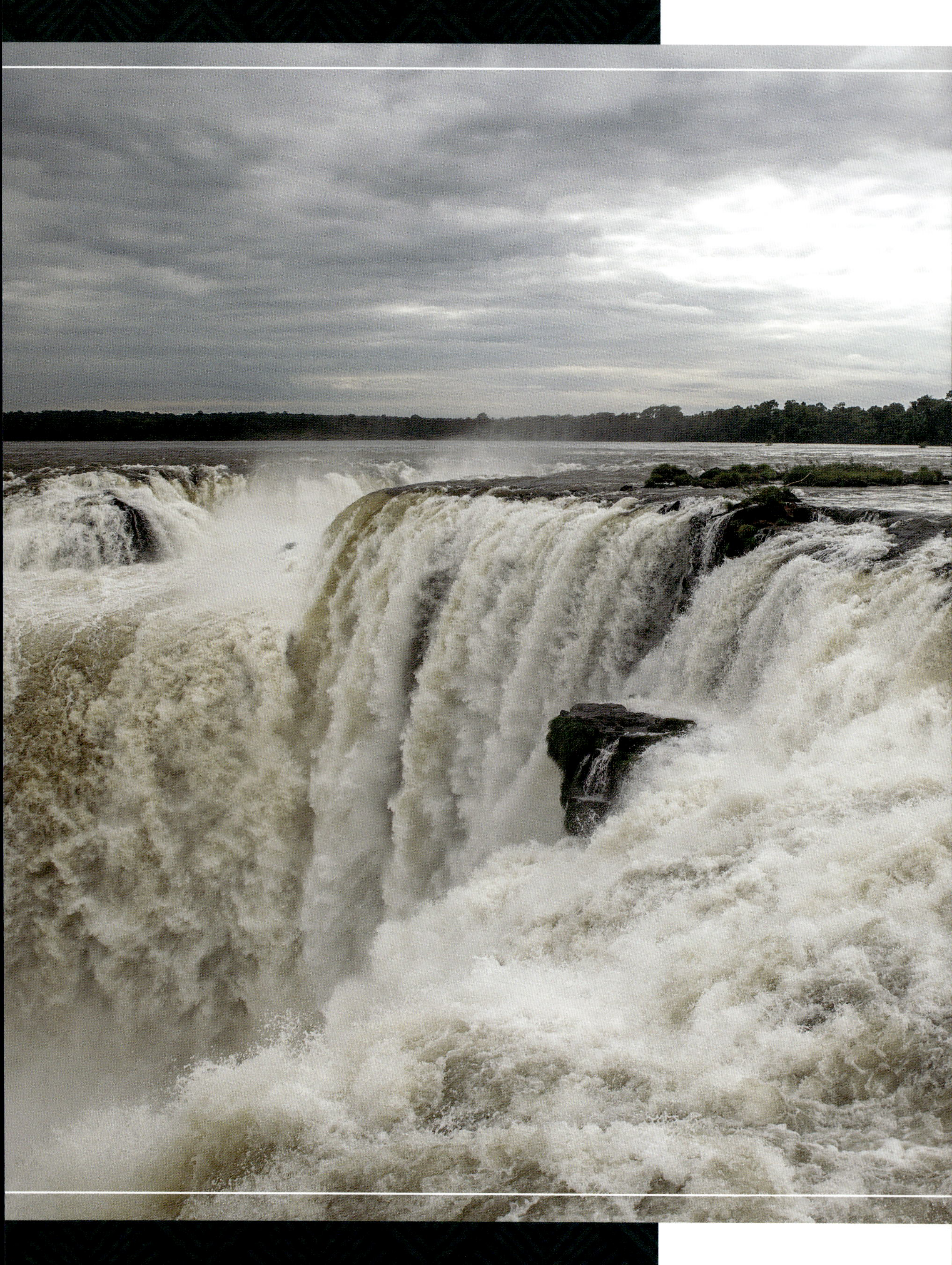

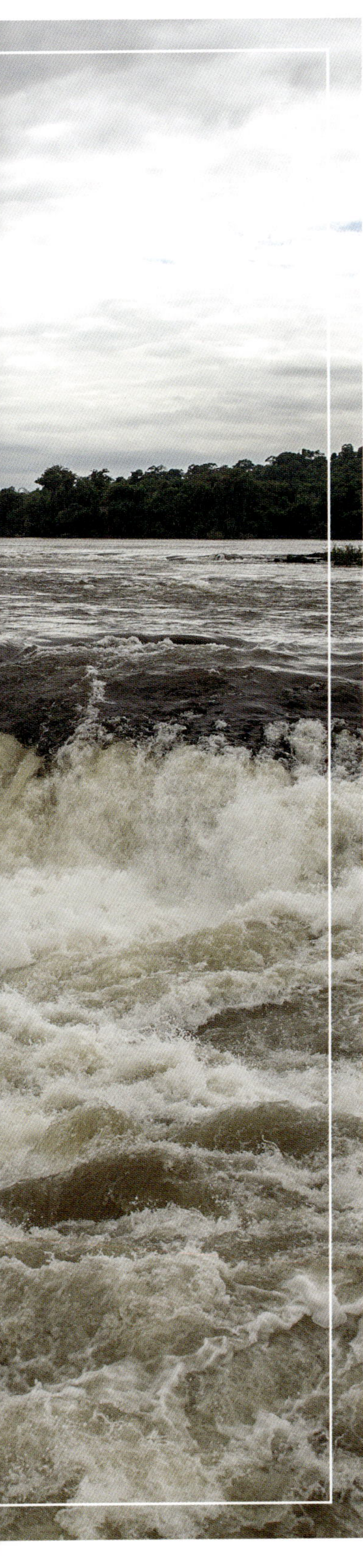

THE INDIGENOUS GUARANI PEOPLE

Spanish seaman Álvar Núñez Cabeza de Vaca is widely credited with "discovering" the Iguazu Falls almost five hundred years ago. But the legacy of the falls began long before the Spanish colonized these lands.[298]

The Guarani are a skillful, resourceful people who flourished in the forests near Iguazu for many hundreds of years before the colonial period.[299] Dubbed by scientists as the "theologians of the forest," the Guarani tribe is the ancient protector of Iguazu Falls. This thunderous wonder was so significant to the Guarani that it shaped their spiritual beliefs and legends, one of which continues to echo through Brazil and Argentina.[300]

THE CREATION OF THE FALLS

A key Guarani folktale revolves around Caroba, an Indigenous warrior who fell for the chief's daughter, named Naipur. Caroba, terrified when he learned that his beautiful young lover was coveted by the serpent god of the forest where they lived, ushered Naipur into a canoe and tried to flee with her down the Iguazu River. They hoped to build a life together. It was not to be.

In a violent rage, the slithering deity fractured the earth's surface, creating the rushing waters of the falls. Naipur tumbled to her death and transformed into a rock, which lies at the base of Iguazu Falls. Caroba morphed into a tree at the cliff's edge, from where he can peer down at his darling. These lovers will always be close, yet never reunited, forever separated by a roaring waterfall forged by a jealous snake.

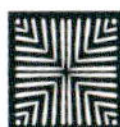

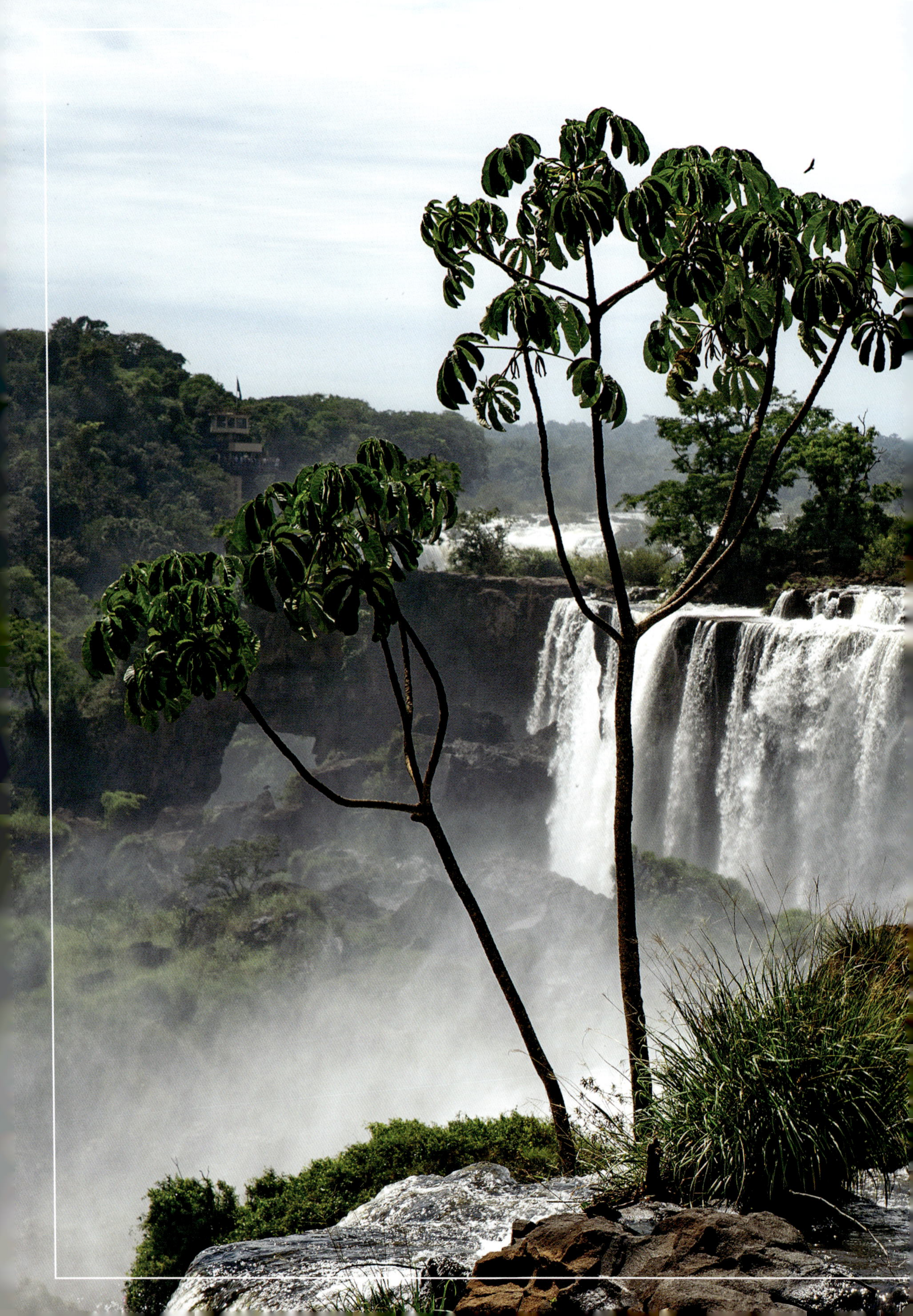

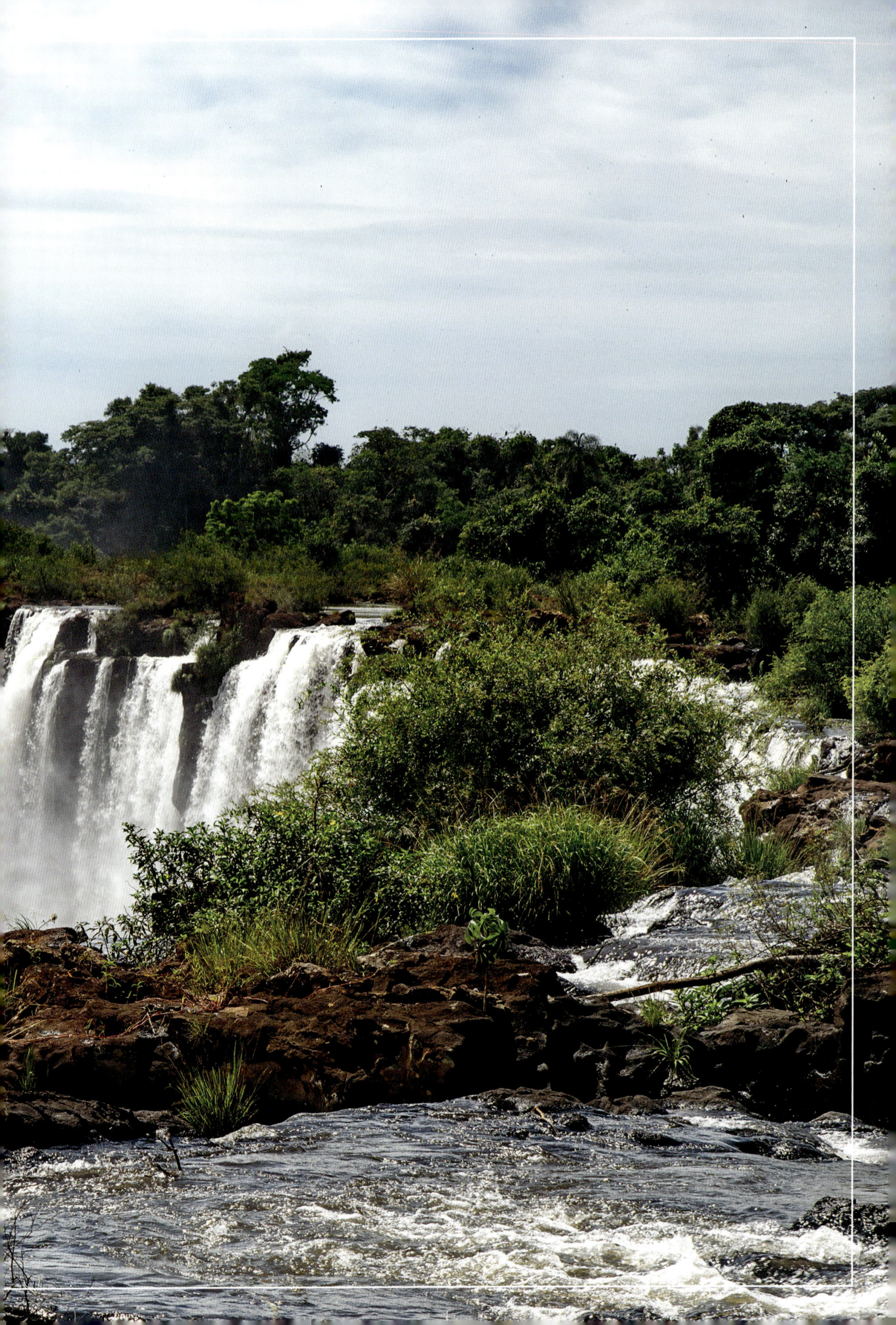

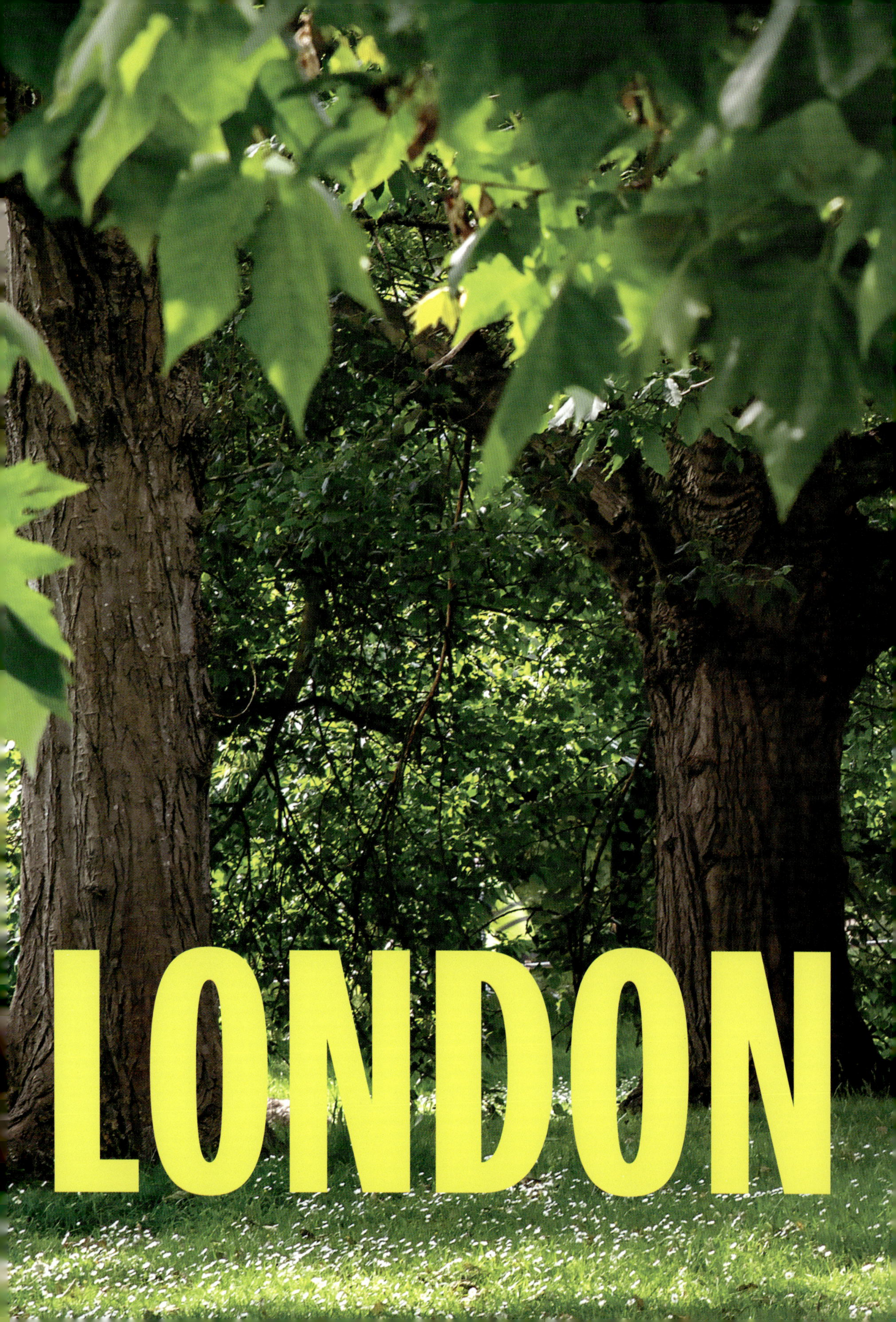
LONDON

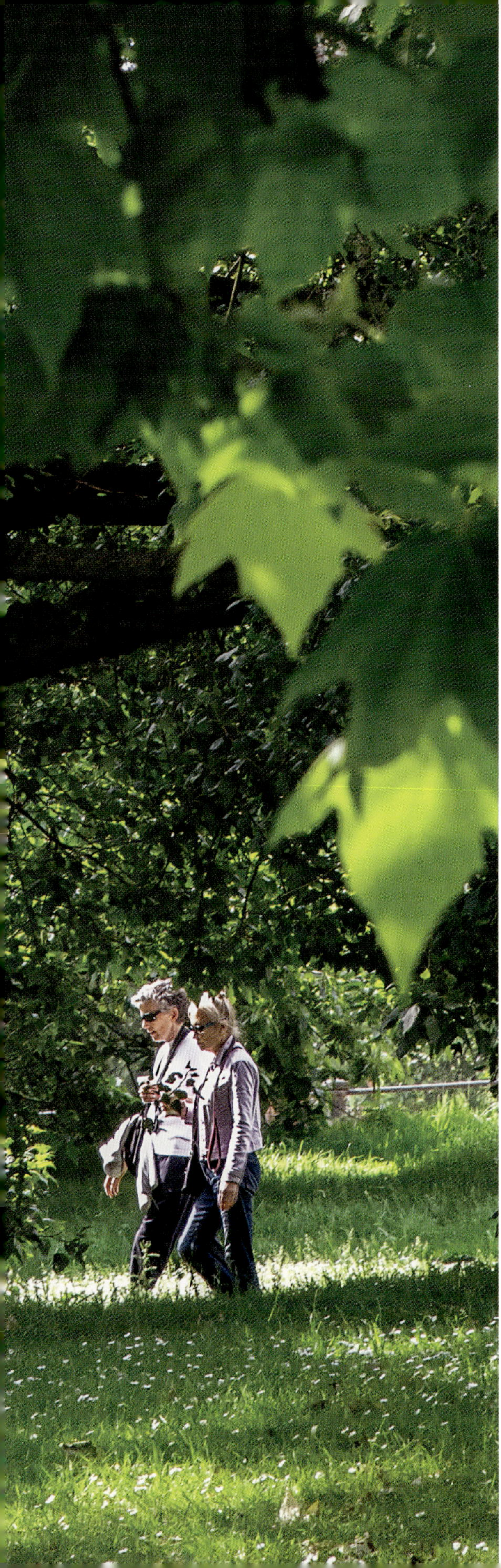

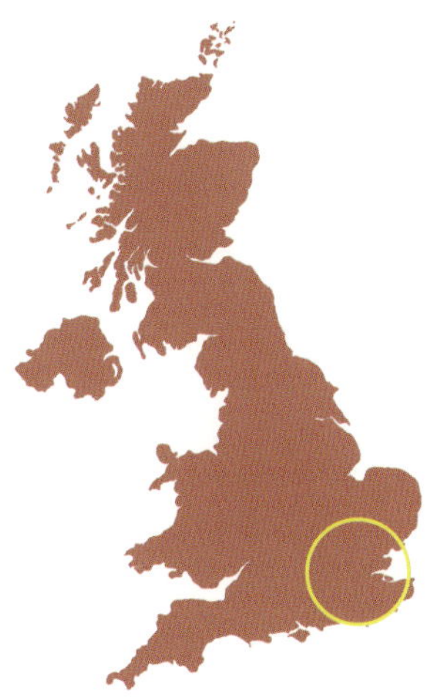

Dead eyes once stared through the trees of London's Hyde Park, which is now among Europe's most popular green spaces. Those emotionless gazes were owned by a breed of ruthless men who could make visiting this park a waking nightmare.

These days, decorated with elaborate statues, glassy ponds, rose gardens, and beautiful landscaping, Hyde Park is an oasis for people seeking respite from the city's ceaseless energy. It's hard to believe that it was once besieged by bloody bedlam.

To blame for the violence were menacing rogues called highwaymen. As recently as the eighteenth century, they would lurk amid Hyde Park's darkened trees, waiting to change someone's life forever.[301]

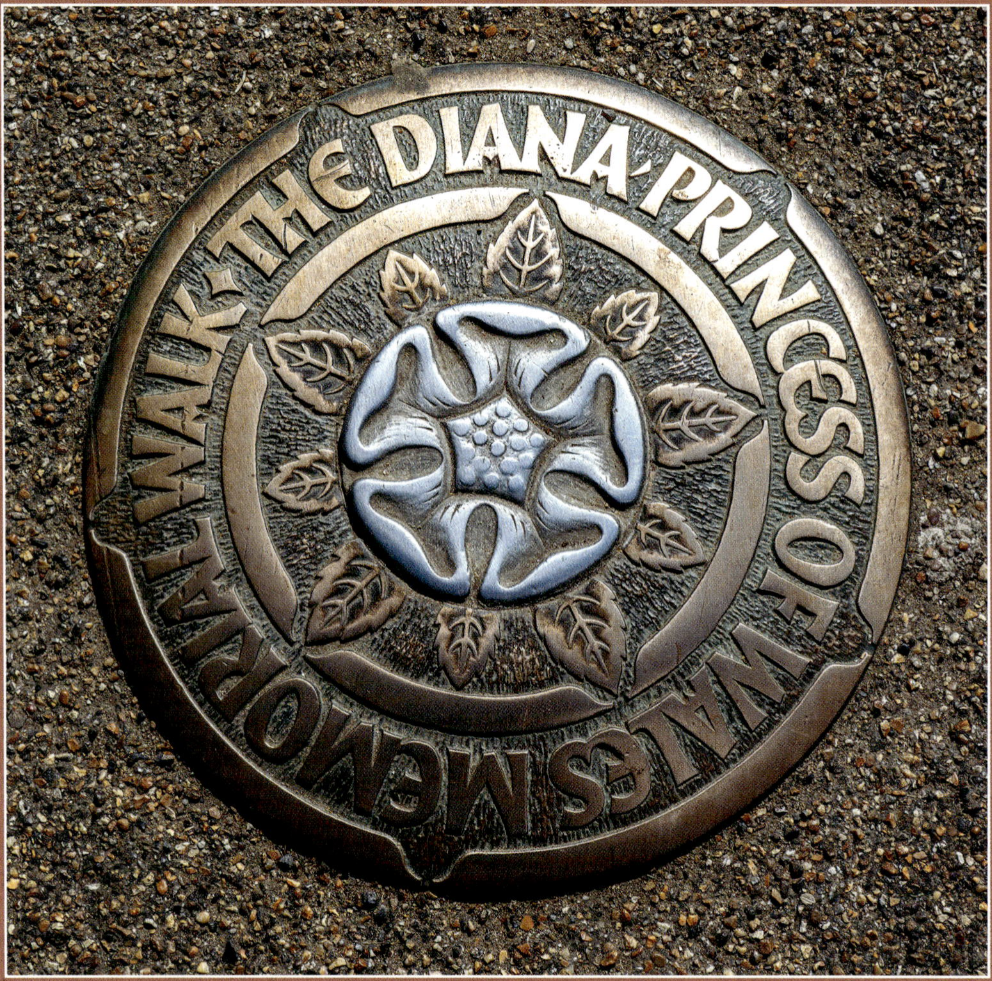

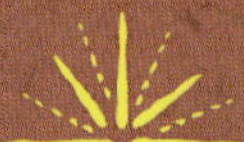

London is one of the world's most verdant cities. More than three thousand green spaces complement the English capital's grand palaces, stately churches, intriguing markets, renowned art galleries, and trove of free museums.[302]

Covering 350 acres, Hyde Park is meticulously landscaped. Many tourists pause in Hyde Park to absorb this tranquility. Others come to see its unique sites, such as Speakers' Corner, where public protests once congregated as orators like Karl Marx and George Orwell addressed the crowd. Some are drawn to visit the Diana, Princess of Wales Memorial Fountain, a spectacular Cornish granite construction dedicated to the late Princess of Wales.[303]

Key landmarks also encircle Hyde Park. To its west is Kensington Palace, tours of which let visitors glimpse its grand interiors and pristine gardens.[304] To the north sits Marble Arch, a splendid eighteenth-century gate that was a key entrance to London's Buckingham Palace before being relocated to its present location.[305] To the south is the Victoria and Albert Museum, one of the world's largest museums, holding more than two million art and design pieces.[306] And east looms Buckingham Palace, the iconic headquarters of Britain's royal family.

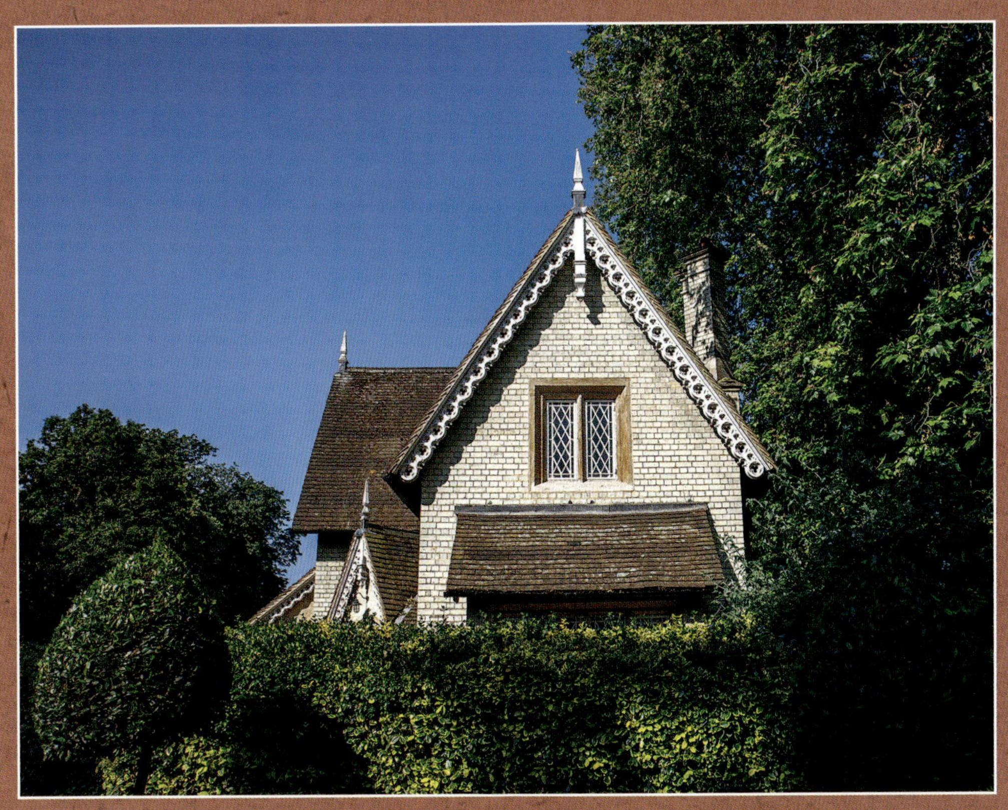

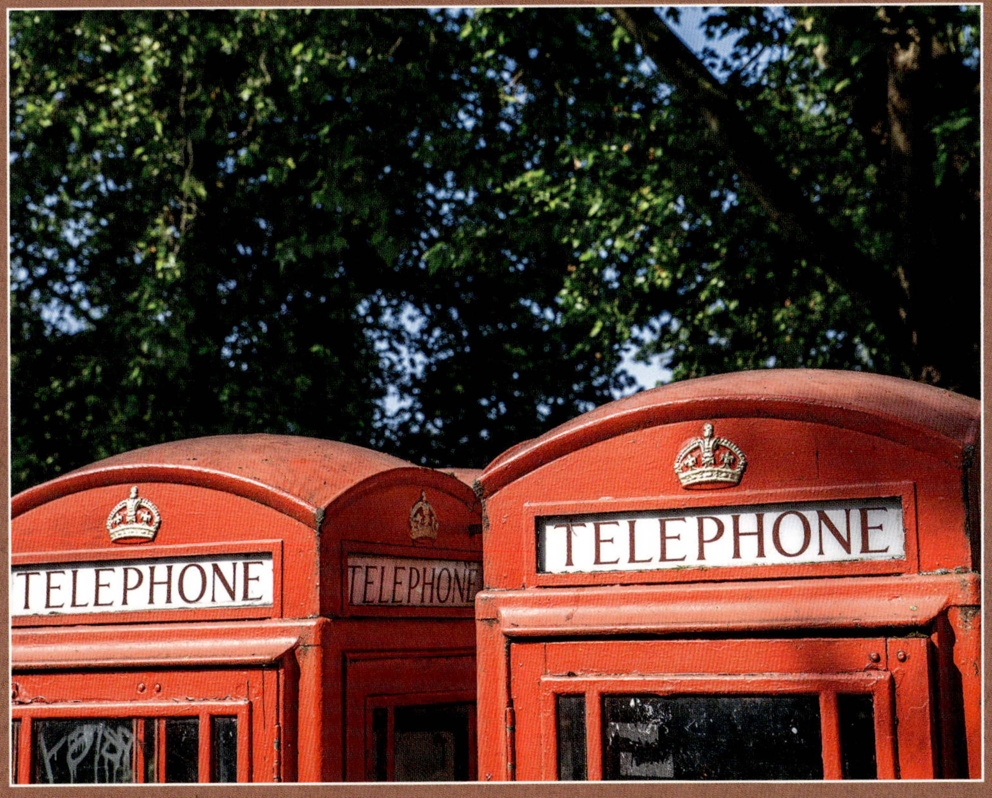
TELEPHONE
TELEPHONE
TELEPHONE

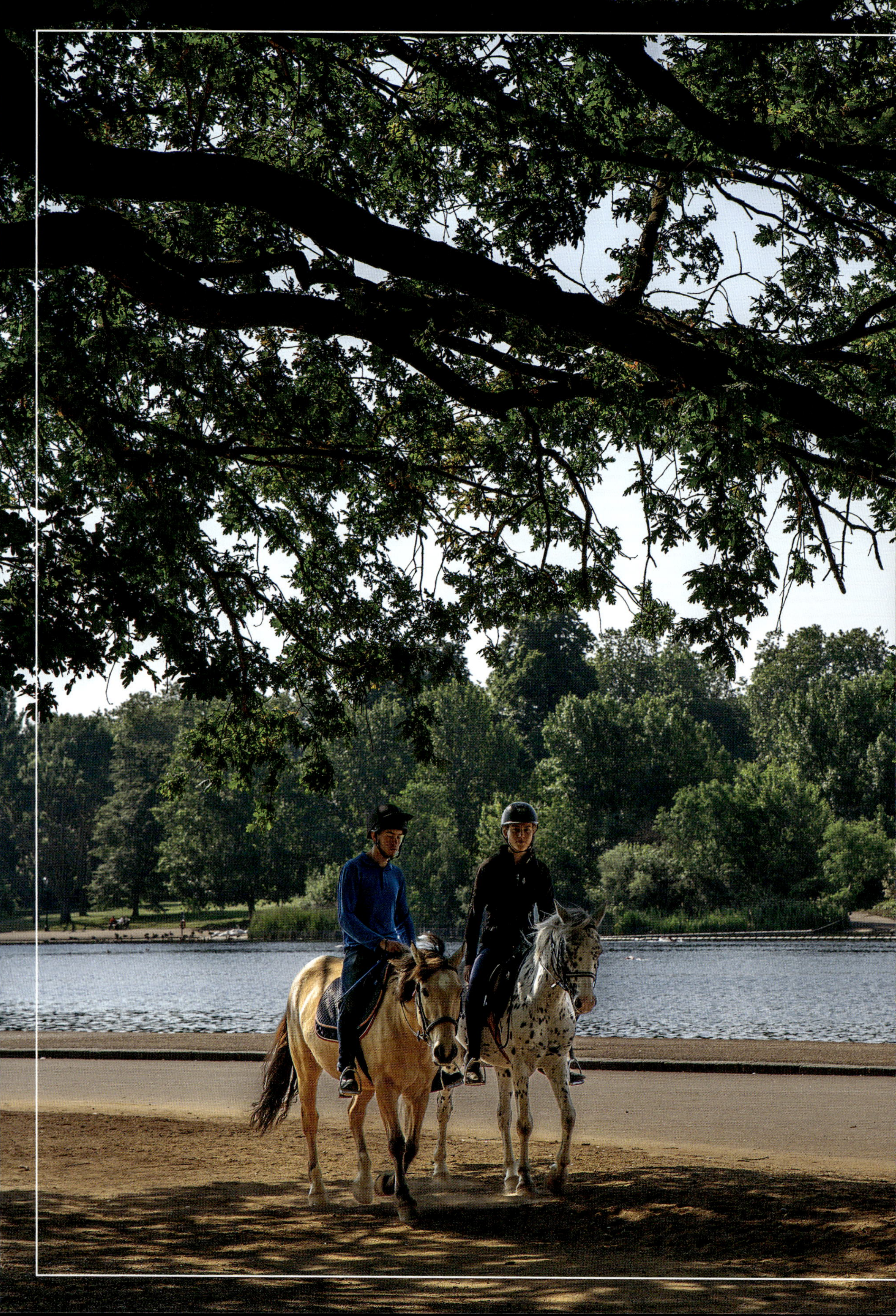

GALLOPING BANDITS PLAGUE LONDON

London in the seventeenth and eighteenth centuries was one of the world's largest, busiest cities. Due to its status as the English capital and a hub of international trade, the city brimmed with affluent residents, royals, celebrities, and business magnates. While this lauded class avoided London's many rundown areas, no degree of wealth or privilege could cocoon them from the highwaymen who roamed London stealing from the rich.[307]

In this way, the highwaymen were continuing a long history of British outlaws, the most famous of whom is Robin Hood.[308] While it is unknown which elements of his twelfth-century legend are true, what is clear is that over the following centuries, countless bandits from the underclasses plagued Britain's wealthy.

Some of these robbers, like Dick Turpin, have been falsely glorified, depicted as noble rebels whose brave heists unsettled the British power structure. Deeper research reveals that, in contrast to Robin Hood's supposed benevolence, their activities were far more cynical. Turpin and his crew, for example, sometimes tortured and murdered strangers simply in the name of profit. Whereas Robin Hood famously robbed from the rich to give to the poor, the highwaymen stole just so they could have more.[309]

Interestingly, this group wasn't the worst of the robbers walking the streets of London. Books and poems give highwaymen a more elevated status among criminals—at least above muggers, burglars, pickpockets, and a robber on foot known as a "footpad." These other lawbreakers often used crude violence to rob small amounts of money from everyday people.

By comparison, highwaymen were much more slick and civil. They worked on horseback, wore masks, picked wealthier victims traveling by carriage, and could afford firearms. This meant they rarely needed to shed blood—only point their barrels in between widened eyes. "Stand and deliver," they would infamously bellow in this moment. Under the threat of a bullet, few travelers refused to hand over their valuables.[310]

BRITAIN'S ROYAL FAMILY TARGETS THE HIGHWAYMEN

So audacious were highwaymen that even the king, William III, felt vulnerable to their ambush. When he and his wife, Mary, were crowned in 1689, they moved into the newly expanded Kensington Palace, which bordered the west of Hyde Park. They frequently needed to pass through this park and the nearby St. James's Park to reach their other home, Whitehall Palace. Security soon became a concern. Since highwaymen often struck under the shadows of darkness, King William III directed three hundred oil lamps to be erected along Rotten Row in 1690. Just like that, Britain got its first illuminated street, the King's Old Road.[311]

One of the few remaining physical traces of this history is a small, round plaque in the middle of Hyde Park giving basic information about the construction of the lamp-lined road. Absent, however, is an explanation that this road needed to be lit to counter the dastardly highwaymen.[312]

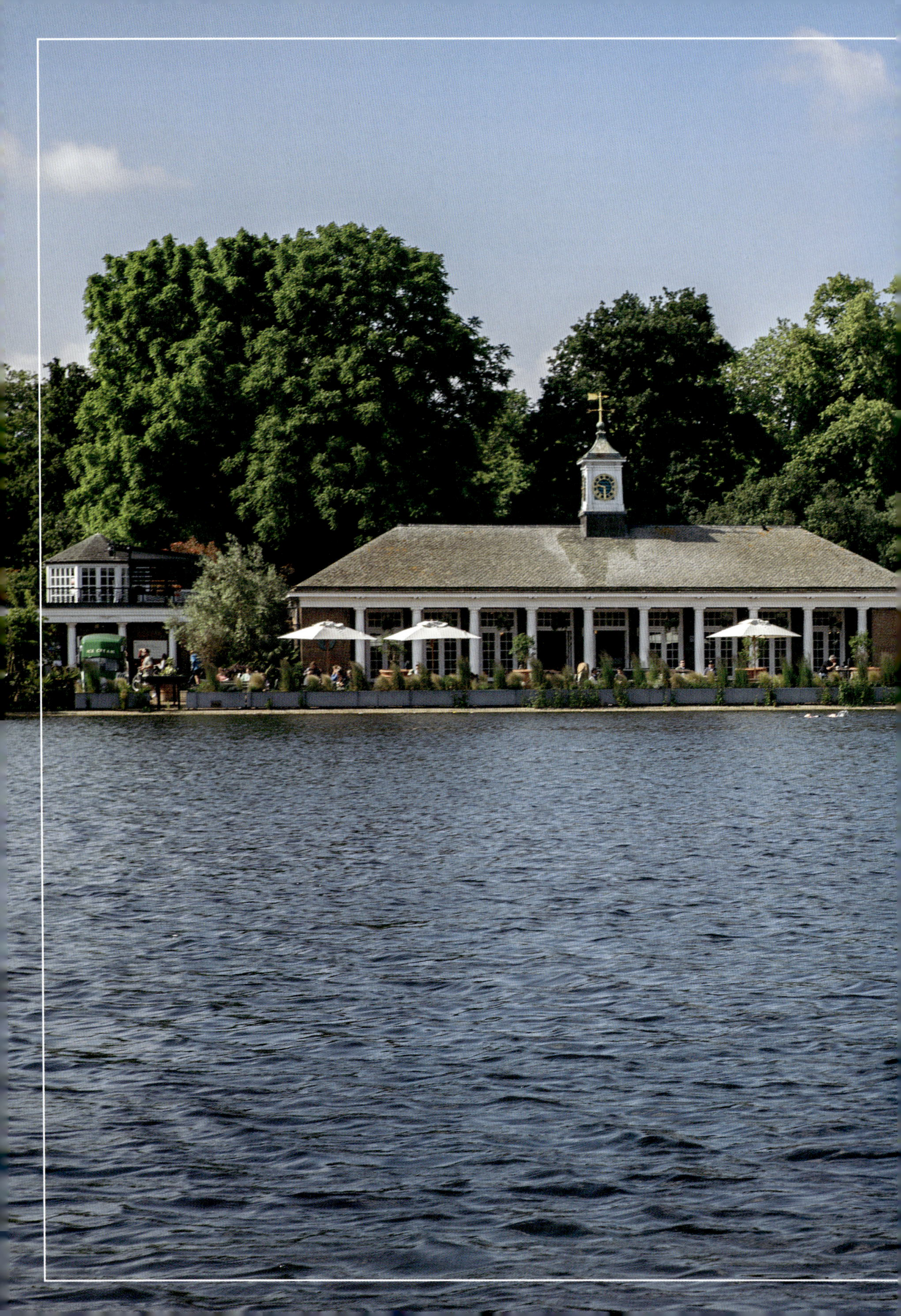

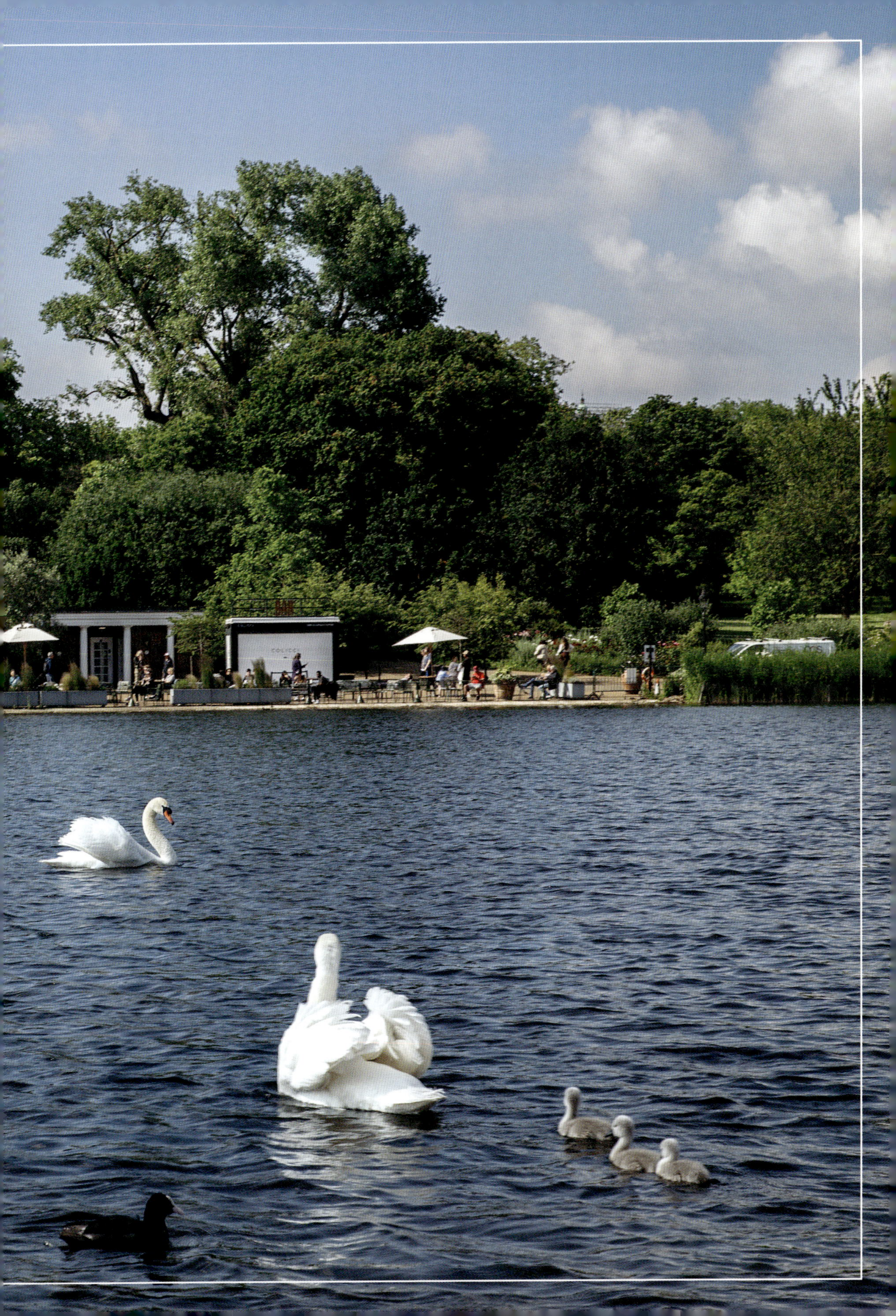

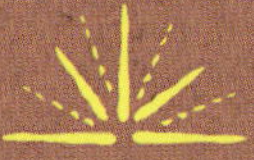

"One is forced to travel, even at noon, as if one was going to battle."[313] This dramatic eighteenth-century quote by an English writer described the extreme danger of visiting Hyde Park due to the threat of its lurking bandits, like James MacLaine.[314]

Handsome and daring, this Scotsman was one of the most prolific highwaymen on record. He brandished a gun on horseback in and around Hyde Park in the 1740s. Stealing loads of loot allowed him to dress like gentry, take overseas holidays, and party with the same rich folk he was likely to rob. Then, one night in 1749, near where people now picnic in Hyde Park, MacLaine entered highwayman folklore.

Horace Walpole sauntered into his crosshairs. Walpole wasn't just rich; he was also the son of Robert Walpole, Britain's first prime minister. The younger Walpole was returning home from Holland House, a mansion in London's Kensington district, when MacLaine and an accomplice materialized from the shadows.

The gloom of Hyde Park was momentarily illuminated by the blast of a pistol. When darkness returned, blood dribbled from Walpole's cheek. MacLaine had skimmed a bullet past his face, a startling act that didn't maim Walpole but did guarantee his cooperation.

Walpole later wrote publicly of this brush with the afterlife. He noted that MacLaine had otherwise been polite, yet no degree of courtesy could let this highwayman escape justice the following year when he robbed a peer. Days after aiming his weapon at England's Earl of Eglington, MacLaine was in handcuffs, his highwayman career over.[315]

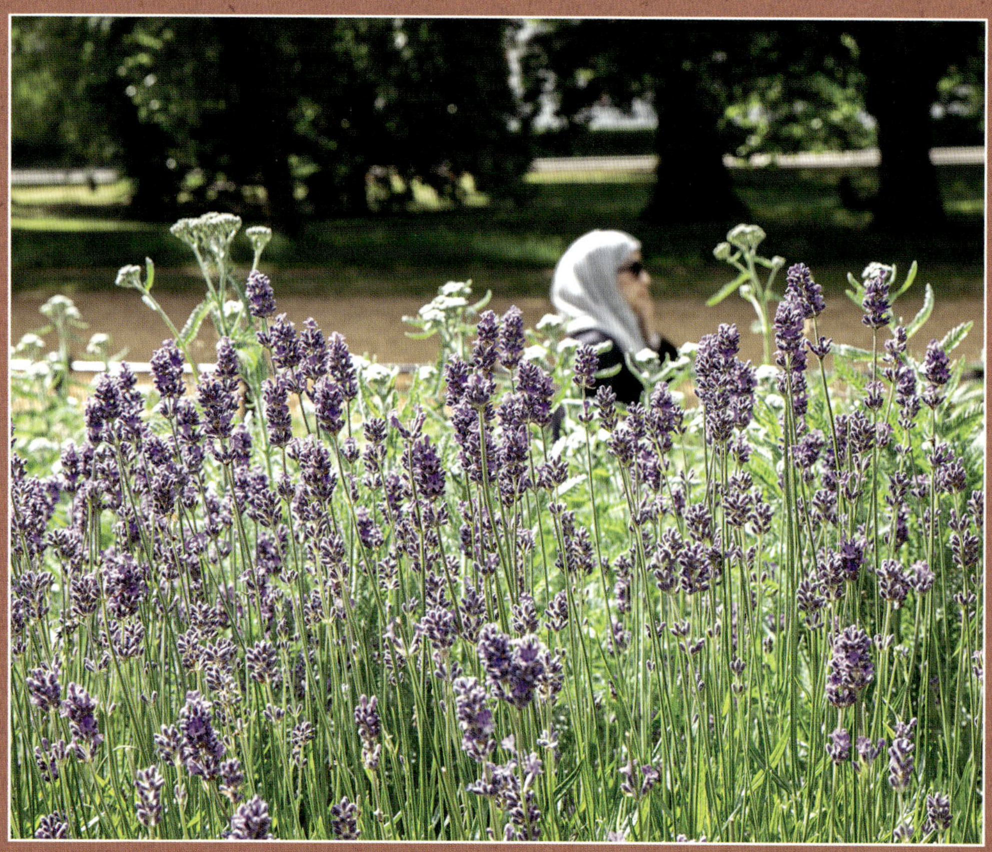

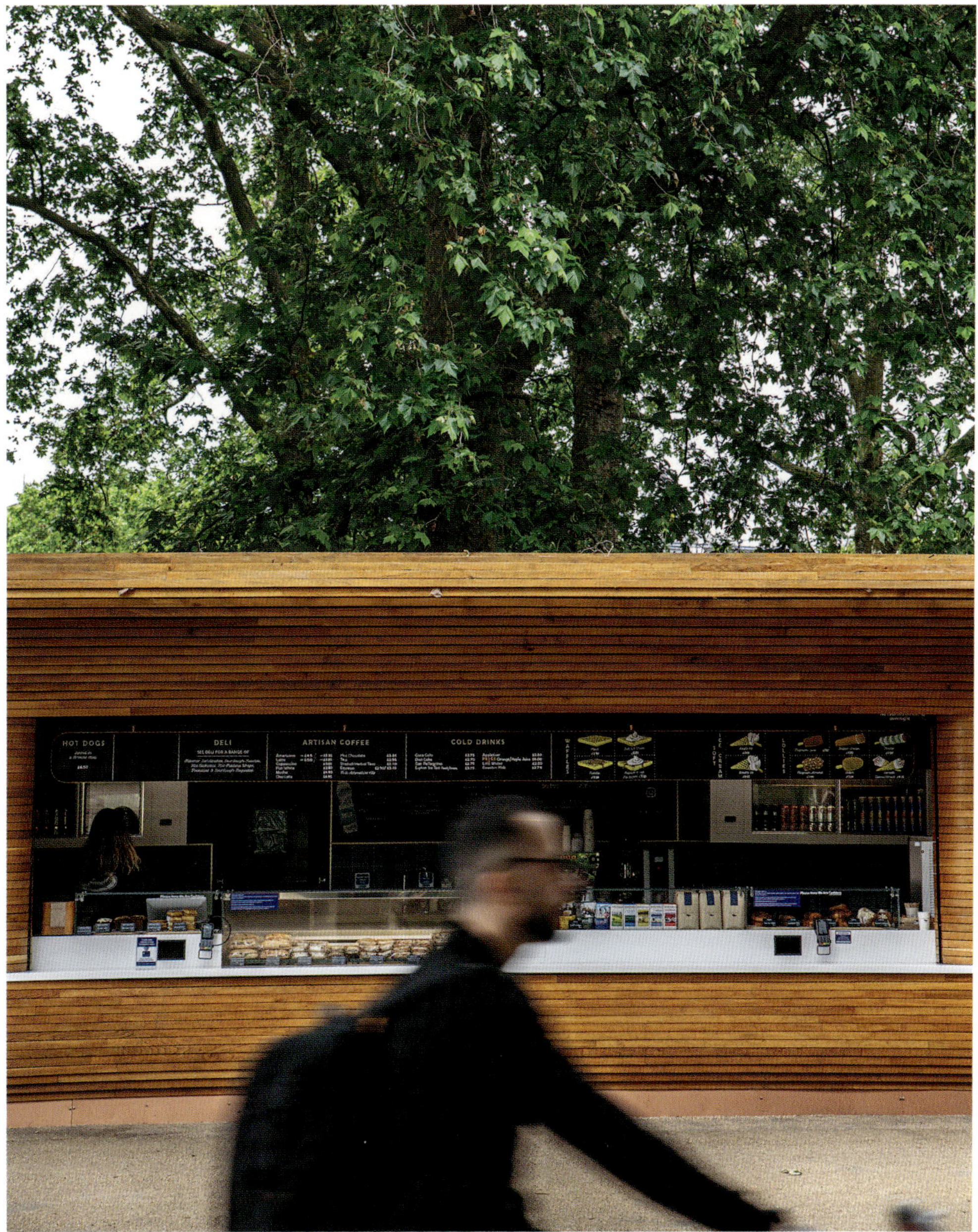

WITH NOWHERE TO HIDE, HIGHWAYMEN DISAPPEAR

With the addition of greater public lighting in Hyde Park and eventually on roads throughout London, highway robbery became a far more perilous career. The increase in lampposts reduced the darkness in which these thieves thrived.

Pulling guns in their favored hunting ground of Hyde Park became increasingly risky, and they were forced into the shadows. They continued to sling pistols and lighten London wallets for another hundred years, until they finally dissolved into obscurity in the early nineteenth century.[316] Being a highwayman was lucrative work while it lasted. And their deeds were so daring and dastardly that they left a permanent imprint on the design of Hyde Park.

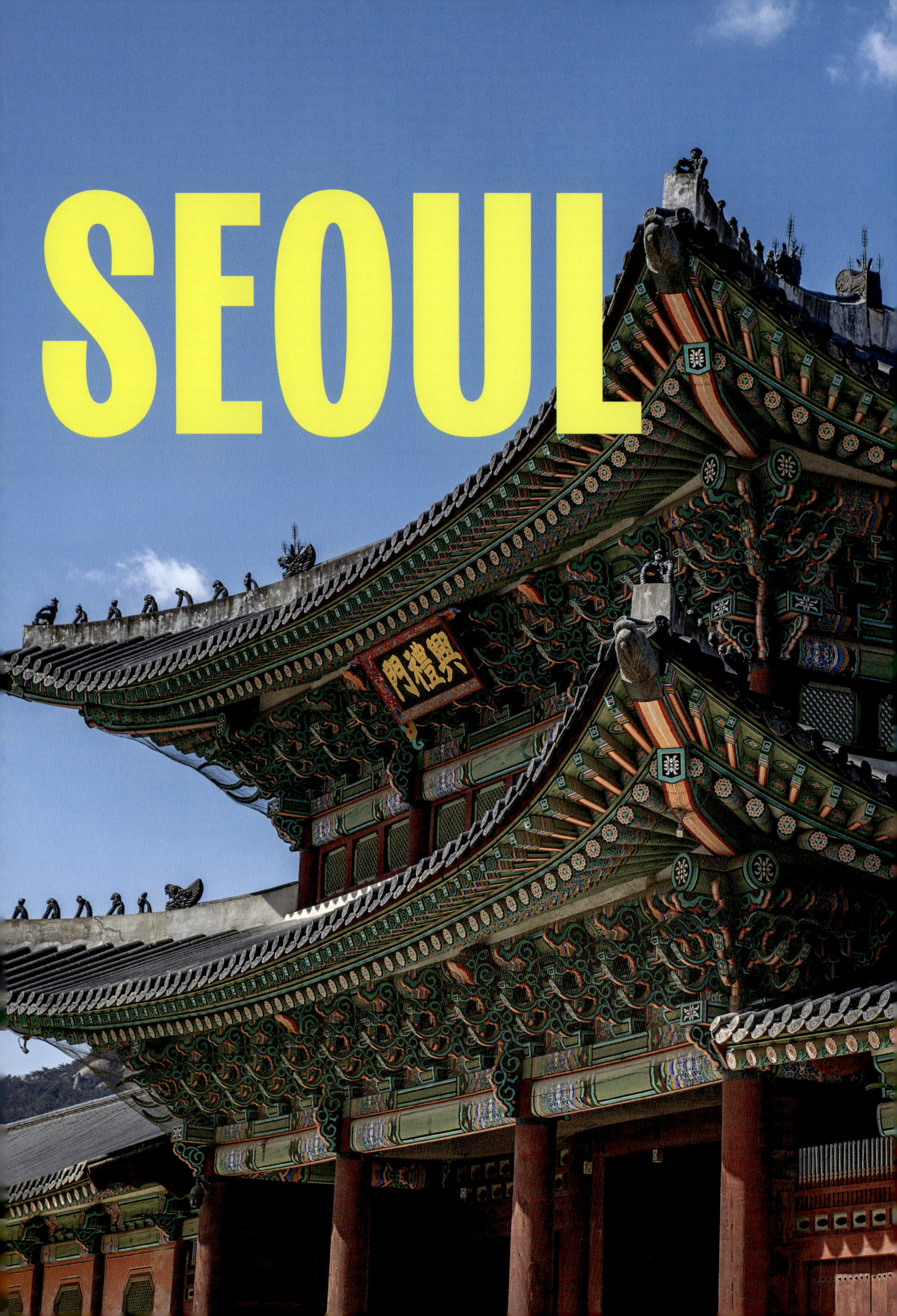
SEOUL
興禮門

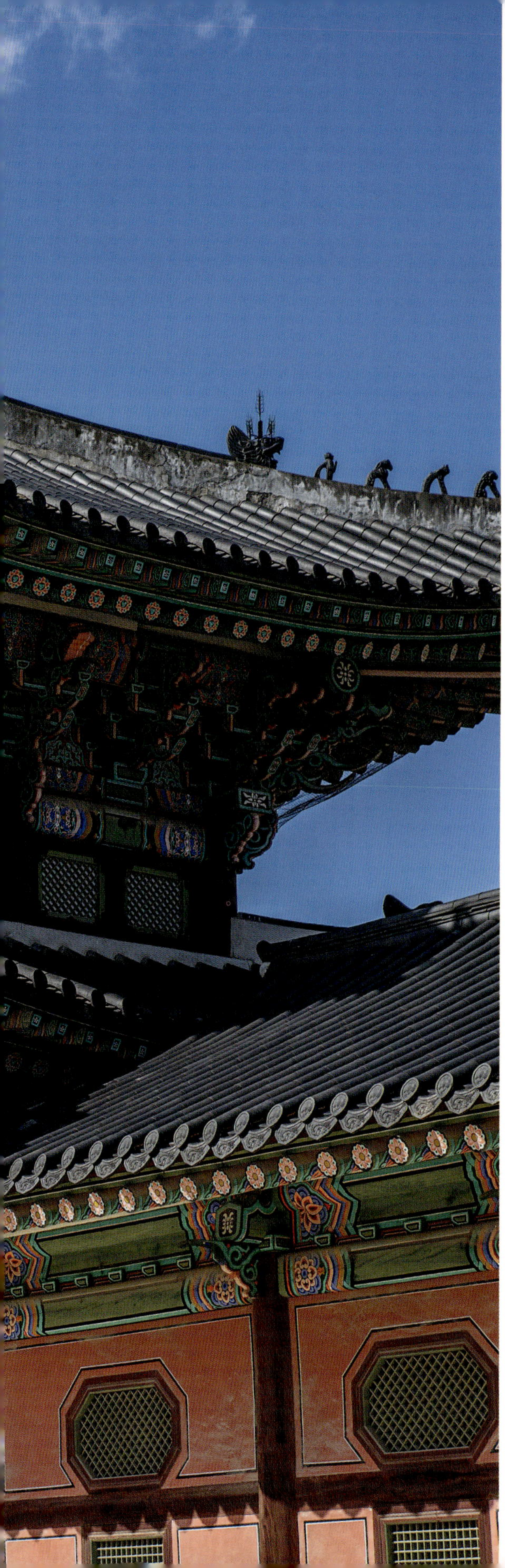

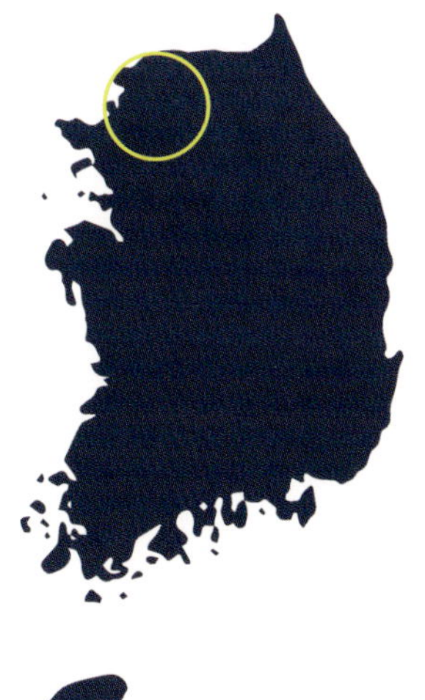

From afar, Gyeongbokgung Palace looms due to its colossal size.[317] But up close, this Seoul landmark hypnotizes with its decoration; the true beauty of this complex is not revealed until visitors get near enough to peer at its cryptic art.

Stare as one might at these vivid embellishments, it is impossible to comprehend the art's significance without knowing the symbolism it contains. Because what the untrained eye spots on the palace's facade, eaves, and pillars is an explosion of colorful patterns—floral forms, geometric motifs, ripe fruits, fluffy clouds, elegant birds.

All of these are, in fact, components of a thirteen-hundred-year-old Korean artistic tradition. Called *dancheong*, this style of decorating employs specific colors, patterns, and images to signifiy a building's history, purpose, and importance. To the discerning eye, these colors and textures hold clues about Gyeongbokgung Palace just waiting to be deciphered.[318]

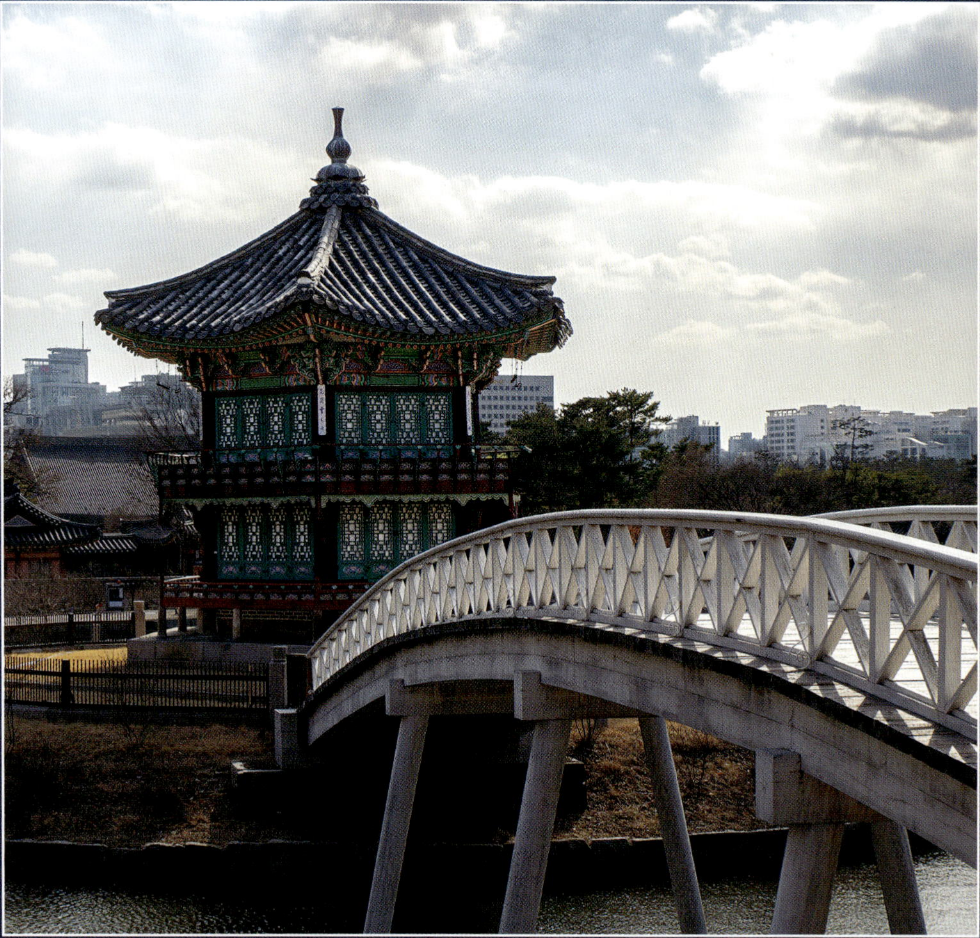

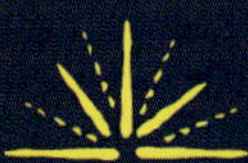

Few cities are as modern as Seoul, a megalopolis of nearly ten million people marked by cutting-edge museums, slick shopping precincts, and a forest of skyscrapers.[319] Yet preserved within this futuristic cityscape is a bedrock of brilliant historic sites, including not one, not two, but five separate royal palaces.[320]

This bounty of imperial marvels is clustered in the downtown area, at the base of Bukhansan National Park, a mountainous, forested expanse that forms Seoul's northern boundary.[321] The easternmost palace is Changgyeonggung Palace, a mid-fifteenth-century structure marked by graceful pavilions, gates, and courtyards. Neighboring Changdeokgung Palace, built in the early fifteenth century, is admired for its sublime classical garden and more than twenty halls and residences.

Further to the west are Deoksugung Palace and Gyeonghuigung Palace. The former is a small compound built as a temporary royal hub in the late sixteenth century, after Seoul's main imperial strongholds were damaged by a Japanese invasion. Gyeonghuigung, too, originated as a backup palace in the seventeenth century, to be used in times of emergency.[322]

Each of these palaces, however, is dwarfed by Gyeongbokgung Palace. Mighty walls one and a half miles long enclose this landmark.[323] Behind those fortifications lie more than a hundred structures: mansions, bridges, pavilions, libraries, temples, banquet rooms, ceremonial halls, and administrative offices.[324]

Entry to Gyeongbokgung is via the three stone arches of Gwanghwamun, the largest of a sequence of hulking gates that form the palace's spine. There, royal soldiers don vibrant gowns, wield long blades, and wave imperial flags all to the percussive rhythm of a Korean gong. Lasting between ten and twenty minutes, these guard changeovers, dispatch ceremonies, and soldier training sessions are captivating re-creations of five-hundred-year-old palace rituals.

In the background, all the while, looms magnificent Geunjeongjeon Hall. The largest of all the palace's buildings, it was here that kings hosted visiting dignitaries and state functions. Seven Korean monarchs were crowned in its dancheong-trimmed interior between the fourteenth and sixteenth centuries. Visitors can peer through its entrances to see the ornate throne on which those kings once sat.

Directly behind Geunjeongjeon are three smaller, yet similarly attractive, halls: Sajeongjeon, Manchunjeon, and Cheonchujeon. Each of these buildings also showcases dazzling dancheong. Walking north, past five more halls and pavilions, leads to tranquil Hyangwonji Lake. Marooned in this petite body of water is a pretty, two-story pagoda, Hyangwongjeong Pavilion, accessible by a narrow bridge. Bukhansan Mountain's looming presence adds to this natural splendor. Here, at the rear of the Gyeongbokgung complex, is one of two terrific museums on the palace grounds.[325]

Via text, maps, and artifacts, the National Palace Museum of Korea explains that Gyeongbokgung was built in the 1390s, constructed as a grand monument to the power of Korea's burgeoning Joseon Dynasty (1392–1910). After warrior Yi Seong-Gye toppled the long-standing Goryeo Dynasty (918–1392), he commissioned the building of a new palace, the largest imperial complex in Korean history. Since then, Gyeongbokgung has been damaged and restored several times.[326]

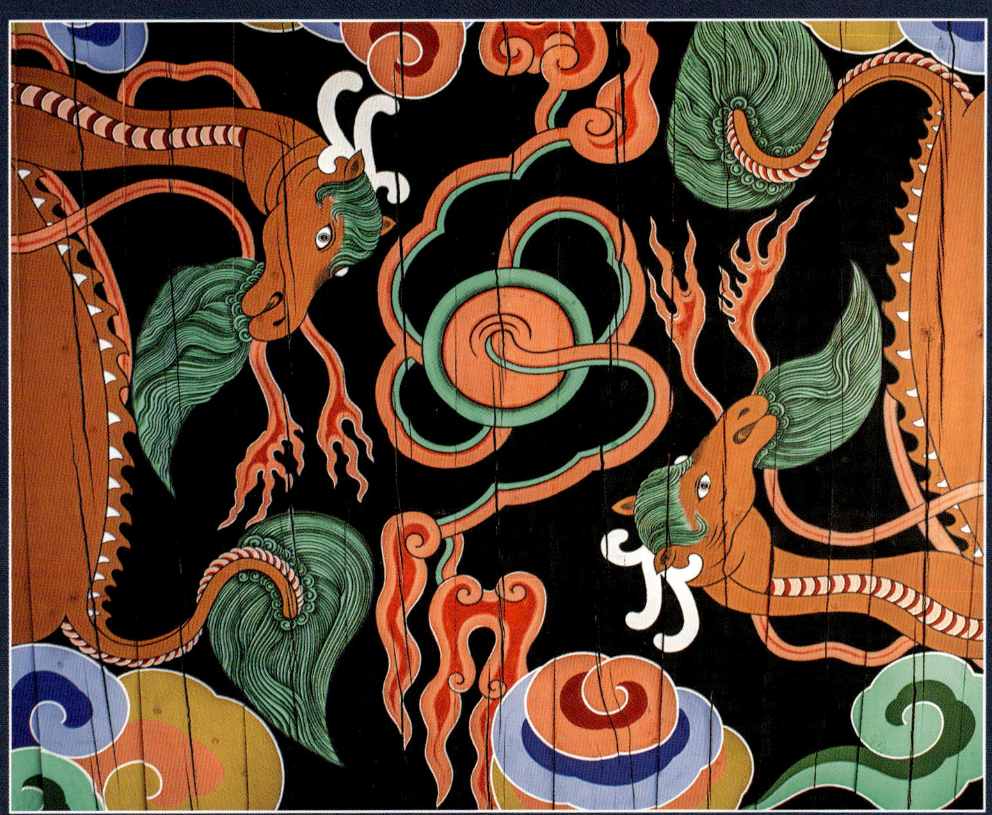

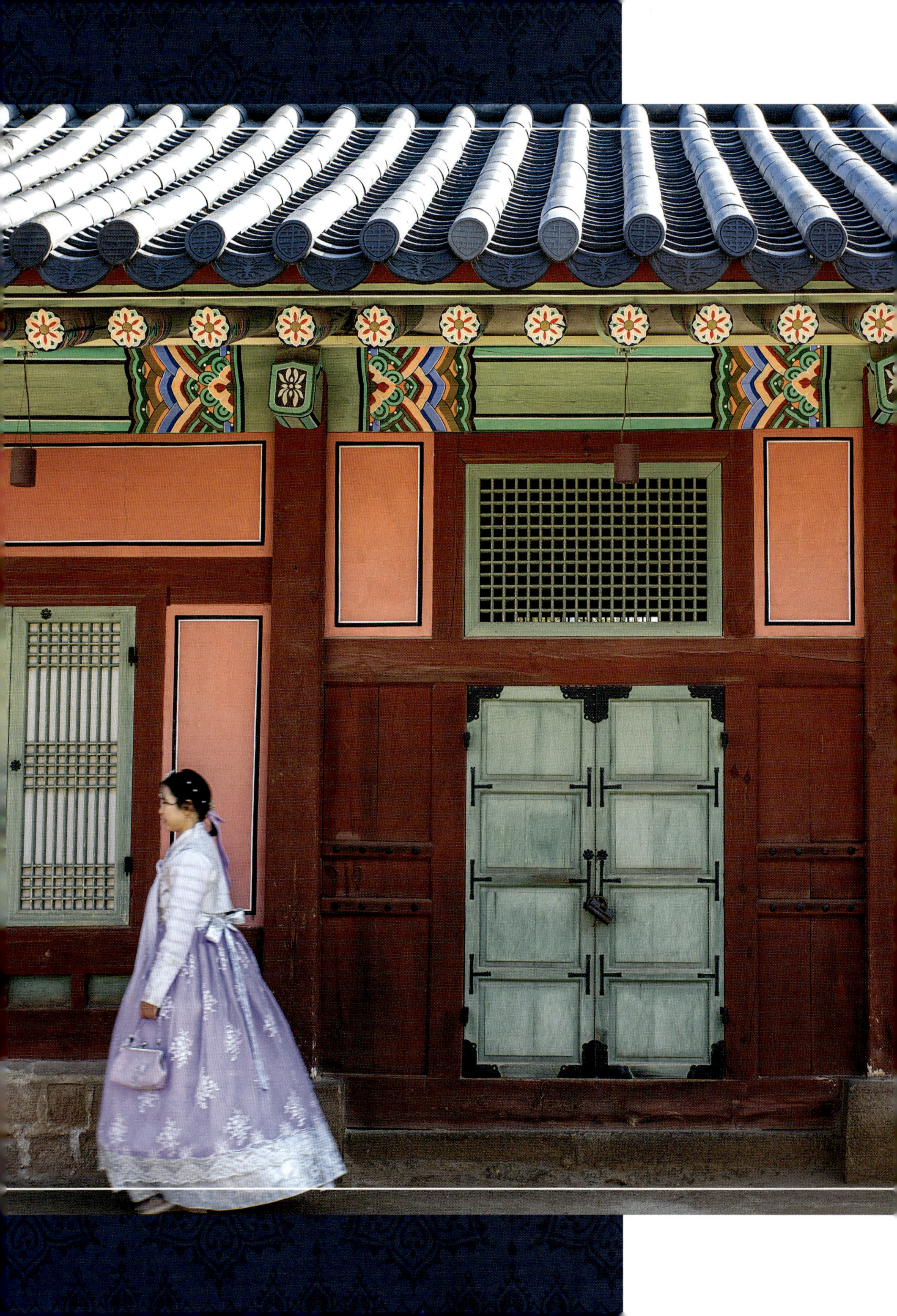

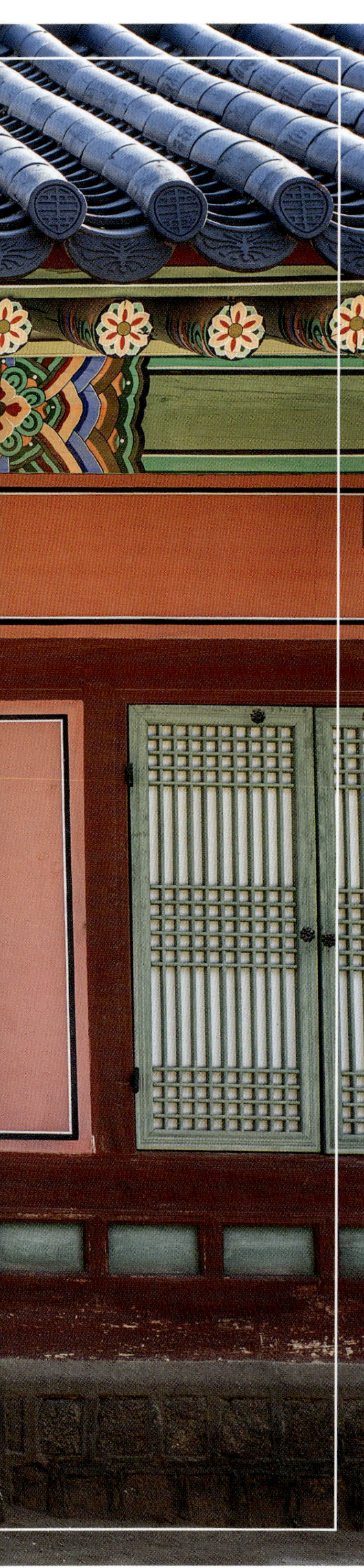

ORIGINS OF DANCHEONG

Dancheong didn't originate here, at Gyeongbokgung Palace. Researchers have found it within weathered murals and lacquerwork of temples from Korea's Three Kingdoms Period (57 BC–AD 668). Dancheong's full vibrancy was reached much later, during the Joseon Dynasty (1392–1910), when this design tradition sprawled to encompass four varied styles, three of which are present at the Gyeongbokgung Palace.

Each style is traditionally reserved for different parts of a building. The *morucho* form of dancheong graces the eaves and support beams at Gyeongbokgung Palace. Feathers, bubbles, pomegranates, water lilies, and green flowers are key motifs of this variety.

Then there's *dandongmui*, the simplest dancheong, consisting of singular images of trees, blossoms, or beasts. And finally, there's the swirling *bidanmunui* form of dancheong. Walls and ceilings within the palace are coated in dozens, or even hundreds, of bidanmunui's geometric and floral patterns. At a distance, the technique creates a soothing repetition. Close proximity turns them mesmeric, almost like staring at a "trick of the eye" painting.[327]

THE CODE OF DANCHEONG

Just one of Gyeongbokgung's dancheong panels can preoccupy an intrigued visitor. Ten minutes could pass as they are entranced by its tangle of acute angles, swirling curves, and concentric patterns.

But dancheong is much more than just a method for painting key Korean buildings. Its colors, motifs, and compositions carefully correspond to the structure's age, function, and importance. Some dancheong also represent influential Korean philosophies. Essentially, dancheong is an artistic code, which can be interpreted by curious onlookers.[328]

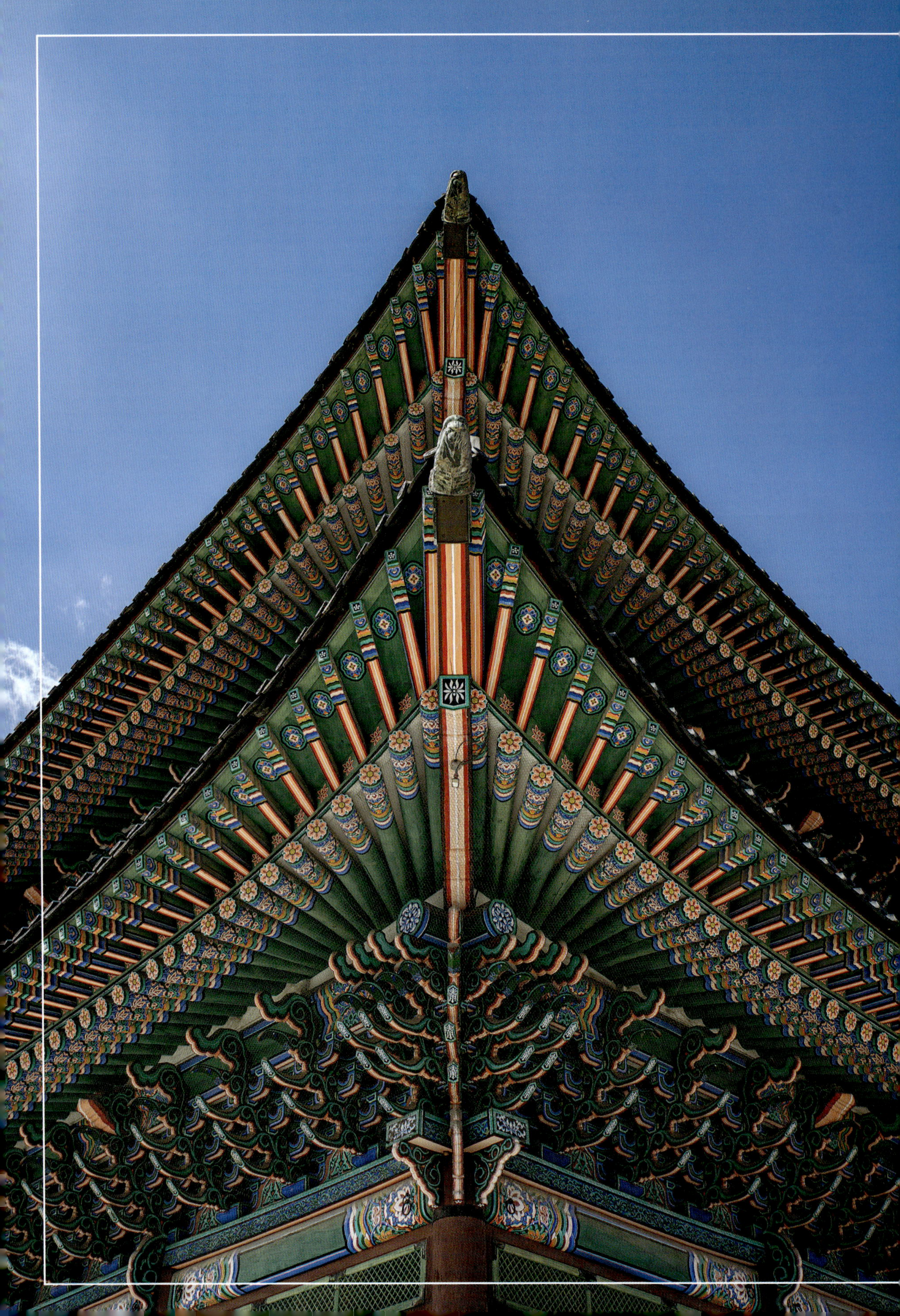

HOW DANCHEONG EXPLAINS A BUILDING

Dancheong designs dominated by blue, green, red, and white indicate that a building was decorated during Korea's Goryeo period. Meanwhile, liberal use of yellow, aqua, pink, maroon, and orange is the calling card of the subsequent Joseon Dynasty. Simply by noting Gyeongbokgung's palette, then, it becomes evident the building was erected during the latter era.[329]

Dancheong elements also underline the purpose of a building. If a structure within Gyeongbokgung features a dragon or phoenix, that means it was formerly a royal abode or throne hall, because those creatures were used to represent the king's supreme authority.[330] They can be seen depicted within Geunjeongjeon Hall and the king's residence, called Gangnyeongjeon.

Meanwhile, visitors can identify the palace's spiritual sites by looking for their painted lotus motifs. This long-stemmed pink-and-white blossom is one of Korea's key symbols of Buddhism.[331] It graces the tranquil lakeside Gyeonghoeru Pavilion, which was once a popular spot for meditation.[332]

DANCHEONG'S SPIRITUAL SYMBOLISM

Near Gyeongbokgung's main entrance are dancheong designs that hint at one of South Korea's key philosophies. These clouds and dragons are painted on Geonchunmun Gate in five colors—blue, red, yellow, white, and black.

Dancheong uses this specific palette to honor Korea's ancient Five Element Theory. Those hues represent the natural elements of wood, fire, water, metal, and earth. According to this theory, those elements must always be kept in harmony to ensure peace within Korean society.[333]

This philosophy is so important to Koreans that Seoul was specifically laid out between mountains and a river to balance the energy of all these elements.[334] As described by Korea's Ministry of Culture, dancheong is "not only a reflection of the Buddhist heaven, but also an attempt to bring the harmony and unity of the cosmos to earth for easy access by humans."[335] What vast ambition to channel into the painting of a structure.

ARTISTIC CHOICES OF DANCHEONG

Beyond their symbolism, dancheong designs also aim to harness natural light. Structural features that are regularly bathed in sun, like columns and facades, were painted in deep hues of red. However, surfaces that received less light, such as ceilings and eaves, featured lighter greens and blues so they still stood out.[336]

Dancheong evolved further during the subsequent Joseon Dynasty, when its traditional palette of black, white, red, blue, and yellow were complemented by many new shades. This explains why some beams within Gyeongbokgung dance with a dozen different colors.[337]

Each such surface is maintained by teams of dancheong artisans. Following in the creative wake of their ancestors, these talented painters ensure that Gyeongbokgung remains fresh and vivid. Collectively, they are entrusted with the preservation of a millennia-old code—one that delights tourists each day, while waiting for them to notice its true character.[338]

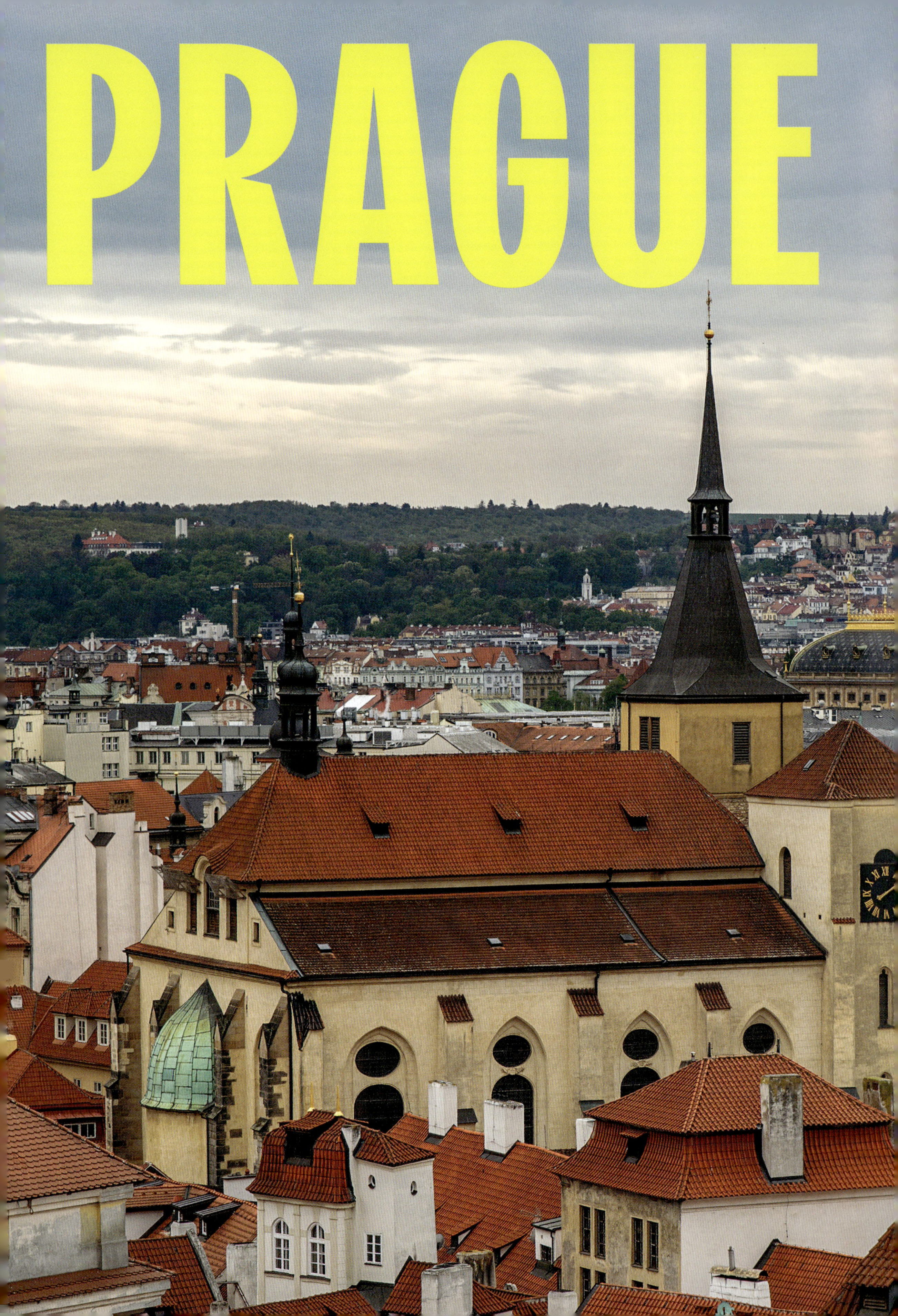
PRAGUE

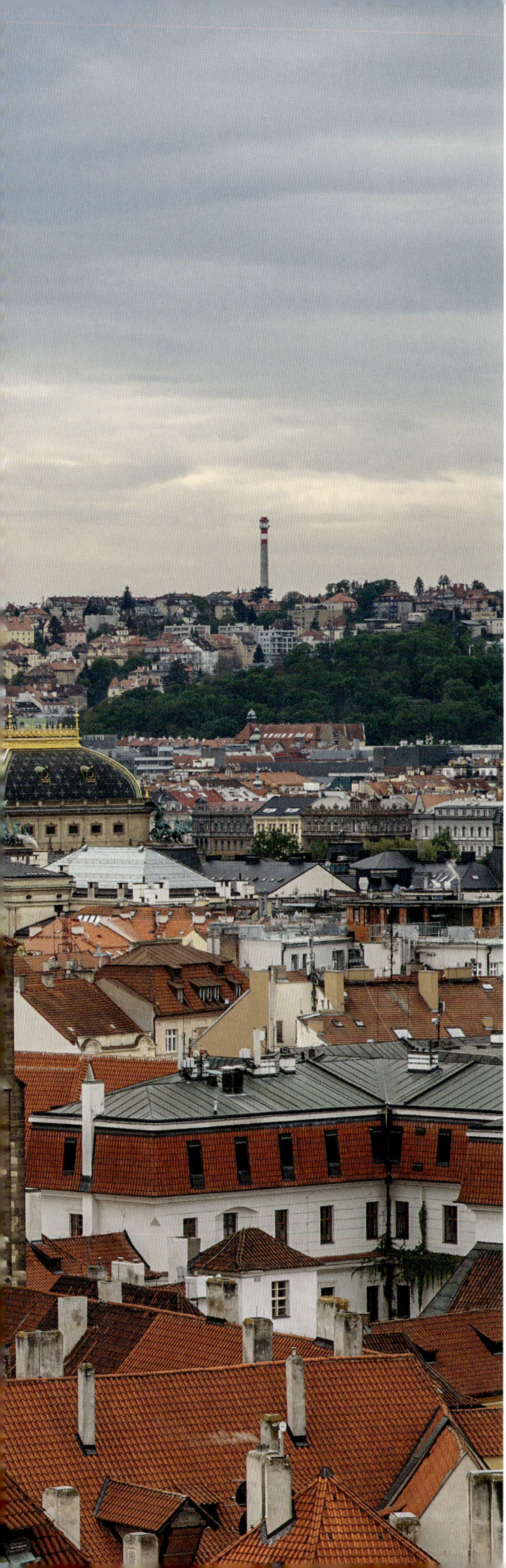

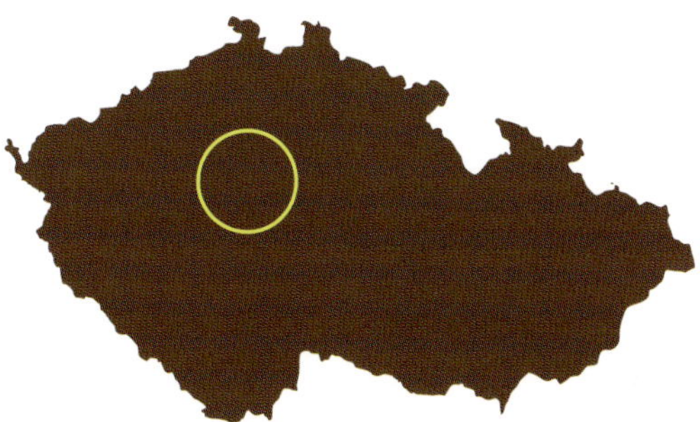

The priest had no head, the Pope had three faces, and while the brothels were ablaze, the judge tried to fly. If that sentence is confusing, imagine living in the reality of this exact chaos that engulfed fifteenth-century Prague. Among the marks time has left on the city's Old Town Hall is damage suffered during that period of bedlam.[339, 340]

Soaring above the hall, an iconic astronomical clock anchors Prague's Staré Město historic quarter. This ticking jewel is a triumph of Gothic architecture, attracting crowds who stand beneath it each day to witness the clock's hourly show. Two trapdoors part, just above the clock's face, to reveal sculptures of the twelve apostles of Jesus. These figures stand alongside kitschier depictions of a skeleton tugging a string, a man shaking a bag of money, and a vain figure staring in a mirror.

In reality, it's an underwhelming show, lasting less than a minute.[341] All the while, tourists stare at a clock that bears scars revealing a tumultuous tale. Few realize that the original design of this structure is forever lost after being vandalized during bloody religious revolts.[342]

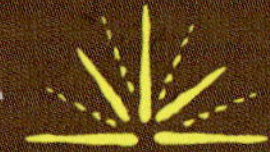

Some of the Czech Republic's finest Gothic structures flank Old Town Square.[343] Standing tall in its center is a statue of Jan Hus, a priest central to the area's medieval religious wars. Tourists often sit on its base to rest, absorb their surroundings, and plan their next move.[344]

Myriad appealing sites ring this square. Behind the delicate stuccowork and evocative sculptures of Kinský Palace awaits the impressive art collection of the National Gallery Prague.[345] Creativity also flows from its next-door neighbor, Prague City Gallery, which specializes in contemporary works.[346]

On either side of the square are two alluring houses of worship. To the west is the graceful eighteenth-century Baroque gem, St. Nicholas Church, with its gilded walls and massive chandelier.[347] Opposite that is the more brutish figure of Church of Our Lady before Týn, a colossal Gothic structure built in the fourteenth century, with a pair of 260-foot-tall bell towers.[348]

The Old Town Hall, meanwhile, is open to those who wish to ascend its tower to see inside the huge timepiece. This cramped, historic building is not equipped to handle many visitors at one time. That is especially true on the ascent to its viewing platform, nearly two hundred feet above street level. A narrow walkway hugs the tower's weathered stone walls and winds up and around. It terminates at a two-hundred-foot-high lookout platform that reveals 360-degree views across Prague's charming cityscape to the green hills and forests that encircle it.

On lower levels, the Hall includes the Chapel of the Virgin Mary, a petite place of worship bathed in kaleidoscopic light filtered through brilliant stained glass windows. Further Gothic glory is showcased in this building's fifteenth-century Old Council Halls.[349] Visitors leave the Old Town Hall with a strong impression of its architectural charm but glean little of its bloody history.

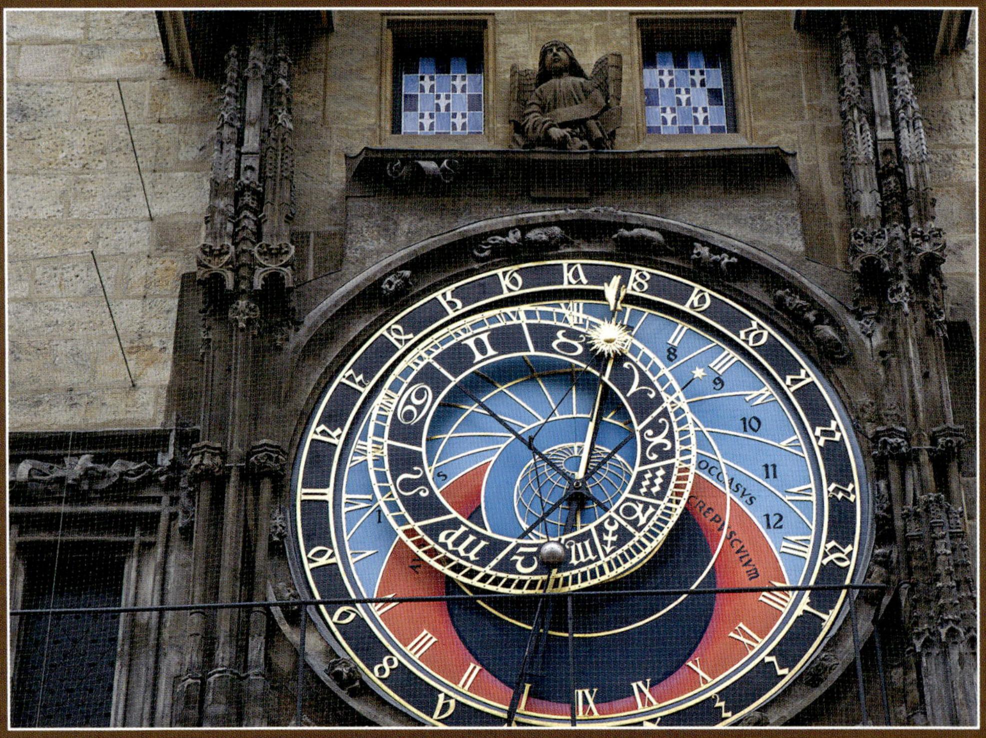

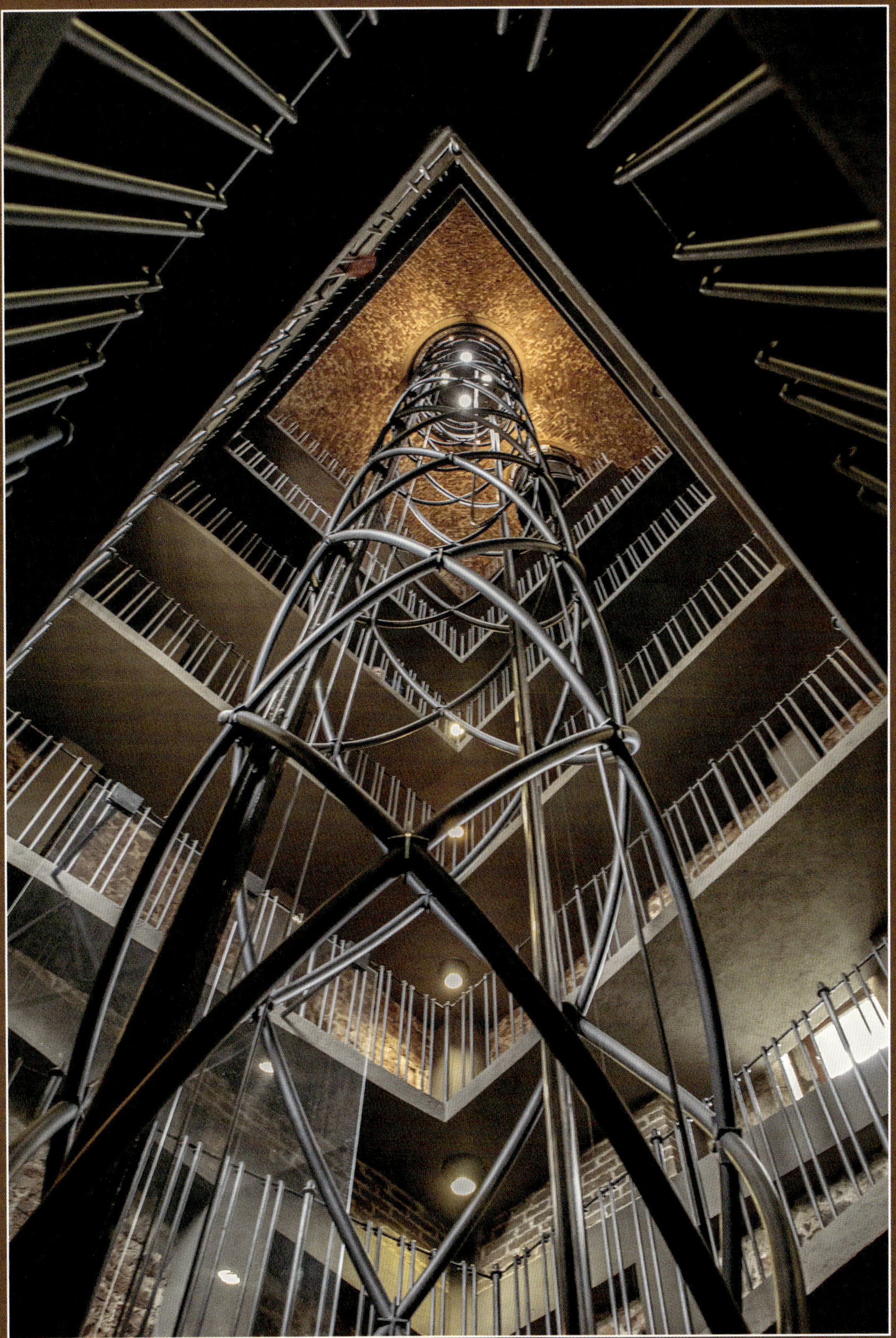

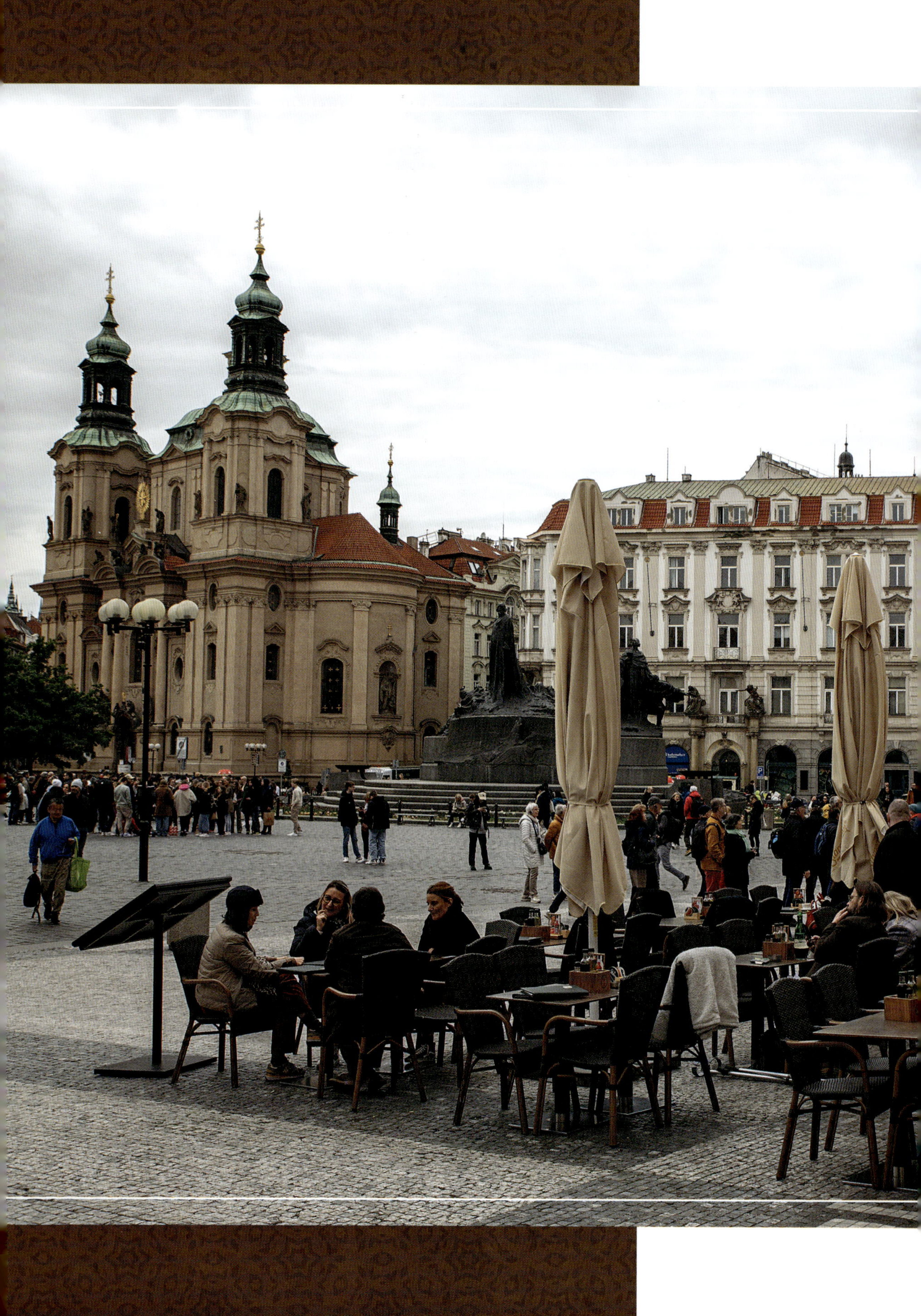

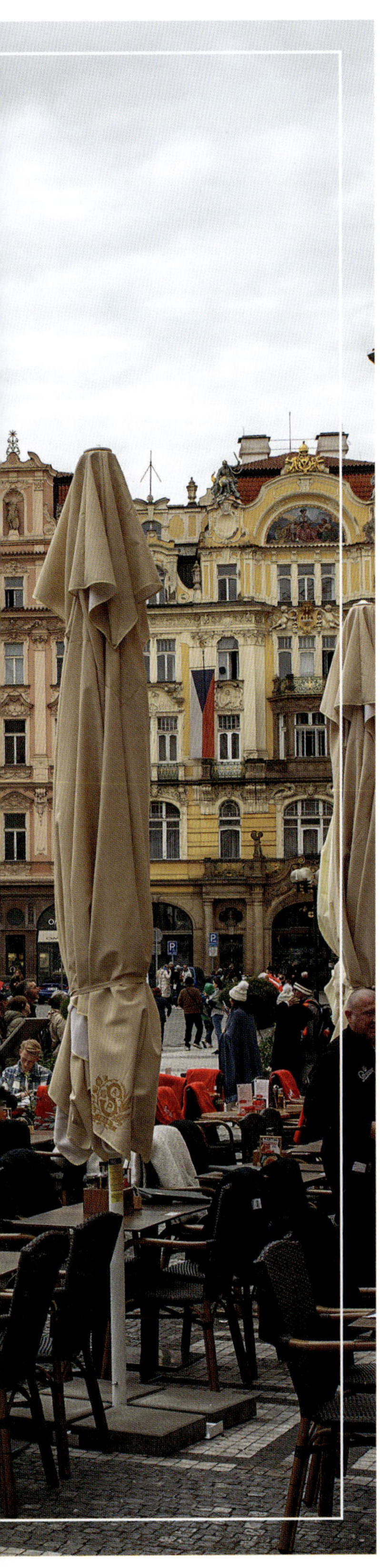

DIVISION IN THE CATHOLIC CHURCH

Three rival popes were central to the hall's violent backstory. Whereas our lived experience is of a singular elected head of the Catholic Church, the late 1300s and early 1400s were comparative mayhem.

Called the Western Schism, this period of Catholic unrest began with the 1378 election of Pope Urban VI. This Italian rose to power with the backing of cardinals from his country. But Urban VI's strict leadership style alienated the French cardinals, who soon abandoned their posts in Rome and returned to France to vote for their own pope: Swiss-born Clement VII.

Even after these two leaders passed away, the Catholic Church remained splintered between two competing popes: one based in Rome, the other in France. The pope who ruled from Rome was commonly acknowledged by England, Hungary, Poland, and the Holy Roman Empire—which included the Czech Republic, then known as Bohemia. Meanwhile, the pope in France typically had the backing of France, Portugal, Scotland, and kingdoms within Spain. Essentially the Church had split in two all across Europe.[350]

BOLD PREACHER IGNITES PRAGUE

Meanwhile, back in Prague, a brazen Czech preacher named Jan Hus was adding fuel to this religious inferno. During his provocative sermons, Hus scolded the Catholic Church. He criticized the warring between its factions, which Hus believed were tarnishing the Church's reputation. Then he targeted its leaders, who he claimed were often greedy and immoral.[351]

Hus strongly supported the 1409 Council of Pisa, a meeting designed to end the Western Schism by deposing the competing popes and voting in a new, singular leader—the Greek Alexander V. But the council failed, as the incumbent popes refused to step aside.[352]

So Europe suddenly had three popes. Hus initially backed Alexander V. His support backfired when the new pope banned preaching in private chapels, which meant Hus was no longer permitted to give his controversial sermons. But Hus ignored Alexander V's order. As a result, he was arrested by Church officials in 1414 and, for the threats he posed to the Church, was burned at the stake the next year.[353]

PREACHER EXECUTION SPARKS A REVOLUTION

Hus's slaying infuriated his army of followers. In response, they launched the Hussite Revolution, a series of civil wars that Hus's disciples waged against Church officials for more than a decade.[354]

At the forefront of this movement was another fiery Hussite leader, Jan Želivský.[355] Like Hus, Želivský also defied the Catholic Church by repeating incendiary criticisms of its hierarchy. In 1419, Želivský's fanatical preaching motivated a gang of Hussites to run amok through Prague. These enraged men ransacked Catholic churches, set brothels alight, and even threw seven Prague city officials, including a judge, from the tower of New Town Hall. The Hussites continued to wreak violent havoc in Prague for years thereafter.[356]

By 1422, Želivský had become such a threat to public order that Prague's Old Town councillors laid a trap. They invited him to a meeting at the Old Town Hall, where he believed he'd get to speak about religious reform. However, soon after Želiviský arrived, he was silenced permanently. The councillors lopped off his head, directly beneath that hall's splendid astronomical clock.

Enraged, the Hussites repeatedly besieged the Old Town Hall.[357] In the process, they caused extensive damage to the astronomical clock, destroying many of its original Gothic sculptures, which had been handcrafted by German-Bohemian architect Petr Parléř.

Of Parléř's design flourishes, the only one that remains is a gray stone angel, which sits just above the clockface. This heavenly figure watched passively as the Hussite Revolution embroiled Prague for another twelve years after Želivský's beheading.

It wasn't until later in the fifteenth century that the scars inflicted on the clock were healed. While the Hussite attacks erased most of Parléř's original artworks, these clock features were replaced by fresh Gothic-style stonework. So what people now see when they visit this Prague landmark is a masterpiece forever altered by a religious revolution.[358]

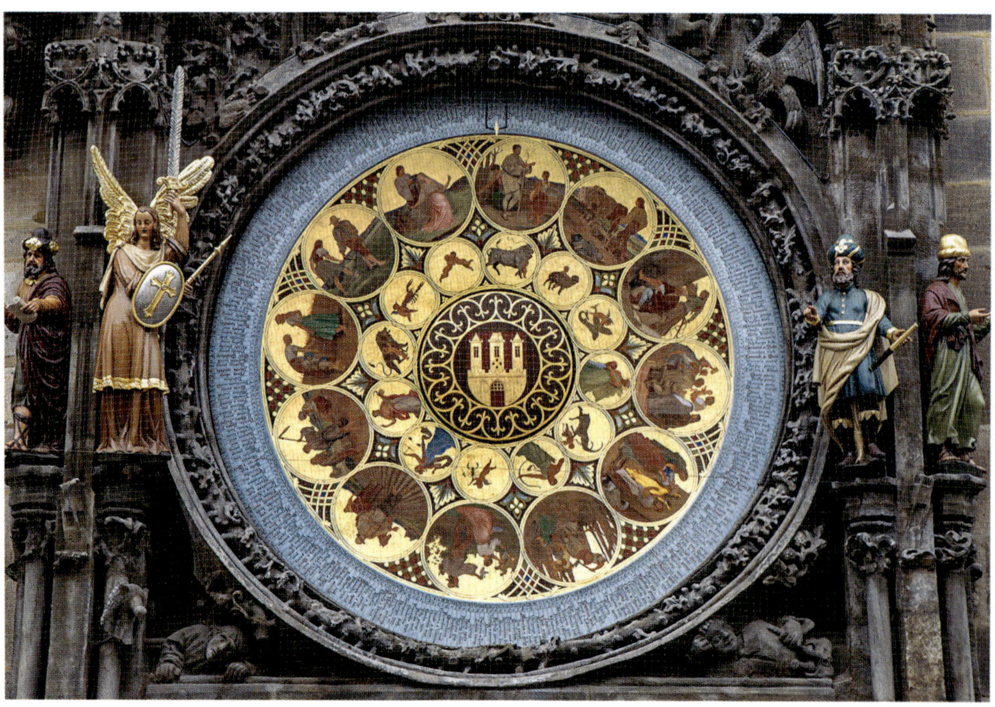

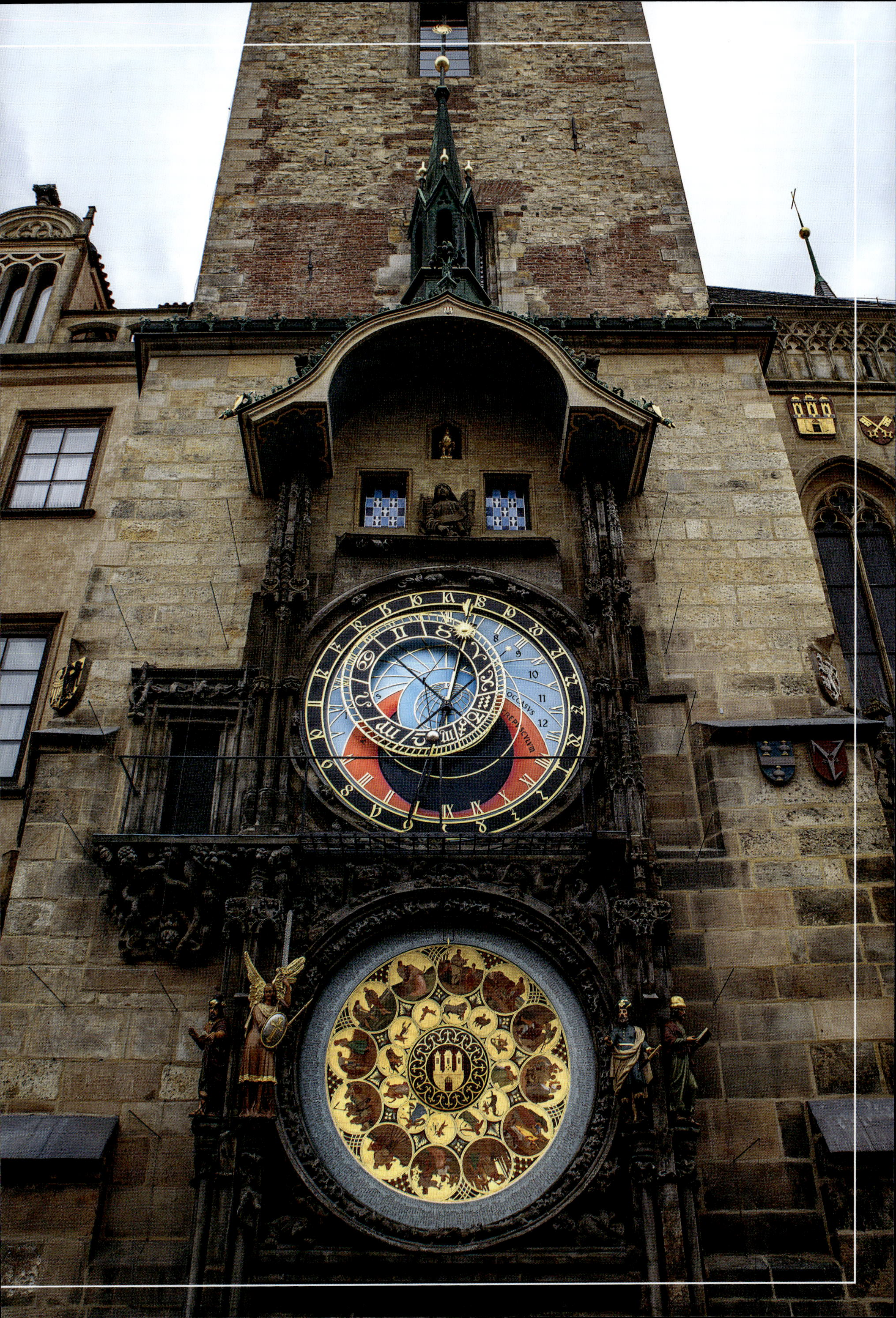
OCCASUS

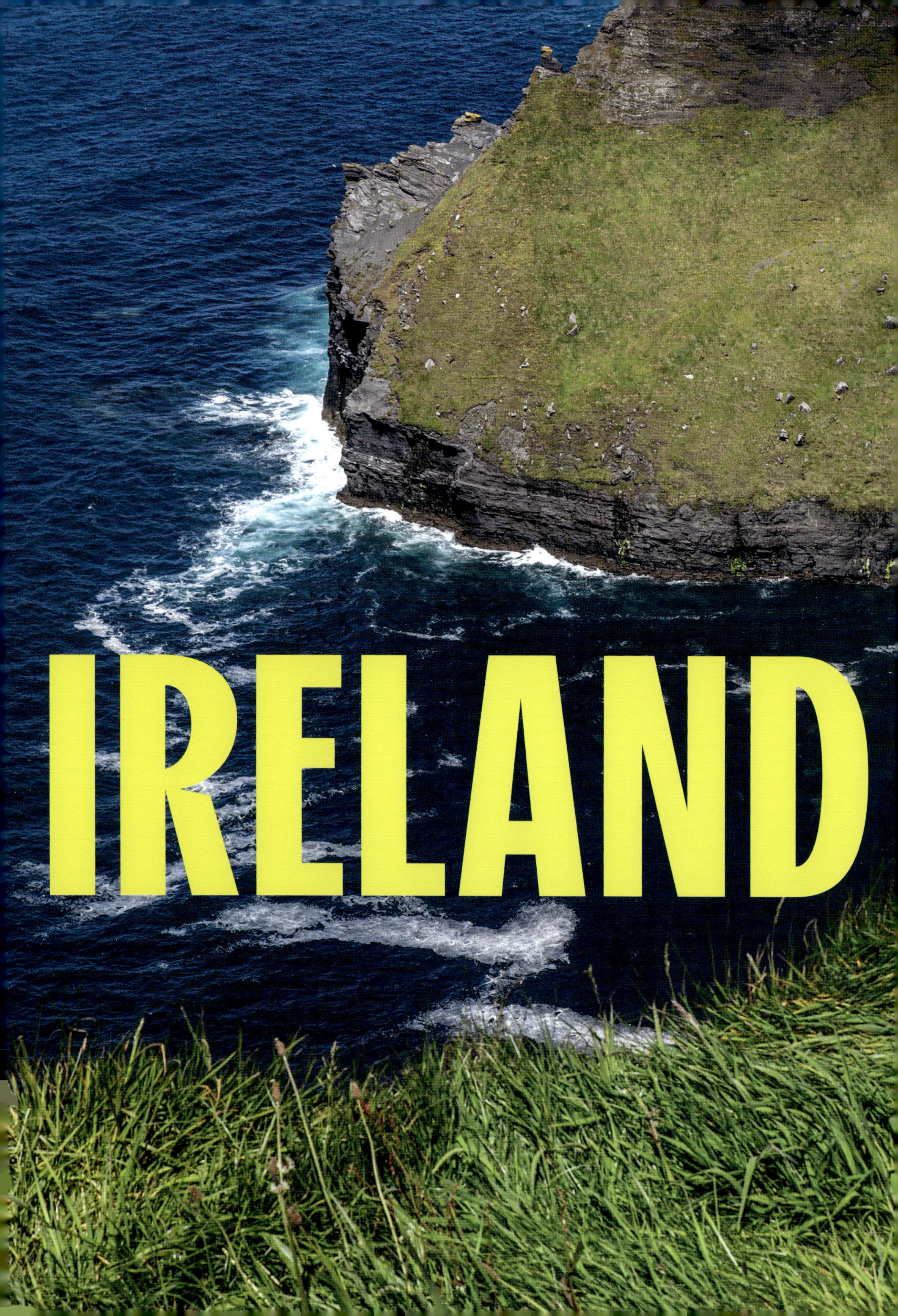
IRELAND

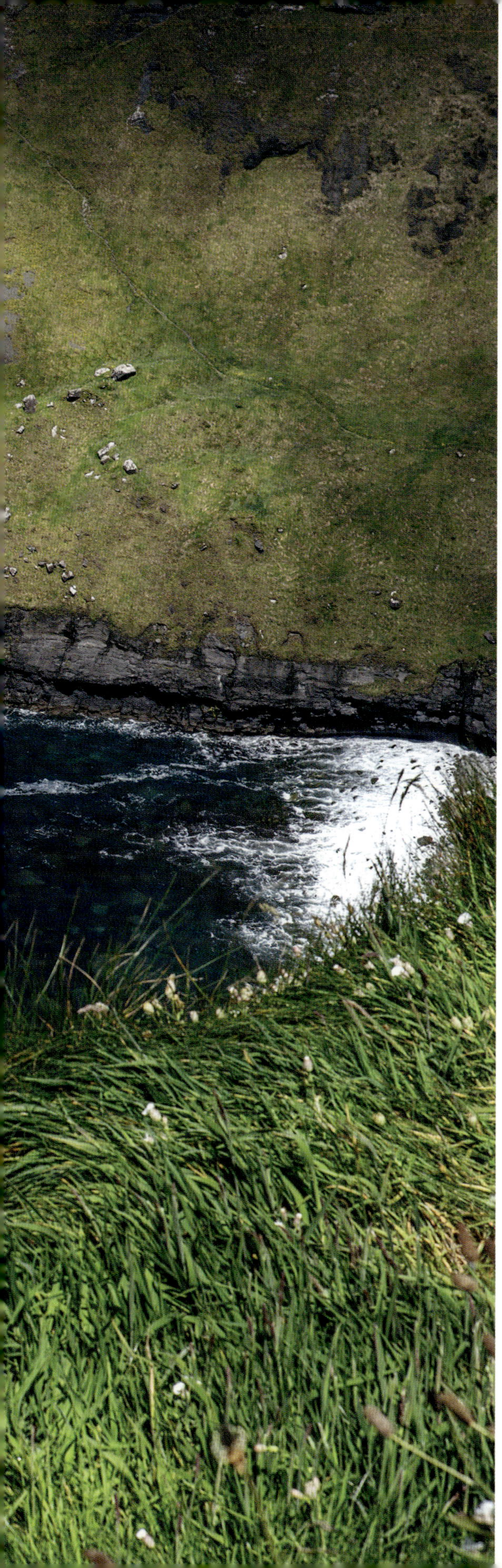

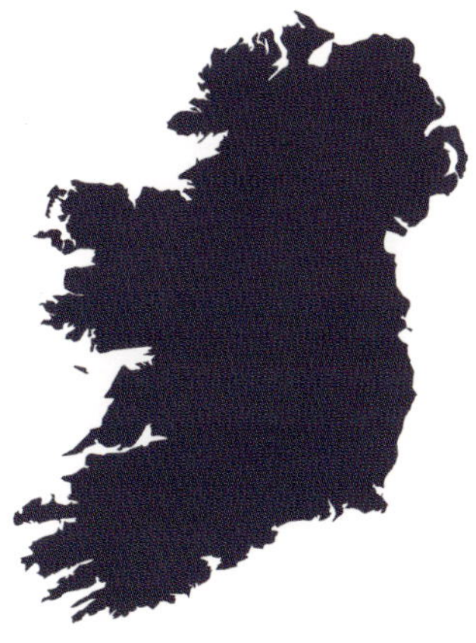

On a clear day, those standing atop the Cliffs of Moher should have been able to peer into the Atlantic Ocean and see it: an island carved by magic, laden with riches, and brimming with fairies.

Today, more than a million people a year visit the Cliffs of Moher. They go to gaze at this seven-hundred-foot tall wonder, where Ireland's strikingly green fields terminate dramatically as cliffs plunge into choppy seas.[359]

Moher was popular in ancient times, too. But back then many of its visitors were drawn not just by its majesty but rather the allure of finding a mysterious nearby island, called Hy-Brasil.[360]

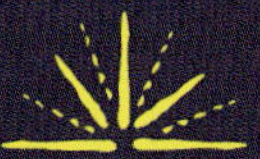

Inhabited for at least ten thousand years, Ireland's raw landscape is embedded with Celtic folklore.[361] Caves echo with tales of shape-shifters. Valleys ring with murmurs of giants. Forests brim with legends of banshees. Some of Ireland's natural landmarks are so spectacular that they inspired multiple legends.[362] The Cliffs of Moher, for example, are woven through with thrilling tales of witches, warriors, mermaids, and shape-shifting horses. Some Irish lore has factual foundations and helps explain this nation's turbulent history,[363] like that of the Irish woman Granuaile, who rebelled against the English forces subjugating her people by becoming a plundering pirate in the seas that flank the cliffs.[364]

Other tales are more fanciful, such as the lost city of Killstiffen, supposedly swallowed by the Atlantic Ocean. Now it sits submerged, near the Cliffs of Moher, waiting to be rediscovered by whoever finds its golden key. Glints from deep in the dark waters have convinced some visitors that they sighted this subsea civilization.[365]

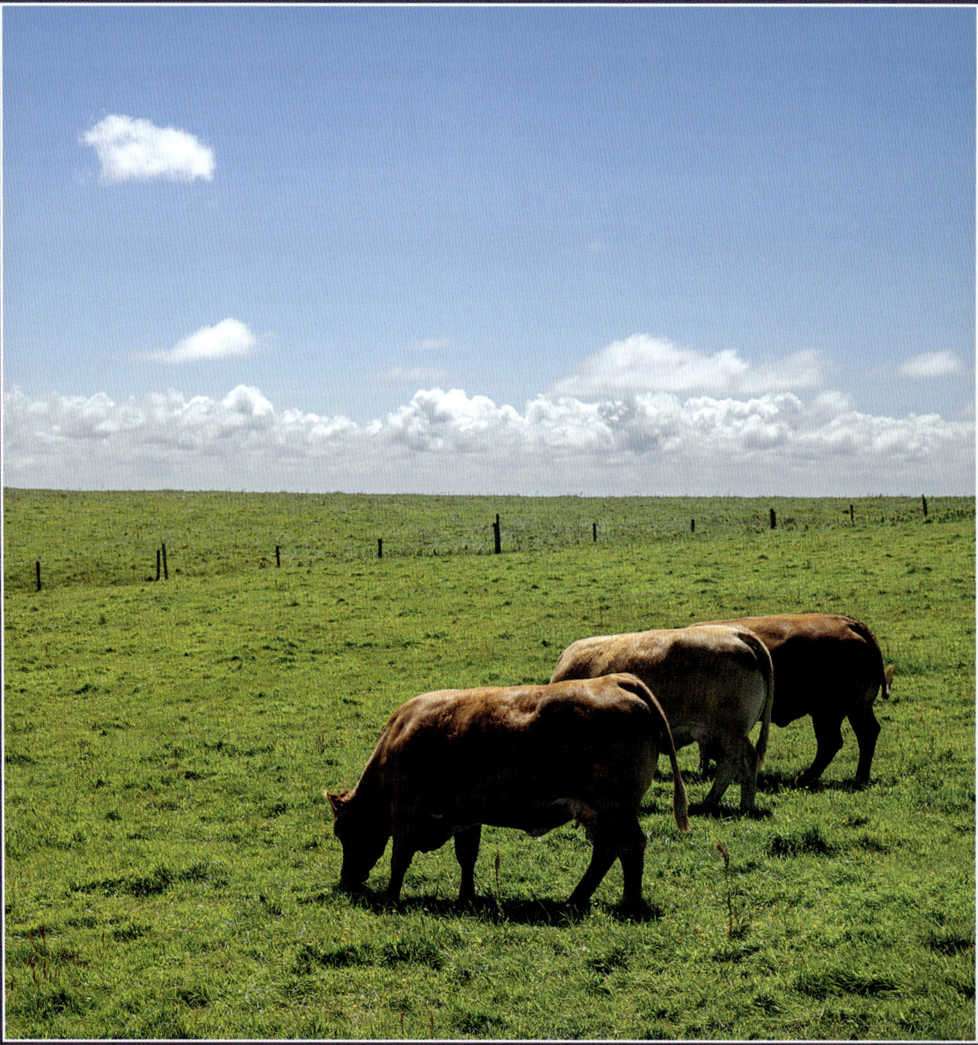

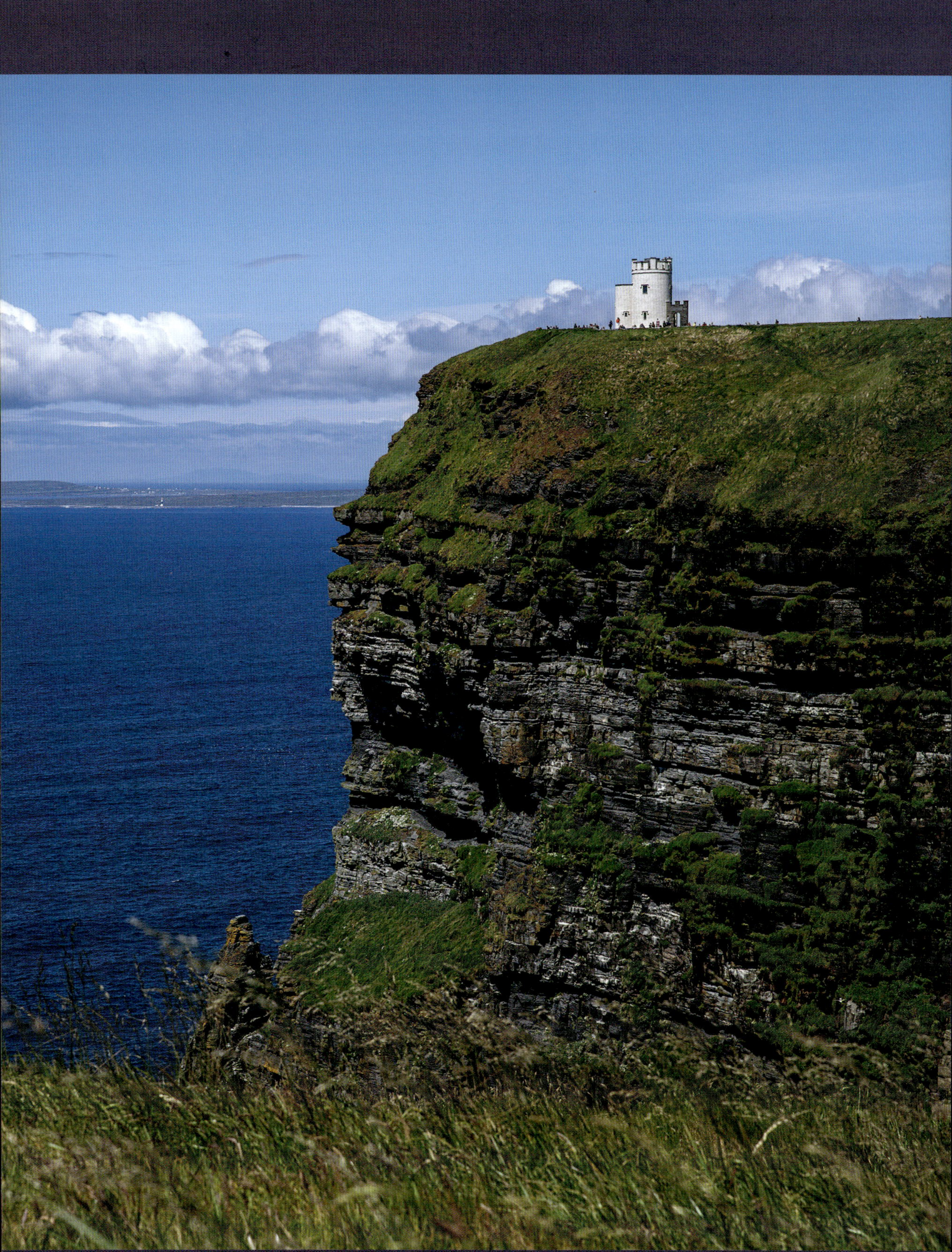

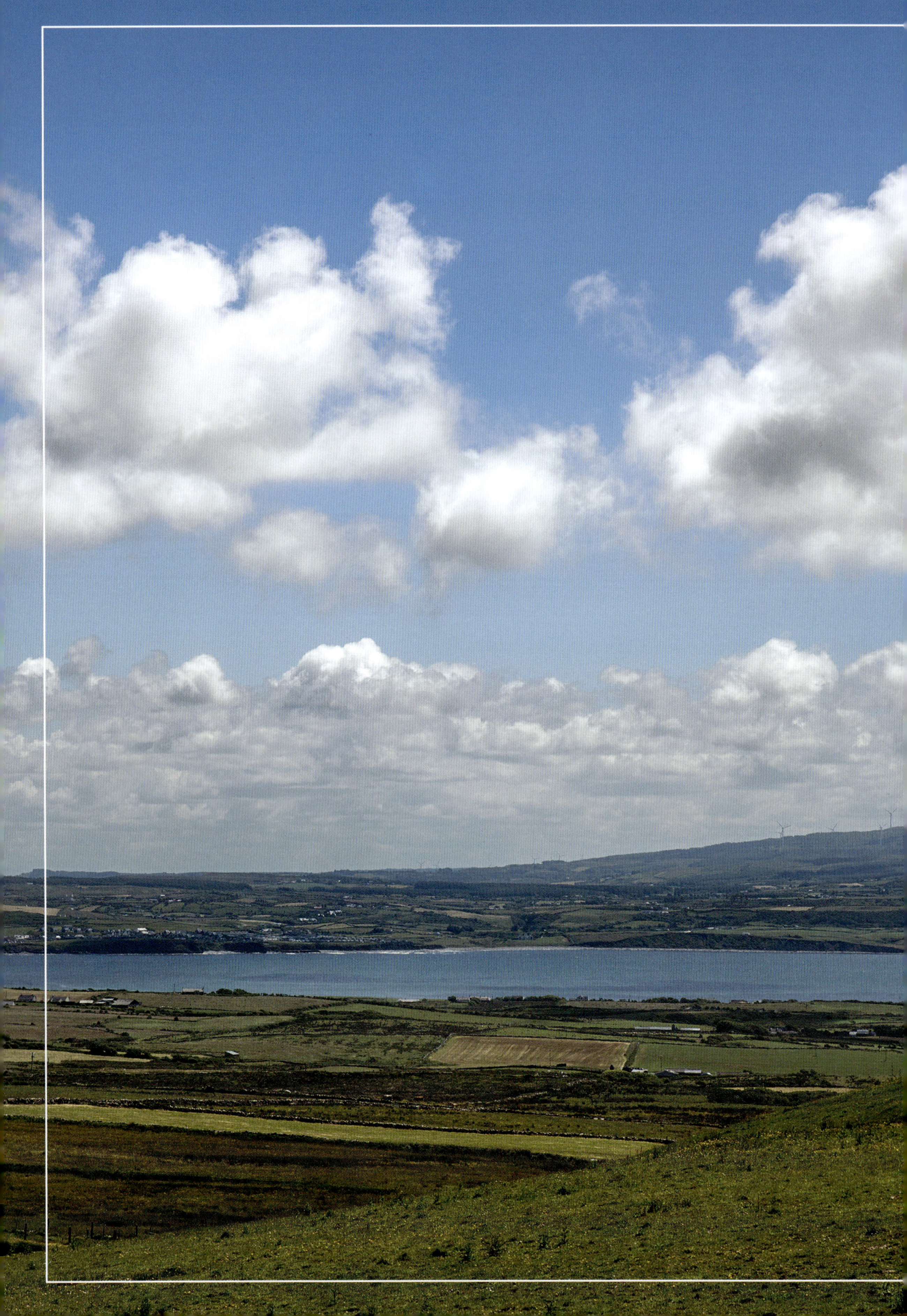

IRELAND'S RUMORED PARADISE

Reputedly located just west of the cliffs, Hy-Brasil was once Ireland's most coveted yet elusive destination. Irish people dreamed of reaching this legendary island, where gold glimmered on beaches, jewels sparkled in meadows, and immortality awaited visitors. Hy-Brasil's promised prosperity was especially enticing in harsh ancient Ireland, where many struggled to survive persistent cold, rain, and hunger.[366]

Local lore described Hy-Brasil as a blissful land connected to Tír na nÓg, a subterranean Celtic otherworld inhabited by fairies, deities, and demons.[367] From the twelfth to the sixteenth centuries, Hy-Brasil was a fireplace legend that thrilled children and gave adults respite from reality. As the story went, once every seven years, the island came out of hiding and became visible from the Irish coastline. But for many centuries, the island's existence was mere hearsay.[368]

HY-BRASIL PUT ON THE MAP

That all changed in 1570, when Belgian cartographer Abraham Ortelius put this fictional island on paper and made it concrete. That year, he released the first-ever atlas, *Theatrum Orbis Terrarum*. It claimed to map the entire world and revealed many new, mysterious lands.[369] And there, off the coast of the Cliffs of Moher, he placed Hy-Brasil. Ortelius's atlas was so well respected that, overnight, it transformed this island from a mythical nirvana, barely known beyond Ireland, into a landmass acknowledged across Europe.[370]

His book also fueled an unprecedented boom in maritime exploration, as European adventurers raced to reach previously uncharted territories. Explorers studied its seventy maps before excitedly setting sail for murky lands like Hy-Brasil. None of these intrepid sailors knew that they were actually chasing geographical ghosts.

THE LURE OF TREASURE

Lives and vessels were lost amid this clamor. Ships scoured the dangerous ocean near the Cliffs of Moher, hoping to find and claim Hy-Brasil.[371] But none of these missions was successful—unless, that is, you believe the word of Scottish captain John Nisbet. According to Nisbet's uncorroborated account, an island emerged from the mist as his ship was sailing along Ireland's west coast in 1674. After docking at Hy-Brasil, Nisbet reported that he and four of his colleagues were greeted by an old sage, who gifted them gold and silver.[372]

Another two hundred years passed before the truth finally emerged about Ireland's version of paradise: Hy-Brasil was not real. Instead it was one of dozens of phantom islands that had been incorrectly pinned to world maps.[373] Researchers gradually realized that these were fictional land masses, which had originated with reports from seafarers that were tainted by lies, miscalculations, or optical illusions.

Across the 1800s, voyagers visited the supposed locations of countless islands. Many times they arrived to find nothing but open seas. As a result, dozens of these ghost islands were soon purged from all new maps. That included Hy-Brasil, which now survives in its original form: as a land whose alluring legend bounces across the rough seas beneath the Cliffs of Moher.[374]

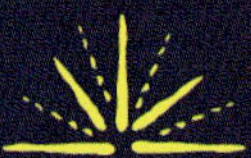

The Cliffs of Moher consistently ranks among Ireland's most visited destinations, alongside Dublin's Guinness Storehouse, which showcases the country's famous stout beer.[375] While that modern facility is situated in the busy Irish capital of Dublin, the Cliffs of Moher are cocooned in bucolic tranquility.

Many tourists head four hours west of Dublin to reach this natural jewel in County Clare. Others visit the cliffs while tracing Ireland's sixteen-hundred-mile Wild Atlantic Way. Since its 2014 launch, this coastal road has become one of the world's most popular driving routes, generating more than $1 billion a year in tourism revenue. Delightfully quaint towns await visitors along whichever route they follow to arrive at the Cliffs of Moher.[376]

More than three hundred million years ago, unrelenting geological forces created this eight-mile strip of cliffs that plummets vertically into the Atlantic. Visitors can hear and feel giant waves detonating on rocks far below as they walk the three-and-a-half-mile clifftop trail. The Atlantic's ceaseless pounding ever so slowly formed one of the cliffs' iconic features, a 220-foot-tall sea stack. It protrudes from the water like the spindly finger of a drowning giant.[377]

Such permanent attractions are enhanced by the cliffs' seasonal features. Although this site is photogenic year-round, its beauty peaks between April and July thanks to both blooming and winged decorations. During this period, when Ireland's days are longer and warmer, wildflowers and seabirds outnumber people.

Lilac, gold, violet, fuchsia, and cream blossoms abound, both in the meadows that adjoin the cliffs and along the edge of these precipices.[378] Meanwhile, up to thirty thousand pairs of seabirds gather to spawn new life at the cliffs, which is a protected bird-breeding site. Summertime visitors may spot dozens of feathered species, including puffins, fulmars, kittiwakes, razorbills, and guillemots. The latter birds lay their eggs in nests hazardously built into the cliffs' face.[379]

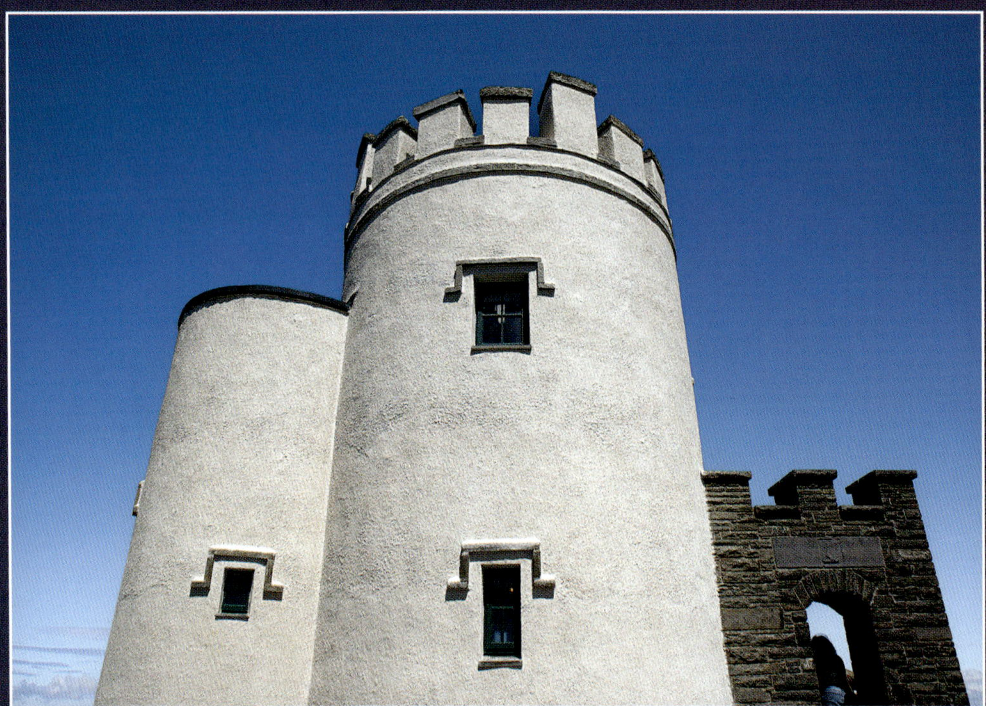

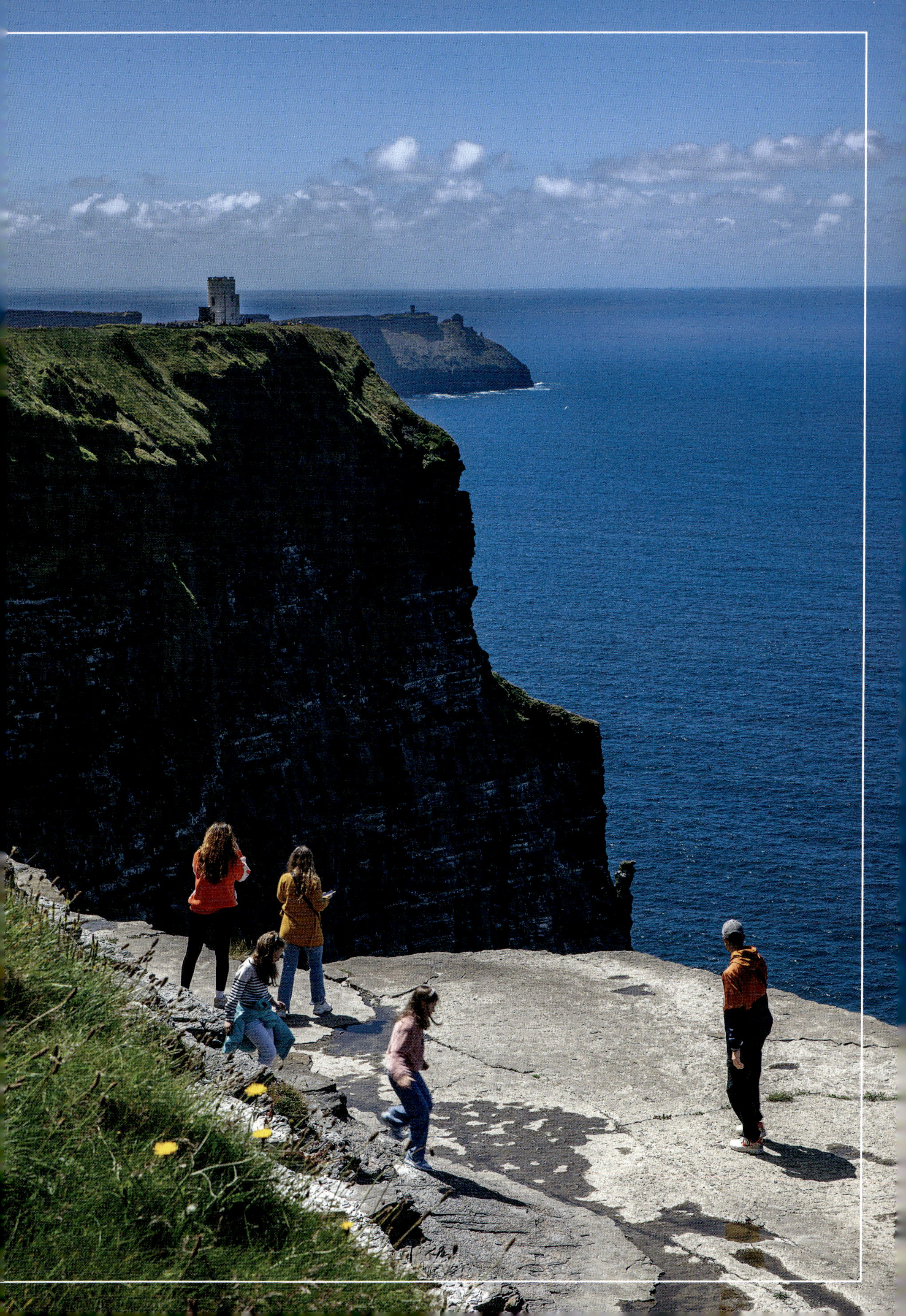

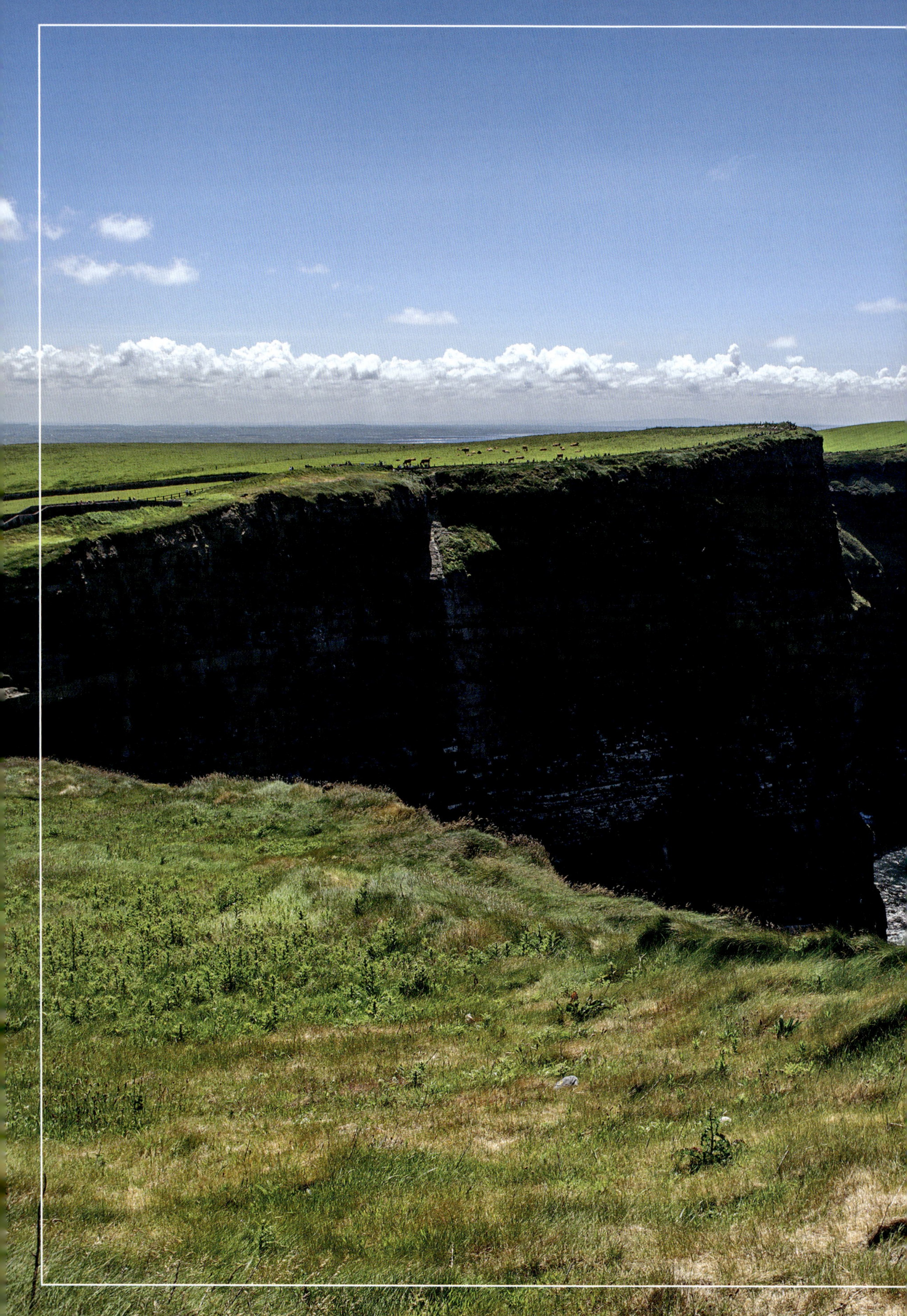

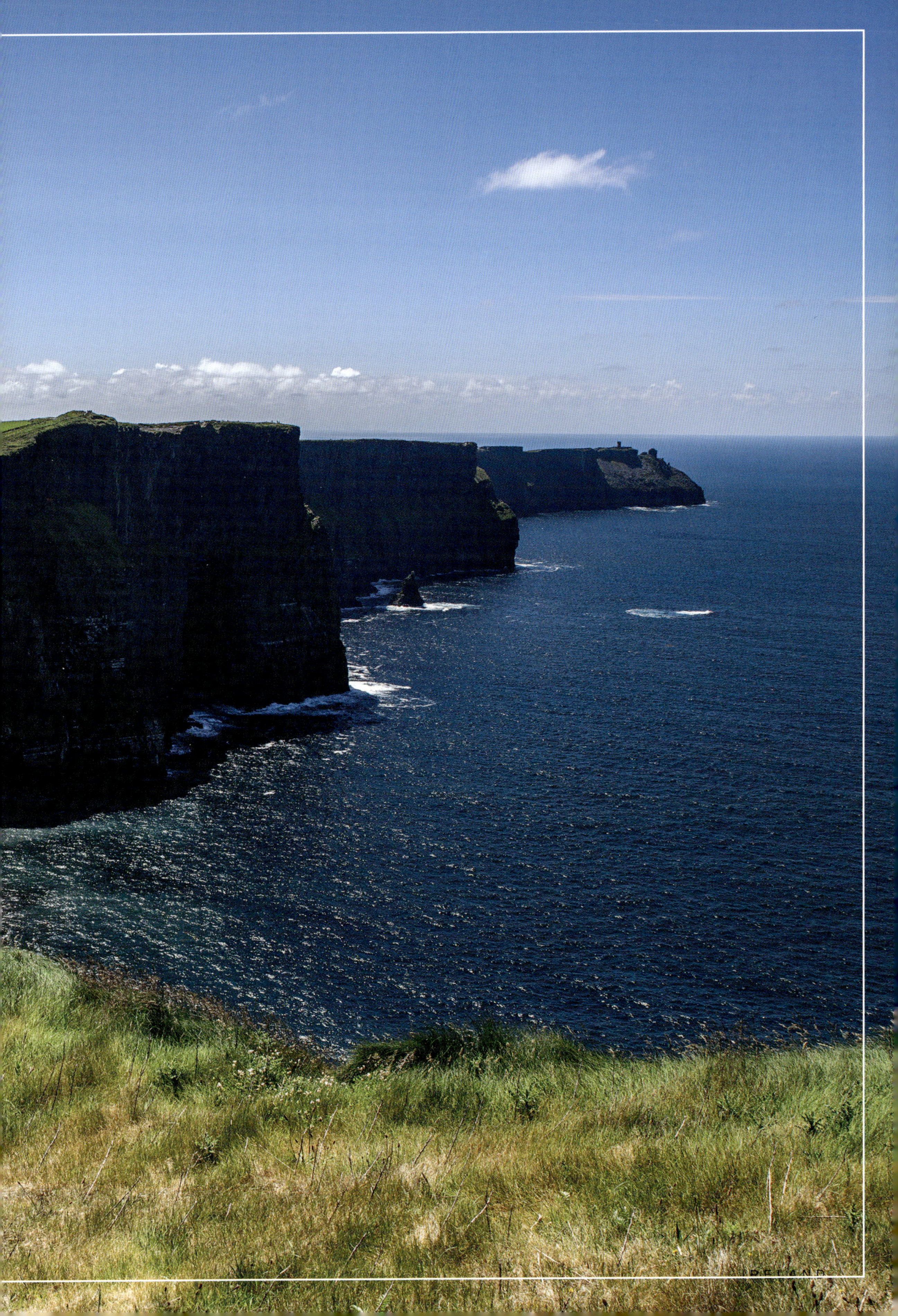
IRELAND

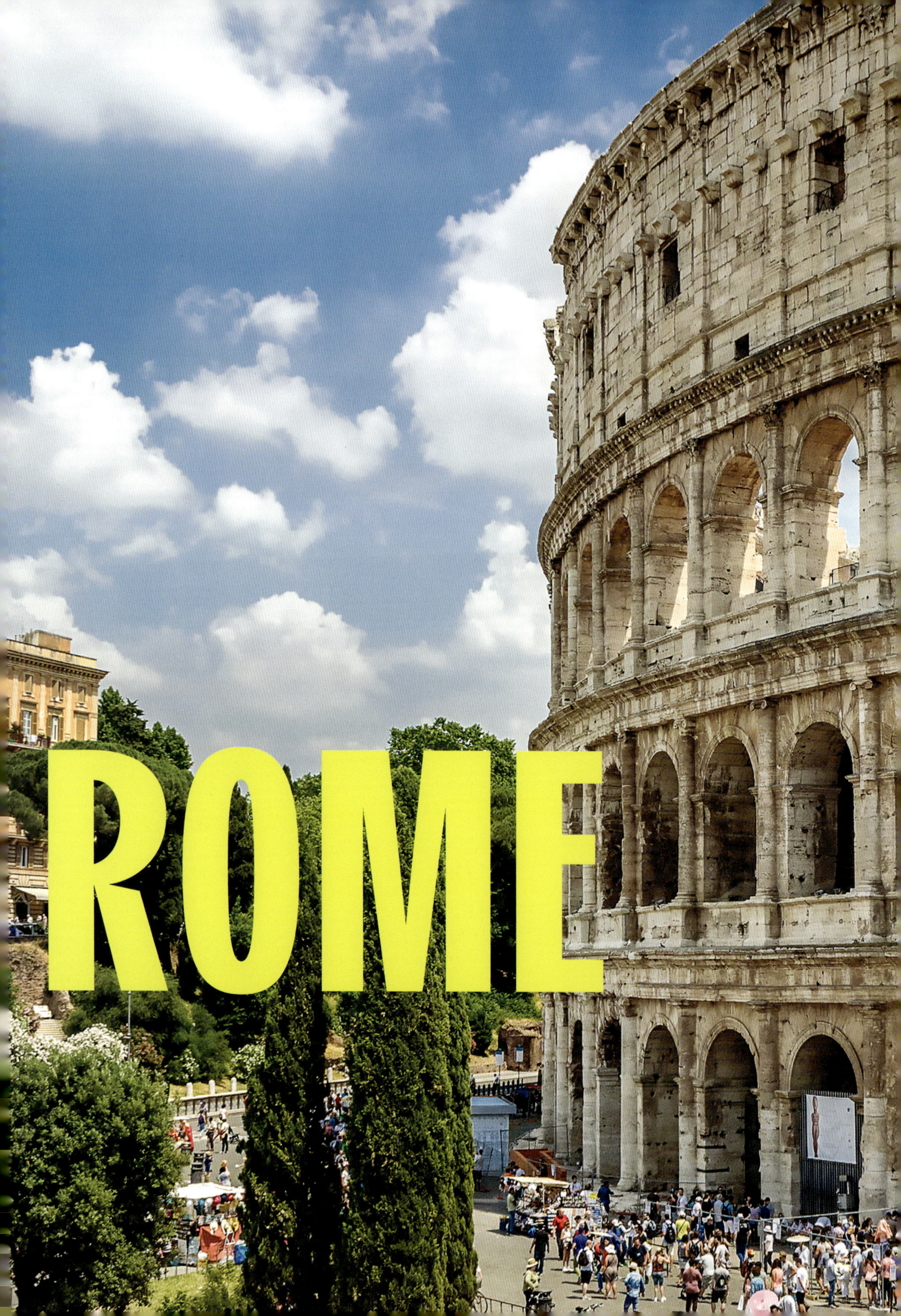
ROME

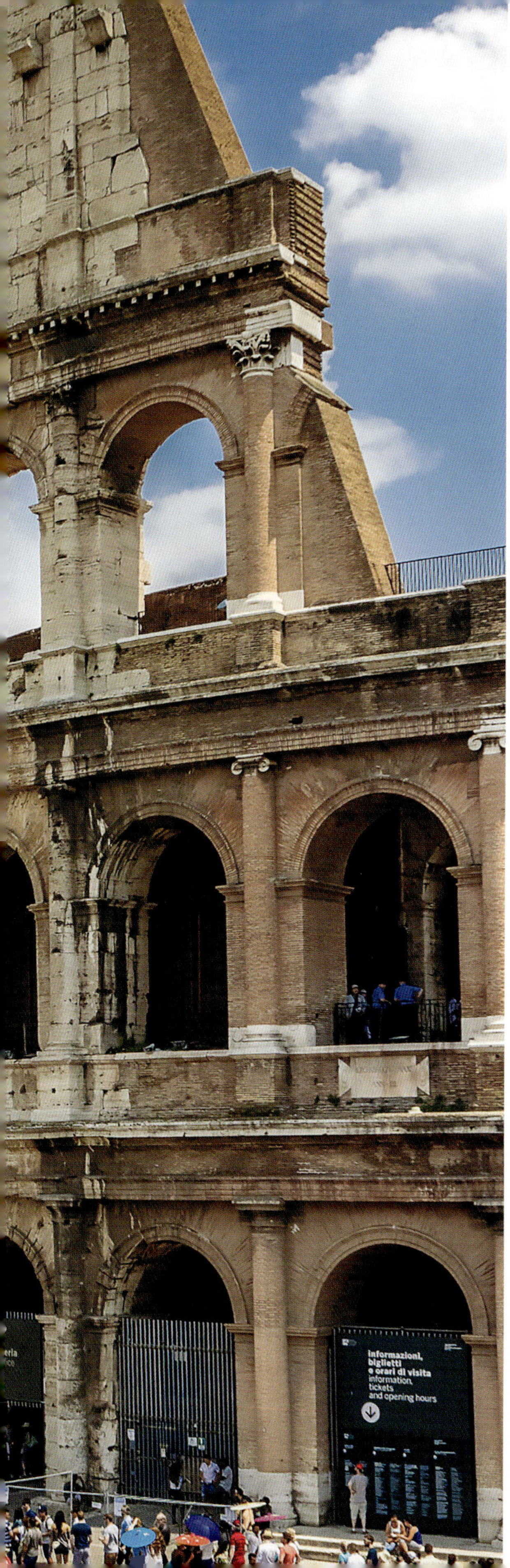

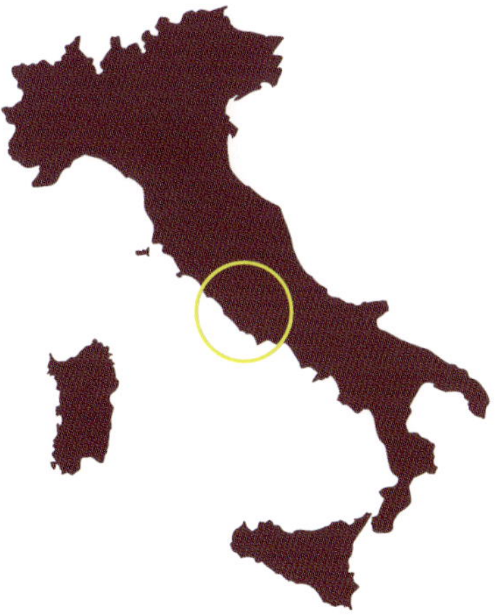

In the Colosseum's shadow, naked men once hid beneath Rome, inspired by an invincible sun and a supernatural bull. Crowds at that giant venue were unaware of the bizarre spectacle unfolding just three hundred meters away. As thousands of spectators watched gladiators battle beasts during the second and third century AD, blood was also being splattered in an underground lair by members of a secret cult.

Nowadays, several million people a year visit the Colosseum, a well-preserved architectural icon of this twenty-seven-hundred-year-old city. While walking toward this landmark, many pass a weathered church, Basilica di San Clemente, which is just a thousand feet from the stadium. The few who pause and descend into its basement find that it holds clues to an eerie puzzle. This damp, subterranean space houses a Mithraeum, the holy temple of an ancient and peculiar religious order. Now, seventeen hundred years after the Cult of Mithras dissolved into obscurity, the group's strange and violent history haunts these walls.[380]

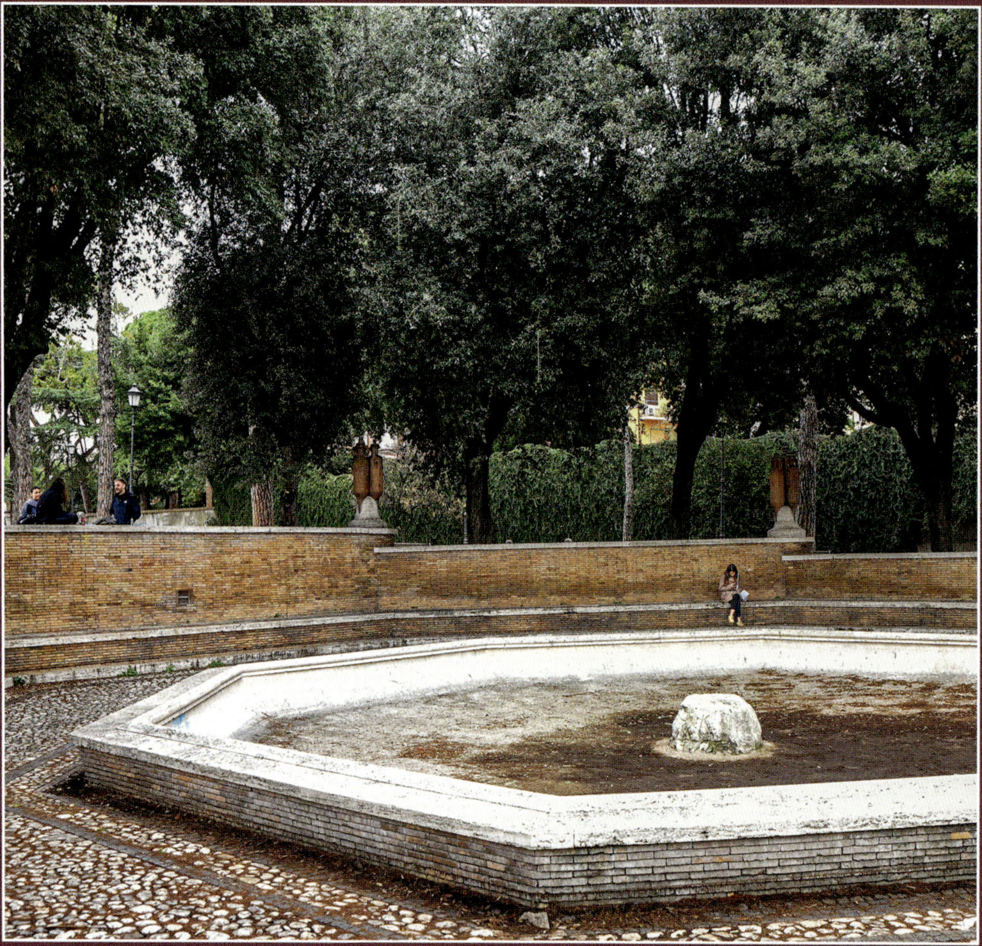

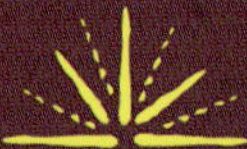

With a history that spans nearly three millennia, Rome is phenomenally dense with landmarks.[381] It is a city where, behind a barbershop, a meandering tourist in a nondescript alley may find a gorgeous thousand-year-old church, empty and overlooked. Although Rome teems with travelers, most follow a similar trail studded by famous sites.

Visitors flood through the towering columns of the Pantheon, a marvelous temple-turned-church built in the second century AD.[382] Their trail converges on Vatican City, seat of the Catholic faith and home to marvels such as St. Peter's Basilica and the Sistine Chapel.[383] They also crowd the photogenic Trevi Fountain, the storied Spanish Steps, the regal Piazza Navona, and the imposing Castel Sant'Angelo.

More visitors still inundate Palatine Hill, where twin infants breastfed by a she-wolf are credited with establishing this city. Cloaked in remains of ancient temples, halls, and palaces, this elevated site is forever linked with those mythical founders of Rome—Romulus and Remus.[384]

IRANIAN ORIGINS OF MITHRAISM

This cult's story begins at least thirty-five hundred years ago—not in Rome but in Persia (or modern-day Iran). There, worshippers gathered to honor the ruler of time, the commander of the cosmos, the god of the invincible sun,[385] each of which was a moniker for the religion's central deity: Mithra.

At the core of Mithra's lore is a beguiling legend that portrays him as the creator of the world. Rather than having parents, Mithra emerged from a rock fully formed. He was naked, except for a Phrygian cap, a style of conical headwear that became an icon of Mithraism. In one hand he held a torch, which he used to give the earth light. In the other he gripped a blade, which he wielded to sacrifice a cosmic bull, an act that furnished the planet with a bounty of food. But this newly formed world was parched. So Mithra splintered a boulder, releasing a torrent of water that nourished the dusty planet. Crisis averted. Humanity saved.[386, 387]

HOW MITHRAISM TOOK ROOT IN ROME

Mithraism is believed to have been brought to Rome by Persian migrants after the collapse of the Persian Empire in the fourth century BC. At that stage, Rome was a largely pagan kingdom. Many of its residents worshipped a wide array of Roman deities, including Jupiter, Venus, Neptune, Minerva, and Juno. Most of these gods and goddesses were inspired by their divine Greek counterparts.

By the time the Colosseum rose in the late first century AD, Mithraism was entrenched in Rome, where the newly formed religion of Christianity was also spreading. Mithras's many thousands of followers were mostly rich and powerful Roman citizens or Roman soldiers.

Devotion to the monarchy was a key tenet of Mithraism, which helps explain why this religion received strong support from several Roman rulers between the first century AD and the fourth century AD.[388] In fact, Emperors Commodus[389] (whose reign encompassed AD 177–192) and Julian (whose reign encompassed AD 361–363) both belonged to this cult.[390]

As the Colosseum swelled in fame across Europe, Mithraism also grew in influence. At its peak, in the third century AD, it is estimated to have had up to sixty thousand members across the Roman Empire. Together the devotees built hundreds of concealed temples on Roman lands.

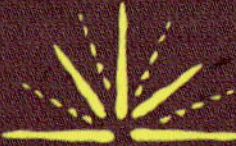

By the time the Colosseum was erected in the first century AD, Rome had morphed from a settlement into a goliath. With as many as one million residents, it was perhaps the world's largest city at the time.[391] This population had just lived through the tumultuous reign of Roman Emperor Nero, a brutal, selfish, and depraved leader who supposedly murdered two wives and even his own mother.[392]

One of his successors, the more humble Emperor Vespasian, destroyed Nero's extravagant monument to himself, the Golden Palace. In its place, Vespasian erected a grand facility to serve and thrill his subjects. Just like that, the Colosseum was born.

Eight years passed as the stadium slowly rose from the ground. By the time the venue opened in AD 80, it stood 620 feet long, 512 feet wide, and 4 stories high. Up to fifty thousand spectators could pour through its eighty entrances. What made the Colosseum's construction even more complex was that it was a free-standing structure, whereas Roman architects typically built amphitheaters into hillsides.

Romans thronged to this new venue to watch cultural performances such as plays, concerts, and historical reenactments. On occasion, the building was even deliberately flooded with water to create a faux ocean in which scaled-down ships could do battle.

Yet it is gory spectacles for which the Colosseum is infamous. Crowds bayed for violence as they watched animals attack one another, be hunted by warriors, or devour unarmed and untrained men called *bestiarri*, who often were criminals thrown into the arena as punishment. Standing a slightly better chance of survival were the Colosseum's iconic gladiators. Highly trained, heavily armored, and wielding swords or spears, these men typically fought one-on-one battles to the death.[393]

Almost two millennia later, visitors lining up to enter the arena see costumed gladiators posing for photos. Inside, meanwhile, they can learn about these ancient warriors at the Colosseum Museum. Located on the second floor, this facility elaborates the tale of the amphitheater via artifacts, maps, drawings, and text displays.[394]

Visitors also absorb the Colosseum's history with each step. They walk through many of the same areas once trod by ancient Roman spectators, who were shaded from the sun by a giant awning that wrapped around the top of this 157-foot-tall stadium.

Public access extends to the arena floor, where chaos once reigned. Formerly the floor was a wooden board, 250 feet long and 150 feet wide, and covered by sand. Now only part of it remains as a flat stone surface where people gather to take photos and take in a 360-degree view of the arena.

Above them, other visitors peer down from the accessible upper levels. Below them, those with exclusive passes weave through the fourteen corridors of the Colosseum's underground.[395] Originally, this was where event organizers and performers prepared. The basement also housed lethal beasts, which at show-time were lifted by winch to the arena floor to face human foes.[396]

The scale of savagery that unfolded in the Colosseum is difficult to exaggerate. One million animals and about five hundred thousand people are estimated to have died during gladiator games. They died for the entertainment of spectators, who ranged from emperors to politicians, soldiers, and peasants.[397] After more than three centuries of carnage, these blood sports were finally abolished around AD 400 by Roman Emperor Honorius.[398]

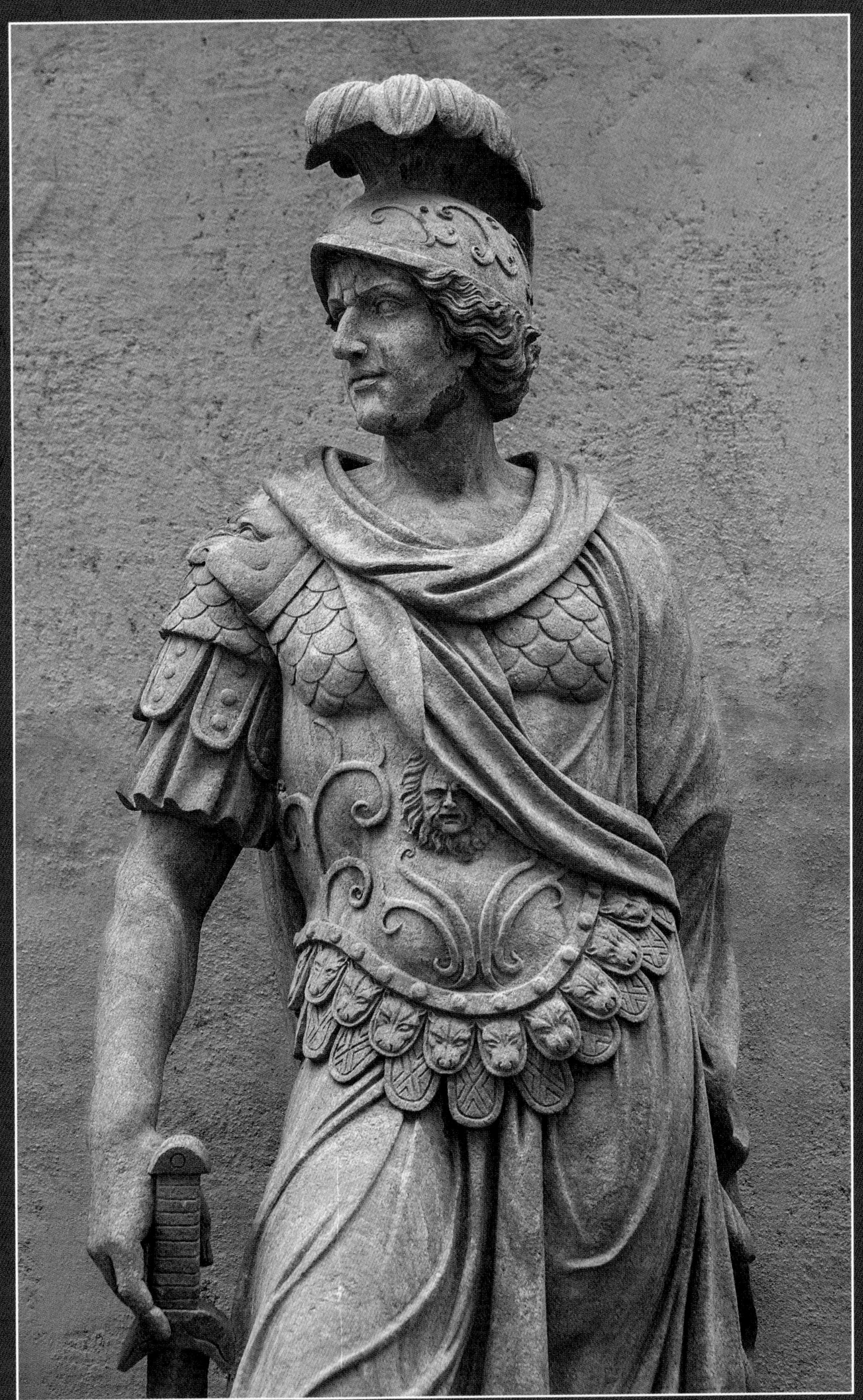

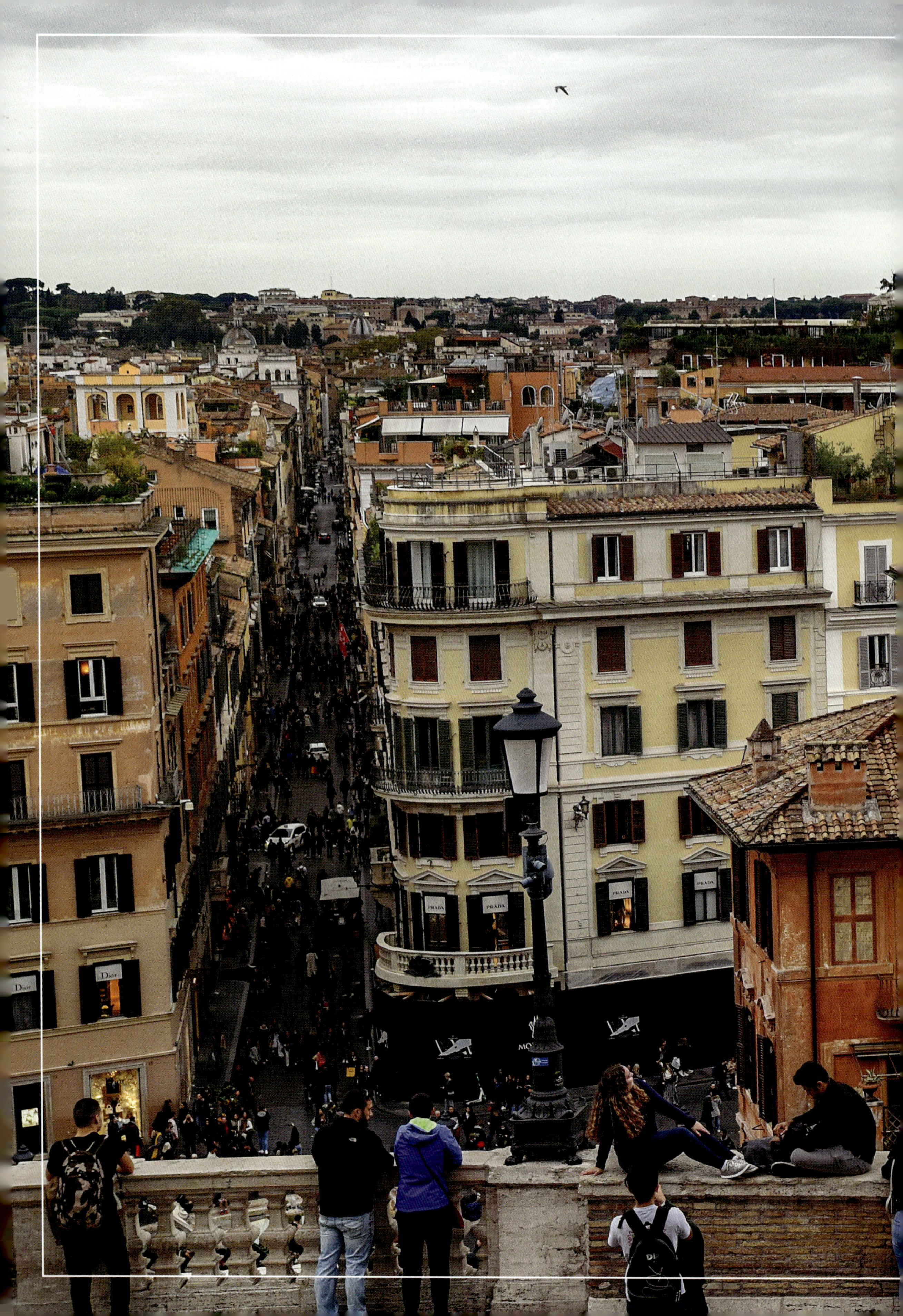
Dior
Dior
PRADA
PRADA
PRADA
PRADA

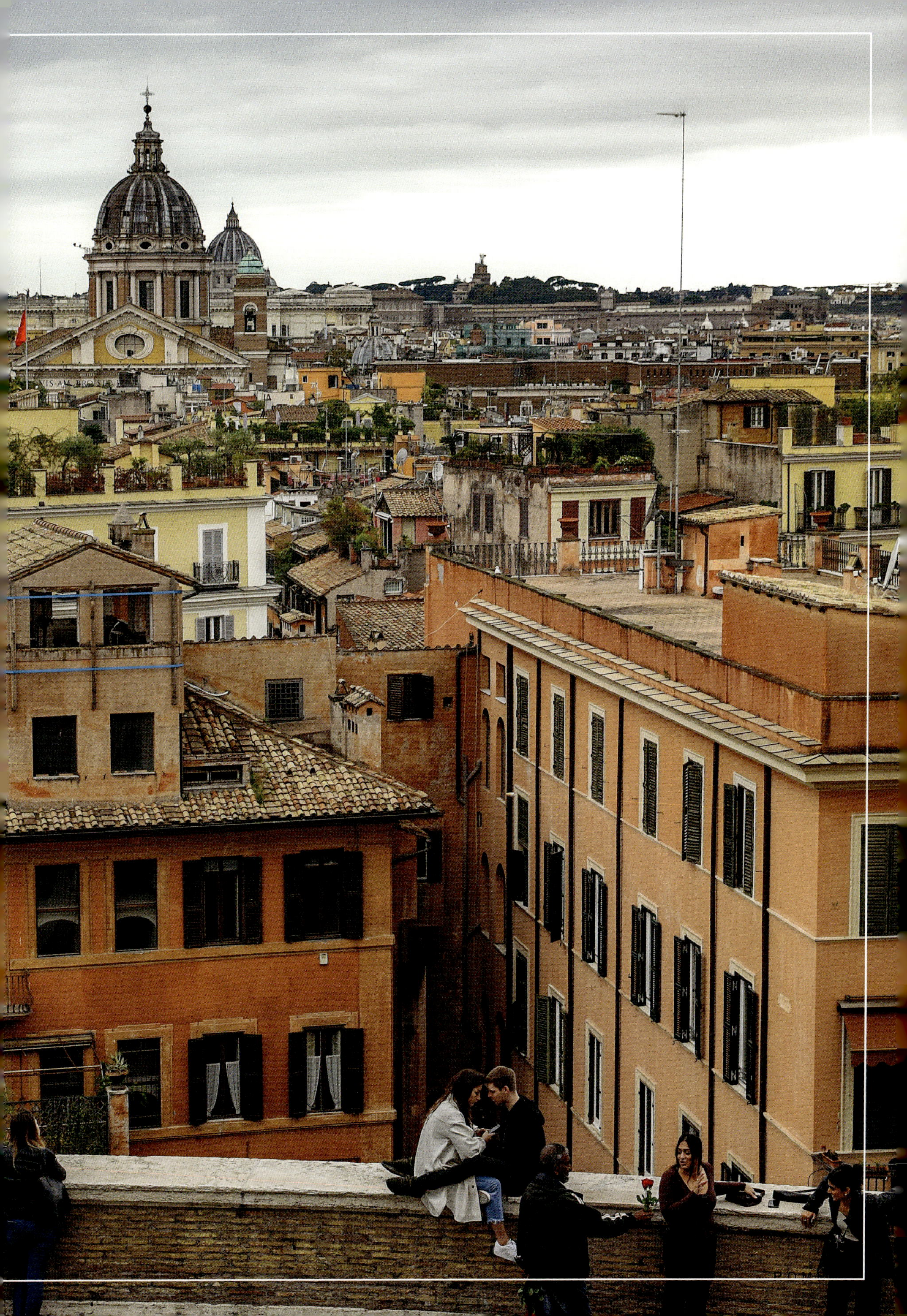

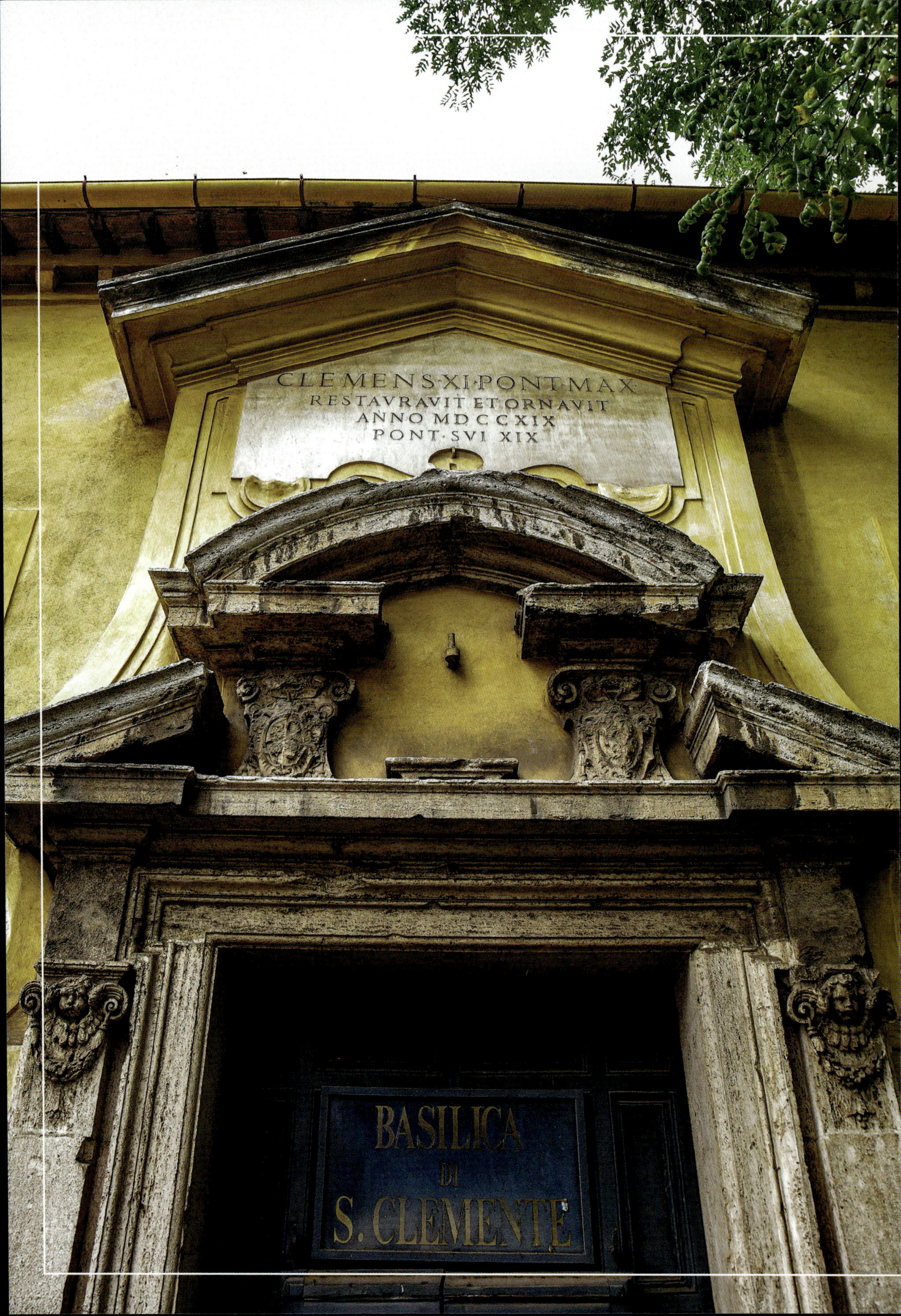
CLEMENS·XI·PONT·MAX
RESTAVRAVIT ET ORNAVIT
ANNO MDCCXIX
PONT·SVI XIX
BASILICA
DI
S. CLEMENTE

STRANGE SUBTERRANEAN RITUALS

Mystery shrouds what exactly Mithras's followers did under the streets of Rome. Written accounts of the cult's customs give limited detail since, upon initiation, each member was sworn to secrecy. But writings do mention debauched ceremonies involving nudity, orgies, and blood sacrifices.[399]

Physical evidence backs up some of these claims. Researchers have identified Roman murals and ceramics decorated by what they believe to be images of Mithras initiation ceremonies. These ancient designs depict nude men with their hands tied and their eyes covered by a blindfold, surrounded by males wearing raven or lion masks.

Due to the bull's significance in the lore of Mithras, sacrificing one of these beasts was a key act of symbolism incorporated into initiations. Whether Mithras's followers actually killed bulls in their temples or merely reenacted this ritual remains unclear.[400]

But just a few steps from the Colosseum, one can observe such artwork at the cult's lair beneath the Basilica di San Clemente. Visitors pass through a colonnaded atrium to enter this cream-colored eleventh-century church, which is built atop a fourth-century chapel. After perusing both those spaces, visitors can descend to the basement Mithraeum.

At the center of this narrow temple is a hand-carved stone altar. Close inspection reveals that it is etched with an image of a man cutting a bull's throat. Cult members once sat nude on the weathered benches that flank the altar while executing odd rituals in secret. Or so the legend goes.[401]

DOWNFALL OF A CULT

In its heyday, Mithraism had so many influential Roman devotees that it could have blossomed into a major global faith. That was the view of Ernest Renan, a revered nineteenth-century French scholar of religion. But Mithraism's spread was slowed by the rapid rise of Christianity, Renan wrote.

Other scholars, meanwhile, suggest that Mithraism was also held back by its unnerving customs and the difficulty of becoming a member. Mithraism did not accept female worshippers, for reasons that aren't clear. It also had a fairly strict screening process for prospective male members, who were required to have a certain level of social status.[402]

Mithraism entered a swift and terminal decline in AD 380, when Emperor Theodosius declared Christianity the official religion of the Roman Empire and soon banned the practice of other faiths. Now Mithraism's legacy in Rome survives in the form of several intact Mithraeums, including this sunken lair next to the Colosseum. There, cult members once engaged in eerie rituals hidden from the public, interrupted only by roars from that famed arena.[403]

ACKNOWLEDGMENTS

My remarkable wife, Rungtiwa, who patiently and lovingly cared for our young son Aidan and maintained our household while I was so frequently overseas producing this book.

My inspiring mother, Maura, for being my sounding board and a wonderful person. Your guidance, encouragement, and constructive criticism are but three of countless things for which you make me thankful.

My siblings, Grainne and Conor, for being thoughtful and caring and putting up with my incessant talk about this book.

My extended family in Ireland and Thailand for your warm hospitality whenever we land.

The editors and designers who worked on this book, including Allison Picard, Jenn McNeil, and Michelle Lenger, and the whole team at Harper Celebrate, especially Danielle Peterson and Michael Aulisio for contacting me to pitch them book ideas and trusting me to both photograph and write this book.

All the many brilliant travel editors I've worked with, and learned from, including Amy Alipio, Catharine Hamm, Carolyn Spencer Brown, Lee Siew Hua, and Mark Footer.

The newspaper editors who gave me opportunities and showed me the ropes when I was a rookie news journalist, including David Hummerston, David Burtenshaw, Ben Harvey, and Mark Mallabone.

The many academics who kindly offered advice on finding quality sources about very niche topics while I was researching this book.

And finally you, the reader, for showing interest in my offbeat book. Feel free to recommend it, perhaps even to every person you meet in the next decade.

NOTES

EDINBURGH

1 "Stone of Destiny Heads South for Coronation," *BBC News*, April 28, 2023, https://www.bbc.com/news/uk-scotland-65411666.
2 "The Stone of Destiny," *Historic Environment Scotland*, accessed May 30, 2025, https://www.historicenvironment.scot/archives-and-research/archives-and-collections/properties-in-care-collections/object/the-stone-of-destiny-13th-century-medieval-edinburgh-castle-6132.
3 "Research Shines New Light on the Stone of Destiny," *Historic Environment Scotland*, April 5, 2023, https://www.historicenvironment.scot/about-us/news/research-shines-new-light-on-the-stone-of-destiny/.
4 "From Fortress to Tourist Attraction," *Edinburgh Castle*, June 28, 2010, https://blog.edinburghcastle.scot/history-tourist-attraction-edinburgh-castle/.
5 Robert Lewis, "Edinburgh Castle," *Encyclopedia Britannica*, May 2, 2025, https://www.britannica.com/place/Edinburgh-Castle.
6 "St Margaret's Chapel," *Edinburgh Castle*, accessed May 30, 2025, https://www.edinburghcastle.scot/see-and-do/highlights/st-margarets-chapel/.
7 Lewis, "Edinburgh Castle."
8 "Edinburgh Castle Siege to Be Brought to Life," *Historic Environment Scotland*, October 6, 2015, https://www.historicenvironment.scot/about-us/news/edinburgh-castle-siege-to-be-brought-to-life/.
9 "Mons Meg," *Historic Environment Scotland*, accessed May 30, 2025, https://www.historicenvironment.scot/archives-and-research/archives-and-collections/properties-in-care-collections/object/mons-meg-jehan-cambier-of-mons-1449-late-medieval-edinburgh-castle-12935.
10 "The Great Hall," *Edinburgh Castle*, accessed May 30, 2025, https://www.edinburghcastle.scot/see-and-do/highlights/the-great-hall/.
11 "The Royal Palace," *Edinburgh Castle*, accessed May 30, 2025, https://www.edinburghcastle.scot/see-and-do/highlights/the-royal-palace/.
12 "Honours of Scotland," *Edinburgh Castle*, accessed May 30, 2015, https://www.edinburghcastle.scot/see-and-do/highlights/honours-of-scotland/.
13 "Crown Jewels of Scotland & the Stone of Destiny," *Visit Scotland*, accessed May 30, 2025, https://www.visitscotland.com/things-to-do/attractions/historic/stone-of-destiny.
14 "Stone of Scone," *Encyclopedia Britannica*, May 3, 2025, https://www.britannica.com/topic/Stone-of-Scone.
15 "Lia Fáil," *Oxford Reference*, accessed 20 May, 2025, https://www.oxfordreference.com/view/10.1093/oi/authority.20110803100103672.
16 Ailbhe Mac Shamhráin, "Fergus Mór," *Dictionary of Irish Biography*, October 1, 2009, https://doi.org/10.3318/dib.003047.v1.
17 "Fergus Mor Mac Erc," *Tartans.com*, https://www.tartans.com/articles/famscots/fergusmor.html.
18 "Genesis 28:10–22," *Bible Gateway*, accessed May 30, 2025, https://www.biblegateway.com/passage/?search=Genesis%2028%3A10–22&version=nkjv.
19 British Geological Survey, "The Stone of Destiny," May 15, 2023, https://www.bgs.ac.uk/news/the-stone-of-destiny/.
20 "Stone of Scone," *Undiscovered Scotland*, accessed May 30, 2025, https://www.undiscoveredscotland.co.uk/usfeatures/stoneofscone/index.html.
21 "The Pharaoh's Daughter Who Was the Mother of All Scots," *The Scotsman*, September 13, 2006, https://www.scotsman.com/whats-on/arts-and-entertainment/the-pharaohs-daughter-who-was-the-mother-of-all-scots-2507668.
22 "The Stone of Destiny," British Geological Survey, May 15, 2023, https://www.bgs.ac.uk/news/the-stone-of-destiny/.
23 "Research Shines New Light on the Stone of Destiny," *Historic Environment Scotland*, April 5, 2023, https://www.historicenvironment.scot/about-us/news/research-shines-new-light-on-the-stone-of-destiny/.
24 British Geological Survey, "The Stone of Destiny," May 15, 2023, https://www.bgs.ac.uk/news/the-stone-of-destiny/.
25 Samuel Wilson, "The Story of the Stone of Destiny," *Historic Environment Scotland Blog*, October 11, 2024, https://blog.historicenvironment.scot/2023/05/the-story-of-the-stone-of-destiny/.

BALI

26 "The Iconic Cliffside Temple of Bali," *Uluwatu Temple*, accessed May 31, 2025, https://uluwatutemple.id/.
27 "Kecak Dance Bali | Book Kecak Uluwatu Ticket | Uluwatu Sunset View," *Kecak Dance Bali*, October 2, 2024, https://kecakdancebali.com/.
28 Margaret Dougherty, "How The Balinese See the Sea: Interpretations of Oceanic Power," *Independent Study Project Collection (ISP)*, 2018, 17–18, https://digitalcollections.sit.edu/isp_collection/2934.
29 "Bali Temples: All You Need to Know," Bali.com, accessed May 31, 2025, https://bali.com/temples-pura/.
30 "Indonesia," *Encyclopedia Britannica*, accessed May 31, 2025, https://www.britannica.com/place/Indonesia.
31 Wendell Cox, "Jakarta Closing Population Gap with Tokyo," *New Geography*, September 20, 2023, https://www.newgeography.com/content/007939-jakarta-closing-population-gap-with-tokyo.
32 Basten Gokkon, "Bali's Rapid Coastal Erosion Threatens Island's Ecosystems & Communities: Study," *Mongabay*, June 22, 2024, https://news.mongabay.com/2024/06/balis-rapid-coastal-erosion-threatens-islands-ecosystems-communities-study/.
33 Ronan O'Connell, "How Homes in Bali Are Designed for Harmony—and to Keep Demons at Bay," *Atlas Obscura*, October 6, 2022, https://www.atlasobscura.com/articles/balinese-traditional-homes-spirits-demons.
34 O'Connell, "Homes in Bali."
35 "History: The Origins of the Fire Dance," *Uluwatu Temple*, accessed May 31, 2025, https://uluwatutemple.id/uluwatu-kecak-dance.

SINGAPORE

36 "Supertree Grove," *Gardens by the Bay*, accessed May 31, 2025, https://www.gardensbythebay.com.sg/en/things-to-do/attractions/supertree-grove.html.
37 "Flower Dome," *Gardens by the Bay*, accessed May 31, 2025, https://www.gardensbythebay.com.sg/en/things-to-do/attractions/flower-dome.html.

38 "Sustainability Report: Greening Singapore Together, Annual Report 2023–2024," *Singapore National Parks*, accessed May 31, 2025, https://www.nparks.gov.sg/portals/annualreport/sustainability-report.html.
39 "Open Spaces and Green Areas," *UN-Habitat Urban Indicators Database*, accessed May 31, 2025, https://data.unhabitat.org/pages/open-spaces-and-green-areas.
40 Scott Hackett, "Singapore Beats 16 Cities With Largest Green Urban Area," *Citygreen* (blog), April 12, 2017, https://senseable.mit.edu/news/pdfs/20170412_Citygreen.pdf.
41 "'Garden City' Vision Is Introduced," *National Library Board Singapore*, accessed May 31, 2025, https://www.nlb.gov.sg/main/article-detail?cmsuuid=a7fac49f-9c96-4030-8709-ce160c58d15c.
42 "Volunteer with Us," *Gardens by the Bay*, accessed May 31, 2025, https://www.gardensbythebay.com.sg/en/support-us/volunteer.html.
43 "Sustainability Efforts," *Gardens by the Bay*, accessed May 31, 2025, https://www.gardensbythebay.com.sg/en/about-us/our-gardens-story/sustainability-efforts.html.
44 "Journey Halfway Round the World to Fill Garden in Singapore," *The Straits Times*, December 13, 2023, https://www.straitstimes.com/multimedia/graphics/2023/12/bay-east-garden-singapore/index.html?shell.
45 "City in Nature: Key Strategies," *Singapore National Parks*, accessed May 31, 2025, https://www.nparks.gov.sg/who-we-are/city-in-nature-key-strategies.
46 "60 Years of Greening," *Singapore National Parks*, accessed May 31, 2025, https://www.nparks.gov.sg/treessg/one-million-trees-movement/.

BERLIN

47 "Victims at the Berlin Wall," *Stiftung Berliner Mauer*, accessed May 31, 2025, https://www.stiftung-berliner-mauer.de/en/topics/victims-berlin-wall.
48 Erin Blakemore, "Why the Berlin Wall Rose—and How It Fell," *National Geographic*, November 8, 2019, https://www.nationalgeographic.com/history/article/why-berlin-wall-built-fell.
49 *Encyclopedia Britannica*, "Berlin Wall," March 30, 2025, https://www.britannica.com/topic/Berlin-Wall.
50 "'...There Is No East, No West..:' Dr. Martin Luther King, Jr. Visits Cold War Berlin," *Rediscovering Black History* (blog), February 19, 2025, https://rediscovering-black-history.blogs.archives.gov/2020/01/20/there-is-no-east-no-west-dr-martin-luther-king-jr-visits-cold-war-berlin/.
51 Olivia B. Waxman, "What Martin Luther King Jr. Said About Walls During His 1964 Visit to Berlin," *TIME*, January 18, 2019, https://time.com/5504826/martin-luther-king-wall-history/.
52 "'...There Is No East,'" *Rediscovering Black History*.
53 Waxman, "What Martin Luther King Jr. Said."
54 "Message from the Director," *The Martin Luther King, Jr. Research and Education Institute*, accessed June 23, 2025, https://kinginstitute.stanford.edu/message-director.
55 Michael P. Steinberg, "Martin Luther King Jr. in East and West Berlin," Cornell University, January 11, 2018, https://www.cornell.edu/video/michael-p-steinberg-martin-luther-king-jr-east-west-berlin.
56 Waxman, "What Martin Luther King Jr. Said."
57 "'...There Is No East,'" *Rediscovering Black History.*
58 "East Side Gallery," *Visit Berlin*, accessed May 31, 2025, https://www.visitberlin.de/en/east-side-gallery.
59 "Brandenburg Gate," *Encyclopedia Britannica*, accessed November 18, 2024, https://www.britannica.com/topic/Brandenburg-Gate.
60 "Berlin Wall Trail—From Potsdamer Platz to Warschauer Strasse," *Berlin.de*, accessed May 31, 2025, https://www.berlin.de/mauer/en/wall-trail/city-route/from-potsdamer-platz-to-warschauer-strasse/.
61 "Berlin Wall Bike Tour," *Visit Berlin*, accessed May 15, 2025, https://www.visitberlin.de/en/berlin-wall-bike-tour.
62 "Berlin Wall History Mile," *Berlin.de*, accessed May 31, 2025, https://www.berlin.de/mauer/en/history/history-mile/.
63 "Berlin Wall Memorial," *Stiftung Berliner Mauer*, accessed May 31, 2025, https://www.stiftung-berliner-mauer.de/en/berlin-wall-memorial.
64 "'Weisse Kreuze' Memorial / German Bundestag," *Berlin.de*, accessed May 31, 2025, https://www.berlin.de/mauer/en/sites/memorials/weisse-kreuze-memorial-_-german-bundestag-479244.php.

ISTANBUL

65 Ann Gibbons, "Why 536 Was 'The Worst Year to Be Alive,'" *Science*, November 15, 2018, https://www.science.org/content/article/why-536-was-worst-year-be-alive.
66 Blake Ehrlich, "Istanbul," *Encyclopedia Britannica*, accessed May 16, 2025, https://www.britannica.com/place/Istanbul.
67 "Hagia Sophia," *Encyclopedia Britannica*, accessed May 17, 2025, https://www.britannica.com/topic/Hagia-Sophia.
68 Procopius, *History of the Wars, Books III and IV: The Vandalic War*, trans. Dewing (The Project Gutenberg, 2020), https://www.gutenberg.org/cache/epub/16765/pg16765-images.html.
69 Becky Little, "Why Much of the World Went Dark for 18 Months in 536," *History*, November 18, 2018, https://www.history.com/articles/536-volcanic-eruption-fog-eclipse-worst-year.
70 Austin A. Mardon, et al., *535–536 AD: The Worst Year in Existence* (Golden Meteorite Press, 2021), 12.
71 John L. Teall and Donald MacGillivray Nicol, "Byzantine Empire," *Encyclopedia Britannica*, last updated August 31, 2025, https://www.britannica.com/place/Byzantine-Empire.
72 Teall and Nicol, "Byzantine Empire."
73 "Myths and Legends," *Ayasofya-i Kebîr Câmi-I Şerîfi*, accessed June 1, 2025, https://ayasofyaikebircamii.gov.tr/en/myths-and-legends/.
74 "Hagia Sophia," *Müze İstanbul*, accessed June 1, 2025, https://muze.gen.tr/muze-detay/ayasofya.
75 "Hagia Sophia," *Encyclopedia Britannica*.
76 Miles Pattenden, "Volcanoes, Plague, Famine and Endless Winter: Welcome to 536, What Historians and Scientists Believe Was the 'Worst Year to Be Alive,'" The Conversation, February 1, 2022, https://theconversation.com/volcanoes-plague-famine-and-endless-winter-welcome-to-536-what-historians-and-scientists-believe-was-the-worst-year-to-be-alive-175654.
77 Little, "Why Much of the World Went Dark."
78 Gibbons, "'The Worst Year to Be Alive.'"
79 "Plague of Justinian," *Encyclopedia Britannica*, March 1, 2024, https://www.britannica.com/event/plague-of-Justinian.
80 Elizabeth Angell, "A Seismic Cityscape: Earthquakes in Istanbul's History," *History of Istanbul*, 2015, https://istanbultarihi.ist/396-a-seismic-cityscape-earthquakes-in-istanbuls-history.

KYOTO

81 Romulus Hillsborough, *Shinsengumi: The Shogun's Last Samurai Corps* (Tuttle Publishing, 2005), 106, https://play.google.com/books/reader?id=jUzRAgAAQBAJ&pg=GBS.PT2&hl=en_GB.
82 "The United States and the Opening to Japan, 1853," Office of the Historian, n.d., https://history.state.gov/milestones/1830-1860/opening-to-japan.

83 Anchi Hoh, "Perry in Edo Bay: The Dawn of the U.S.-Japanese Relationship," *4 Corners of the World* (blog), May 19, 2019, https://blogs.loc.gov/international-collections/2019/05/perry-in-edo-bay-the-dawn-of-the-u-s-japanese-relationship/.
84 Hillsborough, *Shinsengumi: Last Samurai Corps.*
85 Otis Cary, "Kyōto," *Encyclopedia Britannica*, accessed April 27, 2025, https://www.britannica.com/place/Kyoto-Japan.
86 "The Rōnin," *Shinsengume Japan*, accessed February 25, 2024, https://shinsengumijapan.com/en/history/ronins/.
87 Hillsborough, *Shinsengumi: Last Samurai Corps*, 30.
88 Hillsborough, *Shinsengumi: Last Samurai Corps*, 26–27.
89 Hillsborough, "Slaughter at the Ikéda'ya," in *Shinsengumi: Last Samurai Corps*.
90 Chris Rowthorn, "Kyoto Samurai," *Inside Kyoto*, accessed May 8, 2025, https://www.insidekyoto.com/kyoto-samurai.
91 Council on Tall Buildings and Urban Habitat, "Cities by Number of 150m+ Buildings," The Skyscraper Center, accessed June 1, 2025, https://www.skyscrapercenter.com/cities.
92 JAL Editorial Staff, "5 Must-See Temples in Japan's Old Capital," *Japan Airlines*, accessed June 1, 2025, https://www.jal.co.jp/br/en/guide-to-japan/destinations/articles/kyoto/5-must-see-temples-in-ancient-capital.html.
93 Justin McCurry, "Kyoto Bans Tourists From Parts of Geisha District Amid Reports of Bad Behaviour," *The Guardian*, August 1, 2024, https://www.theguardian.com/world/2024/mar/08/kyoto-geisha-district-tourist-ban-gion.
94 *Encyclopaedia Britannica*, "geisha," December 21, 2024, https://www.britannica.com/art/geisha.
95 Kimono Tea Ceremony Maikoya, "Kyoto Geisha Shows and Experiences Gion Maikoya," Mai-ko, n.d., https://mai-ko.com/geisha/.
96 Rowthorn, "Kyoto Samurai."
97 Hillsborough, *Shinsengumi: Last Samurai Corps*, 105–106.
98 Hillsborough, *Shinsengumi: Last Samurai Corps*, 109–11.
99 "Nakaoka Shintaro," National Diet Library, accessed June 1, 2025, https://www.ndl.go.jp/portrait/e/datas/149/.
100 Hillsborough, *Shinsengumi: Last Samurai Corps*, 113–115.
101 "Meiji Restoration," *Encyclopedia Britannica*, accessed April 21, 2025, https://www.britannica.com/event/Meiji-Restoration.
102 Hillsborough, *Shinsengumi: Last Samurai Corps*.
103 "Kodai-ji Temple," Kyoto City Official Travel Guide, n.d., https://kyoto.travel/en/shrine_temple/157.html.

VIETNAM

104 "Mythical Creatures in Vietnamese Culture," *British Library: Asian and African Studies Blog*, April 21, 2016, https://blogs.bl.uk/asian-and-african/2016/04/mythical-creatures-in-vietnamese-culture.html.
105 "Mythical Creatures," *British Library.*
106 Milton Edgeworth Osborne and William S. Turley, "History of Vietnam," *Encyclopedia Britannica*, accessed April 24, 2025, https://www.britannica.com/topic/history-of-Vietnam.
107 "Co Loa—the Oldest Citadel in Viet Nam," *Viet Nam National Authority of Tourism*, April 11, 2017, https://vietnamtourism.gov.vn/en/post/11690.
108 *Encyclopedia Britannica*, "Hanoi," June 23, 2025, https://www.britannica.com/place/Hanoi.
109 *Encyclopedia Britannica*, "Later Le Dynasty," April 16, 2012, https://www.britannica.com/topic/Later-Le-dynasty.
110 Osborne and Turley, "History of Vietnam."
111 "Nguyen Dynasty," *Encyclopedia Britannica*, accessed June 1, 2025, https://www.britannica.com/topic/Nguyen-dynasty.
112 "Imperial Legacy of Huế, Our Ancient Capital in the Nguyen Dynasty," *Consulate General of Vietnam to New South Wales, Queensland and South Australia*, accessed June 1, 2025, http://vietnamconsulate.org.au/en/aboutvn/imperial-legacy-of-hue-our-ancient-capital-in-the-nguyen-dynasty-8.html.
113 "Tet Offensive," *Encyclopedia Britannica*, accessed May 16, 2025, https://www.britannica.com/topic/Tet-Offensive.
114 "Mythical Creatures," *British Library.*
115 Chủ Nhật, "The Most Precious Collection of Vietnam's Sacred Animals," *Public Security News*, October 24, 2016, https://en.cand.com.vn/culture-travel/The-most-precious-collection-of-Vietnam-s-sacred-animals-i409202/.
116 "Beliefs & Religions," *Embassy of the Socialist Republic of Vietnam in the United States*, accessed June 1, 2025, https://vietnamembassy-usa.org/culture/beliefs-religions.
117 Tu Weiming, "Confucianism," *Encyclopedia Britannica*, March 27, 2025, https://www.britannica.com/topic/Confucianism.
118 Vu Hong Van, "Restoration of Confucianism and the Phenomenon of Three Religions of the Homeland Under the Nguyen Dynasty," *Turkish Online Journal of Qualitative Inquiry* 12, no. 3 (July 2021): 1520–33, https://www.tojqi.net/index.php/journal/article/view/1522/795.
119 "Descendants of Dragons and Fairies: Vietnamese History Before French Colonisation," *National Library Singapore*, accessed June 1, 2025, https://biblioasia.nlb.gov.sg/vol-2/issue3/oct-2006/dragon-fairies-vietnamese-french-history/.
120 Nhật, "Vietnam's Sacred Animals."
121 Nguyễn Minh Anh, "The Legend of Hoan Kiem Lake," *Heritage Vietnam Airline* (blog), September 27, 2023, https://heritagevietnamairlines.com/en/the-legend-of-hoan-kiem-lake/.
122 "Mythical Creatures," *British Library.*
123 Nguyen Thi Hoai Chau, "Changing of Ancestor Worship in the Confucian Patrilineal Descent Group in Vietnam: The Case of Ho Chi Minh City," *Journal of Advanced Research in Social Sciences and Humanities* 2, no. 5 (October 17, 2017): https://doi.org/10.26500/jarssh-02-2017-0506.

SYDNEY

124 "Jørn Utzon AC," Sydney Opera House, accessed February 14, 2024, https://www.sydneyoperahouse.com/our-story/jorn-utzon.
125 "The Spherical Solution," Sydney Opera House, accessed February 14, 2024, https://www.sydneyoperahouse.com/our-story/the-spherical-solution.
126 "Interesting Facts About Sydney Opera House," Sydney Opera House, accessed February 14, 2024, https://www.sydneyoperahouse.com/building/interesting-facts-about-sydney-opera-house.
127 "Utzon Departs the House," Sydney Opera House, accessed February 14, 2024, https://www.sydneyoperahouse.com/our-story/utzon-departs-the-house.
128 "The First Fleet Arrives at Sydney Cove," *National Museum of Australia*, accessed June 2, 2025, https://digital-classroom.nma.gov.au/defining-moments/first-fleet-arrives-sydney-cove.
129 "Governor Phillip's Instructions 25 April 1787 (UK)," *Documenting Democracy*, accessed June 23, 2025, https://www.foundingdocs.gov.au/item-did-35.html.

130 Grace Karskens, "Phillip and the Eora: Governing Race Relations in the Colony of New South Wales," *Sydney Journal* 5, no. 1 (September 1, 2017): 39–55, https://doi.org/10.5130/sj.v5i1.5728.
131 Grace Karksens, "Governor Phillip and the Eora," The Dictionary of Sydney, 2017, https://dictionaryofsydney.org/entry/governor_phillip_and_the_eora.
132 Karskens, "Governing Race Relations."
133 Keith Vincent Smith, "Bennelong Among His People," *Aboriginal History Journal* 33 (April 1, 2010): 8–9, https://doi.org/10.22459/ah.33.2010.01.
134 Eleanor Dark, "Bennelong (c. 1764–1813)," *Australian Dictionary of Biography,* January 1, 1966, https://adb.anu.edu.au/biography/bennelong-1769.
135 Keith Vincent Smith, "Woollarawarre Bennelong," *The Dictionary of Sydney*, 2013, https://dictionaryofsydney.org/entry/woollarawarre_bennelong.
136 Smith, "Bennelong Among His People."
137 Smith, "Woollarawarre Bennelong."
138 "Bennelong and Phillip: The Entangled Lives of Two Very Different Men," *University of Technology Sydney*, November 1, 2023, https://www.uts.edu.au/news/2023/11/bennelong-and-phillip-entangled-lives-two-very-different-men.
139 Smith, "Woollarawarre Bennelong."
140 Karskens, "Governing Race Relations."
141 Keith Vincent Smith, "Willemering," *The Dictionary of Sydney*, 2016, https://dictionaryofsydney.org/entry/willemering.
142 "Spearing the Governor," Natural History Museum, n.d., https://www.nhm.ac.uk/nature-online/art-nature-imaging/collections/first-fleet/spearing-governor/index.html.
143 Smith, "Woollarawarre Bennelong."
144 "Profile of First Nations People," Australia Institute of Health and Welfare, July 2, 2024, https://www.aihw.gov.au/reports/australias-welfare/profile-of-indigenous-australians.
145 "Indigenous Australians: Aboriginal and Torres Strait Islander People," *Australian Institute of Aboriginal and Torres Strait Islander Studies*, AIATSIS, accessed June 2, 2025, https://aiatsis.gov.au/explore/indigenous-australians-aboriginal-and-torres-strait-islander-people.
146 "Evidence of First Peoples," *National Museum of Australia*, accessed June 23, 2025, https://www.nma.gov.au/defining-moments/resources/evidence-of-first-peoples.
147 "Aboriginal Flag to Permanently Replace NSW Flag on Sydney Harbour Bridge," *The Guardian*, July 10, 2022, https://www.theguardian.com/australia-news/2022/jul/11/aboriginal-flag-to-permanently-replace-nsw-flag-on-sydney-harbour-bridge.
148 "Bara," City of Sydney, accessed June 2, 2025, https://www.cityofsydney.nsw.gov.au/monuments-and-memorials/bara.
149 "Tourism Australia's Dual Naming Approach," Tourism Australia, March 3, 2023, https://www.tourism.australia.com/en/news-and-events/news/tourism-australias-dual-naming-approach.html.
150 "Acknowledgement of Country and Welcome to Country," Reconciliation Australia, accessed April 29, 2025, https://www.reconciliation.org.au/reconciliation/acknowledgement-of-country-and-welcome-to-country/.
151 Ronan O'Connell, "Australia Hands Control of Its Newest National Parks to Indigenous Peoples," *National Geographic*, October 6, 2022, https://www.nationalgeographic.com/travel/article/australia-hands-control-newest-national-parks-to-indigenous-peoples.
152 Dark, "Bennelong (c. 1764–1813)."
153 Smith, "Woollarawarre Bennelong."
154 "Colonial Frontier Massacres in Australia, 1788-1930," University of New Castle Australia, accessed June 2, 2025, https://c21ch.newcastle.edu.au/colonialmassacres/statistics.php.
155 Dark, "Bennelong (c. 1764–1813)."
156 "Finding Bennelong," City of Ryde, accessed June 2, 2025, https://www.ryde.nsw.gov.au/Finding-Bennelong.

LISBON

157 Ronan O'Connell, "The Long Lost City of Tamão Is Hiding in Plain Sight," *National Geographic*, March 15, 2021, https://www.nationalgeographic.com/travel/article/long-lost-city-tamao-hiding-in-plain-sight.
158 "Baixa," Turismo De Lisboa, accessed June 2, 2025, https://www.visitlisboa.com/en/places/baixa-chiado.
159 "Praça Do Comércio (Terreiro Do Paço)," Turismo De Lisboa, accessed June 2, 2025, https://www.visitlisboa.com/en/places/praca-do-comercio-terreiro-do-paco.
160 "Lisbon Earthquake of 1755," Encyclopedia Britannica, accessed April 30, 2025, https://www.britannica.com/event/Lisbon-earthquake-of-1755.
161 "National Tile Museum," Turismo De Lisboa, accessed June 2, 2025, https://www.visitlisboa.com/en/places/national-tile-museum.
162 "King Manuel I," Castelo De São Jorge, accessed June 2, 2025, https://castelodesaojorge.pt/en/education/schools/educational-content/important-figures/king-manuel-i/.
163 J. M. Braga, *China Landfall, 1513: Jorge Alvares' Voyage to China: A Compilation of Some Relevant Material*, 1955, http://nla.gov.au/nla.obj-239881932.
164 Dan Allosso and Tom Williford, "The World at 1500," *World History*, LOUIS: The Louisiana Library Network, August 1, 2022, https://louis.pressbooks.pub/worldciv2/chapter/chapter-1-the-world-at-1500/.
165 Angus Maddison, *The World Economy: Historical Statistics, Development Centre Studies* (OECD Publishing, 2003), https://doi.org/10.1787/9789264104143-en.
166 Braga, *China Landfall*, 24.
167 Braga, *China Landfall*, 17.
168 Braga, *China Landfall*.
169 Braga, *China Landfall*.
170 Braga, *China Landfall*, 53–55.
171 "Macau," *Encyclopedia Britannica*, accessed May 12, 2025, https://www.britannica.com/place/Macau-administrative-region-China.
172 Lisboa Cultura, "The Squares," Castelo De São Jorge, accessed June 24, 2025, https://castelodesaojorge.pt/en/castle/national-monument/the-squares/.
173 "National Monument," Castelo De São Jorge, accessed June 2, 2025, https://castelodesaojorge.pt/en/castle/national-monument/the-castelo-de-sao-jorge/.
174 "Leisure Area in Praça de Jorge Álvares," Macao Nature, accessed June 2, 2025, https://www.iam.gov.mo/nature/e/facility/rest/detail?id=1b5f9b0e-935c-4d96-ba55-d28224cdc7ba.
175 Braga, *China Landfall*, 54.

DUBAI

176 Irish Eden Belleza, "Burj Khalifa: Towering Challenge for Builders," *Gulf News*, September 15, 2018, https://gulfnews.com/business/property/burj-khalifa-towering-challenge-for-builders-1.561802.
177 Sonja Anderson, "The Never-Ending Race to Build the World's Tallest Structure," *Smithsonian Magazine*, October 26, 2023, https://www.smithsonianmag.com/innovation/race-to-the-sky-the-worlds-tallest-buildings-180983131/.
178 Jane Englefield, "SOM's Burj Khalifa Was the Most Significant Building of 2010," *Dezeen*, January 16, 2025, https://www.dezeen.com/2025/01/16/som-burj-khalifa-21st-century-architecture.
179 "Discover the Burj Khalifa's Incredible Architectural and Design Features," Visit Dubai, August 24, 2020, https://www.visitdubai.com/en/articles/burj-khalifa-architecture-design.
180 Anderson, "The Never-Ending Race."

181 Hiba Alothman, "An Evaluative and Critical Study of Mashrabiya: In Contemporary Architecture" (Graduate Thesis, Near East University, 2017), https://www.dropbox.com/scl/fi/uw8oc697a6c545ivx1rhn/Mashrabiya-study.pdf?rlkey=u06f985vfj7yeor2oar5hm4jh&e=1&st=26icyhr5&dl=0.
182 "In 'City of Shanasheel,' Iraqi Heritage Crumbles from Neglect," France 24, March 26, 2018, https://www.france24.com/en/20180326-city-shanasheel-iraqi-heritage-crumbles-neglect.
183 Demet Taşkan and Alzahraa Ismaeel, "Mimari Bir Eleman: Maşrabiye," Art-Sanat 0, no. 17 (January 27, 2022): 475–96, https://doi.org/10.26650/artsanat.2022.17.841296.
184 Feza Tabassum Azmi, "How India's Lattice Buildings Cool Without Air Con," *BBC*, September 21, 2022, https://www.bbc.com/future/article/20220920-how-indias-lattice-buildings-cool-without-air-con.
185 John Feeney, "The Magic of the Mashrabiyas," *Saudi Aramco World*, 1974, https://archive.aramcoworld.com/issue/197404/the.magic.of.the.mashrabiyas.htm.
186 Hiba Alothman, "An Evaluative Study of Mashrabiya."
187 "Discover the Burj Khalifa's Incredible Features." Visit Dubai.
188 Feeney, "The Magic of the Mashrabiyas."

AMSTERDAM

189 Michael J. Wintle et al., "Amsterdam," *Encyclopedia Britannica*, accessed May 15, 2025, https://www.britannica.com/place/Amsterdam.
190 "Koninklijk Paleis Amsterdam," Paleis Amsterdam, accessed June 2, 2025, https://www.paleisamsterdam.nl/.
191 "National Monument," *I Amsterdam*, accessed June 2, 2025, https://www.iamsterdam.com/en/whats-on/calendar/attractions-and-sights/sights/national-monument.
192 Jamie Doward, "Why Europe's Wars of Religion Put 40,000 'Witches' to a Terrible Death," *The Guardian*, January 13, 2018, https://www.theguardian.com/society/2018/jan/07/witchcraft-economics-reformation-catholic-protestant-market-share.
193 J. B. Russell, "witch hunt," *Encyclopedia Britannica*, January 30, 2025, https://www.britannica.com/topic/witch-hunt.
194 Dries Vanysacker, "Witch Hunts in the Low Countries (1450–1685)," *The Routledge History of Witchcraft*, e-book (Routledge, 2019), 113–24, https://doi.org/10.4324/9781003010296-10.
195 "Haunted Places in Amsterdam for Halloween Lovers," *I Amsterdam*, accessed June 2, 2025, https://www.iamsterdam.com/en/see-and-do/attractions-and-sights/haunted-places-in-amsterdam.
196 "Witch Trials & Witchcraft," Library of Congress Research Guides, accessed June 2, 2025, https://guides.loc.gov/feminism-french-women-history/witch-trials-witchcraft.
197 "De Europese Heksenvervolgingen En Hun Gevolgen," Atria, October 4, 2022, https://atria.nl/nieuws-publicaties/geweld-tegen-vrouwen/europese-heksenvervolgingen/.
198 Machteld Löwensteyn, "Unravelling the Myth and Histories of the Weighing Test at Oudewater: The Case of Leentje Willems," *Cultures of Witchcraft in Europe from the Middle Ages to the Present*, e-book (Springer, 2017), 101–120, https://doi.org/10.1007/978-3-319-63784-6_5.
199 "De Europese Heksenvervolgingen En Hun Gevolgen," Atria.
200 Susan Smit, "You Are Not a Fallen Angel, Never Have Been," Amsterdam Museum, July 11, 2024, https://www.amsterdammuseum.nl/en/topic/women-of-amsterdam/contribution/114032-you-are-not-a-fallen-angel-never-have-been.
201 Vanysacker, "Witch Hunts in the Low Countries (1450–1685)," 113–124, https://doi.org/10.4324/9781003010296-10.
202 George Lincoln Burr, Henry Charles Lea, and Arthur C. Howland, *Materials Toward a History of Witchcraft, Volume 3, (University of Pennsylvania Press*, 1939), https://doi.org/10.9783/9781512820591.
203 "Global Social Progress Index," Social Progress Imperative, 2025, https://www.socialprogress.org/social-progress-index.
204 Kusum Kali Pal et al., "Global Gender Gap Report 2024," *World Economic Forum* (World Economic Forum, June 11, 2024), https://www.weforum.org/publications/global-gender-gap-report-2024/digest/.
205 "Home," Nationaal Heksenmonument, accessed June 2, 2025, https://www.nationaalheksenmonument.nl/.
206 De Mediagraaf, "The Weigh House," Museum De Heksenwaag Oudewater, September 20, 2024, https://heksenwaag.nl/en/.
207 Senay Boztas, "Dutch Feminists Campaign for National Monument to 'Witches,'" *The Guardian*, October 4, 2024, https://www.theguardian.com/world/2024/oct/04/dutch-feminists-campaign-for-national-monument-to-witches.

THAILAND

208 Supin Wongbusarakum, *The Urak Lawoi' of the Adang Archipalego* (Themma Group Co, 2007), https://unesdoc.unesco.org/ark:/48223/pf0000152346/PDF/152346eng.pdf.multi.
209 Erik Nilsson, *Waves of Change: Traditional Religion Among the Urak Lawoi, Sea Nomads of Ko Lanta Thailand*, 2010.
210 Wongbusarakum, *The Urak Lawoi'*.
211 "About Phi Phi Islands," Thai National Parks, accessed June 3, 2025, https://www.thainationalparks.com/hat-noppharat-thara-mu-ko-phi-phi-national-park.
212 "Ko Phi Phi," Amazing Thailand, n.d., https://www.tourismthailand.org/Destinations/Provinces/Ko-Phi-Phi/359.
213 Karla Cripps, "Tourism Killed Thailand's Most Famous Bay. Here's How It Was Brought Back to Life," *CNN Travel*, August 1, 2022, https://www.cnn.com/travel/article/maya-bay-thailand-recovery-c2e-spc-intl.
214 Bloomberg and Bloomberg, "Move Over Singapore, Vietnam Is Now Southeast Asia's Third-Most-Visited Country," *South China Morning Post*, March 25, 2025, https://sc.mp/68u5g?utm_source=copy-link&utm_campaign=3303767&utm_medium=share_widget.
215 Ronan O'Connell, "'The Beach': Witnessing the Heartening Recovery at Thailand's Maya Bay," *The National*, February 16, 2022, https://www.thenationalnews.com/travel/destinations/2022/02/16/the-beach-what-its-like-at-thailands-maya-bay-now-its-reopened-after-four-years/.
216 Nationthailand, "Maya Bay in Krabi to Be Closed to Tourists From August 1," *Nationthailand*, July 26, 2024, https://www.nationthailand.com/news/tourism/40040034.
217 Wongbusarakum, *The Urak Lawoi'*.
218 "Sea People Still Wait for Justice," *Bangkok Post*, accessed May 25, 2024, https://www.bangkokpost.com/opinion/opinion/2799514/sea-people-still-wait-for-justice.

BELFAST

219 "Titanic Belfast—Future Belfast," Future Belfast, July 4, 2016, https://www.futurebelfast.com/property/1-olympic-way-titanic-belfast/.
220 "About Titanic Belfast," Titanic Belfast, accessed June 3, 2025, https://www.titanicbelfast.com/explore/about-titanic-belfast/.
221 "The Titanic Experience," Titanic Belfast, accessed June 3, 2025, https://www.titanicbelfast.com/experiences/the-titanic-experience/.

222 Joel Mokyr, "Great Famine," *Encyclopedia Britannica*, accessed April 22, 2025, https://www.britannica.com/event/Great-Famine-Irish-history.
223 "Harland and Wolff: The Troubled History of Belfast's Shipyard," *BBC News*, August 6, 2019, https://www.bbc.com/news/uk-northern-ireland-49234995.
224 "Harland and Wolff," *BBC News*.
225 "Titanic Quarter Belfast," Titanic Quarter, n.d., https://titanicquarter.com/.
226 Amy Tikkanen, "Titanic," *Encyclopedia Britannica*, accessed May 9, 2025, https://www.britannica.com/topic/Titanic.
227 "Antarctic Iceberg Tracking," US National Ice Center, accessed June 3, 2025, https://usicecenter.gov/Resources/AntarcticIcebergs.
228 Tikkanen, "Titanic."
229 "Titanic in Black and White," Library of Virginia, accessed June 3, 2025, https://www.lva.virginia.gov/exhibits/titanic/newspaper_coverage.php.
230 Tikkanen, "Titanic."
231 The British Government, Report: "Loss of the Steamship 'Titanic,'" *Project Gutenberg*, April 15, 2012, https://www.gutenberg.org/cache/epub/39415/pg39415-images.html.
232 Donald W. Olson J., Russell L. Doescher, and Roger W. Sinnott, "Did the Moon Sink the Titanic?," *Sky & Telescope*, 2012, 34–37, https://www.skyandtelescope.com/wp-content/uploads/Titanic+layout.pdf.
233 "Frequency of Tides," National Oceanic and Atmospheric Administration, accessed June 3, 2025, https://oceanservice.noaa.gov/education/tutorial_tides/tides05_lunarday.html.
234 Olson et al., "Did the Moon Sink the Titanic?"

KUALA LUMPUR

235 "Hindus Unveil Colossal Statue," *Al Jazeera*, January 30, 2006, https://www.aljazeera.com/news/2006/1/30/hindus-unveil-colossal-statue.
236 Robert Lewis, "Batu Caves," *Encyclopedia Britannica*, accessed March 7, 2025, https://www.britannica.com/place/Batu-Caves.
237 "As Greater KL's Population Hits 8.8 Million and Counting, Minister Flags Challenges, Says Pressure Now on DBKL for Proactive City Planning," *Malay Mail*, August 7, 2024, https://www.malaymail.com/news/malaysia/2024/08/06/as-greater-kls-population-hits-88-million-and-counting-minister-flags-challenges-says-pressure-now-on-dbkl-for-proactive-city-planning/146201.
238 "Petronas Twin Towers," Petronas KLCC, accessed June 3, 2025, https://www.petronastwintowers.com.my/.
239 "Merdeka 118," Council on Tall Buildings and Urban Habitat, accessed June 3, 2025, https://www.skyscrapercenter.com/building/merdeka-118/10115.
240 "Murugan," *Encyclopedia Britannica*, accessed April 26, 2025, https://www.britannica.com/topic/Murugan.
241 Carl Vadivella Belle, *Thaipusam in Malaysia: A Hindu Festival in the Tamil Diaspora*, e-book (ISEAS Publishing, 2017), 147–148, http://muse.jhu.edu/chapter/1946806.
242 Bonny Tan, "Thaipusam," National Library Board Singapore, accessed June 3, 2025, https://www.nlb.gov.sg/main/article-detail?cmsuuid=deea4c72-513b-4f08-95a7-3f41b5a0eff0.
243 Max Moseley, "History of Biological Investigations at Batu Caves, Malaysia, and Consequences for the Progress of Tropical Speleobiology: Part 1 - the 19th Century," *Cave and Karst Science* 41, no. 2 (2014): 52–56.
244 Nor Bakhiah Baharim, Ros Fatihah Muhammad, and Ismail Yusoff, "Hydrogeochemical Evolution in a Tropical Cave System; Batu Caves, Peninsular Malaysia," *Journal of Sustainability Science and Management* 13, no. 1 (January 1, 2018): 77–92, https://www.cabdirect.org/cabdirect/abstract/20193256562.
245 "Batu Caves," Visit Malaysia, accessed June 3, 2025, https://www.malaysia.travel/explore/batu-caves.
246 "Thaipusam Festival 2026," Visiting Singapore, accessed June 3, 2025, https://www.visitsingapore.com/whats-happening/all-happenings/festivals/thaipusam/.
247 Benjamin Lee and Ho Jia Wen, "More Than One Million Devotees Throng Batu Caves for Thaipusam," *The Star*, January 25, 2024, https://www.thestar.com.my/news/nation/2024/01/25/more-than-one-million-devotees-throng-batu-caves-for-thaipusam.
248 Dhesegaan Bala Krishnan, "Not Just About 'Kavadi' and Batu Caves: What Is Thaipusam and How Did It Become Massive in Malaysia?" *Malay Mail*, February 10, 2025, https://www.malaymail.com/news/malaysia/2025/02/11/not-just-about-kavadi-and-batu-caves-what-is-thaipusam-and-how-did-it-become-massive-in-malaysia/165864.
249 Tan, "Thaipusam."

BUDAPEST

250 Andor Klay, "Hungarian Counterfeit Francs: A Case of Post-World War I Political Sabotage," *Slavic Review* 33, no. 1 (March 1, 1974): 107–13, https://doi.org/10.2307/2495329.
251 Lásló Péter, "Budapest," *Encyclopedia Britannica*, accessed May 18, 2025, https://www.britannica.com/place/Budapest.
252 "Parliament," *Budapest Info*, accessed June 4, 2025, https://www.budapestinfo.hu/en/parliament.
253 "Budapest, Hungary—Parliament Buildings," University of Pennsylvania, accessed June 4, 2025, https://rees.sas.upenn.edu/about/spotlight/budapest-hungary-—-parliament-buildings.
254 "A Walk Through the House of Parliament," Hungarian National Assembly, accessed June 29, 2025, https://www.parlament.hu/web/visitors/visitor-route.
255 "A Guide to the United States' History of Recognition, Diplomatic, and Consular Relations, by Country, Since 1776: Hungary," Office of the Historian, accessed June 4, 2025, https://history.state.gov/countries/hungary.
256 "Post-war Turmoil and Violence (Hungary)," 1914–1918 Online (WW1) Encyclopedia, July 9, 2024, https://encyclopedia.1914-1918-online.net/article/post-war-turmoil-and-violence-hungary-1-1/.
257 Steven Béla Várdy et al. "History of Hungary," *Encyclopedia Britannica*, accessed March 18, 2025, https://www.britannica.com/topic/history-of-Hungary.
258 Andor Klay, "Hungarian Counterfeit Francs: A Case of Post-World War I Political Sabotage," *Slavic Review* 33, no. 1 (March 1, 1974): 107–13, https://doi.org/10.2307/2495329.
259 Klay, "Hungarian Counterfeit Francs."
260 Klay, "Hungarian Counterfeit Francs."

CAMBODIA

261 Robert Stencel, Fred Gifford, and Eleanor Morón, "Astronomy and Cosmology at Angkor Wat," *Science* 193, no. 4250 (1976): 281–87, http://www.jstor.org/stable/1742346.
262 "Banknotes in Circulation," National Bank of Cambodia, accessed June 4, 2025, https://www.nbc.gov.kh/english about_the_bank/banknotes_in_circulation.php.
263 "Angkor Wat," *Encyclopedia Britannica*, accessed May 21, 2025, https://www.britannica.com/topic/Angkor-Wat.
264 "Cambodia," *CIA World Factbook*, accessed June 4, 2025, https://www.cia.gov/the-world-factbook/countries/cambodia/.
265 Ethan Teekah, "Khmer empire," *Encyclopedia Britannica*, accessed April 12, 2025, https://www.britannica.com/topic/Khmer-Empire.

266 Oliver Wainwright, "Lost Cities #7: How NASA Technology Uncovered the 'Megacity' of Angkor," *The Guardian*, February 3, 2020, https://www.theguardian.com/cities/2016/aug/16/lost-cities-6-angkor-wat-nasa-technology-khmer-megacity.
267 "Angkor," UNESCO *World Heritage Convention*, accessed June 4, 2025, https://whc.unesco.org/en/list/668/.
268 "Angkor Wat," *Encyclopedia Britannica*.
269 Melody Rod-ari, "Angkor Wat," Khan Academy, accessed June 4, 2025, https://www.khanacademy.org/humanities/ap-art-history/south-east-se-asia/cambodia-art/a/angkor-wat.
270 "churning of the ocean of milk," *Encyclopedia Britannica*, October 15, 2024, https://www.britannica.com/topic/churning-of-the-ocean-of-milk.
271 "Angkor Wat," *Encyclopedia Britannica*.
272 Rod-ari, "Angkor Wat."
273 Subhash Kak and Department of Electrical & Computer Engineering, "Time, Space, and Astronomy in Angkor Wat," *Louisiana State University*, August 6, 2001, https://www.ece.lsu.edu/kak/ang3.pdf.

PARIS

274 "Mata Hari," *Encyclopedia Britannica*, accessed March 27, 2025, https://www.britannica.com/biography/Mata-Hari-Dutch-dancer-and-spy.
275 "The Eiffel Tower and Science," La Tour Eiffel, accessed February 28, 2024, https://www.toureiffel.paris/en/the-monument/eiffel-tower-and-science.
276 Saskia O'Donoghue, "Paris Says 'Non' to Tall Buildings—but What's Behind the Ban?" *Euronews*, June 14, 2023, https://www.euronews.com/culture/2023/06/14/paris-says-non-to-tall-buildings-but-whats-behind-the-ban.
276 "Explore the Top of the Eiffel Tower," La Tour Eiffel, accessed October 14, 2024, https://www.toureiffel.paris/en/explore/top.
278 "Explore the First Floor of the Eiffel Tower," La Tour Eiffel, November 19, 2024, https://www.toureiffel.paris/en/explore/first-floor.
279 "Eiffel Tower Key Stats: The Tower in Numbers," La Tour Eiffel, accessed August 21, 2024, https://www.toureiffel.paris/en/the-monument/key-figures.
280 "Ticket Rates and Opening Times," La Tour Eiffel, n.d., https://www.toureiffel.paris/en/rates-opening-times.
281 "The Birth of the Eiffel Tower," La Tour Eiffel (part of the official Eiffel Tower website), accessed November 28, 2024, https://www.toureiffel.paris/en/the-monument/history.
282 "The Eiffel Tower in Lights," La Tour Eiffel (part of the official Eiffel Tower website), accessed March 12, 2025, https://www.toureiffel.paris/en/the-monument/lights.
283 "Mata Hari," *Encyclopedia Britannica.*
284 "The Real Story of Mata Hari," Fries Museum, accessed June 4, 2025, https://www.friesmuseum.nl/en/collection/icons/mata-hari.
285 "Mata Hari," *Encyclopedia Britannica*.
286 "The Real Story of Mata Hari," Fries Museum.
287 Tara Finn, "Mata Hari: The Execution of an Alleged International Spy-Mistress," *History of government* (blog), October 13, 2017, https://history.blog.gov.uk/2017/10/13/mata-hari-the-execution-of-an-alleged-international-spy-mistress/.
288 "The Real Story of Mata Hari," Fries Museum.
289 "Mata Hari," *Encyclopedia Britannica*.
290 "Eiffel Tower," *National Geographic Kids*, July 30, 2024, https://kids.nationalgeographic.com/history/article/eiffel-tower.
291 "The Real Story of Mata Hari," Fries Museum.

IGUAZU FALLS

292 "Iguaçu Falls," *Encyclopedia Britannica*, accessed May 7, 2025, https://www.britannica.com/place/Iguacu-Falls.
293 "Iguaçu National Park," UNESCO World Heritage Centre, accessed June 4, 2025, https://whc.unesco.org/en/list/355/.
294 "Iguazu National Park," UNESCO World Heritage Centre, accessed June 30, 2025, https://whc.unesco.org/en/list/303/.
295 "Discovering the Fauna of the Iguaçu National Park," WWF-Brasil, August 24, 2014, https://www.wwf.org.br/?41025/Discovering-the-fauna-of-the-Iguau-National-Park.
296 "Welcome to the Iguazu Falls National Park!," Iguazú Argentina, accessed June 4, 2025, https://iguazuargentina.com/en/centrodevisitante.
297 "FAQ," Iguazú Argentina, accessed June 4, 2025, https://iguazuargentina.com/en/preguntasfrecuentes.
298 Ramiro Rodriguez, "Who Discovered Iguazu Falls?," iguazufalls.com, accessed March 17, 2025, https://iguazufalls.com/travel-guide/who-discovered-iguazu-falls/.
299 "Guarani—Indigenous Peoples in Brazil," Povos Indígenas No Brasil, November 2011, https://pib.socioambiental.org/en/Povo:Guarani.
300 Rubén Bareiro Saguier, "Guarani Genesis: The Intricate Cosmogony of South America's 'Forest Theologians,'" *The UNESCO Courier*, 1990, https://unesdoc.unesco.org/ark:/48223/pf0000086056.locale=en.

LONDON

301 "Rotten Row," The Royal Parks, accessed September 4, 2024, https://www.royalparks.org.uk/read-watch-listen/rotten-row.
302 Masami Iliffe, "Nature in the City: Explore London's Best Parks and Green Spaces," blog, SOAS University of London, May 13, 2024, https://www.soas.ac.uk/about/blogs/nature-city-explore-londons-best-parks-and-green-spaces.
303 "Diana Memorial Fountain," The Royal Parks, accessed June 4, 2025, https://www.royalparks.org.uk/visit/parks/hyde-park/diana-memorial-fountain.
304 "Kensington Palace," Historic Royal Palaces, accessed June 4, 2025, http://hrp.org.uk/kensington-palace/#gs.g3mkck.
305 "The Story of Marble Arch," Marble Arch, accessed June 4, 2025, https://marble-arch.london/marble-arch-story/.
306 "The Family of Art, Design and Performance Museums," Victoria and Albert Museum, June 4, 2025, https://www.vam.ac.uk/?srsltid=AfmBOoq__aqsM2WSu1A82WmUQWB0P45j9CO_m4coBAiMJ00kx7pO3Ap1.
307 "The Proceedings of the Old Bailey—London, 1674 to 1715," Old Bailey Online, accessed June 4, 2025, https://www.oldbaileyonline.org/about/london-life17th.
308 "Robin Hood," *Encyclopedia Britannica*, accessed March 26, 2025, https://www.britannica.com/topic/Robin-Hood.
309 "Dick Turpin," *Encyclopedia Britannica*, accessed April 3, 2025, https://www.britannica.com/biography/Dick-Turpin-English-criminal.
310 "Highway Robbery in the 18th Century," *BBC Bitesize*, accessed May 30, 2024, https://www.bbc.co.uk/bitesize/guides/z2cqrwx/revision/4.
311 "Rotten Row," The Royal Parks.
312 "Rotten Row," London Remembers, accessed June 4, 2025, https://www.londonremembers.com/memorials/rotten-row.
313 Horace Walpole, *The Letters of Horace Walpole, Earl of Orford*, e-book, The Project Gutenberg, vol. 2 (The Project Gutenberg, 2024), https://www.gutenberg.org/cache/epub/4610/pg4610-images.html.
314 Anthony Holden, "The Capital of Crime," *The Guardian*, February 22, 2018, https://www.theguardian.com/books/2003/apr/13/historybooks.features.

315 Charles G. Harper, "James Maclaine, the 'Gentleman' Highwayman," e-book, in *Half-Hours with the Highwaymen*, vol. 2 (The Project Gutenberg, n.d.), https://www.gutenberg.org/ebooks/53112.

316 "Highway Robbery in the 18th Century," *BBC Bitesize*.

SEOUL

317 "Gyeongbokgung Palace," Korea Tourism Organization Kto, accessed June 4, 2025, https://english.visitkorea.or.kr/svc/whereToGo/locIntrdn/rgnContentsView.do?vcontsId=87740.

318 Lee Eun-yi, "Dancheong," Korea.net, May 2019, https://www.kocis.go.kr/eng/webzine/201905/sub07.html.

319 City Overview Seoul Metropolitan Government, June 4, 2025, https://english.seoul.go.kr/seoul-views/meaning-of-seoul/4-population/.

320 "Traditional Culture: Gyeongbokgung Palace, the Best Palace from the Joseon Dynasty," Seoul Metropolitan Government, accessed June 4, 2025, https://english.seoul.go.kr/service/amusement/traditional-culture/2-five-palaces/.

321 "Bukhansan National Park (Seoul District)," VisitKorea, accessed June 4, 2025, https://english.visitkorea.or.kr/svc/whereToGo/locIntrdn/rgnContentsView.do?vcontsId=81546.

322 "Traditional Culture: Gyeongbokgung Palace," Seoul Metropolitan Government.

323 Salwa Elzeny and Korea.net, "Gyeongbokgung Palace," *Korea Blog*, December 1, 2016, https://koreanetblog.blogspot.com/2016/11/gyeongbokgung-palace.html.

324 "Gyeongbokgung Palace," VisitKorea, accessed June 4, 2025, https://english.visitkorea.or.kr/svc/whereToGo/locIntrdn/rgnContentsView.do?vcontsId=87740.

325 "Gyeongbokgung Palace," Korea Heritage Service, accessed June 4, 2025, https://english.cha.go.kr/html/HtmlPage.do?pg=/royal/RoyalPalaces_4.jsp&mn=EN_02_03_01.

326 "Gyeongbokgung Palace and Its History," Royal Palaces and Tombs Center, accessed June 30, 2025, https://royal.cha.go.kr/ENG/contents/E101010000.do.

327 Korean Culture and Information Service, *Guide to Korean Culture*, e-book (1995; repr., Seoul, Korea, Republic of: Korean Culture and Information Service Ministry of Culture, Sports and Tourism, 2013).

328 Korean Culture and Information Service, *Guide to Korean Culture*.

329 Korean Culture and Information Service, *Guide to Korean Culture*.

330 Korean Culture and Information Service, *Guide to Korean Culture*.

331 Kang Kyung-Nam, "The Lotus, Peony And Chrysanthemum," *National Museum of Korea Quarterly Magazine*, accessed June 4, 2025, https://webzine.museum.go.kr/eng/sub.html?amIdx=15509.

332 "Gyeongbokgung Palace," Korea Heritage Service.

333 Laura Lopez Velazquez, "Korean Cuisine Displays Essence of Traditional Color Palette," Korea.net, January 26, 2021, https://www.korea.net/NewsFocus/HonoraryReporters/view?articleId=194270.

334 Lee Eun-yi, "Dancheong," Korea.net, May 2019, https://www.kocis.go.kr/eng/webzine/201905/sub07.html.

335 Korean Culture and Information Service, *Guide to Korean Culture*.

336 Korean Culture and Information Service, *Guide to Korean Culture*.

337 Korean Culture and Information Service, *Guide to Korean Culture*.

338 Korean Culture and Information Service, *Guide to Korean Culture*.

PRAGUE

339 "Western Schism," *Encyclopedia Britannica*, May 16, 2025, https://www.britannica.com/event/Western-Schism.

340 M. McDonough, "Defenestration: Prague's History of Literally Throwing Authority Out the Window," *Encyclopedia Britannica*, June 13, 2025, https://www.britannica.com/story/defenestration-pragues-history-of-literally-throwing-authority-out-the-window.

341 "Old Town Hall With Astronomical Clock," Prague, accessed June 4, 2025, https://prague.eu/en/objevujte/old-town-hall-with-astronomical-clock-staromestska-radnice-s-orlojem/.

342 *Prague Astronomical Clock: Guide to the Oldest Working Astronomical Clock in the World*, (Prague: Prague City Tourism, 2020), 8.

343 Ivanka Garcia Mancebo, "Staré Město—Old Town, Historic Center of Prague," Introducing Prague, accessed June 4, 2025, https://www.introducingprague.com/stare-mesto.

344 "Jan Hus Monument," Prague, accessed May 9, 2024, https://prague.eu/en/objevujte/jan-hus-monument-pomnik-mistra-jana-husa/.

345 "Kinsky Palace," National Gallery Prague, accessed June 4, 2025, https://www.ngprague.cz/en/about/buildings/kinsky-palace.

346 "Prague City Gallery," GHMP, accessed June 4, 2025, https://www.ghmp.cz/en/.

347 "St Nicholas Cathedral—Old Town," Prague, accessed April 16, 2025, https://prague.eu/en/objevujte/st-nicholas-cathedral-old-town-chram-sv-mikulase-stare-mesto/.

348 "Church of Our Lady Before Týn," Prague, accessed April 14, 2025, https://prague.eu/en/objevujte/church-of-our-lady-before-tyn-chram-matky-bozi-pred-tynem/.

349 "Old Town Hall With Astronomical Clock," Prague.

350 "Western Schism," *Encyclopedia Britannica*.

351 Matthew Spinka and František Bartoš, "Jan Hus," *Encyclopedia Britannica*, accessed May 4, 2025, https://www.britannica.com/biography/Jan-Hus.

352 "Council of Pisa," *Encyclopedia Britannica*, January 24, 2022, https://www.britannica.com/event/Council-of-Pisa-Roman-Catholicism-1409.

353 Spinka and Bartoš, "Jan Hus."

354 "Hussite," *Encyclopedia Britannica*, April 9, 2013, https://www.britannica.com/topic/Hussite.

355 Richard Horseley Osborne et al., "Prague," *Encyclopedia Britannica*, accessed May 9, 2025, https://www.britannica.com/place/Prague.

356 "When Moderation Went Out of the Window: The First Defenestration of Prague," *British Library European Studies Blog*, July 30, 2019, https://blogs.bl.uk/european/2019/07/the-first-defenestration-of-prague.html.

357 Thomas A. Fudge, "Želivský's Head: Memory and New Martyrs Among the Hussites," *The Bohemian Reformation and Religious Practice*, vol. 6, 2007, https://brrp.org/proceedings/brrp6/fudge.pdf.

358 *Prague Astronomical Clock* (Prague City Tourism), 8.

IRELAND

359 "About the Cliffs of Moher | Cliffs of Moher Tourist Attraction in Ireland," Cliffs of Moher, January 17, 2023, https://www.cliffsofmoher.ie/about-the-cliffs-of-moher/.

360 Cynthia Smith, "Hy-Brasil: The Supernatural Island," *Worlds Revealed* (blog), *The Library of Congress*, June 3, 2020, https://blogs.loc.gov/maps/2020/06/hy-brasil-the-supernatural-island/.

361 "Mesolithic—Iron Age," Heritage Ireland, accessed June 4, 2025, https://heritageireland.ie/articles/mesolithic-iron-age-8000bc-400ad/.

362 Jenny Young et al., "Irish Myths," *Upon the Wild Waves: A Journey Through Myth in Children's Books*, Trinity College Dublin, accessed June 4, 2025, https://www.tcd.ie/library/exhibitions/wild-waves/irish_myths.php.
363 "Myths and Legends," Cliffs of Moher, accessed February 14, 2024, https://www.cliffsofmoher.ie/myths-and-legends/.
364 Ronan O'Connell, "On the Trail of Ireland's Legendary Pirate Queen," *National Geographic*, May 21, 2021, https://www.nationalgeographic.com/travel/article/on-the-trail-of-ireland-legendary-pirate-queen.
365 "Myths and Legends," Cliffs of Moher.
366 Smith, "Hy-Brasil."
367 Carl McColman, "The Celts: The People 'at the End of the World,'" Columbia Theological Seminary, May 11, 2017, https:/www.ctsnet.edu/celts-people-end-world/.
368 Barbara Freitag, "Hy Brasil: Cartographic Error, Celtic Elysium, or The New Jerusalem? Early Literary Representations of the Imaginary Brasil Island," *Irish Studies in Europe* IV (2012): 29–39, https://www.efacis.eu/sites/default/files/ISE%204_Huber,%20Mayer,%20Novak%20vol%20IV-29-39.pdf.
369 "Ortelius Atlas," The Library of Congress, accessed June 4, 2025, https://www.loc.gov/collections/general-maps/articles-and-essays/general-atlases/ortelius-atlas/.
370 Smith, "Hy-Brasil."
371 Ronan O'Connell, "These Fabled 'Ghost' Islands Exist Only in Atlases," *National Geographic*, August 24, 2022, https://www.nationalgeographic.com/travel/article/these-fabled-ghost-islands-exist-only-in-atlases.
372 Smith, "Hy-Brasil."
373 Barbara Freitag, "Hy Brasil: Early Literary Representations."
374 O'Connell, "Fabled 'Ghost' Islands."
375 "Visitor Numbers to Attractions Dashboard," Fáilte Ireland, June 4, 2025, https://www.failteireland.ie/Research-Insights/Activities/visitor-numbers-to-attractions-dashboard.aspx.
376 Mark Hilliard, "Wild Atlantic Way Worth €3bn in Annual Tourism Revenue, Says Fáilte Ireland," *The Irish Times*, April 11, 2024, https://www.irishtimes.com/business/2024/04/11/wild-atlantic-way-worth-3-billion-in-annual-tourism-revenue-says-failte-ireland/.
377 "Geology," Cliffs of Moher, August 26, 2022, https://www.cliffsofmoher.ie/unesco-global-geopark/conservation/geology/.
378 "The Wild Flowers of the Cliffs of Moher," Cliffs of Moher, November 30, 2022, https://www.cliffsofmoher.ie/the-wild-flowers-of-the-cliffs-of-moher/.
379 "Clare Birdwatching, Puffins in Ireland," Cliffs of Moher, January 29, 2024, https://www.cliffsofmoher.ie/unesco-global-geopark/conservation/bird-watching/.

ROME

380 "Mithraeum of Saint Clemente," Turismo Roma, March 1, 2025, https://www.turismoroma.it/en/node/43919.
381 Blake Erlich, John Foot, and Richard R. Ring, "Rome," *Encyclopedia Britannica*, accessed May 22, 2025, https://www.britannica.com/place/Rome.
382 "Pantheon," *Encyclopedia Britannica*, accessed March 27, 2025, https://www.britannica.com/topic/Pantheon-building-Rome-Italy.
383 "Vatican City." *Encyclopedia Britannica*, accessed May 19, 2025, https://www.britannica.com/place/Vatican-City.
384 "Palatine Hill," *Encyclopedia Britannica*, accessed January 13, 2024, https://www.britannica.com/place/Palatine-Hill.
385 Reinhold Merkelbach, "Mithraism," *Encyclopedia Britannica*, accessed April 18, 2025, https://www.britannica.com/topic/Mithraism.
386 David Walsh, "The Cult of Mithras," *Lucius' Romans* (blog), January 13, 2018, http://blogs.kent.ac.uk/lucius-romans/2018/01/13/the-cult-of-mithras/.
387 "Mithras, the Invincible God," The New Mithraeum, December 21, 2020, https://www.mithraeum.eu/introductio/mithras-the-invincible-god.
388 Merkelbach, "Mithraism."
389 "Commodus," The New Mithraeum, February 13, 2022, https://www.mithraeum.eu/person/145.
390 "Julian," The New Mithraeum, February 13, 2022, https://www.mithraeum.eu/person/171.
391 Erlich et al., "Rome."
392 Francesca Bologna, "Who Was Nero?," *The British Museum Blog*, April 22, 2021, https://www.britishmuseum.org/blog/who-was-nero.
393 "Colosseum," *Encyclopedia Britannica*, accessed June 4 2025, https://www.britannica.com/topic/Colosseum.
394 "Explore Colosseum Museum & Discover Ancient Rome," www.tickets-rome.com, June 18, 2025, https://www.tickets-rome.com/colosseum/museum/.
395 "Secrets of the Colosseum: Visiting the Colosseum Undergrounds," Journeys to Italy, September 2, 2022, https://www.journeystoitaly.com/secrets-of-the-colosseum-visiting-the-colosseum-undergrounds/.
396 Christopher Klein, "1,500 Years Later, Killer Animal Elevator Returns to Colosseum," HISTORY, March 2, 2025, https://www.history.com/articles/1500-years-later-killer-animal-elevator-returns-to-colosseum. https://education.nationalgeographic.org/resource/colosseum/.
397 "Colosseum," *Encyclopedia Britannica*.
398 James Grout, "The Roman Gladiator," *Encylopaedia Romano*, accessed June 4, 2025, https://penelope.uchicago.edu/encyclopaedia_romana/gladiators/gladiators.html.
399 Csaba Szabó, "Re-interpreting the Mysteries of Mithras," The New Mithraeum, April 2, 2024, https://www.mithraeum.eu/news/re-interpreting-the-mysteries-of-mithras.
400 Merkelbach, "Mithraism."
401 "Mithraeum of Saint Clemente," Turismo Roma, accessed March 1, 2025, https://www.turismoroma.it/en/node/43919.
402 "A Study of Mithraism," The Martin Luther King, Jr. Research and Education Institute, accessed June 4, 2025, https://kinginstitute.stanford.edu/king-papers/documents/study-mithraism.
403 Merkelbach, "Mithraism."

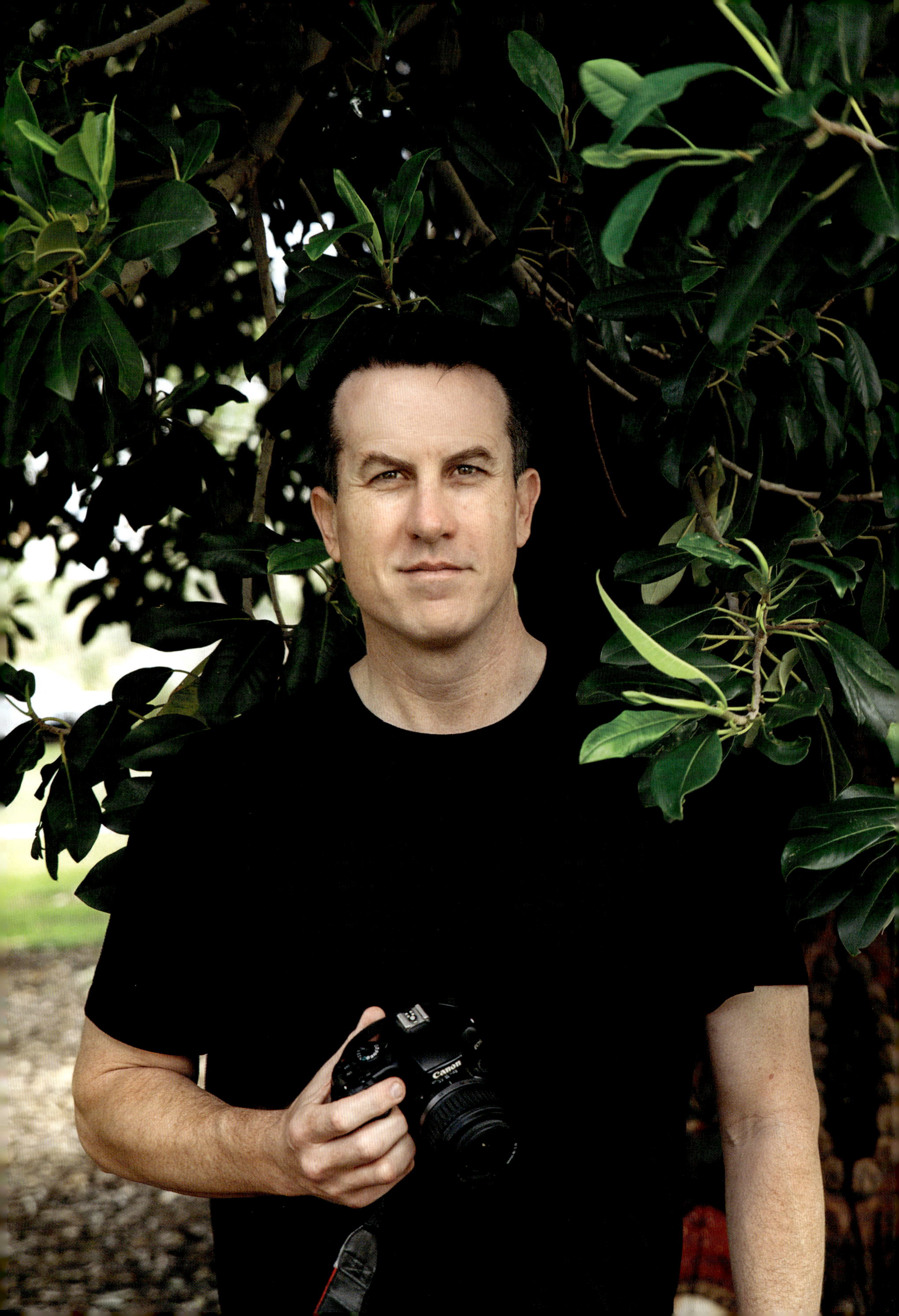
Canon

ABOUT THE AUTHOR

Ronan Patrick O'Connell is a regular contributor to *National Geographic* and a former columnist for *National Geographic Magazine*. A travel journalist and photographer with twenty years of experience, Ronan writes and shoots for major media outlets across the world and has visited more than sixty countries in pursuit of intriguing and compelling stories.

He has contributed stories and photography to *National Geographic*, CNN, the BBC, *Washington Post*, *Smithsonian Magazine*, *Travel + Leisure*, *Conde Nast Traveler*, *The Guardian*, *The San Francisco Chronicle*, *The Toronto Star*, *Forbes*, and more.

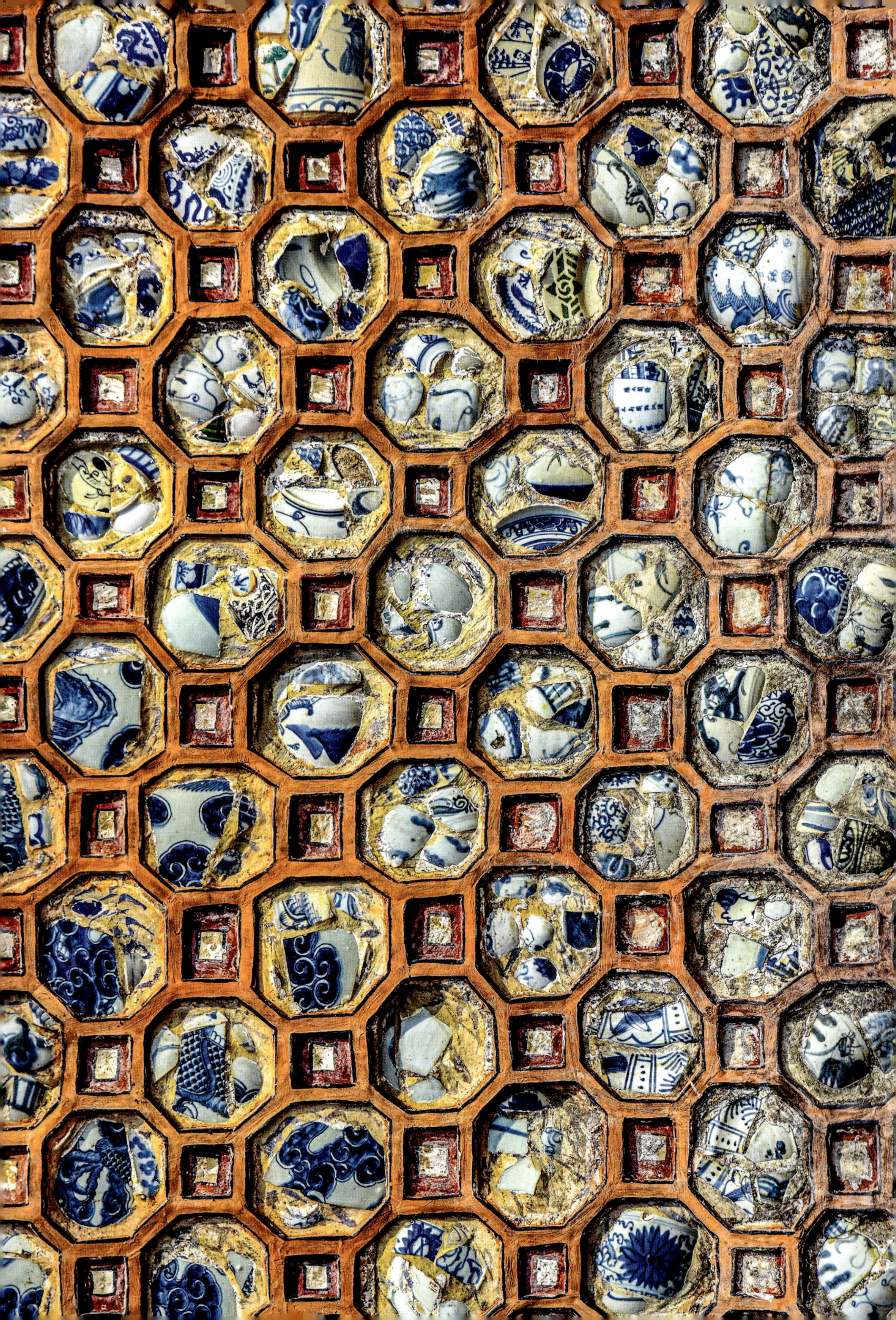